C0-AMS-505

The Past in Perspective

AN INTRODUCTION TO HUMAN PREHISTORY

SECOND EDITION

Kenneth L. Feder

Central Connecticut State University

Mayfield Publishing Company
Mountain View, California
London • Toronto

For Josh and Jacob

Copyright © 2000, 1996 by Mayfield Publishing Company

All rights reserved. No portion of this book may be reproduced in any form or by any means without written permission of the publisher.

Library of Congress Cataloging-in-Publication Data
Feder, Kenneth L.
    The past in perspective : an introduction to human prehistory /
Kenneth L. Feder. — 2nd ed.
        p.   cm.
    Includes bibliographical references (p.   ) and index.
    ISBN 0-7674-1192-7
    1. Prehistoric peoples. 2. Human evolution. 3. Fossil hominids.
4. Human remains (Archaeology) I. Title.
GN766.F43 2000
599.93'8—dc21   99-28265
                                                                      CIP

Manufactured in the United States of America
10 9 8 7 6 5 4 3 2 1

Mayfield Publishing Company
1280 Villa Street
Mountain View, California 94041

Sponsoring editor, Janet M. Beatty; production editor, Lynn Rabin Bauer; manuscript editor, Joan Pendleton; text designer, Jeanne M. Schreiber; cover designer, Laurie Anderson; art manager, Robin Mouat; illustrators, Academy Artworks, Joan Carol, Ann Eldredge, Patti Isaacs, Judith Ogus, and John and Judy Waller; cover photograph © The British Museum; manufacturing manager, Randy Hurst. The text was set in 10.5/12.5 Minion by Thompson Type and printed on 45# Chromatone Matte, PMS 130, by Banta Company. Photograph on pp. 498–499 by the Food and Agriculture Organization, United Nations, photo by H. Null.

The Internet addresses listed in the text were accurate at the time of publication. The inclusion of a Web site does not indicate an endorsement by the author or Mayfield Publishing Company, and Mayfield does not guarantee the accuracy of the information presented at these sites.

Preface

"The past is a bucket of ashes," said the poet Carl Sandburg. Surely he was wrong. The past is not cold, dead, and spent. It is alive in everything we are and will be. We live in a universe filled with its traces. The stars in the night sky shine with a light that began its journey millions of years ago. The fossilized remnants of creatures that once walked the earth lie entombed in the soil beneath our feet. Cooking hearths and food scraps, pyramids and pottery, stone tools and bone awls, cave paintings and ivory sculptures—all date to the ancient human past yet exist in the present. The past is not a bucket of ashes, but rather, as writer L. P. Hartley put it, "the past is a foreign country." In this book, we will visit that country.

The Past in Perspective: An Introduction to Human Prehistory focuses on the dim echoes of the human past, presenting an accessible chronicle of human physical and cultural evolution. The audience for this text is undergraduates who have had no previous coursework in archaeology; for many, it will be their only academic exposure to our prehistoric past. Rather than overwhelm beginning students with an all-inclusive, detailed survey of the human past, this text looks at the major themes of the human evolutionary story. It begins with the evolution of our earliest hominid ancestors, traces the evolution of the modern human species, and follows the various pathways our ancestors took in the development of food-producing societies and complex civilizations. My goal throughout is to instill in readers an appreciation for the long chronicle of humanity and the ongoing processes we use to construct and assess that story.

HOW THE TEXT IS ORGANIZED

Chapters 1–3 provide context and background for the discussion of human prehistory. Chapter 1 places the study of the human past in the context of science, specifically the science of anthropology, using genealogy as a metaphor for the study of human prehistory. Chapter 2 focuses on how a scientific approach to the study of prehistory developed and the role biblical literalism played. Chapter 3 is a brief overview of key methodologies employed by archaeologists and paleoanthropologists.

Following these introductory chapters, Chapters 4–15 present a chronological survey of the human past. Each chapter follows a consistent format with these headings: **Chapter Overview, Prelude, Chronicle, Issues and Debates, Case Study Close-Up, Visiting the Past, Summary,** and **To Learn**

More. My belief is that a consistent format provides a pedagogical advantage; the trajectory of human physical and cultural evolution becomes far more apparent and connected. What we know, what we don't know, and what are still topics of vigorous debate will be clear to the reader.

The **CHAPTER OVERVIEW** introduces the primary topic of the chapter in several brief paragraphs.

The **PRELUDE** represents a conscious attempt on my part to provide a pedagogical "hook" for each chapter. Personal anecdotes or fascinating historical incidents, for example, immediately engage students in the key issue or issues of the chapter, whether it is upright locomotion, the origins of artistic expression, or the power of ancient civilizations.

The **CHRONICLE** presents in narrative form a consensus view of that part of the human past that is the chapter's focus. It represents the heart of each chapter, providing our current understanding of the time period covered, the hominids discussed, and the cultural evolutionary developments reflected in the time period.

ISSUES AND DEBATES sections discuss the answers we have been able to provide for key questions about human physical and cultural evolution as well as the unresolved issues that remain and the ongoing debates. These sections provide differing—and sometimes competing—perspectives. Students are thus exposed to the sometimes messy process of science fraught with disagreements, shifting paradigms, and only hard-won consensus.

The **CASE STUDY CLOSE-UP** is a detailed examination of one or more sites considered diagnostic or emblematic of the time period or primary issue of the chapter.

VISITING THE PAST sections direct readers to key sites mentioned in the chapter that are open to the public, suggest museums where the materials from important sites discussed in the chapter are displayed, and point out computer software "virtual visits" that provide detailed discussions, photographs, videos, and animations related to the chapter topic.

Each chapter **SUMMARY** provides a brief recapitulation of the key issues in the chapter.

TO LEARN MORE is divided into three sections: (1) "Technical Summaries," where students can find primary sources including articles in professional journals and books; (2) "Popular Summaries," including secondary sources like magazine articles and trade books; and (3) "On the Web," providing Internet sources related to the chapter topic.

ADDITIONAL FEATURES

In addition to a consistent chapter format, I've included a number of other features that make this text a more useful learning tool.

- A **timeline** opens every chapter and helps place the key events and sites mentioned in the body of the chapter within a global historical context. The timeline in Chapter 1 shows at a glance the chronological focus of each chapter in the text.
- To help students better orient themselves on the world stage, I've included abundant maps throughout the book. In addition, for Chapters 4–15, I've provided at the beginning of each chapter a **list of sites,** broken out by country, discussed therein.
- A list of **Key Terms** at the ends of chapters identifies important terms that appear in boldfaced type within the chapters; definitions can be found in the end-of-book glossary.
- The text's **visual appeal** enhances its readability. Full-color photographs are cross-referenced to pertinent text discussions. Detailed, colorful charts and drawings, as well as abundant photographs, underscore significant points in the text. Captions for the artwork add information rather than simply label the pictures.
- The **Glossary, References,** and a comprehensive **Index** make information readily accessible.

WHAT'S DIFFERENT ABOUT THE SECOND EDITION

While maintaining the innovative organizational format from the first edition, I have introduced major content changes in the new edition based on the helpful comments of instructors who used *The Past in Perspective.* The text still provides broad coverage of the archaeology of human evolution, but the emphasis has shifted to post-Pleistocene societies, especially relating to the rise of civilization.

Here is a chapter-by-chapter overview of the significant changes:

- **Chapter 1** is now a more straightforward introduction to the field of prehistory. Basic definitions of key terms and concepts—anthropology, archaeology, paleoanthropology, and so on—that did not appear until Chapter 3 in the first edition are now defined and discussed in the first chapter.
- The discussion of modern creationism that appeared in Chapter 1 has been moved to **Chapter 2.** This sets the scene for the historical development of a science of the past. There is now less emphasis on the development of evolutionary thought; greater emphasis is placed on how natural scientists came to the conclusion that the earth was ancient and

changing and that human beings had changed greatly both biologically and culturally during that span of time.

- In **Chapter 3** the material on archaeological epistemology has been expanded with more detailed discussions of dating methods and artifact analysis.

- **Chapter 4** is a combination of Chapters 4 and 5 from the first edition. The material on the Miocene has been condensed, while relevant background information on the evolution of the apes has been retained. Discussion of the australopithecines and *Homo habilis* has been updated.

- **Chapter 5,** on *Homo erectus,* has been thoroughly updated. The chapter includes a discussion of lumping and splitting (a single species—*Homo erectus*—versus multiple species—*Homo ergaster, Homo erectus, Homo antecessor*).

- An expanded discussion of the material from Sima de los Huesos is included in **Chapter 6.** The Neandertal section has been significantly rewritten and updated. The degree of skepticism reflected in the first edition concerning the capabilities of the Neandertals has been tempered with the addition of new material that shows that they were effective hunters (and not just scavengers) and that they produced some items of personal adornment and, possibly, art. It should be more clear to students that Neandertals *were* different, but this difference does not imply that they were inferior to anatomically modern humans.

- **Chapter 7** now includes analysis of Neandertal DNA. New data in the debate concerning the evolution of anatomically modern humans also has been added.

- **Chapter 8** has an expanded explanation of the hunting and gathering practices of the Upper Paleolithic. The hypothesis of a neurophysiological explanation of ancient rock art is discussed.

- The discussion in **Chapter 9** of the earliest settlement of Australia has been rewritten, with a more realistic—and skeptical—appraisal given those sites that are claimed by some to be more than 50,000 years old. The section on the earliest settlement of the New World has been entirely rewritten and includes a possible coastal route. Recently discovered, late-Pleistocene coastal sites in South America are discussed, and the growing consensus concerning the antiquity of Monte Verde is presented. The Kennewick skeleton has been added to the "Issues and Debates" section.

- A key issue concerning the Mesolithic is that of adaptational diversity, which is emphasized and expanded on in **Chapter 10.**

- In **Chapter 11** new molecular data relating to the origins of agriculture are introduced. New evidence of the antiquity of rice cultivation in China, squash domestication in Mesoamerica, and the domestication of cattle in Africa is presented.

- **Chapter 12** is a new chapter on the origins of complexity. A detailed discussion of how and why social, economic, and political complexity developed is included. Stonehenge, Mesopotamia, the Olmec, and Chavin are used as examples, with in-depth discussions of each.

- The development of complex state societies in the Old World is included in **Chapter 13.** Mesopotamia, Egypt, the Indus, China, and Minoan Crete are discussed. The historical Khmer state is presented as a "Case Study Close-Up."
- **Chapter 14** is a new chapter on the later development of non-state complexity. Detailed discussions of the archaeology of the mound builders, Hohokam, Mogollon, Ancestral Puebloan, and Great Zimbabwe are provided. An important theme in the chapter is that complexity does not inevitably lead to state societies.
- New World state societies are discussed in **Chapter 15,** with updated and expanded discussions of the Maya, Teotihuacán, and Aztecs in addition to the ancient states of South America, including the Moche, Tiwanaku, Wari, and Inka.

SUPPLEMENTARY MATERIAL

The **Instructor's Manual** includes a test bank of multiple-choice and short-answer/essay questions, as well as chapter overviews, lists of key words, and suggested sources for videos, CD-ROMS, and Internet sites.

A **computerized test bank** is available free of charge to qualifying adopters. It is a powerful, easy-to-use test generation system that provides all test items on computer disk for IBM-compatible and Macintosh computers. You can select, add, or edit questions, randomize them, and print tests appropriate to your individual classes.

ACKNOWLEDGMENTS

Textbooks, perhaps especially those about human biological and cultural evolution, are themselves evolutionary journeys. My invaluable guides on this voyage included colleagues who have made many useful suggestions concerning my route—both formally as reviewers and informally through letters, phone calls, and e-mails. Also assisting in this endeavor have been students, many of whom were generous with criticism, complaints, encouragement, and assistance. In particular, I wish to thank the reviewers of the first edition: Douglas B. Bamforth, University of Colorado at Boulder; Peter Bleed, University of Nebraska, Lincoln; Christopher DeCorse, Syracuse University; Richard Effland, Jr., Mesa Community College; Douglas R. Givens, Saint Louis Community College; Nicholas Honerkamp, University of Tennessee at Chattanooga; and Paul D. Welch, Queens College, CUNY. I also owe a debt of gratitude to the reviewers of the second edition: Douglas B. Bamforth,

University of Colorado at Boulder; Barry D. Kass, Orange County Community College-SUNY; Carole A. S. Mandryk, Harvard University; Randy McGuire, Binghamton University-SUNY; John Pryor, California State University, Fresno; Michael Stewart, Temple University; William A. Turnbaugh, University of Rhode Island; and Paul D. Welch, Queens College. I also want to thank the many colleagues who provided photographs or line art for this book; they are credited individually in the figure captions. Special thanks to Julie Kasper of the American Museum of Natural History for her help in tracking down the museum's images used here.

It has been my privilege to work with a wonderful group of people at Mayfield. First, I must thank sponsoring editor Jan Beatty. Jan suggested that I might just possibly want to write a prehistory text—I couldn't be happier that it all worked out. Many thanks to Robin Mouat for the wonderful artwork, Brian Pecko for invaluable help with the photo permissions, and Joan Pendleton for a terrific job of copyediting. I have worked several times with production editor Lynn Rabin Bauer, and I cannot imagine there being a sharper, smarter, more dedicated editor.

In the way of personal thanks, I am grateful for having a colleague like Michael Alan Park. My sense of excitement about the world around me was kindled by my parents, and I thank them both. A special thanks to my globe-trotting father for the wonderful photographs. Of course, no acknowledgment is complete without crediting one's immediate family. Thanks to my kids, Josh and Jacob, whose mere existence reminds me of my own very small place in evolution's drama. And expansive thanks to my wife, Melissa, the sweetest person on the planet. I can't lift heavy objects or fix cars, but I can write books. I think she's impressed. Finally, I must acknowledge my two partners in crime, kitties Randolph and Harpo, without whose insistent pestering I might never get up from the computer for dinner.

Contents

FREE COPY FREE COPY FREE COPY FREE COPY FREE COPY FREE COPY FREE COPY FREE COPY FREE COPY FREE

FREE COPY FREE COPY FREE COPY FREE COPY FREE COPY FREE COPY FREE COPY FREE

5 The Human Lineage 100

6 Our Immediate Ancestors:
THE PREMODERN HUMANS 138

15 An Explosion of Complexity:
THE FLOWERING OF CIVILIZATION IN THE NEW WORLD   468

The Past in Perspective

1

Prologue to the Past

CHAPTER OVERVIEW

While genealogists study the roots of an individual family, archaeologists and paleo-anthropologists study the roots of the human species. With evolution as the guiding principle, these scientists investigate humanity's biological and cultural past.

This book focuses particularly on the work of archaeologists. Archaeology is a subdiscipline within the broader field of anthropology—the study of people. Whereas other anthropologists study living groups of people, primates, language, or particular behaviors across cultural boundaries, archaeologists focus on the cultural evolution of our species. Archaeologists concentrate on the physical objects that ancient people made, used, and left behind and that have fortuitously survived, allowing us to investigate them in the present. These objects provide us with a window through which we can gaze back at the past lives and past times of ancient people.

Chronological focus of the chapters				
	25 million	20 million	5 million	2 million
Chapter 1				
Chapter 2				
Chapter 3				
Chapter 4	▬▬▬▬▬▬▬▬▬▬▬▬▬▬▬▬▬▬▬			
Chapter 5				▬▬▬
Chapter 6				
Chapter 7				
Chapter 8				
Chapter 9				
Chapter 10				
Chapter 11				
Chapter 12				
Chapter 13				
Chapter 14				
Chapter 15				
Chapter 16				▬▬▬

Years ago										
1 million	**500,000**	**250,000**	**150,000**	**50,000**	**25,000**	**10,000**	**5,000**	**500**	**Present**	

PROLOGUE

INTELLECTUAL HISTORY

METHODOLOGY

You can see them almost any day in town and county halls, courthouses, libraries, and church basements. Often, they are older, retired people; but they also are young businessmen and -women and middle-aged homemakers, scientists and college students, computer programmers, writers, and carpenters. They all have one interest in common, an all-consuming avocation that occupies their time—the search for their genealogical roots. They peer intently down the dimly lit corridors of their family histories, hoping to illuminate the lives of their ancestors by examining old town and county inventories of births and marriages, school registers and church membership rolls, tax ledgers, land sale and purchase records, immigration files and ship manifests, plantation slave inventories, treaties, and, ultimately, the official documentation of the deaths of their forebears and the disposition of their forebears' worldly possessions.

Genealogical research can be infectious and fascinating. Somehow, you place your own life in a firmer context when you view it as one link in a great chain of ancestors stretching back across generations and centuries. An awareness of your family history changes your perspective drastically, allowing you to view your life as not just an ephemeral thing of the here and now, but also as part of a story that flows through time.

AN ARCHAEOLOGICAL GENEALOGY

This book also is about peering down dimly lit corridors. In a sense, it is about genealogical research, but of a much broader, deeper sort than that conducted by people looking for their relatives in centuries past. This book, about the genealogy of the human species, focuses on the ultimate biological and cultural roots of humanity. The techniques we use, by necessity, differ from those of standard genealogy. Our raw data consist not of documents, photos, and records, but of bones, tools, pots, and pyramids. The time periods on which we concentrate are far different as well. The longest-lived families commonly can be traced back only hundreds of years, but the human family can be traced back millions of years. And our journey of discovery takes us not to local town halls and libraries, but to the sun-soaked savannas of Africa, the frigid caves of Ice Age Europe, the humid rain forests of Mesoamerica, and the fertile floodplains of the Tigris and Euphrates Rivers in southwest Asia (Figure 1.1).

Though our methods and scales are very different, we "genealogists" of all sorts are pursuing the same thing; we are searching for our past in order to understand our present. Where do we come from? How did we become who we are? What challenges confronted our ancestors along the way, and how did they respond to them? Just as genealogists investigate such issues as they apply to themselves and their families, **paleoanthropologists** and **archaeologists** confront these same questions as they relate to the human species as a whole. They go beyond their own personal sagas and focus on the grand sweep of

FIGURE 1.1

While genealogists may rely on local town records to trace an individual family through time, paleoanthropologists and archaeologists often must journey farther afield in their attempt to trace the history of the entire human family. Here are two such places: the North American Arctic, home to the first humans to settle in the New World (top; *see Chapter 9), and the forest of the central Yucatán Peninsula in Mexico, homeland of one of the world's ancient civilizations* (bottom; *see Chapter 15).* (Top: Courtesy of Marc Banks; *bottom:* K. L. Feder)

human **evolution** and history to produce the genealogy of the whole human family. This book will focus on our human genealogy—what we currently know and understand about the roots of us all.

AN ANTHROPOLOGICAL PERSPECTIVE

Paleoanthropology and archaeology are subfields within the broader discipline of **anthropology** (Figure 1.2). Contemporary anthropology is the study of people. Of course, the other social sciences—economics, political science, psychology, sociology—also study people, but from very particular perspectives, focusing on specific aspects of human behavior. Anthropology, on the other hand, attempts to be more holistic and integrative in its approach. If other social scientists specialize in the workings of specific systems within human society, anthropologists tend to be generalists who want to know how

FIGURE 1.2

The major subdivisions of the field of anthropology. While these subdivisions represent distinct approaches, there are numerous connections among them. Moreover, each can be further subdivided into subspecialties.

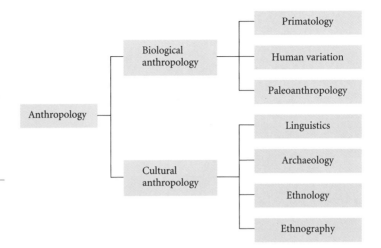

human society, with all its interrelated parts, works as a whole and how it came into existence.

Some anthropologists—called **ethnographers**—study humans by residing in particular societies and observing the behaviors of the people living in them. Margaret Mead, who spent many years among the Samoans (people inhabiting an island chain in the Pacific Ocean), is probably the most famous ethnographer (Figure 1.3). In the past, many ethnographers, most of whom were members of Western societies, chose to focus on exotic, non-Western people. Today, ethnographers study inner-city youth gangs, rural farming communities, factory workers, and even the community of academic anthropologists. Each group, in its own way, represents a society—or a part of a larger society—the study of which can tell us something about the human condition.

Researchers who go beyond examining a particular group of people to compare the behaviors of different cultures are conducting **ethnology.** An ethnologist might take the work of several ethnographers who have conducted detailed studies of specific human groups and investigate, for example, how those various peoples deal with death, discipline their children, choose a mate, or build their houses. A highly specialized subfield of anthropology is **anthropological linguistics.** Here, the focus is language—how it evolved and the historical relationships among the known languages.

Primatologists also live with the groups they study (Figure 1.4). Instead of living among and studying people, these anthropologists focus their attention on the group of animals called the nonhuman **primates.** Prosimians, monkeys, apes, and humans are all primates (see Chapter 4). Primatologists aim to better understand our nearest living relatives. Believing that all primates share a common evolutionary heritage, primatologists hope to gain

FIGURE 1.3

Margaret Mead, in native dress (on the left), poses with a native Polynesian woman. (Courtesy of the Institute for Intercultural Studies, Inc., New York. Photo from the Library of Congress)

FIGURE 1.4

Jane Goodall's work among the chimpanzees has provided enormous insight into the lives of chimps and, indirectly, into the lives of our ancient ancestors (see Chapter 4). (Courtesy of the Jane Goodall Institute. Photo by Ken Regan)

insights into our ancestral line. Jane Goodall, who has devoted much of her life to living among and learning about chimpanzees in the wild, is perhaps the best-known primatologist. Dian Fossey lived and worked with gorillas in the African nation of Rwanda. Her life and work as a primatologist was the subject of a biography by Farley Mowat, *Woman in the Mists* (1987), and the Hollywood movie *Gorillas in the Mist*.

Paleoanthropologists and archaeologists investigate the evolutionary history of humanity, both the biological evolution of our species and its cultural evolution. Paleoanthropologists have as their database the early biological history of our species; they focus on the skeletal remains of our ancient human

FIGURE 1.5

Donald Johanson, whose work in East Africa has revealed the remains of some of our most ancient hominid ancestors, is shown here at Hadar, a fossil locality that has provided the remains of Lucy and other members of the species Australopithecus afarensis *(see Chapter 4).* (Courtesy of the Institute of Human Origins)

ancestors (Figure 1.5). Paleoanthropologists search for and analyze the fossils of our ancestors, and they rely increasingly on the analysis of modern human DNA in an attempt to solve the puzzle of our genetic roots. In a few lucky instances, they have even been able to extract DNA from ancient bones, reading the genetic instructions for some of our ancestors (see Chapter 7).

Archaeologists, on the other hand, rely on the material cultural remains left behind by past peoples, including those same varieties of human beings whose bones the paleoanthropologists unearth (Figure 1.6). Material remains may include the tools and other objects people made and used, from simple stonecutting tools to complex monuments. Although archaeology is often perceived as being a romantic enterprise, it is perhaps more like the study of "other people's garbage," as a PBS TV documentary called it (PBS 1980).

We humans are not only biological organisms whose **adaptation** is rooted in our genes but also cultural organisms whose uniquely great intelligence allows us to invent much of our strategy for survival. As researchers first recognized in the eighteenth century (see Chapter 2), these invented adaptations—our **cultures**—have evolved just as surely as have our bodies and brains. Not only did our human ancestors leave behind their physical remains, which reflected their biological adaptation, but they also left behind the material objects they made and used as part of their cultural adaptation. The study of these two sources of information—their bones and artifacts—allows us to paint a picture of the lives of our ancient human ancestors.

OUR HUMAN GENEALOGY

The saga of human biological and cultural evolution, then, is a genealogy written not in words but in things—in fragmentary skeletons, shattered stone tools, broken pots, charred seeds, elaborate burials, stone carvings, cave paintings, and monumental ruins. Using the methods to be outlined briefly in Chapter 3, paleoanthropologists and archaeologists study the genealogy of humanity that was "written" in the language of these material remains.

This book will chronicle the story of the human past, focusing on the period before the development of writing and describing a journey that began in the furthest reaches of antiquity and continues to the present. We rely on the physical evidence as it has been revealed through the work of paleoanthropologists and archaeologists. The organizing theme of this treatment of the human past will be evolution, here encompassing the physical evolution of our species as well as the evolution of human culture.

We will begin by seeing how our understanding of evolution did not burst spontaneously into our collective consciousness. Like the creatures whose existence and natures it attempts to explain, the evolutionary view itself "evolved." Chapter 2 will focus on the evolution of our scientific perception of the past.

FIGURE 1.6

Archaeologist Melinda Zeder of the Smithsonian Institution has worked extensively in the Middle East, exploring some of the world's most ancient Neolithic sites (see Chapter 11, especially the "Case Study Close-Up"). (Courtesy of Melinda Zeder)

TO LEARN MORE

On the Web

For a comprehensive listing of Internet sites related to the field of anthropology in general, with many sites focusing on archaeology and paleoanthropology, one of the best places to visit is Anthropology Resources on the Internet, located at http://lucy.ukc.ac.uk/afaq.html. Compiled by Allen H. Lutins, this site has many links to sites maintained by university departments, museums, and journals as well as listings of Internet discussion groups (and instructions for how to subscribe to those groups)—all related to anthropology.

KEY TERMS

paleoanthropologist	ethnographer	primatologist
archaeologist	ethnology	primate
evolution	anthropological	adaptation
anthropology	linguistics	culture

2

Perceiving the Past

AN INTELLECTUAL HISTORY

CHAPTER OVERVIEW

In the seventeenth century, some scientists studied the world and saw evidence that physical upheavals characterized the earth's history. Others viewed the earth as the product of slow-acting, ongoing causes. Their view of the world as ancient and ever changing provided the time and context necessary for nineteenth-century thinker Charles Darwin's evolutionary view of life.

Some people decry the evolutionary perspective, believing that it degrades the sanctity of human life. In the evolutionary perspective, however, each life and each culture is precious. Each individual life holds great dignity and enormous value when it is perceived as the unique product of 3.5 billion years of evolution.

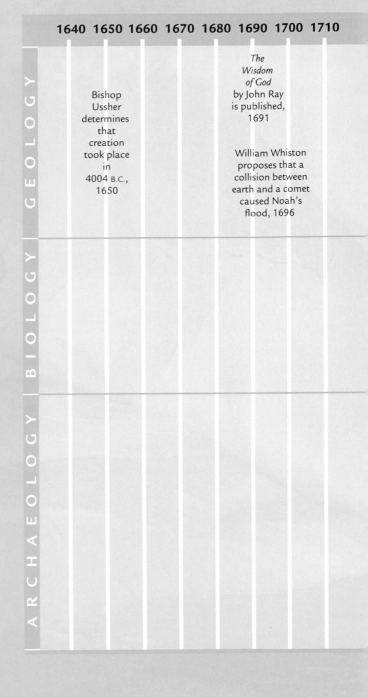

	1640	1650	1660	1670	1680	1690	1700	1710
GEOLOGY		Bishop Ussher determines that creation took place in 4004 B.C., 1650				*The Wisdom of God* by John Ray is published, 1691 / William Whiston proposes that a collision between earth and a comet caused Noah's flood, 1696		
BIOLOGY								
ARCHAEOLOGY								

| 1720 | 1730 | 1740 | 1750 | 1760 | 1770 | 1780 | 1790 | 1800 | 1810 | 1820 | 1830 | 1840 | 1850 | 1860 | 1870 | 1880 |

Row 1 (Geology):

Theory of the Earth by James Hutton published, 1788

William Smith's stratigraphic tables first circulated, 1799

William Smith's stratigraphic tables published, 1815

Principles of Geology by Charles Lyell published, 1830

Row 2 (Biology / Evolution):

Linnaeus publishes his taxonomy for all living things, 1758

Philosophie Zoologique by Jean-Baptiste Lamarck published, 1809

Darwin begins his voyage on the *Beagle*, 1831

Darwin writes a synopsis of his theory of evolution, 1844

The Origin of Species by Charles Darwin published, 1859

The Descent of Man by Charles Darwin published, 1872

Row 3 (Archaeology / Anthropology):

John Frere finds flint tools in soil layer deep in quarry in Hoxne, England, 1797

Flint tools and bones of extinct animals found in Kent's Cavern, England, 1824

Human bones found with bones of extinct animals in French cave, 1828

C. J. Thomsen publishes museum guide and introduces three-age system, 1836

Boucher de Perthes finds ancient flint axes, 1837

Primitive skull found in Neander Valley, Germany, 1856

Geological Evidences of the Antiquity of Man by Charles Lyell published, 1863

Researches in the Early History of Mankind by Edward Tyler published, 1865

Ancient Society by Lewis Henry Morgan published, 1877

Evolution is the organizing theme of this book. The term itself evokes so much emotion and misunderstanding that it is important first to put it in context. I'll begin with the story of a confrontation I had with someone for whom evolution was an obscene concept.

Creationism

I had just attended a lecture given by a sincere but misinformed gentleman who described himself as a **creationist;** he believed that God had created the universe and everything in it exactly as it now appears (Gish 1972; Morris 1974). He rejected completely the theory of evolution, whose proponents view the world and life as the result of entirely natural processes of change over enormous periods of time. He also categorically rejected the idea that evolution might be the process by which God created and continues to create life. Furthermore, he objected especially strenuously when the theory of evolution, in any form, was applied to the human species.

For the lecturer, the only acceptable explanation for the origin of life in general and human life in particular was the biblical version given in the book of Genesis. An all-powerful, all-knowing God, he asserted, created humankind a mere 6,000 years ago. In this view, the history of the universe, including all human history and cultural development, had to be wedged into this incredibly narrow span of time.

It seemed to me that the lecturer based his arguments against evolution on a misinterpretation of evolution as well as his own unfamiliarity with the evidence. Nevertheless, his concern about the implications of evolution—what it signified about the value and importance of human life *if* we had been the product of a natural process rather than the ultimate creation of God—was obviously heartfelt. "What is the value of an individual human life—of *your* life," he asked, "if you are not the personal creation of a divine being but, instead, merely the result of a series of highly improbable chemical and biological accidents?"

These were reasonable concerns articulated by a deeply concerned person, issues we should all perhaps consider. Why should we help to protect or preserve the environment, endangered species, or even the lives of other people if we are just natural creatures living in a cruel world rather than the children of God? According to the theory of evolution, we are not so special, we are not the "crown of creation." Evolution, in the speaker's opinion, was responsible for a view of humanity that led to the seemingly complete devaluation of life and the deification of the self that we have witnessed in the twentieth century.

An Evolutionary View

Biological evolution simply implies a process of systematic change through time. The natural world is vast and diverse, and many living things are born into it. Some of those living things possess, by chance, characteristics that increase the likelihood of their survival and of their having descendants who share those advantageous characteristics. An individual may be faster, stronger, more dexterous, or able to move more efficiently through its habitat. It may be better camouflaged, have better visual acuity, be better at attracting a mate, or possess greater intelligence. These advantages may make it more likely to survive and more likely, therefore, to pass those characteristics on to subsequent generations.

Over vast spans of time, an entire species can be moved toward these advantageous characteristics, because those who lack them tend to die more quickly—often before becoming old enough to mate and produce descendants who also lack them. Through the slow and steady accumulation of advantageous characteristics or as the result of the rapid appearance of a dramatically different and advantageous feature, a species can become so different that it no longer is even the same kind of animal. It has become a new and different species: It has evolved.

The varied and changing natural world provides the context in which an organism must live and to which it must adjust. Biological evolution is not directed; species do not actively develop strategies for survival—called **adaptations.** And biological evolution has no direction; species do not necessarily become bigger, stronger, or faster. In fact, the fossil record shows that most species become extinct. Those that survive do so because at least some individual members are lucky enough to possess physical or behavioral adaptations that allow them to.

For some species, the means of adjustment go beyond the solely biological. Such species are able, as a result of their great intelligence, to develop new adaptations virtually instantly. They can invent new ways of surviving and teach these new ways to other members of their species and to their offspring. These survival methods are not biological; they are cultural. **Culture** represents the nonbiological strategies for survival. Modern human beings rely, as did our ancient human ancestors, on cultural adaptations for survival. A discussion of these adaptations and how they, too, have systematically changed through time makes up a large portion of this book.

With all this in mind, I spoke to the lecturer afterward, not to change his fundamental view, but to point out a basic fallacy in his argument about what the theory of evolution means about the value of life itself. It is true, I admitted, that most evolutionists considered the processes that led to humans as undirected and accidental. But that most definitely did not impel us to denigrate the value of an individual life, I tried to assure him. Each individual life holds great dignity and enormous value when it is perceived as the unique product of 3.5 billion years of evolution, for we are each part of a grand work in progress. From an evolutionary perspective, each life, each person, and each human society is a unique experiment with enormous potential for success. As a result, I maintained, one could argue that the life of the individual was even more precious within a worldview that perceives each of us as the unlikely result of a series of improbable events spread out across such a very long time rather than as the very recent result of a supernatural creation.

AN ANCIENT WORLD?

Most European thinkers in the centuries before our own were, like the speaker I encountered, creationists. They believed that the world and everything in it had been created by God in the not-too-distant past. These same thinkers, for the most part, believed that the proper role of science was merely to illuminate the nature of God's creation, to show the perfection of His plan. The title of an important book written in 1691 by the clergyman and scientist John Ray reflects this perspective precisely: *The Wisdom of God Manifested in the Works of the Creation.* Ray's book was not about the Bible, religion, or even God. It was about nature, including plants and animals, the earth, and the skies above us. In Ray's view and in the view of most European scientists in the seventeenth, eighteenth, and even nineteenth centuries, the job of science was to expose God's wisdom by examining the things He created, using the Bible as a blueprint for His creation.

No Place for Amendments: An Unchanging World

Like Ray, most thinkers before the nineteenth century approached the study of creation by focusing on what they perceived to be its perfection. Following this approach, most of these scientists and philosophers argued that the universe, the earth, and life itself were basically unchanging, having been "fixed" in their perfection at creation. In other words, if the harmony, complexity, and perfection of the world today is evidence of God's work, then the world must be, for the most part, the same as when God created it. In *The Wisdom of God* and in the rest of his career as a naturalist and scientist, Ray was perhaps the most eloquent seventeenth-century proponent of the hypothesis of a fixed creation—the idea that the universe was set during the Genesis creation week and had not changed in any fundamental way since that time. As Ray (1691, 164) put it, "Man is always mending and altering his works: But nature observes the same tenor because her works are so perfect that there is no place for amendments."

Ray admitted that the world around us is not completely static. He allowed for minor changes from the original state of things as God had produced them. There were cyclical changes like seasons, completely random alterations in the world due to accidents or cataclysms, and general change, in the sense of a decline from the original perfection of God's creation. But the concept of fundamental change was not permissible in Ray's natural theology. In his view (1691, Preface), the world around him reflected "the works created by God at first and by him conserved to this day in the same state and condition in which they were first made."

A WRECK OF A WORLD

Even in Ray's own time, there were those who, though agreeing that the study of the natural world was a valid way of glorifying nature's author, disagreed with his interpretation of the fixed nature of God's creation. These thinkers believed that the earth had changed radically from the original creation and that this change had been decidedly for the worse. They agreed with Ray that the world God created had been perfect and that some of that perfection could still be seen and used as an argument for God's existence, but they also viewed the modern world as a pale reflection of the perfect place God had created. In *Sacred Theory of the Earth* (1680), Reverend Thomas Burnet called the modern world "the dirty little planet." Benjamin Franklin summed up this perspective best when he characterized the earth of his time as "this wreck of a world we live on" (Greene 1959, 39).

These men believed that the world God had created was indeed perfect but had been decaying since the time of the creation. They also believed that through the careful, objective study of nature, scientists could reveal the processes God had employed to set the universe in motion, including those that were causing the world to fall apart.

Noah's Flood

One example thinkers in past centuries pointed to as evidence of the process of deterioration of the earth was Noah's flood. The Bible states that God decided to destroy the world and all its living things through a great universal deluge, saving only the family of Noah and representatives of each kind of animal. Edmund Halley (after whom the famous comet is named) proposed in 1694 that a comet crashing into the earth (sent, of course, by God) might have initiated the great flood. Halley feared the reaction if he published such a seemingly mechanical or naturalistic explanation for divine retribution for human depravity, so he circulated his idea only among friends. In 1696, however, another writer, William Whiston, published precisely this hypothesis in *A New Theory of the Earth* (Figure 2.1). To accommodate this physical explanation to theology, Whiston suggested that God had known during the creation week that the human species would descend into a depraved state and immediately set in motion the comet, preordained to encounter the earth at just the right time! Some thinkers began to view Noah's flood as one in a series of catastrophes that had afflicted earth since creation. This argument was based in part on their perception of earth as a "wreck," but not a particularly old one.

The Age of the Earth

It was commonly believed in the sixteenth and seventeenth centuries that the world was only a few thousand years old. For example, in Shakespeare's play *As You Like It*, written in about 1600, one of the characters states, "The poor world is almost six thousand years old." In 1642, John Lightfoot calculated

FIGURE 2.1

Following Edmund Halley, William Whiston suggested that a comet striking the earth had been the cause of Noah's flood. In this illustration, a comet passes by the earth, deforming the planet into an oblong shape. According to Whiston, the flood resulted from water in the comet's tail (shown here on the right) as well as water gushing up from the earth's interior when the surface cracked because of its deformation.
(William Whiston, *New Theory of the Earth*, 1696)

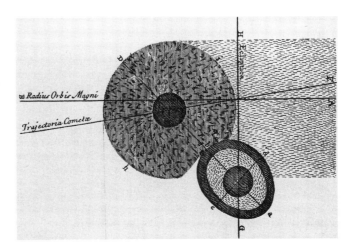

creation's date at 3928 B.C., making the world 5,570 years old at that time (Brice 1982, 19). There were other, similar estimates.

Ultimately, most people came to accept the determination of Irish archbishop James Ussher that the earth had been created in 4004 B.C. and that God had begun the work "upon the entrance of the night preceding the twenty-third day of October" (from Archbishop Ussher's *Annales,* in Brice 1982, 18). This date later became widely accepted; beginning in 1701, it was printed as a marginal note in all English Bibles. Though Ussher's precise figure is often maligned by modern scientists and writers, he arrived at it in 1650 through detailed historical research, analysis of astronomical cycles, and reference to biblical genealogies (Gould 1991).

If Ussher's figure was true, then the earth in 1690 was less than 5,700 years old. Unless a series of cataclysms had occurred, this was quite a short period of time to progress from the perfect place God had created to our imperfect world—with its cracks and crevices (canyons and valleys), imperfect drainage (meandering, rather than straight, rivers), irregular topography (hills and mountains), and assorted other wrinkles and wounds. This scenario, however, is precisely what **catastrophists** proposed.

The Catastrophists

Most naturalists in the late seventeenth through eighteenth centuries moved away from the notion that scientific observation showed the world to be perfect and static. Instead, they believed that the world changed through catastrophic, natural, physical processes that had been set in motion by God at creation and that could be understood through careful study (Figure 2.2).

Catastrophists argued among themselves not about whether catastrophes had occurred, but about what specific, natural processes God had employed. However, catastrophists faced the problem of scale. For example, though

flooding was a common natural phenomenon that often wrought great destruction, and volcanoes were understood as capable of incredible devastation, the power of these processes seemed far too limited to produce, in the accepted time frame provided by Bishop Ussher, the kinds of planetary decay catastrophists believed characterized the earth. Though enormous on a human scale, great floods and powerful volcanic eruptions seemed trifling on a planetary scale. Catastrophists had to posit that calamities—the likes of which human history had never witnessed or recorded—had occurred in the past in order to produce the degree of degeneration they perceived in the physical world.

EQUABLE AND STEADY CHANGE

Clearly, scientists in the seventeenth and eighteenth centuries were wrestling with the issue of the character of God and the essence of nature. Virtually all believed in an all-powerful creative force that used natural processes as tools. They also were firm believers in the notion that through careful observation and the use of logic—intellectual tools granted by God only to humans—they could solve the mysteries of God's creation.

But therein lay a great paradox. For earth to be as young as theologians believed it to be, the scientists who based their intellectual arguments on observation were forced to accept the existence of catastrophic processes that they simply could not observe, because they were no longer occurring. But most scientists were unwilling to risk arguing in direct opposition to theology.

James Hutton and the Radical View of Uniformitarianism

Scottish scientist James Hutton became one of the first proponents of a hypothesis that stood in opposition to catastrophism (Figure 2.3). In his view,

FIGURE 2.2

Catastrophists believed that during its history, the earth had suffered numerous cataclysms, most the result of floods and volcanic eruptions. Clearly such natural catastrophes occur. Here are two recent examples: the 1980 eruption of Mt. St. Helens in Washington state and the Mississippi River floods of 1993. Even natural disasters on this scale are far too small, however, to support the catastrophist perspective. (Mt. St. Helens: Copyright © AP/Wide World Photos; Mississippi River: Copyright © James A. Finley, AP/Wide World Photos)

FIGURE 2.3

Eighteenth-century Scottish geologist James Hutton, one of the first and most persuasive proponents of uniformitarianism. (James Hutton, *Theory of the Earth,* 1795)

first espoused in his seminal and revolutionary work *Theory of the Earth,* "The operations of nature are equable and steady," not unpredictable and catastrophic (1795, 19). This viewpoint, held by others as well, gave rise to the new perspective of **uniformitarianism.**

Hutton viewed the world as a marvelously constructed, perfectly synchronized machine—not merely switched on at creation and destined to run down, but brilliantly conceived to readjust and re-create itself continually. Certainly Hutton believed in God, but not one who would create a perfect world programmed to begin to disintegrate immediately after its creation. Hutton proposed a world designed by a creator so clever that slow and steady processes of decay were eternally offset by slow and steady processes of rejuvenation.

For example, catastrophists interpreted the discovery of the fossil remains of marine organisms at locations hundreds or even thousands of miles from the coast and at elevations of several thousand feet above sea level as evidence for a universal flood as described in the Bible. Hutton viewed these data quite differently. He believed that the presence of fossilized marine organisms on dry land indicated that these places had at one time been under the ocean. He suggested that during earth's history the hardest mountains erode, producing fresh soil in which plants can grow and on which humans can subsist. These soils are continually washed out across the land into rivers and ultimately flow into the oceans, where they become part of the seabed. Marine organisms live and die on these surfaces, depositing their shells. All of the loose materials at the bottom of the sea—including those fossil remains—eventually are consolidated through heat and pressure back into rock again, and through volcanic action the rock is slowly raised up to become mountains once more. Eventually, these mountains also will erode back into soil, the soil will be washed back into the sea, and so on, ad infinitum. Because of this endless cycle, any investigation of the history of the earth reveals "no vestige of a beginning—no prospect of an end" (Hutton 1795, 200).

In Hutton's view, it is unnecessary to propose rare, irregularly occurring catastrophes to explain the appearance of the modern world. We can best understand the history of the earth, Hutton suggested, if we study those regular, uniform, natural processes of destruction and renewal that operate and are observable in the present and then extrapolate their impacts backward through time. As he put it, "In examining things present, we have data from which to reason with regard to what has been" (1795, 19). Processes like **erosion** and **weathering**—seen every day in rivers cutting their channels, in tides resculpting the shore, or in wind carving canyons—could have produced the present appearance of the earth, if afforded sufficient time. In a conceivably indirect criticism of Bishop Ussher's calculation, Hutton maintained that "time, which means everything in our ideas and is often deficient in our schemes, is to nature, endless" (1795, 15). Hutton argued that once it was accepted that these ordinary processes were responsible for earth's alteration since creation, earth's actual age could be deduced. Through the careful scientific study of the rates and patterns of ordinary processes of erosion and weathering, "we find . . . means for concluding a certain portion of time to have necessarily elapsed, in the production of those events of which we see the effects" (1795, 19).

For the earth to have attained its appearance, modern observable phenomena must have been operating long enough to have produced mountain chains, meandering rivers, great canyons, and eroded valleys. Because the rates of erosion and weathering could be measured, one needed only to ask how long such processes must have been operating in order for modern features to have formed.

FIGURE 2.4

Two views of one of the flint implements discovered and reported on in 1797 by John Frere. Frere believed that the great depth at which the implements were found, as well as their position in a soil layer beneath one in which the bones of extinct animals had been located, indicated great antiquity for the makers of such tools. (From John Frere's "Account of Flint Weapons Discovered in Hoxne, Suffolk," *Archaeologia,* 1800)

ANCIENT HUMANS?

In 1797, only two years after the publication of Hutton's expanded version of *Theory of the Earth,* John Frere, a young Englishman, found some curious stone tools in a brick-earth quarry in the small English village of Hoxne (Figure 2.4). His letter describing the artifacts to the London Society of Antiquaries was read before the group in the same year and printed in its journal in 1800 (Frere 1800).

Some of the objects Frere reported on were finely made, as were other stone tools of sharp flint previously found throughout England and elsewhere in Europe. With Hutton's concept of an ancient earth still quite controversial, however, all of human history—including previous cultures that apparently made stone tools instead of metal ones—had to be shoehorned into a very short period of time.

This time frame resulted in some remarkable suggestions about the primitive-looking stone objects that had been found. Some seventeenth-century observers proposed that they had been fashioned, not by ancient people, but by modern elves and fairies! In the mid-1600s, in a more naturalistic but equally improbable explanation, Ullisses Aldrovandi suggested that such objects were produced by nature through "the admixture of a certain exhalation of thunder and lightning with metallic matter . . . which is coagulated by the circumfused moisture and conglutinated into a mass" (Daniel and Renfrew 1988, 29–30).

Other scientists in the seventeenth century were not quite so enamored of explanations that relied on fairies and elves or thunder and lightning. They suggested that these flint objects had been made by people in the past. But this explanation still was hampered by the restriction that a previous race of stone-tool-using humans could be no more than about 6,000 years old because that was the age of the earth and the universe that God had created. Some scientists suggested that the tools were made by pre-Adamites (literally, people "before Adam," created by God in a previous construction of the world not mentioned in the Bible). Another approach that conformed better to the

6,000-year restriction and a more standard biblical view was to credit the manufacture of the implements to a race of barbaric people who had lived after Adam and before Noah's flood.

The Implications of Frere's Discovery

What made Frere's discovery so significant was that for perhaps the first time, primitive stone tools could be shown to have originated at great depth (in this case, 10 ft below the surface) and that the bones of extinct animals were found *above* the tools, in more recent soil layers. Frere recognized that from a uniformitarian perspective, this placement implied a great age for the tools and, in turn, a significant age for the humans who made them.

Frere's argument for the antiquity of the artifacts he found was based on their **stratigraphic** position in the quarry. Frere and members of the society may have been aware of the work of surveyor William Smith, who a few years earlier had recognized that the soil beneath the earth's surface occurred in layers and that the layers produced ordered and regular groups of fossils. Smith showed that the layers could be identified and distinguished by their population of fossil species, with sequentially lower layers representing increasingly ancient time periods. In 1799 Smith circulated a handwritten table showing the order of strata he had encountered, but he did not publish a detailed report until 1815, laying the groundwork for the analysis of **stratigraphy** (see Chapter 3; Grayson 1983).

Frere's excursion to Hoxne may have put him at the right place to add to the mounting evidence for the uniformitarian perspective of an ancient earth—and to show that the human species was a part of that story—but he surely had made his discovery at the wrong time. Smith's stratigraphic work was quite new, and Hutton and his supporters were in the midst of the first skirmishes of a battle to defend uniformitarianism against the attacks of a hostile scientific and religious community. Hutton and his followers were more interested in evidence related directly to the age of the earth than in other, somewhat incidental, and even more controversial evidence confirming a human presence on an ancient earth. As scholar A. Bowdoin Van Riper (1993) points out, even many ardent uniformitarianists continued to maintain that humans were a recent addition to an ancient earth that had passed through a series of stages leading up to the modern world. Sadly, Frere's letter to the society about the stone tools and their apparent great age was promptly forgotten.

More Stone Tools . . . and Bones

Additional evidence discovered in the early 1800s also failed to convince most scientists of the great antiquity of the human species. For example, in 1828, in the town of Narbonne, France, a museum curator reported the discovery of human bones together in the same cave deposit with the bones of extinct animals. The gentleman who made the discovery, however, elected not to make any connection between the human and animal remains, suggesting that their co-occurrence was a result of chance (Daniel and Renfrew 1988, 33).

At about the same time, Father John MacEnery announced the discovery of flint tools and the bones of extinct animals in Kent's Cavern in Torquay in southern England. MacEnery's evidence, gathered between 1824 and 1829, strongly suggested that the tools and animal remains were of equal age; they were found together, sealed beneath a stalagmite in the cavern. MacEnery's writings show him initially to have been quite excited about the implications of his discovery as it related to the antiquity of humanity. Nevertheless, MacEnery ultimately backed off from any claim of association between the tools and the bones of extinct animals (Grayson 1983). Most scientists believed, despite the lack of evidence, that the stone tools had gotten under the stalagmites only recently, when humans dug out ovens in the cave floor (Daniel and Renfrew 1988, 33–34).

These and other discoveries made in the early years of the nineteenth century implied a greater antiquity of the human species than was allowed for in Bishop Ussher's biblically based chronology. The unearthing of tools and bones seemed to place our species deep in time in Hutton's uniformly changing, ancient earth. Yet none of these discoveries separately or together were viewed as compelling by most scientists.

The denial of great human antiquity might be ascribed to pressure applied by the church or simply to a stubborn refusal to accept the evidence. But, as Donald Grayson (1983) shows, this is an unfair assumption. Certainly, there was a desire to reject the claim of great age for our species, but until about 1859 the evidence supporting this claim just wasn't that strong. Stratigraphy was a new approach, and archaeological excavation methods were not well developed. In the court of scientific opinion, the physical association between artifacts and the bones of extinct animals could not be proven beyond a reasonable doubt.

THE SLOW AGENCY OF EXISTING CAUSES

Hutton had fired the first salvos in a revolution in thinking about the processes responsible for the physical features of the earth and the age of the planet. But in the intellectual battle that ensued, Hutton barely was able to hold his position. The human place in time could not be established when time itself was still a point of such great contention. It became the task of the brilliant British geologist Charles Lyell (Figure 2.5) to continue this revolution in thinking about the past and to provide time enough for an ancient humanity. The subtitle of Lyell's seminal work, *Principles of Geology,* first published in 1830, conveys the essence of his approach: "An attempt to explain the former changes of the earth's surface by reference to causes now in operation" (Lyell 1830).

To come to a rational understanding of the earth, Lyell felt it necessary to dispense entirely with "imaginary pictures of catastrophes and confusion such

FIGURE 2.5

Nineteenth-century English geologist Charles Lyell. Lyell was the most eloquent and thorough of the uniformitarianists. (Charles Lyell, *Principles of Geology,* 1830)

as haunted the imagination of the early cosmogonists" (1830, 72). His fundamental assertion was that "all past changes on the globe had been brought about by the slow agency of existing causes" (1830, 63).

Perhaps the most revolutionary and problematic deduction from such a hypothesis concerned the time necessary to produce the kinds of geological features seen on the earth if only the "slow agency of existing causes" was considered. Lyell himself admitted, "The imagination was first fatigued and overpowered by endeavoring to conceive the immensity of time required for the annihilation of whole continents by so insensible a process" (1830, 63). But he went on to apply his fundamental axiom of uniformitarianism to estimate the ages of significant geological features. In a work published in 1863, for example, Lyell calibrated the modern rate at which the Mississippi Delta was growing and concluded that at its current rate of growth it must have taken 100,000 years to have attained its size.

Needless to say, such an estimated age for the Mississippi Delta was shocking to those who accepted Bishop Ussher's determination for the age of the entire earth. Lyell was viciously attacked in print and charged with heresy, but such allegations rang hollow. Though the Bible measures the period of creation as six days, it does not place that creation week in time; nowhere does the Bible actually record the age of the universe, earth, or life. Hutton's and Lyell's view and that of uniformitarianism may have contradicted the interpretation of an archbishop, but it did not disclaim the word of God.

Lyell was a great scientist and a persuasive proponent of the uniformitarian perspective. His work resonated in the minds of many geologists, biologists, and archaeologists and freed them from the perspective of a recent earth into whose chronology all of their observations and deductions had to be crammed. Charles Darwin later was to state, without too much exaggeration, "The science of geology is enormously indebted to Lyell—more so, as I believe, than to any other man who ever lived" (Barlow 1958).

ANCIENT HUMANS REVISITED

With Lyell, uniformitarianism was to become the orthodox perspective in geology. The earth was old, and its story could be read in its ancient layers. Discoverers of primitive-looking stone artifacts found at a great depth began to suggest great antiquity for humanity as well—how old was still a matter of conjecture, but certainly far greater than Bishop Ussher's calculation of 5,700 years. With the discovery of clusters of such stone tools and with no evidence of the use of metals found alongside, it became increasingly obvious that human cultures had changed dramatically since the makers of those stone tools had lived.

Cultures Ancient and Changing

Just six years after the initial publication of Lyell's *Principles of Geology*, a guidebook was published describing the artifacts that could be seen in the

Danish National Museum in Copenhagen. Written by Christian Jurgensen Thomsen, the guidebook organized the museum's collection chronologically into three prehistoric ages—stone, bronze, and iron—based on the most-favored raw materials used to make tools during each of the three epochs.

Inherent in Thomsen's **three-age system** was the notion that culture had changed through time, in a predictable sequence. The three ages were developmental as well as chronological. There was an implied succession of increasing technological sophistication, an evolution toward tools that were better (more effective, more durable) but also more difficult to manufacture.

That culture had been undergoing great change during human tenure on the planet was no more evident in the nineteenth century than was the notion of an ancient earth. In fact, it was surprising to some thinkers that the very oldest traces of human culture did not include metal tools. They assumed that metallurgy had simply always been around. Thomsen deserves credit for recognizing and making explicit in his guidebook that the archaeological record clearly shows great changes in human technological abilities.

More Stone Tools

In 1837 a French customs official, Jacques Boucher de Perthes, initiated a long and detailed search for flint axes. In 1839 he began publishing volumes about the tools he had found, concluding that they represented an ancient and culturally primitive period of human history from long before Noah's flood. Boucher de Perthes was not taken seriously by most scientists. Another two decades would pass before mounting evidence led to a fundamental shift in the view of those studying human antiquity. This shift would accompany one of the most momentous events in the history of science: the 1859 publication of Charles Darwin's great work, *The Origin of Species by Means of Natural Selection.*

FIGURE 2.6

Charles Darwin, the father of modern biological evolutionary theory. (Negative no. 108781, courtesy of Department of Library Services, American Museum of Natural History)

CHARLES DARWIN AND THE ANTIQUITY OF LIFE

In 1828, a bright, young Englishman entered Cambridge University in pursuit of a degree in theology. His name was Charles Darwin (Figure 2.6).

Darwin took a natural science course at Cambridge under a brilliant scientist and charismatic professor, John Stephens Henslow, a remarkable teacher who became a mentor to many of his students. Henslow regularly took his students on long geological tours and on botanical and zoological field trips; and he often invited his students to parties attended by some of the most brilliant scientists of the time, where discussions of astronomy, geology, and biology continued long into the evening. It was in the heady atmosphere of Henslow's world that the young theology student Charles Darwin began to reconsider the course mapped out for his life as a simple country parson.

Henslow genuinely liked Darwin and felt that he had a real knack for observing nature. He recommended his young student to the post of naturalist aboard a British government survey ship, the *Beagle,* which was to produce detailed sailing charts of the coast of South America and then circumnavigate the world. The voyage would begin in 1831 when Darwin was just 22 years old. The task of the ship's naturalist was to collect geological, botanical, and zoological specimens in all areas visited by the ship. Despite some initial misgivings on the part of his father, who was still supporting him financially, Darwin agreed to the position and began a mission that was supposed to last 2 years but actually lasted closer to 5. Thus, events had conspired to push the young theology student to collect the data that would, 28 years later, lead to one of the most important books ever published in the name of science.

The Voyage of the Beagle

Darwin kept a detailed journal of all that he saw during that remarkable five-year expedition (Darwin 1845)—arguably the most significant travel log ever kept. During frequent port stops and landfalls, Darwin walked or rode on horseback across some 3,000 mi, collecting thousands of specimens, which he sent back to England for further study by experts in botany, zoology, and geology. Indeed, Darwin's collection and investigation of the plants and animals of these previously unexplored territories (unexplored by a Western naturalist, anyway) opened the eyes of many Europeans to the immense and often unrecognized diversity of life present in the world.

A Paradigm for Life

During Darwin's time the commonly accepted explanation for life's diversity, commonalities, and interrelationships was the will of God. Life was seen as having been "fixed" (or set) by God at creation. In fact, Karl von Linné, the well-known eighteenth-century Swedish biologist better known as Carolus Linnaeus, had developed a **taxonomy** of living things that we still use today (dividing all life into branching categories of kingdom, phylum, class, order, family, genus, and species). This taxonomy assumed that each species was immutable and had been fixed at creation. Similarities and differences among various species were explained by Linnaeus as simply reflecting the way God made them in the beginning. As a popular saying maintained, "God created and Linnaeus arranged."

Darwin was certainly aware of the Linnaean taxonomic system, but his observations during the voyage made it increasingly difficult for him to accept the tenet of the immutability (or "fixity") of species. Darwin was not the first to question this concept. In fact, his grandfather, Erasmus Darwin, had written about the evolution of life, and a French naturalist, Jean-Baptiste Lamarck, had developed a detailed explanation of how organisms evolved by sensing a change in their environment, acting in some new way in response to that change, and then passing those changes down to subsequent generations.

Darwin, ever the empiricist, was not all that interested in his grandfather's largely speculative approach. He also felt that Lamarck's mechanism was simply unsupported by real data. Though he came to no definite conclusions of his own during the voyage (at least not in anything he wrote), Darwin collected some provocative information on this subject that set the stage for the evolutionary drama he ultimately was to unfold.

The Mutability of Species

Although he didn't think it was important at the time, Darwin recognized that animals he encountered on islands off the coast of South America resembled, but were not identical to, animals found on the mainland, where they must have originated. The island descendants of mainland species seemed to have altered from their original state after migrating. The descendants must have become better adjusted, or **adapted,** to the different environmental conditions in their new habitats. Even on different islands within island chains, individual kinds of animals resembled each other, though differing in significant attributes from island to island.

For example, on the Falkland Islands, off the southeast coast of South America, foxes were recognizably different from one island to the next. All these island foxes must have come from the mainland, so why were they different from mainland foxes, why did they vary from island to island, and how could this variety have occurred? On the Galápagos Islands, 500 mi west of the northwestern coast of South America, Darwin found that tortoises living on each of the dozen large islands could be differentiated, and so could finches—small birds whose source was certainly the mainland. The finches did not look precisely like any other South American finch, and they differed in form and behavior among islands. How had each type of finch become uniquely adjusted to the particular features of its island, if the finch species (like all species in the Linnaean view) was immutable and fixed at creation? This mystery simply could not be explained within the accepted paradigm of the fixity of species.

In 1836, after a long and successful voyage, Darwin and the *Beagle* returned triumphantly to England. Many of Darwin's reports and specimens had preceded him, and he returned to find his work roundly praised by the scientific community. Darwin met and was befriended by geologist Charles Lyell, who was extremely grateful that Darwin's geological observations matched precisely his uniformitarian view of the evolution of the earth.

Darwin's Conversion to Evolution

Darwin's theoretical edifice was to be constructed with the brick and mortar of his own scientific observations and those of his colleagues. Lyell supplied the uniformitarian perspective, which provided eons of time. Economist Thomas Malthus, in his *Essay on the Principle of Population* (1798), which Darwin read in 1838, provided the raw numbers when he pointed out the ability of animals to reproduce at a rate far greater than that necessary to maintain a steady population. Darwin's own observations of the incredible diversity within and among species provided evidence of the extreme range of variation of life on the planet. And Darwin's growing understanding of **artificial selection** in agriculture and animal breeding—where people decide which individual animals or plants will be allowed to live and reproduce in order to pass down traits viewed as preferable by the human breeders—provided an analogous mechanism for how change within a species might be wrought without human intervention. With this information as his foundation, Darwin began building his theory of **descent with modification,** based on the process he called **natural selection.**

In 1844, Darwin wrote a synopsis of his new theory, explaining "the simple way by which species become exquisitely adapted to various ends" (Bowlby 1990, 254), but he was not ready to go public with his revolutionary idea. First, he felt he needed an enormous data set to support his radically new perspective. He also wished to answer all possible criticisms before they were posed. Further, throughout his life he had been subject to horrible attacks of nausea, heart palpitations, and other symptoms that seem to have been brought on by unpleasant events in his life. As a result, Darwin was not ready to submit for publication the discussion of his theory or to submit himself to the intense controversy and personal criticism it was certain to generate. This reluctance to go public changed only in 1858 on learning that Alfred Russel Wallace, a younger man who was not a trained scientist but a professional collector of botanical and zoological specimens, was circulating a paper he had written in which he proposed almost precisely the same mechanism for change that Darwin had theorized.

THE ORIGIN OF SPECIES

So, in 1859, Darwin's masterpiece, *The Origin of Species by Means of Natural Selection,* at last was published. In the introduction to the book, Darwin succinctly articulates the essence of his theory:

> As many more individuals of each species are born than can survive; and as, consequently, there is a frequently recurring struggle for existence, it follows that any being, if it vary, however slightly in any manner profitable to itself, under the complex and sometimes varying conditions of life, will have a better chance of surviving, and thus be *naturally selected.* From the strong principle of inheritance, any selected variety will tend to propagate its new and modified form. (Darwin 1859, 7)

As Darwin saw it, variation within a species provided some individuals with characteristics that allowed them a better chance for survival under the conditions established by nature. Those individuals were "selected" by nature to survive and pass along their advantageous characteristics to their offspring.

Given the time allowed for by Lyell, the vast numbers of organisms that pass through this world as calculated by Malthus, and the huge amount of variation seen by Darwin, a process of selection analogous to that maintained in breeding programs could produce not just a new, improved version of the same species, but a new species!

In this way, for example, finches of a single species might lose their way in a storm and get blown to an island where conditions were quite different from those at their mainland home. Many of the finches would die, unable to survive in their new circumstances; but a few might, by chance, possess characteristics that would enable them to endure. They would pass those features on to their offspring; and over many generations, birds with those qualities would continue to be selected for—that is, to survive. After a time, the island finches would no longer resemble the mainland finches. Given sufficient time, they might become so different that they would be a different species entirely.

Human Evolution

As astounding as Darwin's suggestions were, perhaps what bothered people most was the deduction that this process could be applied to the evolution of human beings. An ape with a slightly larger brain and greater intelligence might be more apt to survive than his or her slower cousins. Over time, through natural selection, large brains would be increasingly selected for, and eventually the ape would become human. The implication so shocked Charles Lyell that, though by and large a supporter of Darwin and a close personal friend, he never quite accepted that human intellect could be produced via such a mechanism.

Darwin knew how delicate the subject of human evolution might be. In 1857 he wrote Wallace: "You ask whether I shall discuss 'man.' I think I shall avoid the whole subject, as so surrounded with prejudices; though I fully admit that it is the highest and most interesting problem for the naturalist" (Bowlby 1990, 325). He hinted at the applicability of natural selection to humanity in *Origin* when he concluded that, by the application of the theory, "Much light will be thrown on the origins of man and his history" (Darwin 1859, 243). As we will see throughout this book, Darwin was right.

The Human Factor

In 1856, the year before Darwin indicated to Wallace his desire to steer clear of any mention of humanity in his discussion of evolution, a partial fossil skull was found in the Neander Valley in Germany (see Figure 6.10). At least two similar skulls had been found previously in Europe (in Belgium and on Gibraltar), but these largely were ignored. The Neander Valley skull, like those found previously, was as large as a modern human skull, though it looked quite different. As we will see in Chapter 6, while some scientists declared the large, flat skull with great ridges of bone above where the eyes had been to be a pathological oddity, others saw it as representative of an ancient race of humans.

Discoveries related to the question of human antiquity accelerated in the late 1850s. A few months before the November 1859 publication of Darwin's *The Origin of Species,* the respected geologist John Prestwich delivered an address to the Royal Society of London announcing his belief that flint tools he had seen in France, which had been excavated by Boucher de Perthes, provided convincing evidence of the great antiquity of humanity. The archaeologist John Evans had accompanied Prestwich to France and had come to the same conclusion. The week after Prestwich's speech, Evans delivered a speech to the Society of Antiquaries—the same society John Frere had written to 62 years earlier—in which he asserted that Frere had been right after all. The sites he saw in France convinced him of the great age of the flint artifacts he saw there—they looked just like the artifacts Frere had discovered, and they were in a similar stratigraphic position. Evans concluded: "This much appears to be established beyond doubt, that in a period of antiquity remote beyond any of which we have hitherto found traces, this portion of the globe was peopled by man" (Daniel and Renfrew 1988, 37).

With the notion of a uniformly changing, very ancient earth in place, the new artifactual and skeletal evidence began to convince many people of the great antiquity of the human species. There still was substantial debate over what "great antiquity" meant on any kind of a fixed time scale. No date could be assigned to the early humans who had made the stone tools, nor could any age be assigned to the German skull. But scientists were clearly shifting their opinion and beginning to view the earth and the human species as ancient—far older than 6,000 years.

Also in 1859, the venerable Charles Lyell announced that he was now convinced of the chronological length of the human presence on the earth, which he knew to be ancient (Daniel and Renfrew 1988, 37). His publication of the *Geological Evidences of the Antiquity of Man* would come four years later (1863), providing a massive compendium of the evidence for ancient human traces. Lyell's initial statement of support for great age for humanity and especially the publication of *Geological Evidences* meant the previous heresy of a greatly ancient human species now bore "the stamp of scientific orthodoxy" (Van Riper 1993, 9).

CULTURES EVOLVING

Led first by Hutton and then Lyell, the uniformitarianists had shown that the earth was old; the pages of its ancient history were the strata that lay beneath our feet. Archaeologists had discovered human-made objects on those ancient pages, proving the great antiquity of humanity within the stratigraphic history of the planet.

Darwin had gone on to show that within the lengthy history of the earth, plants and animals had changed dramatically; they had, in fact, evolved. And now, the ancient human-made objects found by the early archaeologists—the stone tools—provided clear evidence that human culture had evolved as well. As Charles Lyell himself pointed out (1863, 379), if culture had remained constant throughout human history, then archaeologists should have been finding "buried railways or electrical telegraphs" along with other scientifically advanced artifacts in ancient stratigraphic layers. Instead, archaeologists were finding stone tools, admittedly finely made but essentially and fundamentally primitive, associated with the bones of extinct animals in ancient stratigraphic levels. Clearly, this was evidence of great change from the culture of the earliest humans to that of the modern (nineteenth-century) world. As surely as geologists had shown that the earth had sustained enormous change over a vast expanse of time and as surely as biologists now were showing that life itself had experienced great change, so archaeologists were showing that human behavior had also changed greatly during our species' history on earth.

The recognition of great cultural changes from earliest times to the present lent support for the three-age system and its identification of all that had happened in between. What Christian Thomsen understood and made concrete others now began to build on in constructing broad theories of cultural evolution. For example, Edward Tyler's *Researches into the Early History of Mankind and the Development of Civilization* (1865) expanded on Thomsen's chronology, subdividing his stone age into an "unground stone" phase (in which tools were produced by the presumably more primitive method of flaking or striking) and a "ground stone" phase (in which tools were produced by the presumably more advanced method of grinding and polishing).

For most thinkers in the nineteenth century, the cultural evolution they perceived in the archaeological record was synonymous with cultural progress. Tyler (1871, 198) characterized culture change as "in the main, an upward development." Tyler and others assumed that if the world and even human beings were not the stable, safe, reassuring entities they had once been presumed to be, at least the human past told a story of continual, if slow, improvement. And not surprisingly, nineteenth-century European scientists assumed that the pinnacle of cultural development was nineteenth-century Europe. To them, the archaeological record presented a long and remarkable tale of a species hoisting itself up from its original primitive state to an ever increasing level of civilization.

Some scholars suggested specific sequences of culture change that most of humanity had passed through in the long ascent toward modern civilization. For example, Lewis Henry Morgan (1877, 8) theorized that "the experience of mankind has run in nearly uniform channels." In Morgan's view, cultures evolve through stages he labeled savagery, barbarism, and civilization (with each stage involving substages) and are marked by increasingly complex material culture and greater sophistication in how people feed themselves. Where Thomsen's sequence dealt only with the advancement in the raw materials used to make tools, Morgan's included the invention of fire and pottery, the development of farming and animal husbandry, the use of iron tools, and, finally, the invention of a written, alphabetic language. In Morgan's view, virtually all cultures in human history had passed through his various stages, and those that were still in one of the more primitive levels by the nineteenth century had simply become "stuck" at some stage in this universal sequence as the result of something lacking in their society—for example, an important invention like metal or an alphabet.

We now view culture as adaptation, as the fundamental way in which people adjust to their surroundings. Cultures change as conditions change, and there is no necessary "upward" movement or progress. Cultures survive not because they become better, but because they become better adapted to their world. Nevertheless, thinkers like Thomsen, Tyler, and Morgan made the important observation, not self-evident in the nineteenth century, that human behavior has vastly changed through time. This behavior became translated into the material record, which provided the data the early archaeologists used to frame their cultural evolutionary constructs. That same material record—now much expanded—continues to provide much of the data on which this book is based. The methods by which data gathering is accomplished are the focus of the next chapter.

OUR MODERN VIEW

We began our historical discussion with a belief in an unchanging universe that was created less than 6,000 years ago by an omnipotent God and that was populated by plants, animals, and people whose forms and qualities were for-ever fixed at creation. That universe was simple, predictable, and reassuring.

We now hold the modern scientific view of the universe and life, initially es-poused by Lyell and Darwin, as ancient and dynamic, unpredictable and seren-dipitous, awesome and awful. It is no wonder, therefore, that so many people are terrified by the modern scientific perspective and retreat to creationism.

What we have lost in terms of a pleasant and comforting view of the world and the human species' place in it is more than made up for in the infinitely fascinating story we can now tell of the evolution of our species. And, as seventeenth-century scientist and clergyman John Ray stated, "Those who scorn and decry knowledge should remember that it is knowledge that makes us men, superior to the animals and lower than the angels, that makes us capable of virtue and happiness such as animals and the irrational cannot attain" (Raven 1950, 251).

SUMMARY

Most thinkers in the seventeenth century believed that the world and all life within it had been established during the creation week and that their world was just as God had made it and reflected the perfection of creation.

Some natural scientists, on the other hand, saw the world as a "wreck," which had decayed since the time of creation. Viewing the world as quite young, perhaps no more than 6,000 years old, these thinkers suggested that the history of the earth had been marked by a string of catastrophes.

James Hutton and Charles Lyell were spokesmen for a different perspective. Rejecting claims of hypothetical catastrophes, they explained the appearance of the earth on the basis of observable, slow, steady, and uniform natural processes. They asserted that such observable natural phenomena could produce the current state of the earth if afforded sufficient time. They measured the age of the earth not in thousands of years but in hundreds of thousands and even millions of years. Especially during the nineteenth century, researchers began uncovering tantalizing bits of evidence—in the form of flint implements together with the bones of extinct animals and even those of human beings—that suggested this ancient earth had been populated by early forms of humanity.

Charles Darwin viewed the biological world as the result of natural processes of change. His theory of natural selection provided an overarching explanation for the diversity of life on the planet. With the amount of time provided by Hutton's and Lyell's perspective of earth history, the process of natural selection could have produced the great diversity of life seen on the planet, the differences and similarities among different kinds of organisms, even the evolution of humanity.

TO LEARN MORE

Technical Summaries

For a firsthand glimpse of how the scientists discussed in this chapter worked out the problems presented by the study of the origins of life and the planet and of how they reached the conclusion that the earth was ancient and changing, there is no better place to go than the original works. These sources are cited in the text.

Popular Summaries

Two excellent sources on the history of archaeological and paleoanthropological thoughts are Glyn Daniel and Colin Renfrew's *The Idea of Prehistory* (1988) and William Stiebing Jr.'s *Uncovering the Past: A History of Archaeology* (1993). For more detailed coverage of the early history of the discipline, see Donald Grayson's *The Establishment of Human Antiquity* (1983) and A. Bowdoin Van Riper's *Men Among the Mammoths: Victorian Science and the Discovery of Human Prehistory* (1993). If you are interested in a detailed discussion of the life of Charles Darwin, John Bowlby's 1990 monograph, *Charles Darwin; A New Life,* is simply terrific. Charles Raven's 1950 biography, *John Ray, Naturalist: His Life and Works,* shows how a great seventeenth-century thinker accommodated both his religious faith and his scientific perspective.

On the Web

One of the best places on the Web to learn more about the creation-evolution debate is the site called TalkOrigins found at http://www.talkorigins.org/. This site has an extensive archive of articles, which often respond in great detail to the claims made by people opposed to the theory of evolution. How the second law of thermodynamics does *not* contradict evolution, the impossibility of Noah's ark, how the Piltdown hoax exemplifies the self-correcting nature of science—all are on this Web site.

KEY TERMS

evolution

creationist

adaptation

culture

catastrophist

uniformitarianism

erosion

weathering

stratigraphic

stratigraphy

three-age system

taxonomy

adapted

artificial selection

descent with
modification

natural selection

3

Probing the Past

CHAPTER OVERVIEW

Paleoanthropologists and archaeologists study the physical remains of human beings and our evolutionary ancestors. They also examine the material remains that result from the behavior of these ancient ancestors: the things they made and used and then lost or discarded. Through analysis of ancient and modern human bones as well as ancient artifacts, paleoanthropologists and archaeologists hope to better understand the ways in which our ancestors evolved and adapted. This chapter summarizes some of the many techniques used by these scientists to paint a picture of the human past.

Applicable range of major dating techniques

	1 million	900,000
Radiocarbon Radioactive decay		
Archaeomagnetism Alignment with changes in location of the earth's magnetic pole		
Dendrochronology Counting of annual growth rings of trees		
Uranium series Radioactive decay		
Obsidian hydration Chemical process: accumulation of weathering rind on artifact		
Fission track Radioactive decay leaves microscopic tracks in crystals at known rate		
Luminescence Radiation damage: accumulation of TL in crystals		
Electron spin resonance Radiation damage: accumulation of unpaired electrons in crystals		
Potassium argon (K/Ar) Radioactive decay		
Paleomagnetism Alignment of particles with the earth's magnetic field		

800,000	700,000	600,000	500,000	400,000	300,000	200,000	100,000	Present

Every field of scientific study presents its own set of challenges. Researchers in each branch of science must, of necessity, develop a specific set of methods for data collection as well as techniques of data analysis and interpretation. Archaeology and paleoanthropology are no different. Our data are the objects that ancient humans and human ancestors made, used, lost, abandoned, or discarded, along with the physical remains of the species themselves. Archaeologists and paleoanthropologists have developed procedures for finding these ancient remains along with techniques for extracting from them information about the lives of our ancient ancestors. This chapter summarizes some of the more significant methods used in archaeology and paleoanthropology for data collection and analysis. (For a more detailed discussion of archaeological or paleoanthropological methodology, see any of the works listed in "To Learn More" at the end of this chapter.)

The "Science" in the Study of the Past

Science often begins with objective observation of the world or universe. For example, biologists examine living things; astronomers focus on other planets, stars, and galaxies; and geologists observe the earth itself. Anthropologists, on the other hand, concentrate on humanity, with paleoanthropologists and archaeologists focusing more specifically on the human past.

All scientists observe the world and look for patterns or correlations, cause-and-effect relationships, trends, and trajectories in an attempt to puzzle out the rules that govern how the world works—how the earth was formed, how rivers flow, how life originated, how humanity evolved, or how people adapt through their cultures. From the things they observe and the patterns they perceive, scientists come up with general explanations, or **hypotheses,** for what they have observed.

Scientists are not content, however, just to generalize about the world. They also need to test these hypotheses by predicting what other data will be found if a hyothesis is valid, if it accurately explains how things work. Paleoanthropologists and archaeologists accomplish these tasks by applying the procedures outlined in this chapter and by a rigorous adherence to the scientific method.

Our goal may be to understand the mysteries of life, but science is a process as much as a result and rarely provides absolute answers to our questions in any field. With our imperfect knowledge and incomplete understanding, usually we can expect no more than increasingly better approximations about how things are—or were. Certainty is a rare commodity in any of the sciences.

In archaeology and paleoanthropology we are examining our own human past and time periods enormously distant from our own. It is one thing for a chemist to examine a chemical reaction and suggest a rule that governs how those reactions progress; it is one thing for a microbiologist to focus on a colony of bacteria and suggest a hypothesis for how those bacteria react to heat or an overabundance of food. These chemical reactions and bacteria are of the here and now, and they are apart from us. It is quite another thing for paleoanthropologists and archaeologists, who gaze back across the centuries, millennia, and eons of human history where the data are ancient, elusive, and rare and where our interpretations impinge on how we view ourselves. Did we humans begin our journey as a "killer ape," and what does it mean to us if we did? Were the world's first civilizations dependent on slavery and warfare, and if so what does this knowledge tell us about our twentieth-century civilization? As scientists, we must always be aware of and try to transcend our own preconceptions of what we think the past *should* tell us—or what we would like it to tell us—about ourselves. Our constructs of the past should be objective and free of our own temporal and cultural biases. This ideal is not easy to achieve, and we archaeologists and paleoanthropologists have sometimes fallen short of these goals. Further, we must recognize that our interpretations of the human past are approximations subject to continual refinement, major overhaul, or even complete abandonment as new data and new ways of looking at the same data come to the fore.

PALEOANTHROPOLOGICAL AND ARCHAEOLOGICAL SITES

Paleoanthropological and archaeological **sites** are places where physical evidence of a past human presence can be recovered. Such evidence consists of (1) the skeletal remains of human beings or human ancestors, (2) **artifacts**— objects made and used by past peoples (Figure 3.1), and (3) **ecofacts**—environmental elements that exhibit traces of human use or activity, such as the bones of butchered animals (see Figure 9.18, for example).

Wherever people lived or worked, they used material from the surrounding environment: stone, clay, metal, wood, bone, plant fiber, seeds, antler, animal hides, and so on. These materials ultimately are lost, used up and discarded, abandoned, or hidden away for future use. Where conditions in the soil allow for their preservation, these items can be found and recovered for analysis by scientists who study the human past. Together, these physical remnants make up the archaeological site.

Sites are defined not only by the recovered objects themselves, but also by the physical arrangement of the remains. The preserved spatial context of archaeological remains—where things were used and left by an ancient people—allows us to reconstruct the activities that took place at a site. Most reconstructions of past times are based on analysis of human remains, artifacts, and ecofacts, as well as their spatial arrangement at sites where people lived or performed special tasks. Sites can be small and short-term, like hunting

FIGURE 3.1

Artifacts, features, and sites are primary elements of archaeological analysis. For example, all of these 1,500-year-old stone blades from Connecticut are artifacts: objects that ancient people made and used (top). This 4,000-year-old stone platform represents a cooking feature: it is the physical manifestation of an activity conducted along the banks of the Farmington River (middle). Hovenweep, located in southwestern Colorado, is a nearly 1,000-year-old site, a place where people lived and worked (bottom). (K. L. Feder)

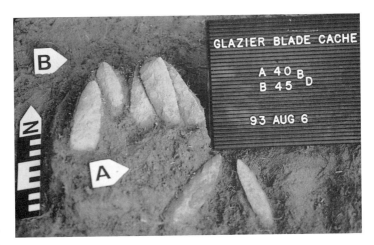

camps, or large and permanent, like the sites of the world's first cities in Mesopotamia (see Chapter 13).

How Sites Are Formed

Sites come into existence through a series of site formation processes: Tools can be discarded or lost; food remains can be thrown in a trash pit or pile; dead bodies may be casually abandoned or intentionally and ceremonially buried; valuable objects may be "cached," or hidden away, for a future retrieval that never takes place; human ancestors may be killed by animals and their remains dragged into a lair, and so forth. The study of how paleontological remains ended up in a particular place is called **taphonomy;** we can also apply this term to the study of how paleoanthropological or archaeological remains came to rest in their place of discovery. Recognition of how items became part of the paleoanthropological or archaeological record provides insights into the behavior of the human beings who left those artifacts behind.

Archaeological artifacts and ecofacts used or produced together to accomplish a task—to make stone tools, to prepare food, to carry out a ceremony—often are deposited together on the ground in a pattern that reflects the spatial arrangement of the activity. These clusters of archaeological material are called **features** and can be analyzed in our attempt to reconstruct a particular activity or set of behaviors. When areas of activity are intact—in other words, where the items used together and deposited together are left exactly where they fell by ancient people—we use the term **primary refuse.** Just like us in the modern world, however, ancient people also often cleaned up the places where they carried out tasks, removing the objects used and produced from their primary contexts to a designated refuse area or areas. Just as we use refuse dumps and recycling facilities in our towns and cities, people in the past often took their trash to a pile or pit, removing from the immediate vicinity of their living quarters material that might be dangerous, that might attract wild animals or noxious insects, or that might simply otherwise be a nuisance (perhaps because of its smell). We call such deposits **secondary refuse.**

How Sites Are Preserved

Once material objects are laid on or in the earth, natural processes may cover, protect, and preserve them. Volcanic ash or lava, silt from a flooding river, sand blown by the wind, a collapsed cave roof, an avalanche—all may cover the objects left behind by people, preserving them until nature or anthropologists uncover them many years later. Some of the materials used by people, especially stone tools and pottery, preserve very well under most circumstances. Other materials, like bone and plant remains, require special conditions for preservation. When archaeologists and paleoanthropologists are lucky, an archaeological site is itself like a fossil, a preserved physical representation of a past people and way of life.

FIGURE 3.2

At Skara Brae, in the Ork-ney Islands north of Scot-land, an ancient site a few thousand years old was ex-posed by the winds and waves of a North Atlantic storm. (K. L. Feder)

How Sites Are Found

Archaeological sites are found in a number of ways. While some natural pro-cesses may preserve sites, other such processes may expose them. Rivers cut-ting into their banks, wind blowing sand away from an area, or waves eroding a beach may bring to light ancient, buried remains (Figure 3.2). Many of the sites related to the earliest history of humanity have been exposed by these processes of erosion. Places such as Olduvai Gorge in Tanzania and the Hadar region of Ethiopia (see Chapters 4 and 5) present naturally exposed layers of ancient geological deposits (Figure 3.3). By walking over these places sys-tematically, paleoanthropologists and archaeologists found many of the im-portant ancestral human fossils discussed in this book.

In other cases, archaeologists do not have the luxury of naturally exposed ancient layers in which to search for artifacts, ecofacts, or human skeletons. In these areas, scientists search for sites through a process of subsurface sam-pling, placing **test pits** at regular intervals in an attempt to locate ancient material buried by natural processes (Figure 3.4). In some cases, sophisticated **remote-sensing** devices—ground-penetrating radar, proton magnetometers, electrical resistivity meters—can help in the search for sites by probing for anomalous readings under the surface that may indicate the presence of bur-ied cultural material or soil disturbance by ancient people. Aerial photography can help identify large-scale land modifications or buried remains that affect the growth of vegetation.

FIGURE 3.3

The ancient soil levels and many sites of Hadar have been revealed through the slow-acting process of erosion. Much of Don Johanson's work on the fossil species Australopithecus afarensis *(see Chapter 4) has been conducted at Hadar (see also Figure 1.5 and Color Plate 1).* (Courtesy of the Institute of Human Origins)

FIGURE 3.4

In areas of the world where natural processes have not exposed ancient sites, archaeologists must dig to reveal buried cultural deposits. Test pits are often excavated to explore an area for buried archaeological material. (K. L. Feder)

How Data Are Recovered

Once a site has been found, the arduous task of extracting the physical evidence from the ground begins. Paleoanthropological and archaeological evidence is rare, precious, and often fragile, so the methods used to unearth it have been designed accordingly.

We must recover our data with great care. Though we may use power equipment and picks and shovels to remove the culturally sterile overburden, once within the zone of a site, we ordinarily rely on handheld trowels, dental

FIGURE 3.5

To maintain the spatial relationships among the materials found at a site, archaeologists often excavate in square units, slowly peeling away soil layers. (K. L. Feder)

FIGURE 3.6

The stones lining the bottom of a 4,000-year-old earth oven demarcate this archaeological feature. The stones were heated in a fire and then placed in the bottom of a pit, where the heat radiated by the stones was used for cooking. (K. L. Feder)

picks, and brushes to remove the soil enclosing site materials (Figure 3.5). Material may be left exactly where found in order to expose the possible **associations** among the remains. For example, a single stone, found and then tossed in a bag, is not nearly as informative as a series of stones, each one left in place, that together denote an earth oven (Figure 3.6).

As careful as we are in excavating a site, we can miss small fragmentary remains. All excavated soil ordinarily is sifted through wire screening of ¼-in, ⅛-in, or even smaller mesh, to ensure 100% recovery. In some cases, the soil matrix may be taken to an on- or off-site lab, where standing water may be used to help in separating artifacts, ecofacts, or human bone from the surrounding soil.

ANALYZING ARCHAEOLOGICAL DATA

How Artifacts Are Analyzed

In analyzing artifacts, at a minimum we want to know where the raw materials for the objects came from, how the items were manufactured, and how they were used.

The Sources of Raw Materials   Raw material sources—where a particular rock type for making stone tools or clay for making pots was obtained—can be traced by analyzing small amounts of impurities in those raw materials. The percentages of particular impurities often are unique and diagnostic of specific sources and can serve as a fingerprint for place of origin when re-searchers apply techniques that fall under the heading **trace element analysis.** Artifacts are examined for their particular percentages of these trace elements. Possible sources for the raw material from which the artifact was made are also examined for their trace element percentages. If a raw material source and the artifact have matching trace element profiles, a scientist can usually suggest that the raw material for the artifact derived from that source.

For example, obsidian is a volcanically produced natural glass found throughout the world. It can be chipped into extremely sharp-edged tools, and virtually everywhere it was available, ancient people used it as a raw material for cutting, scraping, or piercing tools. The trace element signatures of obsidian spearpoints found at the 11,000-year-old Lindenmeier site in Colorado were determined through a procedure called **neutron activation analysis** (Wilmsen 1974). The trace element percentages for the obsidian spearpoints were then compared to those determined for a number of natural obsidian sources in the western United States. As a result, the obsidian used to make the spearpoints found at Lindenmeier could be traced to two partic-ular obsidian sources: one in northeastern Wyoming, the other in central New Mexico. Most likely, the inhabitants of Lindenmeier either passed through these regions during their seasonal migration or traded with groups who lived near the obsidian sources.

Tool Manufacture and Use   Through **experimental replication,** the process of attempting to authentically re-create ancient artifacts, researchers can assess how an item was made. They also examine historically described groups that possessed a technology analogous to that of the ancient people being studied. Scientists can deduce the use an artifact served from its **morphology**—its

FIGURE 3.7

Burials are archaeological features. They represent a moment in time when a community laid to rest a companion, friend, loved one—or ruler. Burials often reflect the social and economic status of the deceased and, of course, the religious beliefs of the community, especially as these relate to the meaning of death. This museum representation of the main burial of Mound 72, at Cahokia (see Chapter 14) reflects the care with which the residents of this complex community disposed of the remains of an important ruler. (Courtesy of Cahokia Mounds Historic Site)

form, what it looked like—and by the evidence of **wear patterns.** Different actions (piercing, cutting, scraping, engraving, chopping) performed by different tools on different raw materials (stone, wood, leather, bone, antler) leave distinctive and diagnostic wear traces, or "edge damage" (striations, polish, scars) that can be assessed through replication (Shea 1992). In an experiment conducted by archaeologist Lawrence Keeley (1980), stone-tool replicas were used to perform different tasks on particular raw materials. For example, some tools were used to cut animal hide, some were used to saw wood, some were used to scrape meat off of bone, while others were used to drill in antler. Each tool used was then examined carefully under a microscope, and the particular kinds of resulting polish, damage, or wear on each were catalogued. This experiment essentially defined the damage or wear that accompanies each kind of use so that these tools and those from subsequent experiments and experimenters can serve as models for stone-tool wear patterns in the analysis of ancient specimens. If the ancient wear patterns match those seen on a particular experimental tool, researchers can conclude that the archaeological implement was used in much the same way.

Social Patterns   Along with providing insights into technology and use, artifacts can sometimes help illuminate less concrete aspects of ancient lifeways. The particular style of an artifact made by an individual may tell us something about who taught the maker. How people learn to make objects within a culture is a social decision. For example, they may learn from a parent who is passing down a family tradition of spearpoint or ceramic styles. The style seen in the archaeological remains, therefore, embodies this aspect of an ancient social system.

Some archaeological features even more directly reveal the nonmaterial practices of a people. Most obvious here are burials, which often directly reflect a group's religious ideology as it relates to recognition of the significance of death as well as possible belief in an afterlife (Figure 3.7). Neandertals (see Chapter 6) interred their dead with tools and food 60,000 years ago, and what we uncover may tell us much about their perspective on life and death. Egyptian pharaohs were laid to rest in sumptuous splendor (see Chapter 13), and what we unearth in their pyramids informs us of their beliefs about the meaning of death.

How Ecofacts Are Analyzed

Animal bones, charred seeds, nut fragments, the shells of marine organisms, and fruit pits recovered at sites may represent the food remains of past people. Since diet is an important part of a culture, scientists would like to reconstruct the subsistence practices of prehistoric people.

Because the skeletons of different animal species are usually distinctive, the kinds of animals present in an archaeological deposit can often be identified if remains are not too fragmented. Cut marks on bone and charring from a fire are good indicators that the animal was used for food. Many archaeology labs possess **osteological comparative collections,** or bone libraries, where ancient specimens can be compared to known, labeled specimens to help identify the species recovered in excavation.

The minimum number of animals represented in the **faunal assemblage** at a site can also be reconstructed. Because most animals exhibit two distinct forms on the basis of sex—that is, **sexual dimorphism**—scientists often can distinguish male from female animals. In addition, because animals go through a number of **osteological** developmental stages—changes in their bones as they grow and mature—the age at death of an animal hunted, killed, cooked, and eaten by a prehistoric people can often be determined. Furthermore, the bones of wild animals can be differentiated from those of domesticated animals: Domesticated animals frequently are smaller than their wild ancestors; the teeth of domesticated dogs are more crowded than those of their wolf progenitors; and the bones of wild animals are often denser than those of their domesticated descendants. We can learn much about the subsistence strategies of an ancient people if we can determine the species of an animal and its sex and age, whether the people hunted only older animals, and whether they avoided killing females or killed most of the young males but allowed females to survive to adulthood (a common pattern among domesticated animals).

Plant remains, including seeds, nuts, and wood, can be recovered and analyzed, and the contribution of plant foods to the diet can be assessed. Since plants are available seasonally, the yearly schedule of a people can be reconstructed based on which plant foods are present at a site and which are absent. We usually can differentiate the seeds, grains, or fruits of wild species from those that have been altered by humans through **artificial selection** (see Chapter 11) in the process of domestication.

How Human and Prehuman Skeletal Remains Are Analyzed

The bones of human ancestors are an invaluable resource to paleoanthropologists and archaeologists. To begin with, the fact that archaic forms of human beings existed is shown most clearly by the presence of their bones, which are different from those of either apes or modern humans. (See the many photographs in Chapters 4–6 of creatures who were ancestral to us but, at the same time, were not quite us.) These bones can inform us about how human ancestors walked, the kinds of climates to which they were adapted, the foods they ate, their general level of nutrition, and the diseases and traumas from which they suffered. Comparing the bones of ancient human ancestors to those of modern people can help us place these specimens accurately in the human evolutionary line.

The Species Represented by a Bone   Ordinarily, the first question scientists ask about a bone concerns its species. When bones are complete, species identification is relatively straightforward because the precise form of each of the bones in an animal's body is unique to its species. For example, each of the 212 bones of the human body is uniquely human and cannot be mistaken for the bones of any other animal species. As a result, for the most part, the species of an intact bone found at an ancient archaeological site can be identified with great accuracy.

Species identification can be far more difficult when, as is often the case, a paleoanthropological or archaeological specimen is badly fragmented. Luckily, however, many bones exhibit landmarks, or features, that are species-specific; and so even if a bone is badly broken up, a very small fragment bearing one of those uniquely configured features can reveal its species. Human beings and our ancestors have many such features, and their presence helps in identifying a bone as human. In the case of ancestral forms of humanity, the degree of similarity as well as the amount of difference exhibited in their bones when compared to ours allows us to at least begin the process of assessing the overall similarities and differences between us.

Along with similarities and differences in their form, in a few cases, bones have provided researchers with intact segments of DNA, the biochemical blueprint for each species of animal. Where DNA has been preserved, the species of the individual who left the bone behind can sometimes be identified with great certainty even with only the tiniest of fragments.

The Sex of a Skeleton   This book will refer to specific fossils as being male or female. This identification is possible because of the recognition of sexual dimorphism. Human and ape males, for example, have skeletons that often are readily distinguishable from those of females of the same species. Among humans and apes, males tend to be larger, with heavier, denser, and rougher bones than females.

In addition, males tend to have larger, heavier skulls, with larger and rougher areas for muscle attachment. In some ape species, males have a bony crest on the top of their skulls, while females lack this feature. Also, in some species, males have a large ridge of bone above the eye orbits (sockets). Females either lack this feature or have a smaller bony ridge.

Among human beings, all of the various angles of the pelvis that control the overall size of the birth canal are, of necessity, larger in the vast majority of females than in males. With enough skeletal elements recovered, anthro-

AGES OF EPIPHYSEAL UNION

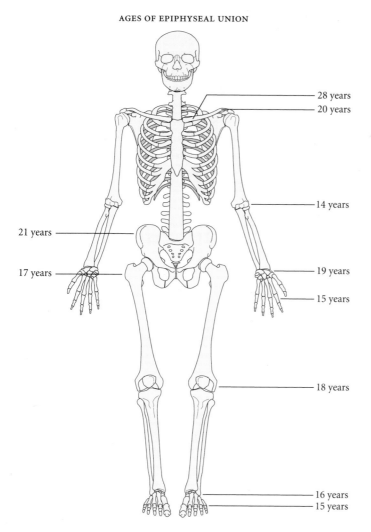

21 years

17 years

28 years
20 years

14 years

19 years

15 years

18 years

16 years
15 years

Age at which the epiphyses in the indicated area fuse to the shafts.

AGES OF TOOTH ERUPTION

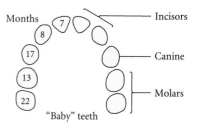

Months

7
8
17
13
22

Incisors

Canine

Molars

"Baby" teeth

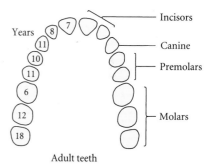

Years

7
8
11
10
11
6
12
18

Incisors

Canine

Premolars

Molars

Adult teeth

FIGURE 3.8

These diagrams show epiphyseal fusion for human beings and the age order of tooth eruption. Careful analysis of skeletal remains can reveal species, sex, age at death, nutritional status, cause of death, and geographic origin of the individual.

pologists can correctly distinguish males and females more than 95% of the time (Krogman 1973).

The Age at Death   Our discussion of human skeletons will occasionally mention the approximate age at death of an individual. As with animals, the bones of human children go through a series of developmental changes during the course of their lives. For example, tooth eruption and replacement provide developmental time-posts in human maturation. The **deciduous dentition**—the baby teeth—erupt above the gum line in a regular order and at fairly well established times (Figure 3.8). The permanent teeth then replace the baby teeth, also in a regular pattern, at reasonably well fixed ages until, finally, the wisdom teeth—the 18-year molars—come in. Using a chart like that shown in Figure 3.8, one can estimate the age of a child under 18, based on which teeth have already erupted above the gum line and which teeth have yet to appear.

Another developmental time-post can be found on the long bones—the various bones of the arms, legs, hands, and feet. When we are born, each of the long bones in our extremities is in three sections: a shaft, or **diaphysis,** and two endcaps, or **epiphyses** (*sing.,* epiphysis). In a process called **epiphyseal fusion,** the shafts and endcaps fuse to one another during growth at more or less set times during our teen years; this fusion reflects maturity and full growth (see Figure 3.8). Once again, by reference to the time range when each of the individual epiphyses fuses to its respective diaphysis, the age at death of an immature individual can be estimated fairly accurately.

Later in life, changes come less regularly and are subject to greater variation than are tooth eruption or epiphyseal fusion; and so determining the age of an adult's skeleton can be much trickier. For example, **cranial sutures**—the places where the different cranial plates come together—fuse through time. Young adults usually exhibit well-defined sutures, whereas aged people may have had their sutures disappear entirely. The region where the pubic bones come together—the **pubic symphysis**—can also be used to estimate the age at death of an individual. At their point of articulation, the faces of the left and right pubic bones go through a fairly regular, age-dependent sequence of changes.

Geographic Origin   We all recognize that people's physical features differ based on the geography of their origins; humans from different parts of the world possess a constellation of physical traits—skin color, nose shape, hair texture, body proportions—that distinguish them from people from other parts of the world. Skeletal traits also vary geographically; so, in some instances, the skeletal remains of individuals can be traced to the part of the world from which they came. For example, one reason we know that Native Americans originated in Asia is that the oldest skeletal remains in North America share a group of skeletal characteristics with Asian people (see Chapter 9).

Pathology and Disease   The bones in a human body are like a book on which some of that human's life experiences are written. Healed bone breaks, episodes of malnourishment during growth, specific dietary deficiencies, the ingestion of certain poisons, arthritis, tuberculosis, syphilis, cancers, and many other conditions leave recognizable traces on bones. These marks can be read by the specialist in **paleopathology.** Even the primary vegetal foods in a diet can be detected in bones, under certain circumstances. The paleopathological evidence on the bones of European Neandertals will be discussed in Chapter 6; the high level of malnutrition evident on their bones may explain why the Neandertals became extinct.

Preserved Bodies   Human skeletal remains are poignant reminders of our own mortality as well as valuable sources of information about the lives of ancient people. It is not so hard to imagine flesh on the bone and to consider that the dry, hard "specimen" analyzed by the archaeologist was once part of a living human being. But on rare occasions, the human being behind the osteological remains does not have to be imagined. Some complete—or nearly complete—bodies of ancient humans have been remarkably preserved. These rare discoveries offer the archaeologist a uniquely clear window on the past.

Nearly intact bodies 2,000, 3,000, even 4,000 years old have been recovered from Danish peat bogs (Glob 1969). The anaerobic character of the bogs—the complete lack of oxygen—prevents the survival of bacteria that eat flesh. Several partially complete bodies have been removed from the bogs, with internal organs intact, the skin—including fingerprints and body markings such as tattoos—fully preserved, facial expressions clearly discernible, and even the hair on their heads and eyebrows and eyelashes preserved virtually completely. The equivalent of autopsies conducted on the modern deceased can be performed on these ancient corpses. Diseases, traumas, parasites, and even the immediate cause of death can be diagnosed. Some of the bog bodies were the remains of people who had been executed by strangulation; in at least one case, the rope used was preserved along with its victim and was discovered intact and in place around the deceased's neck.

Even a person's final meal can be ascertained. In the case of the so-called Lindow Man found in a bog in England, the stomach contents revealed a final meal that was known to be a ceremonial offering ingested by sacrifice victims in an ancient Druid ceremony some 2,000 years ago (Ross and Robins 1989). Lindow Man, a probable Druid prince, ate a ceremonial charred cake before he was garroted and then interred in that peat bog.

Recently, another well-preserved ancient body was found. This so-called Ice Man was essentially freeze-dried beneath a glacier in the Italian Alps (Roberts 1993; Sjøvold 1992; Spindler 1994). When discovered accidentally by two German hikers, his body was just peeking out from the ice; they first thought it was a doll. Officials who arrived on the scene presumed the body was the remains of one of the many hikers who had died in recent, unexpected blizzards. Only when the body was removed from the ice and the surrounding area searched for evidence were ancient tools and clothing found: grass-lined shoes, a hafted copper axe, an ash-handled flint knife and woven grass sheath, an antler-tipped stick for sharpening the flint tool, twelve unfinished arrows, an unfinished bow, and a deerskin quiver. Radiocarbon dating (see the next section) indicates that the Ice Man lived about 5,000 years ago, yet his organs are intact and his flesh preserved; enigmatic tattoos—consisting of a series of parallel lines on his body—are still visible.

A detailed analysis of the Ice Man's body currently is under way. Preliminary results show that he probably was in his 40s or 50s when he died. X-rays show clearly that he suffered from arthritis in the neck as well as the lower back and right hip. His body also displays evidence of a number of traumas sustained during his life: Eight ribs show evidence of healed or healing fractures; the bones of at least one toe exhibit evidence typical of frostbite; the single preserved fingernail shows furrows that probably represent periods of reduced nail growth attributable to malnutrition or other bodily stress. Much more analysis remains to be done. The remarkable preservation of the Ice Man allows scientists to conduct a postmortem more than 5,000 years after his death.

DETERMINING THE AGE OF A SITE OR SPECIMEN

Until fairly recently in the history of paleoanthropology and archaeology, dating fossils and sites depended on sequences based on **stratigraphic** layering of the earth's surface—and a lot of guesswork. The fundamental technique had changed little since William Smith recognized its applicability in the late eighteenth and early nineteenth centuries (see Chapter 2). Dating was not absolute, but relative; scientists could determine whether a fossil or site was older or younger than another fossil or site depending on whether it was in a higher or lower stratigraphic layer. Fossil specimens and archaeological sites were assigned to particular stratigraphic layers. Though no certainty could be achieved, dates were derived based on assumed rates of formation of the layers above and below, on the guessed ages of fossils of extinct species found in association with human remains, and on a bit of intuition.

Dating Techniques Based on Radioactive Decay

Stratigraphic sequences, fossil associations, and even intuition are still used by paleoanthropologists and archaeologists in dating specimens, but these are no longer the only or primary methods of dating. Researchers can now rely on **radiometric** dating techniques based on the known rates of decay of several radioactive (unstable) **isotopes** (varieties) of common elements such as carbon (^{14}C dating), uranium (uranium series dating), and potassium (potassium/argon, or K/Ar, dating). These techniques provide **absolute dates** rather than **relative dates.** This does not necessarily mean they are accurate. The term *absolute* means only that we can associate a year or range of years with an object or site rather than place the sites or objects only in chronological order, as is the case in relative dating.

K/Ar Dating   One technique that has been particularly useful when applied to early human ancestors is **K/Ar dating** (Dalrymple and Lanphere 1969). A newer version of the technique, $^{40}Ar/^{39}Ar$, is more accurate and is used more often than the older procedure, but it is still based on measuring the amount of argon 40 buildup in volcanic rock (Deino, Renne, and Swisher 1998). Potassium, a common element found in volcanic deposits, decays into argon gas. When a volcanic layer is deposited, all of the argon already present from previous potassium decay bubbles off into the atmosphere. In a sense, the atomic clock in the ash or lava is set to zero and there is no argon left in the deposit. When the volcanic rock solidifies, the unstable potassium continues its slow decay to argon, which is trapped in the rock. Because we know the rate at which potassium decays to argon—its **half-life** is 1.250 billion years—by measuring how much argon has accumulated in the rock, we can determine how long the argon has been building up since the rock was last liquefied (that is, since the volcanic eruption deposited the lava) and, therefore, when that rock was deposited.

This method dates the rock and, usually, not the fossil, unless the creature was actually found within a lava flow. In the case of the Laetoli footprints featured in the "Prelude" in Chapter 4, dating the ash layer directly dates the footprints and, hence, the creature that made the prints. Ordinarily, however, human fossils are found above or below a datable layer. When a fossil is found above a dated layer, the fossil must be younger than that layer; that is, the creature was alive at some point after the volcanic layer was deposited. When a fossil is found beneath a dated layer, we can be sure it is older than that deposit; that is, the creature was living in the area before the dated layer was deposited. Under the best of circumstances, the fossils can be associated with layers both above and below them, enabling us to bracket their age.

^{14}C Dating   Carbon is an extremely abundant element and one of the building blocks of life on earth; every living thing contains carbon. The most common and stable isotope of carbon is ^{12}C. The numeral 12 refers to the number of particles in the carbon atom's nucleus: 6 positively charged particles, or protons, and 6 neutral particles, or neutrons. A radioactive isotope of carbon is produced when free neutrons originating in the sun stream toward earth and collide with nitrogen atoms in the earth's atmosphere. In some cases, these swiftly moving neutrons strike protons in the nuclei of atmospheric nitrogen atoms, ejecting them from the nuclei, while the neutrons stop, remaining in the nucleus (like a cue ball stopping still after it has struck another pool ball, sending it toward the corner pocket). Once this occurs, the nucleus is left with only 6 protons (one less than before the collision) and 8 neutrons (one more than previously). Because nitrogen must have 7 positively charged particles to be nitrogen, these atoms that have lost a proton have been transformed into another element, carbon, which has 6 protons. Unlike the standard and stable carbon atom with 12 nuclear particles—6 protons and 6 neutrons—the carbon atoms created by neutrons colliding with nitrogen atoms have 14—6 protons plus 8 neutrons. This configuration is what gives ^{14}C its name.

Because ^{14}C and ^{12}C are nearly identical chemically, they combine equally with oxygen to produce carbon dioxide, which is taken into plants through respiration. Plants exhale oxygen and keep the carbon atoms—both ^{14}C and ^{12}C—which they then use in the production of leaves, branches, roots, nuts, seeds, or fruits. Again, because ^{12}C and ^{14}C are so similar chemically, the proportion of ^{12}C to ^{14}C in grasses, trees, and bushes is the same as it is in the atmosphere (one trillion ^{12}C atoms for every one ^{14}C atom). When animals eat the products of these plants and again when other animals eat these animals, the ratio of ^{12}C to ^{14}C across the food web remains the same. In fact, all living things on earth are part of the carbon cycle and maintain the same proportion of stable ^{12}C to unstable ^{14}C during their lifetimes—a proportion that is, in turn, the same proportion as is seen in the atmosphere.

As an unstable isotope, ^{14}C ultimately decays, reverting back to the nitrogen atom from which it was produced. Like radioactive potassium, ^{14}C decays at a regular, naturally fixed half-life—in its case, 5,730 years. Once an organism dies, no new carbon is respired or ingested, and so the constantly decayfjing ^{14}C is no longer replenished. When an organism has been out of this carbon cycle for a substantial amount of time—measured in the hundreds, thousands, or tens of thousands of years—it contains significantly less ^{14}C than it did when it was alive. How much less can be measured and the amount of time it must have taken for that much loss to have occurred can be determined based on the known rate of decay.

So the decay of ^{14}C provides a natural clock, a kind of hourglass where the rate at which the sand pours into the bottom of the glass is known. One need only determine how much sand (^{14}C) was present initially in the hourglass (organism) and how much now remains to establish approximately when the glass was overturned (when the organism died). For the **radiocarbon dating (carbon dating,** ^{14}C dating) to produce accurate results, the item being dated needs to be at least a few hundred and ordinarily less than about 40,000 years old. **Accelerator mass spectrometry (AMS),** another method of ^{14}C dating, may ultimately extend the viable dating range back 10,000 to 30,000 years beyond this. For now, AMS dating allows for much smaller samples to be radiocarbon-dated.

Fluctuations in solar radiation cause changes in the production of ^{14}C in the atmosphere over broad stretches of time, and this variation has an effect on the dates derived through radiocarbon dating. During periods when ^{14}C was being produced at a slightly higher rate, dated items will produce dates that are a little younger than their actual, or "calendar," age. On the other hand, during periods when ^{14}C was being produced at a lower rate, dated items produce dates that are a little older than their actual age. A partial solution to this complication is provided by dendrochronology.

Dating Techniques Based on Biology

Dendrochronology, or tree-ring dating, is an extremely accurate biological dating technique, though its use is geographically limited. Its usefulness in dating archaeological sites results from four factors that apply in some areas of the world:

1. Trees add one growth ring every year.
2. The width of each year's tree ring is controlled by an environmental condition or set of conditions such as spring rainfall amount or temperature.
3. Any sequence of varying tree-ring widths over a long period of time is unique.
4. All trees in a given area reflect the same pattern of changes through time in tree-ring width.

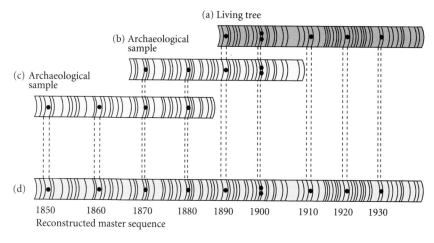

(a) Living tree

(b) Archaeological sample

(c) Archaeological sample

(d)

1850   1860   1870   1880   1890   1900   1910   1920   1930

Reconstructed master sequence

FIGURE 3.9

Cross section of tree rings from a living tree (a) over-laps the ring sequence from an archaeological sample (b), which, in turn, over-laps part of the sequence of another archaeological sample (c). The overlapping of many samples allows for the construction of a "mas-ter sequence" of tree-ring patterns (d). (From *Archae-ology: Discovering Our Past,* by Robert J. Sharer and Wendy Ashmore, Mayfield Publishing, 1993, p. 320)

By overlapping ring sequences of living trees with those of old dead trees, a **master sequence** of tree-ring width variation over many years has been developed. By analysis of bristlecone pine trees, a master sequence greater than 9,000 years has been produced for the American West. The master sequence constructed in England extends to 7,000 years ago. When an archaeological site is located that contains wood or even entire cross sections of logs, the succession of thick and thin rings in the ancient specimens can be compared to the master sequence. By determining where the individual sequence overlaps with the master sequence, the life span of the tree can be fixed in time (Figure 3.9). By seeing in what year these archaeological specimens were cut down—the actual year in which the tree's final ring was added—an exact date can be associated with the site.

Individual tree rings have been carbon-dated. Old rings are no longer growing and are, therefore, removed from the carbon cycle; ^{14}C is not being replenished in them. A ring laid down 1,000 years ago in a *living* redwood tree, for example, will produce a carbon date of about 1,000 years. A very large sample of carbon dates derived from old tree rings has been carefully compared to the actual calendar age of each ring as determined by dendrochronology. The resulting **calibration curve,** now extending back to 11,000 years ago, allows a radiocarbon date within this period to be converted to a calendar year date (Figure 3.10).

Dating Techniques Based on Radiation Damage

Electron spin resonance dating (ESR) is one of a number of techniques that date materials through the measurement of radiation damage—in this case, the buildup of electrons trapped in crystalline materials at a site (Grün 1989, 1993; Grün and Stringer 1991). When, for example, a tooth is formed, the

FIGURE 3.10

Calibration curve for radio-carbon dates. The vertical axis represents the radiocarbon dates derived for a large number of tree-ring samples, and the horizontal axis represents the actual dendrochronologically de-rived dates for those same tree rings. As you can see, for tree rings that are more than about 3,000 years old, radiocarbon dates generally understate the true age of a sample.

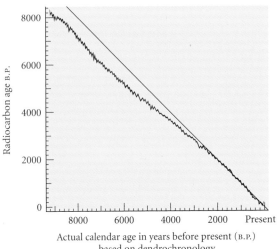

Actual calendar age in years before present (B.P.) based on dendrochronology

electrons in the atoms of that tooth are technically in an unexcited state, or "ground state." As a result of natural radioactivity in the tooth itself, as well as in the soil in which the tooth is deposited, some of those electrons get transferred to higher energy levels and get "trapped" there. The number of trapped electrons is a function of characteristics of the material (in this case, tooth enamel), the amount of background radiation, and time—how long since the tooth formed. Because the trapping characteristics of different materials as well as background radiation levels can be measured and accounted for, the number of electrons trapped in a sample can be used to determine the age of the sample. ESR can date teeth that are more than a few thousand years old, but its key contribution is in dating sites that are too old for radiocarbon dating—in other words, sites more than 50,000 years old. The upper limit for ESR is unknown; it has been estimated at somewhere between 10 million and 100 million years (Gürn and Stringer 1991, 165). Even the lower limit renders the technique applicable to sites directly related to human evolution. Greatest success has been achieved on mollusk shells, speleothems (cave deposits), corals, volcanic rock, and tooth enamel. ESR does not, however, work well on bone (Grün and Stringer 1991, 155).

Luminescence dating, like ESR, measures the amount of energy that is trapped in material recovered at archaeological sites as a result of natural radioactive decay in the surrounding soil. Again, such energy is released at a set rate in a given soil, so the amount captured in site materials reflects their age. The amount of energy captured by the archaeological material over time and, hence, its age can be measured after releasing the energy by heat (in the application called **thermoluminescence,** or **TL**) or by laser light (in the application called **optically stimulated luminescence,** or **OSL**).

Luminescence dating has been applied successfully to fired clay objects, especially pottery, as well as to stone that has been heated to a high temperature—for example, the rocks lining a fireplace. In both cases, the application of heat—the firing of the pot or the heating of the stone in a fire—releases all of the energy previously trapped in the material. This effectively sets the trapped-charge clock to zero. Then, once the pot or stone is returned to the earth, it again begins to accumulate energy at the set rate produced by the natural radioactivity of the surrounding soil. Knowing that rate allows calculation of how much time has elapsed since the object was heated and, therefore, when people were present at the site making pots or banking their hearths with stones.

Fission-track dating, another radiation-damage measurement, bases age estimates on the number of visible "tracks" left by radioactive decay in site materials; these microscopic tracks build up at a regular rate.

Dating by Measuring Chemical Processes

Obsidian hydration measures the regular buildup of a "hydration layer" on freshly exposed volcanic glass; a fresh surface is exposed when a human hammers off a stone flake while making obsidian tools. The exposed surface immediately begins to combine chemically with water in the air around it or in the soil in which it is deposited. The thickness of the layer on an exposed obsidian surface is a function of time, the moisture level and temperature of its environment of deposition, and characteristics of the particular obsidian. Where that moisture level can be measured and controlled for, the age of the flake can be determined. Where the rate of hydration-layer development can be determined, an absolute date can be derived for the artifact. In other cases, only relative dates can be determined; we can figure out which objects are older than others on the basis of their thicker hydration layer.

Dating by Measuring Paleomagnetism

Paleomagnetic dating is based on the fact that the position of magnetic north has fluctuated over time. The orientation of naturally magnetic particles in a lava flow is measured to determine the direction of magnetic north when the flow was hot. Because the location of magnetic north has been determined for long periods of time, volcanic layers that preserve evidence of the location of north when the deposits were laid down can be dated (Kappelman 1993).

SUMMARY

Archaeologists and paleoanthropologists apply a broad array of techniques in their investigation of the human past. This chapter has briefly surveyed some of the more important procedures for recovering and analyzing the data on which the rest of this book is based.

How sites are formed, how they are preserved, and how they are discovered are key questions for archaeologists and paleoanthropologists. Once found, data can be analyzed to determine the age of the materials, how tools were made and used, the subsistence base of the people, and aspects of their social and even religious lives. Past peoples can also be investigated directly through analysis of their physical remains, which determines the age, sex, health status, and geographic origin of ancient individuals. The evolutionary relationship between a prehistoric person and modern human beings can therefore be determined.

Using the general procedures outlined in this chapter, and many other very specific analytical techniques mentioned throughout this book, archaeologists and paleoanthropologists can reveal the chronicle of the human past. We begin that chronicle in Chapter 4.

TO LEARN MORE

Technical Summaries

Many fine textbooks describe the methods of archaeology and paleoanthropology; see especially Wendy Ashmore and Robert Sharer's brief introduction, *Discovering Our Past* (1995), and their longer *Archaeology: Discovering Our Past* (Sharer and Ashmore 1993); Brian Fagan's *Archaeology: A Brief Introduction* (1997) and his longer *In the Beginning: An Introduction to Archaeology* (1997); Colin Renfrew and Paul Bahn's *Archaeology: Theories, Methods, and Practice* (1996); and David Hurt Thomas's short work, *Archaeology Down to Earth* (1997) as well as his longer *Archaeology* (1998). For the analysis of human skeletal material, see Wilton Marion Krogman's *The Human Skeleton in Forensic Medicine* (1973) for a classical treatment. There is probably no better recent source than Tim White and Pieter Folken's *Human Osteology* (1991).

Popular Summaries

Brian Fagan has written two wonderful treatments of archaeology and its history: *Quest for the Past* (1994), which focuses on several famous discoveries in archaeology (such as King Tut's tomb) and *Eyewitness to Discovery* (1997), which consists of more than 50 original, first-person accounts of archaeological discovery. Two anthologies of popular articles discussing archaeological method and meaning are available: *Annual Editions: Archaeology* (1998; edited by Linda Hasten) and *Lessons from the Past: A Reader in Introductory Archaeology* (1999b; edited by Kenneth L. Feder).

On the Web

You can find lots of specific information about the methodology of archaeology and paleoanthropology on the Internet. A useful set of links to resources on archaeology can be found at http://www.academicinfo.net/archsub.html. One of the most useful Internet sites devoted to archaeology is ArchNet, located at http://archnet.uconn.edu/. Along with a wealth of material on archaeology in northeastern North America, ArchNet also provides numerous links to archaeology museums, university programs, virtual digs, and all manner of other sites devoted to the science of humanity's ancient past.

KEY TERMS

hypothesis
site
artifact
ecofact
taphonomy
feature
primary refuse
secondary refuse
test pit
remote sensing
association
trace element
    analysis
neutron activation
    analysis
experimental
    replication
morphology
wear pattern

osteological comparative
    collection
faunal assemblage
sexual dimorphism
osteological
artificial selection
deciduous dentition
diaphysis
epiphysis
epiphyseal fusion
cranial suture
pubic symphysis
paleopathology
stratigraphic
radiometric
isotope
absolute date
relative date
K/Ar dating

half-life
radiocarbon dating
carbon dating
accelerator mass
    spectrometry (AMS)
dendrochronology
master sequence
calibration curve
electron spin resonance
    dating (ESR)
luminescence dating
thermoluminescence
    (TL)
optically stimulated
    luminescence (OSL)
fission-track dating
obsidian hydration
paleomagnetic dating

4

African
Roots

CHAPTER OVERVIEW

Though human beings are distinguished by large brains, great intelligence, and reliance on culture, fossil evidence shows that these were not characteristic of our earliest ancestors. The first steps of the hominids were literal first steps; upright locomotion differentiated them from the other apes.

The oldest hominids date to more than 4 million years ago. Scientists have identified several different species, with varying brain sizes and body configurations, but all share an anatomy suited to walking on two feet.

A fork in the hominid road appeared about 2.5 million years ago. The fossil record shows a new hominid form, *Homo habilis,* who had a brain size beyond the range of the apes and produced stone tools, showing a greater reliance on culture to survive. *Homo habilis* and some of the australopithecines were contemporaries. While the latter were highly specialized and became extinct, the former are direct ancestors of modern humans.

Millions of years ago

	5	4	3	2	1
Ardipithecus ramidus					
Australopithecus anamensis					
Australopithecus afarensis					
Australopithecus africanus					
Australopithecus robustus					
Australopithecus boisei					
Australopithecus aethiopicus					
Homo habilis					

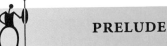
PRELUDE

Wearing shoes most of the time, few of us think about the actual mechanics of walking. Our feet are ordinarily enclosed in footwear with stiff, hard soles, and we walk on even harder pavement.

Walking barefoot on the soft sand of a beach, however, reminds us with each step of the natural process. No longer is walking a matter of two flat slabs of leather or rubber alternately clomping down on the pavement. Instead, we can sense our feet actually interacting with the earth, gripping into the soil beneath them, pushing us ever forward in our desire to get from here to there. In the instant of each step, our heels strike first, leaving deep impressions as the sand compresses beneath our weight, all of it focused on that small point at the heel of the foot. Then, the foot rolls forward, the arch lightly curving over the sand and leaving a thin, sharp indentation with the side of the sole. Next, all in a fraction of a second, we rock up onto the balls of our feet, thrusting our center of gravity forward, as we push our alternate leg in front of us. Finally, our toes push down, gripping into the earth, with sand squishing up between and around them, as we propel our bodies further forward, ready to catch ourselves in the next step with the other foot.

Most of us have, at one time or another, walked barefoot on wet sand in this way, leaving a uniquely human trail of footprints behind us. I remember in particular one time when I walked on a beach with my then six-year-old son Josh and glanced back at our two sets of footprints, one big, one small, as the waves began the inevitable process of erasing them from the sand.

Our disappearing trail of footprints reminded me of another such trail, made in a far distant time by two people who passed together across a landscape. Those footprints, however, were not washed away by the tide or blown away by the wind. Those prints, left in a fine volcanic ash on an East African plain in a place called Laetoli, in the modern nation of Tanzania, were preserved because a rare ash type known as carbonatite was spewed out by a nearby volcano (Hay and Leakey 1982; Leakey and Hay 1979; White and Suwa 1987).

CHAPTER SITES

AFRICA
Allia Bay
Aramis
FLK
Gona
Hadar
Kanapoi
Koobi Fora
Laetoli
Olduvai
West Turkana

The conditions and sequence of events had to be perfect for those footprints to be preserved. First, a thin ash layer had to be deposited. Soon after, a mild rain had to fall, turning the ash into the consistency of wet cement. Immediately following this, and before the ash had hardened, the two people (and, perhaps, another) had to walk across its surface, leaving their footprints in the still damp ash. Then the sun needed to come out to dry the ash bed to the hardness of rock before another rainfall might wash it all away. Finally, another ash layer had to be deposited, covering the footprint trail and protecting it from the natural erosion that might otherwise have destroyed it. Even stolid scientists have characterized the preservation of the Laetoli footprint trails as "miraculous" (Johanson and Edey 1981).

Those footprints were found more than 3.5 million years after the two people, possibly a child and an adult, and perhaps a third person, strode across the surface (Leakey and Lewin 1992; Figure 4.1). We will never know their

names or why they were walking, apparently in cadence and, perhaps, giving our imagination free rein, hand in hand across the ash bed. Yet in taking those steps, they achieved a kind of immortality. Perhaps most remarkably, their footprints show that those anonymous folk, whose life journey occurred so many years ago, walked in a fashion that is nearly indistinguishable from the way modern humans walk (Charteris, Wall, and Nottrodt 1981; Day and Wickens 1980; T. White 1980; White and Suwa 1987; see Figure 4.1). Those people were among the earliest **hominids,** with whom all living people share a temporally distant but biologically intimate connection. This chapter is about the first people and the world in which they lived.

Imagine a 2-hour movie representing the history of the universe; the very first moment of the film represents the first instant of the beginning of everything, the event cosmologists call "the Big Bang." In our imaginary movie, everything happens proportionally to when it actually happened in the history of the universe. In such a movie, the earth does not form until more than 80 minutes after the first flash on the screen, the first living things make their appearance at about 90 minutes into the film, dinosaurs briefly flash across the screen at the 118-minute mark, and, finally, the earliest members of the human family do not appear until 1 hour,

 **CHRONICLE**

FIGURE 4.1

On the left is the Laetoli pathway, the fossilized footprints of at least two human ancestors who walked in a remarkably modern fashion. On the right is the recent pathway of a father and his six-year-old son. Though separated in time by more than 3.5 million years, the two sets of footprints clearly show the continuity of bipedal locomotion in the hominid family. (Left: Peter Jones; right: K. L. Feder)

59 minutes, and 58 seconds into the movie. The entire human story, in other words, is contained in the final *2 seconds* of the film! Though this period may not seem very important from a universal perspective, in human terms we are talking about more than 4 million years, or 200,000 generations of human ancestors. These metaphorical final 2 seconds are the focus of paleoanthropologists and archaeologists.

MIOCENE PREFACE

The world of the **Miocene** (from about 25 million to 5 million years ago; Figure 4.2) is one we can scarcely imagine. During this epoch, our planet was a matchless place for forest-dwelling creatures like apes, and many species evolved to fill the varied **niches** offered by this rich world. Places that today are covered with grassland, prairie, and agricultural crops were then fertile forests, populated by an astounding bestiary of tree-loving species.

Fossil Apes of the Miocene

In 1988, primatologist John Fleagle enumerated 39 distinct species of extinct fossil apes, all of whose remains date to the Miocene, and several more species have been added since Fleagle's listing was published. More significant than

FIGURE 4.2

Humans appear extremely late on this standard time scale for earth history. The earliest hominids date no further back in time than the Pliocene epoch.

ERA	PERIOD	EPOCH	MILLION YEARS AGO
Cenozoic	Quaternary	Holocene	0.01
		Pleistocene	1.7
	Tertiary	Pliocene	5
		Miocene	25
		Oligocene	38
		Eocene	55
		Paleocene	65
Mesozoic	Cretaceous		135
	Jurassic		190
	Triassic		225
Paleozoic	Permian		270
	Carboniferous		345
	Devonian		400
	Silurian		425
	Ordovician		500
	Cambrian		600
Precambrian	Proterozoic		1,000
	Archeozoic		3,000
	Azoic		4,600

actual number of ancient ape species is the great geographical range and the broad diversity reflected among these apes.

For example, when we consider the natural habitats of apes in the modern world, we most often think of Africa and southeast Asia; but the Miocene apes flourished in a far broader area of the world; their fossil remains are spread throughout much of Europe and Asia, as well as Africa. Fossil apes dating to the Miocene epoch have been found in Spain, France, Italy, Greece, Turkey, Hungary, India, Pakistan, and China, far from where we find apes today (Andrews 1985; Andrews and Stringer 1989). Fossil remains of many of these extinct apes have been found in areas that were tropical forests during the Miocene, but some have been found in areas that were temperate woodlands, much cooler and drier than the tropical rain forests where apes currently reside.

Miocene apes had a greater size range than do modern ape species. For example, *Micropithecus clarki* was the size of a small monkey, weighing just a bit more than 4.5 kg (7.5 lb), smaller than even the smallest of the living lesser apes. On the other hand, scientists have estimated that the aptly named *Gigantopithecus blacki* tipped the scales at 300 kg (660 lb), which is quite a bit heavier than even the mean weight of adult male gorillas, which average only about 180 kg (400 lb) in the wild. The other species of Miocene apes, such as *Dryopithecus, Oreopithecus, Pliopithecus, Laccopithecus, Sivapithecus,* and so on, all fall somewhere in between these extremes of size (Figure 4.3, p. 64).

Based on their reconstruction from skeletal and dental remains, the many Miocene apes also exhibited a very broad range in their anatomical features. In fact, during the Miocene, apes attained their highest level of diversity in morphology, habitat, and adaptation, varying far more broadly than modern apes in their form, where they lived, and what they ate. *Dendropithecus macinnesi,* for example, was small, with quite long, thin arms, ideal for **brachiating** (Andrews 1985). Its skeletal anatomy suggests that members of this species were capable climbers and leapers in their East African tropical forest. Their teeth indicate they subsisted on a diet that consisted primarily of fruits. On the other hand, *Proconsul nyanzae* was chimplike in appearance but had rather short arms and squatter proportions, which indicate that it likely was more at home on the ground than in the trees of its dry forest residence (Pickford 1983). *Oreopithecus,* found in Italy, was likely a leaf-feeder in the swamp-forest it inhabited. Its long arms and hooklike hands enabled it to move around in the forest canopy in a manner similar to that of tree sloths and unlike that of any living apes (Andrews and Stringer 1989). One recently discovered species of *Oreopithecus* may have possessed the ability to walk upright regularly. The 3-ft tall, 8-million-year-old *Oreopithecus bamboli* possessed a highly divergent big toe, set at an angle of greater than 90 degrees from the other toes, so that its foot had the appearance of a bird's. This feature allowed *Oreopithecus bamboli* a certain degree of stability when walking upright that other apes, who walk on two feet only occasionally, lack. *Dryopithecus* was adapted to the temperate woodlands of Europe—recent paleontological research has suggested that *Dryopithecus* may have shared a common ancestor with the

FIGURE 4.3

An artist's conception of a small segment of the diversity of Miocene apes.
(Courtesy of John G. Fleagle/ Academic Press; drawn by Stephen Nash)

gorilla (Begun 1992). *Kenyapithecus* was adapted to the subtropical forest of East Africa; and *Sivapithecus,* who appears to be ancestral to the modern orangutan, was at home in the seasonal woodlands of southeastern Europe and south-central Asia (Fleagle 1988).

Though only a small sample of Miocene apes has been discussed here, it should be clear that apes were varied and widespread during the Miocene,

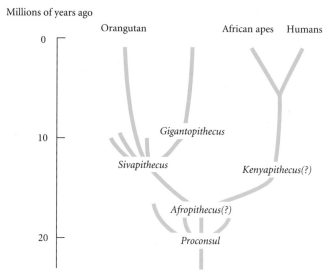

FIGURE 4.4

Phylogeny for apes and humans, based on the fossil record.

much more so than they are today. See "To Learn More" in this chapter for sources of more information.

Why the Study of Apes Is Relevant to the Study of Humanity

We are not descended from chimps, bonobos, gorillas, or orangutans. They have been evolving separately from us for as long as we have been evolving separately from them. But we share with them a common ancestor, as yet unrecognized in the paleontological record, but almost certainly dating to no more than 5–7 million years ago. Figure 4.4 presents a general phylogeny for the fossil and modern apes, showing how we currently conceive of their evolutionary relationships. The figure also shows how we view the human position on this phylogeny, and we will focus our energies on that branch in the rest of this book.

By studying modern apes in a natural setting, we can catch glimpses of behaviors they share with us: A chimp infant runs to its mother when it is frightened, and two adults embrace and pat each other's backs; chimps live in tightly knit social groups, make and use tools, and occasionally walk on two feet while carrying objects in their hands. In these shared elements we likely are recognizing behaviors we have inherited from a common ancestor who lived more than 5 million years ago and from whom both chimpanzees and humans descended.

By studying modern fossil apes, therefore, primatologists are able to get a glimpse, however fleeting and indirect, of our own distant past. To comprehend the environmental and evolutionary context in which our human ancestors first appeared, we have to understand what preceded them and, in essence, where they came from.

Today, the surviving ape species—gorillas, orangutans, chimpanzees, bonobos (pygmy chimpanzees), gibbons, and siamangs—are threatened with extinction as a result of habitat destruction at the hands of humanity. As the tropical forests of Africa and Asia that are home to the apes are cleared for agriculture to support the burgeoning human population, the apes are pushed into smaller and smaller enclaves. Without a concerted effort by our species, the same species that is responsible for their current precarious position, our nearest living evolutionary relatives may become extinct except in zoos and animal parks.

At the end of the Miocene, the many species of apes that are represented in the fossil record also faced extinction, but not by any human agency; our direct ancestors had not yet evolved. Instead, a natural environmental change began to shrink the rich forest world. Though paleoclimatologists and paleobotanists disagree about how and why this change took place, almost all agree that large areas of the extensive forest lands began to contract sometime during the middle or late Miocene, to be replaced largely by grasslands, or **savannas,** by the beginning of the next epoch, the Pliocene, about 5 million years ago. And with the contraction of the forest, most of the ape species that had thrived there became extinct.

For example, geologists Thure Cerling, Yang Wang, and Jay Quade (1993) have shown that soils and fossil teeth in south-central Asia (Pakistan) and North America (the western United States) exhibit a simultaneous, dramatic increase between 7 million and 5 million years ago in their concentration of the ^{13}C **isotope** (variety) of the element carbon (Figure 4.5). The ^{13}C found in carbon dioxide in the atmosphere is involved far more readily in the particular photosynthesis process used by many grasses and sedges (those following the so-called **C4 pathway**) than it is in that of trees, virtually all of which follow a different photosynthesis pathway (**C3 pathway**). As a result, most grasses have a higher concentration of ^{13}C than do trees. The ^{13}C concentration in the plants growing in an area becomes reflected in local soils as that vegetation decays, as well as in the bones and teeth of the herbivorous animals ingesting those plants. Because we know the relative concentrations of ^{13}C in most trees (C3 pathway) as compared to many grasses (C4 pathway), then by measuring the concentration of that isotope in soil and fossil bones and teeth in an area, we can deduce which kind of plants (in simplest terms here, trees or grasses) were most abundant in that area during a particular time period.

Cerling and co-workers interpret the overall and dramatic increase in ^{13}C concentration at the end of the Miocene as an indication of "a rapid expansion of C4 biomass [that is, grasses] in both the Old and the New World starting 7 to 5 million years ago" (1993, 334). They further point out that the "synchronous expansion of C4 ecosystems in both the New and Old World suggests a change in global conditions rather than local development" (345). More recent research (Morgan, Kingston, and Marino 1994) in Pakistan and Kenya

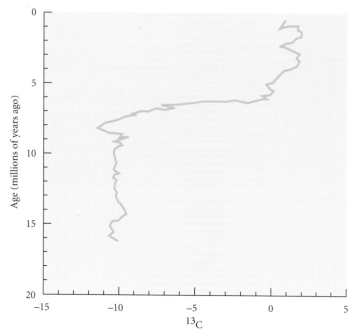

FIGURE 4.5

This graph shows the dramatic proportional increase of ^{13}C in fossil teeth and soils at the end of the Miocene. (From Cerling, Yang, and Quade 1993)

questions the rapid rate the previous study suggested for the expansion of savannas and contraction of the forests worldwide but still supports the general contention that this was a significant, worldwide phenomenon. As Morgan and colleagues have said, "We agree that significant environmental changes occurred around 7 million years ago, near the time when the first hominids appeared" (quoted in Bower 1994d, 38).

Cerling and colleagues (1997) suggest that the late Miocene spread of C4 plants resulted from a planet-wide decrease in carbon dioxide in the atmosphere. The concentration of this gas dropped from 1,000 parts per million during the reign of the dinosaurs 100 million years ago to about half that amount by the end of the Miocene. This drop, Cerling and colleagues suggest, inhibited the growth of C3 plants, including trees—which do not use carbon dioxide as efficiently as C4 grasses—and paved the way for the spread of the savanna.

The Irony of Extinction

Evolution and extinction are serendipitous and unpredictable. Extinction is, in fact, the norm; it is estimated that 99% of the plant and animal species that have existed during the 3.5-billion-year history of life on earth are extinct. The role of extinction in evolution also is sadly ironic. Sometimes it is the extinction of one species, genus, or family of animals that opens up the evolutionary field to another. In fact, it was the extinction of the dinosaurs that allowed a previously insignificant class of animals, the mammals—of which we are one—to explode into prominence. Just as surely, the massive wave of ape extinctions resulting from the great climatic and habitat changes that accompanied the end of the Miocene provided the catalyst for the florescence of the small number of ape species that were able to adapt, adjust, and survive (Gingerich 1986; Pickford 1983).

Remember, environmental change does not cause evolution, and evolution is not progressive or directional. Changing environmental conditions simply set up situations in which some physical or behavioral characteristics, previously of little use to their possessors, become highly advantageous. Through natural selection, as suggested by Darwin (see Chapter 2), these advantageous features allow those members of a species that possess them a better chance at surviving under the new environmental regime.

This appears to be precisely what happened at the Miocene-Pliocene boundary. Unfortunately, the fossil record is so poor for this period of upheaval that we cannot be certain in reconstructing what transpired. Almost certainly, those species that survived the terminal Miocene possessed some characteristics that, by chance, gave them an advantage in the very different world that was establishing itself. Perhaps it was their remarkable ability for brachiation that ensured the survival of the ancestors of today's gibbons and siamangs when forests were shrinking and competition for remaining space was fierce. Maybe it was the strength, size, intelligence, and social systems of the ancestors of modern gorillas that allowed for their survival. The intelligence and behavioral flexibility of the ancestors of chimps and bonobos probably provided them with an advantage as the myriad Miocene ape species vied for space in the diminishing forests of 7 million years ago.

The modern apes, therefore, can be viewed as the descendants of the winners of this evolutionary struggle. The losers were those who, at the end of the Miocene, found themselves in an alien habitat in which their physical and behavioral characteristics, honed by millions of years of evolution to life in a thick, humid forest, were useless—those who could not survive on the savannas.

One ape species at the end of the Miocene possessed a different, uniquely advantageous characteristic, one that may also have been beneficial for life in the forest: the ability to walk on two legs, which all living apes can do with varying degrees of success. But **bipedal locomotion** is inefficient and tiring for them; the bones and muscles of their hips and legs simply are not compatible with that form of locomotion. The same was probably true for the apes of the Miocene.

But one Miocene species could stand up and walk on two legs better than the others. While providing some advantage in the forests, this ability was particularly valuable in the expanding grasslands that replaced the Miocene woodlands. Natural selection, as discussed in Chapter 2, feeds on variability. The nascent ability for upright locomotion within one Miocene ape species provided natural selection with the raw material needed to produce a creature fully capable of bipedal locomotion, one that habitually and efficiently walked on two feet. The species that had this ability was the first human ancestor.

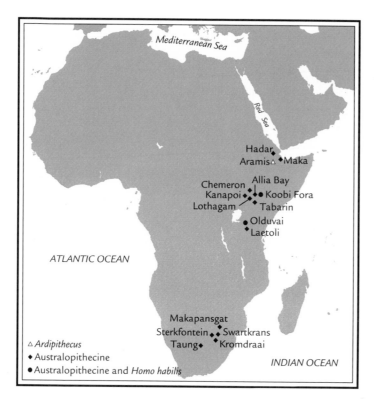

FIGURE 4.6

Fossil localities of early hominids.

THE FIRST HOMINIDS

Ardipithecus

The oldest fossils that reflect a species with this ability to walk regularly on two feet—and, therefore, the first hominids—have been labeled *Ardipithecus ramidus* (White, Suwa, and Asfaw 1994). Discovered initially in Ethiopia in 1992, the fragmentary remains include a child's lower jaw, parts of an adult **cranium,** upper and lower arm bones, and a few teeth (Figure 4.6). These remains have been dated to 4.4 million B.P. Though quite fragmentary, details of the arm bones and teeth show some similarities to those of human beings. Most important, the cranial fragment recovered in 1992 provided researchers with part of the **foramen magnum,** the large hole at the bottom of the skull through which nerves and blood vessels pass, connecting the brain to the rest of the body. The bony ridge circling the foramen magnum represents the place where the skull rests on top of the vertebral column. The location of the foramen magnum dictates whether a creature is a quadruped or a biped. A cat, for example, has a foramen magnum toward the back of the skull, and the vertebral column lies horizontally toward the rear. In a bipedal human, the foramen magnum is located at the very bottom of the cranium, and the

FIGURE 4.7

Two fragments of a tibia (the larger, lower leg bone) belonging to a member of the species Australopithecus anamensis. *The top part of the tibia, shown on the right, exhibits two concave surfaces on the left and right condyles that meet the upper leg (femur) at the knee, typical of upright walkers and unlike the convex surfaces of an ape tibia.*
(Copyright © Kenneth Garrett/ National Geographic Society Image Collection)

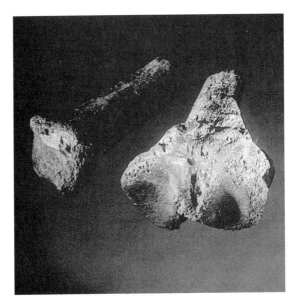

vertebral column sits in a vertical position below. There was enough of the foramen magnum preserved on the *Ardipithecus* specimen to indicate that it was positioned more toward the bottom of the skull than the back. This implies that *Ardipithecus* was upright and, in fact, the oldest hominid yet discovered. The environment in which it lived appears to have been a closed woodland. So, though bipedal, *Ardipithecus* appears not to have moved out onto the expanding savanna.

The Genus Australopithecus

Dating to sometime between 4.17 and 4.07 million years ago are the exciting discoveries made in Kanapoi and Allia Bay, Kenya (Leakey et al. 1998). The 12 specimens from Allia Bay and the 9 from Kanapoi, including teeth, cranial fragments, and some bones below the skull, have been assigned the species name *Australopithecus anamensis* (Figure 4.7).

The *anamensis* jaw fragments and fossil teeth are apelike. The configuration of the jaw is boxlike in both apes and *anamensis*. Human jaws, on the other hand, expand or open up toward the back of the mouth. An upper arm bone found 30 years ago—now assigned to this species based on its stratigraphic position—exhibits many humanlike features. In addition, and more significantly, both ends of a tibia (shin bone) that were recovered are very humanlike; its discoverers identify this bone as clearly indicating bipedal locomotion nearly half a million years before the Laetoli footprints. The environment in which *Australopithecus anamensis* lived was characterized by open woodland or bushland conditions.

The discoverers of *anamensis* suggest that it provides the clearest picture of a human ancestor from about 4 million years ago. As such, this recently discovered fossil may represent the species ancestral to all of the later hominids to be discussed here (Leakey and Walker 1997).

Australopithecus afarensis

Far better known and with a far larger sample of remains is a later, somewhat less apelike form of the same genus, *Australopithecus afarensis*—most likely the creature that left the footprint trail described in this chapter's "Prelude." A significant number of *afarensis* fossils have been discovered. The great majority of these fossils date to the period from 4 million to 3 million years ago. The most significant *afarensis* fossils were found in the Afar geographical region of Ethiopia, where the first and most complete specimens were discovered at the site of Hadar (Figure 4.8), highlighted in this chapter's "Case Study Close-Up."

Some individuals are critical of the evolutionary conclusions of paleoanthropology because they believe the data always to be quite scanty and equivocal. As paleoanthropologist Richard Leakey (Leakey and Lewin 1992, 81) points out, however, the fragmentary remains of close to 1,000 individuals have been recovered that date to the early period of hominid evolution. *Afarensis* alone has produced more than 300 individual specimens. Among the key elements of the *afarensis* skeleton that have been found and used to define the species are the pelvis, vertebrae, leg bones, fingers, feet, jaws, skull fragments, a nearly complete cranium, and teeth. Together, these skeletal elements allow us to paint a reliable picture of a creature that, beginning about 4 million years ago, was not becoming bipedal but already was fully upright (see this chapter's "Issues and Debates").

The **postcranial** skeleton (everything below the skull) of *afarensis* is diagnostic of a creature far more like a human than an ape. The feet of *afarensis* were quite modern, lacking the divergent big toe of the apes. The ape big toe is positioned on its foot just as our thumbs are positioned on our hands, allowing the ape to grasp objects with its feet (for example, to grasp tree branches when climbing) far better than we can. *Afarensis* possessed the foot of a walker, not that of a climber. Also, the pelvis was quite similar to ours and is easily distinguished from an ape's (see Figure 4.18); the configuration of the pelvis is an accurate indicator of a creature's mode of locomotion (see this chapter's "Issues and Debates").

A recent computer simulation of *afarensis* locomotion tested various models, including a chimplike gait and a more fully upright, humanlike mode of walking (Crompton et al. 1998). Using the shapes of the preserved bones of the fossil called Lucy in the computer simulation of *afarensis* locomotion, these researchers concluded that a humanlike gait was far more likely. Though Lucy certainly possessed some apelike characteristics, she walked on two feet, not clumsily like a chimp, but efficiently like a modern human being. (See this chapter's "Case Study Close-Up" for more on Lucy.)

FIGURE 4.8

This 45% complete skeleton of the fossil known as Lucy plus a series of 13 other Australopithecus afarensis specimens have been dated to 3.18 million years ago. (Copyright © 1995 John Reader, Science Source/Photo Researchers, Inc.)

Compared to human beings, the apes have proportionally very long arms in relation to their trunk and legs. Long, powerful arms allow the apes to climb or swing through trees as well as to walk quadrupedally on the ground. Human arms are, by comparison, quite short in relation to human legs; try walking on your hands and feet, and you will soon discover that either your legs are far too long, or your arms are simply too short. Analysis of the proportions of upper and lower limbs in *afarensis* shows quite clearly that in this respect as well, the species was proportioned far more like modern humans than like apes (Shreeve 1996).

On the other hand, *afarensis* had not left its ape heritage behind entirely. In some specimens, the finger bones were long and curved, like an ape's (Susman, Stern, and Jungers 1984). This evidence may indicate that *afarensis* retained some of the **arboreal** ability of its ape ancestors at the same time that it walked bipedally on the ground.

Though *afarensis* may have been a proficient climber, recent evidence shows clearly that this first hominid species had moved away from the heavily arboreal adaptation of apes. Paleoanthropologist Tim White (see Bower 1993d) excavated fragments of an upper and lower arm from a deposit dated to 3.4 million years ago at the site of Maka in Ethiopia. The upper arm bone (the **humerus**) is proportionally short, like a modern human's and unlike the relatively long arm of the ape, with its adaptation for life in the trees. The recent discovery of one of the lower arm bones (**ulna**) of an *afarensis* specimen lends further support to the notion that the arms were more like a human's than an ape's. The specimen exhibits some apelike characteristics, but in general the pattern is more like that of a modern human (Kimbel, Johanson, and Rak 1994; Aiello 1994).

All of the essentially human qualities of the postcranial skeleton of *Australopithecus afarensis* must be contrasted with the almost entirely apelike features of its skull, as exhibited in the nearly complete cranium recently discovered at Hadar (Kimbel, Johanson, and Rak 1994). This cranium, labeled A.L. 444-2 by its excavators, is the most complete *afarensis* skull yet found. It dates about 3 million B.P., making this specimen one of the youngest yet identified in the *afarensis* fossil species. Its discovery is quite recent, and a detailed description has not yet been published. Nevertheless, it is apparent that, in its overall form, A.L. 444-2 is certainly more apelike than any subsequent human ancestor, including other, later versions of *Australopithecus* we will discuss. Cranial capacity is apelike, in the range of 400–500 ml—like that of a modern chimpanzee and about one-third the human mean for brain size (see Figure 4.17). The upper portion of the face is small when compared to the lower part (as in apes), which is the opposite of the pattern seen in modern human beings. The jaws jut out and are snoutlike—they are said to be **prognathous**—just like those in an adult ape and again quite different from the relatively flat face of a modern human being.

The *afarensis* jaw presents a combination of apelike and humanlike features (Figure 4.9). Humans and apes have the same numbers and kinds of

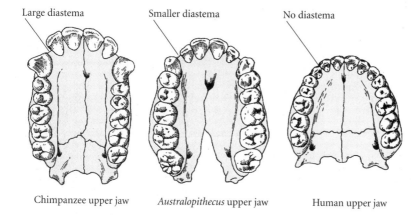

Large diastema   Smaller diastema   No diastema

Chimpanzee upper jaw   *Australopithecus* upper jaw   Human upper jaw

FIGURE 4.9

From this comparison of the maxillae (upper jaws) of chimps, Australopithecus, *and modern human beings, it is clear that the teeth in a chimp's mandible are arranged in a boxlike pattern, like those of* Australopithecus. *Modern human teeth form a curve, or arch.* (Adapted from drawings by Luba Dmytryk Gudz from *Lucy: The Beginnings of Humankind.* Copyright © 1981, Donald C. Johanson and Maitland A. Edey)

teeth: two incisors, one canine, two premolars, and three molars in each quadrant of the adult mouth. Human teeth, however, in both the upper jaw— the **maxilla**—and the lower jaw—the **mandible**—are positioned in a curving arch that expands to the rear of the mouth; ape teeth present a more boxlike appearance, with the premolars and molars set in nearly parallel rows perpendicular to the incisors. Also, apes have proportionally much larger canine teeth and a gap in the teeth of the opposing jaw to allow room for the large canines when the mouth is closed. This gap, or **diastema,** is not present in the human jaw; our canines are much smaller, and so no gap in the opposing jaw is needed. The *afarensis* jaw is not quite like an ape jaw but not quite like a human jaw either. The configuration of the teeth is more like a box than an arch; there is a small diastema; and tooth size, including that of the canines, is more apelike than human.

The evidence, then, is quite clear: *Australopithecus afarensis* seems to have been a bipedal ape living between 4 million and 3 million years ago. It looked like a chimpanzee standing on two short but otherwise humanlike legs, with no diverging big toe (Figure 4.10). What we share with *afarensis* is a mode of locomotion, but not a level of intelligence or a reliance on culture.

A FORK IN THE HOMINID ROAD

In the consensus view presented here, *Australopithecus afarensis* was the only representative of the hominid line from about 4 million years ago until about 3 million years ago (for a quite different view, see Leakey and Lewin 1992). At about 3 million years ago, *afarensis* seems to have evolved into a somewhat different form of hominid. We call these new fossils by the taxonomic name *Australopithecus africanus.* Like its evolutionary progenitor, *africanus* was bipedal and still walked in an essentially modern human fashion. It also retained

FIGURE 4.10

This artist's conception of Australopithecus afarensis *shows the ability of this ancestral hominid to walk on two feet and also to climb trees.* (Courtesy of John Fleagle/ Academic Press; drawn by Stephen Nash)

FIGURE 4.11

The cranium of Australopithecus africanus, *a lightly built, or "gracile," australopithecine form that followed* afarensis *in southern Africa.* Africanus *flourished after 3 million years ago and appears to have become extinct by 2.2 million years ago.* (Transvaal Museum, D. C. Panagos)

a basically apelike skull and brain (Figure 4.11). There are a number of fairly well preserved *africanus* crania, all apelike, with a sloping forehead and large ridges of bone above the eyes. On the other hand, the jaw and its teeth are a bit more humanlike and the face not quite so prognathous as *afarensis,* so in some ways it seems a little more human in appearance. Nevertheless, its brain size still falls into the range of the great apes (see Figure 4.17).

Australopithecus africanus dates to no more than 3 million years ago and seems to fade out of the picture by about 2.2 million years ago. At that point,

FIGURE 4.12

The cranium of Australopithecus robustus. Robustus *appears to have been a highly specialized hominid, with extremely powerful jaws adapted to processing a diet of hard, gritty foods.* Robustus, *which may have replaced* africanus, *became extinct around 1 million years ago.* (Transvaal Museum, D. C. Panagos)

a larger bipedal form seems to have taken its place (Figure 4.12). Called *Australopithecus robustus,* it was a biped, and its brain size was a bit greater than in *africanus.* More significant is the difference in the cranial architecture of *robustus:* Where the top of the *africanus* skull is round and smooth, the top of the *robustus* skull sports a thin ridge of bone called a **sagittal crest.** Such a crest allows for a much larger, stronger temporalis muscle, which powers the movement of the mandible while chewing.

This feature of the *robustus* skull, along with its much larger surfaced molars and microscopic evidence of wear on the molar surfaces (Figure 4.13), is a pretty good indication of a shift in dietary emphasis in *robustus,* when compared to *africanus,* toward a diet of hard foods such as seeds and nuts rather than roots, fruits, or leaves (Grine 1987). Recent analysis of the mineral content of their bones indicates that the *robustus* diet may have included meat as well (Bower 1992a). *Robustus* fossils disappear from the paleontological record by about 1 million years ago.

The *robustus* pattern of powerful cranial architecture is even more pronounced in another fossil hominid, *Australopithecus boisei,* whose specimens date from 2.2 million years ago to 1.4 million years ago, making it partially contemporaneous with *robustus* (Suwa et al. 1997). *Boisei* is different enough from *robustus* to warrant separate species status. In other words, there was more than one distinct hominid species living in Africa during the same period, a situation similar to the modern situation for **pongids,** in which there are two extant species of chimp (the common chimp and the bonobo).

To complicate matters further, there is a well-preserved, virtually intact cranium (specimen designation KNM WT-17000), called "the Black Skull"

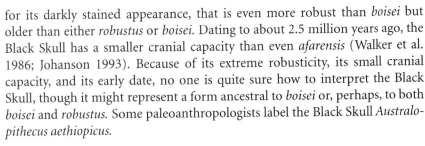

for its darkly stained appearance, that is even more robust than *boisei* but older than either *robustus* or *boisei*. Dating to about 2.5 million years ago, the Black Skull has a smaller cranial capacity than even *afarensis* (Walker et al. 1986; Johanson 1993). Because of its extreme robusticity, its small cranial capacity, and its early date, no one is quite sure how to interpret the Black Skull, though it might represent a form ancestral to *boisei* or, perhaps, to both *boisei* and *robustus*. Some paleoanthropologists label the Black Skull *Australopithecus aethiopicus*.

A FOREST OF HOMINIDS

A more lightly built variety of *Australopithecus*, dating to about 2.5 million years ago, has recently been identified in East Africa. Called *Australopithecus garhi* by its discoverers (Asfaw et al. 1999), the fossils—among which are limb bones and a fragmentary cranium—provide us with another possible descendant of *afarensis*. Some features of the bones suggest to the discoverers that *garhi* may be a link between *afarensis* and the hominid to be discussed next. And, as they put it, "It is in the right place, at the right time" (Asfaw et al. 1999, 634).

FIGURE 4.13

Teeth tell the story of a significant difference in the diets of the gracile and robust australopithecines. A photomicrograph of an africanus *molar (top) provides evidence of a diet of soft foods, perhaps roots and meat. A photomicrograph of a robustus molar (bottom) shows clear evidence of a diet rich in such foods as hard seeds and nuts. (Courtesy of F. E. Grine)*

To be sure, it is difficult to decide how all these different-named fossil species are related in evolutionary terms. Nevertheless, based on the dating of the specimens, detailed comparative analysis of the fossils themselves, and some guesswork, several models have been constructed to express how the various early fossil hominids relate in terms of evolutionary connections: which are ancestral, which are descendant forms, which are contemporaries, which are evolutionary offshoots that became extinct, and which led more directly to the modern human species. Though no general consensus exists, Figure 4.14 presents a common view of how the **australopithecines** are related in evolutionary terms (Grine 1993; Skelton and McHenry 1992).

In the view favored here, based on the highly detailed analysis by paleoanthropologists Randall Skelton and Henry McHenry (1992) of 77 skeletal traits and on new information discovered since their analysis, *Australopithecus anamensis* may be descendant from *Ardipithecus ramidus* and ancestral to all later hominid forms. The far better known *Australopithecus afarensis* descended from *anamensis* and was the sole hominid species for about 1 million years. *Australopithecus africanus* represents a population descendant from *afarensis*, with both the diet-specialized *robustus* and *boisei*, in turn, splitting off from its line. The Black Skull—*Australopithecus aethiopicus*—here represents another australopithecine evolutionary pathway branching off from *afarensis*. At about the same time that the robust australopithecines start to head down their evolutionary pathway with their physical adaptation to a highly specialized diet, another line emerges from *africanus*. That line is different, with a far greater reliance on culture for survival. (The next section will focus on this evolutionary line.)

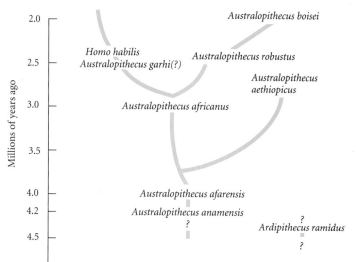

FIGURE 4.14

This phylogeny shows the possible evolutionary relationships among the fossil hominids discussed in this chapter.

New discoveries will no doubt force us to revise our models. But some facts almost certainly will not be amended: The six named species subsumed within the genus *Australopithecus* shared the fundamental, original hominid adaptation—they walked on two feet.

Ultimately, no matter which view you subscribe to, what the fossil record shows is change through time within the *Australopithecus* genus, with a burst of change and a proliferation of types occurring after 2.5 million years ago. This burst of change is the source of much of our confusion, since it resulted in a host of new hominid types whose evolutionary relationships are proving difficult to resolve. But how we resolve the confusion is, at least for our purposes here, not nearly as interesting as the fact that there was the proliferation in the first place. We will be discussing a possible explanation for this evolutionary burst in this chapter's "Issues and Debates."

Finally, how we divide up the various kinds of australopithecines is not vital to the rest of our discussion. Most of the australopithecines were evolutionary dead ends. Today, we simply do not see any bipedal, sagittally crested, apelike creatures walking around with brains slightly larger than one-third of our brain size. Any arguing we might do about them remains a debate about extinct species.

A DIFFERENT PATH—*HOMO HABILIS*

Soon after 2.5 million years ago, and just as the australopithecines were experiencing great changes in their evolutionary pathway, another hominid seems to have branched off from the main line of the *Australopithecus* genus (see Figure 4.14). This breakaway group followed a different evolutionary route, one in which its survival on the African savanna was not the result of an increasingly specialized diet but, instead, was due to an increase in intelligence made possible by an expanding brain. This creature first appears in the fossil record about 2.4 million years ago (Bower 1993b,c; Hill et al. 1992; Schrenk et al. 1993), a little before *africanus* became extinct, which makes it a contemporary of *Australopithecus robustus* and *aethiopicus*. But this new form cannot be mistaken for any variety or form of *Australopithecus*. With a much flatter face, a steeper forehead, and a larger brain—a mean size close to 700 ml, larger than any ape brain and just about one-half the modern human mean—this clearly is a new and different hominid. It is called *Homo habilis* (Figure 4.15).

Sharing the same genus as modern humans means that *Homo habilis* was much more like us than were any of the australopithecines. Whereas taxonomically *Homo sapiens* might live in the same neighborhood as the australopithecines, we live on the same street as *Homo habilis*.

The skull of *Homo habilis* was not just larger than that of the australopithecines, but was shaped differently as well, with significantly less prognathism, a taller, steeper forehead, and a more rounded profile. All of these features seem to presage modern human beings.

Once again, however, this "new and improved" hominid retained some pongid features in its postcranial skeleton. Though postcranial remains of *habilis* are scanty, what has been found shows that from the neck down the members of this species can be safely characterized as upright apes. Unlike some earlier australopithecines, their arms are still long and the legs short in proportion to each other, much like an ape's but unlike a human's short arms and long legs (Johanson et al. 1987).

The Ability to Make Stone Tools

The species we label *Homo habilis* on the basis of its skeletal characteristics exhibits another key feature not previously seen in the archaeological record: Its members made stone tools. We do not know whether any of the australopithecines made tools out of soft material such as wood or animal hide that would have decayed long ago. Modern chimps are known to manufacture tools by stripping the bark off of twigs, which they then poke into termite mounds (Goodall 1986). The termites adhere to the sticky residue on the stripped wood. The chimps pull out the twigs after a suitable wait and then feast on termites. Australopithecines were probably capable of similar work.

It also seems possible that at least some of the later australopithecines were physically capable of making stone tools. Researcher Randall Susman (1994) compared the hand bones of specimens of *Australopithecus afarensis*, *Australopithecus robustus*, *Homo erectus* (see Chapter 5), *Homo sapiens neanderthalensis* (see Chapter 6), and modern humans. While the *Australopithecus afarensis* hand Susman examined was similar to that of a chimp, all of the other specimens examined, including that from *Australopithecus robustus*, were more similar to a modern human's hand. *Australopithecus garhi* was

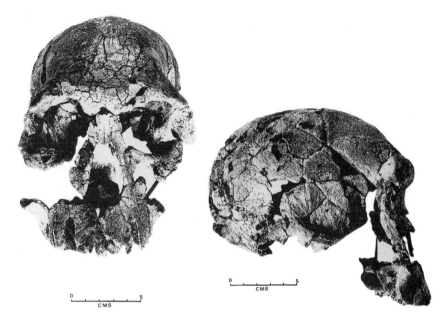

FIGURE 4.15
The cranial capacity of this fragmentary cranium of Homo habilis *shows that* habilis *possessed a brain larger than any ape's. Dated at 2.4 million years ago,* habilis *represents the first hominid with an expanded brain.* (Copyright © National Museums of Kenya)

found at the same level as stone tools; they may have used the tools to slice meat off bone (Heinzelin et al. 1999).

However, the first appearance of the oldest stone tools closely coincides with the earliest appearance of *Homo habilis.* As archaeologists Kathy Schick and Nicholas Toth (1993, 103) point out, the relatively small brain of the robust australopithecines and the small number of presumed stone tools found at their sites argue against their being proficient tool makers. The massive cranial architecture of *Australopithecus* further suggests to these researchers that they didn't need a cultural assist in the form of stone tools to process food in the first place. Although the question of exactly who made the first stone tools—and who did not—is still open to debate, it is certain that *Homo habilis* possessed both the hand anatomy and the increased intelligence needed to carry out the sophisticated process of forethought and action in the production of permanent tools.

Oldowan Technology

These oldest stone tools date back to about 2.5 million years ago at Gona, Ethiopia (Semaw et al. 1997). Tools like these were first recognized, defined, and described by the famous paleoanthropologist team of Louis and Mary Leakey (Leakey 1971). They called the tools **Oldowan,** after the place where they were first found and where the Leakeys had devoted so much of their research energy, Olduvai Gorge in Tanzania (see Color Plate 1).

The Leakeys originally defined Oldowan tools as a series of specifically shaped, sharpened rocks that served as chopping tools. Mary Leakey (1971)

FIGURE 4.16

The process by which flakes were removed from a stone core in the Oldowan tradition: A hard stone was struck with another stone in just the right locations to allow for the removal of sharp, thin flakes. (From "The First Technology" by Nicholas Toth. Copyright © 1987 by Scientific American, Inc. All rights reserved; drawing by Edward L. Hanson)

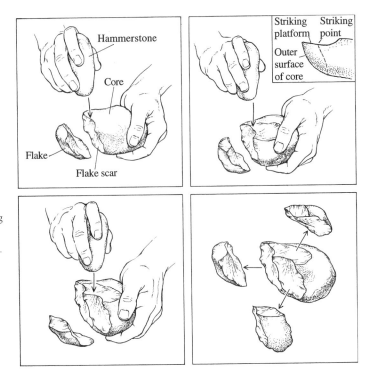

classified Oldowan choppers into a number of types based on shape and inferred function—cutting, chopping, scraping, and so forth. More recent work, however, by Nicholas Toth (1985) and Kathy Schick (Schick and Toth 1993) shows clearly that, though some of the "Oldowan choppers" may have been used as tools, the vast majority functioned as **cores** from which **flake** tools were produced.

The maker of the tool, or the **knapper,** begins with a more or less spherical nodule of stone. Holding this **object piece** in one hand, the knapper strikes it with a **hammerstone,** usually a fortuitously shaped harder rock (or just one less likely to break as a result of its particular geometry). Without much trouble, the knapper can knock a flake off the stone (Figure 4.16). Then the knapper turns the object piece around in his or her hand so the interior surface of the rock that was just exposed with the first hammerstone blow is facing up. Next, using that surface as a **striking platform,** the knapper strikes down on it with the hammerstone, thereby removing a stone flake from the opposite side of the object piece. Repeating this several times can produce a number of sharp, relatively straight-edged flakes useful for cutting, scraping, sawing, chopping, and the like. Microscopic analysis of a large collection of Oldowan flakes shows that many were used for these purposes (Keeley and Toth 1981; Toth 1985). The flakes exhibit a polish on their edges that is typically caused by cutting plant material, butchering animals, and woodworking.

Stone flakes are sharper, stronger, and more durable than the teeth or nails nature provided our ancestors. Although you don't need to be a genius to figure out how to make stone tools, it does take what researcher John Gowlett calls an "appreciation of the properties of stone" (1986, 251). The production of Oldowan tools took some knowledge of the characteristics of different rocks, an understanding of their breakage patterns, forethought in planning the sequence of blows, a bit of hand–eye coordination, and flexibility to change the planned sequence when problems cropped up. More fundamentally, this process takes enough intelligence to recognize that a round, dull rock can be transformed into a large number of straight, thin, sharp pieces of rock suitable for many different uses. Clearly, this is the thought process of an intelligent being.

Even the oldest known Oldowan tools from Ethiopia show the relative sophistication of the toolmakers. Most of us would not know what kinds of rock would be useful in making stone tools; most of us might think, in fact, that any rock would do, but this is far from true. The hominids at Gona selected the best stone in their territory, rock that fractures readily and regularly to produce sharp, thin flakes. Flaking was not random but done according to a sensible pattern of removal from a core. In fact, the Gona researchers propose that the 2.5-million-year-old tools found there almost certainly do not represent the first or even a very early attempt by these hominids to make stone tools. These researchers suggest that further study may likely reveal evidence of even older toolmaking, more representative of the initial experimentation performed by our ancestors as they literally invented stone toolmaking (Semaw et al. 1997).

To Schick and Toth (1993), the archaeological record at *Homo habilis* sites suggests quite a bit of forethought and planning in the manufacture of stone tools. In their view, Oldowan was not a simple and "expedient" technology in which tools were made only to fill an immediate need from whatever happened to be available. If this had been the case, then flakes and the cores from which they originated would all be found together where they were made and used, and they would have been produced from raw materials found nearby.

Instead, the archaeological record shows that cores were transported, sometimes several kilometers from their point of origin. *Homo habilis* was willing to travel some distance for a source of stone known to be superior for the production of sharp, durable tools. The cores themselves appear to have been moved around to wherever flakes were needed; it is common to find flakes, but not their source cores, at a site. The cores, apparently, were carried to the next place tools might be needed. This process shows a high level of planning and intelligence. As Schick and Toth (1993, 128) maintain, "This is a much more complicated pattern than many would have suspected from this remote period of time. It bespeaks to us an elevated degree of planning among these early hominids than is presently seen among modern nonhuman primates."

The Fate of Homo habilis

The existence of *Homo habilis* was rather short in evolutionary terms: Occurring first in deposits that are about 2.4 million years old, their remains disappear entirely sometime after about 1.8 million years ago. But the evidence does not imply that *Homo habilis* simply became extinct, leaving no evolutionary descendants. In fact, *habilis* appears to have evolved into another hominid species. This evolutionary jump and the new species that resulted is the focus of the next chapter.

ISSUES AND DEBATES

WHAT WERE THE FIRST STEPS IN HOMINID EVOLUTION?

The evidence regarding how the hominid family began is unequivocal. The first hominids were, fundamentally, bipedal apes; the first steps of our evolution were literally "first steps." The physical evidence shows that creatures dating to at least 4.4 million years B.P. had a skeletal anatomy suitable for walking on two feet, in a manner similar, if not identical, to the way modern human beings walk. At the same time, these creatures possessed brains of a size and configuration virtually indistinguishable from those of some species of fossil and modern apes (Figure 4.17). The consensus on this is clear.

FIGURE 4.17

A comparison of brain size and body weight in a number of different ape and hominid species.

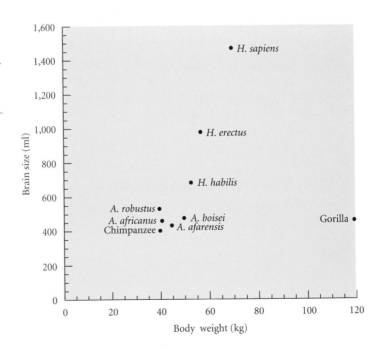

This scenario of the origin of the human line, based on locomotor patterns rather than growth in brain size and intelligence, was not what most nineteenth-century evolutionary scientists expected and may seem to contradict common sense even today. After all, the hallmark of our species, the characteristic that seems to distinguish us the most from other animals, including the apes, is our great intelligence. Chimps and bonobos, for all their great intelligence, their inventiveness, and even their capacity for communication, have brains less than one-third the size of the modern human brain (about 450 ml compared to about 1,450 ml). In other words, our brains are a quantum leap larger in volume, more than three times larger than those of chimps and bonobos.

We might expect, therefore, that our brain has been evolving the longest and was the first characteristic that differentiated us from the other primates—and that its growth is what initiated the split between the pongid and hominid families. In fact, many scientists held this view in the late nineteenth and early twentieth centuries. For example, Grafton Elliot Smith, a renowned British scientist who published extensively on human evolution, expressed the perspective of many others when he characterized the then hypothetical earliest human ancestor as "merely an ape with an overgrown brain" (1927, 105–6). The belief that the fossil record should provide specimens that looked like apes with "overgrown" brains made many people susceptible to a hoax. The famous fossil found at Piltdown in southern England seemed to be that big-brained early ancestor. Many scientists suspended their usual skepticism and accepted the Piltdown finding. But the fossil turned out to be a modern human skull planted with an ape jaw that was doctored so as to appear to belong to the skull (see Feder 1999).

WHAT CAUSED THE PROLIFERATION
OF HOMINID SPECIES?

The answer to the question "What caused the proliferation of hominid species?" is far from clear. The work of paleoanthropologist Elisabeth Vrba (1985, 1988, 1993) shows a proliferation of new grassland animal species after 2.5 million years B.P., including arid-adapted creatures such as gazelles, antelopes, and wildebeests. She interprets this change as the result of an expansion of savanna habitats and the creation of new grassland niches because of the overall cooling of the planet. As commonly happens when new niches open up (new ways to make a living in an environment), evolution moves quickly to fill those niches with life. Because natural selection is fueled by environmental conditions, when those conditions diversify, selection accelerates for species with characteristics advantageous for the newly created conditions. Vrba calls this process a **turnover-pulse** (1993, 50).

However, more recent analysis of the faunal record, while showing a definite increase in grassland-adapted species through time, calls into question

Vrba's notion of a dramatic change coinciding with the appearance of *Homo habilis* (Behrensmeyer et al. 1997).

Paleoecological evidence collected in association with the earliest hominids shows that our ancestors were not restricted to living in the grassland. *Ardipithecus, Australopithecus anamensis,* and *Australopithecus afarensis* have been shown to have lived in diverse environments with both savanna and open woodlands in their territories. Remember the features they retained for climbing trees at the same time they had become bipedal: curving toes and long, hooklike hands. Paleoanthropologist Richard Potts (1996) suggests that rather than adapting to one specific set of ecological circumstances, our ancestors seem to have proliferated and prospered in environments characterized as **mosaic**—a diverse mixture of habitats. Perhaps it was their adaptive flexibility that gave them an evolutionary advantage in the diverse and inconstant world of 3 to 5 million years ago. An animal that could both readily climb trees *and* walk on two feet in the expanding grasslands might have possessed a significant adaptive advantage over those species that could only climb trees. It makes sense and it establishes a pattern we will see throughout later human biological and cultural evolution: The flexibility to adjust to a diverse and uncertain environment has long been the hallmark of the hominid family.

HOW DO WE KNOW THE HOMINIDS WERE UPRIGHT?

The configuration of the skeleton is quite different for creatures who walk quadrupedally and for those who are habitual bipeds. The most important part of the skeleton in this regard is the pelvis, made up of a left and a right **innominate** bone (Figure 4.18). The innominate bones of a primate quadruped—for example, a chimpanzee—have a long and narrow top blade (the **ilium**) that connects to the base of the pelvic bone (the **ischium**), creating a flat plane. A human innominate, on the other hand, has an ilium that is short and broad and, when compared to a chimp's, flares out at the top and seems twisted to the side, producing a complex curve away from the plane of its ischium (Lovejoy 1988).

The configuration of the innominate bone in an animal determines the position of the large gluteal muscles, which in turn determines how the creature could most easily get around. Thus, the position of the ilium on the innominate bone of an extinct animal allows us, with some accuracy, to deduce how that creature walked—in other words, whether it got around on four legs or two.

There really is very little argument about the pelvis of *Australopithecus afarensis* as well as of the other australopithecines; they have an innominate bone very similar to that of a modern human being (Lovejoy 1988; Lovejoy, Heiple, and Burnstein 1973; see Figure 4.18). Scientists who have examined

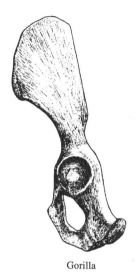  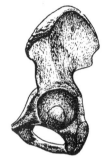

Gorilla   *Australopithecus*   Modern human being

FIGURE 4.18

A comparison of the pelvis of a gorilla, an Australopithecus, *and a modern human. Despite some differences, the pelvises of the extinct and the modern hominid are far more similar to each other than either is to that of the ape. This is because the pelvis determines the configuration of the muscles that attach to the upper leg, which, in turn, determines how an animal walks: Apes are quadrupeds;* Australopithecus *and modern human beings are bipeds.* (From "The Antiquity of Human Walking" by John Napier. Copyright © April 1967 by *Scientific American*, Inc. All rights reserved; drawing by Enid Kotschnig)

the bones disagree about whether *afarensis* differed in some of the particulars of walking; for example, Stern and Susman (1983) suggest that, though bipedal on the ground, *afarensis* shuffled more in the way a chimp does. However, most of these scientists maintain that *afarensis* walked much in the way we do (Lovejoy 1988).

IS THERE OTHER EVIDENCE FOR BIPEDALITY?

Though the pelvis is the best place to look for evidence of locomotion, other parts of *Australopithecus afarensis* anatomy further support bipedality. The Laetoli footprints (see Figure 4.1) are virtually indistinguishable from footprints of a modern human; individually they exhibit the typical pattern of a human foot, and together they match the human stride (Charteris, Wall, and Nottrodt 1981; Day and Wickens 1980; T. White 1980; White and Suwa 1987). The prints display a humanlike arch and lack any hint of the divergent big toe that characterizes the apes.

As we saw earlier, the location of the foramen magnum determines the position of the vertebral column, which in turn indicates whether a species is quadrupedal or bipedal. All fossil hominid crania possess a foramen magnum at the base of the cranium, in nearly the same position as in modern human beings, who, of course, are bipedal.

Other skeletal evidence of upright locomotion includes the bones around the knee. Fragments of the **femur** (upper leg) and **tibia** (lower leg) of *afarensis* show clearly that its upper and lower leg joined at an angle more like that in modern human beings than in apes (Johanson and Shreeve 1989). The preserved foot bones of *afarensis* are longer and more curved than the modern human form, but, like the footprints, they exhibit a modern arrangement of the big toe. In fact, when the large, well-preserved foot from the site of Hadar (see the "Case Study Close-Up" in this chapter) is scaled down to the size of the Laetoli prints, it is a perfect match (Johanson and Shreeve 1989, 197).

WHY BIPEDALISM?

Though the environmental change hypothesized by Vrba shows how evolution in general, and for hominids in particular, may have accelerated on the grass-lands as new niches opened up, it does not address the fundamental question of what advantages a bipedal ape might have had over its quadrupedal cousins.

As anatomist Owen Lovejoy (1984) points out, we can't explain the suc-cess of bipedalism on the basis of its current utility. The question must be asked in an evolutionary framework and placed within the context of natural selection: If you are an ape, what is it about walking on two feet in the savanna that increases your likelihood of survival and, in turn, the probability that you will reproduce and pass on the genetic disposition for bipedal locomotion to another generation, for whom greater proficiency for that mode can be fur-ther acted on by natural selection?

Seventeenth-century natural historian John Ray believed that upright walking was an endowment from God, giving human beings a unique advan-tage, enabling them to see for greater distances—to spot resources as well as dangers—and to carry objects.

Modern explanations of why this ability was the key selective factor in early hominid evolution are a bit more complex, though they often build on Ray's assertions. Modern hypotheses elaborate on how the ability to walk on two feet allowed our ancestors to survive at the end of the Miocene when so many other ape species became extinct and why it continued to be the central adaptive trait of the hominids until brain expansion took over more than 1.5 million years later.

The Upright Provider

Consider the hypothesis proposed by anatomist Owen Lovejoy (1981, 1984), who suggests that the key advantage to bipedal locomotion was that it freed the hands to carry things. Specifically, it freed the hands of males to carry food back to a camp or village where females and their offspring could be provisioned.

Among modern primates, chimp females raise their children alone. They are often quite good mothers, devoting much time and energy to the health and well-being of their offspring. From an evolutionary perspective, they are doing all they can to ensure that these children—individuals carrying half their genes—will survive to reproduce and pass on those genes. Male chimps, on the other hand, generally have little to do with infants. Since chimp society is sexually promiscuous, the males don't know which, if any, infants they have sired. So, from an evolutionary perspective, why should they waste time providing for offspring that probably do not carry their genes?

Obviously, for a female the more offspring she gives birth to, the greater the likelihood that one or more will survive to adulthood and continue passing on her genes. But there's a trade-off in a species like chimps (and especially humans), where offspring are dependent on their mothers for extended periods (chimps commonly stay with their mothers for 8 to 10 years). With each new baby, the female can spend less and less time caring for older children, which may lower their chances for survival. Any help she can get, especially if she has more than one young child, will improve the likelihood of survival of all of her children. It makes sense for her to solicit assistance from a concerned adult male.

But how can she convince a male to do this? In Lovejoy's view, she must assure him that the offspring are his and that, by helping them, he ensures that half his genes get passed along as well. Only a pattern of sexual fidelity—in other words, monogamy—can do this. Basically, it's a trade: Females increase the likelihood their children will survive by remaining sexually faithful to one male. The male receives exclusive sexual access to a female and an increased probability that he will father offspring. All he has to do is faithfully provision the female and the children he has sired with her. This ability to bring food and other resources back to the female and the young is made feasible, in Lovejoy's view, by the freeing of the hands—which, in turn, is made possible by walking on two feet.

Remember, individual animals are not making a conscious choice to enhance their contribution to the evolutionary gene pool. Females merely are choosing to associate with males who help them care for their children, and males help females who provide them with sex. These behaviors increase the probability that offspring survive to adulthood. In terms of natural selection, it should be apparent that those late Miocene apes who were pushed out onto the savanna and who acted in a way that increased the likelihood of their offspring's survival were more successful than those who did not: Their population increased while other groups became extinct. Since the provisioning behavior was made possible by upright walking, that ability would be strongly selected for.

Lovejoy's hypothesis explains bipedality, sexuality, and the development of monogamous family structure all at the same time. However, it has been criticized for being male-oriented and generally mistaken about modern primate behavior and the prevalence (or actual lack) of monogamy in modern human foraging societies (Tanner 1981; Zihlman 1979). There is at least one glaring problem here: When a male is away gathering food, what is to prevent a female from copulating with other males? In fact, such behavior may be to her advantage, because it would increase the number of males willing to provision her and her offspring. Sex is used in many of the social primates to make alliances and maintain friendships. In such a scenario, sexual fidelity might even

FIGURE 4.19

This micrograph of fossil bone from FLK Zinj at Olduvai Gorge shows tool marks on the bone (the horizontal lines and the diagonal line beginning at the top of the photo) and a carnivore tooth mark (beginning on the right side and angled toward the center). The carnivore mark overlies the tool mark, indicating that the hominids sliced meat off of this part of the bone before a scavenger began eating. (Photo by Pat Shipman)

be disadvantageous, particularly if the male doesn't do a good job of provisioning. Ultimately, it is difficult to understand how a more rigid pattern demanding sexual fidelity actually could have been maintained in ancient hominid societies.

The Upright Scavenger

Anthropologist Pat Shipman (1984, 1986) has proposed another hypothesis. Using the scanning electron microscope, Shipman has examined the remains of animal bones recovered at early hominid sites. She found microscopic evidence of tooth marks from predators and scavengers, as well as cut marks from stone tools, made when hominids removed the meat (Figure 4.19). In some instances she found carnivore and stone-tool marks on the same bones, either with the tool marks superimposed on the carnivore tooth marks or with the tool marks made first. In other words, sometimes the hominids got at the bones after carnivores had already chewed on them (indicating hominid scavenging behavior), and sometimes carnivores had access to the bones only after the hominids had processed them (indicating hominid hunting behavior). There are too few marks, however, to come to any conclusion regarding the relative contribution of hunted versus scavenged meat.

As we will discuss later in this chapter, archaeologist Lewis Binford (1987a) has shown that the animal bones found at ancient hominid sites usually are from meat-poor parts of the carcass. This finding suggests to Binford, as well as to Shipman, that the early hominids largely were scavengers of meat, chasing off large carnivores after a kill or simply waiting for them to leave after they had filled their stomachs.

Walking on two feet was highly advantageous to hominids who were opportunistic scavengers rather than habitual hunters. Hunters need to run, and an animal can run faster on four feet than on two. Scavengers, however, don't need to run; their prey isn't going anywhere. But scavengers still need to find their quarry, and that means walking great distances and scanning a broad territory for evidence of a predator kill. Bipedalism is highly energy-efficient, in part because it involves only two limbs, and yields greater endurance for walking long distances. It also is advantageous in the treeless and shadeless savanna; wandering, upright scavengers reduce the surface area of skin exposed to the burning African sun (Wheeler 1991).

In addition, since scavengers always need to be wary of the return of the predator who did the killing in the first place, as well as of other large, aggressive scavengers—like hyenas or jackals, who might compete for the same kill—it is wise to get in and out quickly: Cut the meat off the bone as fast as possible, and carry it back to a safe place to eat. The free hands of a bipedal hominid can carry both the tools for extracting the meat from the carcass and the meat.

The Efficient Walker

Primatologist Peter Rodman and anthropologist Henry McHenry (Johanson, Johanson, and Edgar 1994) have proposed what may be the simplest and most elegant hypothesis of all. After analyzing the energy expended by chimps when they walk quadrupedally and by humans with their upright gait, Rodman and McHenry determined that human locomotion was simply more efficient than chimp locomotion, meaning we expend less energy to accomplish the same task. As the Miocene forest shrunk and ape species were pushed out onto the growing savanna, where food resources were more dispersed, a more efficient way of moving across increasing distances in the search for food became adaptively advantageous.

All of the accumulated evidence of twentieth-century paleoanthropology basically brings us back to John Ray's seventeenth-century suggestions for the advantages of bipedalism. Though the modern hypotheses are more elaborate, they all suggest that ability to carry things, to move around in a more energy-efficient way, and perhaps to see across greater distances was crucial in the selection process. Hominids, who could walk upright, had advantages that afforded them a better chance of survival in their grassland habitat.

WHAT DO WE KNOW ABOUT THE EARLY HOMINID BRAIN?

Under the very best of circumstances, paleoanthropologists are limited to the direct study of the hard parts of a hominid's anatomy—those that lend themselves to preservation: teeth (which are the hardest parts of our bodies and so the most abundantly preserved ancient hominid remains) and bones (which, though not as hard as teeth, under the right circumstances will fossilize and be preserved for millions of years). But if we want to know about early hominid intelligence, we are usually limited to hypothesizing on the basis of brain size as determined from the volume of the preserved skull.

The cranium is the vessel in which the brain resides. Where the cranium is well preserved, we can measure its volume to determine the size of an early hominid brain—in some cases, using sophisticated computer imaging technology (Conroy et al. 1998). Most of the early hominid brains turn out to be about the size of a chimpanzee's. The mean size of a chimp brain is about 400 ml. Compare this to the mean size of a modern human brain, which measures about 1,450 ml. Though we do not have enough cranial fragments to accurately assess the size of the *Ardipithecus* or *Australopithecus anamensis* brain, the *afarensis* brain can be measured; its mean is about 413 ml, marginally larger than a chimp's. *Australopithecus africanus* possessed a brain about 440 ml in size, and the more robust and larger australopithecines had brains that were closer to 500 ml in size. *Homo habilis*, the first member of our genus, possessed a brain with a mean size of close to 650 cc, still less than half the size of the modern human brain.

The brain itself is soft tissue and quickly decays, usually leaving no trace. However, under rare circumstances a cast of the brain, showing features of its exterior surface, can survive when minerals replace the brain as it decays, filling the skull like Jell-O in a mold. Called **endocasts,** these natural models of ancient brains can show us what the exterior surface of an ancient brain looked like.

Anthropologist Dean Falk (1984) has examined the seven known cranial endocasts of *Australopithecus africanus.* The exterior surfaces of all these casts are virtually indistinguishable from the brains of modern apes. They display none of the characteristics of the exterior of the human brain that distinguish it from that of an ape's brain. Specifically, the brains of the australopithecines are symmetrical: The left and right halves appear to be mirror images of each other. Modern human brains are decidedly asymmetrical: The left and right halves look different and actually are associated with different functions. Considering our view of the australopithecines as a series of bipedal apes, we should expect them to lack this feature of the human brain.

Where nature has not provided endocasts, they can be manufactured by coating the inside of a fossil skull with liquid latex or a similar material that, when dry, can be peeled off. This artificial endocast reflects the form of the interior surface of the skull and, it is hoped, shows features of the exterior of the brain with which the skull was in constant contact for an individual's lifetime. The artificial endocast of a *Homo habilis* specimen (ER 1470) shows a far more humanlike, asymmetrical morphology, providing further evidence of the ancestral connection they share with us.

WERE THE EARLY HOMINIDS HUNTERS?

From the physical remains of ancient hominid skeletons, we can reconstruct what they looked like and how they walked. We also know about their stone tools. These artifacts are quite durable and show in a direct way the technological abilities of the first toolmaking hominids. Every stone tool is a fossil of a series of actions, and we can fairly accurately reconstruct those actions and, hence, a technology.

When we are dealing with ancient sites and fossils, however, more detailed questions of lifestyle are often extremely difficult to answer. For example, the nature of the hominids' **social systems**—how they related to each other within groups, how they defined "family," whom they considered suitable mates—is, perhaps, forever out of reach. We are relegated to using living primates or hunting-and-gathering groups of human beings, neither of which should be considered truly reliable as models for prehistoric hominid behavior. Using modern primate models, R. A. Foley and P. C. Lee (1989) make an interesting attempt to construct early hominid social systems. They suggest that savannas encourage relatively large group size because of the greater risk of predators in a grassland environment. They maintain that large groups based on male kin alliances are adaptive under these circumstances. Applying this scenario specifically to *Australopithecus afarensis,* they see a social organization consisting of related males who interacted with females and their off-spring and for whom they provide protection from predators. Of course, it is extremely difficult to find data to test such a hypothesis.

Subsistence, that part of a culture's economic system that supplies the necessities for survival, is something that archaeological research can often illuminate more directly. For instance, as we saw in Chapter 3, the dietary pattern leaves physical remains in the form of bones, seeds, nuts, and so on that can be studied. So the diet of the earliest members of the human family is, at least potentially, reconstructable.

In the past, many paleoanthropologists assumed that the first humans were hunters and that any tools found would relate to a hunting adaptation. Actually, there is very little evidence to support this view. Neither the Oldowan choppers nor the used flakes would have been all that handy as spearpoints. Moreover, a detailed **taphonomic** analysis conducted by archaeologist Lewis Binford (1987a) has shown that animal bones found at early hominid sites typically are not those we would expect to find at the hunting camps of proficient hunters. The animal skeletal elements found are not those that would have been associated with the best cuts of meat, such as upper limbs. Binford determined that the excavated animal bones were mostly lower limbs and parts of skulls and mandibles, among the least meaty of animal parts. Moreover, many of the tools found at *Homo habilis* sites would have been more suitable for extracting marrow than for removing meat from bones; marrow inside the shafts of long bones, typically left behind by carnivores, is a staple for many scavengers. Binford's analysis indicated that early hominids were probably not proficient hunters at all but, instead, opportunistic scavengers of the carcasses of animals killed by large carnivores.

Electron microscope analysis conducted by Pat Shipman (1983, 1984, 1986) along with Richard Potts (Potts and Shipman 1981), which we discussed in connection with the origins of bipedality, further supports the hypothesis that scavenging played a major role in the diet of early hominids. For example, the cut marks on animal bones Shipman examined from *habilis* sites in Olduvai Gorge tend to be near the midshaft of the bones (Shipman 1983). For later groups known to be butchering entire carcasses rather than just scavenging them, the cut marks are almost always located near the joints, where the best meat is available. The location of the cut marks on the Olduvai animal bones seems to conform better to a scavenging than a hunting mode of subsistence.

Though scavenging might seem an unreliable mode of subsistence, under certain circumstances it is a reasonably low-risk strategy that yields an abundance of food. Using as a model modern ecosystems broadly similar to those in which the early hominids found themselves, a number of analyses have shown scavenging to be a productive subsistence strategy (Blumenschine 1989; Blumenschine and Masao 1991). Hyenas are virtually the perfect scavenger; they are powerful and intelligent, and they prowl their territory looking for fresh kills in organized social groups. A large group of hyenas can run a pride of lions off of their kill, and they would have provided fierce competition for any other species, including hominids, that might have relied on scavenging. On the other hand, where hyenas occurred in small numbers and posed little threat, it may have made sense for hominids to wait for large predators such as lions to make their kills and then take advantage of what they left behind—or even run them off and "steal" the meat in what is called "confrontational scavenging." In fact, a decrease in the number of hyenas seems to coincide with the appearance of *Homo habilis* (Blumenschine 1987).

Though scavenging clearly was important in the early hominid quest for food, other research shows that hunting also was a part of early hominid subsistence. Henry Bunn and Ellen Kroll (1986) analyzed stone flakes and bones from the 1.8-million-year-old FLK site in Olduvai Gorge in Tanzania and found substantial evidence for reliance on meat; bones representing the meatiest parts of animals bore ample evidence of stone-tool cut marks. The evidence for hunting seems a bit stronger for small animals, with a pattern of scavenging but also some hunting of larger animals.

If animals are being scavenged, the scavenger grabs whatever portion of the killed animal can be obtained and takes it to a secure place. The archaeological sites that develop in such secure places produce lots of small portions of animals, bones reflecting whatever pieces of the animals the scavenger was able to grab. On the other hand, hunters carry most, if not all, of an animal back to a place where the food can be shared; they have complete control of the animal from the time of its killing to the time of its being eaten. At FLK, large sections of animals were found, suggesting that hunting was a primary mode of subsistence there.

We needn't be too concerned about the finer points of early hominid subsistence. All researchers would probably agree that hunting was not predominant in the subsistence base of the australopithecines or in *Homo habilis*. Though we have to be careful when generalizing from nonhuman primates, we do know that chimpanzees in the wild occasionally engage in cooperative hunts (Goodall 1986). In questioning the hunting abilities of early hominids, many archaeologists and paleoanthropologists are reacting to previous, overly romantic versions of a human past populated by killer apes (see Robert Ardrey's 1961 book *African Genesis* for his now discounted view that the killer instinct is what allowed our ancestors to thrive). But, in reacting to the killer-ape hypothesis, as paleoanthropologist Daniel Stiles (1991) has pointed out, there is no reason to believe our hominid ancestors were less capable than chimps in their ability to plan, coordinate, and carry out a hunt. The first hominids were not born killers, but they probably did rely on meat to a certain degree, some of it scavenged, some from hunting. The early hominids probably were opportunistic foragers, taking whatever food they could, whenever the opportunity presented itself.

SINGLE OR MULTIPLE SPECIES?

Defining species on the basis of fragmentary bones is a difficult task. Assigning a new discovery to a particular, previously recognized species or identifying a new species is an even more difficult job. Interfertility—the ability of fertile males and females to produce fertile offspring—is a major criterion applied in defining the boundaries of a living species. This criterion is obviously of no use to the paleoanthropologist. These scientists must rely on detailed similarities and differences in skeletal anatomy and behavioral characteristics reconstructed from the archaeological record to assign a particular specimen to a known species or to decide that it represents a new, as yet unrecognized, group. Essentially, paleoanthropologists must carefully measure every possible feature on a newly discovered bone or skeleton. If these measurements are a reasonable match for those same measurements for an already defined fossil species, the new find is placed within that group. If, on the other hand, the new bones fall outside of the range of measurements for any previously defined group, a new species may be defined and a new name assigned.

For example, when researchers discovered the bones from Kanapoi and Allia Bay, Kenya, mentioned earlier in this chapter, there were a number of previously defined and named hominid species to which the new bones might have been assigned: *Australopithecus afarensis* or *africanus,* for example. The detailed measurement of these new specimens showed, however, that they simply were too different from those of the already named species. As a result, the researchers decided to assign the bones to a new species with a new name: *Australopithecus anamensis* (Leakey et al. 1995).

The problem is that there is no objective yardstick by which one can know for certain whether the measurements of a new specimen are close enough to warrant inclusion in a previously defined species or far enough outside of the range to justify the naming of a new species. We must remember that some living species, humans included, exhibit quite a bit of variation, and there is no reason to believe ancient hominid species were less diverse than modern people.

All living human beings are members of the same species, *Homo sapiens,* despite wide variability within the species. Would a paleoanthropologist from another planet, confronted with the fragmentary skeletal remains of a number of different kinds of modern human beings, recognize that the small, light skeletons of Mbuti pygmies, for example, and the large, heavy bones of Athapaskan Indians belong to the same species?

Assigning a fossil to an existing species or naming a new species based on its measurements is not an entirely objective enterprise, and scientists debate this process all the time. Some paleoanthropologists are lumpers, allowing for great variation within a species, "lumping" lots of specimens into individual species categories. Others are splitters, dividing the lumpers' large and diverse species, "splitting" them into several species. For example, Bernard

Wood (1992a,b) suggests that *Homo habilis* reflects too much variability to represent a single species. Since a rather large number of contemporary, different species of *Australopithecus* are recognized, might not such complexity characterize the first representatives of the genus *Homo?* Specifically, Wood agrees that all of the specimens from Olduvai Gorge currently assigned to the taxon *Homo habilis* should remain as members of the species along with some, but not all, of the specimens from Koobi Fora (see Figure 4.6). These fossils have in common a larger cranial capacity than any of the australopithecines (and smaller than the species *Homo erectus,* to be discussed in the next chapter) but a postcranial skeleton that is similar, if not identical, to that of *Australopithecus.* The rest of the Koobi Fora specimens currently contained in *Homo habilis,* according to Wood, should be placed in a separate species and called *Homo rudolfensis.* Like *Homo habilis, Homo rudolfensis* had a larger brain than *Australopithecus,* but its postcranial skeleton is more modern in appearance.

Most researchers still adhere to the single-species model, including paleoanthropologist Philip Tobias, who helped define *Homo habilis* more than 35 years ago (Leakey, Tobias, and Napier 1964; Tobias 1991). A recent analysis of brain size differences within the known *habilis* specimens shows a range similar to those of other fossil species and even within modern ape species, supporting the one-species model (Miller 1991). But the sample size for early *Homo* is quite small, so this issue cannot be decided with any confidence. Only more research and larger sample sizes will help solve this problem.

RATES OF CHANGE IN EVOLUTION

As paleontologist Stephen Jay Gould (1994) points out, most people think that evolution proceeds along a steady, even course, with small, incremental changes leading to large changes across the vast expanse of time. Yet, when we look at the evidence for the fossil species *Australopithecus afarensis,* we see something quite different. The oldest commonly accepted *afarensis* specimen is the Belohdelie frontal bone from a skull dated to 3.9 million years ago. The youngest is the nearly complete Hadar cranium, A.L. 444-2, dated to 3 million years ago. Separated by nearly 1 million years, these two specimens are remarkably similar, where comparisons can be made. They imply fundamental stability in the species during this period, not accretional change.

Gould and his colleague Niles Eldredge proposed a perspective on evolution called **punctuated equilibrium** (Eldredge and Gould 1972). In this view, species tend to remain stable for long periods of time before undergoing—perhaps in response to a dramatic change in their environment—a period of relatively rapid change ("rapid" in geological time is still rather slow by human standards). Long periods of stability—"equilibrium"—marked by rapid bursts of change—"punctuations"—seem to characterize the history of many species, including our own. If Gould is right, and if Elisabeth Vrba is right in her conclusion of a period of rapid and dramatic environmental change, then the extinction of *afarensis* and the proliferation of a number of new hominid forms after 3 million B.P. are directly connected.

Hadar, located in the Afar triangle of northeastern Ethiopia, is one of the most spectacular fossil hominid sites ever excavated. All by itself, the Hadar site disproves the notion that the pronouncements of paleontologists are based on a tiny handful of unrecognizable bone fragments or indistinguishable teeth. This one site produced 250 hominid fossil bones representing 14 individual members of the species *Australopithecus afarensis* (Johanson and Shreeve 1989, 21). Perhaps most significantly, Hadar produced Lucy.

The remains of the fossil that her discoverers named Lucy were found in 1974. Close to one-half of her skeleton was recovered, including parts of the skull, the lower jaw, ribs, vertebrae, arm bones, left innominate, left femur (upper leg), and parts of the lower right leg (see Figure 4.8). The following year, fragmentary remains of 13 more individuals were found, including 9 adults and 4 children. Dubbed "the First Family," all these individuals were deposited at the same time and seem to have died together.

The Hadar fossils provided the name for this hominid species, *Australopithecus afarensis,* after the Afar region of Ethiopia where the site is located. Lucy and the First Family fossils constitute solid support for the interpretation presented in this chapter: Dating to more than 3.18 million years ago, these early hominids were, essentially, bipedal apes.

Lucy has received most of the attention as a result of her remarkable degree of preservation, but her size is not typical of the group found at Hadar. Lucy, an adult, was tiny by modern standards, standing only a little over 110 cm (3½ ft) tall, with an estimated weight of about 30 kg (65 lb), small even by *afarensis* standards. But Lucy is a female in a species that exhibits a large measure of **sexual dimorphism**—that is, a big difference between males and females. For example, among gorillas—a species with strong dimorphism—males are commonly twice the size of females. A recent analysis shows that sexual dimorphism among the known *afarensis* specimens is less than that exhibited by gorillas and orangutans but more than in chimpanzees and much more than in modern human beings (McHenry 1991). Lucy falls within the broad range of sizes represented in the First Family fossils. Though she is a small female, she is clearly a female.

The Hadar specimens show what these ancient hominids looked like: They were bipedal. Their arms were proportionally longer than those of modern humans, with hands quite modern in appearance except for fingers that curled more like an ape's fingers. Their jaws were an amalgam of ape and human. They had ape-sized brains housed in skulls that exhibited large, ape-like bony ridges above the eyes and a highly prognathous profile.

Hadar presents an astonishing picture of more than a dozen individuals who probably knew each other and perished together in the dim mists of our own beginnings. Like the footprints at Laetoli, they have achieved a kind of immortality as a result of the lucky accident of the preservation of their bones. And like the Laetoli prints, that lucky accident affords us, 150,000 generations later, the luxury to contemplate where and how we began.

 **VISITING THE PAST**

Unfortunately, most of you reading this book will probably not be able to visit Africa anytime soon, so you won't be visiting any of the fossil localities discussed here. Even if you were able to, most of the sites are nondescript, without any on-site museum or display. The Laetoli footprints, for example, were left in place and, after casts of the individual hominid prints were made, were covered up. Recently, the footprints were stabilized and covered in an attempt to preserve them for the future. The site is not open to visitors (Agnew and Demas 1998). Some of the sites are in areas where tourists are not welcome. For example, Donald Johanson, Lucy's excavator, was unable to return to Hadar for some time because of political turmoil in that part of Ethiopia (Johanson and Shreeve 1989).

Most of the significant early hominid fossils are housed in museums, particularly the National Museum of Tanzania in Dar es Salaam and the National Museum of Kenya in Nairobi, in eastern Africa, and in various museums in southern Africa. However, very few of the actual original specimens are on display. Almost all are locked away, to preserve them for future research as new techniques of analysis are developed—for example, the extraction and analysis of minute quantities of DNA left in fossil bone.

The good news is that many natural history and science museums, especially those in big cities in the United States and Canada, have displays showing casts of some of the original fossils, replicas of the Laetoli pathway, dioramas showing artists' reconstructions of ancient hominids, and even some actual stone tools. Many of these exhibits are quite well done and certainly worth a visit. Recently, the American Museum of Natural History in New York City refurbished its human evolution exhibit, relying extensively on fossil casts, computers, holograms, and other high-tech tools.

SUMMARY

Humanity began its evolutionary journey more than 4 million years ago as an "upright ape." Bipedal locomotion and not brain size or intelligence first distinguished us from the apes. The 4.4-million-year-old *Ardipithecus ramidus* may have been the first upright hominid. Its fossil remains are scanty, and so we are not certain. By 4.2 million years ago, *Australopithecus anamensis* certainly was upright and likely was ancestral to all later forms of hominids. The ability to walk on two feet was advantageous in many ways: Hominids could travel with greater energy efficiency, which assisted in scavenging. With the hands freed, they could carry tools to where they were needed and bring back food to provision the young and possibly the females with children.

Around 2.5 million years ago, an environmental change in Africa, sparked by worldwide cooling, induced a burst of evolution in the hominid family. A number of varied species branched off from *Australopithecus afarensis* after this time. One branch, *Homo habilis,* had a brain size larger than any ape's. With its larger brain, *Homo habilis* was able to produce the first stone tools—simple, but revealing a level of planning and forethought that reflects the great intelligence of this first member of our genus.

TO LEARN MORE

Technical Summaries

See Donald A. Savage and Donald E. Russell's *Mammalian Paleofaunas of the World* (1983) for a listing, with maps, of Miocene fossil species. To read more about ape species, see Peter Andrews and Chris Stringer, *Human Evolution* (1989), which includes paintings of a broad sample of reconstructed Miocene ape species. For detailed discussions of the Miocene fossil apes, see John Fleagle's *Primate Adaptation and Evolution* (1988) and F. Szalay and Eric Delson's *Evolutionary History of the Primates* (1979). For a broad presentation about the modern apes, see J. R. Napier and P. H. Napier's *A Handbook of Living Primates* (1967).

Popular Summaries

For very well written, less technical, and broader discussions of the paleoanthropology and archaeology of the first hominids, books written by some of the best-known scientists in the field are good choices: Donald Johanson and Maitland Edey's *Lucy: The Beginnings of Humankind* (1981), Donald Johanson and James Shreeve's *Lucy's Child: The Discovery of a Human Ancestor* (1989), and Richard Leakey and Roger Lewin's *Origins Reconsidered: In Search of What Makes Us Human* (1992). Donald Johanson, Lenora Johanson, and Blake Edgar's book, *Ancestors: In Search of Human Origins* (1994) is quite good. It brings the reader up-to-date on the latest discoveries in Africa and beyond and covers the entire story of human evolution. The book was a companion to a series on PBS with the same name. The videos are available at many libraries and anthropology departments. For a broad, all-encompassing, popular treatment of human evolution, see the beautiful coffee-table book written by Donald Johanson and Blake Edgar called *From Lucy to Language* (1996). There is no better source for artistic photographs of fossil hominid remains (taken by well-known photographer of paleoanthropological specimens, David Brill).

National Geographic magazine has remained very current on the latest hominid discoveries and newest interpretations in an ongoing series titled "The Dawn of Humans" that has appeared in many individual issues over the past few years. Look through back issues of the magazine starting with September 1995 for well-presented information—and, of course, fantastic graphics—on any of the periods of human evolution discussed in this book.

Some authors outside of paleoanthropology have chronicled the search for and analysis of the earliest hominids—and exposed the humanity behind the scientists involved in the search. See Delta Willis's *The Hominid Gang: Behind the Scenes in the Search for Human Origins* (1989) and noted science writer Roger Lewin's *Bones of Contention: Controversies in the Search for Human Origins* (1987).

On the Web

For summaries of the place of the australopithecines and *Homo habilis* in human evolution and also for lots of photographs of the fossils—and maps indicating the locations where these fossils were found—visit the following Internet sites:

http://dekalb.dc.peachnet.edu/~pgore/students/s97/bonetgar/austra.htm

http://citd.scar.utoronto.ca/ANTD15/Shan/title.html

KEY TERMS

hominid	ulna	striking platform
Miocene	prognathous	turnover-pulse
niche	maxilla	mosaic
brachiating	mandible	innominate
savanna	diastema	ilium
isotope	sagittal crest	ischium
C4 pathway	pongid	femur
C3 pathway	australopithecine	tibia
bipedal locomotion	Oldowan	endocast
cranium	core	social system
foramen magnum	flake	subsistence
postcranial	knapper	taphonomic
arboreal	object piece	punctuated equilibrium
humerus	hammerstone	sexual dimorphism

5

The Human Lineage

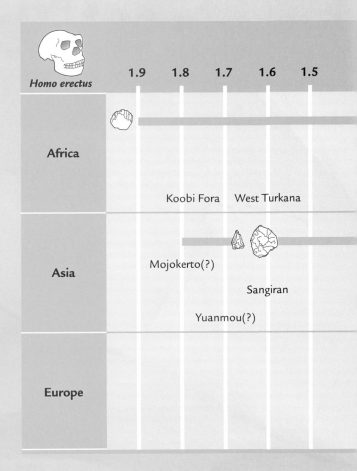

Homo erectus

	1.9	1.8	1.7	1.6	1.5
Africa					
		Koobi Fora		West Turkana	
Asia					
	Mojokerto(?)				
				Sangiran	
	Yuanmou(?)				
Europe					

CHAPTER OVERVIEW

Close to 1.8 million years ago, a new hominid—*Homo erectus*—made its appearance on the evolutionary stage. *Homo erectus* possessed a brain larger than that of *Homo habilis*, from which it evolved; the *Homo erectus* brain was two-thirds the size of a modern human brain.

Homo erectus exhibited increased intelligence as well as an increased reliance on cultural adaptations. Though born in an African nursery and possessing an anatomy best suited to life in the tropics, culture allowed *Homo erectus* to expand into other regions by at least 1 million and perhaps 1.5 million years ago. *Homo erectus* was the first hominid to leave remains in Europe and Asia. A sophisticated stone-tool technology, cooperative hunting, the controlled use of fire, clothing, and the possible construction of shelters were all a part of the *Homo erectus* adaptation. A reliance on culture is a hallmark of this human ancestor.

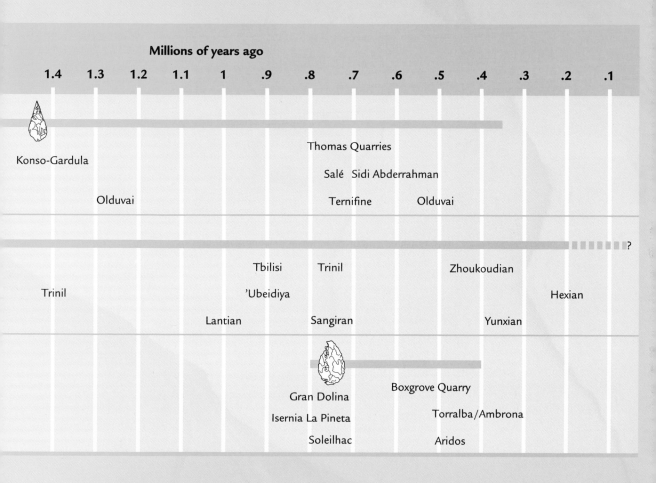

Millions of years ago

| 1.4 | 1.3 | 1.2 | 1.1 | 1 | .9 | .8 | .7 | .6 | .5 | .4 | .3 | .2 | .1 |

Konso-Gardula

Thomas Quarries

Salé   Sidi Abderrahman

Olduvai

Ternifine   Olduvai

Tbilisi   Trinil   Zhoukoudian

Trinil   Hexian

'Ubeidiya

Lantian   Sangiran   Yunxian

Gran Dolina   Boxgrove Quarry

Isernia La Pineta   Torralba/Ambrona

Soleilhac   Aridos

PRELUDE

As famed paleoanthropologist Richard Leakey (Leakey and Lewin 1992) admits, it sometimes is easy to forget that the bits and fragments, shards and slivers of fossilized bone paleoanthropologists hold in their hands, place under their microscopes, and mount in museum displays were connected to actual, thinking, feeling beings. Perhaps such small fragments make it easy to forget. But sometimes paleoanthropologists get lucky and recover the nearly complete skeleton of an individual—then it becomes impossible to forget they are looking at the remains of once-living creatures. The remains of the boy from Nariokotome, west of Lake Turkana, in Kenya, is one case that makes it impossible to forget (Leakey and Walker 1985a; Walker and Leakey 1993; Figure 5.1).

Based on the degree of his skeletal development, at the time of his death the boy was the equivalent of an 11- or 12-year-old modern child (Walker and Shipman 1996). Ironically, the age of the West Turkana boy is estimated the same way today's parents gauge the physical development of their own children. The loss of the deciduous teeth and the appearance of the permanent teeth occur at fairly set times during an individual's life, so we can gauge our children's level of maturation by the timed loss of baby teeth and the fixed appearance of their 6-year molars, their 12-year molars, and their 18-year molars (the "wisdom teeth").

By the time of the Nariokotome boy's death, his first (6-year) and second (12-year) permanent molar teeth had already erupted; that is, they were above where the gum line would have been and, therefore, must have been exposed in his mouth. Both of his upper deciduous canines were still in place, and his permanent upper canine on the right side was just erupting (Brown et al. 1985, 789; B. H. Smith 1993). None of his third molars had yet broken through. Thus, by using the rate of dental maturation for modern humans as a guide (Moorrees, Fanning, and Hunt 1963), it would seem that the Turkana boy was about 12 years old at the time of his death (B. H. Smith 1993)—if he were a modern human child. Other broad skeletal indicators, however, show that *Homo erectus* likely matured more quickly than modern humans, so the boy may actually have been no more than about 9 at the time of his death (Walker and Shipman 1996, 188).

The cause of death of the West Turkana boy is a sad mystery. What we do know is that he was struck down in his youth, leaving a remarkably well preserved, nearly complete skeleton that shows little except great health and vigor. Alan Walker, one of the fossil's excavators, describes him as a "strapping youth" and estimates his height at between 5 feet 4 inches and 5 feet 8 inches (Leakey and Lewin 1992). Except for some evidence of infection where he had lost a deciduous tooth, there is no sign of pathology on the skeleton, no evidence of disease, and no indication of trauma.

The West Turkana boy died on the edge of a lagoon near a lake. The position of his bones indicates that his body floated face down in the shallow water after he died. Fortunately, no scavengers picked at his corpse as it decayed, so most of the body remained pretty much in place, if not intact.

Animals coming to the lagoon for a drink may have walked on the body, breaking one of the legs and scattering the rest of the bones as the flesh, muscle, and tissue that had once been a boy were washed away. After the soft parts had decayed, a gentle current dispersed the bones across a linear distance of about 7 m (slightly more than 21 ft). The bones were then covered in the mucky lake bottom by waterborne silt and ash from a nearby volcano, where they rested for close to 1.6 million years.

In August 1984, Kenyan paleontologist Kamoya Kimeu was scouting for fossils in Nariokotome, in an area that is now a dry lake bed. Kimeu was looking for fossils on his day off before the camp of paleontologists moved to another locality as planned because so little of importance had been found in the area. Within a short time, he spotted a skull fragment, and an excavation

CHAPTER SITES

EUROPE
Isernia La Pineta
L'Escale
Mauer
Saint-Acheul
Schöningen
Soleilhac
Torralba

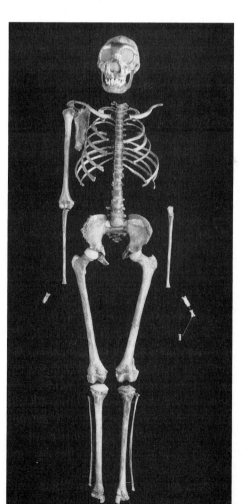

FIGURE 5.1

One of the most complete fossil hominid skeletons ever found: WKT-15000, the 9-year-old Homo erectus *boy from Nariokotome.* (Copyright © David L. Brill 1985/Atlanta, National Museums of Kenya)

was initiated. Soon the nearly complete skeletal remains of a boy were uncovered, revealing, with unprecedented clarity, an enormously ancient ancestor.

It is ironic that by dying in the right place at the right time, a young boy achieved an immortality that none of us will probably attain. Even 1.6 million years after he lived, in a time and world we can barely imagine, people still ponder his life. We place him in the taxonomic category *Homo erectus,* and his people are the focus of this chapter.

 **CHRONICLE**

As indicated by a series of new fossil specimens, soon after 1.8 million B.P. in Africa, and somewhat later in Asia and Europe, an acceleration of human evolution took place. The new fossils are different enough from *Homo habilis* to warrant a new name or names for the reasons enumerated in our discussion of species designation in Chapter 4. The new specimens have skeletal anatomies so different from that of *habilis* that they simply cannot reasonably be placed in the same group. But what to name the new fossils, and should they all be placed together in the same group?

Many paleoanthropologists believe that all of the hominids that follow *Homo habilis* and predate *Homo sapiens*—from after 1.8 million B.P. until about 300,000 B.P. or even later—belong to a single species: *Homo erectus.* When the sample of specimens recovered for this group was small and anatomical variation seemed quite limited among those fossils found from Africa all the way to east Asia, this assumption was reasonable. A recent spate of discoveries has convinced others, however, based on highly technical analyses of the morphology of the various specimens, that this period of human evolution instead presents us with a number of related, but more or less geographically separate, species: *Homo ergaster* in Africa, *Homo erectus* in central and east Asia, and *Homo antecessor* in Europe. In other words, a population of fossils that had all been placed within a single species is now seen by some to exhibit enough variation to separate them into three.

Though consensus is growing that these fossils should be separated into at least two and possibly three or more individual species, the jury is still out on this. For the sake of clarity and to make this part of the human story more straightforward, we will take the simpler approach here, labeling all of the specimens to be discussed in this chapter *Homo erectus.* (Figure 5.2 presents two different phylogenies, one based on the simpler view followed here and one on the multispecies model.) Of course, the number of hominid species alive at any given time is of enormous importance. But for our purposes, it is not as important as understanding that—one species, two, three, or more—during the period from 1.8 million to after 300,000 B.P., populations of intelligent hominids, relying upon cultural adaptations, spread throughout much of the Old World, using their intelligence to successfully adjust to a series of widely different environments.

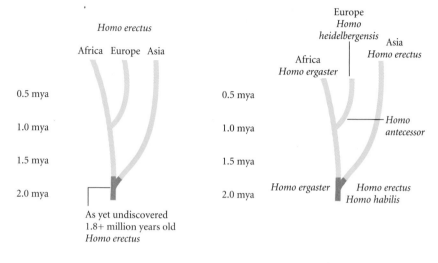

Europe
Homo
heidelbergensis
Asia
Homo erectus
Africa
Homo ergaster

0.5 mya
1.0 mya
Homo
antecessor
1.5 mya
Homo ergaster   *Homo erectus*
2.0 mya   *Homo habilis*

Homo erectus
Africa Europe Asia

0.5 mya
1.0 mya
1.5 mya
2.0 mya

As yet undiscovered
1.8+ million years old
Homo erectus

FIGURE 5.2

Two competing models for the number of species, evolution, and spread of hominids after 2 million years ago. In the more traditional model (left), Homo habilis *gave rise to* Homo erectus *in Africa sometime after 2 million years ago. From there,* Homo erectus *populations quickly spread into Asia and, later, Europe. In the competing model* (right), Homo habilis *gave rise to* Homo ergaster *in Africa sometime after 2 million years ago.* Homo habilis *or a descendant also spread into Asia soon after 2 million years ago, where it evolved into* Homo erectus. Homo ergaster *may have spread into Europe, where it gave rise to yet another hominid species,* Homo antecessor, *which later evolved into* Homo heidelbergensis.

HOMO ERECTUS

Soon after 1.8 million B.P., a new form of hominid appeared in the fossil record of eastern Africa. Potassium/argon dating has placed the oldest specimen—a skull labeled ER 3733 (Figure 5.3) from a rich fossil locality called Koobi Fora, east of Lake Turkana (Leakey and Walker 1985b)—at about 1.78 million years ago (Feibel, Brown, and McDougal 1989). The species is given the name *Homo erectus*. Physically and culturally, *Homo erectus* is recognizably human, yet it is intriguingly different from us.

The cranium of this new member of the human lineage was quite different from that of its evolutionary antecedent, *Homo habilis* (Figure 5.4). To begin with, its skull, and by implication its brain, was significantly larger. Most specimens have cranial volumes in excess of 800 ml, and the species as a whole has a mean cranial capacity of close to 1,000 ml (Table 5.1). The Nariokotome boy's cranial capacity was 880 ml; it is estimated that his brain size, had he lived to adulthood, would have been a little over 900 ml (Begun and Walker 1993, 346). The largest members of the species have skulls with volumes of over 1,200 ml. This measurement places the brain size of the species far above that of *Homo habilis* and within the lower range of modern human beings.

The skull of *erectus* was not just larger than that of *habilis,* but it was also differently configured and differently proportioned in ways that signify a shift toward a more modern human appearance. For example, the forehead of *erectus* is somewhat flatter and less sloping than that of *habilis,* a bit more similar to the modern, virtually vertical human forehead. The back, or **occipital,** portion of the *erectus* skull is rounder than that of *habilis,* with a much larger area for muscle attachment. Larger and stronger muscles were needed to support its much larger, heavier skull.

FIGURE 5.3

This fossil cranium designated ER 3733, at nearly 1.8 million years of age, is the oldest known specimen of the fossil species Homo erectus. (Copyright © National Museums of Kenya)

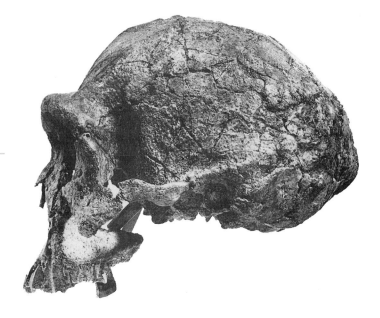

FIGURE 5.4

In this comparison of the skulls of Homo habilis *and* Homo erectus, *the skull of* erectus *is seen to be larger and more modern (less apelike) than that of* habilis.

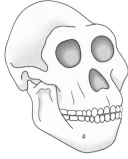

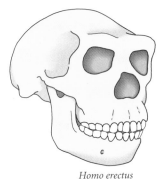

Homo habilis   *Homo erectus*

   Analysis of cranial endocasts (see Chapter 4) of a number of *Homo erectus* specimens (Holloway 1980, 1981) shows intriguing similarities to the modern human brain. Most significantly, anthropologist Ralph Holloway discovered hemispheric asymmetry in the *erectus* brain, similar to that seen in modern human beings. The different halves, or hemispheres, of the human brain regulate different tasks; in particular, human speech is ordinarily controlled by the left hemisphere. As a result, the two halves of a human brain are of slightly different shape, proportion, and size. Whether the asymmetry in the endocasts of the *erectus* brain means they were capable of humanlike speech cannot be determined. But the configuration of the *erectus* brain was definitely

TABLE 5.1

Major *Homo erectus* Fossils Discussed in *Chapter 5*

COUNTRY	LOCALITY	FOSSILS	CRANIA	AGE	BRAIN SIZE (ML)
Java	Trinil	Skull cap, femur	"Java Man"	<1 million yrs	940
	Sangiran	Cranial and postcranial fragments from approx. 40 individuals	S-2	0.7–1.6 million yrs	800
			S-4	0.7–1.6 million yrs	900
			S-10	0.7–1.6 million yrs	850
			S-12	0.7–1.6 million yrs	1,050
			S-17	0.7–1.6 million yrs	1,000
			1993 Cranium	1.1–1.4 million yrs	856
	Ngandong	Cranial and postcranial fragments from over a dozen individuals	N-1	<1 million yrs	1,170
			N-6	<1 million yrs	1,250
			N-11	<1 million yrs	1,230
			N-12	<1 million yrs	1,090
	Sambungmachan		Sambungmachan	<1 million yrs	1,000
	Mojokerto	Child's cranium		1.8 million years?	
China	Zhoukoudian	Cranial and postcranial remains of over 40 individuals	II	<0.46 million yrs	1,030
			III	<0.46 million yrs	915
			VI	<0.46 million yrs	850
			X	<0.46 million yrs	1,225
			XI	<0.46 million yrs	1,015
			XII	<0.46 million yrs	1,030
			Locality 13	0.7 million yrs	
	Hexian (Longtandong)	Partial skull	"Hexian Man"	0.27 million yrs?	1,000

(continued)

TABLE 5.1 (continued)

COUNTRY	LOCALITY	FOSSILS	CRANIA	AGE	BRAIN SIZE (ML)
China (cont.)	Lantian (Gongwangling)	Cranial fragments, mandible	"Lantian Man"	0.7–0.8 million yrs	800
	Yunxian	Two crania		>0.35 million yrs	
Tanzania	Olduvai	Cranial and postcranial fragments, including mandibles and pelvis and long-bone fragments	OH 9 OH 12	1.25 million yrs 0.6–0.8 million yrs	1,060 800
Kenya	East Turkana	Cranial and postcranial fragments including mandibles and pelvis and long-bone fragments	KNM-ER 3733 KNM-ER 3883	1.78 million yrs 1.57 million yrs	850 800
	West Turkana	Nearly complete juvenile individual	KNM-WT 15000	1.5 million yrs	880
Algeria	Ternifine	Three mandibles and a skull fragment		0.5–0.7 million yrs	
Morocco	Thomas Quarries	Mandible and skull fragments		0.5 million yrs	
	Sidi Abderrahman	Two mandible fragments			
	Salé	Skull fragments	Salé	0.4 million yrs	880
Georgia	Tbilisi	Mandible fragment, 16 teeth		0.9–1.6 million yrs	
England	Boxgrove Quarry	Tibia		0.48–0.51 million yrs	
				Mean	971.96
				Standard Deviation	116.50

Data from Walker and Leakey (1993); Freibel, Brown, and McDougal (1989); Holloway (1980, 1981); Rightmire (1990).

more like that of modern human beings, and different from that of the chimp, gorilla, orangutan, australopithecine, and *habilis* specimens to which Holloway compared them.

Beneath the intriguingly humanlike brain, the *erectus* face itself is somewhat flatter, projecting less than the *habilis* face, though it still is far more prognathous than that of a modern human. Above the eye orbits, *Homo erectus* crania display a massive ridge of bone called a **supraorbital torus.** This "brow ridge" is present in the skulls of all ape species and is generally absent in the modern human form, though some people, especially males, exhibit relatively smaller but discernible ridges above their eyes.

From the front, the *erectus* skull presents a flattened trapezoidal shape as opposed to the corresponding very round appearance of a modern human skull. The sides of the *erectus* skull begin nearly parallel at the base and then angle inward toward the top. This provides a keel, but not a bony crest, at the apex of the skull. Also, preserved nasal bones indicate that *erectus* was the first of our ancestors to possess the modern human form of a projecting nose, rather than the inset nostrils that characterize the living apes and earlier hominids (Franciscus and Trinkaus 1988).

Below the skull, the bones of *Homo erectus* bear witness to a creature that indisputably walked upright, in a manner similar, if not identical, to that of modern human beings. To be sure, the West Turkana boy and other, more fragmentary, postcranial remains exhibit a skeletal architecture indicative of great muscularity and strength, probably outside the range of modern human beings. Nonetheless, as more than one paleoanthropologist has stated, you would not be alarmed if a *Homo erectus*, with a cap pulled down low over his or her forehead and face and appropriately dressed, were to sit down next to you in class. (In fact, he, or she, might appear to be an ideal candidate for the football team!)

It had long been assumed that nonmodern hominids were smaller in stature than modern humans. Certainly, Lucy was tiny (see Chapter 4), and many of the Neandertal fossils indicate a short, stout body shape for these extinct hominids (see Chapter 6). The Nariokotome boy, however, shows that relatively short stature was not universal among our ancient ancestors. At about 5½ ft in height at only 9 years of age, he was tall, even by modern standards. Since he was still developing (see "Issues and Debates" later in this chapter), he certainly would have grown even taller; at full growth he might have reached 6 ft.

The Evolutionary Position of Homo erectus

Current consensus is that *Homo erectus* is the direct evolutionary descendant of the African hominid species *Homo habilis*. The oldest *erectus* fossils are found in Africa, often in the same areas where *habilis* remains have been recovered (Figure 5.5). Fossils such as the Nariokotome boy (officially designated

FIGURE 5.5

Fossil localities of Homo erectus.

KNM-WT 15000), ER 3733, ER 3833, and OH 9 share the standard suite of *erectus* cranial characteristics and date to between 1.78 million years ago and 1.25 million years ago (Figure 5.6; Rightmire 1979a, 1990). Later African *erectus* remains, dating from 500,000–800,000 years ago, include the OH 12 calvarium from Olduvai Gorge in Tanzania, a skull fragment and three mandibles from Ternifine (now called Tighenif) in Algeria, and skull and mandible fragments at Thomas Quarries, a braincase from Salé, and two mandibles from Sidi Abderrahman, all in Morocco. (The **calvarium** is the top part of the cranium, minus the facial bones and the base of the skull.) These later fossils are quite similar, where comparisons can be made, to the older African material.

In terms of cranial capacity and morphology, all of the African *erectus* fossils reflect a position midway between *Homo habilis* and anatomically modern human beings. *Erectus* is interpreted as representing, therefore, an "evolved" *Homo habilis*. However, notice that the oldest *erectus* fossil is very close in time to, and perhaps even overlaps slightly, the youngest *habilis* fossils. This may mean that the situation is a bit more complex than the current consensus view would have it.

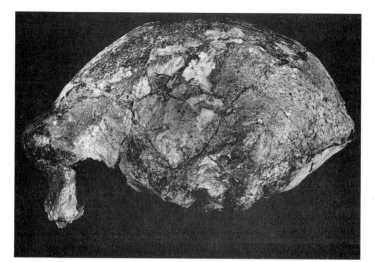

FIGURE 5.6

Crania of Homo erectus *from Sangiran, Java* (top), *and Zhoukoudian in China* (bottom). (*Top:* Courtesy of Ralph L. Holloway; *bottom:* Negative no. 315446, courtesy of Department of Library Services, American Museum of Natural History, photo by Charles H. Coles)

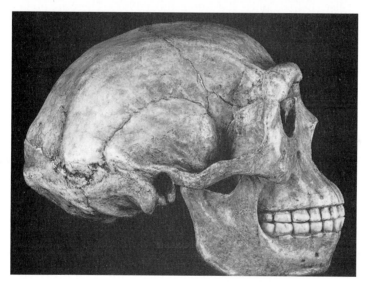

HOMINIDS CONQUER THE WORLD

Homo erectus, like its hominid predecessors, evolved in Africa. Unlike its forebears, however, *Homo erectus,* or perhaps an immediate evolutionary descendant, was not restricted to that continent. Fossils very similar to *erectus* have been found in Asia and date to soon after the appearance of *erectus* in Africa, 1.8 million years ago.

Africa is viewed as the cradle of human evolution for the simple reason that the oldest hominid fossils have been found there. The australopithecines

and *Homo habilis* are known only from Africa. *Homo erectus* is the first hominid species found outside of Africa. One might reasonably suggest that the
Homo erectus route out of Africa would take it to the north and east, into and
through the Middle East and eventually into east Asia. If this is the case, the
oldest specimens of *Homo erectus* migrants should be found in northeastern
Africa or the Middle East itself.

Unfortunately, the fossil record for this period is not as extensive as we
might like for northern Africa or the Middle East. We do not have a geographically continuous trail of the expansion of *erectus* out of Africa to the north
and east.

There is a well-preserved, 1-million-year-old *Homo erectus* cranium from
Eritrea, in northern Africa, near the Red Sea (and, therefore, close to Saudi
Arabia; Abbate et al. 1998). In the Middle East itself, there are very few sites
that date to the period before 1 million B.P.

Perhaps the oldest and most important site is 'Ubeidiya in the Jordan
Valley (Belfer-Cohen and Goren-Inbar 1994). There are no hominid remains
at the site, but there is a recognizable *Homo erectus* tool assemblage consisting
of stone choppers, picks, and bifaces (see the discussion of *Homo erectus*
toolmaking later in this chapter). 'Ubeidiya is estimated to be close to 1 million years old.

Farther north, on the east coast of the Black Sea, a well-preserved hominid
lower jaw and 16 teeth have been found at the Tbilisi site in Georgia (Bower
1995). The remains have been dated to an astonishing 1.6 million B.P. The
anatomy of the remains indicates quite clearly that they belonged to a representative of *erectus*. Because of the age and location of the Tbilisi mandible,
it is the closest specimen yet discovered of the earliest hominid migrants out
of Africa.

East Asia

Eastern Asia is the farthest point in the Old World from the African source
for *Homo erectus* populations; it is at the end of the migration pipeline. Ironically, however, *Homo erectus* specimens were found there before they were
found in Africa. And now, remarkably, recent redating indicates that some of
the east Asian *Homo erectus* specimens rival in age even the oldest *Homo
erectus* fossils in Africa.

The fact that *Homo erectus* fossils were found first in east Asia—Java,
to be more specific—is no mystery. It is simply a factor of where a scientist
first looked. In a remarkable instance of intuition, Dutch physician Eugene
Dubois (1894) traveled to the island of Java in the western Pacific in the late
nineteenth century expressly to seek out evidence of human origins in the
Asian tropics. In 1891, along the Solo River in the vicinity of the town
of Trinil, he came upon a calvarium that looked not quite human but not
quite apelike (Figure 5.7). It possessed large brow ridges like those of apes.

FIGURE 5.7

The first Homo erectus *skull fragment found was this skullcap recovered in Java in the late nineteenth century by Dutch scientist Eugene Dubois.* (Copyright © National Museum of Natural History)

But the cranial capacity, as best as could be judged at the time, was far larger than an ape's while still smaller than a modern human's. Dubois labeled the find *Pithecanthropus erectus,* meaning "upright ape-man." Still popularly referred to as "Java Man," we now include Dubois's discovery in the *Homo erectus* species. Its estimated cranial capacity of 940 ml and its age (still uncertain but probably about 1 million years old) place it firmly in the *erectus* species.

Also along the Solo River, northeast of Trinil, is the site of Ngandong. About a dozen crania were found here in the 1930s (Santa Luca 1980; Bartstra, Soegondho, and Wijk 1988). Though their skulls are quite large when compared to the other *Homo erectus* specimens, Philip Rightmire (1990) in his summary monograph on the species provides a detailed analysis that indicates that the Ngandong fossils belong in the same taxonomic group.

Just 65 km (40 mi) east of Trinil, another important fossil locality, called Sangiran, was found in 1937. The cranial remains of about 40 individuals have been recovered (see Figure 5.6). Some of the crania are more complete than the Trinil calvarium and share its form and size (Holloway 1981).

Most of the Javanese hominid remains were found more than 50 years ago—primarily by local farmers and other workers and not in controlled archaeological excavations. As a result, dating the specimens is a bit problematical, for it is difficult to be certain in which geological deposit, and precisely where in the deposit, the material originated. Scientists are pretty sure that the geological formation from which they were recovered is the **Kabuh Formation;** its estimated age is about 700,000–800,000 years, so the hominid remains are presumed to be about this old.

A recent discovery may change this assumption. Paleoanthropologist Donald Tyler has identified another skull unearthed by farmers at Sangiran (Rose 1993). It is clearly a *Homo erectus,* with a cranial capacity of 856 ml. In this case, however, Tyler has been able to associate the skull with a specific geological deposit more precisely than was possible with the earlier Sangiran discoveries. He has dated the age of the deposit to between 1.1 million years ago and 1.4 million years ago. Either of these dates would push back the *Homo erectus* expansion out of Africa fairly significantly. Tyler is excavating at the site in hopes of finding additional evidence of the *Homo erectus* occupation and of more confidently dating the newly found specimen.

Redating of three *Homo erectus* crania from Java, one found in 1936 (the Mojokerto child) and two at Sangiran in 1974, has excited and perplexed virtually everyone in the field. The dates (determined by the ^{40}Ar/^{39}Ar technique) are 1.8 million years for the Mojokerto child's skull and 1.6 million years for the Sangiran crania (see Bower 1994a and Swisher et al. 1994). The first date, if valid, not only puts *Homo erectus* in Asia substantially earlier than expected, but also makes the species at least as old as it is in Africa.

Do these dates support the notion that *Homo erectus* may actually have appeared first in Asia and migrated to Europe and Africa, rather than the other way around? This is extremely difficult to accept since no older, more primitive hominid from which *erectus* could have evolved has ever been found outside of Africa. Could the very early appearance of the species in Java signify that even older specimens will be found in Africa, since all other evidence indicates that they evolved there? Possibly, but as we push *erectus* further back, it becomes increasingly difficult to accept the consensus scenario that it evolved from *Homo habilis;* instead, they would have been contemporaries.

As is typically the case in paleoanthropology, the dates for the extremely old Java crania are derived not from the skulls themselves, but from the deposits in which they were recovered. It is possible that the deposits are older than the skulls, the hominid remains having settled into a stratum lower than their original place of deposit. It likely will take an *in situ* discovery—found in place—by a trained excavator before such an old date will become broadly accepted.

China

One of the most important *Homo erectus* sites ever discovered is in the village of Zhoukoudian, about 50 km (35 mi) southwest of Beijing. The cave at the site and the surrounding area produced the remains of about 45 *Homo erectus* individuals in a region possessing a continental climate (typified by hot summers and cold winters with ample precipitation spread more or less evenly throughout the year), then and now, not unlike that in the northern United States—obviously a far cry from tropical Africa, where the species originated. Occupation of the main site (Locality 1) by "Peking Man" has been dated through thermoluminescence, electron spin resonance, uranium series, and fission track dating to between about 600,000 and 230,000 B.P., though a maximum date of 462,000 B.P. is considered more accurate for the earliest occupation of the site (Pope 1992). Another site, located about 1 km south of the original Peking Man cave site, Locality 13, has been dated to 700,000 B.P. (Jia and Huang 1990).

More details concerning the site, its discovery, and its significance—and the tragic mystery of the disappearance of the fossils more than 50 years ago—are provided in this chapter's "Case Study Close-Up."

Chinese paleoanthropology has produced a number of other important *Homo erectus* discoveries. The Lantian skull from Gongwangling Hill of Shensi Province in east-central China has been dated to at least 500,000 years ago; new dating indicates it may be a bit more than 1 million years old (Chen and Zhang 1991). The Lantian cranium had a capacity of about 800 ml (Woo 1966). Its large brow ridges and broad face are very close in appearance to those of the Zhoukoudian fossils.

The remains of at least three individuals, including the nearly complete calvarium of a young male, were found near the village of Longtandong in Hexian County, Anhui Province, in eastern China. The calvarium has an estimated cranial capacity of about 1,000 ml (Wu and Xingren 1982). The Hexian material seems to include the youngest *Homo erectus* specimens yet discovered; thermoluminescence and uranium series dating place the specimen at somewhere between 150,000 and 270,000 years old (Pope 1992). This late date, if it holds up, indicates that late populations of *Homo erectus* were contemporary with early groups of *Homo sapiens* in China (see Chapter 6).

The latest discoveries of *Homo erectus* in China are the crania of two individuals found in Yunxian in Hubei Province in the east-central part of the country (Li and Etler 1992). These crania are quite large and complete, though very distorted. The researchers estimate a minimum age of 350,000 years for the two crania, which present an interesting mix of features similar to those of both the Zhoukoudian material and later, more modern-looking, human ancestors. Much work needs to be done restoring these very important fossils before their significance can be fully assessed.

Siberia

A site on the Lena River in Siberia in Russia, recently excavated, may represent the farthest extent of *Homo erectus* to the east and its adaptation to the coldest climate (Bower 1994c). Called the Diring site, it may date to about 500,000 years ago. No hominid fossils have been found here, but a large assemblage of stone tools has been recovered. Since the climate in and around Diring is far colder than anything previously known for *Homo erectus* and since no other sites in Siberia are known to date to before 35,000 years ago, most paleoanthropologists are intrigued by, but skeptical about, the site and its association with *erectus*. Additional research now being carried out at the site should help to verify or reject its age.

Homo erectus: *Ocean Explorer?*

As distant as any of the *Homo erectus* sites are from their ultimate source in Africa, all of these places are within "walking distance" of their point of origin—at least over many generations of wandering and expansion. It now appears that *Homo erectus* also had, at least to some degree, the ability to travel by sea. Stone tools have been found on the Indonesian island of Flores in the western Pacific in a stratigraphic layer dated to as much as 900,000 years ago (Morwood et al. 1998). Flores is separated from the mainland of southeast Asia by a natural underwater trench. Even during periods of lowered sea level, Flores would still have been separated from that mainland by approximately 19 km (almost 12 mi) of open sea. Though it was previously assumed that only anatomically modern human beings were capable of such feats, if the dates on Flores hold up, then in all likelihood *Homo erectus* had much earlier developed the capacity to make boats or canoes and to navigate and explore far from shore and, at least in the instance of Flores, to colonize islands.

Europe

The oldest unequivocal hominid remains found in western Europe were recovered at the site called Gran Dolina in the Atapuerca Mountains in Spain (Carbonell et al. 1995). The Gran Dolina finds show that humans were present in western Europe by at least about 800,000 years ago, and perhaps as much as 1 million years ago (Parés and Pérez-González 1995).

The Gran Dolina hominid fossils include the remains of at least four individuals, including two adults, one teenager, and one 10- to 12-year-old child. The preserved lower portion of the child's body is entirely modern in its morphology and, therefore, quite different from that seen in *Homo erectus* fossils dating to the same period. As a result, the Gran Dolina researchers have assigned these fossils to a new species, *Homo antecessor* (Bermúdez de Castro et al. 1997). As a result of the mosaic of primitive and modern traits of the Gran Dolina fossils, the researchers suggest that *antecessor* represents a descendant of *Homo erectus* (see Figure 5.2). Whether *antecessor* possesses features sufficiently different from those of *erectus* to justify the naming of a new hominid species becomes an argument between the lumpers and the splitters again, and the details need not concern us here. Following the practice established at the beginning of this chapter, we will label these specimens as *Homo erectus*. Whatever we call them, it is reasonable to say that African hominids had entered Europe by at least 800,000 years ago.

Other hominid fossils in Europe are more recent. At Boxgrove Quarry, in England, a hominid tibia has been dated to about 515,000 years ago (Bahn 1994). Of similar age is the so-called Mauer mandible, found in Heidelberg, Germany, in 1907. It has been less firmly dated to about 500,000 years ago.

There also are at least a few middle Pleistocene sites in Europe where artifacts—but no hominid bones—have been found. One of the oldest of these sites is Isernia La Pineta, in central Italy. Here a stone-tool industry of limestone choppers and unmodified flint flakes was found in association with the remains of bison, deer, elephant, rhinoceros, and hippopotamus (Coltorti et al. 1982). The site was found under a volcanic deposit K/Ar-dated to 730,000 years ago. At Soleilhac, in France, artifacts and faunal remains have been dated to 800,000 years ago (Weaver 1985).

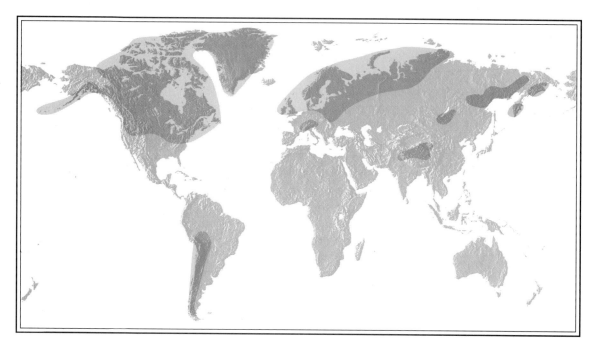

FIGURE 5.8

Worldwide glacial coverage during the peak periods of glaciation in the Pleistocene epoch.

THE AGE OF ICE

In 1991, one of the largest volcanic eruptions of the twentieth century occurred on Mt. Pinatubo in the Philippines. The eruption had an impact on worldwide climate as tons of fine ash wafted into the upper atmosphere and circled the globe. The ash cloud actually blocked out sufficient sunlight to drop the earth's temperature by a few degrees, enough to be the probable cause of the long, cold winter experienced in the northern hemisphere after the eruption.

As significant as the eruption of Mt. Pinatubo was, and as serious as its climatic impact may have been, it pales in comparison to the change in worldwide climate whose first impacts were felt about 3.2 million years ago (see Chapter 4) and which accelerated after 2.5 million and then again at about 1.6 million or 1.7 million years ago (Shackleton et al. 1984). For reasons that are still uncertain, beginning at this time the earth became a significantly colder place, particularly after about 900,000 years ago, with northern latitudes and higher elevations becoming covered by huge, expanding ice fields called **glaciers** (Shackleton and Opdyke 1973, 1976; Figure 5.8). Some of the proposed explanations blame the descent into colder temperatures on a decrease in solar output, interplanetary dust, or a change in the earth's orbit.

This colder period of time is called the **Pleistocene epoch** (see Figure 4.2 for a time chart placing the Pleistocene chronologically in the history of the earth). By convention, its inception is marked at 1.7–1.6 million years ago, though some push it back to the sharp worldwide temperature decrease that occurred 2.5 million years ago (Stipp, Chappell, and McDougall 1967). Researchers mark the end of the Pleistocene at 10,000 years ago, when worldwide temperature rose and glaciers shrunk. The modern period is called the **Holocene epoch.** Many climate experts believe that the Holocene is simply a relatively warm period that is destined to end in only a few thousand years, with glacial conditions nearly certain to return.

Though initially conceptualized and still commonly thought of as an "Ice Age" of unremitting cold, the Pleistocene actually was an epoch of fluctuating climate, with periods called **glacials** much colder than the present. These glacials were characterized by widespread ice and snow cover—imagine most of the central and northern United States and Canada and much of northern Europe looking and feeling like Greenland. But within the glacials themselves were colder and warmer periods, with attendant glacial advances (**stadials**) and retreats (**interstadials**). Between the glacials were relatively long **interglacial** periods, during which temperature often approached, sometimes equaled, and rarely may even have exceeded the modern level. If the Ice Age is, in fact, not over, then we are probably currently in an interglacial.

The pattern of temperature fluctuation and glacial advance and retreat can be studied in a number of ways. Glaciers leave significant and recognizable features as they cover the land. If you live in the northern third of the United States or virtually anywhere in Canada, then you can still see the effects of the huge, moving continental sheets and rivers of ice, some a few kilometers thick, as they rode over everything in their path. Glacial geologists can read a landscape for its glacial deposits, which can then be dated to develop a chronology of glaciation, as each subsequent expansion of ice overrode the previous one. (See Richard Foster Flint's *Glacial and Quaternary Geology,* 1971, for the classic work on the New World Pleistocene.)

The Oxygen Isotope Curve

The worldwide sequence of glacial advances and retreats can also be studied indirectly, via the ratio of two isotopes of oxygen ($^{16}O{:}^{18}O$) present in the preserved, datable shells of ancient marine microorganisms called **foraminifera.** The foram shells reflect the $^{16}O{:}^{18}O$ ratio in seawater when they were alive. That ratio changes, depending on how much of the ocean's seawater evaporates, falls on the land as snow, and then does *not* melt back into the ocean as worldwide temperature declines. Because ^{16}O is lighter than ^{18}O, water (H_2O) molecules containing ^{16}O are lighter and, therefore, evaporate more readily than water molecules with ^{18}O. During cold periods, water evaporates from the oceans and falls as snow in higher elevations and upper latitudes, and less of the snow melts off in the spring. The ocean, therefore, becomes somewhat depleted of ^{16}O relative to ^{18}O. The curve representing the relative proportion of $^{16}O{:}^{18}O$ has been determined by Shackleton and Opdyke (1973, 1976). Their results are presented in Figure 5.9. Covering the last

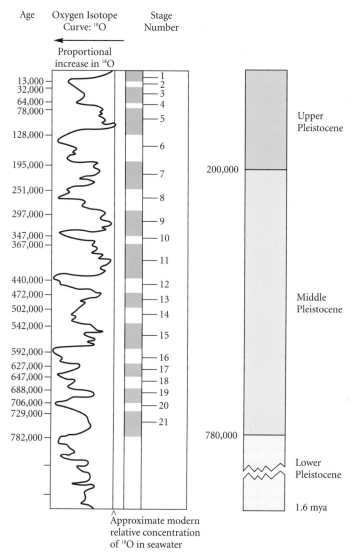

Age Oxygen Isotope Stage
Curve: ^{18}O Number

Proportional
increase in ^{18}O

^
Approximate modern
relative concentration
of ^{18}O in seawater

Odd-numbered stages (in yellow) = warmer periods, less glacial ice cover
Even-numbered stages = colder periods, more glacial ice cover

FIGURE 5.9

The Shackleton and Opdyke curve of ^{18}O concentration in fossil foraminifera is an indirect reflection of glacial expansion and contraction during the past 780,000 years.

780,000 years, a bit less than the last half of the Pleistocene, the Shackleton and Opdyke chronology exhibits 10 periods of drops in ^{16}O and, therefore, significantly colder temperatures and greater ice cover on the earth's surface. Further research has indicated at least 10 additional such periods in the first half of the Pleistocene.

All of this climatic instability must have affected our hominid ancestors. Chapter 4 discussed the key role the climate change of around 2.5 million years ago may have had in the evolution of *Homo habilis*. Though *Homo erectus* did not penetrate into areas where there were large continental ice sheets after 1.7 million B.P., all of the earth was influenced during the Pleistocene. Sea level dropped substantially, perhaps by as much as 125 m (more than 400 ft), during glacial maxima. Such a drop altered the configuration of most of the world's coasts, exposing as dry land thousands of square kilometers that previously were and presently are under water. The climate of areas even far south of the farthest extent of the glaciers changed, as low-pressure systems altered their usual flow patterns. These changes certainly altered the conditions to which *Homo erectus* needed to adapt. Adaptive flexibility seems to have been a hallmark of the members of this species. Their ability to inhabit new regions with environmental conditions far different from their tropical source, as well as their ability to change as their surroundings altered, bear witness to their great intelligence and, in fact, their humanity (see "Issues and Debates").

HOMO ERECTUS: THE TOOLMAKER

The great advance in toolmaking represented by *Homo erectus* as compared to *Homo habilis* is made clear by the following anecdote.

In a class I teach called "Experimental Archaeology," we spend a lot of time trying to replicate, as authentically as possible, various stone tools made by prehistoric people. We follow a chronological, evolutionary sequence, first replicating the Oldowan tools of *Homo habilis* and then making copies of the **Acheulean handaxe** (named for the French site of Saint-Acheul, where they were first identified) that typifies *Homo erectus*, at least in Africa and Europe (Figure 5.10). The earliest and simplest handaxes have been found in Africa and can be dated to about 1.4 million years ago. Earlier tools (prior to 1.4 million years ago) made by *Homo erectus* give the appearance of advanced Oldowan choppers. There seems to have been a slow development of the far more complex handaxe from the simpler Oldowan chopper after the first appearance of *erectus* in Africa sometime after 1.8 million B.P. Interestingly, the handaxe is found nearly exclusively in Africa and Europe. It is rarely—some claim never—found at eastern Asian *Homo erectus* sites. *Homo erectus* probably spread out of Africa and into Asia before the handaxe's invention in Africa, which would explain why the early *Homo erectus* sites in eastern Asia lack that tool. It is still a mystery why the tool didn't make it into Asia later on.

Students generally have little trouble making impressive versions of Oldowan choppers and flake tools—with a little elbow grease and after mastering the proper striking angle of hammerstone on core. This is not the case, however, for the *Homo erectus* handaxe, which is not easy to make, at least not without lots of practice, knowledge, and time. Very few of my students ever develop proficiency in handaxe production.

This comes as no surprise. To produce an Oldowan tool takes very few steps, and the process affords wide latitude for variation: With only three or

FIGURE 5.10

The Acheulean handaxe, a tool of Homo erectus *in Europe and Africa. These two examples were found in France.* (K. L. Feder)

four blows from a hammerstone and little precision in placing the blows, you can make such a tool. A handaxe is another thing entirely. Handaxes are symmetrical, finely flaked, and often aesthetically exquisite (see Figure 5.10 and Color Plate 2). Dozens of flakes are removed from the core, not just a few (Figure 5.11). Even quite simple handaxes, such as the earliest known examples, from the site of Konso-Gardula in Ethiopia (Asfaw et al. 1992) and dated to 1.4 million B.P., can take 25 individual hammer strikes. The best-made examples, which date to after 1 million B.P., in Africa and more recently in Europe, took nearly three times that number (Constable 1973, 128). Each flake blow must be located precisely in order to allow for the proper positioning of the next strike. The stone must be turned over again and again between hammer strikes, to maintain symmetry and to keep the edge of the tool straight. All—or, at least, most—of the exterior rind, or **cortex,** of the object piece was removed in order to keep the tool relatively thin and light, so flakes needed to shoot across the face of the axe at the same time that the edge was being maintained. This takes great skill, precision, and strength.

Experimental archaeologist Mark Newcomer (1971) has replicated handaxes, determining that at least some were made in three separate steps. First, a blank, or **preform,** was roughed out with a stone hammer into the general shape of the desired end product. Then, the preform was refined via a second stage of percussion with a softer stone or even a piece of antler used in thinning the tool. Finally, the edges were straightened and sharpened in one last application of percussion. All the work was worth it: For the same mass of stone, a handaxe produces about four times more cutting edge than an Oldowan chopper and, at the same time, yields far more usable, sharp flakes.

FIGURE 5.11

Through a process of bifacial flaking, a symmetrical, finely made handaxe was produced. Compare this to the process for producing Oldowan tools (see Figure 4.16). (Noel G. Coonce)

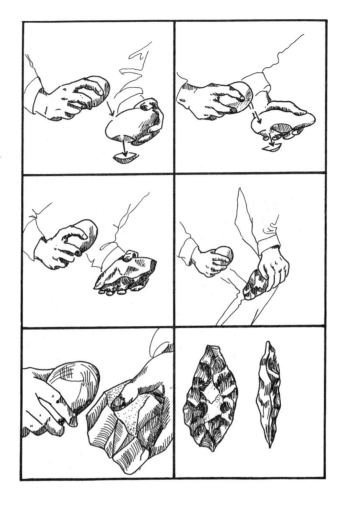

During the production of a single handaxe, Newcomer produced more than 50 flakes usable for cutting or scraping.

The handaxe appears to have been an all-purpose tool (a colleague of mine calls them the "Swiss Army rocks" of the Pleistocene). Its sharp tip was used for piercing, the thin edges for cutting, and the steeper-angled edges toward the butt of the tool for scraping or chopping. Archaeologist Patricia O'Brien (1984) even suggests that it may have been used as a projectile, thrown like a discus at fleeing game animals. The flakes removed during manufacture were used on the basis of their form and thickness.

Handaxes have been found at many *Homo erectus* sites in Africa and Europe dating from between 1.4 and 0.5 million years ago. They are, as previously mentioned, extremely rare or entirely absent from *erectus* sites in Asia east of India, where nonsymmetrical, less morphologically consistent, chipped stone tools made from stone nodules predominate. This geographic division is so clear between the makers of handaxes in the West and the less formal tradition of stone choppers and flakes in the East that a name is applied to this division: the **Movius Line,** named for the researcher (Hallam Movius) who first articulated this geographic distinction. As mentioned, the existence of the Movius Line may be explained by the fact that the hominids left Africa and arrived in eastern Asia long before the handaxe was developed back in Africa.

SUBSISTENCE

Remember one major issue concerning the subsistence base of *Homo habilis:* Did the members of this species hunt big game or merely scavenge remnants of kills left by carnivores? As a whole, the evidence supports the view that *Homo habilis* had a broad and opportunistic subsistence strategy: Big-game hunting was probably not preeminent, but hunting, scavenging, and gathering wild plants together provided subsistence for *Homo habilis.*

The evidence regarding the hunting abilities of later hominids is stronger than for *Homo habilis.* For example, the sites of Torralba and Ambrona in Spain, which date to about 350,000 years ago, are located on two hills over-looking a valley that served as a natural pass for large game animals on their seasonal migrations during the Pleistocene. Though no hominid remains were found at the site, lots of tools and the remains of 55 elephants, 26 horses, 25 deer, 10 wild cattle, and 6 rhinoceroses were recovered (Freeman 1973).

It seems clear from the evidence of tools as well as cut marks on the bones (Shipman and Rose 1983) that hominids were present at the site and cut some meat off the animal carcasses. However, because the bones themselves were so badly weathered, it cannot be concluded that the animals were hunted, killed, and then systematically butchered by the hominids (Binford 1987b).

Better evidence, at least of butchery, comes from the nearby sites of Aridos 1 and 2, 18 km (11 mi) southeast of Madrid, Spain (Villa 1990). Both sites produced an apparently butchered elephant, dating to probably about 350,000 years ago. Mixed in with the bones were the tools used to cut off the meat, as well as the waste flakes produced in sharpening the cutting and scraping tools.

While there is no evidence of hunting at either Aridos site—no spear-points were found, for example—there also is no evidence that *Homo erectus* gained access to the carcasses after carnivores had their fill—there are no tooth or gnaw marks on the bones.

That the flint that served as the raw material for the tools at Aridos came from deposits at 3 km distance and that much of the toolmaking occurred away from the butchery site, with mostly sharpening conducted on-site, offers evidence for what researcher Paola Villa calls "planning depth." In other words, the hominids who butchered the elephant carcasses at Aridos knew that elephants roamed the area and that there was always a chance one or more of them might die at any given time—the Aridos 1 elephant was a

5 cm

0

FIGURE 5.12

This 400,000-year-old throwing spear was one of three found at the Schöningen site in Germany. These spears are evidence of hunting on the part of their makers and represent a hint of the role organic materials—which preserve only under extraordinary circumstances—played in ancient tool technology.

juvenile and Aridos 2 was an old male, both part of subpopulations with high natural mortality rates. The *Homo erectus* population in the area seems to have planned for the lucky occasions when a carcass became available by collecting the raw material and making the tools in advance. Planning ahead for a future eventuality is a human behavior, and the evidence at Aridos suggests that *Homo erectus* was capable of such behavior.

Evidence for the hunting abilities of the earliest European hominids is clear at Boxgrove Quarry. The remains of four butchered rhinoceroses found there show cut marks made by stone tools. The researchers at Boxgrove have demonstrated that these butchering marks were made on the animals' vertebrae, just where you would expect for the most efficient dismembering of the animal (Bower 1997b).

While the evidence from the bones can be equivocal concerning the hunting abilities of *Homo erectus,* recently discovered artifacts leave little doubt that hunting played a role in its subsistence. Three remarkably well preserved, very ancient wooden spears have been recovered from a coal mine in Schöningen, Germany (Thieme 1997). Found in a well-understood stratigraphic sequence, the spears are approximately 400,000 years old and range in size from 1.82 to 2.30 m (about 6 to 7.5 ft) in length (Figure 5.12). These artifacts are thought to be spears, in part, on the basis of gross morphology (they have sharpened tips and certainly resemble more recent spears). Beyond this, all three spears were made the same way; each was produced from a spruce sapling with the harder, denser, and heavier wood from the base of the tree used for the spear tip, which was sharpened. The butt ends of the spears taper gently, and the balance point of each spear is located about one-third the spear length from the tip, just as it is in a modern javelin. Their form seems a clear indication that the spears were meant to be thrown, and their size implies that large game animals were the target.

ISSUES AND DEBATES

DID THE PLEISTOCENE CAUSE THE EVOLUTION OF *HOMO ERECTUS?*

We saw in the case of the earliest split between pongid and hominid at the end of the Miocene, between 5 and 7 million years ago, as well as with the initiation of the *Homo* line 2.5 million years ago, that a significant change in climate predated and may have inspired the evolution of our ancestors. It is tempting to suggest that the changes produced by the Pleistocene are at the root of the apparently rapid divergence of *Homo erectus* from *Homo habilis* sometime soon after 2 million years ago. However, the timing of the climate changes during the Pleistocene seems to rule out this possibility. Though the first appearance of *erectus* and the accepted beginning of the Pleistocene epoch are roughly contemporaneous, significant global cooling and the growth of continental ice sheets predate the appearance of *erectus* as well as its expansion into Asia and Europe. This conclusion may change if older specimens of *Homo erectus* are found.

Even if the Pleistocene is not at the root of the development of *erectus* as a new species of hominid, it remains an important consideration in our reconstruction of *Homo erectus*'s intelligence and cultural capability. *Homo erectus* was able to thrive and expand geographically despite the unsettled climatic and geographic conditions produced by the Pleistocene. Its adaptability and flexibility are hallmarks of the human cultural adaptation and show how similar to us members of this different species must have been.

WHAT ENABLED THE GEOGRAPHIC EXPANSION OF *HOMO ERECTUS?*

The spread of members of *Homo erectus* out of Africa into new habitats with different climates, resources, and challenges was not made possible by or accompanied by any change in their physical adaptation. The earliest hominids in Asia or Europe were not cold-adapted version of African *Homo erectus.*

Intelligence

It seems clear that what enabled *Homo erectus* to survive where human ancestors had not previously been able to penetrate was intelligence and the ability to invent new adaptations as needed. While *Homo habilis* was a cultural creature, as shown by its invention, manufacture, and use of stone tools, *Homo erectus* seems to have been the first human ancestor to rely for survival on the invented, learned, and passed-down adaptations of culture. In the use of sophisticated tools and ultimately in the taming of fire (see the next section), *Homo erectus* exhibits how similar the species was to us. Its reliance on culture was an adaptive strategy that would define forever what it means to be a human being, and it is the most important thing we modern humans share with *erectus.*

Control of Fire

There is something very compelling, even to us twentieth-century humans, about a simple open flame: the smell of wood smoke, the crackling and popping of dry tinder, the warmth of the fire. For countless generations of our human ancestors, fire was more than just a diversion; it meant warmth and light, power and strength—in fact, survival itself. When did the first human ancestors make the great leap from fear of this elemental natural force to understanding and controlling it?

The best available evidence indicates that *Homo erectus* was our first ancestor able to control fire. The timing of the earliest use of controlled fire, however, is a point of contention within paleoanthropology; see James (1989) for a skeptic's perspective.

An analysis performed by Andrew Sillen and C. K. Brain (1990) at the site of Swartkrans in South Africa, for example, shows that controlled fire may have been present as long ago as 1.3 million years. That there was fire at Swartkrans is indisputable: There is evidence of burned bones, though there are no hearths. But fire can be produced naturally, by lightning or by extremely hot, dry conditions. Sillen and Brain have shown, through experimentally burning bone to different temperatures, that the bones at Swartkrans had been heated to a temperature of perhaps 800°C, far higher than expected for a natural grass fire and more in keeping with an artificially produced and maintained flame. The jury is still out on their conclusion, though the possibility is intriguing.

The controlled use of fire may have been the key cultural adaptation that enabled members of this tropically derived and adapted species to survive outside the tropics. Fire gives warmth and protection from animals and enables cooking, which renders meat more digestible and makes it safer by killing bacteria. Fire also produces light and, therefore, probably played an important role in extending the usable part of the day for members of a species who, like us and most other primates, relied primarily on vision for their sensory input but who, also like us, did not see well in the dark.

It had long been thought that Zhoukoudian presented the best evidence for the use of fire by *Homo erectus*. Fire certainly would have been a valuable asset in the long, cold winters of northern China. The most recent analysis, however, shows no confirming evidence for this supposition (Weiner et al. 1998). In fact, though some of the animal bones found in the same level as the oldest *Homo erectus* remains recovered at Zhoukoudian do show evidence of burning, there is no direct evidence of a fire in the cave itself. No hearths nor ash or even charcoal remains have been found in the cave. So, though it would seem reasonable to suggest that the control of fire would have been a significant cultural achievement and might have enabled hominid expansion outside of the tropics, evidence is equivocal about exactly where or when control of fire was achieved—and even which of our ancestors was responsible for this development.

THE "ART" OF MAKING TOOLS

An important point should be made about the handaxes we discussed previously: They were better made than they had to be. That is to say, the Acheulean handaxes—at least many of the later ones—have a symmetry, balance, precision, and beauty that took a lot of work, but work that was not absolutely necessary from a utilitarian perspective (see Color Plate 2). A high level of consistency in handaxe form can be found within sites, as if the makers were adhering to a particular standard. For example, paleoanthropologist John Gowlett (1984) found a remarkable consistency and uniformity in the ratios among length, width, and thickness of the handaxes he studied from the 700,000-year-old Kilombe site in Kenya.

That such extra care was taken in their production implies that their makers were interested in more than simple utility. *Homo erectus* toolmakers must have been producing beautiful objects for the sake of displaying their great skill or for the pleasure of producing a thing of beauty. Though the first true art is usually associated with anatomically modern humans of a much later period—the cave paintings of the European Upper Paleolithic (see Chapter 8) are clearly recognizable as art—for producing stone tools more artfully than they needed to, some of our much earlier ancestors may well deserve the credit, if not for being the first true artists, then at least for being the world's first craftspeople (Gowlett 1984).

RAISING *HOMO ERECTUS*

My understanding of the care necessary for raising human babies as compared to the young of other species has been forged on the anvil of experience: I've got two kids and two cats, and there simply is no comparison. We adopted the cats when they were 7-week-old kittens, ready to leave their mothers. They could walk, could feed themselves, were litter-box trained, knew how to manipulate human beings to get anything they wanted, and were fierce hunters of blowing leaves and dust bunnies. My kids, like all baby humans, are another story. Immediately following birth and for an extended period thereafter, my kids were capable of crying, filling their diapers, sleeping, and little else.

Whereas after just several weeks of life, animals such as cats attain a reasonable level of competence at moving around, eating, and defending themselves, human children are utterly dependent on adults to satisfy all their needs for a very long time—usually years, even decades. Some specialists characterize even full-term human babies (nine months of gestation) as inherently premature and little more than embryos living outside the womb. The term **altricial** is used to characterize baby birds who are completely dependent on their parents for fulfilling their needs. Intellectually, human babies are anything but altricial; almost from birth they begin to gather and process sensory information, and they are quickly insatiably curious and experimental about their world. Physically, however, they are born and remain immature for longer than the offspring of other species; human babies are said to be **secondarily altricial.**

There are a number of reasons why evolution would have selected for a seemingly dangerous situation in which human children are born at an early stage of physical development. A reconfiguration of the human pelvis was necessary to allow our first hominid ancestors to stand up. This change in pelvic form provided for a change in muscle positioning and shape necessary for bipedal locomotion. It also had an incidental effect: It greatly narrowed the pelvic outlet in females, making it far more difficult for a baby's body to pass through the birth canal. This difficulty can be shown by a simple statistic: Average birth labor time for a chimpanzee is about 2 hours; for a human mother it is more than 14 hours (Rosenberg 1992, 99; see this study for an informative discussion of the evolution of human childbirth).

A detailed comparison by Robert Tague and Owen Lovejoy (1986) of the reconstructed pelvis of the fossil Lucy (*Australopithecus afarensis*) with the pelvises of a chimpanzee and a modern human female indicates that, though bipedality probably complicated birth for *Australopithecus* females, it still was not as problematical as it is for modern human women (Figure 5.13). The brains of the various *Australopithecus* species were still quite small, so while there may have been a tighter fit at birth, this probably presented little problem since their heads were still no bigger than those of chimp babies.

However, as natural selection began to favor greater intelligence in the hominids—made possible by an increase in brain and, therefore, head size—a problem did develop: A smaller pelvic outlet was forced to accommodate an increasingly large head at birth. Nature's solution, still hardly perfect, as witnessed by the often difficult time women have in childbirth, was twofold. The first strategy was to maximize pelvic outlet size in females by fine-tuning the configuration of the pelvis. Male and female human pelvises became readily distinguishable because the pelvis exhibits **sexual dimorphism.**

The second strategy of natural selection was timing the birth of human babies at an earlier stage in fetal development, when the head, though large, was still small enough to pass through the birth canal. Today, this timing is reflected in the fact that the human newborn has a smaller head, proportional to its ultimate adult size, than do any of the living apes. A human newborn's brain is less than 25% of its ultimate adult size (Jordaan 1976, 274). Compare this to the great apes, in whom a newborn's brain is more than 40% of its adult size. Most human brain growth occurs outside the womb, after birth. This is fundamentally different from the situation for all the apes. For example, while the rate of brain growth declines dramatically in chimpanzees immediately after birth, human babies maintain what is essentially a relatively fast fetal rate of brain growth for an entire year after they are born (Rosenberg 1992, 106; Martin 1989). The proportionally small size of the human baby's head at birth is what enables the baby to be born at all, given the constraints of pelvic outlet size necessitated by upright walking. But this situation presents problems, for the less developed a newborn of any species is, the more susceptible it is to trauma, infection, cold, and death.

Birth at an early stage of development for an organism with a large and complex brain has some advantages. Stimulation and learning begin earlier, while the brain is still experiencing rapid growth, and bonding between parents and children is, of necessity, stronger. This timing can be advantageous in a species that depends for its survival so thoroughly on learned behavior

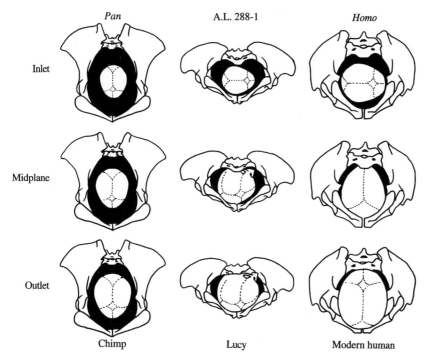

Inlet

Midplane

Outlet

Pan

A.L. 288-1

Homo

Chimp

Lucy

Modern human

FIGURE 5.13

The birth canals of apes and modern human beings and the fossil pelvises of extinct hominids allow for a comparison in the birth process of these three kinds of creatures. (Courtesy of Robert Tague)

and social relations. It is beneficial for humans to be born at an immature stage of development and to have an extended childhood; the learning curve is simply a lot steeper and longer for us than it is for cows, cats, or even other primates.

An additional hypothesis holds that one of the key changes that characterized ancient hominids from *Homo habilis* onward is **neoteny,** or the "holding on" to features that are typical of newborn apes (Gould 1977). And modern human adults resemble baby chimps more than they resemble adult chimpanzees. Our lack of body hair, rounded skulls, flat faces, and even the point of articulation between the base of our skull and backbone are all things we share with fetal or newborn, but not adult, chimpanzees.

This brings us back to the boy from West Turkana. Though his cranial capacity and that of his species was substantially larger than that of *Homo habilis*, the size of the *Homo erectus* skull—and, therefore, the size of the brain—in proportion to the size of its body was really no different from the proportion for *Homo habilis* (Walker and Shipman 1996, 215–216). In other words, the *Homo erectus* brain was larger to control a larger body, but it falls right in line with what would have been expected based on the brain-size to body-size ratio for *habilis*. There was no great, disproportional increase in brain size for *Homo erectus*. As paleoanthropologists Alan Walker and Pat Shipman (1996, 212) point out, if you want an impression of what the Nariokotome boy looked like at the age of about 9 years, picture a 15-year-old modern human boy (based on the Nariokotome boy's height) with the head of a 1-year-old modern human child (based on cranial capacity)! Recognizably human, but alien indeed.

Nevertheless, when the pelvis of *Homo erectus* is reconstructed, it is clear that the size of the birth canal had been so diminished to accommodate upright locomotion that even the proportional increase in *Homo erectus*'s brain size would have seriously compromised an infant's ability to pass through the mother's body. During birth, the Nariokotome boy's head size surely challenged the size of his mother's birth canal. Almost certainly, natural selection was already at work, favoring survival of infants born at an earlier stage of fetal development. This selective process, however, would work only if adults—particularly mothers, but potentially fathers and other adults—could spend an enormous amount of time caring for the newborns. This must have been the case for the West Turkana boy.

The immature nature of a *Homo erectus* child at birth can be added to another human characteristic exhibited by the West Turkana boy: an extended period of physical development and delayed maturation. A 9-year-old cat is an older adult, and even a 9-year-old chimp is close to being an adult. But the 9-year-old West Turkana boy was still physically immature, as evidenced by his dental development and the development of the bones of his arms, legs, hands, and feet—none of the **epiphyses** (see Chapter 3) of the West Turkana boy had yet fused at the time of his death. He was just a boy.

As Brown et al. (1985) point out, the West Turkana boy shows clear evidence of an extended period of immaturity that is characteristic of modern human beings. This long period of childhood allowed him, 1.6 million years ago, and all *Homo erectus* children to learn what they needed to know. A long period of learning is emblematic of the human species.

WHEN DID *HOMO ERECTUS* BECOME EXTINCT?

It should be clear by this point that human evolution was not a simple, progressive process with each species thriving during its time and then giving way to the next in line, repeating this process as a series of steps leading directly to modern human beings. The human story is, instead, far more complex, characterized until fairly recently by geographically separated, multiple contemporary hominids (Figure 5.14).

We will begin the next chapter talking about a new, more modern-looking, hominid species that can be dated to about 400,000 years ago. The appearance of this new species does not mean that all older species conveniently disappeared from the scene at that time. In fact, in the scenario presented in this book, only one of the *Homo erectus* populations—that in Africa—is directly ancestral to us. That African *Homo erectus* line evolved into another hominid that looked and behaved more like modern humans, while other branches of

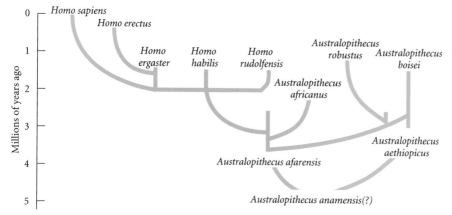

FIGURE 5.14

One alternative phylogeny proposed for the fossil hominids. (From Bernard Wood 1992a,b)

Homo erectus, particularly those in Europe and Asia, almost certainly continued on more or less the same as they always had.

It should not surprise anyone, then, that there is evidence for temporal overlap after 400,000 years ago between, on the one hand, Africa's more modern-looking hominids and Europe or Asia's later *Homo erectus* populations on the other. What is stunning is the degree of temporal overlap that some researchers suggest. According to scientists who have recently redated *erectus* fossils from Ngandong and Sambungmachan on Java, *Homo erectus* may have survived until as recently as 27,000 to 53,000 years ago (Swisher et al. 1996). If either of these dates can be upheld with further evidence, it would mean that long after completely modern-looking human beings had evolved in Africa and spread into Europe and Asia, pockets of an ancient, more primitive variety of humanity still lived—at least on the island of Java. Considered from the vantage point of the present world—where all human beings are members of a single species, *Homo sapiens,* with equal intelligence, abilities, and potentials—this scenario seems especially remarkable.

STABILITY OR CHANGE?

How much change is exhibited in *Homo erectus* fossils included in the species but separated by an extraordinarily long time span? Lasting from 1.78 million years ago to 0.4 million years ago, *Homo erectus* is one of the longest-lived of the hominid species. If evolution is thought of as a gradual, steady process (see the discussion of punctuated equilibrium in Chapter 4 and "Issues and Debates" in Chapter 6), then we might expect *erectus,* if it was the direct ancestor of humanity, to exhibit such steady evolution toward the anatomically modern condition over its lengthy existence on the planet. As evidence for this view, some researchers point to certain changes through time within

FIGURE 5.15

This graph of the trend in Homo erectus *brain size through time shows a rather remarkable stability from the first appearance of the species some 1.8 million years ago to the most recent specimens, dating to 400,000 years ago.*

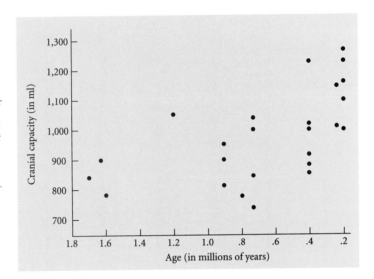

the *Homo erectus* species: The back teeth get smaller, and the anatomical structure of the face and lower jaw decrease (Wolpoff 1984).

On the other hand, Philip Rightmire (1981, 1985, 1990) argues that such changes are extremely minor and that, especially when considering the enormous amount of time involved and the geographical breadth of *Homo erectus,* the evidence is overwhelming for great stability within the species over its entire existence. As Rightmire points out, all of the *Homo erectus* specimens, from the very oldest to the most recent, are "built on a common plan" (1990, 190).

Even brain size within the species can be shown to be fundamentally stable through time: There is no significant increase in cranial capacity within *erectus* from its earliest appearance in Africa 1.78 million years ago until it is replaced by *Homo sapiens* sometime after 400,000 years ago (Figure 5.15). Rightmire (1981, 1990) applies the statistical procedure of regression analysis to the data and finds no statistically significant temporal trend in brain size. Though researcher Steven Leigh (1992) disputes this result, maintaining that, at least within the Asian subsample of *erectus,* the increase in brain size through time is statistically significant, that increase is extremely small. As Figure 5.15 shows, statistical significance issues aside, there appears to be little change in cranial capacity through time until about 400,000 years ago.

Interestingly, this period of relative stability in brain size is also a period of great cultural stability regarding stone tools. The handaxes made by *Homo erectus* change only slightly from 1.4 million to 400,000 years ago. One million years of relatively little change in a technology is in stark contrast to the modern situation, in which technologies change virtually overnight. That stability lends further support to the notion of *Homo erectus* as a fundamentally unchanging species representing a long period of evolutionary equilibrium.

At about 400,000 years ago, however, a steep increase in brain size over a short interval is seen. This jump in brain size, in fact, is how the earliest appearance of members of our species is identified.

So it seems that *Homo erectus*, like *Australopithecus afarensis* (see Chapter 4), was a stable, long-lived species. The fossil evidence again supports the evolutionary model of punctuated equilibrium—with *Homo erectus* representing a long period of equilibrium in the hominid line. Major changes in brain size and cranial morphology did not occur until around 400,000 years ago. Those changes produced and defined the first *Homo sapiens* in what is seen here as being a punctuational event (see Chapter 6).

CASE STUDY CLOSE-UP

In 1918, a fossil locality southwest of Beijing, China, was explored by Swedish geologist Johan Gunnar Andersson. Andersson took advantage of a local Chinese belief that fossil bones were actually the remnants of dragons and that powder made from ground-up "dragon bones" was a cure-all. Many local druggists collected such bones for use in their medicines. Even today, paleontologists rely on local druggists for leads in their search for fossil ("dragon") bones (Jian and Rice 1990).

In 1918, Andersson was directed by a druggist to a hill called Jigushan (Chicken Bone Hill) near the village of Zhoukoudian (Jia and Huang 1990). Convinced there was a rich array of fossil bones in the surrounding region, he began excavating on another hill, called Longgoshan—Dragon Bone Hill. In 1926, two humanlike teeth were recovered; in 1929, with the dig now led by British scientist Davidson Black, a nearly intact skull was encountered in a cave at the top of the hill (Locality 1). The fossil was recognizably different from almost everything that had been found previously, with the possible exception of Java Man. A new species was named and defined: *Sinanthropus pekinensis*. The specimens from Zhoukoudian are now included in the species *Homo erectus*, but in the popular mind both then and now, they may forever be known as "Peking Man."

The cave at Dragon Bone Hill was spectacularly productive by any standards. By the time excavations were finished at Zhoukoudian, the expedition had recovered, along with thousands of specimens of ancient animals, 15 fragmentary skulls, 6 more complete crania, 13 fragmentary mandibles, 3 upper jaws, some postcranial bones (including pieces of femur, upper arms, toe bones, numerous teeth), and a single vertebra of Peking Man (Jia and Huang 1990, 161–62). All told, the remains of more than 40 hominid individuals were recovered from deposits in the cave dated to between 462,000 and 200,000 years ago (according to fission-track dating as reported by Jia and Huang 1990, 111). Being so numerous and discovered so early in our thinking about human evolution, the Peking Man fossils played an important historical role in the scientific conceptualization of human evolution and in interpretations of the culture of ancient human beings.

Tragically, the Zhoukoudian hominid assemblage was lost during World War II when the fossils were being removed from China by U.S. Marines in an attempt to keep them away from Japanese invaders, coincidentally on the same day that Pearl Harbor was attacked. The Marines were captured and imprisoned, and to this day no one knows what became of their precious fossil cargo. (It may have been destroyed by Japanese troops or simply lost, or it may have been found later by Chinese druggists who ground the bones up for medicine. There is even a very slight possibility that some are still hidden away in China, Japan, or the United States.)

VISITING THE PAST

Just as with the fossils and sites related to *Australopithecus* and *Homo habilis* discussed in the previous chapter, you need to travel a great distance to visit the *Homo erectus* sites discussed here. Even then, the important fossil remains usually are unavailable for viewing by all but researchers in the field. Again, however, most large museums in major American cities have displays on human evolution that cover some of the important discoveries and issues dealt with in this chapter.

China has a fine museum display at Zhoukoudian. Upgraded in 1979, the museum is devoted to the finds made at the Peking Man site as well as the area surrounding Zhoukoudian. On display are casts of the now-lost original hominid fossils, tools, and the bones of animals killed and eaten by the ancient inhabitants of the locality; there is also a general display on human evolution. Zhoukoudian, being close to Beijing, is reasonably accessible to tourists.

In Kenya, the Olorgesailie sites, containing a number of excavated localities, are open to tourists. The sites date to after 400,000 B.P.; numerous, sometimes finely made handaxes have been left exactly where they were found by the excavators (including Louis and Mary Leakey) and, presumably, where they were left by *Homo erectus*. The monograph by Glynn Isaac (1977) provides details on the excavation and analysis of the Olorgesailie sites.

One of the most interesting of the Olorgesailie localities is Site B. The remains of many stone tools and the smashed bones of an extinct species of baboon were found there; some have been left in place for viewing. The bones appear to have been broken for marrow extraction. Because so many of the stone tools have been left in place, the visitor can gain a unique insight into the appearance of a 400,000-year-old *Homo erectus* site as it was discovered by the archaeologists who excavated it.

SUMMARY

Sometime after 1.8 million years ago, *Homo habilis* was replaced by a new hominid species, *Homo erectus*. *Erectus* possessed a larger brain than *habilis;* its mean brain size of about 1,000 ml is two-thirds the modern human mean. With its larger brain and attendant greater intelligence, *Homo erectus* was able to adapt to the changing environmental conditions posed by the Pleistocene epoch. Its greater intelligence is evidenced by its more sophisticated stone tools. Reliance on a cultural rather than a physical adaptation enabled members of this species to expand into new habitats in Asia and, later, Europe and to adjust to environmental conditions far different from those presented in its African birthplace.

Homo erectus was a stable and long-lived species. Fossils from Africa to east Asia show a consistent morphology from close to 1.8 million to 400,000 years ago. After 400,000 years ago, brain size, relatively stable during the existence of *erectus,* exhibits a rapid increase, signifying the evolution of the first *Homo sapiens* from an *erectus* base.

TO LEARN MORE

Technical Summaries

The definitive work on the Nariokotome 9-year-old *Homo erectus* boy has been edited by two of its excavators, Alan Walker and Richard Leakey: *The Nariokotome* Homo erectus *Skeleton* (1993). A good, very descriptive, general technical work on *Homo erectus* is G. Philip Rightmire's *The Evolution of* Homo erectus: *Comparative Anatomical Studies of an Extinct Human Species* (1990).

Popular Summaries

Richard Leakey and Roger Lewin's (1992) *Origins Reconsidered: In Search of What Makes Us Human* discusses the discovery, excavation, and interpretation of the Nariokotome skeleton. Much information about *Homo erectus* is offered in *Ancestors: In Search of Human Origins* by Don and Lenora Johanson and Blake Edgar (1994). A very helpful, popular summary of evolution with quite a bit of information on the Lower Paleolithic is provided in Alan Walker and Pat Shipman's *The Wisdom of the Bones* (1996). For a good popular summary of the latest work on *Homo erectus* in Europe, see Robert Kunzig's "Atapuerca: The Face of an Ancestral Child," in *Discover,* December 1997. Paleoanthropologist Harry Shapiro's *Peking Man* (1974) provides a riveting account of the discovery and loss of Peking Man. See *The Search for Peking Man,* by Christopher Janus and William Brashler (1975) for an interesting, if unreliable, account of an attempt to track down the present whereabouts of the bones, replete with stories of clandestine meetings atop the Empire State Building and multimillion-dollar ransom demands. Also, see *The Story of Peking Man* (1990), by Jia Lanpo and Huang Weiwen, for a detailed telling of the story of Peking Man by one of its excavators (Jia Lanpo).

On the Web

If you would like to see more photographs of *Homo erectus* specimens, learn more about the stone tools they made and the distribution of the sites where their remains have been found, or read summaries of the fossils and discussions of their place in human evolution, visit the following site on the Internet:

http://www.wsu.edu:8001/vwsu/gened/learn-modules/top_longfor/timeline/erectus/erectus-a.html

KEY TERMS

occipital	glacial	preform
supraorbital torus	stadial	Movius Line
calvarium	interstadial	altricial
Kabuh Formation	interglacial	secondarily altricial
glacier	foraminifera	sexual dimorphism
Pleistocene epoch	Acheulean handaxe	neoteny
Holocene epoch	cortex	epiphysis

6

Our Immediate Ancestors

THE PREMODERN HUMANS

CHAPTER OVERVIEW

The fossil record from about 400,000 years ago shows a great change in the hominids. Brain size expanded, and the fossils from the period look so much more modern that they are categorized as *Homo sapiens*, though of a type called "archaic," or "premodern."

The best-known of the archaic *Homo sapiens* are the Neandertals. Represented by the skeletons of hundreds of individuals, the Neandertals seem to have been physically highly adapted to life in the Arctic cold of Pleistocene (Ice Age) Europe and west Asia. They may have been too specialized; the last of the Neandertals died out about 30,000 years ago.

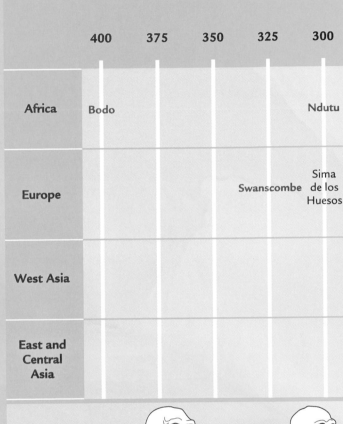

	400	375	350	325	300
Africa	Bodo				Ndutu
Europe				Swanscombe	Sima de los Huesos
West Asia					
East and Central Asia					

Premodern *Homo sapiens*

Neandertal and pre-Neandertal

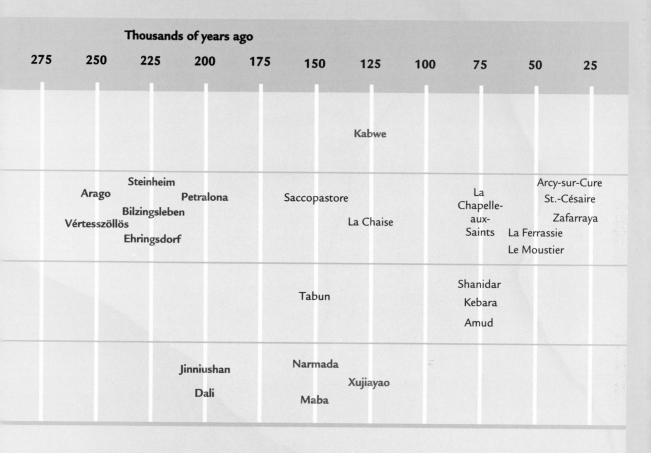

Thousands of years ago

275	250	225	200	175	150	125	100	75	50	25

Kabwe

Arago

Steinheim

Petralona

Bilzingsleben

Vértesszöllös

Ehringsdorf

Saccopastore

La Chaise

La Chapelle-aux-Saints

Arcy-sur-Cure

St.-Césaire

Zafarraya

La Ferrassie

Le Moustier

Tabun

Shanidar

Kebara

Amud

Jinniushan

Dali

Narmada

Maba

Xujiayao

PRELUDE

What would have happened if not one, but two separate and unequal species of human beings had somehow survived to the present? This fascinating concept is the basis for the 1953 novel *You Shall Know Them*, by Jean Bruller, a French author who wrote under the pen name Vercors. In the novel, a group of explorers investigates a secluded, pristine valley in the highlands of New Guinea in the mid-twentieth century.*
The explorers discover a population of a presumedly extinct variety of human being—*living* hominids, more advanced than Peking Man (*Homo erectus*) yet less advanced than modern human beings. Called "tropis," these creatures make stone tools, speak a simple language, have fire, and bury their dead.

In actuality, of course, all modern human beings belong to a single species, *Homo sapiens sapiens,* and all of us are more alike than different in our physical appearance, intellect, and emotion, no matter what our geographic origin or family heritage. But this situation was not inevitable. There could today be different, coexisting species of human beings with different physical and intellectual capacities, just as there are different species of bear, antelope, elephant, and camel—and just as there were different, contemporaneous, and coexisting species of hominids in the past (see Chapter 4).

In Vercors's novel, the primitive people discovered in New Guinea are treated quite badly. They are essentially enslaved. On the one hand, they are not true "people," so no law prevents their exploitation (just as there is no law against harnessing a horse to a plow). On the other hand, they are far more intelligent than any other nonhuman animal and can be trained to do things modern humans can do but find degrading, boring, or dangerous.

Considering the amount of mistrust and hatred that exists today among the empirically minimally different individuals of our single species, it is frightening to consider what the world would be like if there were truly different, coexisting species of human beings. In a broad sense, however, this might have been.

The Neandertals to be discussed in this chapter are an extinct variety of human beings that come chronologically closer to the modern era than do any other nonmodern hominid; they became extinct only a little more than 30,000 years ago, a mere tick on the evolutionary clock. As we will show here and in Chapter 7, there may well have been an overlap of tens of millennia during the waning years of the Neandertals and the ascendance of the earliest anatomically modern human beings.

As we will see, the Neandertals were not only similar to us in many ways, but also quite different. Though often depicted as apelike or subhuman, they managed to survive for tens of thousands of years during an extremely harsh period of the Pleistocene, or Ice Age. They did so through their great intelli-

*As late as the 1930s such places existed on New Guinea, completely unknown to Europeans. Perhaps 1 million people lived there, people who were truly the last substantial aboriginal population on the planet, untouched by European disease, missionaries, exploitation, or cultural hegemony. Their story is chronicled in a PBS documentary and companion book, both titled *First Contact* (Connolly and Anderson 1987).

gence, inventing sophisticated stone tools for hunting, producing clothing and shelter, and using fire. Neandertals are also noted for another behavior that contradicts their modern stereotype: They buried their dead. In recognizing the enormity of death and in ceremonially disposing of the mortal remains of their comrades, they exhibited a behavior that shows their close kinship to us. Despite their intelligence, Neandertals were surely quite different from us. Considering how badly we humans treat one another—and that we are more similar to one another in how we look and how we think than we would be to living Neandertals—the Neandertals probably would have ended up like the primitive hominids in Vercors's book, doomed by us to lives of confinement, drudgery, and pain (Gould 1988).

The Neandertals, however, did not survive to the present. Who they were, how they were related to other nonmodern human beings, why and how they became extinct, and what place, if any, they had in the evolution of **anatomically modern *Homo sapiens*** are questions addressed in this chapter.

As we saw in Chapter 5, after about 1 million B.P., the tapestry of human evolution seems to have been characterized by

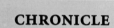 **CHRONICLE**

a single primary thread made up of three generally similar strands in Africa, Asia, and Europe. Then, about 400,000 years ago, there is a burst of change, with new hominid varieties appearing on the evolutionary stage. Though regional differences are maintained among the fossils seen in Africa, Asia, and Europe, these hominids all appear to have been more modern in appearance than previous hominid species, so much more modern in cranial capacity and shape that some researchers call these new hominds **premodern,** or **archaic,** *Homo sapiens* (Figure 6.1, p. 142).

The archaics shared a bigger, more modern brain than previous hominids had. The mean cranial capacity of the archaics (excluding the Neandertals, who will be treated separately) was a little over 1,200 ml—more than 20% larger than their evolutionary antecedents (Table 6.1, p. 143). Most of the premodern fossil specimens still possess large brow ridges. But more like the modern form, they also exhibit steeper foreheads, generally (though not universally) thinner cranial bones, and flatter faces than *erectus*. However, there is a lot of variation among the premodern *sapiens* specimens: Some have relatively thin cranial bones, others thick; some have nearly vertical foreheads, while others' foreheads slope back more severely.

PREMODERN HUMANS: FOSSIL EVIDENCE

Versions of archaic *Homo sapiens* are known from Europe, Africa, and Asia, where they appear to have evolved in place from previous populations of hominids.

CHAPTER SITES

EUROPE (NEANDERTALS)
Regourdu
Saccopastore
Saône-et-Loire
Sima de los Huesos
   (Atapuerca)
Slovenia
Spy

WEST ASIA (NEANDERTALS)
Amud
Kebara
Kobeh
Shanidar
Tabun
Teshik-Tash

FIGURE 6.1

Fossil localities of premodern Homo sapiens.

Africa

In Africa, it appears that native populations of *Homo erectus* gave rise to a new and a more modern form of hominid sometime after 600,000 years ago. Three specimens from East Africa—Bodo, Ileret, and Ndutu—are representative of the African archaics. Bodo, from Ethiopia, exhibits a round cranial profile and dates to as much as 600,000 years ago. The cranial capacity of the Ileret specimen, found in Kenya, may be as much as 1,400 ml, which is entirely modern in brain size, though it dates to about 300,000 years ago (Bräuer et al. 1997). It also exhibits large brow ridges, like other archaic specimens. The Ndutu cranium, from Tanzania, has a brain size of over 1,100 ml and exhibits a more rounded profile than that seen in earlier *Homo erectus* skulls (Clarke 1990). It is likely more than 200,000 years old.

Other ancient archaic *Homo sapiens* remains found in Africa and dating to more than 200,000 years ago include the Jebel Irhoud remains found in Morocco, the Florisbad remains in southern Africa (with a pretty firm date of 259,000 years old; Grün et al. 1996), and Ngaloba from Tanzania.

One of the best-preserved archaic specimens found in Africa is the Broken Hill, or Kabwe, cranium from Zambia (Bräuer 1984). The Kabwe brow ridges are huge—larger, in fact, than in many *Homo erectus* specimens. On the other hand, the Kabwe cranium is more rounded, as it is in modern humans; and

TABLE 6.1

Major Archaic Homo sapiens *Fossils (Exclusive of the Neandertals)*

COUNTRY	LOCALITY	FOSSILS	AGE (YEARS)	BRAIN SIZE (ML)
Germany	Steinheim	Cranium	200,000–240,000	1,200
	Bilzingsleben	Cranial fragments	228,000	
	Ehringsdorf	Cranial fragment	225,000	
	Mauer	Mandible	<450,000	
England	Swanscombe	Occipital cranium	225,000	1,325
Greece	Petralona	Cranium	160,000–240,000	1,400
France	Arago	Cranium and fragmentary remains of 7 individuals	250,000	1,200
Hungary	Vértesszöllös	Occipital fragment	200,000	1,250
Zambia	Kabwe (Broken Hill)	Cranium, additional cranial and postcranial remains of several individuals	>125,000	1,280
Tanzania	Ndutu (Olduvai)	Cranium	200,000–400,000	1,100
Kenya	Ileret	Cranium	300,000	1,400
Ethiopia	Bodo	Cranium	200,000–400,000	
South Africa	Elandsfontein	Cranium		
India	Narmada	Cranium	150,000?	1,300
China	Jinniushan	Nearly complete skeleton	200,000	1,350
	Dali	Cranium	200,000	1,120
	Maba	Cranium	130,000–170,000	
	Xujiayao	Fragments of 11 individuals	100,000–125,000	
			Mean	1,265.91
			Standard Deviation	83.55

Data from Day (1986); Pope (1992); Rightmire (1990).

its volume is 1,280 ml, far beyond that seen in *erectus* and within the modern human range (Figure 6.2). Unfortunately, Kabwe's date is uncertain, with estimates ranging from as much as 250,000 to 40,000 years ago. Most accept a date of about 125,000 years.

Taken together, these fossils show that bigger-brained, rounder-skulled hominids had appeared in Africa by as much as 600,000 and certainly by about 300,000 years ago. They most likely had evolved from *Homo erectus* and, as we

FIGURE 6.2

Premodern Homo sapiens *from Africa include the Kabwe (formerly called Broken Hill) specimen, one of the best-known examples.* (Copyright © The Natural History Museum, London)

will see, very well may have served as the parent population in the evolution of anatomically modern human beings (see Chapter 7).

Asia

In Asia, a number of fossils can be placed within the archaic category. From central India comes the Narmada hominid, with its cranial capacity of 1,200–1,400 ml and a morphology reminiscent of the African and European archaics (Kennedy et al. 1991). Dating is unclear, though artifacts associated with the skull are probably no more than 150,000 years old. The Narmada cranium, though distinctive, has more in common with other examples of European and African archaic *Homo sapiens* than it does with *Homo erectus.*

A substantial and growing list of sites in eastern Asia is providing testimony for the presence there of archaic *Homo sapiens* (Brooks and Wood 1990; Chen and Zhang 1991; Pope 1992). Perhaps of greatest interest because of its antiquity and the relative completeness of the skeleton is the so-called Jinniushan Man from Yingkou County, Liaoning Province (Figure 6.3; Lu 1987). The cranial capacity, estimated at about 1,330–1,390 ml, is large for an archaic *Homo sapiens,* and the cranial bones are very thin, like a modern human's and unlike the thick cranial bones of other archaics. Its general shape and form, however, are a mixture of primitive and modern; it doesn't look quite like anything from anywhere else. Animal teeth found in the same cave and from the same layer as the hominid have been dated by electron spin resonance to about 165,000–195,000 years ago and by uranium series to 200,000 years ago (Chen, Yang, and Wu 1994).

These dates for Jinniushan suggest that early archaic *Homo sapiens* was contemporary with late *Homo erectus* in China; the Jinniushan dates overlap the final dates at Zhoukoudian and Hexian (Chen and Zhang 1991; and see Chapter 5). Additional fragmentary remains at Chaohu, located just 50 km from Hexian, appear to represent premodern *Homo sapiens*. Chaohu is the same age as the *Homo erectus* remains at Hexian, further evidence of the two species' partial contemporaneity in east Asia. The implication is that while one or more *Homo erectus* populations in east Asia made an evolutionary jump and evolved into a more modern form, other populations remained static, retaining their more primitive morphology.

Other archaic or premodern *Homo sapiens* from China include the Dali cranium from northern Shaanxi Province. Its cranial capacity has been estimated at 1,120 ml; its form has been described as intermediate between that of *erectus* and that of modern *sapiens* (Pope 1992). The site has produced a uranium series date of about 200,000 years old. In southern China, the Maba specimen, a partial skullcap, is reminiscent of the European Neandertals. It has been dated to 130,000–170,000 years ago. Xujiayao in Shanxi Province has produced hominid remains that seem to belong with the archaic *Homo sapiens*. Dating from about 100,000 to 125,000 years ago, the 11 individuals in the fossil record exhibit a form midway between that of Chinese *Homo erectus* specimens from Zhoukoudian and that of modern *Homo sapiens* (Pope 1992).

Europe

The earth is often stingy in giving up the remains of our ancestors. Paleoanthropologists usually feel themselves lucky to find the remains of even a single ancient individual. They are understandably ecstatic when, as was the case at the site where Lucy was recovered, more than a dozen individuals are found (Chapter 4). With this in mind, the excavators of Sima de los Huesos in the Atapuerca Mountains in northern Spain must view themselves as among the most fortunate paleoanthropologists ever (Bahn 1996; Arsuaga et al. 1993). The 1,600 bones they have recovered represent the remains of more than 30 and perhaps more than 50 ancient people (Figure 6.4).

The fossils were recovered beneath a stratum that has been dated to more than 300,000 years ago; the bones must be at least that old. Volumes have been measured at 1,125 and 1,390 ml for the two adult crania recovered and 1,100 ml for the juvenile, all within the range of the premodern humans we have already discussed from Africa and Asia.

Several other well-preserved premodern human remains have been found in Europe. For example, the Steinheim skull from Germany dates to between 200,000 and 240,000 years ago (Ikeya 1982; Figure 6.5). The skull is long and relatively narrow with a large brow. The face is flat and rather small, as in modern humans. There is no occipital torus, giving the rear of the skull a modern appearance. The cranial capacity has been estimated at just below 1,200 ml.

The Swanscombe cranial fragments found in England are probably another example of pre-modern *Homo sapiens* (Howell 1960; Ovey 1964). The

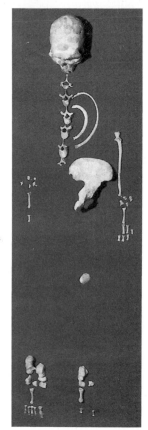

FIGURE 6.3

Archaic Homo sapiens *from Asia include this specimen from Yingkou in the Jinniushan Mountains, one of the most complete archaic human fossils outside of Europe.* (Copyright © China Pictorial Photo Service)

FIGURE 6.4

Cranium of one of the more complete pre-modern Homo sapiens *specimens from Sima de los Huesos (the Pit of Bones) in the Atapuerca Mountains, Spain. The Sima de los Huesos hominids have been dated to 300,000 years ago and have been shown to possess many of the same anatomical features as the later, so-called classic Neandertals.* (Copyright © Javier Trueba/Madrid Scientific Films)

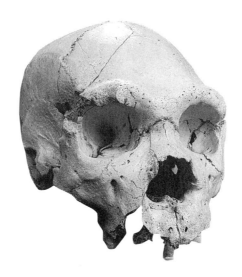

FIGURE 6.5

The Steinheim cranium from Germany, one of the most complete archaic Homo sapiens *specimens found in Europe, falls within the lower range of cranial capacity of modern humans. The form of the skull, however, is far from modern in appearance.* (Copyright © State Museum for Nature, Stuttgart, Germany)

Swanscombe find includes three major skull fragments: the back (occipital) and both sides (parietals). The skull has an estimated cranial capacity of over 1,300 ml, which places the brain size of "Swanscombe Man" well within the modern human range, though, it must be said, the skull's general appearance is a mosaic of primitive and modern traits. A radiometric date for material associated with the Swanscombe remains was calculated at 326,000 B.P. (Szabo and Collins 1975). Flint tools, including handaxes and flakes, were found in the same deposit.

The Petralona skull found southeast of Thessalonika, Greece, possesses very large brow ridges, but it is rounder and the face is flatter than in earlier hominids. The cranial capacity is judged to have surpassed 1,200 ml (Poulianos 1971–72). Electron spin resonance performed on an encrustation on the skull resulted in a date of between 160,000 and 240,000 years ago (Henning et al. 1981).

Material associated with a small occipital fragment found in Vértesszöllös, Hungary, has produced a uranium series date of between 250,000 and 475,000 years ago (Gamble 1986). The bone is rather thick, and there is an indication of an occipital torus, but the extrapolated cranial capacity is larger than in older specimens. At Arago, near the the village of Tautavel, France, the fragmentary remains of at least four adult and three juvenile hominids were found (Cook et al. 1982). The best preserved of these is a distorted face with large, thick brow ridges. The Arago fossils appear to represent archaic *Homo sapiens* dating to more than 250,000 years ago (Gamble 1986).

In Germany the Bilzingsleben site produced two occipitals, two frontal bones, and a molar. These were found together with about 60,000 flint flakes that reflected a range of scraping tools, awls, points, and chopping tools (Gamble 1986). A minimum age of 228,000 B.P. has been calculated (Harmon et al. 1980). An adult skull fragment was also found in Ehringsdorf, Germany, and dated to 225,000 B.P. (Cook et al. 1982). Bifacially worked points and scrapers were also found at this site.

PREMODERN HUMANS: CULTURAL EVIDENCE

There is no great cultural break or jump seen in the archaeological record of the archaic humans. Handaxes similar to those manufactured by *Homo erectus* are common at archaic *Homo sapiens* sites in Europe and Africa; east Asia shows continuity in the stone toolmaking tradition as well. In fact, it was not until about 200,000 years ago that a new and more efficient industry developed.

Called **Levallois,** the new industry involved a shift in emphasis from the production of core tools to the production of flake tools. Instead of sculpting a large, multipurpose tool from a stone nodule and using only the waste flakes that fortuitously fit a given need, emphasis now shifted to the flakes themselves, whose form and size were controlled by careful preparation of the core (Figure 6.6). The stone nodule, or core, was no longer the object to be shaped into a tool, but, instead, became the source from which flakes of given sizes and shapes were produced. The flakes were used as blanks to be refined into tools intended for specific tasks. The Levallois technique enabled flakes of predetermined size and form to be produced (Figure 6.7).

FIGURE 6.6

In the toolmaking technology called Levallois, a stone core was prepared so as to produce flakes of a consistent size and form. (After J. Bordaz. 1970)

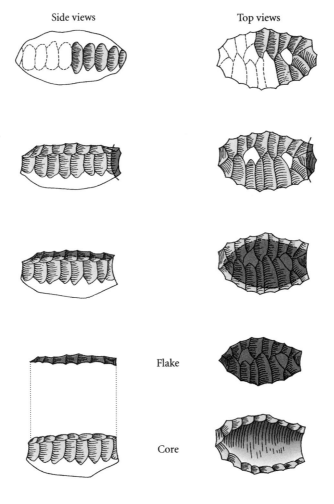

Flake

Core

Modern experts in stone-tool replication often perform the following remarkable feat: They take a stone nodule in hand and draw an outline on it in the precise shape of the flake they want to remove by striking the core with a hammerstone. A good knapper can remove a flake whose edges closely approximate the drawn outline. The key is knowing how a particular rock type breaks and preparing the rock beforehand in order to control how it will break when struck. The Levallois technique involves this kind of careful preparation of the stone core for patterned and predictable flake removal.

Preparing the core allowed archaic humans finer control of flake removal than had previously been possible. The right shape for tools with particular functions like cutting, piercing, or perforating could be ensured. The technique was also far more efficient in its use of stone than either Oldowan or Acheulean. A greater amount of sharp, usable edge is produced per unit weight of core. A replicative study by Bruce Bradley (Gamble 1986) showed that four or five predictable flakes could be removed from a single Levallois core.

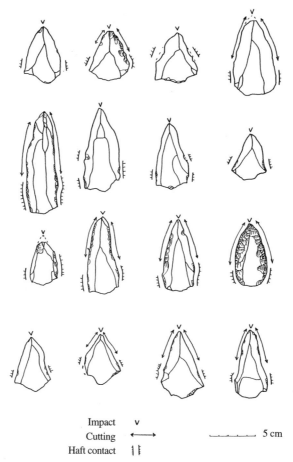

FIGURE 6.7
These triangular Levallois flakes from sites in Israel may have been used as stone tips on wooden spear shafts. (Courtesy of John Shea)

Impact   v
Cutting   ←——→   _ _ _ _ _ _ 5 cm
Haft contact   ⌡ ⌡

THE NEANDERTALS

In popular parlance, a "Neandertal" is an individual who is stupid, crude, boorish, animalistic—a real "throwback." For many people, the Neandertals represent all of our human ancestors, icons of our primitive and brutal past. The first artistic reconstruction of a Neandertal in a natural setting, ostensibly based on a Neandertal skeleton, appeared in 1909 in the French magazine *L'Illustration* (Figure 6.8); see the discussion of the meaning of artistic representations of Neandertals in Moser (1992). The image is a grotesque caricature of a hairy ape-man beast. Neandertals have been the archetype of "cavemen" ever since: ugly, apelike, violent, brutish, and stupid (Hager 1994). A famous diorama at the Field Museum of Natural History in Chicago, now maintained for its historical significance but not its scientific accuracy, depicts the Neandertals as hairy, dirty creatures with crudely sewn animal pelts for clothing, barely standing upright, with knees bent, heads thrust forward, and a vacant

FIGURE 6.8

This artist's conception of a Neandertal, first published in the French magazine L'Illustration *in 1909, was not the result purely of artistic speculation. The illustrator, Kupka, produced this image under the watchful eye of paleoanthropologists who were working on Neandertal skeletons. This drawing set the precedent for many subsequent depictions of Neandertals as animal-like and bestial.* (Illustrated London News, March 6, 1909. Artist: Kupka)

FIGURE 6.9

Fossil localities of Neandertals.

expression on their faces. Misleading images of Neandertals have, until fairly recently, shown up in newspapers, books, and magazines; and unintelligent, animalistic Neandertals have been depicted in movies as villains out to kill modern human beings. For a detailed and lively discussion of the history of scientific—and not so scientific—thinking about the Neandertals, see paleo-anthropologists Erik Trinkaus and Pat Shipman's (1993) *The Neandertals: Changing the Image of Mankind.*

In reality, the Neandertals were just another group of premodern human beings. They happen to be better known because of a number of historical accidents. For example, they were abundant in Europe (Figure 6.9), and most early paleoanthropological research was undertaken there because most of the world's paleoanthropologists have come from Europe. Also, Neandertals used caves extensively, and archaeological remains are better preserved in cave settings. The Neandertals deserve an in-depth look, if only because so much is known about them by both paleoanthropologists and the general public.

In many ways the Neandertals were similar to us. Their brain size was equal to or even larger than our own (Table 6.2). But their brain configuration was different from ours, with less of their brain in the front and more to the rear. Their skulls were marked with huge brow ridges like those of older hominid species, their faces protruded in an apelike fashion, and there was an enormous mass of bone at the rear (occipital) portion of the skull, where large muscles were attached that enabled the Neandertals to balance their large, heavy heads. They were physically far more powerful than modern human beings, and their pelvises were configured differently.

The Neandertal* name comes from the Neander Valley in Germany, where, in 1856, not the first such fossil was found, but the one that first caught the attention of the scientific community (see Chapter 2 and Figure 6.10). The recovered skull exhibited both modern human and primitive, nonhuman features. Though it was big, indicating a brain size at least as large as that of a modern human being, the shape was all wrong, with protruding, apelike bony ridges above the eyes, a face that projected forward like that of an ape, and a flattened profile rather than the rounded profile of a modern human skull.

Researchers of the time had difficulty explaining the Neandertal skull. (One scholar even suggested that its peculiar appearance was the result of "stupendous blows" with a heavy instrument sustained during the individual's lifetime.) However, as more Neandertal specimens—as all such similar fossils

---

*You will sometimes find *Neandertal* spelled *Neanderthal.* The original German spelling included an *h,* though it was (and is) pronounced as if no *h* were present. Modern German spelling has removed the *h,* so it is not used in this text. To complicate matters further, according to the rules of biological nomenclature, under most circumstances the original name given to a species cannot be changed. Since the Neandertals were originally given the species name *neanderthalensis,* with the *h,* we are obliged to leave the *h* when using the taxonomic name.

TABLE 6.2

Major Neandertal Specimens Discussed in Chapter 6

COUNTRY	LOCALITY	FOSSILS	CRANIA	AGE (YEARS)	BRAIN SIZE (ML)
Spain	Atapuerca	Remains of at least 24 individuals	Adult	>300,000	1,125
			Adult	>300,000	1,390
			Juvenile	>300,000	1,100
Germany	Neandertal	Skullcap			1,250
France	La Chappelle	Skeleton	"Old man"		1,620
	Fontéchevade	Cranial fragments of several individuals		100,000	1,500
	La Ferrassie	8 skeletons		>38,000	1,680
	La Chaise	Cranium		126,000	
	St.-Césaire	Skeleton		36,000	
Belgium	Spy	Cranium			
Italy	Mt. Circeo	Cranium			
	Saccopastore	Cranium			1,350
Yugoslavia	Krapina	Cranial and postcranial fragments of >45 individuals		Isotope stage 5	1,300
Israel	Tabun	Skeleton, mandible, postcranial fragments		60,000	1,270
	Amud	Skeleton		70,000	1,740
	Kebara	Postcranial skeleton		60,000	
Iraq	Shanidar	9 partial skeletons		70,000	1,600

With Atapuerca		
Mean		1,410.42
Standard Deviation		181.34
Without Atapuerca		
Mean		1,478.89
Standard Deviation		165.68

Data from Day 1986; Arsuaga et al. 1993.

were labeled—were discovered in Europe, it became clear that the Neandertal skull form represented a distinct and extinct variety of humanity.

In the attempt to assess the precise relationship between the Neandertals and modern humans, a major error crept into the discussion. In 1913, French scientist Marcellin Boule produced a reconstruction of the entire Neandertal

FIGURE 6.10

This skullcap of the specimen that gave the Neandertals their name was discovered in the Neander Valley in Germany in 1856. (Copyright © Landschaftsverband Rheinland)

skeleton that was rife with error (Boule and Vallois 1923). Assuming, on the basis of the form of the skull, that the Neandertals were apelike, Boule's reconstruction showed a bent-over, splayed-toe, apelike creature.

It probably didn't help that the specimen Boule chose to focus on had had a bad case of arthritis that may have caused the individual to bend over when walking. As Erik Trinkaus (1985) points out, however, Boule had two other, perfectly normal Neandertal specimens in his lab at the time, and the disease present in the one he chose to work on did not justify the apelike appearance Boule imparted. Most likely, Boule made the reconstruction apelike from the neck down because it fit his preconception of what it would have looked like based on its appearance from the neck up. Later, when Boule helped the French artist produce his drawing and when others, like the designers of the diorama at the Field Museum of Natural History, put flesh on Boule's skeletal creation, they compounded the error by giving the Neandertals an open-mouthed, dazed expression that could not even have been implied by the bones. It is from this incorrect reconstruction that our modern, insulting use of the name derives.

But who were the Neandertals, really? The evidence now is quite extensive that they were not club-toting caricatures; neither, as Erik Trinkaus and Pat Shipman put it, were they "simply funny-looking humans" (1993, 385). They were a distinctive, now-extinct variety of human beings, in some ways like us and in some ways very different (Figure 6.11). Most paleoanthropologists apply the taxonomic label *Homo sapiens neanderthalensis* to them, though some want to place them in a species separate than modern human beings: *Homo neanderthalensis* (Gould 1988).

Their roots in Europe can now be traced back to more than 300,000 years ago, an age equivalent to that of some of the other European archaics already mentioned (Arsuaga et al. 1993; Stringer 1993). However, true, or "classic," Neandertals possessing all the typical traits (to be discussed) were confined to Europe and west Asia and date from about 130,000 to 33,000 years ago.

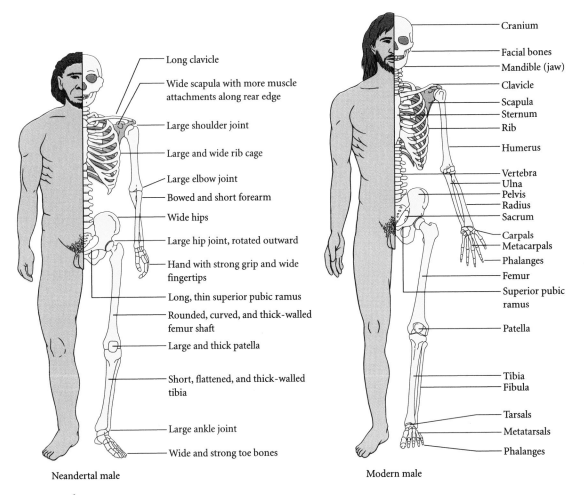

Long clavicle

Wide scapula with more muscle attachments along rear edge

Large shoulder joint

Large and wide rib cage

Large elbow joint

Bowed and short forearm

Wide hips

Large hip joint, rotated outward

Hand with strong grip and wide fingertips

Long, thin superior pubic ramus

Rounded, curved, and thick-walled femur shaft

Large and thick patella

Short, flattened, and thick-walled tibia

Large ankle joint

Wide and strong toe bones

Neandertal male

Cranium

Facial bones

Mandible (jaw)

Clavicle

Scapula

Sternum

Rib

Humerus

Vertebra

Ulna

Pelvis

Radius

Sacrum

Carpals

Metacarpals

Phalanges

Femur

Superior pubic ramus

Patella

Tibia

Fibula

Tarsals

Metatarsals

Phalanges

Modern male

FIGURE 6.11

In this comparison of the skeletons of a modern human being and a Neandertal, the so-called musculoskeletal hypertrophy of the Neandertals is readily apparent. (After Stringer and Gamble 1993)

Morphological Evidence

Though we now recognize the Neandertals as being closely related to modern humanity, controversy persists concerning the precise place of the Neandertals in the human family: Were they our evolutionary grandparents or just distant cousins? (See Trinkaus 1983a,b, 1986, 1989; Trinkaus and Shipman 1993; Wolpoff 1989b; and especially F. Smith 1991.) On this issue, paleoanthropologists seem to suffer from the ironic disadvantage of a wealth of data: Whereas other fossil species are represented by samples of just a few to a dozen or so, more than 400 separate Neandertal individuals have been excavated and are represented by thousands of bones. A limited database presents less to argue about than does a more substantial body of evidence.

Cranial Morphology   Neandertal brain size often surpassed that of modern human beings. Skull sizes range from about 1,300 ml to more than 1,600 ml, with a mean of nearly 1,480 ml (see Table 6.2); modern human mean cranial capacity is about 1,450 ml. However, the configuration of the Neandertal cranium—long and low in profile, with a steeply sloping forehead—is far different from the round, high profile of a modern human with its virtually vertical forehead. The Neandertal face was large, with the lower portion far forward of the eyes and brows. The Neandertal nasal bridge was wide and flaring, and Neandertals lacked the thin, pointy chin that typifies modern human beings. The robust features of the Neandertal head and face can be seen even in young Neandertals, including a 3-year-old Neandertal child from Gibraltar (Dean, Stringer, and Bromage 1986) and a ten-month-old infant from Amud Cave in Israel (Bower 1994b).

From the Neck Down: Designed for Cold   Contrary to Boule's reconstruction, below the head the Neandertal skeleton is essentially modern in appearance, but with some crucial differences. One morphological pattern is consistent with a physical adaptation to cold: Neandertals were big—relatively wide with broad, squat torsos and short extremities (see Figure 6.11; Trinkaus 1983a; Ruff et al. 1993), a body form associated in modern humans with cold environments because it retains heat better than does a body with a small torso and long limbs. Christopher Ruff (1993) compares the Neandertal body to that of a modern Inuit (Eskimo). This adaptation probably reflects the fact that the Neandertals flourished during isotope stage 4 (see Figure 5.9), a glacial maxima in Ice Age Europe. Another likely adaptation to cold was the Neandertal's large, projecting nose, beyond the size range of the modern human nose, valuable in cold, dry climates for conserving moisture during vigorous physical activity (Trinkaus 1989). In the architecture of the nasal cavity itself, Neandertals possessed a feature not present in modern human beings: triangular peninsulas of bone projecting into the nasal opening from both sides of the nasal margin. Researchers have suggested that these bony knobs may have provided additional surface area for mucus-producing nasal membranes, which, in turn, may have aided in warming and humidifying the cold, dry air of the Neandertal environment (Menon 1997).

From the Neck Down: Built for Strength   Not all skeletal features of the Neandertals are directly related to their adaptation to life in a cold climate. A suite of characteristics seems to reflect their enormous strength and endurance and shows them to be strikingly different from modern humans.

Specifically, in about every area on the skeleton where researchers have looked, the Neandertals exhibit what is called **musculoskeletal hypertrophy.** Paleoanthropologist Erik Trinkaus and a number of his co-workers have produced a detailed body of evidence on this very point. For example, the Neandertals were generally short and stocky when compared to modern humans, and the bones of their lower legs reflect this build (Gibbons 1996a). The breadth of their scapulae (shoulder blades) and the length of their clavicles (collar bones), along with the robusticity of areas of muscle attachment on those bones, are indicative of broad, powerful shoulders (Churchill and Trinkaus 1990).

The great size and robusticity of their upper arm bones (Ben-Itzhak, Smith, and Bloom 1988) and the large areas for muscle attachment on their forearms (Trinkaus 1983a) are clear indications that the Neandertals had tremendous upper-body strength. Trinkaus and co-worker Chris Ruff recently X-rayed and performed computerized tomography on the fossil bones of Neandertals and anatomically modern human beings (Gibbons 1996a). The upper arms of the Neandertals had more bone and reflected far greater strength than did those of anatomically modern humans who lived at the same time as the Neandertals.

Even in their ribs, vertebrae, and fingers, Neandertal bones show areas for muscle attachment far larger than what is seen in modern humans. The bones of the Neandertal hand are indicative of an extremely powerful grip (Trinkaus and Villemeur 1991). Paleoanthropologist Fred Smith succinctly summarized the data: "Neandertals seem to represent the high-water mark for the genus *Homo* in favoring the brawn approach to environmental adaptation" (1991, 225). Put another way, a spear-wielding Neandertal would have been an imposing adversary.

It is difficult to know for certain if all of these differences were the result of a fundamental biological difference between Neandertals and anatomically modern people. Trinkaus used to think that it did but now leans toward the explanation that the differences seen in arm strength resulted from differences in lifestyle. He and Ruff have suggested that the Neandertals relied more on strength than did those contemporaries of theirs who were modern-looking (see Chapter 7). A heavier reliance on brawn on the part of the Neandertals would have resulted, in their view, in the buildup of muscle and in the strengthening of those bones where the larger muscles attached. Clearly, the Neandertals were physically powerful. The degree of strength exhibited in Neandertal bones almost certainly reflects an adaptation for and a subsistence strategy based, at least in part, on the hunting of large and powerful game animals (see the section on Neandertal subsistence later in this chapter).

While the Neandertals certainly were capable of upright posture and bipedal locomotion, evidence exists that they may have walked somewhat differently than modern humans. The nearly complete right half of a Neandertal pelvis from Kebara Cave in Israel is very different from that of a modern human, which has been interpreted as signifying differences in posture and locomotion (Rak 1990; see this chapter's "Case Study Close-Up").

Fossil Evidence

Neandertal Origins   The hominids mentioned earlier in this chapter whose remains were recovered at Sima de los Huesos in the Atapuerca Mountains of northern Spain are more than twice as old as the so-called classic Neandertals to be discussed next. Nevertheless, the researchers characterize the morphol-

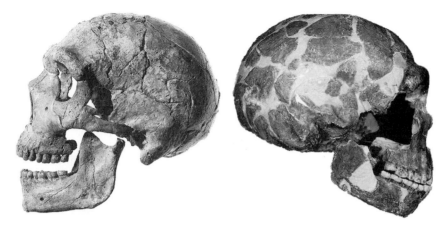

FIGURE 6.12

These typical Neandertal skulls are from (left) *Amud, Israel, and* (right) *Tabun, Israel.* (*Left:* Copyright © Israel Antiquities Authority; *right:* Copyright © The Natural History Museum, London)

ogy of the crania of the two adults and one child thus far recovered as "Neandertal-like" and as anticipating the Neandertal cranial form (Arsuaga et al. 1993, 535). Preliminary analysis by paleoanthropologist Chris Stringer indicates that of 15 typically Neandertal cranial and postcranial characteristics, the Atapuerca hominids exhibited 10, or two-thirds (Stringer 1993). They had less in common with either *Homo erectus* or modern *Homo sapiens.*

These very early (or pre-) Neandertals from northern Spain shared some features in common with the other premodern *Homo sapiens* from Europe already listed. Christopher Stringer (1993) proposes that the Atapuerca specimens and most, if not all, of the other European premoderns represent a single, variable group of hominids, whose differences are the result of geographic distance and time. The excavators propose that the morphology of the Atapuerca fossils implies a gradual evolution in Europe through time.

"Classic" Neandertals While these oldest Neandertal-like fossils can now be dated to more than 300,000 years ago, "classic" Neandertals are less than half that age. The site of La Chaise, France, has produced typical Neandertal remains dating to 126,000 years ago (Cook et al. 1982), and the site of Fonté-chevade, also in France, is probably more than 100,000 years old (Gamble 1986). Because the earliest Neandertal sites are in Europe, and because their physical characteristics originated in an environment marked by the ice and cold of the Pleistocene, it seems clear this marks their origin. They spread into southwest Asia only later, retaining their unsuitable (for the Middle East) physical adaptation to a cold climate.

The great florescence of the Neandertals in Europe and southwest Asia occurred between 80,000 and 40,000 years ago. Sites that have produced important Neandertal remains that are closely similar in morphology (Figure 6.12) include Le Moustier, La Chappelle-aux-Saints, and La Ferrassie in France; Spy in Belgium; Saccopastore and Mt. Circeo in Italy; Krapina in Yugoslavia; Amud, Kebara, and Tabun in Israel; and Shanidar in Iraq.

FIGURE 6.13

These typical Mousterian tools are produced by a core-and-flake technology practiced by the Neandertals. (Reprinted with permission from F. Bordes. 1961. Mousterian cultures in France. *Science* 134:803–10. Copyright © 1961 American Association for the Advancement of Science)

NEANDERTAL CULTURE

Stone Tools

Without guidance, many people attempting to replicate stone tools rely on brawn. They take one rock in each hand, close their eyes, smash the stones together, and hope that useful flakes wind up in the rubble at their feet. Though Neandertals were brawny, their toolmaking relied at least as much on brain power as on physical prowess.

Named for the French Neandertal site of Le Moustier, the **Mousterian** toolmaking tradition of the Neandertals represents not a replacement of the Levallois technique but a refinement. The Mousterian is a **Middle Paleolithic** industry; it is more sophisticated than the Oldowan (Chapter 4) or Acheulean (Chapter 5) industries of the **Lower Paleolithic** and less so than the Aurignacian industry of the **Upper Paleolithic** (Chapter 7).

Mousterian flakes were smaller and more precisely made than the earlier Levallois flakes: The Neandertals were capable of producing flakes whose size and shape matched more precisely the form needed for a predesignated purpose. Instead of a single all-purpose tool like a handaxe or a few particular kinds of tools as in the earlier Levallois industry, dozens of different task-specific, standardized Mousterian tool types are recognized. French archaeologist François Bordes (1972) defined 63 specific Mousterian tool types for cutting, slicing, piercing, scraping, sawing, and pounding (Figure 6.13). Archaeologists disagree about how to interpret these types. Bordes broke them down into five groupings that he interpreted as representing five separate, coexisting European Neandertal cultures. Lewis Binford and Sally Binford (1966; S. Binford 1968) viewed the five groupings of tools as five different sets of **tool kits** made and used at different sites by the same, not different, groups. Harold Dibble (1987) considers both of these views incorrect, suggesting that Bordes's groupings represent only different stages in the use-life of the tools; that is, they look different as they wear out and are resharpened. Whatever the case, the complexity of the Neandertal stone-tool assemblage clearly is the result of the complexity of what the Neandertals were doing with those tools.

Each Mousterian flake received more precise treatment once it was removed from the core. Whereas an Acheulean handaxe may have required as many as 65 blows of a hammerstone, the production of a highly specialized Mousterian tool required an additional hundred or more blows to shape and sharpen the edge once the flake was removed from its core (Constable 1973).

Subsistence

One kind of stone tool in particular implies a sophisticated element of Neandertal behavior: spearpoints. Archaeologist John Shea (1998) has examined stone spearpoints found at 58 caves in the Middle East. Some of these sites are known to have been occupied by Neandertals, others by contemporary, anatomically modern human beings. The stone tips made by the Neandertals and those by the anatomically modern humans were technologically quite similar and likely had been hafted onto wooden shafts by both groups of humans.

Shea found high frequencies of stone spearpoints at the Neandertal sites in his sample. In fact, these stone spear tips were *more* frequent at the sites of Neandertals than at sites of the modern humans living at the same time. The fact that the Neandertals had manufactured spearpoints is, by itself, strong evidence that they hunted for a part of their subsistence. The frequencies may indicate that, at least here, Neandertals relied on hunting to an even higher degree than contemporary anatomically modern humans in the same region.

Beyond this, Shea (1988, 1993, 1994) has noted the presence of a set of diagnostic patterns of damage he calls **impact wear** on some Mousterian triangular points found in southwest Asia, including those recovered at Kebara Cave. This damage is represented by clusters of small fractures on the point and nearby edge of the tool. Shea has shown experimentally that this is the probable result of using these tools as projectiles—as in hunting spears. When the stone-tipped spear enters an animal's body—by thrusting or throwing—it will often strike a bone. That impact removes the kinds of damage flakes Shea has recognized. Shea has found the scars left by damage flakes knocked off of spearpoints to be fairly common on Mousterian points in southwest Asian Neandertal sites.

It is still unclear just how reliant the Neandertals were on hunting for their subsistence. As seen previously, fragmentary animal bone remains can be very difficult to assess. Are the bones the remains of animals killed by carnivores, with only their leavings salvaged and returned to camp by the ancient humans? Or, are the bones the remains left behind by capable hunters fully reliant on the success of such expeditions?

Some evidence shows clearly that hunting contributed an important element to Neandertal diet. For example, investigators at Kebara Cave in Israel (Bar-Yosef et al. 1992) found evidence of an abundance of gazelle and fallow deer in the Neandertal diet. Evidence of burning and cut marks on their bones, as well as on those of elephant, horse, and several other mammalian species, shows the breadth of the animal subsistence base of the cave inhabitants. An abundance of carbonized seeds of wild peas found in the fireplaces is a direct indicator that the Kebara Neandertals also ate locally available vegetable foods.

Recent meticulous work conducted by Curtis Marean and Soo Yeum Kim (1998) at Kobeh Cave, in Iran, shows that many of the bones found are the upper and lower limbs of wild goats. These limb bones are meat-rich portions of the creatures, unlikely to have been left behind by predators for Neandertals to scavenge. Further, few of these limb bones showed animal bite marks, again supporting the notion that the animals were killed by people and not by lions or other predators. The bones do exhibit much evidence of cut marks made by stone tools precisely where one would expect them if hunters had been cutting off the best cuts of meat. In addition, there are plenty of percussion marks on the limb bones, most likely representing blows from stone hammers in the process of removing protein-rich marrow. Evidence seems clear here that Neandertals had first crack at the meat on these bones, that they were hunters of the meat, not scavengers. Marean and Kim conclude that the Neandertals were quite capable hunters, at least at this site.

Archaeologist Lewis Binford has been an important researcher in the field of **ethnoarchaeology,** in which anthropologists residing with living groups of people study them from an archaeological perspective. One focus of ethnoarchaeology is to examine how behavior is transformed into what we find in the archaeological record. By investigating the data's journey from behavior to archaeological evidence, anthropologists hope that insights will be gained on how to interpret backward from archaeological evidence to behavior.

Lewis Binford's (1978) classic study among the Nunamiut, a living Inuit (Eskimo) group in Alaska, focused on patterns of hunting, butchering, preparing, and disposing of animal resources. Binford has used what he learned among the Nunamiut to interpret the archaeological record at the Neandertal site of Combe Grenal in France (Binford 1987a). In examining the remains of animals processed by the Neandertal inhabitants of the site, he recognized butchering patterns in the cut marks preserved on the bones he had seen in the fresh kills of the Nunamiut. Cut marks similar to those made by the Nunamiut on caribou jaws to extract the tongue, for example, were seen by Binford on the mandibles of horse, reindeer, and aurochs (wild cattle) at Combe Grenal. From his comparisons he concluded that the Neandertals had a similar pattern of behavior designed to extract the tasty delicacy of tongue meat.

Based on his analysis of the animal bones at Combe Grenal, Binford is unconvinced that the Neandertals were great hunters. He did not find an abundance of butchering marks on those parts of the bones of animals at the site reflecting the best cuts of meat. Binford understood this to mean that the Neandertals were probably opportunistic scavengers, subsisting on the poorer meat left over by carnivores. If so, it was a successful strategy, allowing Neandertals to flourish during extremely cold periods of the Pleistocene, when meat may have been the only reliably available source of food.

Though the precise relative importance of hunting and scavenging in the Neandertal diet is not yet certain, some hunting and some scavenging is almost certain. The extent of the faunal deposits at some Neandertal sites clearly indicates that they were proficient at obtaining meat for their diet. That they likely were successful hunters should not be surprising considering the enormous skeletal and muscular strength that would have provided Neandertal hunters the stamina necessary to walk great distances in tracking animals— and in Pleistocene Europe, in the snow and cold. After tracking down animals across great distances, their great physical strength and their sophisticated tool kit would have made them formidable hunters indeed.

Compassion

It is often said that a society can be judged by how it treats its sick or injured. Ironically, evidence shows that the Neandertals, whose intelligence is so often maligned and who are used as a symbol for brutality, may actually have been compassionate and caring. This suggestion stems from evidence of the survival of Neandertal individuals who had significant health problems or who had suffered severe trauma sometime during their lives. Some of these individuals had been in such bad shape that they probably could have survived only with the help of comrades.

The best, though not only, example comes from the skeleton of an adult male (Shanidar I) found in Shanidar Cave in Iraq (Solecki 1971; Trinkaus 1983b). This Neandertal had lived a rather eventful life, to judge by his skeleton, which showed several serious, but healed, bone fractures. There was evidence of severe trauma to the left side of the head: The left eye orbit had been fractured so badly that it is likely the blow blinded his eye. His right arm had been so severely smashed that the lower part had been amputated (perhaps by the blow, perhaps intentionally in an early example of surgical amputation). The right leg showed signs of disease and possible trauma.

It is clear this individual had sustained a heavy trauma at some time in his life and that, rather remarkably, he had survived. Such survival would have been a virtual impossibility without the help and care of his companions. As K. A. Dettwyler (1991) points out, he still could have made a significant contribution to his society, so we should not interpret his and other remains as indicating absolutely selfless acts of compassion; he was not an individual who, once healed, necessarily would have been a physical "burden" to society. Nevertheless, the survival of Shanidar I does show a level of care, at least during the healing process, that is usually associated only with modern human beings. That the Neandertals may have cared for the sick and wounded merely shows how similar they may have been to us.

Burial of the Dead

In at least one essential area, Neandertals behaved much as we do: They buried their dead. At sites such as Le Moustier, La Chappelle-aux-Saints, and La Ferrassie in France; Teshik-Tash in Uzbekistan; Shanidar in Iraq; and Amud, Tabun, and Kebara in Israel, the evidence indicates that Neandertals interred their dead in the ground, most often in an intentionally flexed position, knees drawn up toward the chest, and even with some simple items such as stone or bone implements, ochre, or unmodified animal bone (Figure 6.14; Harrold 1980).

Archaeologists Anna Belfer-Cohen and Erella Hovers (1992) surveyed burial data for the Middle Paleolithic period of the Neandertals and counted 59 intentional burials. They point out that these burials make no sense as a mere hygienic way to dispose of a dead body. Why put that much time into digging a hole if a dead body can be far more unceremoniously dumped in

FIGURE 6.14

This intentional burial site found at La Ferrassie in France shows the Neandertals' affinity with the modern human practice of burying their dead. (Courtesy of the Musée de l'Homme, Paris, M. Lucas, photographer)

the woods, allowing scavengers to do the work? They conclude that the Neandertals were burying their dead in recognition of the significance of death.

More than that is difficult to tell. It is impossible to know, for example, if Neandertals regarded the tightly flexed position of many of the bodies the way some modern people have, as mimicking a fetus in the womb. Archaeologist Frank Harrold (1980, 200) found that 14 of 20 bodies examined (70%) were in this flexed position. Did the Neandertals use the fetal position to symbolize death as the end of the circle of life? Were the bodies tied into this flexed position to confine the spirit to the grave? Or was such a position simply most convenient because it minimized the size of the hole that had to be dug? Were grave goods intended for use in a perceived afterlife? Or were they remembrances for a dead friend? We simply do not know the answers.

We should not conclude that Neandertals were just like us—had funerals, memorial services, and formalized cemeteries; L. Binford (1987a) and Gargett

(1989) debunk some of the more fanciful reconstructions of Neandertal burial ceremonialism. But the questions raised by the intentional disposal of the dead practiced by the Neandertals are more important than the answers we might suggest. Clearly, Neandertals understood the significance of death and recognized it through burial. Here again, these very different human ancestors exhibit their kinship to us.

WHY ARE THE NEANDERTALS EXTINCT?

ISSUES AND DEBATES

The Neandertals and other archaic humans are extinct, having been replaced by anatomically modern human beings. In the consensus view presented in this book, the Neandertals were not the immediate ancestors of modern people, but a side branch of human evolution, at least partially overlapping in time with anatomically modern human beings (see Chapter 7). What significant advantages did the early anatomically modern humans have over the archaics that led to the survival of the modern humans and the extinction of the archaics? The European fossil record may shed light on this question.

Some evidence indicates that the Neandertals were having a rough time in Pleistocene Europe. For one thing, the Neandertals were rather short-lived as compared to even ancient anatomically modern humans. Erik Trinkaus and D. D. Thompson (1987, 126) have shown that, in a sample of 246 Neandertals, 4 out of 10 died before reaching adulthood. And of those that survived childhood, less than 10% were more than 40 years old at death (1987, 127). Paleoanthropologist Olga Soffer (1992, 252; 1994, 103–4) has shown that, in her Neandertal sample of about 200, 43% died at less than 12 years of age, while less than 30% of early modern humans in a similar-size skeletal sample (about 150) died that early in life.

As alluded to in Chapter 3, the human skeleton preserves a record of dietary deficiencies suffered during its developmental years. For example, **Harris lines,** cracks on the ends of long bones (arm and leg) that result from dietary deficiency during the developing years, and **enamel hypoplasia,** zones of thin tooth enamel that result from unmet nutritional needs during early childhood, are present to a far greater degree in Neandertal remains than in the remains of early anatomically modern human beings. Marsha Oglivie, Bryan Curran, and Erik Trinkaus (1989), for example, found evidence of hypoplasia in the enamel of 36% of 669 Neandertal teeth, reflecting an estimated incidence of 75% in the individuals represented. This is more than double the incidence in nutritionally stressed recent human samples (Oglivie, Curran, and Trinkaus 1989, 30). Other studies have produced similar results (Molnar and Molnar 1985; M. Brennan 1991). As Olga Soffer (1994) points out, this paleopathological evidence indicates that Neandertal children suffered far more physical stress than did their anatomically modern contemporaries.

Finally, Erik Trinkaus (1989) points to a notable decrease in evidence of trauma when early anatomically modern fossils are compared to Neandertals: fewer broken bones among the early moderns than in Neandertal skeletons.

Together this evidence has been interpreted as indicating that the Neandertals were, perhaps, too highly specialized in their physical, genetically determined adaptations to the harsh climates of the Ice Age and in their great size and strength. As Erik Trinkaus (1983a) points out, massive and heavily built individuals like the Neandertals incur a higher energy cost than do those more lightly built. Where Neandertals needed to burn more calories by ingesting greater amounts of food to keep their heavily built bodies warm, anatomically modern humans could get by with less, simply because they were smaller and more lightly built. The paleopathological evidence cited may have resulted from the Neandertal inability to procure enough food under the harsh conditions of Ice Age Europe.

Moreover, anatomically modern humans may have possessed better cultural buffers against the climate of the Pleistocene. According to archaeologist Richard Klein (1994), when compared to the cultures of Middle Paleolithic Neandertals, anatomically modern humans produced more complex tools with a greater number of types, obtained better raw materials from greater distances to make those tools, used bone as a source of raw material for tool manufacture, built more complex structures, buried their dead in more complex graves, and produced indisputable works of art. As Klein puts it, a "very substantial behavioral gulf" separates the Neandertals from anatomically modern humans (1994, 11; see Chapter 7).

Furthermore, and importantly, rather than having to burn calories to keep warm, anatomically modern humans could more efficiently burn wood than could their Neandertal cousins. As pointed out by Klein (1994), Neandertal hearths were simple and did not exhibit the more sophisticated design and better heat retention of fireplaces constructed by anatomically modern human beings. At Kebara Cave, for instance, Neandertal hearths were round or oval and used no stone and, therefore, had no banking of the heat as was typically found in the hearths of early modern humans. Additionally, Arthur Jelinek (1994) suggests that some of the artifacts made by modern human beings—but not by Neandertals—were part of a tool kit for the manufacture of more effectively tailored cold-weather clothing; Jelinek calls this clothing "personal insulation" (1994, 83). Because cultural adaptations are faster, more flexible, and often less energy-expensive than physical adaptations that accomplish the same thing, anatomically modern humans would have had an enormous advantage over the Neandertals.

Statistical models based on these probable advantages indicate just how easily the extinction of the Neandertal could have been accomplished. Ezra Zubrow (1989), a mathematician turned archaeologist, has determined that under certain circumstances, when Neandertal mortality exceeds that of anatomically modern humans by between only 1% and 2%, the complete extinction of the Neandertals can occur in only thirty generations—less than a thousand years. So it is ironic: The very physical features that allowed Neandertals to survive and even thrive for a time under the harsh conditions of Pleistocene Europe ultimately led to their extinction. They appear to have become too massively built, too specialized, for life in the cold. This specialization put them at a distinct disadvantage when conditions changed and food became harder to obtain.

COULD NEANDERTALS TALK?

This question may appear to be almost impossible to answer. After all, sound does not fossilize, and the next best source of information about oral communication—the muscles and tissues that make up the human vocal tract—leave no direct physical trace. Fortunately, however, such muscles and tissues are connected to bone, in particular at the base of a hominid's cranium. Analysis of the **basicranium** may give us information about an extinct hominid's ability to speak.

The work of Philip Lieberman (1984; Lieberman et al. 1992) and Edmund Crelin (1987), both separately and together (Lieberman, Crelin, and Klatt, 1972), has served as a lightning rod in the debate about Neandertal speech. Based on their analysis of the basicranium of Neandertal, they reconstructed the soft parts of Neandertal vocal anatomy and then used a computer to simulate the sounds a Neandertal might have been capable of making and the speed with which they could be made. In their reconstruction of Neandertal vocal tract anatomy as implied by the morphology of the base of the skull, the larynx was positioned high up in the throat, and the pharynx lacked the sharp bend that typifies modern humans. In fact, the reconstructed Neandertal vocal tract resembled that of a chimpanzee or a newborn human more than that of an adult human being. They concluded that, while the Neandertals could make sounds, they were incapable of producing anything close to the range of sounds that characterizes human speech. Lieberman (1992) has gone so far as to suggest that the great differences he postulates between the speech of Neandertals and that of early anatomically modern humans may have served as one of the key factors to keep these groups apart. This might explain how Neandertals and modern humans maintained separate evolutionary trajectories though they were contemporaries and, in some cases, living in close proximity to each other (see Chapter 7).

Many, if not most, paleoanthropologists are highly critical of Lieberman and Crelin's conclusions. Even if the Neandertals were physically incapable of producing the complete range of sounds we are capable of making, no modern human language requires all those sounds anyway. Neandertal brains are so large and their culture so complex, it is difficult to believe that their linguistic abilities were as elementary as some researchers have suggested. In addition, the recent discovery of a very modern-looking hyoid bone (a horseshoe-shaped bone in the throat) at Kebara Cave (Arensburg et al. 1990) has led some researchers to conclude that the Neandertals were physically capable of fully human speech. There this debate stands.

DID NEANDERTALS WORSHIP CAVE BEARS?

You may still find in popular literature the claim that the archaeological record shows that the Neandertals regularly killed the large species of European Ice Age bear, *Ursus spelaeus,* and then built shrines for the skulls of these huge beasts.

Unfortunately, the notion of bear-worshipping Neandertals simply doesn't hold up under careful taphonomic analysis. As shown by paleontologist and cave bear expert Björn Kurtén (1976), the supposed archaeological features used to support this notion—a stone chest filled with bear skulls at the site of Drachenloch, Switzerland; a stone cubicle with 20 skulls at Regourdu in France; and other accumulations of cave bear skulls at Les Furtins and Saône-et-Loire—were more in the minds of the excavators than in reality. Kurtén has shown in these and other cases that key data concerning the positioning of the bones are contradictory in the various sketches made by the excavators and further contradict some of their notes on the discoveries. Moreover, if Neandertals cut up the bear carcasses with stone tools, they were very neat about it; no stone tools have been found in association with the bear remains, and no cut marks have been found on the bear bones.

The bears likely died natural deaths in the caves, where there is clear evidence of their having lived. Scavengers then came in, removing some of the body along with some of the bones. Commonly in such a situation, the large skull is left in place. Any other bear who subsequently moves into the cave simply pushes the skull against a wall, out of the way. After a time, a group of skulls can accumulate. It might appear to be intentional and cultural, but it is not. It can be explained as the result of taphonomic processes that involve no human agency. And the stone chests the researchers reported were nothing more than piled-up rock, fallen from the roof of the caves, covering the bones of the bears who lived and died there. The image of the lone hunter, with nothing more than a spear in hand, facing off against an angry bear well over 10 feet tall when on its hind legs, hoping to claim its cave home and then to propitiate its dead spirit, is evocative indeed. The extant evidence, however, simply does not support this romantic image.

DID NEANDERTALS PRODUCE ART AND MAKE MUSIC?

The creative or artistic impulse and the desire to use symbols in expressing that impulse might seem to be uniquely human traits. Did the Neandertals have that same desire?

Examples of grooved or perforated bones, perforated animal teeth, polished ivory, and even geometrically incised bone and ivory found at Neandertal sites are the closest things yet found that could reflect an artistic impulse on the part of the Neandertals (Bahn 1998; Chase and Dibble 1987; Simek 1992). At one site in France, Arcy-sur-Cure, there are more than 142 such objects (Hublin et al. 1996). Some of these, especially the perforated objects, may have been used in personal ornamentation—for example, as pendants.

What might the use of such ornamentation tell us about the Neandertals? Even today, along with simply providing beautiful decoration, our jewelry may be intended to convey messages to others concerning our marital status, our economic position, our membership in a particular social group, or even our religion. It is an intriguing possibility that in wearing items of personal adornment, Neandertals may also have been conveying messages like these in a symbolic way.

There even is some evidence that the Neandertals were musically inclined. A small bone fragment found in a Slovenian cave had four round holes punched or drilled into one of its sides. Researchers believe the object may have been part of a Neandertal flute (Folger and Menon 1997). Hole placement suggests a standard musical scale, though some are skeptical about the artifact and have suggested the holes resulted from an animal bite.

The supposed Neandertal artwork and musical abilities, if supported by subsequent research, nevertheless appear relatively late in the Neandertals' tenure on earth. Virtually all of it dates to after 50,000 B.P., so it certainly was not part of their repertoire for the greater part of their existence. Nonetheless, though the art objects and possible musical instrument made by Neandertals are less sophisticated than those seen later on, produced by anatomically modern human beings, in the desire to scratch symbols on a stone or polish a bit of ivory, in wearing such items suspended around their necks, wrists, or fingers, and maybe even in playing a simple tune, the Neandertals exhibited a striking similarity to us. Such evidence, perhaps more than any of the other material presented in this chapter, belies the stereotype of the Neandertals as subhuman beasts.

WERE NEANDERTAL BABIES LESS ALTRICIAL THAN MODERN BABIES?

As shown in Chapter 5, the configuration of the female pelvis can be used to estimate the degree of development of a hominid newborn. For some time, no intact Neandertal pelvis had been found, and the available fragments seemed to indicate a Neandertal pelvic inlet that was quite a bit larger than in modern human females. This led Erik Trinkaus to suggest that Neandertal babies were born at a more developed fetal stage than modern humans. He postulated that a larger birth canal would have allowed the birth of Neandertal babies of a year or more's gestation, significantly more than the nine-month gestational period of modern humans (Trinkaus 1983a, 1984). This implied that Neandertal babies would have been less altricial than modern human newborns. This would be another, highly significant difference between them and us.

While no well-preserved female Neandertal pelvis has yet been found, the recent discovery and analysis of a complete right pelvis of a Neandertal male at Kebara Cave has caused Trinkaus to withdraw his suggestion of a longer gestation for Neandertals (Bar-Yosef et al. 1992). Analysis of the pelvis by researcher Yoel Rak (1990) shows some significant differences from that of modern human beings, but has also shown that the Neandertal pelvic inlet would have been no different in size from that of modern human females. Robert Tague (1992) concludes that, based on the Kebara pelvis, Neandertal babies could have been proportionally no larger than those of modern humans without making birth even more difficult than it is among modern human females. So the relatively large size of Neandertal children when compared to anatomically modern children of the same age is probably related to accelerated development after birth, not faster or longer prenatal development (Dean, Stringer, and Bromage 1986).

CASE STUDY CLOSE-UP

Kebara Cave is located on Mt. Carmel in Israel, in a region rich in Middle Paleolithic sites in general and Neandertal fossils in particular. The first excavation in the cave occurred in 1927, and researchers have returned intermittently in the ensuing years. Most recently, between 1982 and 1990, previously unexcavated parts of the cave were meticulously excavated. A detailed summary of all of the work conducted in the cave can be found in Bar-Yosef et al. (1992).

The extensive artifact and faunal assemblages recovered from the cave provide a detailed picture of life in southwest Asia in the Middle Paleolithic. As mentioned previously, the Neandertal inhabitants of the cave subsisted on the meat of a wide range of animals, especially gazelle and fallow deer. They also collected and ate plant foods that abounded near the cave.

The artifact assemblage is typically Mousterian. Most of the lithic raw materials for tool production were obtained locally, from no more than 5 km away from the cave. All stages of the reduction sequence, from core preparation to final flake sharpening, were found in the cave. Wear-pattern analysis carried out by archaeologist John Shea (1989) shows that the tools were used for various activities, including woodworking, butchering animals, bone and antler carving, and hideworking.

The skeleton of a Neandertal male was excavated at Kebara in 1983. He was 25–35 years old when he died some 60,000 years ago. We do not know how he died—there is no sign of significant disease or trauma on his skeleton, though it does display some enamel hypoplasia so common among the Neandertals. We do know that he was intentionally buried, having been laid on his back in an east–west orientation, his head facing west. Based on the positioning of his bones, the excavators concluded that in his grave, his right arm had been laid across his chest, with his hand on his left breast. His left arm and hand had been placed on his stomach. Though the vast majority of animal bones in the cave bore evidence of gnawing by carnivores and scavengers, there were no gnaw marks on the Neandertal's bones. His body had been placed in a trench by his comrades, leaning up against the north wall of the grave. This leaning of the body against a wall of earth, and the infilling of the trench after placement, served to preserve much of the skeleton in correct anatomical sequence.

In a most unfortunate but equally intriguing turn of events, the otherwise largely intact skeleton was missing the head; no cranial fragments whatsoever were found in the thorough excavation of the burial. The mandible was in place, which seems to rule out animal disturbance as the cause of the head's disappearance. The researchers suggest that the head was intentionally removed by the deceased's cohorts after sufficient decay, to render the task minimally disruptive to the rest of his remains (Bar-Yosef et al. 1992, 529). Why this would have been done is a mystery, though some ceremonial treatment of the skull of a dead comrade is a reasonable possibility.

As mentioned previously, the Kebara skeleton has provided significant information concerning the Neandertal ability to speak, in the recovery in anatomical position of the hyoid bone of the throat (Arensburg et al. 1990). It has also cleared up the question of Neandertal pelvic inlet size (Rak 1990), showing a pelvic form different from that of anatomically modern humans, but not larger. For many researchers, the image of nearly mute Neandertals giving birth to large, relatively mature babies at 12 or more months' gestation has been put to rest by the Kebara adult burial.

Among the museums that display the most significant array of archaic and, in particular, Neandertal material is the Musée de l'Homme (Museum of Man) in Paris. If you are not planning to visit France, virtually any large natural history museum in the United States or Canada has displays on the Neandertals. It would be an interesting project to see how many of these museums continue to present old and inaccurate depictions of Neandertal life.

VISITING THE PAST

SUMMARY

Beginning some 400,000 years ago, existing hominids gave way to more modern-looking hominid forms. With a mean cranial capacity reaching past 1,220 ml, the brain size of these premodern humans falls well within the modern human range.

One sort of premodern human, the Neandertal, is the best known of these. Present in large numbers in Europe and southwest Asia, Neandertals were successful and intelligent hominids. Their tool technology, called Mousterian, was far more efficient and sophisticated than the Acheulean technology of *Homo erectus*. There also is evidence that they cared for their sick, buried their dead, and were the first human ancestor to produce art.

The preponderance of evidence seems to indicate that the Neandertals were physically specialized to life in Ice Age Europe and represent an extinct side-branch of human evolution. This interpretation, however, leaves us in a bit of a quandary. If the Neandertals were a side-branch off the main evolutionary line, which, if any, of the other, non-Neandertal, archaic humans were directly ancestral to us? That question is the focus of the next chapter.

TO LEARN MORE

Technical Summaries

For the most up-to-date perspectives on the Neandertals, see the articles in the supplement to the June 1998 edition of the journal *Current Anthropology*. The articles reflect the current and growing consensus that the Neandertals were not inferior human beings, but instead a different and extinct kind of human being. A richly detailed summary of the Neandertals has been provided by Paul Mellars in *The Neanderthal Legacy* (1996). Mary Stiner's book, *Honor Among Thieves: A Zooarchaeological Study of Neandertal Ecology* (1994) presents an interesting perspective on Neandertal subsistence strategies.

Popular Summaries

Erik Trinkaus and Pat Shipman's *The Neandertals: Changing Images of Mankind* (1993) is an enormously informative and well-written history of the discovery and interpretation of the best-known, yet most controversial of the varieties of premodern humans, the Neandertals. Paleoanthropologist Christopher Stringer and archaeologist Clive Gamble have written *In Search of the Neanderthals* (1993), a terrific book on the modern arguments and consensus regarding the significance of the Neandertals and their role in the evolution of anatomically modern people. One of the best popular treatments of the Neandertals is paleoanthropologist Ian Tattersall's *The Last Neanderthal* (1995). Joshua Fischman summarized the controversies surrounding the Neandertals in *Discover* magazine's February 1992 issue.

On the Web

The Atapuerca site in Spain has its own homepage with a substantial amount of information about the fossils found there. Its address is http://atapuerca.geo.ucm.es/.

An abundance of material on the Internet is related to the Neandertals. One site that links to many other sites dealing with issues related to the Neandertals is located at http://thunder.indstate.edu/~ramanank/index.html. I recommend it highly.

The original Neandertal site now has a museum and a homepage on the Internet. The Web address is http://www.neanderthal.de/e_thal/fs_1.htm.

Computer technology allows us to imagine what living Neandertals looked like. To see modern human models (an adult woman, an adult man, and children) "morphed" into Neandertals, visit the fascinating site at the address http://www.bvl.uic.edu/bvl/ng/slides/slide07.html.

KEY TERMS

anatomically modern
  Homo sapiens
archaic *Homo sapiens*
premodern *Homo
  sapiens*
Levallois

musculoskeletal
  hypertrophy
Mousterian
Middle Paleolithic
Lower Paleolithic
Upper Paleolithic

tool kit
impact wear
ethnoarchaeology
Harris lines
enamel hypoplasia
basicranium

The Evolution of Us

THE ORIGINS OF MODERN HUMANS

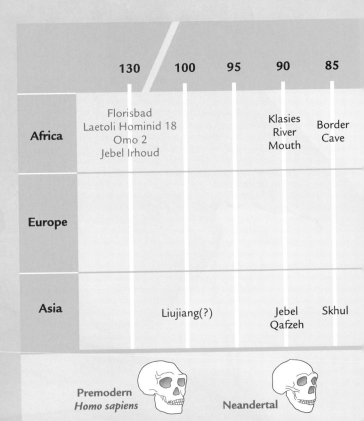

CHAPTER OVERVIEW

Anatomically modern human beings appear in the fossil record about 100,000 years ago. Three competing models—the population and genetic replacement hypotheses and the multiregional approach—have been proposed to explain their evolution. In the replacement hypotheses, modern humans evolved once in one place—probably southern Africa—and spread out from there. In the multiregional approach, modern human beings evolved from their premodern antecedents in various world areas more or less simultaneously. Anatomically modern human beings replaced premodern humans wherever the two came in contact. A deductive test of the evidence lends some support to the replacement views.

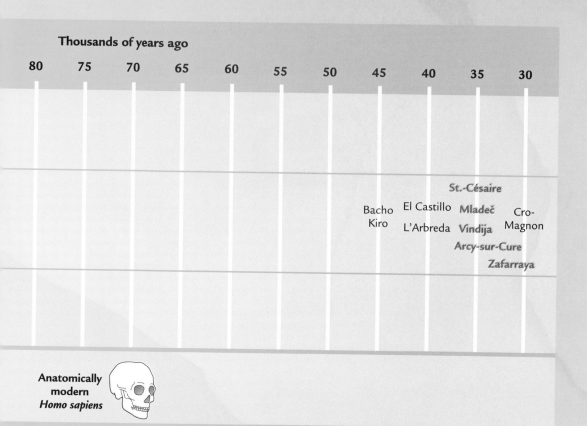

Thousands of years ago

80 75 70 65 60 55 50 45 40 35 30

St.-Césaire

Bacho   El Castillo   Mladeč   Cro-
Kiro   L'Arbreda   Vindija   Magnon

Arcy-sur-Cure

Zafarraya

**Anatomically
modern
*Homo sapiens***

PRELUDE

How do we know in what ways the ancient hominids discussed in this book were related to living human beings? Which hominids were most like us, which were most different? Which were our direct ancestors? Which were offshoots from the evolutionary line that led to us?

Much of our understanding about ancient human ancestors and, in fact, about all other extinct animal life ultimately has been based on the analysis and interpretation of the size, shape, and internal architecture of their fortuitously preserved bones. The many photographs of skulls you find in this book reflect the simple fact that often these have been our best source of information about the human biological past.

But stunning research conducted over the past two decades has begun to change how we know and what we know. The morphological analysis of bone is still and always will be important, of course, but a new avenue of study allows us, when we are lucky, to read the actual genetic instructions encoded in those ancient bones.

MITOCHONDRIAL DNA AND MOLECULAR ARCHAEOLOGY

Nuclear DNA, the so-called double helix of two parallel, connected strands of chemicals, looking much like a twisted ladder, serves as the blueprint for an individual and a species and is present in most cells of an organism. Most cells also contain another kind of **DNA** called **mitochondrial DNA (mtDNA).** Mitochondria (*sing.,* mitochondrion) are usually referred to as the cells' energy factories.

There are major advantages to using mtDNA instead of nuclear DNA in tracing the evolutionary connections between and among organisms. To begin with, mitochondrial DNA consists of a much shorter set of genetic instructions than does nuclear DNA. For example, instead of the human nuclear DNA's double helix, coding for more than 100,000 genes, human mitochondrial DNA comes in small, two-strand rings and codes for only 37 genes that control the mitochondrion (Wilson and Cann 1992). The human mitochondrial genome (the entire mitochondrial DNA sequence for humanity) is already completely known (Stoneking 1993); the entire sequence of genes in the human nuclear genome will not be known until sometime during the first decade of the twenty-first century.

Furthermore, while the DNA contained within the mitochondria of an organism's cells is unique to that individual and species, it plays little if any role in coding for the characteristics of the individual. The appearance of the mtDNA within a population is largely the result of accumulated accidents that otherwise have little impact. Observation indicates that mutations or errors build up at a relatively rapid and constant rate in the mtDNA when compared to nuclear DNA. MtDNA can be viewed, therefore, as a clock, where the number of changes (mutations) from a previous state is primarily a function of time. This aspect of mitochondrial DNA has enabled its use in the investigation of the nature and timing of the evolution of modern human beings (see the discussion later in this chapter).

Another advantage of using mtDNA in assessing evolutionary connections rests in the fact that it is inherited only through the female line. As a result, it is less complicated to use as an evolutionary marker. You do not get mixing of the mtDNA of two different individuals in each generation, so it is much easier to trace back through generations than is ever-recombining nuclear DNA. MtDNA evolutionary analysis is analogous to genealogically tracing a family name that remains pretty much the same as far back as you go, with only random, regular changes in the spelling occurring through time. Using nuclear DNA for the same purpose would be like trying to trace back a lineage of people where in each generation the family name changes to a random combination of letters in the mother's and father's names.

RESURRECTING EXTINCT SPECIES

The last quagga, a beautiful species of striped wild equines, died in an Amsterdam zoo in 1883. With no living examples to study and no behavior to observe, conclusions concerning where the quagga fit into the living world were necessarily based on fading black-and-white photographs, paintings, written descriptions, and preserved museum specimens. The quagga, however, has been able to tell us its story in a new way; it was one of the first extinct animals to have its mtDNA extracted from a preserved specimen (Higuchi et al. 1984).

When this mtDNA was compared to that of modern species, the quagga's place relative to them was secured. Its mtDNA was much more similar to that of a particular kind of zebra (the Burchell zebra) than to that of a horse or wild ass.

More recent projects have extracted DNA from an extinct Siberian woolly mammoth whose 40,000-year-old remains were preserved in ice. Not surprisingly, its DNA was quite similar to that of modern elephants (Pääbo, Higuchi, and Wilson 1989). A 14,000-year-old saber-toothed tiger, recovered from Los Angeles's La Brea tar pits, produced DNA similar, but not identical, to living species of large wild cats (Grimaldi 1993). And yes, a key element in the plot of the book and movie *Jurassic Park* is actually true; DNA has been successfully retrieved from insects caught in amber dating to more than 25 million B.P. (Grimaldi 1993). Unfortunately, no dinosaur DNA has been recovered from the guts of biting insects dating to the Jurassic, so you won't be visiting a real Jurassic Park anytime soon. But the DNA of insects preserved in amber has been used to accurately assess the evolutionary relationships of extinct bees and termites.

MOLECULAR ARCHAEOLOGY AND THE EVOLUTION OF HUMAN BEINGS

DNA has also been recovered from some ancient human remains. A 2,400-year-old Egyptian mummy (Pääbo 1985), 500- to 800-year-old Chilean mummies (Rogan and Salvo 1990), some well-preserved 7,000-year-old human brains (found in waterlogged conditions at archaeological sites in Florida; Pääbo, Gifford, and Wilson 1988), and human bones from Illinois dated to A.D. 1300 (Stone and Stoneking 1993) have all provided ancient human DNA that can be compared to modern human DNA. When the genetic makeup of an ancient person can be compared directly to that of modern individuals, the relationship to modern people can be assessed.

Most recently, in a stunning research result, a fragment of mitochondrial DNA was extracted from a small Neandertal bone fragment, allowing scientists for the first time to compare the genetic instructions for an extinct form of humanity with the DNA of our own species. The bone was one of those recovered in 1856 at the original Neandertal site in Germany. The research project was led by Svante Pääbo, one of the world's leading investigators of ancient DNA (Krings et al. 1997).

This "molecular archaeology" of the Neandertals shows that they were genetically distinct from modern humans. In the DNA segment recovered (379 base-pairs of a total mitochondrial DNA length of about 16,500 base-pairs in humans), there are more than three times the number of differences between Neandertals and modern humans than are found when comparing any two groups of living humans. This degree of difference supports the hypothesis that the Neandertals were not our immediate ancestors but instead were evolutionary cousins, plying their own separate course through ancient history.

If other attempts to extract the genetic blueprint from extinct hominid bones are successful, we may be able, ultimately, to construct the genealogy of the human species more precisely than ever before by reading the DNA of our ancient ancestors. By being able to directly compare DNA among various human ancestors, our evolutionary trees will no longer be based only on morphological characteristics as reconstructed from fragmentary fossil remains. Our evolutionary models will be based on the actual genetic instructions that determine what we are, whether it's *Homo sapiens*, *Homo erectus*, or *Homo habilis*. And, perhaps, at last, we will be able to resolve one of the most vexing of riddles about human evolution: How did anatomically modern *Homo sapiens* evolve? That question is the focus of this chapter.

 **CHRONICLE**   Whereas the "Chronicle" sections in previous chapters have presented the consensus opinion on each chapter's topic, there is, unfortunately, no consensus on the origins of anatomically modern *Homo sapiens*. Instead, there are three competing models for explaining the source and timing of the evolution of modern human beings and numerous approaches somewhere between the three opposing explanations.

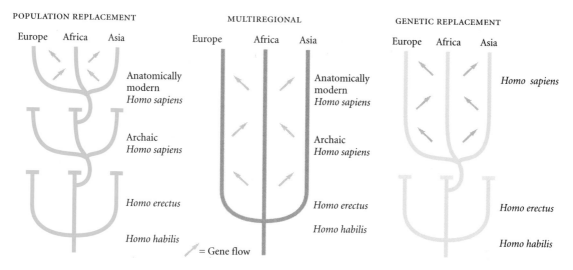

FIGURE 7.1

Schematic depiction of competing models of the evolution of anatomically modern Homo sapiens.

One explanation is called the "population replacement" model. The second is the "multiregional" or "regional continuity" view. The third is called the "genetic replacement" hypothesis (Figure 7.1).

THE POPULATION REPLACEMENT MODEL

In the **population replacement model,** whose chief proponent is British paleoanthropologist Christopher B. Stringer (1990, 1992a,b, 1994; Stringer and Andrews 1988), nearly all of the fossils of premodern humans described in Chapter 6 (at least those from Europe and Asia) represent extinct forms of human beings that contributed nothing to the evolution of modern humanity. Instead, the evolution of anatomically modern human beings is considered to have occurred just once, in one place—currently believed to be Africa, perhaps in the south of that continent—and fairly recently—between 100,000 and 200,000 years ago.

In this view, the first anatomically modern human beings spread out from their African homeland, first into southwest Asia and then east to the rest of Asia and north and west to Europe (Figure 7.2, p. 178). There, these African-originating modern humans encountered populations of premodern humans—those discussed in Chapter 6—including remnant groups of *Homo erectus.* For a time they were contemporaries, perhaps living virtually next door to each other. The anatomically modern humans possessed some fundamental advantage, as yet poorly understood, over their premodern neighbors—perhaps they were smarter or could communicate more effectively. The modern-looking humans replaced premoderns wherever they came into contact. Premoderns could not successfully compete for resources with the modern humans and so became extinct, leaving no genetic endowment to modern humanity.

FIGURE 7.2

The geography of the evolution of modern humans implied by the population replacement model.

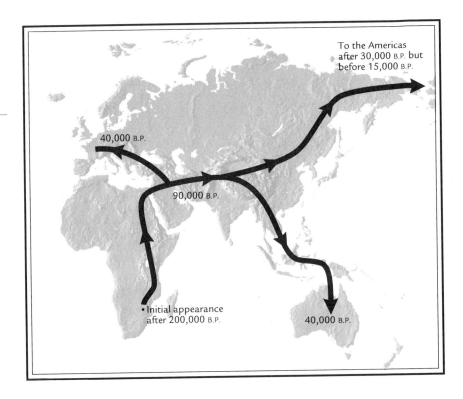

FIGURE 7.2 *The geography of the evolution of modern humans implied by the population replacement model.*

THE MULTIREGIONAL MODEL

In the **multiregional** (or **regional continuity**) **model,** whose champion is American paleoanthropologist Milford Wolpoff (Frayer et al. 1993; Thorne and Wolpoff 1992; Wolpoff 1989a, 1992; Wolpoff and Caspari 1997; Wolpoff, Wu, and Thorne 1984; Wolpoff et al. 1994), the evolution of modern human beings was a geographically broad process, not an event restricted to a single place. Various geographically separated groups of archaic humans—representing many regions—together evolved toward the modern form. Enough contact between groups in Africa, Europe, and Asia was maintained to allow for **gene flow** among them. This gene flow was sufficient to keep the archaics as a single, variable species. Through migration and intermarriage among the different groups, new, advantageous modern traits, originating in various places and among different archaic groups, rippled through the population of premodern humans (Wolpoff et al. 1994, 178). Together and simultaneously, not separately and independently, all these groups evolved into the modern form while still maintaining some relatively minor regional traits traceable back to their premodern ancestors. Gene flow among groups was not so great as to wipe out such local, regional, or "racial" characteristics. So *Homo erectus* and archaic *Homo sapiens* in east Asia evolved into the modern people of Asia; even though their DNA was quite different from ours, in this view, the Neandertals of Europe and west Asia evolved into modern Europeans and west Asians; and the archaic humans of Africa evolved into the modern people of Africa. All groups remained part of the human species, yet all maintained their own unique physical features.

A MIDDLE GROUND: GENETIC REPLACEMENT

The population replacement and multiregional views have been tempered by scholars searching for a middle ground in this debate. The middle ground can be called the **genetic replacement model.**

Günter Bräuer (1992), for example, agrees with Stringer that Africa was the source of modern humanity at a fairly late date but does not accept the notion of complete replacement. He believes that as the first anatomically modern human beings spread from Africa, they did not replace the archaics they encountered; instead, they mated with them, producing hybrid populations that, ultimately, were pulled along to modernity. Also falling somewhere in between is Fred Smith (1991, 1992), who holds that modern human traits developed in a single population (maybe Africa, maybe someplace else) and then spread primarily through gene flow (as opposed to migration) into archaic groups.

In the genetic replacement model, populations of premodern humans living in Europe and Africa were not simply eliminated by a wave of anatomically modern human beings as they spread from their African homeland. Instead, the replacement that occurred was on a genetic level. Modern human genes spread throughout the world by interbreeding. In this view, it was the modern genes that replaced premodern ones.

The deductive implications of the genetic replacement model fall between those of the multiregional and population replacement models. As in the population replacement model, we might still expect that modern humans appeared first in a single source area. If Bräuer is correct, outside of the source area for modern humans we might still expect some degree of temporal overlap between the newly arrived moderns and the indigenous premodern humans. This hypothesis resembles the population replacement model. But, unlike that model, the genetic replacement view expects to see some continuity of regionally restricted traits in each area, as the genes of modern and archaic humans combine in hybrid populations. This aspect of the genetic replacement model is like the multiregional model.

Because there is so much debate on the issue of the evolution of modern human beings, this "Chronicle" must end here. Because virtually all data are interpreted differently depending on which model is being used, the evidence for each model will be presented in "Issues and Debates." As yet there are no definitive answers to the questions to be raised. The issues are complex and the debate is unresolved, which makes this part of the human story both exasperating and exciting.

ISSUES AND DEBATES

REPLACEMENT OR CONTINUITY?

As both Christopher Stringer and Milford Wolpoff agree, the competing views of modern human evolution must be tested deductively with data. Here we will lay out the predictions of the population replacement, multiregional, and genetic replacement models—those things we expect to find in the fossil and genetic records if one or the other hypothesis is correct—and then examine the record to see how well it matches those predictions. The predictions are taken largely from Stringer and Andrews (1988), Wolpoff (1992), and Wolpoff et al. (1994).

What We Would Expect on the Basis of the Population Replacement Model

If the population replacement model is correct—if early anatomically modern humans evolved in Africa from earlier archaic roots and then spread from there, replacing indigenous hominids in Europe and Asia—then the fossil record should show the following:

1. The oldest anatomically modern human fossils should be found in Africa and nowhere else.
2. There should be continuity only in Africa. That is to say, fossil forms intermediate between archaics and moderns should be found only in Africa.
3. Outside of Africa, the emigrant moderns should be contemporaries of indigenous archaics until the nonmodern humans become extinct.
4. There should be a distinct break in the form of archaic and modern human fossils outside of Africa as African moderns replaced indigenous archaics. The first anatomically modern humans in Europe and Asia should look like the early anatomically modern humans in Africa, since that is where they originated. The earliest modern-looking humans in Europe and Asia should exhibit no specific skeletal continuities with the premodern human fossils of their regions.
5. The archaeological record is expected to show the sudden appearance of nonlocal, African-originating artifact types in Europe and Asia as the early anatomically modern African population spread from its place of origin.

What We Would Expect on the Basis of the Multiregional Model

If the multiregional hypothesis is to be upheld, then the following, quite different, predictions can be made about the fossil record:

1. Early versions of anatomically modern *Homo sapiens* should be found in many different regions. No one region should have anatomically modern fossils substantially older than any other region.

2. Intermediate forms—advanced archaics—should be found in each region, since evolution from premodern to modern occurred everywhere.
3. Because local archaics are everywhere ancestral to modern humans in their regions, there should be no or very little chronological overlap between the archaic and modern forms.
4. Local skeletal traits should show continuity between archaic and modern humans because in each region local archaics evolved into modern people.
5. The archaeological record should show a continuity in regional artifact types, for as local premodern humans evolved physically into modern humans, their archaic toolmaking traditions evolved into more sophisticated modern traditions.

What We Would Expect on the Basis of the Genetic Replacement Model

If the genetic replacement model is to be upheld, then the following predictions can be made about the fossil record:

1. The oldest anatomically modern human fossils should be found in Africa and nowhere else.
2. Outside of Africa, at least in some areas, there should be chronological overlap between indigenous premodern humans and emigrant moderns.
3. There should *not* be a distinct break between premodern and modern forms. Premodern forms will grade into modern forms everywhere that hybridization occurred.
4. There should be continuity of regional traits seen in local premodern groups wherever they mated with bearers of modern human genes. Local characteristics seen in modern human regional populations can be traced back to the premodern of these regions.

Testing the Implications of Replacement and Continuity

1. Are the oldest anatomically modern human fossils found in Africa and nowhere else, or are early versions of anatomically modern Homo sapiens *found in many different regions?*

Those who support either replacement model view a number of fossil sites in Africa as supporting their hypotheses. They see the hominid fossils from these sites as being the earliest anatomically modern human beings yet found and demonstrably older than the earliest moderns found in Europe or Asia. Key sites in this interpretation are Border Cave and Klasies River Mouth in South Africa, Omo in Ethiopia, and Singa in the Sudan (Figure 7.3).

The Border Cave site, for example, produced the remains of four hominids from different layers in the cave deposit: a complete mandible, a partial mandible, a fragmentary infant skeleton, and a fairly complete cranium (Figure 7.4). The cranium looks quite modern (Rightmire 1979b): It has a modern

FIGURE 7.3
Fossil localities of early anatomically modern Homo sapiens.

FIGURE 7.4
This nearly complete skull from Border Cave in South Africa has a suggested date of 100,000 B.P. If this is correct, the Border Cave hominid is an early anatomically modern human being. (Courtesy of Professor P. V. Tobias, University of the Witwatersrand, Johannesburg, South Africa)

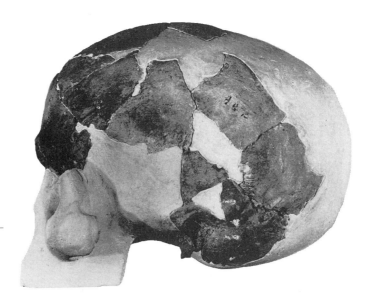

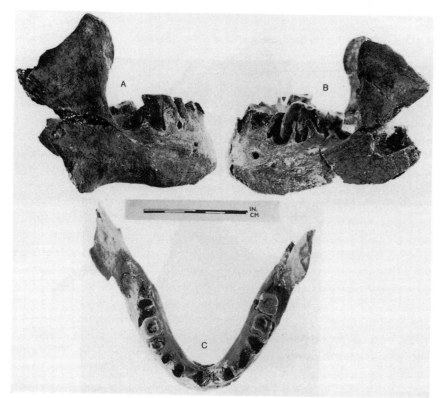

FIGURE 7.5

This mandible from Klasies River Mouth, though fragmentary, is rather lightly built and, therefore, relatively modern in appearance. The hominids found at this site are firmly dated to around 100,000 years ago. (From *The Middle Stone Age at Klasies River Mouth, South Africa*, by Ronald Singer and John Wymer, University of Chicago Press, 1982)

cranial capacity and no appreciable brow ridges; it is round in profile; and the face is flat (Beaumont, de Villiers, and Vogel 1978; Bräuer 1984). Electron spin resonance dates on animal teeth found in association with the hominid remains indicate that the cranium and partial mandible are probably more than 70,000–80,000 and less than 90,000 years old; the complete mandible is 50,000–65,000 years old; and the infant skeleton is 70,000–80,000 years old (Grün, Beaumont, and Stringer 1990). Unfortunately, the cranium was not excavated professionally, so precisely where it came from in the cave is not certain and therefore the date may not apply.

At Klasies River Mouth (KRM; see Figure 7.11), the hominid material can be assigned more confidently to a stratigraphic layer and, therefore, to a date; but the bones are more broken up and, as a result, more difficult to assign to a particular taxonomic category. The site itself was meticulously excavated in 1966–68 and produced thousands of artifacts and several fragmentary human remains (Figure 7.5; Singer and Wymer 1982). The bones, including several lower jaws and some cranial fragments, were analyzed by their excavators as well as by paleoanthropologist Philip Rightmire (1984). They agreed that the Klasies River Mouth fossils were essentially modern in appearance. A modern human chin was clearly apparent in at least one of the mandibles, and the bits of cranial bones, though large and robust by modern standards, nevertheless looked more modern than archaic. For example, there is no evidence of a brow ridge. The hominid remains were firmly dated to about 100,000 years ago by reference to stratigraphy.

Along with their skeletal remains, some of these ancient, anatomically modern people also left a short path of footprints that, like the Laetoli trail discussed in Chapter 4, has luckily been preserved. Dating to about 117,000 years ago, the trail, found in South Africa, was originally made in soft sand that hardened to rock over the millennia (Bower 1997a). Not unexpectedly, the footprints reflect an anatomy and pattern of walking that is indistinguishable from that of a modern human being.

Recent research has served to confirm both the identification of the hominid material at KRM as modern and the great antiquity of the site. Fragments of two upper jaws, some individual teeth, and a broken lower arm bone (ulna) were recovered in 1984–89. Detailed analyses of the upper jaws indicate that they are quite modern (Bräuer, Deacon, and Zipfel 1992). Additional analyses of these newer finds and the original discoveries at KRM provide further confirmation of the modern aspects of the material (Deacon and Shuurman 1992; Rightmire 1991a). Philip Rightmire and Hilary Deacon compared the KRM material directly to European Neandertal specimens and noted fundamental differences. Finally, recent ESR dating of animal teeth found in the same layer as the hominid fossils places the age of the specimens at about 90,000 years (Grün, Shackleton, and Deacon 1990).

On the other hand, Geoffrey Pope (1992), an expert on Chinese paleoanthropology, has suggested that the well-preserved and absolutely modern hominid specimen from Liujiang, China, may be as old as some of the African specimens mentioned; it has been uranium series dated to more than 100,000 years ago (Pope 1992, 275). This supports the multiregional view that anatomically modern humans appeared in several places more or less simultaneously.

Altogether, the preponderance of evidence seems to support the view that the first anatomically modern human beings have been found only in Africa. It should be clear, however, that a definitive answer is not yet possible.

2. Is there continuity only in Africa, or are forms intermediate between archaic and modern humans found in many regions?

Supporters of the population replacement model maintain that Africa is the only continent that has produced fossils intermediate in form between its earliest modern specimens and older archaic humans. Multiregionalists and genetic replacement advocates see intermediate forms in other places.

As mentioned in Chapter 6, African fossils such as Kabwe, Ndutu, and Bodo are clearly archaic in appearance and generally have been dated to before 200,000 years ago (see Figure 6.2; again, Kabwe's dating has been a problem). Another set of African fossils, however, seems to be less archaic but not quite modern either and appears to fit the morphological gap between purely archaic and anatomically modern forms. The Florisbad, Ngaloba (Laetoli hom-

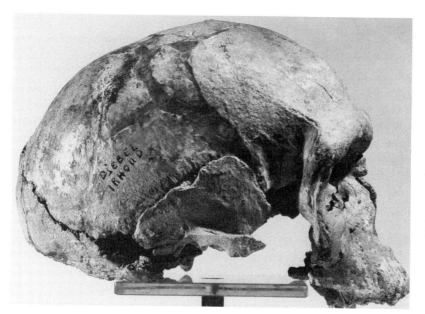

FIGURE 7.6

This cranium from Jebel Irhoud in north Africa has been interpreted as representing a form intermediate between archaic and modern Homo sapiens. *Some researchers contend that such intermediate forms are found only in Africa, lending support to the population replacement model (see Figure 7.1).* (Courtesy of the Musée de l'Homme, Paris)

inid 18), Omo 2, and Jebel Irhoud crania all appear to represent forms transitional between premodern and modern humans (Figure 7.6; Smith, Falsetti, and Donnelly 1989). Supporters of the population replacement model contend that such intermediate forms are not found outside of Africa, which is precisely what this view predicts, because it assumes that archaic humans outside of Africa did not evolve into modern humans but instead became extinct and were replaced by moderns who had evolved in Africa and then spread from there (see Figure 7.2).

Supporters of the genetic replacement model interpret a 24,500-year-old fossil found in Portugal as a hybrid between Neandertals and anatomically modern humans (Holden 1999). The bones are those of a young child. The intact lower jaw is modern in appearance with a uniquely human chin. However, the body proportions—especially the broad trunk, short lower legs, and lower arms—are similar to the Neandertal form. More analysis is needed to support the idea that the fossil is a hybrid and not just a heavily built modern.

Some researchers interpret the fossil remains from several eastern European sites—including Mladeč, Kůlna, Sipka, and especially Vindija—as transitional or hybridized forms between the classic Neandertals and anatomically modern Europeans (F. Smith 1994). These crania are lighter and less robust than those of classic Neandertals. As Fred Smith states, while the Vindija remains are "clearly still Neandertals, it is difficult not to recognize Vindija as a transitional sample between most Neandertals and early modern Europeans" (1994, 232). If these Neandertals represent such a transition, multiregionalism or genetic replacement would be supported; the evolution of modern people from premoderns would have taken place both in Africa and Europe. Though this interpretation of some skeletal remains as morphologically transitional between classic Neandertal and modern was dealt a blow by the DNA analysis cited earlier in this chapter that indicated a wide chasm between Neandertals and modern human beings, some paleoanthropologists still adhere to this view. They point out that there has, as yet, been no successful recovery of DNA from anatomically modern human beings who lived at the same time as the Neandertals. Perhaps their DNA would also be greatly different from our own. Simply put, some supporters of the multiregional view believe the jury is still out on the meaning of the Neandertal DNA analysis. They choose to focus on the morphological similarities between the two groups. Of course, they recognize that there are differences; they simply interpret these differences as representing steps in the evolution of modern humans from Neandertals. On the other hand, Günter Bräuer (1992) suggests that populations like those of Vindija represent hybrids between local Neandertals and immigrant (from southwest Asia) anatomically modern humans. This interpretation matches one of our expectations if the genetic replacement model is correct.

Though recognizing the less robust form of these fossils, many researchers dispute both of these interpretations. Certainly not all Neandertal skulls must fit the stereotype; some are more robust, some less so without implying an evolution toward modern humans. As paleoanthropologist Ian Tattersall (1998, 158) states, these supposedly transitional specimens are still "distinctively Neandertal." As Erik Trinkaus (1983a) points out, postcranially, there is little evidence of these or any other Neandertals slowly evolving into the modern form. While brow ridges in some populations like that of Vindija are smaller, the crania more rounded, and the face less prognathous, the bones below the head retain the typical suite of robust Neandertal features. Though we must recognize some degree of variability within the Neandertals, it is difficult to conclude that these eastern European Neandertals represent an overall transition to the modern form. These specimens do not supply good evidence for the multiregional model. Truly transitional forms from premodern to modern *Homo sapiens* are, as yet, confined to Africa.

3. Were archaic and anatomically modern human beings contemporaries?

The replacement models predict that outside of Africa, fossil evidence will show the contemporaneity of locally evolved archaic humans and immigrant groups of African moderns; southwest Asia is pointed to as verification. There, in caves that are sometimes in quite close proximity to each other, the remains of Neandertals and anatomically modern humans have been found. Dating techniques place the archaic and modern humans in their respective caves during the same periods and may even indicate that the modern humans are *older* than some of the Neandertals.

For example, classic Neandertals have been excavated at Kebara Cave, featured in the Chapter 6 "Case Study Close-Up," as well as at the sites of Amud and Tabun (see Figure 6.12), in Israel. With their large, heavy skulls, large brow ridges, flattened occipitals, sloping foreheads, and prognathism,

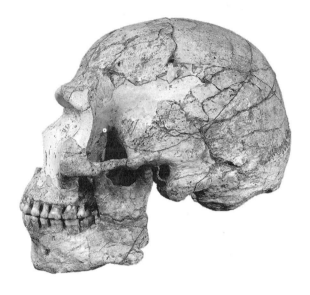
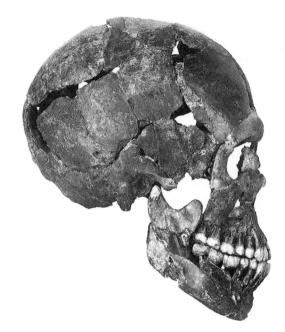

FIGURE 7.7

These Skhul (left) and Qafzeh (right) skulls from Israel are quite modern in appearance and are clearly dated to the period of around 100,000 years ago. Neandertals lived in Israel at the same time, supporting the replacement models. (*Left:* Courtesy of the Peabody Museum, Harvard University, photograph by Hillel Burger; *right:* Laboratory of Vertebrate and Human Paleontology, Paris, Bernard Vandermeersch)

their form is unmistakably Neandertal. The Kebara site dates to 60,000, Amud is closer to 70,000, and Tabun has now been dated to about 100,000 years ago (McDermott et al. 1993).

Quite robust but otherwise rather modern-looking specimens have been excavated at the sites of Skhul and Qafzeh, also in Israel. Skhul, on Mount Carmel, is not even 100 m (300 ft) from Tabun, with its Neandertal fossils, and Qafzeh is less than 30 km (18 mi) east of those two cave sites. Kebara Cave is also close by, about 10 km (6 mi) south of Mount Carmel. It is remarkable that such different-looking, generally contemporaneous hominids have been found in such a restricted area (see Figures 6.9 and 7.3).

The 10 or so individuals represented in the fossil record at Skhul and the 20 hominids at Qafzeh are generally categorized as anatomically modern or near modern. The crania present round profiles, nearly vertical foreheads, and flatter faces than do the Neandertals, though their brow ridges, small by Neandertal standards, are quite marked when compared to most modern humans (Figure 7.7). A detailed comparison of 82 fossil hominids from Africa, southwest Asia, and Europe, including Neandertals as well as the Skhul and Qafzeh materials, showed that the latter were primarily anatomically modern, with certain specimens from these sites showing some similarities to Neandertals (Bräuer and Rimbach 1990, 805).

The Skhul and Qafzeh sites are now judged to be broadly contemporaneous with the new date for Tabun. Thermoluminescence conducted on burned flints at Qafzeh has produced a date of 92,000 years ago (Valladas et al. 1988), ESR produced an age of more than 90,000 years (Stringer 1988), and a

FIGURE 7.8

This Neandertal skull from Saint-Césaire, France, is among the more recent of the Neandertal specimens, dating to about 36,000 years ago, which is long after anatomically modern Homo sapiens *evolved, making problematic any hypothesis that modern humans evolved from the Neandertals.* (Transparency A11, courtesy of Department of Library Services, American Museum of Natural History)

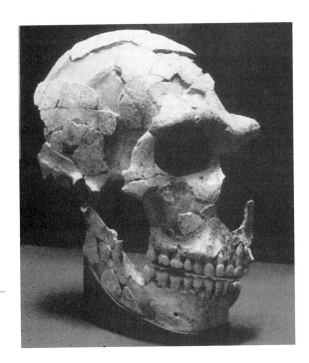

uranium series date further confirms this with a range of 85,000–110,000 years (McDermott et al. 1993). Skhul has been dated with ESR to between 81,000 years ago and 101,000 years ago (Stringer et al. 1989) and more recently by uranium series to about 80,000 years ago (McDermott et al. 1993).

The issue of the contemporaneity of premodern and modern forms outside of Africa comes up again in the European fossil record. The Neandertal fossil from the site of Saint-Césaire (Figure 7.8) in France is dated to 36,000 B.P. (Mercier et al. 1991; Stringer and Grün 1991), and the Neandertal mandible from Zafarraya, Spain, is 33,400 years old (Rose 1995). The earliest anatomically modern human fossils from Europe are those from the French site of Cro-Magnon, dated to less than 30,000 years ago. However, artifacts of a tradition called **Aurignacian** (see Chapter 8) and associated only with modern humans and never with Neandertals have been found in western Europe; they are contemporary with or even predate the Saint-Césaire and Zafarraya Neandertals (Klein 1994). For example, Aurignacian tools have been recovered at the El Castillo and L'Arbreda sites in Spain from levels dated to 38,000 years ago (Bischoff et al. 1989; Valdes and Bischoff 1989; and see the discussion later in this chapter).

Overall, the data from Africa, the Middle East, and Europe confirm the replacement models. Neandertals seem too different to have been directly ancestral to modern humans in Europe or southwest Asia and certainly cannot have been ancestral to modern humans if they were contemporary with them, living in nearby caves or adjacent valleys in the Middle East and Europe.

4. Is there a break in the form of premodern and modern human fossils outside of Africa, or do local skeletal traits show continuity between premodern and modern humans in each region?

If anatomically modern humans evolved in Africa and spread from there, replacing premoderns in all regions, locally derived, region-specific traits should have disappeared in each area as the indigenous premoderns became extinct. The modern in-migrants in Europe and Asia should have looked like the earliest anatomically modern Africans and not at all like the local premoderns they were replacing. Local traits presently seen among modern people (skeletal features that are the equivalent of "racial" characteristics) would have evolved only very recently, after the replacement occurred.

If, instead, there was regional continuity or genetic replacement in Africa, Europe, and Asia, then region-specific traits of the skeleton might be expected to be maintained within populations evolving from premodern to modern. In other words, skeletal traits specific to a particular region would show continuity from *Homo erectus* through premodern *Homo sapiens,* through the earliest anatomically modern humans, right up to the population of human beings living in an area today (at least among those individuals who can trace their ancestry back deeply in the area).

Paleoanthropologist David Frayer (1992) lists specific Neandertal skeletal features found (admittedly in lower numbers) in anatomically modern human fossils in Europe. For the most part, however, the first anatomically modern humans in Europe—the so-called Cro-Magnon people from France dating to between 25,000 years ago and 30,000 years ago—were proportioned entirely differently than the Neandertals. Tall and thin, with long extremities, they looked, as Christopher Stringer has said, "as if they walked straight out of Africa" (Ross 1991, 47).

But there is one area in which the evidence seems most strongly to support the multiregional view, since continuity, at least in a number of traits, is the rule. Even the strongest proponents of the population replacement model agree there is evidence for continuity of traits, at least in east Asia (Stringer 1994). More than 50 years ago, physical anthropologist Franz Weidenreich (1943) listed 12 very specific features of *Homo erectus* skeletons found in Asia and dating from about 500,000 years ago that matched those seen among modern, twentieth-century Asians. More recently, as Wolpoff et al. (1994) point out, general traits present in modern Asians, including overall cranial robusticity and detailed features of the face, have been seen in east Asian fossils dating all the way back to Java Man. Paleoanthropologist Andrew Kramer (1991), in comparing the mandibles of the Sangiran *Homo erectus* specimens and the lower jaws of modern Australians and Africans, found evidence for continuity between Javanese *erectus* specimens and those of local modern humans. Specific traits like a shovel shape in the maxillary (upper jaw) incisors, which is found throughout modern Asian populations, are exhibited in every east Asian fossil hominid where those teeth are preserved (Wolpoff et al. 1994, 187).

This evidence for continuity, however, does not convince everyone. Lahr and Foley (1992) point out that some of the supposed continuities in form between premodern and modern Asian humans are simply the result of the size of their crania and teeth. Stringer (1992b) sees many of the supposedly regionally diagnostic traits as far more widespread in ancient times. In other words, many of the east Asian traits that show continuity between *Homo erectus* and the modern residents of Asia were also present in other premodern populations in Africa and Europe. In a recent statistical comparison of premodern and modern humans performed by Christopher Stringer (1992a), little continuity could be seen between fossil premodern and modern populations in Asia. Stringer went on to show high levels of skeletal traits, putatively restricted to European, Asian, and Australian populations, present in a late Pleistocene sample of African crania.

Colin Groves (1989) and Phillip Habgood (1992) have analyzed the claim of morphological continuity from *Homo erectus* to modern Asians. In their view, many (though not all) of the features that show continuity in Asia are merely primitive retentions—features seen in many ancient hominids in Asia, Africa, and Europe that coincidentally have been maintained to a higher degree in modern Asians. Even the presumably diagnostic Asian trait of shovel-shaped incisors turns out not to be so diagnostic; Habgood (1992, 279) provides an extensive list of European and African fossils exhibiting shovel-shaped incisors (including australopithecines, *Homo erectus*, Neandertal, and early and relatively late anatomically modern humans from Europe and Africa).

If these claimed Asian traits are not uniquely Asian traits at all, but are features once widespread, the case for regional continuity is seriously weakened. It would be entirely possible, in this view, for those supposedly regionally restricted traits to have been present in the earliest anatomically modern African migrants to Asia and Europe. Based on the work of Stringer and especially of Groves and Habgood, the case for regional continuity of traits seems only weakly supported by the Asian evidence and even less strongly by the European evidence.

5. Does the archaeological record show the sudden appearance of nonlocal, African-originating artifact types in Europe and Asia as the early anatomically modern African population spread out from its place of origin, or is there continuity in regional artifact types as local premodern humans evolved into modern ones?

While the European Neandertals were making their Mousterian tools, anatomically modern humans in Africa were producing assemblages categorized as Middle Stone Age. Though the makers of Middle Stone Age tools are supposed to have been anatomically modern human beings, there is little in these assemblages to indicate greater technological sophistication or intelligence on their part when compared to European Neandertals. There is evidence for somewhat more sophisticated stone tools at Klasies River Mouth (Figure 7.9; see this chapter's "Case Study Close-Up"), including long stone

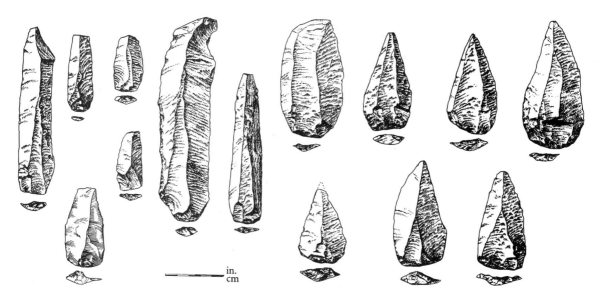

blades. (Blades generally require more preparation of the stone core from which they are produced and represent a more efficient use of the stone, which produces proportionally more sharp cutting edge than in the Mousterian technology.) But, by and large, African Middle Stone Age lithic assemblages do not clearly reflect any great technological leap forward coinciding with the evolution of modern humans.

Recently, however, evidence—not in stone, but in bone—for increased technological complexity associated with early anatomically modern human beings in Africa has been found at three sites at Katanda in eastern Zaire. Dating to about 90,000 years ago, the lithics recovered at these sites reflect a fairly typical Middle Stone Age assemblage and, as such, are similar to European Mousterian industries (Yellen et al. 1995). The excavators of these sites also recovered very sophisticated bone tools, including barbed and unbarbed points and a dagger-shaped object of unknown function (see Color Plate 3). They suggest that the technological sophistication of these bone tools indicates "modern behavioral capabilities" of the early anatomically modern inhabitants of Africa, distinct from the capabilities of contemporaneous premodern humans of Europe (Yellen et al. 1995, 555). This evidence is the first clear artifactual support for the notion that human beings possessing a modern level of intelligence evolved in Africa first, as much as 90,000 years ago.

Unfortunately for the population replacement model, these Middle Paleolithic African blade and bone tools do not appear to have accompanied their makers on their migration to Asia. In fact, there is no archaeological evidence in the form of an alien or invasive tool technology in Asia dating to the Middle Paleolithic that might mark the arrival of immigrant, anatomically modern Africans. The earliest modern-looking hominids in southwest and

FIGURE 7.9

These long blade tools dating to close to 100,000 years ago from the site of Klasies River Mouth, South Africa, were associated with fragmentary remains of anatomically modern human beings (see Figure 7.5).
(From *The Middle Stone Age at Klasies River Mouth, South Africa,* by Ronald Singer and John Wymer, University of Chicago Press, 1982)

east Asia practiced the same stone-toolmaking tradition as the local, indigenous archaic-looking people. The stone-tool assemblages from Skhul and Qafzeh, with their modern-looking fossils, and nearby Tabun, with its contemporary, archaic-looking fossils, exhibit the same stone-tool tradition: They were all making Mousterian tools (Shea 1990; Thorne and Wolpoff 1992).

The population replacement model would be bolstered if there was some evidence of an African-looking tool assemblage accompanying the supposedly immigrant anatomically modern humans in Asia. In other archaeological cases where migration is claimed, the confirming evidence of the sudden appearance of a new and exotic way of making tools, traceable to the source of the immigrants, is demanded or, when such evidence is lacking, the hypothesized immigration is usually rejected.

The situation in Europe, on the other hand, is quite different. Though African blades are not found at the earliest modern human sites, there is, as archaeologist Francis Harrold (1992) points out, a close correspondence between different-looking hominids and tool traditions on that continent: Neandertals in Europe are almost always associated with tools of the Mousterian tradition (described in Chapter 6), while the first anatomically modern humans in Europe are associated with the more sophisticated Aurignacian tradition (to be described in detail in Chapter 8).

The earliest sites exhibiting the Aurignacian tradition in Europe include L'Arbreda Cave in eastern Spain, El Castillo Cave in northern Spain, Istallöskö in Hungary, and Bacho Kiro Cave in Bulgaria (Straus 1989). As mentioned previously, the Spanish sites date to about 38,000 years ago (Bischoff et al. 1989; Valdes and Bischoff 1989); the Hungarian and Bulgarian sites date to about 43,000 years ago. James Bischoff and his colleagues, who analyzed the Spanish sites, characterize the appearance of Aurignacian tools in the Spanish caves, as well as the other European sites mentioned, as "abrupt" (Bischoff et al. 1989, 573). The Mousterian and Aurignacian technologies are quite different, and, in the case of the Spanish sites, the raw materials used are different: The Mousterian flakes are almost all made of locally available quartz and quartzite, whereas the Aurignacian tools are almost all made of a more distantly available flint. There is no evidence there of a slow, steady transition from a Mousterian to an Aurignacian tradition, no sign of an evolution of the simpler Mousterian tradition of the Neandertals to the more sophisticated Aurignacian tradition of the first anatomically modern humans in Europe. Bischoff and his colleagues take this to support the population replacement model; when a new toolmaking tradition appears abruptly in the archaeological record, with no evidence of its having evolved from an earlier way of doing things, it is often concluded that the new tradition arrived from the outside, the product of a new group's migration into the area.

To be sure, the oldest European sites with Aurignacian tools, as previously mentioned, have produced no hominid remains. To date, Neandertals have never been found with such tools, and few expect that they will be. Unless such a surprising discovery is made, there seems to be a good correspondence

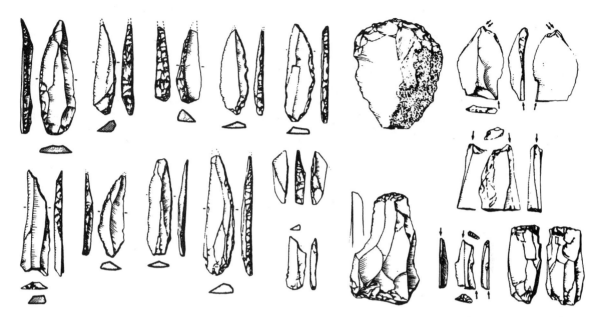

FIGURE 7.10

Tools of the Châtelperronian tradition, such as these, were found with the Saint-Césaire Neandertal. This tradition may represent a cultural blending of the Neandertal Mousterian and the anatomically modern human tradition called Aurignacian. (Adapted from Bordes and Labrot 1967)

between the appearance of physically modern people and a new tool tradition in Europe: Both the people and their toolmaking tradition show up rather suddenly, about 40,000 years ago.

Certain data complicate this conclusion. Just as there is support for the notion of biological hybridization between Neandertal and anatomically modern humans in Europe, there also is support for a melding of their different tool traditions. The so-called **Châtelperronian** tradition had been thought to have been produced by anatomically modern human beings because of the presence of long, narrow stone blades, a hallmark of the modern humans in Europe (Figure 7.10). But this was only an assumption, since Châtelperronian tools had not been found in direct association with the bones of the people who made and used them. The tradition was a bit mysterious because, aside from the blade component, it looked rather like Mousterian. Châtelperronian tools were finally found in firm association with skeletal remains of a Neandertal, not of a modern human being: the Saint-Césaire Neandertal, dated to 36,000 years ago. They also have been found in association with Neandertal remains at Arcy-sur-Cure, also in France. This discovery has led to a dramatic reassessment of the significance of the Châtelperronian. If, as seems to be the case, the tradition is fundamentally Mousterian, with elements of the Aurignacian grafted on (Harrold 1989), then it would appear that an indigenous Mousterian flake industry in Europe produced by Neandertals added bladelike tools beginning sometime after 40,000 years ago, just when anatomically modern humans show up in the fossil record. Since the timing is right and the Aurignacian industry of anatomically modern humans has a major component of blade tools, it may be the source. In other words, flake-tool-manufacturing

Neandertals may have shifted, at least in part, to blade tools as a result of contact with anatomically modern people who were making such tools. Neandertals living side by side with anatomically modern human beings, and even borrowing the idea behind some of their more effective tools, supports the population replacement model.

On the other hand, a careful analysis of the Châtelperronian blades shows that their production was somewhat different from Aurignacian. In other words, Neandertals had not simply watched anatomically modern humans produce blade tools and then unquestioningly copied each of the steps (Bahn 1998). But whatever the case—Châtelperronian was copied from Aurignacian or Châtelperronian was developed independently—the two separate and temporally overlapping industries present further evidence that Neandertals and anatomically modern human beings were separate evolutionary lines. This finding supports the population replacement model.

Châtelperronian is rather short-lived, dated between about 36,000 and 33,000 years ago. Châtelperronian artifacts are sometimes found in the same sites as Aurignacian but separated stratigraphically; they are sometimes even interdigitated, with Châtelperronian tools in layers sometimes above Aurignacian tools, sometimes below (and sometimes both), such as at Le Piage in France (Simek 1992). This indicates fairly clearly that they were produced by separate groups who inhabited these sites at different times. The Châtelperronian, therefore, can be interpreted as supporting the population replacement model in Europe.

On a related matter, paleoanthropologist Geoffrey Pope (1992), who strongly supports regional continuity in human evolution, has wondered how, if the replacement model is valid, newcomers to a region who were highly intelligent but with no experience in a new and alien habitat could outcompete and cause the extinction of local, indigenous hominids, who had developed a cultural adaptation to that territory over millennia? It would help the replacement case if a new and much advanced tool assemblage accompanied the newcomers, one so far superior to that of the less intelligent and less capable premoderns that it enabled the newcomers to displace the indigenous group. It can be argued that the European evidence supports this scenario exactly, with anatomically modern humans and their more sophisticated Aurignacian tools replacing Neandertals with their simpler Mousterian technology. Clearly, however, such a claim cannot be made for the archaeological record of Asia, where continuity in the stone-toolmaking tradition is the rule.

HOW CAN MODERN HUMAN GENETICS INFORM US ABOUT THE ANCIENT ORIGINS OF HUMANITY?

The use of modern mitochondrial DNA to illuminate the question of human origins has been reported in the popular media since 1988, even getting a cover story in *Newsweek,* headlined "The Search for Adam and Eve" (Tierney, Wright, and Springer 1988). The media attention initially was generated by the work of geneticists Rebecca Cann, Mark Stoneking, and Allan Wilson (1987), who examined the mitochondrial DNA of a sample of living human females (as mentioned in the "Prelude" to this chapter, we all inherit our mtDNA from our mothers—the mtDNA present in sperm is jettisoned at conception and so is not passed down).

Given that mtDNA accumulates mutations relatively faster than nuclear DNA, Cann, Stoneking, and Wilson were struck by the fact that the modern human mtDNA they analyzed was quite homogeneous across populations from different regions and even among people who had no genetic admixture with individuals from other areas. The population that exhibited the relatively highest degree of diversity within its mtDNA was the African sample. The researchers drew two main conclusions.

First, since the mtDNA showed so little overall diversity, modern human beings must have evolved relatively recently. Diversity in mtDNA develops as a result of mutations that build up quickly relative to nuclear DNA. A lack of diversity across widely separated populations indicates a lack of time for this diversity to have developed. Humans have only a small fraction of the mtDNA diversity seen, for example, among modern chimpanzees. If chimps have been a separate species for 5–7 million years, and assuming that mutations accumulate in the human mtDNA genome at the same rate as in chimps, then human beings must have been a separate species for only a much shorter span of time. In fact, the rate of mutation has been shown to be the same for a wide variety of animals, including apes, monkeys, rats, birds, and rhinoceroses (Cann, Stoneking, and Wilson 1987, 34).

Second, the oldest modern human mtDNA and, therefore, the source of the rest of the world's mtDNA, was African. The African mtDNA had accumulated more mutations and so exhibited greater diversity and looked different from the rest of the world's mtDNA. Mutation accumulation is a factor of time, so the African mtDNA must have been the oldest.

From here, Cann and her co-workers got more specific. Using the known age of the establishment of a number of human populations as a standard, they derived what was effectively an mtDNA clock, a measurement of the rate of mtDNA accumulation. For example, knowing that New Guinea and Australia had first been settled between 40,000 years ago and 50,000 years ago (see Chapter 9), they measured the amount of mtDNA mutation accumulation among modern New Guineans and aboriginal Australians during those years. Then they compared modern African mtDNA to that from New Guinea and Australia and discovered about three times more mutations in the mtDNA from Africa. This means that about 120,000–150,000 years have passed since the African mtDNA began accumulating mutations; this they interpreted as the age of the first anatomically modern *Homo sapiens* (Wilson and Cann 1992). Cann and her colleagues even argued that all modern mtDNA could be traced statistically back to a single female living in Africa about that time. The news media and some skeptical paleoanthropologists dubbed this woman "Eve."

Clearly, this interpretation supports the replacement models. It seems to indicate that modern humans evolved first in Africa after 200,000 years ago, and only later were populations established in Europe and Asia.

Unfortunately, Cann, Stoneking, and Wilson's methodology had major problems. Their initial sample was very small, only 147 women. The "African" sample consisted of African Americans and not actual Africans, so the possibility of the admixture of mtDNA from Asians, Native Americans, and Europeans existed. Finally, a reanalysis has shown that their results were affected by the order in which the data were input by the researchers; a different order would have yielded a different geographical center for the origin of modern mtDNA (Templeton 1992).

In reanalyzing the same data, biologist Alan Templeton (1993) comes to conclusions directly opposite to those of Cann, Stoneking, and Wilson. He views the mtDNA of modern humans as indicating an equal age in Europe, Asia, and Africa, as well as low levels of consistent genetic contact between groups in those areas. In other words, Templeton's interpretation of the mtDNA of modern humans supports the multiregional model. Research by French geneticists Laurent Excoffier and André Langaney (1989) using a much larger sample than Cann and her co-workers found that modern African mtDNA exhibits less, not more, diversity than Asian and European DNA.

In a different approach, the work of geneticist Tom Kocher (as cited in Cann, Richards, and Lum 1994, 144–45) has shown that the diversity within a sample of chimpanzee mtDNA is 40 to 50 times greater than that seen within the human sample. Again, applying some simple mathematics, if the chimp and human evolutionary lines diverged some 5–7 million years ago, then mtDNA variation within the chimps has been accumulating for that long. Because modern human mtDNA exhibits only $\frac{1}{40}$ to $\frac{1}{50}$ the variation seen among chimps, modern humans must have been accumulating that variation for $\frac{1}{40}$ to $\frac{1}{50}$ as long as the chimps have. This places the origin of the modern human line at somewhere between 100,000 years ago and 175,000 years ago.

Altogether, genetic research into the origins of modern humanity, which was intended to solve the problems presented by the vicissitudes of fossil bones, has merely added to the muddle. Rebecca Cann and others have recognized some of the mistakes made in the original research and have gone on to conduct additional work on the mtDNA of living humans. This new work, now based on a combined sample of more than 5,000 women, including Africans in Africa, seems to lend support, though admittedly not very much, for an African source for modern human beings (Cann 1992; Cann, Richards, and Lum 1994; Long et al. 1990; Stoneking 1993; Vigilant et al. 1991). However, the various mtDNA arguments are still being sorted out (Hedges et al. 1992); the mitochondrial DNA research of Cann and her colleagues alone can no longer be viewed as strong support for the replacement models.

Another study looked at a genetic marker on the Y chromosome among 900 males and found the most ancient form of that gene, shared by other primates. Only a few modern men possess that form, and they are all Africans. All men outside Africa, and most Africans, carry a different version of the gene (Gibbons 1997). A second study surveyed 1,544 men and found a particular Y chromosome DNA sequence variant that appears to be ancestral since it is also found in chimpanzees. That variant occurs only in some Africans. Other Africans and all non-African men have another variant. Using average mutation rates for nuclear DNA, the new variants of both these markers were calculated to have arisen between 200,000 and 100,000 years ago (Gibbons 1997).

WHICH EVIDENCE IS BETTER: GENES OR BONES?

In assessing the origins of modern humans, it is reasonable to ask which kind of evidence ultimately will be more important in the debate between those who support the replacement models and those who stand behind the multiregional model. Milford Wolpoff et al. (1994) maintain that the genetic evidence of modern humans can only suggest ways that human evolution may have occurred, while the paleontological record provides the hard data to test those suggestions. Allan Wilson and Rebecca Cann, on the other hand, believe that genetic interpretation will inform us more precisely about modern human origins than will any analysis of bones, since "paleontologists cannot be sure that the fossils they examine do not lead down an evolutionary blind alley" (1992, 68). Ultimately, we can hope that one day soon, the genetic information preserved in the bones themselves will enable us to answer directly the vexing questions raised here.

CASE STUDY CLOSE-UP

Looking out from the Klasies River Mouth caves, you can see the huge expanse of the Indian Ocean. Inside the cave, looking with the mind's eye back through the ancient layers deposited at your feet, you can see the story of the earliest beginnings of modern humanity (Figure 7.11).

The caves near where the Klasies River empties into the Indian Ocean may have been first explored scientifically in 1923 during a survey of caves and rock shelters along the South African coast. The geological, paleontological, paleoanthropological, and archaeological work accomplished at the cave in the major excavations of 1966–68 are reported in Ronald Singer and John Wymer's (1982) *The Middle Stone Age at Klasies River Mouth in South Africa.* Because of the caves' significance to questions of the origins of anatomically modern human beings, additional excavations were carried out there in 1984–89. The human remains recovered at Klasies River Mouth (KRM) have already been discussed in this chapter, so the focus here will be on the stone-tool assemblage and the faunal remains.

FIGURE 7.11

The area around the caves at Klasies River Mouth, South Africa. (From *The Middle Stone Age at Klasies River Mouth, South Africa,* by Ronald Singer and John Wymer, University of Chicago Press, 1982)

An extensive array of stone tools was recovered at KRM. The vast majority of the tools were made from locally available beach cobble quartzite. Cobbles used by the cave's inhabitants to make tools were available virtually at the doorstep of the Klasies River Mouth caves.

The technology represented at KRM is, in the vernacular of African archaeology, a Middle Stone Age (MSA) industry, which means that it is essentially Mousterian in its technology. For the duration of the Late Middle Paleolithic occupation of the caves, the inhabitants were removing flakes of various shapes and sizes from carefully prepared nodules of stone in a manner not unlike that of their European contemporaries.

Compared to European Mousterian industries, however, KRM technology exhibits a number of more finely made long flakes, called blades, with parallel or slightly subparallel (gently converging) sides (see Figure 7.9). Some blades with converging edges had been further flaked, after removal from their cores, into apparent spearpoints. Some of these tools seem, in a general way, to anticipate later, more advanced Late Stone Age industries in Africa and even the Aurignacian industry of the European Upper Paleolithic, to be discussed in Chapter 8. It is probably not coincidental that these more advanced-looking tools are found associated with modern-looking humans.

Faunal analysis of the bone assemblage at KRM supports the notion that hunting played a major role in the inhabitants' subsistence. We know that the inhabitants of KRM and other Middle Paleolithic sites in coastal South Africa were among the first people in the world to exploit aquatic resources, including shellfish, seals, penguins, fish, and sea birds (Klein 1977).

A detailed analysis by Richard G. Milo of the Klasies River Mouth faunal assemblage shows that the inhabitants were active hunters of large game animals (Bower 1997c). About 20% of the 5,400 animal bones examined showed signs of butchery, often in areas that indicate the humans at Klasies were extracting prime cuts of meat, not just scavenging what carnivores had left behind (there are few signs of carnivores gnawing on the bones). Beyond this, a stone spearpoint was found embedded in the cervical vertebrae of a giant buffalo. Milo's analysis indicates that anatomically modern human beings were hunting in a behaviorally modern way by 100,000 years ago in South Africa.

Virtually any large natural history museum will have displays on the origin of anatomically modern human beings. Some may be out of date, having been made when the French site of Cro-Magnon was presumed to represent the oldest evidence of anatomically modern human beings anywhere in the world. But many others, including the American Museum of Natural History in New York City, present an updated display where the vexing question of modern human origins is touched on. The important sites discussed here are located all across the face of the earth. The key fossils are housed in various museums and research facilities.

VISITING THE PAST

SUMMARY

Three models have been proposed to explain the evolution of anatomically modern human beings. The population replacement model maintains that modern humans evolved once, in Africa, sometime between 100,000 years ago and 200,000 years ago. From there they spread throughout the rest of the world, replacing indigenous groups of premodern humans and even, possibly, *Homo erectus.* The multiregional model hypothesizes that anatomically modern humans evolved across all of Africa, Europe, and Asia, together and simultaneously. Gene flow resulting from mating was sufficient to move newly evolved modern traits throughout the many premodern populations. This gene flow, however, was not sufficient to swamp, or wipe out, local physical features, which are maintained even into the present era as so-called "racial" characteristics. The genetic replacement model maintains that anatomically modern human beings evolved just once, probably in Africa. Through contact and interbreeding, modern human genes were introduced into non-African populations of premodern humans. Eventually, the premodern genes were replaced with those of modern humans.

The data discussed in this chapter, consisting of skeletal evidence, artifacts, and modern genetics, provide only ambiguous support for either extreme or for any intermediate formulation. The question of modern human origins continues to be a source of often-bitter debate among paleoanthropologists and geneticists.

TO LEARN MORE

Technical Summaries

Obviously, this book can only briefly summarize aspects of the often contentious debate over modern human origins. If you wish more information about current thinking regarding the origins of anatomically modern people, the citations contained here are a good place to start. Specifically, for technical summaries of the debate over modern human origins from the perspective of the multiregional position, see volume 95, number 1, of the journal *American Anthropologist* (1993 articles by Frayer et al. and Templeton) as well as a more replacement-oriented position by Leslie Aiello (1993). Another nice summary favoring replacement is an article by Richard Klein (1992) in the journal *Evolutionary Anthropology*. If you are interested in biology, the remarkable work that led to the extraction of Neandertal DNA from a preserved bone is summarized in the July 11, 1997, issue of the journal *Cell* (volume 90, pp. 19–30, written by Matthias Krings et al.).

Popular Summaries

A fascinating book on the mitochondrial DNA evidence, revealing the personalities of many of the scientists involved in the ensuing debate, is Michael Brown's *The Search for Eve* (1990). Also, see any of the articles by Christopher Stringer, especially his 1994 summary, "Out of Africa: A Personal History," for a strong presentation of the population replacement model. His most recent book, *African Exodus* (1996), written with R. McKie, is a forceful and convincing defense of the population replacement model (with a little wiggle room left for some genetic admixture between anatomically modern and premodern humans). Another well-written book on human evolution in general, where the population replacement model is championed, is *The Fossil Trail: How Do We Know What We Know About Human Evolution?*, by Ian Tattersall (1995). There also is a wonderful and dramatic piece of speculative fiction, *Dance of the Tiger,* by paleontologist Björn Kurtén (1980), focusing on the shared world of Neandertals and anatomically modern human beings.

On the Web

For issues and controversies related to the evolution of anatomically modern *Homo sapiens* with detailed presentations related to the various models of that evolution—especially the replacement and multiregional approaches—both of the following sites related to university courses are good resources:

http://www.as.ua.edu/ant/bindon/ant101/syllabus/mod_hum/mod_hum.htm#top

http://ampere.scale.uiuc.edu/anth102/lect21.html

KEY TERMS

nuclear DNA	multiregional (regional continuity) model	Aurignacian
DNA		blade
mitochondrial DNA (mtDNA)	gene flow	Châtelperronian
population replacement model	genetic replacement model	

Expanding Intellectual Horizons

ART AND IDEAS IN THE UPPER PALEOLITHIC

CHAPTER OVERVIEW

The Upper Paleolithic is marked by dramatic changes in human culture the world over. Beginning after 50,000 B.P., we see a shift toward a lithic technology based on the production of blade tools; an expansion in the subsistence quest; an increase in site size; use of raw materials such as bone, shell, and antler; the production of nonutilitarian objects; the use of exotic materials; the elaboration of burials; and the production of true art in the form of cave paintings and portable sculptures.

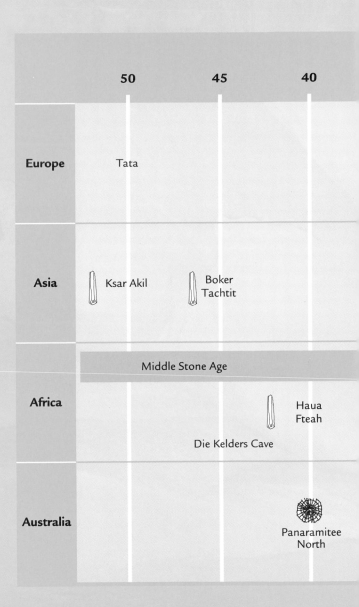

	50	45	40
Europe	Tata		
Asia	Ksar Akil	Boker Tachtit	
	Middle Stone Age		
Africa			Haua Fteah
		Die Kelders Cave	
Australia			Panaramitee North

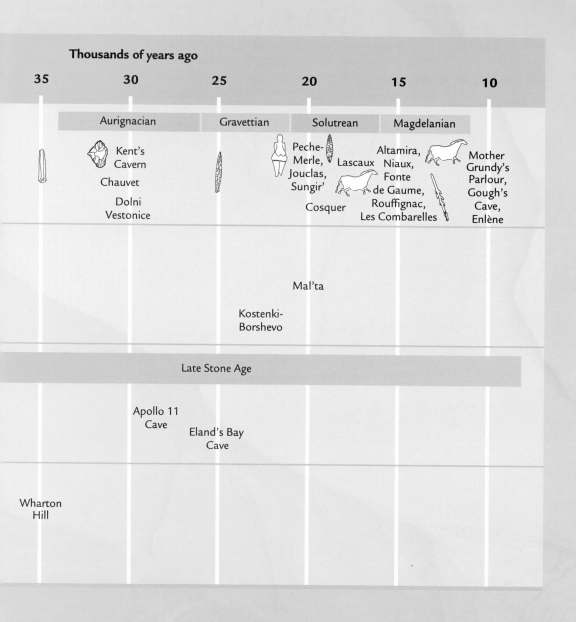

Thousands of years ago

| 35 | 30 | 25 | 20 | 15 | 10 |

Aurignacian   Gravettian   Solutrean   Magdelanian

Kent's Cavern

Chauvet

Dolni Vestonice

Peche-Merle, Jouclas, Sungir'

Cosquer

Lascaux

Altamira, Niaux, Fonte de Gaume, Rouffignac, Les Combarelles

Mother Grundy's Parlour, Gough's Cave, Enlène

Mal'ta

Kostenki-Borshevo

Late Stone Age

Apollo 11 Cave

Eland's Bay Cave

Wharton Hill

PRELUDE

Across all of North America and, likely, other parts of the world as well, the broad, blank, metal panels along the fronts and sides of our refrigerators serve as personal art galleries upon which we display the creative work of our kids. On canvases of oaktag, construction paper, photocopier paper, and recycled computer printouts, their boldly colored images in crayon, pencil, ink, paint, chalk, and marker gaily decorate our kitchen appliances.

Who could deny the obvious talent of these young artists?

More to the point, who could deny their humanity? While there have been some silly attempts to get zoo animals to produce works of art (chimpanzees and elephants, at last count), which then sell for ridiculous sums (though at least they raise money for financially strapped zoos), only human beings possess the desire, the ability, and even the *need* to produce art.

Educational psychologists have long pondered the significance of the universal and unique human behavior of producing art, which seems to manifest itself even while we are still young (DiLeo 1970; Gardner 1980; Thomas and Silk 1990). For Freud (1976), children's drawings represent a safety valve, allowing them to express deep, largely unconscious fears by safely reliving them on paper. According to Freud, art also provides a way for children to express unconscious wishes. For the best-known child development researcher, Jean Piaget (Piaget and Inhelder 1969), drawings reflect the developmental stages a child's intellect passes through on the road to adulthood.

Other researchers have emphasized the sensory pleasure (both motor and visual) of producing a picture; still others (Arnheim 1956) have suggested that drawing and painting are simply "universally satisfying." Ultimately, however, as psychologists Glyn V. Thomas and Angèle M. J. Silk (1990, 70) point out: "It is not easy to give a totally convincing answer to the question of why children draw.... While all these proposed motivations [those just listed] seem plausible, it is rare to find independent evidence for their validity."

I am certain that most of you passed through the well-established stages of symbolic/artistic achievement, unaware of the arguments among psychologists over the significance of your accomplishments. Each of you has been a link in a long chain of human beings—first as children, later as adults—who have applied pigment to metaphorical canvases and produced something that was initially just in their heads but now resides outside them. This chain begins perhaps 50,000 years ago with our anatomically modern ancestors and continues to the present. The period when we see the initial appearance of uniquely modern human capacities like artistic, symbolic expression—the Upper Paleolithic—is the focus of this chapter.

CHRONICLE

Though the earliest anatomically modern human beings date to more than 100,000 years ago, they do not become culturally differentiable from their archaic contemporaries for a long time. As we have seen in Europe, for example, about the same time that anatomically modern humans were making blade tools in their Aurignacian tradition,

Neandertals were also making blade tools in their separate but not necessarily inferior Châtelperronian tradition. We have also seen simple items of personal adornment, initially not all that different, at sites inhabited by modern-looking humans and at least one Neandertal site (Arcy-sur-Cure; Hublin et al. 1996).

In fact, it is not until after 50,000 B.P. and perhaps as late as 40,000 B.P. that the archaeological record begins to exhibit the remnants of a material culture—and, by inference, a spiritual, artistic, and intellectual culture—previously unknown and recognizably modern (Chase and Dibble 1987; Chase 1991). In Europe prehistorians call the period when modern behavior becomes manifested in the archaeological record the Upper Paleolithic. The behavior of Upper Paleolithic people can be distinguished absolutely from the behavior of their Middle Paleolithic predecessors. As archaeologist Anthony Marks (1990, 56) characterizes it, the evidence from the Upper Paleolithic indicates "at least dramatic and, at most, a profound and fundamental change in both behavior and human potentials."

CHAPTER
SITES

ASIA
Boker Tachtit
Ksar Akil
Mal'ta

AUSTRALIA
Koonalda Cave
Panaramitee North
Wharton Hill

THE UPPER PALEOLITHIC GREAT LEAP FORWARD

Archaeologist Randall White (1982) has contrasted the cultures of the Middle and Upper Paleolithic. Using as guides his list and the lists of archaeologist Richard Klein (1989) and Heidi Knecht, Anne Pike-Tay, and Randall White (1993), we can examine the following cultural evolutionary "disconformities," or breaks, between the Middle and Upper Paleolithic:

- A dramatic shift in stone-tool technology, from a reliance on flake tools to the production of stone blades
- A broadening of the subsistence base to include a greater range of animal and plant species in the quest for subsistence
- Much larger sites
- A dramatic increase in the production of bone, antler, ivory, and shell tools (Color Plate 4)
- A shift from very few nonutilitarian items to an abundance of them
- A greater use of imported, "exotic" goods—raw materials obtainable only from great distances away from habitation sites
- Much more elaborate burials
- A shift from virtually no works of art to the highly characteristic use of symbol and the production of art

We will now discuss in detail each of these changes from Middle Paleolithic to Upper Paleolithic culture.

Stone Blades of the Upper Paleolithic

Blades are commonly defined as flakes that are at least twice as long as they are wide. The regular and efficient production of blades from a prepared stone

FIGURE 8.1

These stone blades from the site of Ksar Akil in Lebanon date back to before 40,000 years ago and may be as old as 52,000 years. (Reprinted from Paul Mellars, ed.: *The Emergence of Modern Humans: An Archaeological Perspective.* Copyright © Edinburgh University Press. Used by permission of the publisher, Cornell University Press)

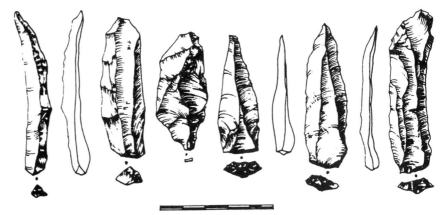

core was a fundamental characteristic of the stone-tool industries of the Upper Paleolithic. As we saw in the last chapter, the Aurignacian blade technology of early anatomically modern humans overlapped in time with a different blade-making tradition practiced by the Neandertals: the Châtelperronian. Châtelperronian disappeared with the extinction of the Neandertals sometime before 30,000 B.P., while Aurignacian blade tools became increasingly sophisticated, efficient, and complex.

Aurignacian blade technology dates back to before 40,000 B.P. (Figure 8.1). In the Near East, for example, at the sites of Boker Tachtit in Israel (Marks 1990, 1993) and Ksar Akil in Lebanon (Ohnuma and Bergman 1990), the shift from Levallois technology (prepared core and flake; see Chapter 6) to a stone-tool technology based on the production of elongated blades occurred by at least 45,000 years ago at Boker Tachtit and perhaps as much as 52,000 years ago at Ksar Akil (Marks 1993, 12). In Africa, sites like Haua Fteah Cave show this shift to have occurred by about 40,000 B.P. (Van Peer and Vermeersch 1990). In central and southeastern Europe, the shift from Mousterian flake to Upper Paleolithic blade production occurred before 40,000 B.P. (Svoboda 1993); in western Europe, the shift seems to have occurred a bit later, about 38,000 B.P. (Allsworth-Jones 1990).

In reconstructing stone-core reduction sequences at these and other sites, researchers have concluded that although removal of just a few flakes would exhaust a Levallois core, removal of blades was more efficient—many more blades could be removed from the same core, producing far more cutting edge from the same mass of stone. The Aurignacian represents a far more efficient use of stone, with more than five times the amount of usable edge generated from the same quantity of stone than when regular flakes were being produced.

The blade technologies of the Upper Paleolithic are short-lived, and change is greatly accelerated (Figure 8.2). In western Europe, for example, the **Aurignacian** tradition, which consisted of a specific set of tools that included

FIGURE 8.2

Tools from the Aurignacian tradition (left), *a blade-based industry of the European Upper Paleolithic dating from 34,000 B.P. to 27,000 B.P. The long spear-points of the descendant Solutrean tradition* (right), *dating from 21,000 B.P. to 16,000 B.P., are beautifully crafted and were highly effective.* (Transparencies 610, *left,* and 609, *right,* courtesy of Department of Library Services, American Museum of Natural History)

retouched blades, engraving tools called burins, and stone scrapers, is dated to between 34,000 B.P. and 27,000 B.P. From 27,000 B.P. to 21,000 B.P., the **Gravettian** tradition developed, with its emphasis on smaller blades and denticulate knives. The **Solutrean** tradition, dated from 21,000 B.P. to 16,000 B.P., is the most striking of all, characterized by finely made, bifacially flaked, symmetrical, leaf-shaped projectile points. Solutrean points are among the most finely made stone tools ever found (Color Plate 5). The Solutrean was followed by the **Magdelanian,** from 16,000 B.P. to 11,000 B.P., where the emphasis was not on stone tools at all, but, rather, on bone and antler, with the attendant production of microblades.

Together, artifacts from these various industries of the Upper Paleolithic reveal two very important facts. First, lithic technology had jumped forward, with a number of different manufacturing techniques that used stone more efficiently; produced more effective tools for cutting, scraping, piercing, and so on; and yielded objects far more symmetrical and balanced than those of the Middle Paleolithic. From our twentieth-century Western vantage point (or, perhaps, bias), European Upper Paleolithic industries produced tools that are more aesthetically pleasing, more artfully rendered, than those of earlier traditions.

Second, and equally as important, the profusion of specific tool-tradition names points to one of the most salient differences between the Middle and Upper Paleolithic: Whereas Middle Paleolithic technology was marked by relative homogeneity temporally and geographically, Upper Paleolithic technology was marked by relatively rapid change and far greater geographic variability.

Broadening the Subsistence Base

Undeniably, the hunting of big game—**megafauna**—made a significant contribution to the subsistence of Upper Paleolithic people. In central and eastern Europe, for example, sites dating between 28,000 B.P. and 10,000 B.P. reflect the major role of the woolly mammoth in the subsistence base of Upper Paleolithic people. At a single site, Dolni Vestonice I, the remains of more than 100 mammoths butchered by the inhabitants have been identified (Soffer 1993). At this same site, butchering marks have been located on the remains of horse and reindeer as well. Also in Europe are the Kostenki-Borshevo sites located along the Don River in the eastern part of European Russia. The list of game animals present at these Upper Paleolithic sites is extensive; included in archaeologist Richard Klein's (1969, 64) enumeration are mammoth, woolly rhinoceros, horse, cattle, musk ox, red deer, elk, reindeer, and saiga antelope, among others. Klein also points out the extensive presence of the butchered bones of carnivores such as brown bear, arctic fox, lynx, and wolf and suggests that they are significant not so much for food, but for the rich, warm fur they would have provided for people living in a cold, tundra environment.

The situation is much the same in Africa and western Europe, where Upper Paleolithic inhabitants exploited local large game animals. In Siberia, the site of Mal'ta near Irkutsk shows extensive hunting of woolly mammoth and reindeer. In South Africa, at Late Stone Age sites such as Die Kelders Cave and Eland's Bay Cave, remains of eland (a large antelope) are abundant, and there is evidence of the hunting of the Cape buffalo, a far more dangerous animal and one avoided during the Middle Paleolithic (Klein 1983). In the Upper Paleolithic of western Europe, at sites such as Abri Pataud in France, the bones of reindeer, elephant, horse, and wild cattle were found (R. White 1982). At Mother Grundy's Parlour, a cave occupation site in Great Britain dating to about 12,000 B.P., the remains of woolly rhinoceros and mammoth, reindeer, and wild horse were found (C. Smith 1992). Also in Great Britain, Gough's Cave shows extensive use of wild horse and red deer more than 12,200 years ago (C. Smith 1992).

The faunal remains of fish and bird food species, virtually absent in Middle Paleolithic contexts, are far more common at Upper Paleolithic sites. The same South African sites just mentioned, for example, show evidence of the extensive reliance on seals, penguins, mollusks, and flying shore birds (Klein 1983, 43). The bones or shells of these organisms have been found, along with grooved-stone net weights used in fishing and possible early fishhooks (called "gorges") that were baited and attached to lines.

Small mammals also contributed to the food quest. At one of the mammoth hunting sites mentioned, Dolni Vestonice, and at the nearby site of Pavlov, there is indirect evidence of the use of nets in hunting small game (Pringle 1997). Fragments of netting made by the inhabitants of these sites, dating from between 29,000 and 22,000 years ago, had accidentally been pressed into the clay floors of the inhabitants' houses. In a few cases those houses burned and the impressions of the netting were preserved in the baked clay.

The nets were sophisticated, indicating a probable long tradition of net weaving (Adovasio, Soffer, and Klima 1996). The netting mesh was too fine to have been used to capture large animals, but there are plenty of bones of smaller creatures, including hare and fox, at these sites. A large hare can produce six pounds of meat and a pelt. Driving small mammals like hares into nets is an efficient hunting technique that all members of a social group can participate in—the very young and the aged, pregnant or nursing females, and, of course, strong males in their prime. It seems likely, therefore, that net hunting played a substantial role in subsistence at these and other sites that date to the same period (Pringle 1998a).

Human beings are omnivores, not carnivores. As much as some of us may like to eat meat, we cannot survive on meat alone; fruits, vegetables, and grains make up important components of our human diet. Unfortunately, seeds, fruit pits, and starchy roots usually do not preserve as well as large animal bones. As a result, the role of big-game hunting in Upper Paleolithic subsistence has most likely been exaggerated. Furthermore, archaeologists often don't find what they are not looking for. Unfortunately, there has been a self-fulfilling prophecy at work here. Archaeologists have focused on the search for animal bones, and they have found them, reinforcing the notion that big-game hunting was the key form of subsistence in the Upper Paleolithic. At the same time, many researchers assumed that plant foods were not as important—and wouldn't have preserved anyway—so they didn't look for these remains, at least not very closely.

Researchers are beginning to remedy this omission by applying intensive techniques for recovering and analyzing plant remains; and, not surprisingly, now that they are looking for them, they are finding these kinds of food remnants. For example, researcher Sarah Mason has found the burned residue of edible taproots in hearths at Dolni Vestonice (Pringle 1998a). And berries have been found in hearths at other Upper Paleolithic sites.

It is highly unlikely that Upper Paleolithic people overlooked important sources of protein, carbohydrates, or vitamins available in their territories. Portrayals of ancient hunters fighting a daily duel to the death with huge, aggressive beasts may offer us a romantic image, but it seems an unlikely strategy for survival. It is far more likely that the people of the Upper Paleolithic subsisted on a broad spectrum of foods, including the meat from animals both large and small, birds, fish, seeds, nuts, berries, and starchy roots. Archaeological evidence is finally beginning to support this sensible reconstruction.

Larger Sites of Aggregation

Middle Paleolithic sites tend to be small, representative of the encampments of nomadic, **opportunistic foragers,** who took whatever resources they could wherever they became available, without much planning in advance

FIGURE 8.3

This reconstruction of a dwelling made of mammoth bone is evidence that in the Upper Paleolithic in Siberia, trees were not generally available for construction but the bones of large game animals were. (Negative no. 69368fr15, courtesy of Department of Library Services, American Museum of Natural History)

(Binford 1984). Though Upper Paleolithic sites include similarly small foraging camps, much larger sites also date to the Upper Paleolithic. Randall White (1982) interprets these as places of aggregation, localities where numerous small bands of people would come together seasonally. The site of Mal'ta, in Siberia, for example, covers an area of some 600 m² (about 7,500 ft²; Chard 1974, 20); it includes the remains of numerous dwellings whose frames were made from the large bones of woolly mammoth (Figure 8.3). This size is far larger than that of the standard Middle Paleolithic site.

The **settlement pattern** of the Middle Paleolithic reflects a strategy of opportunistic foraging within a pattern of unrestricted wandering. Here, the nomadic band moves in no particular pattern, following resources wherever they might become available. The pattern of subsistence in the Upper Paleolithic appears to be different, at least in part. During the Upper Paleolithic, the settlement pattern seems to indicate a shift to a fixed seasonal round as part of a strategy of **logistical collecting** (Binford 1984). People still lived in nomadic bands, but the movement of the band was no longer unrestricted, instead following a fixed yearly pattern where at least some seasonally occupied sites were returned to each year, perhaps by members of several bands. Subsistence and movements were planned out in advance as people gained a detailed knowledge of their territory, seasonality, and the behavior and shifting locations of the plants and animals on which they subsisted.

Some sites were continually visited by aggregations of related people during fixed and known times of the year when resources may have been particularly abundant at these places—for example, at a topographic bottleneck on a migration route for large animals. Some of these sites, perhaps, became ritually sanctified through the use of artwork to denote the significance of a particular place to the members of the group. This possibility will be discussed in the section on the appearance of artwork in the Upper Paleolithic and in "Issues and Debates."

Branching Out in Raw Materials

Expanding their raw material base beyond stone, Upper Paleolithic toolmakers also used bone, antler, shell, and ivory for such tools as sewing equipment (awls, punches, and needles) and hunting equipment (projectile points). Along the Dnestr River in Russia, Upper Paleolithic sites have produced slotted daggers of reindeer antler. At the Kosoutsy site in this same region, reindeer antler was also used as a raw material to manufacture spearpoints for use in the hunt, and thin slivers of reindeer bone were used in the production of eyed needles (Borziyak 1993).

Eyed needles are indirect evidence of sewing and the inferred manufacture of sewn clothing during the Upper Paleolithic. More direct evidence of the production of tailored clothing comes from the 22,000-year-old site of Sungir', just north of Moscow, in Russia. Beads used for fastening were found in a pattern in the ground, outlining what appears to have been pants, a shirt or jacket, a cap, and shoes (Klein 1989; R. White 1993).

Eyed needles of ivory have been found at Jouclas, in France, dating to 21,000 years ago (Dennell 1986). Eyed needles allowed for more precisely tailored and sewn clothing. The production of protective outergarments that were, at least to a degree, windproof and waterproof, with seams stitched tightly through the use of such needles, would have been extremely important as people spread into colder climates, fundamentally inhospitable to our tropically evolved and adapted ancestors. In no small measure, tight, weatherproof seams enabled by thin, eyed needles made expansion into places like the Arctic a more reasonable possibility for ancient humans.

Long, pointed bone spearpoints with inserts of small, sharp flint blades have been reconstructed at the Amvrosievka sites in eastern Europe (Krotova and Belan 1993). Barbed bone harpoons (like those from Kent's Cavern in Great Britain; C. Smith 1992), antler hammers, wrenchlike bone "shaft-straighteners" (like the one recovered at Gough's Cave in Great Britain and often called *bâtons de commandement*), and bone awls all have been found in Upper Paleolithic sites from western Europe to east Asia.

The **spear-thrower** was an innovation of the Upper Paleolithic. This tool is an elongated, hooked handle that attaches to the butt of a spear and effectively increases the length of the arm of the person throwing the spear. A longer arm increases the contact time between the inception of the throw and the release, allowing for greater accuracy, speed, and distance; it works for the same reason a baseball pitcher with a long arm can often throw the ball harder and faster than can someone with a shorter pitching arm.

The spear-thrower is a remarkable example of applied physics practiced by ancient humans. By artificially extending the arm—and by exploiting the

FIGURE 8.4

This necklace, made of antler and bone beads, was found in Siberia at the Upper Paleolithic site of Mal'ta. The site has produced a wealth of beautifully made pieces of artwork, including sculpted pieces of bone, antler, and ivory, dating to around 15,000 B.P. (Courtesy of Department of Archaeology, The Hermitage Museum)

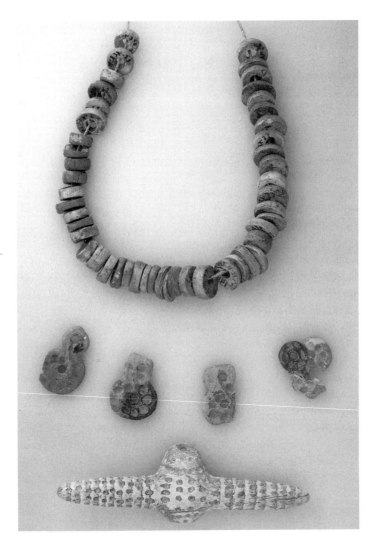

stored energy in the bending shaft of the dart as it is thrown—our ancestors were able to dramatically increase the accuracy as well as the power with which they could launch a spear in the quest for food.

Recent experiments have compared the force of various methods of propelling a projectile. The force of a dart thrown with a spear-thrower far exceeds that generated by a hand-thrown spear, a traditional bow, or even a modern compound bow (Karl and Bruchert 1997). A computer-designed spear-thrower recently produced a record throw of 250 m (over 800 ft)!

Spear-throwers date back to as much as 30,000 years ago. The bearers of this technology certainly had an advantage in the hunt over those who needed to get much closer to large, dangerous animals in order to successfully spear them.

A 13,000-year-old spear-thrower from Enlène Cave, France, was carved from reindeer antler (Dennell 1986). Along with being a useful tool, this spear-thrower is far more beautiful than it had to be; the handle was finely carved into the image of two ibexes (mountain goats) locked in combat (see Color Plate 4).

Clearly, the Upper Paleolithic represents a period when our human ancestors perfected technologies that previously they had barely experimented with, branching out into the use of raw materials other than stone for the unique benefits and special qualities afforded by bone, ivory, and antler.

Abundance of Nonutilitarian Objects

In my classes I see many students, men and women, wearing nonutilitarian items of personal adornment: necklaces, earrings, nose rings, ear cuffs, finger rings, bracelets, anklets, hairpins. Some have gold and silver draping every extremity and dangling from a multitude of pierced body parts.

All our bodies look basically the same, built along one of two fundamental models: male or female. But we have invented numerous ways of decorating ourselves—defining, identifying, and distinguishing ourselves—with objects of adornment. Artifacts interpretable as items of personal adornment are rare at Middle Paleolithic sites. they are only infrequently found in association with premodern humans; the Neandertal site of Arcy-sur-Cure is one of the very few places where multiple objects of personal ornamentation can be traced to premodern humans. Upper Paleolithic sites, however, are replete with such objects. Stone, bone, antler, shell, and ivory jewelry is common, often found as grave goods. Other Upper Paleolithic nonutilitarian objects include engraved animal bones that may have served as objects of personal or group identity (Conkey 1980) and even as items for keeping track of lunar phases (Marshack 1972).

One site where such items are abundant is Mal'ta in central Asia (Chard 1974). Dated to sometime after 15,000 B.P., the site has produced a wealth of items of adornment. A small child was found buried at Mal'ta with a necklace made of bone and antler beads (Figure 8.4). Also found were schematic carvings of birds, a carved bone plaque with designs consisting of dots and wavy lines etched or punched into the surface of the bone, and depictions of human beings (Figure 8.5).

A spectacular necklace was recovered from Rocher de la Peine in France. There, 13,000 years ago, an Upper Paleolithic jewelry maker strung together beads of dentalium shell, three large bear teeth, and one tooth from a late Pleistocene European lion (Dennell 1986). The shells came from the coast, about 160 km (100 mi) from the site.

As Randall White (1982) points out, the appearance of items of personal adornment that were often painstakingly made, frequently out of exotic material that must have been difficult to obtain—and therefore "expensive" in terms of time and effort to obtain it—is significant. In White's view, such

FIGURE 8.5

This figurine is one of some 30 such artifacts carved from the bone of woolly mammoth found at the site of Mal'ta, in Siberia. (Courtesy of the Musée de l'Homme. J. Oster)

objects imply increasing awareness and importance of individual identity in Upper Paleolithic society.

Archaeologists Heidi Knecht and Anne Pike-Tay, writing along with Randall White (1993, 3), have suggested that the use of personalized ornaments may signify the existence of hierarchical social systems in the Upper Paleolithic, with such ornamentation symbolizing the social position and role of the wearer. Whatever the significance of the development of items of personal adornment, it seems clear that people in the Upper Paleolithic were much like ourselves.

Use of Exotic Raw Materials

The ability to obtain raw materials and manufactured goods from great distances might seem to be a feature strictly of modern societies. Look around your house and try counting up the goods that originated in other countries—stereo equipment and camera manufactured in Japan, clothing made in China or the Philippines, car from Germany, dishware from Great Britain, backpack fromIndia, wristwatch from Switzerland, calculator from Singapore, and on and on.

But the expansion of economic systems to connect places at great distances from each other actually has a long history. As far back as the Upper Paleolithic, the expansion of the geography of economies can be seen, as raw materials and manufactured goods began traveling far greater distances than in the Lower or Middle Paleolithic.

Whereas Middle Paleolithic people relied on raw materials whose source was close to their habitations, in the Upper Paleolithic we see far more extensive use of raw materials available only at great distances from living sites. For example, at the Kostenki-Borshevo sites in Russia, local lithic materials (quartzite and brown and yellow flint) were used in making stone tools. Also used, however, was a black flint that possessed superior chipping qualities (it chipped more regularly) but was not available in the Kostenki-Borshevo region. Its nearest possible source was about 150 km (97 mi) away. Analysis of the raw materials recovered at the site suggests that the flint obtained by the inhabitants of the Kostenki-Borshevo region for their artifacts actually came from a source 300 km (176 mi) distant (Klein 1969, 227).

The situation is much the same throughout the geographical extent of Upper Paleolithic cultures. For example, in Moravia, in south-central Europe, flint commonly was moved across distances of 100 km (65 mi) from its source (Oliva 1993, 52). In rare instances, apparently highly valued material like obsidian (volcanic glass) from Hungary is found in Paleolithic sites up to 500 km (325 mi) away (Oliva 1993, 52). Even where quite serviceable stone was available locally, material obtainable only from great distances was often used. Archaeologist Martin Oliva (1993) suggests that maintaining long-distance contacts through trade seems to have been more important than the specific qualities of the lithics themselves and that the stone and its trade took on more of a ritual meaning than just a utilitarian significance.

The use of raw materials from great distances away by Upper Paleolithic peoples implies a greater reliance on trade with distant groups and, perhaps, also implies broader social networks (hypothetically maintained by seasonal get-togethers evidenced at the aggregation sites) than anything seen in Middle Paleolithic contexts.

More Elaborate Burials

If the modern folktale is true, a woman in California (sometimes the story has it in Florida) was buried in a nightgown, seated at the wheel of her brand new Jaguar (or Porsche, take your pick). Other modern examples include the burying of married people wearing their wedding bands or the burying of devout Christians with a cross around their neck. Burying the dead with treasured personal items is a long-standing human tradition. Egyptian pharaohs were buried with food, jewelry, furniture—even other people (see Chapter 13). The emperors of imperial China were buried with chariots and entire life-sized ceramic armies of soldiers and horses. We see this pattern repeated over and over. Whether because it is believed that the deceased will need such items in the afterlife or simply because of the desire to place some items of personal identification with a departed friend, the practice of burying the dead with objects that were meaningful to them and their loved ones seems nearly universal.

Clearly, the first human burials are associated with Middle Paleolithic archaic humans—that is, European and southwest Asian Neandertals (see Chapter 6). However, fundamental differences exist between Middle and Upper Paleolithic burials. For example, archaeologist Frank Harrold (1980) has compared a series of 36 Middle Paleolithic Neandertal burials with 96 Upper Paleolithic burials of anatomically modern humans. Only about 40% of the Neandertal burials included **grave goods,** objects intentionally buried with the dead (as objects of remembrance or, perhaps, as needed in an afterlife). Virtually all such objects were simple tools or animal bones. On the other hand, about 90% of the Upper Paleolithic burials contained grave goods, and these items were far more elaborate than the material included with the Middle Paleolithic interments. Upper Paleolithic burials included some of the same items of personal adornment mentioned previously: necklaces, bracelets, stone and bone artifacts (see the "Case Study Close-Up" in this chapter).

Production of Art

We can imagine many compelling scenes from the human past—for example, australopithecines walking side by side on an African ash bed (Chapter 4) or beetle-browed Neandertals mourning over the remains of a fallen comrade placed in a crudely dug grave. But perhaps none of these is more evocative than an imagined scene of two cave painters from the Upper Paleolithic.

In the dark and distant recesses of a cave's narrow passageway, a flickering oil lamp smears dancing shadows on a flat rock wall. A young woman, tall and muscular, her arms coated with a thin layer of grime and sweat, carefully places a dark slurry in her mouth. Next, she holds a hollow reed to her lips and places her other hand palm down on the rock face. Aiming the reed at the area around her hand, she begins puffing up her cheeks, spraying a fine mist of pigment out of the end of the reed. Some of the paint thinly coats her hand, but much of it covers the cave wall immediately around the area hidden by her palm and fingers. After a few puffs through the reed, she removes her hand from the cave wall, and we see in our mind's eye her remarkable artistic creation: a negative image of her own hand, a signature some 20,000 years old calling out across time.

By her side, a tall and broad young man with a deeply lined face belying his years dips a frayed twig into a thick red paste. Using skills of observation and artistry developed during his short life, he conjures up a vision held in a part of his memory as deep as where he now labors breathlessly in the cave: The horse, wild and free, runs across his mind, her legs leaving the ground as she gallops in her desperate but doomed attempt to flee from the hunters. A deep red gash on her belly where a stone-tipped spear pierced her hide leaks her lifeblood. Soon, he remembers, very soon, she falls, and his comrades are upon her, thrusting their spears deep into her viscera. Then, at last, she is quiet and still. He shudders, thinking of her spirit now returned to the sky. Then he remembers the taste of her flesh in his mouth. Her life lost, the life of his people maintained. It is the way of life and death in the world that he knows.

Now long dead and no longer of this life but of another world, a world of stories and magic, the mare lives again in a creation of pigment, memory, awe, and sorcery. Once a creature of blood and bone, of sinew and muscle, she is now a creature of color and binder. No longer running across the plains of western Europe, she now runs and bellows on a flat sheet of rock, straining against her fate and bleeding eternally in the deep recesses of a dark cave. In this incarnation she has lived for 20,000 years now; and in her life of pigment and memory and magic, she will live forever.

THE MEANING OF UPPER PALEOLITHIC ART

It is abundantly clear that it is in the past 40,000 years that humanity experienced what more than one author has likened to an "explosion" of artistic and symbolic creativity (Conkey 1978, 74; Pfeiffer 1982, who titles his book *The Creative Explosion*). From incised bone to carved statues to cave paintings, the period beginning 40,000 years ago is marked by the beginning of human artistic and symbolic expression (Figure 8.6). The roots of such expression may be traced back to the Middle Paleolithic, but only dimly. It is after 40,000 B.P. that we see the uniquely human capacity—and perhaps need—to mark our existence through the creation of permanent, symbolic works of art.

COLOR PLATE 1

Ancient hominids began crafting stone tools—the technology is called Oldowan—about 2.5 million years ago. Thin, sharp stone flakes struck off cores like this one were used for cutting and scraping, while the remaining cores could be used as chopping tools. (Chapter 4) *Copyright © Institute of Human Origins*

COLOR PLATE 2

A finely chipped, symmetrical Lower Paleolithic handaxe. First occurring in the archaeological record nearly 1.5 million years ago, handaxes were sophisticated, multipurpose tools made by *Homo erectus* in Africa, Europe, and western Asia. (Chapter 5) *Copyright © Boltin Picture Library*

COLOR PLATE 3

Barbed bone artifacts found in Katanda, Zaire. These sophisticated implements date to more than 90,000 years ago and may reflect the greater intelligence and technological sophistication of the first anatomically modern *Homo sapiens* when compared to premodern members of our species. (Chapter 7) *Copyright © Alison Brooks, George Washington University*

COLOR PLATE 4

Two ibexes wrestle on this fragment of a spear-thrower. The fine carving of this artifact is diagnostic of the Upper Paleolithic and is an example of the great skill and artistic abilities of this period. (Chapter 8) *Courtesy Musée de l'Homme, photo by D. Destable*

COLOR PLATE 5

The stone-tool technology of the Upper Paleolithic included the production of beautifully flaked, symmetrical, spearpoints shaped like a willow leaf. Solutrean spearpoints like these, made more than 18,000 years ago, represent, in an aesthetic sense, some of the finest stone tools ever made. (Chapter 8) *K. L. Feder*

COLOR PLATE 6

The so-called Chinese Horse from Lascaux Cave, France, is one of the best-known and most beautiful of the Upper Paleolithic cave paintings. Viewing these pieces of art allows us, at least in a small way, to look at the Upper Paleolithic world through the eyes of those who lived in it. (Chapter 8) *Copyright © Art Resource*

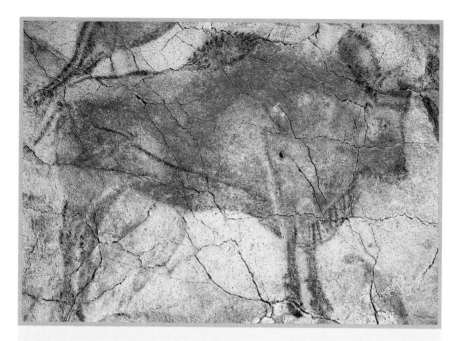

COLOR PLATE 7

This painting of a bison was found in Altamira Cave, Spain. Its detail of form, three-dimensionality, and color testify to the remarkable observational and artistic skills of the Upper Paleolithic artist who created it. (Chapter 8) *Copyright © Scala/Art Resource*

COLOR PLATE 8

An array of finely flaked fluted points from the Richey Clovis Cache discovered in Washington State and dating to 11,200 years ago. Fluted points, exhibiting distinctive "flutes," or channels, were hafted onto wooden shafts and used by Paleoindians to prey on the abundant populations of large game animals at the end of the Pleistocene. (Chapter 9) *Copyright © R. M. Gramly/Great Lakes Artifact Repository*

COLOR PLATE 9

Stonehenge is emblematic of the ability of early, complex, non-state societies to organize large labor forces to engage in communal, monumentally scaled construction projects. (Chapter 12) *Joshua Max Feder*

COLOR PLATE 10

Stonehenge consisted of upright sarsens forming a circle 100 ft in diameter; adjacent sarsens were connected by horizontal stone lintels. Five sets of trilithons—two upright stones and one stone resting horizontally on top—were set in a horseshoe pattern inside the sarsen circle. (Chapter 12) *Copyright © Martin Gray, www.sacredsites.com*

COLOR PLATE 11

This spectacular mask was carved by an Olmec artisan from a single piece of jadeite. (Chapter 12) *Copyright © Boltin Picture Library*

COLOR PLATE 12

These splendid Olmec figurines found at La Venta were made of jade and serpentine. They were discovered just as displayed here, with a central figure carved in stone encircled by the other individuals. The figurines are between 15 and 25 cm (6 and 10 in) in height. (Chapter 12) *Copyright © Boltin Picture Library*

COLOR PLATE 13
Built more than 4,000 years ago, the impressive ziggurat at the Mesopotamian city of Ur is a testament to the ability of early state societies to conscript the labor of a large population to produce monumental public works. (Chapter 13)
Copyright © Comstock

COLOR PLATE 14
From the 4,000-year-old tomb of Puabi in ancient Sumeria, this gold bull-head harp exemplifies a number of elements unique to state societies. Clearly the product of a specialist and made from rare and precious materials, this object served to symbolize the standing of a member of the ruling class in a stratified society. Full-time specialists and social stratification are hallmarks of the state. (Chapter 13) *Copyright © Lee Boltin/Boltin Picture Library*

COLOR PLATE 15

Crafted from gold and lapis lazuli (the bands of dark-blue stone), the coffin lid of Egyptian pharaoh Tutankhamun is among the many splendid objects recovered from his tomb. The tomb symbolizes the wealth and power held by leaders of the world's ancient civilizations. (Chapter 13)

Copyright © Lee Boltin/Boltin Picture Library

COLOR PLATE 16

Constructed more than 4,500 years ago, the sphinx of ancient Egypt is an integral part of the Giza Necropolis, which includes the largest pyramids built by the ancient Egyptians. (Chapter 13) *M. H. Feder*

COLOR PLATE 17

One of the defining characteristics of civilizations is the development of a class of full-time artisans. This sculpted stone bust from Mohenjo-daro almost certainly was crafted by a specialist, likely for a member of the Indus Valley civilization's elite class. (Chapter 13) *Copyright © Archivo Iconografico, S. A./Corbis*

COLOR PLATE 18

Bronze metallurgy played a significant role in the development of ancient Chinese civilization. This charming casting of a baby elephant perched atop an adult elephant was found at An-yang, a capital city of the Shang civilization. (Chapter 13) *Courtesy of the Freer Gallery of Art, Smithsonian Institution, Washington, D.C.*

COLOR PLATE 19

Hopewell artisans carved these pipes, which were recovered from Tremper Mound, Ohio. The stone Hopewell pipes are often whimsical, with bowls carved into the shapes of animals or birds. (Chapter 14) *Copyright © Ohio Historical Society*

COLOR PLATE 20

The Square Tower House ruin, nestled in a niche at the base of a cliff in Mesa Verde in Colorado. With names such as "Cliff Palace," "Balcony House," and "Square Tower House," the cliff dwellings of Mesa Verde were the product of a sophisticated complex society that flourished more than 500 years ago in the American Southwest. (Chapter 14) *K. L. Feder*

COLOR PLATE 21

The impressive Temple I (Temple of the Giant Jaguar) at the Maya site of Tikal in Guatemala. Built around A.D. 700, it towers 45 m (145 ft) above the Great Plaza in this pre-Columbian city of 50,000 people. (Chapter 15) *Cris Wibby*

COLOR PLATE 22

The Pyramid of the Magician (far right) at the Maya site of Uxmal in the central Yucatán Peninsula. Uxmal reached its peak at the end of the Classic period of Maya history. (Chapter 15) *K. L. Feder*

COLOR PLATE 23

A computer-graphic reconstruction of the main pyramid located in the central part of the Aztec capital of Tenochtitlán conveys a sense of the beauty and majesty of the brightly painted architecture of this ancient New World city. (Chapter 15) *Copyright © Taisei Corporation*

COLOR PLATE 24

The Moche produced beautiful works of art in clay. Pictured here is a pot made to look like the head of a Moche priest or lord wearing a bird headdress. The part of the pot sticking up out of the head is the spout of the vessel. (Chapter 15)
Copyright © Gianni Dagli Orti/Corbis

COLOR PLATE 25

Finely crafted works of art made from rare or precious raw materials are a hallmark of complex societies. This engaging gold alligator was made by an ancient Inka artist. (Chapter 15)
Copyright © Boltin Picture Library

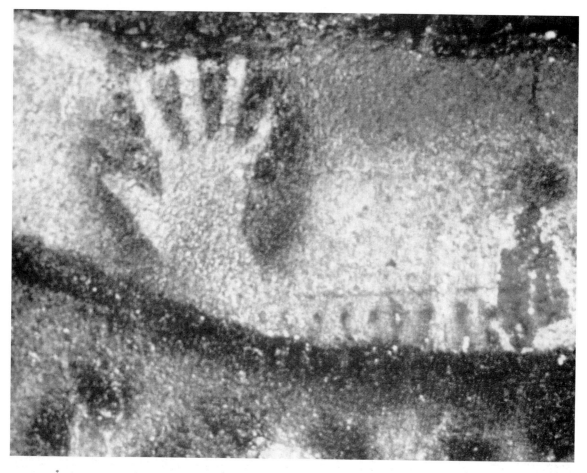

FIGURE 8.6

This image of a human handprint from the cave wall of Peche-Merle in France is an eternal signature of a human being who lived more than 20,000 years ago. (Courtesy of the Musée de l'Homme. B. G. Dellue)

The Earliest Art: Australia and Africa

Though we may not know what the images and objects mean, many artifacts dated to the period beginning about 40,000 years ago clearly denote the use of symbol and the production of art. For example, at Wharton Hill in Australia (Figure 8.7), more than 36,000 years ago, an aborigine etched an oval shape into the abutting rock face (Bednarik 1993, 5; see Chapter 9 for a discussion of the human presence in Australia). To derive a radiocarbon date, organic material was recovered from inside the groove. Encased in the rock varnish (a weathering rind of rock that builds up on an exposed surface) of the **petroglyph** (literally, "rock-writing"), the organic deposit could have gotten into the groove only after the groove was made, providing, therefore, a minimum possible age for the carved oval shape. At the nearby site of Panaramitee North, a curvilinear petroglyph has been dated via the same technique, to 43,000 B.P. (Bednarik 1993, 6). These dates, if correct, render the Australian petroglyphs the earliest evidence of art in the world.

FIGURE 8.7

Upper Paleolithic sites in Australia, Africa, Asia, and Europe.

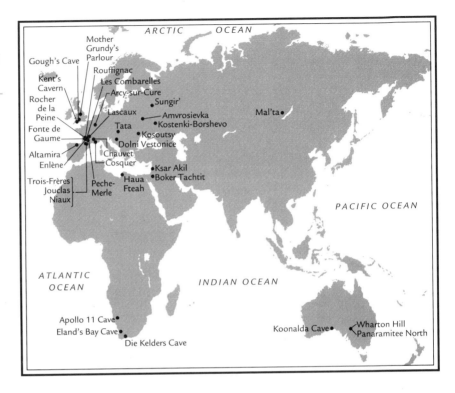

The first African art has been dated to as early as 28,000 B.P. (Phillipson 1993). Stone slabs with painted and engraved images of animals have been excavated from deposits dating to this time at the Apollo 11 cave site in southern Namibia (see Figure 8.7; Wendt 1976). The images are natural renderings of the fauna of southern Africa for the time period of their production.

Upper Paleolithic Art in Europe

The artwork of late Pleistocene Europe is far better known than the Australian or the African artwork, partly as a result of geography—it is found in an area where extensive archaeology has been conducted—and partly because of placement—its location in caves has kept it better preserved. In the cave paintings (**parietal art**) and in carved statues and inscribed bone, antler, and ivory (**mobiliary art**), Upper Paleolithic Europeans produced an astounding amount of art (see Figure 8.7). Some of the paintings and inscribed artifacts incorporate geometric designs and abstract images whose meanings are difficult to interpret. In many of the paintings and carvings, though we may never be certain of the artist's intent (see "Issues and Debates"), we cannot help but recognize the images they were producing. Cave walls in France and Spain especially, but also others scattered throughout Europe, are adorned with realistic depictions of the animals of the Upper Paleolithic. Images of prehistoric horse and bison, woolly mammoth and rhinoceros, reindeer and wild cattle flow across cave-wall canvases at places like Lascaux and Altamira, Les Combarelles, Niaux, Les Trois-Frères, Peche-Merle, and Fonte de Gaume (see Color Plates 6 and 7; Leroi-Gourhan 1982).

Southwestern Europe alone has more than 200 caves with Paleolithic artwork, and more caves are found fairly regularly. The most exciting recent find, Chauvet Cave (Hughes 1995), near Avignon, France, contains an amazing array of paintings. Most people who have seen them consider them some of the most beautiful examples of Paleolithic artwork ever discovered. The dates derived for the artwork at Chauvet are stunning: The two oldest dates of the eight derived from carbon samples taken from the paintings were earlier than 31,000 B.P., making the Chauvet artwork the oldest cave paintings yet discovered in Europe (Chauvet, Deschamps, and Hillaire 1996).

In their paintings, produced from 31,000 years ago to 10,000 years ago, the artists of the Upper Paleolithic have willed to us evocative images of their natural surroundings and, at the same time, whispered to us of their intellectual world. At Niaux, France, a detailed image of a bison includes two spears penetrating its body. At Rouffignac, also in France, two outlined woolly mammoths appear to confront each other in an apparent dance for dominance. At Chauvet, a group of overlapping, stiff-maned horses rendered in shades of gray seem to be relaxing on the cave wall surface. At Lascaux, a badly wounded bison, its viscera hanging from its wounded belly, is confronting its attacker, knocking over an outlined hunter.

Upper Paleolithic artists also depicted themselves, though commonly more schematically and less realistically (Figure 8.8). Researchers Patricia Rice and Ann Paterson (1988) analyzed more than 100 human images from 32 caves in western Europe. Their statistics are provocative: More than three-quarters of the images are men, who tend to be depicted singly, in an active mode—running, walking, throwing spears. Females tend to be portrayed at rest and in close proximity to other females. What does this mean in terms of the roles of males and females in Paleolithic society? This glimpse into the sexual division of labor in societies that existed more than 15,000 years ago simply is not based on a sample large enough to allow us to draw any conclusions.

Though largely enigmatic in the meaning of their images, these caves were clearly not art galleries. In the more than 150 mostly western European caves where significant numbers of paintings have been found, some images overlap, and the strange juxtapositioning of the animals—some floating above others, some upside down in relation to others—shows quite clearly that individual paintings and panels were not intended as part of a single tableau.

The relative frequency of species depicted and their locations are not random. Carnivores, for example, are often placed in the least accessible parts of the caves, and the herbivores seem to be depicted in proportion to their significance in the diet of the people who painted them (see "Issues and Debates"). While at some caves animal species that served as food for Paleolithic hunters predominate, the newly discovered Chauvet cave has quite a

FIGURE 8.8

The cave walls are haunted by the cryptic images of the people who produced the remarkable artistic legacy of the Upper Paleolithic. This image appears at the site of Le Portel in France.

FIGURE 8.9

These two examples of the so-called Venus figurines— the famous Venus of Willendorf (left) *and a relief carving from a cave in France* (right)*—fit the common stereotype of such figurines: broad hips, large breasts, fat bellies, and vague faces.* (*Left:* Negative no. 326474, courtesy of Department of Library Services, American Museum of Natural History; photo by Lee Boltin. *Right:* Courtesy of the Musée de l'Homme. D. Ponsard)

few paintings of carnivores: three cave lions, a panther, and a bear. Chauvet also presents us with the single largest concentration of paintings of woolly rhinoceroses—50 of them.

The Venus Figurines

Then there are the so-called **Venus figurines.** Most of them, across much of Europe, date to the period between 25,000 and 23,000 years ago—some were made nearly 27,000 years ago, and a few date to 20,000 years ago (Gamble 1986). One group, but by no means all, of these statuettes depicts obese females, usually without faces but with enlarged breasts and buttocks (Figure 8.9). This particular variety of the female figurines has become the stereotype of this class of artifacts, perhaps, as archaeologist Patricia Rice (1981) points out, because these are the ones most often depicted in books on prehistoric art. Many researchers have suggested that they were fertility symbols, realistic depictions of pregnant females, or portrayals of women with various medical conditions.

However, these suggestions are difficult to support when large samples are examined. Patricia Rice (1981) looked at a group of 188 Venus figurines and found their shape, size, and form to be quite varied. There were depictions of thin and fat women, women with large breasts and women with small breasts, pregnant and not pregnant women, and women who were, by Rice's estimation, old, middle-aged, and young (based on the depiction of physical appearance, especially the presence or absence of lines in their faces and in how flat or saggy breasts, stomachs, hips, and buttocks looked).

Rice (1981, 408) proposes that the deduced age spread of the Upper Paleolithic female figurines in her large sample was remarkably similar to the actual age distribution in historical hunter-gatherer populations. So in her view, the Venus figurines depict women of all shapes and sizes, all ages, and all states of fertility. More recently, Jean-Pierre Duhard (1993) has examined Upper Paleolithic depictions of human beings. While he questions some of Rice's methodology, he agrees with her most general conclusion: "The women depicted display every variation and accurately reproduce the forms encountered among living people" (Duhard 1993, 87). Duhard also points out that some males are depicted among the figurines, although most are female and many of the females are pregnant.

The precise meaning of the cave paintings as well as of the figurines is elusive. But what is key here is that in painting their images in caves, in engraving designs on antler, and in sculpting depictions of women, the artists of the Upper Paleolithic were doing something that we recognize as human behavior. They were creating images from their memory, filtered through the lens of their imagination. In doing this they left us wonderful works to ponder.

WHY IS THERE NO CORRELATION BETWEEN ANATOMICAL AND BEHAVIORAL MODERNITY?

ISSUES AND DEBATES

At the chronological boundary between the Middle and Upper Paleolithic, prehistorians are faced with a riddle. As we saw in Chapter 7, anatomically modern human beings with presumably physically modern brains encased within demonstrably modern crania perched atop modern postcranial skeletons appear in the archaeological record more than 100,000 years ago. But though these first human beings represent a jump to modern morphology from their physically archaic roots, the archaeological record shows no such great leap in their behavior at this time. Though minor differences exist in the kinds of tools made, the way fireplaces were constructed, and so forth, the material culture of Middle Paleolithic premodern humans is quite similar—in some cases, virtually identical—to the material culture of the earliest anatomically modern humans living at the same time.

In fact, the great leap forward to a more modern culture does not appear to have occurred until sometime after 50,000 B.P.—more than 50,000 years after the first appearance of humans whose cranial morphologies suggest they had brains capable of modern adaptations right from the start.

We still do not understand why this extended temporal gap exists between the first appearance of ostensibly modern humans and the first appearance of a modern-looking material culture. Archaeologist Richard Klein (1989, 1994) even suggests that, though we call them anatomically modern *Homo sapiens* on the basis of skeletal features, perhaps the hominids represented at Border Cave, Klasies River Mouth, Skhul, and Qafzeh (see Chapter 7) were only superficially modern, retaining a fundamentally archaic neuroanatomy. In other words, though we can't prove it archaeologically, perhaps their modern-looking skulls housed brains that were not yet modern and so they were not yet intellectually capable of producing the material culture that characterizes the Upper Paleolithic. Klein suggests that what amounts to a rewiring of the human brain occurred sometime between 40,000 and 50,000 years ago, allowing for a great leap to modern intelligence. As of now, this remains an untested—perhaps untestable—hypothesis.

WHAT DOES THE ART OF THE UPPER PALEOLITHIC MEAN?

It is difficult not to be moved by the images that adorn the cave walls of ancient Europe and elsewhere. With twentieth-century-A.D. eyes we can appreciate the visual beauty and movement of the artwork. But what did these works mean to the twentieth- (and thirtieth-) millennium-B.P. eyes of their creators? And why did they create them?

There are as many answers to these questions as researchers who have contemplated them. Some have argued that the art of the Upper Paleolithic explains itself: It is (and was) beautiful and, just like modern art, was produced for the simple joy of creating something of beauty and power. It was "art for art's sake" (Halvorson 1987).

Most researchers, though, eschew such an explanation as no explanation at all and have sought deeper meaning in the art. There has long been a "just-so" explanation, proposing that when a hunting people depict animals in their artwork, they are necessarily practicing what is called sympathetic magic. The hunters paint the animals and show them being speared or captured in the magical, symbolic realm to ensure their capture and slaughter in the real world.

French researcher André Leroi-Gourhan (1968) championed a popular hypothesis that the cave art was filled with sexual symbolism, with phallic spears piercing vulva-like wounds on the animals. So the animal depictions of the Upper Paleolithic were not about animals or hunting at all; instead, they were about sex and gender.

Other researchers have suggested that cave paintings depicted actual historical events, hunts symbolically and artistically recorded for posterity. And still others have likened the paintings to mounted animal-head trophies hung on walls by their modern hunters.

Recent researchers, delving more deeply, see the artwork as part of a system of communication of ideas—a system that uses animals and geometric patterns as symbols, the specific meaning of which may be lost forever. Archaeologist Meg Conkey (1980) views the 1,200 bones engraved with abstract geometric patterns at Altamira Cave, Spain, as the identifying symbols—the "flags"—of different groups of people who came together at the cave during periods of population aggregation. Michael Jochim views the cave paintings of northern Spain and southern France—the so-called Franco-Cantabrian region—as symbols marking territory. Social stresses that accompanied population influx into the region during the period after 25,000 B.P. may have resulted in the need to mark territory with symbols of ownership. Painting animals—probably the most important resources of a territory—within a sacred place in the territory like a cave might have served to announce to all interlopers the rightful ownership of the surrounding lands. Clive Gamble (1982, 1986) views the Venus figurines as a symbolic social glue, helping to maintain social connections between geographically distant groups through a common religion and art style.

More recently, researchers Patricia Rice and Ann Paterson (1985, 1986) have returned to a more economic perspective. Their statistical analysis of the numbers and kinds of animals seen on cave walls in the European Upper Paleolithic shows interesting correlations with the faunal assemblages of habitation sites in Spain and France. Small, nonaggressive animals such as reindeer and red deer were important in the diet of the cave painters and seem to have been depicted on cave walls in proportion to their economic importance. On the other hand, animals less often seen in faunal assemblages, but impressive, dangerous, and productive of large quantities of meat when they were successfully procured, also were commonly included in the artwork. However, the newly discovered Chauvet Cave contradicts this pattern, with its stunning depictions of animals not known to have been exploited for food by Paleolithic Europeans, including carnivores like lions, bears, and panthers, as well as woolly rhinoceroses.

A fascinating neuropsychological approach has been applied by researchers J. D. Lewis-Williams and T. A. Dowson (1988) to explain at least some of the less naturalistic cave art. They note that there are six basic geometric forms that people who are placed into an altered state of consciousness under experimental conditions report seeing: dots, wavy lines, zigzags, cross-hatching or grids, concentric circles or U-shaped lines, and parallel lines (Bower 1996). Interestingly, these geometric forms are precisely those seen in some ancient cave art dating to more than 30,000 years ago.

Lewis-Williams and Dowson's approach is cross-cultural. In other words, they surveyed a wide variety of historical and archaeological cultures, finding common images in artwork all over the world. Lewis-Williams and Dowson point out ethnographic records of shaman or priests who, in an attempt to communicate with spirits or to see into other worlds, induce a trancelike state by fasting, dancing, hyperventilating, going into isolation in absolute darkness, undergoing sleep deprivation, or even ingesting natural hallucinogens. When these shamans produce an artistic representation of what they have seen in their trances, they often include the geometric shapes induced in modern experimental subjects that also are seen in Upper Paleolithic artwork.

These trance-induced images are not culturally controlled but result, in part, from the structure of the optic system itself and are therefore universal. Perhaps through sleep deprivation, staring at a flickering fire, or the ingestion of drugs, ancient shamans or priests induced these images in their own optic systems. They then translated these images to cave walls as part of religious rituals.

The art of the Upper Paleolithic has been depressingly resistant to any comprehensive explanation for its existence. That we cannot even fathom the reason for our own children's scribblings (see this chapter's "Prelude") does not bode well for our attempt to illuminate the motives for and meanings of the artwork of our Upper Paleolithic ancestors. Perhaps we are destined merely to enjoy the cave paintings and Venus figurines, much as we delight in those crayon, pencil, and paint images we attach with magnets to our refrigerators. That would not be so terrible, so great is the aesthetic enjoyment we might derive from them. Then again, there are insights yet to be extracted from these beautiful puzzles that, when solved, will tell us much about what it means to be a human being.

DOES THE PALEOLITHIC HAVE A GENDER?

On many levels, gender issues are part of our ideas about human behavior, both in the past and in the present (Gero and Conkey 1990; Spencer-Wood 1991). For example, the discussion of the origins of upright walking in Chapter 4's "Issues and Debates" presented the hypothesis of Owen Lovejoy that bipedalism arose to enable males to provision females. Issues of sex roles, monogamy, and paternity—for *Australopithecus* as well as their modern descendants—are bound up in his hypothesis.

Gender issues are just as pertinent to our discussion of the Upper Paleolithic. Consider cave art. I intentionally tried to surprise you in the "Chronicle" section's vignette of two Paleolithic artists: One of them was female. Many people think, on the basis of virtually no data, that men were the ancient artists of the Paleolithic. But why?

Archaeologist Diane Gifford-Gonzalez (1993) points out that in most popular reconstructions of ancient life, virtually all of the important and exciting behaviors reflected in the archaeological record have been ascribed only to ancient males. Surveying the work of 88 modern artists, Gifford-Gonzalez determined the proportions of Paleolithic males and females depicted performing a number of different tasks (Figure 8.10). Her results are truly amazing. For example, in her sample of 331 images of individual ancient people, all of the individuals depicted performing a ritual, hunting, or carrying game were males. And 90% of those depicted producing Paleolithic artwork were males. In the same sample, not one male was shown holding a baby or touching a child.

From illustrations in coffee-table books to diorama kits for kids to professionally produced museum dioramas, images abound of ancient men hunting, creating art, and performing ceremonies, while women are shown in the background with children, performing drudge work like scraping hides or cooking.

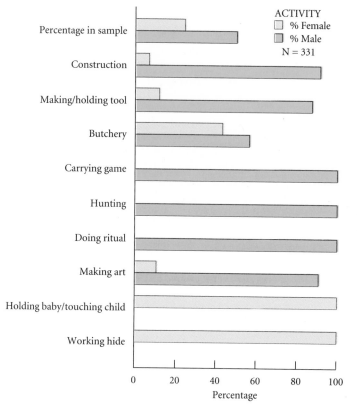

FIGURE 8.10

In this graph, archaeologist Diane Gifford-Gonzalez shows the kind of sex-role stereotyping modern artists have engaged in when depicting Paleolithic people. Women are commonly shown caring for children and working animal hides; men are shown hunting, using tools, carrying game, performing rituals, and producing art. (Adapted with permission from Diane Gifford-Gonzalez 1993)

So it is not surprising that many people assume that the role of ancient women focused on cooking food, making clothing, and, of course, bearing and raising children. These same people assume it was men who, by wit, sinew, and intelligence, fed their families by tracking, killing, and bringing animals back to the cave. Then, though exhausted from providing sustenance for their families, they worked the evenings away, producing great works of art, as fresh and vibrant today as they must have been 25,000 years ago when they were painted. In this view, men were involved in all of the exciting, intellectually stimulating, and physically challenging activities, while women got to clean up.

In truth, we must admit our ignorance; we don't know who produced the cave art in the Upper Paleolithic or who performed rituals. We must not allow our twentieth-century preconceptions about the sexual division of labor to bias our view of the ancient past. It could have been women as easily as men who applied those remarkable images onto the cave walls, carved the figurines, and held positions of ritual importance. At the same time, we should not presume that Paleolithic men played out a 1950s-style fatherhood: stiff, distant, and uninvolved. It is far more likely that survival during the Pleistocene required all members of a group to contribute in many different ways;

FIGURE 8.11

This skeleton of an older man who lived more than 25,000 years ago is one of five burials excavated at the Upper Paleolithic site of Sungir' near Moscow. More than 3,000 ivory beads were sewn into his burial garments. (Courtesy of the Musée de l'Homme. O. Bader)

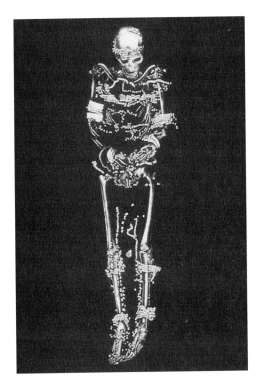

Paleolithic people probably could not have afforded to restrict the contributions of individuals on the basis of sex. Perhaps at some point we might recognize the same thing.

CASE STUDY CLOSE-UP

The site of Sungir' is located about 150 km (100 mi) northeast of Moscow, in Russia (R. White 1993). Five burials dating to at least 25,000–30,000 years ago (and possibly as much as 38,000 years ago) have been excavated at the site; the burials are of an older male, an adult female, a young girl, a teenage boy, and an individual of undetermined sex.

The Sungir' graves are loaded with grave goods, primarily items of adornment (all data on the Sungir' graves are taken from R. White 1993, 287–96). The older male was adorned with nearly 3,000 finely worked ivory beads; some apparently were part of a beaded cap, and the rest were positioned in strands around his body (Figure 8.11). A flat stone pendant was located on his neck. On his arms were 25 finely carved bracelets made from the ivory of a woolly mammoth. The young boy's body was surrounded with more than 4,900 ivory beads. A carved ivory pendant had been placed on his chest. He wore a belt decorated with 250 polar fox teeth. There was an ivory pin at his throat, an ivory lance and carved ivory disk at his side, an ivory sculpture of a woolly mammoth under his shoulder, and by his left side a human femur (not his own) whose cavity was filled with red ochre. Next to the adolescent boy lay the young girl, buried with more than 5,200 strung beads, an ivory pin at her throat (perhaps a clasp for a garment long since decayed away), small ivory lances, and three ivory disks carved with intricate latticework.

An enormous amount of time must have been invested in preparing these items for burial. Replication of the beads has indicated that 45 minutes were needed to make just *one* of the ivory beads in the Sungir' burials (R. White 1993, 296). If this estimate is accurate, then 2,000 hours of work were needed just for the beads in the older man's burial, and more than 3,500 hours per child were needed for their beadwork.

We cannot say why such items turn up in Upper Paleolithic burials, nor what such items meant to the people of that period. Nevertheless, that such labor, care, and—yes—love was invested in remembrances for the dead means that the emotional and spiritual world of the Upper Paleolithic must have been remarkably similar to our own, more than 30,000 years later.

Of all the site visits suggested so far in this book, none is as dramatic as the painted caves of Paleolithic Europe. Unfortunately, some of the best-known sites are now closed to the public. Years of tourist visits have taken their toll on the artwork. Lights and especially the increased humidity produced by breathing and perspiring have harmed many of the precious painted images.

VISITING THE PAST

Spain and France have come up with an innovative solution to this problem: Replicas of some image groups from Altamira and Lascaux Caves have been produced. The actual contours of the ceiling of Altamira Cave were measured and copied in an artificial material. The cave paintings were then copied on this surface. The artificial cave with its replica artwork is on display at the Archaeological Museum in Madrid.

A more ambitious project is ongoing at Lascaux. Here, in a concrete blockhouse about 200 m (650 ft) from the actual cave, a new cave has been constructed to the exact measurements of the original. Modeled concrete precisely replicates the cave surfaces, and teams of artists attempt to produce perfect copies of the originals. Lascaux II re-creates two of the main galleries of Lascaux I, artificially placing most of the major paintings together. Hundreds of thousands of tourists have visited Lascaux II since it opened in 1984, providing a wonderful opportunity to visit the past, even when the original is off-limits.

SUMMARY

For 50,000 years—from 100,000 years ago to 50,000 years ago (virtually half the duration of the existence of the modern species *Homo sapiens sapiens*)—the material culture of human beings as reflected in the archaeological record was remarkably similar to that of our archaic contemporaries. Then, sometime after 50,000 years ago, a remarkable transformation occurred that resulted in cultural systems with a decidedly modern cast. This period of intellectual upheaval is called the Upper Paleolithic. The cultures of the period are characterized by the production of blade tools; a broadening of the subsistence base; an increase in the size of some sites (implying a practice of temporary population aggregation); the use of bone, antler, ivory, and shell in toolmaking; the manufacture of nonutilitarian items, some of which served as items of personal adornment; the extensive use of nonlocal, exotic raw materials; the regular placement of elaborate grave goods in burials—including items of personal adornment; and the first appearance of artwork, in the form of naturalistic paintings, fanciful sculptures, and engraved bone and antler. In the material culture of the Upper Paleolithic we see a recognizably "modern" human pattern.

TO LEARN MORE

Technical Summaries

Many useful works detail the significant changes seen at the boundary between the Middle and Upper Paleolithic. For technical reports, see many of the individual articles in *The Emergence of Modern Humans: An Archaeological Perspective*, edited by Paul Mellars (1990).

Popular Summaries

For splendid photographs of cave paintings from a variety of caves take a look at André Leroi-Gourhan's *The Dawn of European Art* (1982). For a detailed photographic treatment of Lascaux, don't miss Mario Ruspoli's *The Cave of Lascaux: The Final Photographs* (1986). It is a magnificent coffee-table book, but it is also much more, with lengthy discussions of the painted images. Another coffee-table book that offers informative text as well as compelling photographs is Jean-Marie Chauvet's 1996 work (written with Éliette Brunel Deschamps and Christian Hillaire) *Dawn of Art: The Chauvet Cave*. Yet another book with terrific photographic images of cave art, but which also has much to say about the significance of the art itself is *Dark Caves, Bright Visions*, by Randall White (1986), the archaeologist whose work on the Middle Paleolithic/ Upper Paleolithic transition provided a framework for part of this chapter's "Chronicle." For another beautiful art book depicting Paleolithic cave paintings, see *The Cave Beneath the Sea: Paleolithic Images at Cosquer,* by Jean Clottes, Jean Courtin, and Marilyn Garner (1996). Today, Cosquer can be reached only through an underwater passageway and provides a unique context for Upper Paleolithic artwork.

For thoughtful discussions of the meaning of Upper Paleolithic artwork there is no better place to start than John Pfeiffer's *The Creative Explosion: An Inquiry into the Origins of Art and Religion* (1982). Though a bit dated now, Pfeiffer's book is always a good read. For a more recent and more technical book-length treatment, see the thought-provoking *The Dawn of Belief: Religion in the Upper Paleolithic of Southwestern Europe,* by Bruce Dickson (1990). One of the best and most succinct popular articles is archaeologist Pat Shipman's "Old Masters" in *Discover* (1990). For another article not aimed at scientists, this time by one of the most thoughtful researchers in the field of Paleolithic art, see Margaret Conkey's "A Century of Paleolithic Cave Art" in *Archaeology* (1981). For the most recent popular summary of the meaning of cave art with a focus on the "altered states of consciousness" hypothesis, see the article by Mary Roach in the June 1998 issue of *Discover*.

On the Web

The cave paintings and other artwork of the Upper Paleolithic are wonderful subjects for the Internet. To see far more than the small handful of photographs of cave paintings that I can present in this book, visit the homepages devoted to Chauvet, Lascaux, and Altamira Caves at the following addresses:

http://www.culture.fr/culture/arcnat/chauvet/en/gvpda-d.htm

http://www-sor.inria.fr/~pierre/lascaux/

http://www.unican.es/arte/Ingles/prehist/paleo/b/Default.htm

Wonder at the remarkable world we live in where the products of 30,000-year-old human imaginations are made accessible by a technology made possible by the modern human imagination.

KEY TERMS

Aurignacian

Gravettian

Solutrean

Magdelanian

megafauna

opportunistic foragers

settlement pattern

logistical collecting

spear-thrower

grave goods

petroglyph

parietal art

mobiliary art

Venus figurine

9

Expanding Geographical Horizons

NEW WORLDS

CHAPTER OVERVIEW

Beginning after 45,000 B.P. human population expanded into much of the rest of the habitable world. Sahul (Australia–New Guinea–Tasmania) exhibits evidence of human occupation by 40,000 years ago. Western Melanesia was populated by 30,000 years ago.

Northeast Asians crossed the Bering Land Bridge into the New World, possibly by about 20,000 years ago. Some migrants may have traveled along the coast and reached as far south as Chile by 13,000 years ago. Others migrated through the interior, where the evidence of their presence is substantial after 12,000 B.P.

The islands of Micronesia and Polynesia also show evidence of occupation after 3500 B.P.

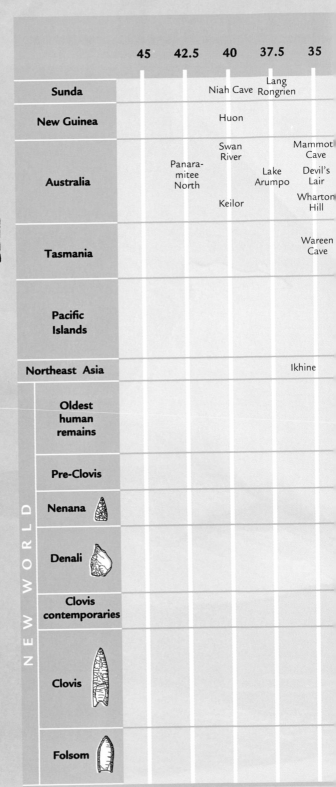

	45	42.5	40	37.5	35
Sunda			Niah Cave	Lang Rongrien	
New Guinea			Huon		
Australia		Panaramitee North	Swan River / Keilor	Lake Arumpo	Mammoth Cave / Devil's Lair / Wharton Hill
Tasmania					Wareen Cave
Pacific Islands					
Northeast Asia					Ikhine
NEW WORLD: **Oldest human remains**					
Pre-Clovis					
Nenana					
Denali					
Clovis contemporaries					
Clovis					
Folsom					

32.5	30	27.5	25	22.5	20	17.5	15	12.5	10	7.5	5	2.5	Present
	Leang Burung						Timor						
	Kuk		Nombe										
		Kosipe											
			Mandu-Mandu		Nullarbor								
Lake Mungo				Puritjarra									
		Hamersley											
	Willandra Lakes 50		Koonalda										
	ORS7, Acheron, Bone, Nunamira			Cave Bay Cave									
					Kutikina, Beginner's Luck								
	Solomon Islands										Fiji	Hawaii	
											Society, Cook, Samoa		
												Easter Island	
												New Zealand	
						Dyuktai	Ushki						
								Midland					
									Kennewick				
								Tepexpán, Marmes,					
								Pelican Rapids					
							Arlington						
								Meadowcroft					
							Bluefish Caves						
							Monte Verde						
								Dry Creek I					
							Moose Creek						
							Walker Road						
								Dry Creek II					
								Usibelli, Slate Creek,					
								Donnelly Ridge, Campus Site,					
								Healy Lake, Teklanika River,					
								Panguingue Creek II					
								Mesa					
							Quebrada Jaguay						
								Quebrada Tacahuay					
								Templeton					
								Debert					
								Murray Springs, Dent, Lehner,					
								Anzick					
								Clovis, Richey, Colby, Domebo,					
								Vail					
								Casper					
								Olsen-Chubbuck					
								Folsom					
								Lindenmeier					

Sunday, July 20, 1969, was a momentous day in human history: For the first time in the existence of our species, a human being walked on the soil of another world. On that day, American astronaut Neil Armstrong left the relative safety of the lunar lander, climbed down the ladder, took a final step off, and became the citizen—if only temporarily—of another world.

NASA, leaving nothing to chance, had scripted a weighty but succinct statement to be intoned by the first human to walk on the moon. But wouldn't you know it, he blew his lines. As Armstrong made his first contact with the lunar surface, he uttered the following words: "That's one small step for man, one giant leap for mankind." But this statement is redundant and basically meaningless; "man" and "mankind" are synonymous in this context. He meant to say, "That's one small step for *a* man, one giant leap for mankind." In other words, though the step off the lunar lander was literally a "small step" for an individual, it represented a giant figurative leap forward for the human species.

The literal and figurative step Armstrong took that day was a significant one, but really just one stride in the great march of human history, a history marked by uncounted steps, both small and big, and leaps, both modest and great. From our literal first steps onto the African savanna to Armstrong's first step onto the lunar surface, human history has been filled with small steps that collectively have added up to giant leaps. One thing that surely characterizes our species is the desire to take those steps and to explore both new vistas of the imagination and actual vistas of new lands. This chapter focuses on the exploration of such new horizons by our anatomically modern ancestors as they spread into the new worlds of Australia, the islands of the Pacific, and the Americas.

CHRONICLE

When British explorer Captain James Cook's ship made landfall on the east coast of Australia in 1770, he had no professional speechwriters to help commemorate the occasion. The record of his first impressions on encountering native Australians is more mundane than Neil Armstrong's remarks: "Sunday 29th April. Saw as we came in on both points of the bay Several of the natives and a few hutts. Men, women and children on the south shore abreast of the Ship, to which place I went in the boats in hopes of speaking with them" (Price 1971, 65).

When the first British settlement of the Australian continent was established at Sydney harbor in 1778, the colonists also arrived by oceangoing vessels, as had Cook. Cook and those who followed found a land populated by more than a quarter million people and perhaps as many as 1 million. Those natives were the descendants of settlers who had also arrived by sea. Lacking a written language, the original settlers left no record of their reaction to their "giant leap" to a new continent. Only the archaeological record speaks to us about how they survived as a people in their new world.

THE SETTLEMENT OF GREATER AUSTRALIA

The original Australians, called Aborigines, were an enigma to the European colonizers. In the Europeans' biased view, the Aborigines seemed primitive in their material culture, a Stone Age people with few material advances, throwbacks to a distant time in human history. Yet what these people lacked in things, they more than made up for in ideas. They possessed a range of sophisticated social systems; the individual Aborigine had a far denser web of relations and was far more knowledgeable of his or her social connections than was the average European. These supposedly primitive people also had a richly detailed mythology and oral history and a sophisticated knowledge of their natural surroundings. Australian Aborigines also produced a richly textured artistic tradition, painting fantastical images of the animals they encountered in their environment, as well as the ancestors, heroes, and spirits that inhabited their spirit world (Gray 1996).

As different as they were from the European settlers, these native Australians shared at least one thing with the newcomers; as already mentioned, they had arrived by watercraft (Birdsell 1977; Jones 1989, 1992; J. White and O'Connell 1982). Their voyages of exploration and migration—a series of small steps adding up to one giant leap to a new world—occurred some 50,000 years before the arrival of the Europeans.

Paleogeography in the Western Pacific

During the height of the Pleistocene, ice covered much of the northern latitudes and higher elevations of the world, locking up a prodigious quantity of the earth's water in permanent ice fields—so much water that sea level was lowered by at least 100 m (325 ft) and perhaps as much as 150 m (500 ft). During glacial maxima, the islands of Java, Sumatra, Bali, and Borneo were connected to each other in a single landmass called **Sunda** (or **Sundaland**) (Figure 9.1, p. 234). Sunda, in turn, was connected to mainland southeast Asia. The oceans separating these islands from one another, as well as from Asia proper, are not as deep as the amount by which sea level was depressed during glacial maxima. Wide swaths of land connecting these territories, now many meters under the ocean's surface, were exposed during periods of lowered sea level.

During these same periods of depressed sea levels, Australia, New Guinea, and Tasmania were similarly connected as a single landmass, called **Sahul,** or "Greater Australia" (see Figure 9.1). Unlike Sunda, however, Sahul was never connected to mainland Asia. Even when the Pleistocene glaciers were at their most extensive and sea level was at its lowest, Sahul was still separated from

Asia by a water barrier. In fact, Greater Australia has been separated from Asia since the two were separated through continental drift more than 100 million years ago. This long-standing isolation of Australia has resulted in that continent's unique native fauna of kangaroos, wallabies, wombats, and koala bears—which are marsupials (primitive mammals that give birth to very immature young who complete their gestation in pouches)—and platypuses, echidnas, and spiny anteaters—which are monotremes (egg-laying mammals). Only a very small number of Asian mammals, including some rodents (rats and mice) and bats, were able to cross the gap and populate Australia in prehistory (Diamond 1987a). Bats flew across the water, and rodents were probably washed out to sea from Asia on matted vegetation, which fortuitously washed up on the shores of Sahul.

The **Wallace Trench,** located between New Guinea–Australia and Java–Borneo, is an enormous undersea chasm, nearly 7,500 m (25,000 ft) deep. Though the distance between the shores of Sunda and Sahul lessened as sea level became depressed during glacial maxima at 65,000 years ago, then 53,000 years ago, and again at 35,000 years ago, the islands never coalesced, kept apart by the deep waters of **Wallacea,** the sea over the Wallace Trench (Glover 1993).

The Road to Sahul

Oceanic islands in Wallacea, like Timor and Sulawesi (formerly called the Celebes), would have served as stepping-stones between Asia and Australia

FIGURE 9.1

The current coastlines of Australia, New Guinea, and southeast Asia, as well as the coastline during glacial maxima. Arrows show proposed migration routes from Sunda (the combined landmass of the islands of southeast Asia) to Sahul (Greater Australia).

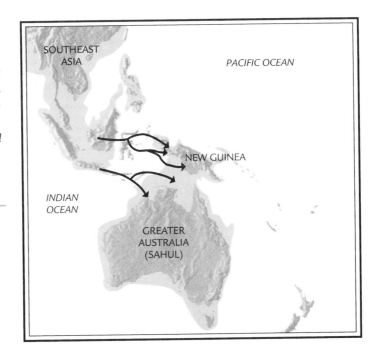

during the Pleistocene. Anthropologist Joseph Birdsell (1977) has suggested a series of possible routes from Sunda to Sahul during periods of lowered sea level (see Figure 9.1). During glacial maxima and the concomitant lowering of sea level, one viable route starts on the eastern shore of contemporary Borneo, continues east through Sulawesi, and includes several island hops to northwest New Guinea. The longest inter-island gap would be about 70 km (43 mi); the mean of the eight gaps in this route is only about 28 km (17 mi) (Birdsell 1977, 127). An alternate route suggested by Birdsell is more southerly, beginning in Java, traversing the Indonesian archipelago, crossing south to Timor and then south to Australia proper. This route also contains eight ocean crossings, with a maximum of 87 km (54 mi) and a mean of a little more than 19 km (12 mi) between landfalls (Birdsell 1977, 127). When sea level is not as low as the proposed maximum, the distances become greater and the trip more difficult.

As Birdsell points out, this voyage likely did not take place all at once, but transpired, perhaps, over several generations, as people with a marine adaptation explored the islands in their vicinity and discovered more distant islands accidentally by being blown off course during storms. These people might then have settled on some of the islands, and the process would have been repeated, pushing the limits of their world ever farther out along its edges.

The Discovery of Greater Australia

The timing of the original human discovery and settlement of Greater Australia has long been disputed. It cannot have preceded a human presence on coastal southeast Asia (which is the most logical source for the native Australian population), and it must have followed the development of a coastal adaptation and the invention of seaworthy watercraft.

The archaeology of tropical southeast Asia, unfortunately, is not well known enough for us to trace with confidence the aboriginal inhabitants of Sahul to their Sunda source. Only a few early sites have been found in the most logical source areas, and most of these sites are younger than the oldest sites now known from Sahul (Figure 9.2).

For example, one of the older sites in southeast Asia is located in Niah Cave on the island of Borneo. The lowest levels in the cave produced stone flakes, bone tools, and the remains of several animal species, including tapir, pig, monkey, deer, and porcupine (Jones 1989). One of the larger stone tools recovered at the site exhibits a distinct notching or grooving around its middle—in essence, a "waist." This form turns up again on the other side of Wallacea, in New Guinea and Australia, and may indicate a cultural connection between the peoples who made this tool form on both sides of the Wallace Trench. Radiocarbon dates place the earliest occupation of Niah Cave at around 40,000 years ago. A fully modern, lightly constructed human skull was recovered from this same level in the cave.

Most of the rest of the sites in southeast Asia date to after 40,000 B.P. For example, Lang Rongrien, in Thailand, dates to 37,000 years ago (O'Connell

FIGURE 9.2

Sites representing the earliest occupation of Greater Australia.

and Allen 1998). The oceanic island of Sulawesi in Wallacea has produced archaeological evidence of human occupation dating to 31,000 years ago at the Leang Burung cave site (Jones 1992). The oldest occupation of Timor is more recent still, dating to within the last 15,000 years. As indicated, these islands may have been used as stepping-stones from Sunda to Sahul. But again, the archaeological record has not provided sites old enough to represent the earliest migrants in transit.

THE EARLIEST OCCUPATION OF GREATER AUSTRALIA

The Archaeology of Sahul

The earliest-known settlement of New Guinea, then a part of Greater Australia, was located on an ancient, exposed coral reef on Bobongara Hill on the north coast of Papua New Guinea, at the southeastern terminus of the Huon

Peninsula. The site has been dated by thermoluminescence to 40,000 B.P. (Groube et al. 1986). Recovered from the site were a number of axe heads with a distinct narrowing or notching toward their middles (thus the name "waisted axes" and the similarity to the waisted tool found at Niah Cave in Borneo), a couple of stone cores for making flake tools, and a small number of flakes. Waisted axes have been found in archaeological contexts elsewhere in New Guinea, most notably at the Kosipe site, dating to 26,000 years ago, and at Nombe, dating to 25,000 years ago (J. White and O'Connell 1982). The waist was probably produced to aid in hafting the stone axe onto a wooden handle. Groube et al. (1986) suggest that these axes were used in forest clearing, an activity that, according to Rhys Jones (1989, 764), would have encouraged the growth of wild foods like yams, taro, and sugarcane by opening up the thick forest canopy and allowing more sunlight to reach the ground. The Kuk site in the New Guinea highlands, consisting of some carbon and **fire-cracked rocks,** is dated to a little before Kosipe and Nombe and may be as old as 30,000 years.

Some archaeologists believe that a very few Australian sites are substantially older than any of the sites in New Guinea or, for that matter, on the southeast Asian coast or on the islands leading to Australia. For example, it has been proposed that the Malakunanja II site in northwestern Australia, which has produced more than 1,500 artifacts—including stone flakes, a grindstone, and pieces of ground hematite and ochre (used in producing yellow and red pigment for paints)—is more than 45,000 and may be more than 60,000 years old (Roberts, Jones, and Smith 1990, 154). The Nauwalabila I site, located just south of Malakunanja II, has also produced dates of over 50,000 years ago.

Perhaps the most stunning claims about human antiquity in Australia come from the Jinmium site, also in northwestern Australia. There, it has been claimed that tools and even artwork were found in stratigraphic layers dating to 58,000, 75,000, 116,000, and even 176,000 years ago (Bahn 1996). If these dates were accurate, not only would we need to rewrite the early history of Australia, we would also have to reconfigure our scenarios about the evolution of modern human beings and their spread from Africa (O'Connell and Allen 1998).

All three of these anomalously early Australian sites were dated with the thermoluminescence (TL) method, and all the dates have been seriously questioned as a result of a possible problem in the technique. Thermoluminescence dating is based on the regular accumulation of energy in the material being dated. If we know the rate at which the energy is being accumulated in a given environment and if we can accurately measure how much has built up, we should be able to date the material.

TL dating always relies on the assumption that the material being dated has been thoroughly bleached, or "zeroed," before it was deposited in an archaeological context. It appears, for example, that the initial Jinmium dates were based on the analysis of sediments that had not been sufficiently bleached prior to deposition at the site. In other words, the very ancient dates did not relate to the site's occupation, but were based on the measurement of energy trapped in the crystal lattice of grains of the sediment prior to occupation of the site. In fact, a new analysis of the Jinmium material, applying carbon dating as well as optical luminescence, has shown that the human occupation of the rockshelter is actually no more than 22,000 and likely closer to 10,000 years old (Roberts et al. 1998).

Many other early sites in Australia, on the other hand, date to the period after about 40,000 B.P. and seem to support the belief of many archaeologists that this was the period of earliest occupation of the island continent (O'Connell and Allen 1998).

For example, the Upper Swan Bridge site in the southwestern part of the country has produced radiocarbon dates of 39,500 B.P., 37,100 B.P., and 35,000 B.P. in association with about 200 artifacts, including stone chips, worked flakes, and flakes with edges exhibiting wear patterns (Jones 1992). The chert used to make some of the Swan River artifacts was available only during the Pleistocene, when sea level was low enough to allow access to the source. Also in southwest Australia is Devil's Lair, with a series of hearths, stone and bone artifacts, and the remains of kangaroos that had been killed, butchered, and eaten by the cave's human inhabitants. Radiocarbon dates place occupation of the cave at before 32,000 years ago and perhaps as much as 38,000 years ago (Jones 1992). Eleven kilometers (7 mi) northwest of Devil's Lair is Mammoth Cave, where burned bones, possible stone artifacts, and charcoal have been dated to between 31,000 years ago and 37,000 years ago. The Keilor site, near the city of Melbourne in southeastern Australia, has produced some quartzite flakes that were intentionally struck off a core. The soil layer in which the artifacts were recovered is estimated to be more than 36,000 years old and less than 45,000 years old (J. White and O'Connell 1982).

Willandra Lakes

A number of important aboriginal sites have been found in the Willandra Lakes region of western New South Wales, in southeastern Australia. This section of the country is characterized by a succession of ancient Pleistocene lakes that have been dry for as much as 10,000 years (Figure 9.3). At Lake Arumpo, for example, a midden of freshwater mussel shells has been dated to 37,000 years ago.

Perhaps the archaeologically richest of the Willandra Lakes is Lake Mungo, occupied as early as 32,000 years ago. Five discrete sites were identified around the now dry lake bed (Barbetti and Allen 1972). Archaeologists located numerous ancient fireplaces, some stone cores and flakes, steep-edged scraping tools, an earth oven, and the burned eggs of emu (large, flightless birds indigenous to Australia). Charcoal from the fireplaces produced radiocarbon ages ranging from 24,020 to 32,750 years (Barbetti and Allen 1972, 48).

One of the Lake Mungo localities produced the remains of a cremated human female dated to 26,000 years ago (the "Mungo I" skeleton; Bowler,

FIGURE 9.3

Willandra Lakes, the fossil lake region of southeast Australia, have produced some of the oldest skeletal evidence of a human presence on the continent.

(Institute of Human Origins. Donald Johanson, photographer)

Thorne, and Polach 1972). After her death, her body was burned and the bones were pulverized and then interred. About 25% of the Mungo I skeleton was recovered, and enough recognizable cranial fragments were found to partially reconstruct the skull; the young woman was fully anatomically modern and rather **gracile** physiologically, lacking the large brow ridges or heavy buttressing bone typical of modern Australian natives (Bowler et al. 1970). Mungo II consists of 30 small fragments, and not much can be determined about its morphology. The more complete Mungo III skeleton, dated to between 28,000 and 30,000 years ago, looks quite similar to Mungo I (J. White and O'Connell 1982, 37). Buried in an extended position and not cremated, Mungo III was an adult male, again showing a cranial architecture far lighter than that of more **robust** modern natives.

Just north of Lake Mungo, the Willandra Lakes skeleton was recovered. Dating to between 20,000 and 30,000 years ago (and, therefore, conceivably more recent than the Lake Mungo remains) Willandra Lakes 50 (as the skeletal remains are designated) is far different in appearance, exhibiting enormously thick cranial bones (some seven times thicker than the Lake Mungo remains). As Australian archaeologist Rhys Jones (1992) has pointed out, in these three specimens (Mungo I and III and the Willandra Lakes 50 cranium) from sites just a few miles apart, there is a greater difference in cranial bone thickness than within and among all modern human populations! For Jones, such a difference is not possible within a single population. He sees two biologically distinct populations inhabiting the same region of Australia at different times. However, as J. Peter White and James O'Connell (1982) point out, this conclusion is difficult to support with such a small sample of crania for an entire continent and with so many differing habitats that people adapted to over such an extensive period of time. In their view, variations in cranial form merely reflect regional differentiation among native Australians, who can be derived from a single population wave from Asia more than 40,000 years ago.

THE SPREAD THROUGH AUSTRALIA

The Australian sites discussed so far are located in a ring around the perimeter of the continent (see Figure 9.2). As archaeologist Sandra Bowdler (1977, 1990) points out, the initial human population entered Australia from the north and then spread primarily east and to a lesser degree west along the coast, focusing on those areas with tropical coastal environments most like those of the source areas from which it migrated. When the migrants moved inland, they always did so along major river systems, enabling a shift in their subsistence foods from marine to riverine resources.

This pattern makes sense when you consider that the first inhabitants of Australia were almost certainly a coastally adapted people. This coastal adaptation, including the use of watercraft, enabled their discovery of Sahul and their migration onto its land mass in the first place. People with a history of coastal subsistence would have been wise to spread along the coast of their newly found home. And, as shown, the oldest human sites in Australia are located along the modern coastal rim or in formerly wetter interiors drained by rivers or dotted with lakes (the Lake Mungo area, for example).

The Australian Interior

The earliest inhabitants of Australia seem to have avoided, at least initially, the vast, harsh, dry interior of the continent (J. White 1993). Not until 20,000–25,000 years ago did human groups begin to penetrate the dry core of central Australia. Evidence from the Puritjarra Rockshelter in the Cleland Hills of central Australia shows that the cave was occupied intermittently between 22,000 and 12,000 years ago (M. A. Smith 1987). The stone-tool assemblage included primarily large flake tools but also some small flakes and cores. Other interior sites of similar antiquity include two rockshelter sites from the Hamersley Plateau in western Australia—dated at 21,000 B.P. and 26,000 B.P., respectively—and evidence of flint mining in the Nullarbor Plain dated to 20,000 years ago (Jones 1987).

TASMANIA

Tasmania is the last "new world" in Sahul to be occupied by human beings. A human population first entered what is today the island of Tasmania when it was still connected to the Australian continent. The earliest people of Tasmania lived farther south and closer to Antarctica than did any other human group to that point. The environment was entirely different from any faced previously by Australian Aborigines—a frozen tundra not unlike that of Upper Paleolithic Europe (see Chapter 8).

Tasmania shows archaeological evidence of occupation as early as 35,000 years ago at Wareen Cave and 30,000 years ago at the ORS7 site as well as at Acheron, Bone, and Nunamira Caves in south-central Tasmania (Cosgrove, Allen, and Marshall 1990). Archaeologists Richard Cosgrove, Jim Allen, and Brendan Marshall (1990) conducted a survey of south-central Tasmania, locating 41 sites occupied between 30,000 and 11,000 years ago. Sites like Cave Bay Cave, located on Hunter Island off the northwest coast of Tasmania, date to about 23,000 B.P. (Bowdler 1974). On Tasmania proper there is Beginner's Luck Cave and Kutikina Cave (formerly Fraser Cave), both initially occupied at 20,000 years ago. Kutikina is extraordinarily rich, with over 75,000 stone flakes and tools recovered from less than a 1% sample of the site (Kiernan, Jones, and Ranson 1983). Most of the tools are steep-edged scrapers, similar in appearance to those recovered at Lake Mungo. The faunal assemblage is dominated by the remains of the large wallaby, which is a member of the kangaroo family, and the wombat, a sizable, heavyset, burrowing marsupial (Kiernan, Jones, and Ranson 1983, 30). Interestingly, there are no remains of the larger, now extinct animals that typified the Pleistocene of Australia. This Australian Pleistocene megafauna probably was already extinct by the time humans first penetrated Tasmania.

GREATER AUSTRALIA: A BROAD RANGE OF ADAPTATIONS

In the stereotype, the Australian Aborigines were a homogeneous group, possessed of a simple technology, barely eking out a living in the great arid desert of central Australia. In this view, they had become stuck in time, holdovers from a primitive Stone Age society, forever limited by their harsh environment. But the archaeological record shows clearly that such a stereotype is inadequate to characterize Aboriginal culture. Rather, the ancestors of the native people of Australia arrived by watercraft by about 40,000 years ago in what had to have been, at least in part, a planned, intentional migration. Beginning with an adaptation to a tropical, coastal environment, they managed by 20,000 years ago to have adapted to the myriad habitats of Greater Australia. Coastal people maintained many of their original maritime adaptations, but others adjusted to the temperate regions of the interior, and some even developed cultural strategies for coping with environments as diverse as the Great Sandy Desert in the interior—one of the hottest, driest places on earth—and the sub-Antarctic tundra of south-central Tasmania. And the lives of these people extended far beyond the quest for subsistence. In Koonalda

Cave, located near Australia's south-central coast, is preserved some of the world's oldest artwork, a series of meandering lines made by human fingers as much as 24,000 years ago—a sort of finger painting in the soft limestone of the cave's ceiling (Johanson, Johanson, and Edgar 1994). As mentioned in Chapter 8, potentially even older art has been dated at Wharton Hill and Panaramitee North, where microscopic vegetable matter recovered from within the grooves of petroglyphs of geometric figures has been dated to 36,000 B.P. and 43,000 B.P., respectively (Bednarik 1993). If these dates hold up (and the methodology is a bit controversial), this Australian aboriginal art will be the oldest known from anywhere in the world.

The lesson of the earliest settlement of Australia is not one of the persistence of a primitive, backward people, but of the nearly infinite capacity of human groups for adaptive flexibility. It is a lesson we will see repeated in the initial discovery of and migration to the Americas.

COMING TO AMERICA

On Thursday, October 11, 1492, a sea voyager had an encounter that forever affected the trajectory of human history—another of those small steps that became a giant leap. Documenting the ship's arrival, the journal of the captain of that momentous voyage reads: "When we stepped ashore we saw fine green trees, streams everywhere and different kinds of fruit. . . . Soon many of the islanders gathered around us. I could see that they were people who would be more easily converted to our Holy Faith by love than by coercion" (Cummins 1992, 94). Thus begins Christopher Columbus's narrative of the first contact between Europeans and American natives since the series of short-lived, brutal incidents on Newfoundland in Canada that were recorded in the Viking sagas about 1,000 years ago (Magnusson and Paulsson 1965).

Thinking he had discovered a series of islands off the coast of Asia, Columbus called the people he encountered *los Indios*, or Indians. After his initial voyage, Columbus returned three more times, always expecting that the Asian continent lay just beyond the limits of his previous exploration. Though Columbus never accepted it, most European scholars concluded that he had happened on, not a cluster of islands immediately off the coast of south Asia, but, as Amerigo Vespucci was to characterize it in 1503, a "new world," populated by peoples unknown to and not even conceived of by Europeans.

This New World consisted of two entire continents that make up almost 28.5% of the world's land surface, with a native population estimated to have been in the tens of millions and speaking more than 1,500 different languages and dialects. Individual groups had adapted to nearly all of the countless habitats of the Western Hemisphere, from frigid arctic tundra to arid sandy deserts, from luxuriant tropical rain forests to temperate woodlands, from seacoasts to mountains, from river valleys to plateaus. And they lived ways of life as varied as did people inhabiting the "known" continents: hunters and gatherers in small, nomadic bands foraging for food in a seasonal round; fisherfolk in established villages, harvesting the plentiful natural resources of river and shore; farmers in huge adobe apartment complexes, tending the kinds of crops that even today feed the population of the planet. There were great kingdoms with impressive cities, splendid monuments of pyramids and palaces, and powerful hereditary rulers, not unlike King Ferdinand and Queen Isabella of Spain, the monarchs who had funded Columbus's expedition.

THE SOURCE OF *LOS INDIOS*

Almost as soon as it was recognized that Columbus had "discovered" a new world with people unknown to his benefactors, questions were raised concerning the origins of those "new" people. True to the spirit of the period, the answers had to conform to biblical interpretation: American natives had to be derived, ultimately, from Adam and Eve and then more recently from those few people who had survived Noah's flood.

Despite broad speculation concerning the source of the Native American population (see Feder 1999 and Williams 1991), quite early on some scholars recognized a connection between the natives of the New World and the people of Asia. In 1555, for example, the Portuguese traveler Antonio Galvão noted physical similarities between Asians and Native Americans in their eyes, noses, and general body shape.

Jesuit missionary Friar Joseph de Acosta (Huddleston 1967) used the Bible to come up with a precociously accurate hypothesis concerning the geographic origins of Native Americans. Acosta pointed out in 1590 that all animals on earth except those onboard Noah's ark had been killed in the great flood. After the flood, he reasoned, the many animals present in the New World must have descended from the animals saved onboard Noah's ark. That is, animals native to the New World must have arrived after the flood by walking into the Americas from the landing place of Noah's ark—according to the Bible, someplace in southwest Asia on "the mountains of Ararat." Acosta argued that what animals could accomplish, people could have done as well.

Thus, there must have been a land connection between the Old and the New Worlds to allow animals descended from those saved on the ark to walk into the Western Hemisphere, Acosta argued. He knew where such a connection could *not* have been, based on sixteenth-century exploration of the American coastline. By a process of elimination, he suggested that the Old World and the New World were probably joined somewhere in northwestern North America and northeastern Asia. That is, the first Americans must have come from Asia, having walked into the New World from the Old World at a point where they were joined. It was not until about 150 years later that Russian

FIGURE 9.4

The modern coastlines of northeast Asia and northwest North America as well as the projected coastline of Beringia during glacial maxima.

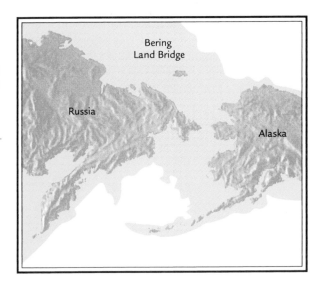

explorer Vitus Bering verified what the native people of northeastern Siberia and northwestern North America had long known: The Old World and the New World are separated by only about 90 km (55 mi) of sea, called the Bering Strait (Figure 9.4).

Today the Bering Strait is only 30–50 m deep (100–165 ft). But during periods of glacial maxima in the Pleistocene, sea level was depressed by far more than this, exposing a platform of land connecting Russia and Alaska that was as wide, perhaps, as 1,500 km (1,000 mi) from north to south. During long periods in the Pleistocene, people in northeast Asia could have walked into the New World across the body of land today called **Beringia,** or the **Bering Land Bridge** (see Figure 9.4).

Early thinkers like Galvão and Acosta were correct. Geographically, a northeastern Asian origin for Native Americans makes sense. Gross anatomical characteristics such as those cited by Galvão have long shown the biological connection between Asians and Native Americans. Modern analysis of the mitochondrial DNA of Native Americans also supports the idea that the aboriginal human population of the New World was derived wholly from Asia (Gibbons 1993; Stone and Stoneking 1993; Wallace, Garrison, and Knowler 1985).

WHEN DID THE FIRST MIGRANTS ARRIVE?

Though anthropologists agree on the geographic and genetic sources of Native American populations, there is still great controversy over the timing of the arrival of the first settlers of the New World. To find out when people first entered the Americas from Siberia we need to know three things:

1. When was Beringia exposed and open for travel?
2. When was eastern Siberia first inhabited (the source population for New World migrants)?
3. What is the age of the earliest New World sites?

When Was Beringia Exposed and Open for Travel?

Actually, the land bridge idea might not be necessary to explain aboriginal migration patterns. If Australia's first settlers could have populated that "new world" as early as 40,000 years ago (remember, there was no land bridge between Sunda and Sahul; they had no choice but to arrive by boat), then northeast Asians might have done the same thing during periods when no land bridge was present between Asia and North America. And even without a land bridge, during periods of extreme cold the Bering Strait would have frozen, producing an ice bridge between the two hemispheres.

Nonetheless, a wide land connection between the two continents would have facilitated the movement of animals and people either through the interior of northeast Asia, then through the middle of the exposed land bridge, and then into the interior of Alaska, or else along the Pacific coast of northeast Asia, then along the southern Beringian coast, and finally south along the coast of northwest North America (see Figure 9.4). Anthropologists know that Beringia was exposed several times during the Pleistocene and was above water more or less continuously from the period beginning about 35,000 years ago until its final inundation about 11,000 years ago (Elias et al. 1996). This range may represent the key interval for migration into the Americas, based on what little is known about the timing of the earliest human presence in Siberia, the population source for the first settlers of the Americas.

When Was Eastern Siberia First Inhabited?

Just as the most likely source area for the original migration of people into Australia is poorly known archaeologically, so too is the most likely source area for the original migration of people into the New World poorly known. Eastern Siberia is a difficult place to do archaeology, and relatively little work has been done there. Archaeologist David Meltzer (1989) points out that we simply do not know when it was first inhabited.

The oldest human occupation of Siberia may have been found at the Diring Yuriakh site. The site has been controversial since it was discovered, with dates in excess of 2 million years ago suggested by some (Bower 1994c). More recently, the site has been carefully excavated and dated to 260,000 years ago (Waters, Forman, and Pierson 1997). The site may represent an occupation of Siberia by *Homo erectus* during a relatively warm interglacial period.

Radiocarbon dates indicate a more certain human presence in central Siberia by at least 20,000 years ago and possibly as much as 34,000 years ago, the latter at the Ikhine site on the lower Aldan River (Table 9.1).

TABLE 9.1

Sample of Sites in Eastern Russia Occupied at Times of Possible Human Population Movement into North America

SITE NAME	LOCATION	AGE	ARTIFACTS
Dyuktai Cave	Central Siberia	After 18,000 B.P.	Wedge-shaped cores, simple bifaces
Ust'-Mil II	Central Siberia	11,500–35,000 B.P.	Wedge-shaped cores
Ikhine	Southern Siberia	31,000–34,000 B.P.	Burins, cores
Ezhantsy	Central Siberia	35,000 B.P.	Wedge-shaped cores, biface fragments
Berelekh	Lower Indigirka Valley	12,000–13,000 B.P.	Bifaces
Ushki Lake	Kamchatka	13,000–15,000 B.P.	Bifaces, burins, microblades, unifaces

Data from F. H. West (1981).

What Is the Age of the Earliest New World Sites?

On the question of the earliest settlement of the Americas, one of the most important sites on the west side of Beringia is Dyuktai Cave, on the Aldan River in central Siberia (Yi and Clark 1985). The radiocarbon method dates the site to about 18,000 B.P. Though some distance from Beringia itself, the site is important for the artifact assemblage it has produced. There are some striking similarities between the small **wedge-shaped cores** and **microblades** struck off those cores at Dyuktai—and at a number of similar, more or less contemporaneous sites in central Siberia—and tools found in Alaska several thousand years later as part of a complex known as the **Paleo-Arctic tradition** (Figure 9.5). Microblades can be set into bone, antler, or wooden handles, producing very sharp, highly effective cutting tools.

Though the area of the earliest Siberian sites is still only poorly known, there appears to be no substantial evidence for human occupation much before 30,000 B.P.; even evidence much before 20,000 B.P. is weak (Meltzer 1993b, 161). Jelinek (1992) may be correct in asserting that until about 25,000 years ago, prehistoric people simply had not yet developed an adaptation for life in arctic regions, so they could not have survived in Siberia. And without adapting to Siberia, they could not have had access to the Bering Land Bridge and the two continents that lay on the other side.

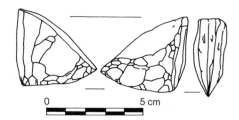
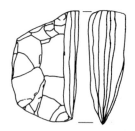

0   5 cm

FIGURE 9.5

These stone tools from the Dyuktai culture, eastern Russia (about 18,000 B.P.), exhibit a preponderance of so-called wedge-shaped cores, small stone cores of the implied shape from which sharp microblades were removed. (From Seonbonk Yi and Geoffrey Clark 1985)

Beringia: Avenue to the New World

Earlier in this chapter, we discussed the initial movement of people into Australia approximately 40,000 years ago: Because Australia has been separated from Asia for millions of years, the first migrants to the island continent must have arrived by boat. They almost certainly were a coastally adapted people who would have been capable of crossing long stretches of ocean, hopping from island to island, until they reached Australia. It is not surprising that migrants who were adapted to life on the southeast Asian coast would expand initially in their new territory along its coast, moving into the interior only later.

The question of the earliest settlement of the Western Hemisphere is complicated by the existence of the Beringian land connection between the Old and the New Worlds. When Beringia became exposed as sea level fell, people adapted to the interior habitats of northeast Asia would have been able to expand their territories by moving east through the interior of the land bridge and then into the interior of northwestern North America. At the same time, people living along the Pacific coast of northeast Asia could have moved along the coast of the land bridge as it became exposed. As sea level continued to fall, the growing coasts of northeast Asia and northwest North America finally coalesced, creating a single coast from northeast Asia, across the newly exposed land bridge coast and then along the coast of northwestern North America. Over several generations, northeast Asians expanding east along this coast would have found themselves in the New World, where they might have continued the process of expansion south along its coast. These migrants, moving through the interior as well as along the coast, would have had no sense that they were moving into a "new world": They merely would have been taking advantage of additional territory (Figure 9.6).

THE FIRST HUMAN SETTLEMENT OF AMERICA

The legend of the midnight ride of Paul Revere tells us that one or two lamplights placed in the window of the Old North Church steeple would signal the mode of the British attack on Boston: "One if by land and two if by sea." Regarding the first "invasion" of America by human beings, there also are two

FIGURE 9.6

Sites representing the earliest occupation of North America and South America.

possible modes of movement; the first migrants may have been an interior-adapted people taking an interior land route, or they may have been a coastally adapted people taking a sea route along the coast. Obviously, to assess which of these is correct—or whether both routes were used simultaneously by different groups—we need to locate the oldest sites in the New World.

It would be convenient if the oldest sites in the New World were located near the point of entry, either in the interior of Alaska for a group arriving by land or along the Alaskan coast for a group arriving by sea. Unfortunately, the Alaskan interior can be a very inhospitable place to conduct archaeology, and many places along the coast that might have provided shelter for a people living and moving within sight of the sea have been inundated by sea-level rise after the last glacial period.

One If by Land

A few ancient sites in northwestern North America have provided evidence of an interior adaptation. The inhabitants of these sites may represent the descendants of people who came from the interior of northeast Asia and then crossed through the interior of the land bridge. For example, Bluefish Caves in western Canada, reasonably close to the Beringian point of entry, has produced artifacts in a level that has been dated to between 15,000 and 12,000 years ago (Cinq-Mars 1978).

Most of the evidence for the late Pleistocene occupation of the interior of the New World, however, has been found far to the south of Alaska. Before we can bring the transplanted Asians from Alaska, south into the rest of the New World, there is an additional environmental issue that must be considered. During the Pleistocene, there were two primary centers of glacial expansion: the **Laurentide** ice sheet in northeastern North America, which spread south, east, and west and covered much of the northern latitudes of this continent, and the **Cordilleran** ice sheet, whose center was in the Rocky Mountains. During glacial maxima, when sea level was at its lowest and the land bridge at its largest, the Laurentide continental glacier reached its western limit, and the Cordilleran mountain glacier reached its eastern limit. Though the two major ice bodies did not wax and wane in synchrony (Catto and Mandryk 1990), it is likely that they coalesced, at least in some places, for periods of time as they simultaneously expanded (Figure 9.7). We know, for example, that at about 18,000 B.P. the two major ice fields coalesced near the present border of British Columbia and Alberta, Canada, across a linear distance of close to 1,200 kilometers (750 miles; Wright 1991).

In other words, the periods when it was easiest for human groups to migrate into Alaska from northeast Asia may have coincided with the periods when it was impossible for them to spread farther south because their way was blocked by an impenetrable ice barrier a few kilometers high. The overall timing and extent of this barrier is still uncertain, but even where and when coalescence did not occur, the so-called **ice-free corridor,** or **McKenzie corridor,** may not have been particularly hospitable for large game animals and, therefore, of little interest to human hunters; much before 14,000 B.P. the corridor was likely a place to avoid rather than enter (Wright 1991). For example, pollen studies indicate that when an ice-free corridor was available for travel, vegetation was too poor to support large populations of animals (Mandryk 1990)—and without animals, humans would have had no reason to be there. Indeed, there is no archaeological evidence of an early human presence in the corridor until about 11,000 years ago (Burns 1990).

The challenges that must have accompanied any attempt to move south of the ice sheets make interpreting the occupation of the Meadowcroft Rockshelter

FIGURE 9.7

Map showing the proposed boundaries of the Cordilleran and Laurentide ice sheets of North America. Though the two may have coalesced in some localized areas during glacial maxima, for long periods an ice-free corridor may have existed by which people south of Alaska could have migrated into North America south of the ice sheets.

(Courtesy of David Meltzer)

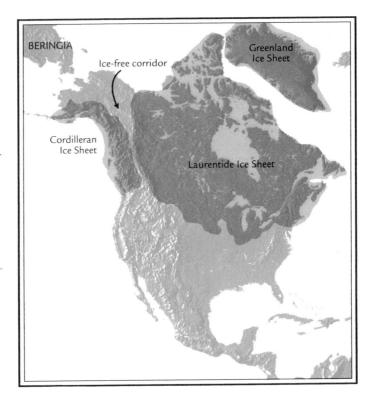

so difficult. Located in western Pennsylvania, south of the ice sheets and thousands of miles from Beringia, it is one of the oldest and most deeply stratified archaeological sites ever excavated in North America. Within the natural rock enclosure, human beings made tools, cooked food, and threw away trash, taking advantage of the natural protection afforded by the small cave. Moving back in time, the excavators of Meadowcroft have chronicled the human occupation of western Pennsylvania, covering a time span of thousands of years (Adovasio et al. 1979–80a,b; Adovasio, Donahue, and Stuckenrath 1990; Carlisle and Adovasio 1984). And at the base of the sequence brought to light by these researchers may be the oldest radiocarbon dates associated with human-made material south of Alaska. Six dates earlier than 12,800 B.P. have been associated with stone tools near the base of the Meadowcroft sequence. Sealed beneath a rock fall from the roof of the shelter dated to 12,000 B.P. were some 400 lithic artifacts, including blades, knives with retouched edges, and an unfluted, bifacial projectile point (Figure 9.8).

As you know, western Pennsylvania isn't anywhere close to Beringia. Since the inhabitants of Meadowcroft could not have parachuted into their habitation, the necessary implication is that we should be able to find an extensive archaeological trail of sites successively older still, leading from Pennsylvania

FIGURE 9.8

Stone tools from the earliest indisputable cultural layer at the Meadowcroft Rock-shelter in western Pennsylvania. The layer in which these tools were found dates to more than 12,800 years ago. (Courtesy of James Adovasio, Mercyhurst Archaeological Institute)

back to Beringia, reflecting the movement of people through an ice-free corridor, south of the glaciers, and then east—but such a trail simply does not exist. It has been suggested that patterns of erosion and deposition in the late Pleistocene in North America were not at all conducive to site preservation, so the discovery of undisturbed early sites in stratigraphic context is unlikely (Butzer 1991). Perhaps we simply haven't looked in the right places or the sites are barely visible archaeologically. The other possibility, of course, is that we have found no trail of sites because there is none, suggesting that Meadowcroft is younger than we think.

Two If by Sea

The Monte Verde site in Chile is located on Chinchihuapa Creek and exhibits a remarkable degree of preservation (Dillehay 1987, 1989, 1997a,b; Dillehay and Collins 1988). In addition to hundreds of stone artifacts, including long, slender spearpoints and cutting and scraping tools, the excavators of the site, led by archaeologist Tom Dillehay, also found wooden lances and stakes that likely held down the bases of the inhabitants' hide-covered tents (Figure 9.9). The wet peat that covered the site produced an environment in which the bones of animals killed and butchered at the site and even pieces of meat and skin tissue (identified as mastodon) and fragments of almost 70 different plant species were preserved. Thirty radiocarbon dates firmly date the site to 12,500 years ago.

Located near the coast, Monte Verde might best be explained as the remains of a community whose distant ancestors had entered the New World along the Beringian coast, obviously long before 12,500 B.P.. Archaeologist David Meltzer suggests that the age of the Monte Verde site implies a time of entry into the New World along the Beringian coast before 20,000 B.P. (1997,

FIGURE 9.9

These stone tools from Monte Verde, in Chile, date to as early as 12,500 B.P. (Courtesy of Tom Dillehay)

755). These people traveled south along the Pacific coast of the New World—virtually all of their sites would have been submerged by rising sea level and cannot be found. Eventually, these people reached the southern coast of South America, where they then moved into the interior, leaving the remains at Monte Verde.

New and very important data from the South American coast offer evidence for an ancient, coastally adapted people (Pringle 1998b). At one section of the southern Peruvian coast, the floor of the sea slopes away sharply from the shore. As a result, and unlike most stretches of the coast, when sea level rose at the end of the Pleistocene, the shoreline did not move much. Two archaeological teams, working independently, have located two sites—Quebrada Jaguay (Sandweiss et al. 1998) and Quebrada Tacahuay (Keefer et al. 1998)—that are among the oldest sites found in South America.

Dating to 11,100 B.P., Quebrada Jaguay presents clear evidence of a maritime adaptation by its occupants. Hunting was not a significant contributor to the diet at Quebrada Jaguay, and the remains of very few terrestrial mammals have been found. On the other hand, the bones of numerous, quite small drumfish, most likely caught by nets, and a large assemblage of the shells of wedge clams indicate that the inhabitants of the site depended on the sea for subsistence. At 10,700-year-old Quebrada Tacahuay, the sea was the major source for subsistence. Close to 100% of the bones recovered at the site were those of marine creatures, with a focus on anchovies and cormorants (a sea bird).

Though both of these sites are substantially younger than Monte Verde, they are clear indications of an early coastal occupation of the New World. Their ancestors—and the ancestors of the inhabitants of Monte Verde—were most likely coastally adapted northeast Asians who took a coastal route across the Bering Land Bridge into the New World.

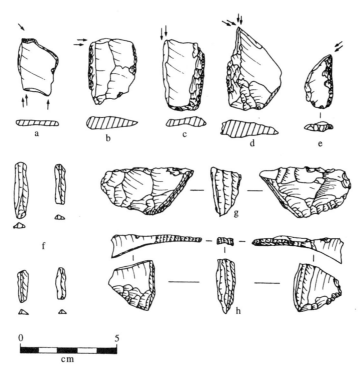

FIGURE 9.10

These stone tools from the Denali Complex of Alaska, dating to after 11,000 B.P., include some wedge-shaped cores (g and h), suggesting a derivation from the older wedge-shaped cores in Asia (see Figure 9.5). (Courtesy of William Powers)

ALASKA

Back in Alaska, close to the Beringian point of entry, are a number of sites dating to before 11,000 B.P. As archaeologists William Powers and John Hoffecker (1989) point out, it is now clear that there was a widespread tradition of producing small blades from wedge-shaped cores in northeast Asia and northwest North America at the end of the Pleistocene. Sites with wedge-shaped cores and microblades have been excavated in Siberia, China, Japan, and Mongolia, as well as in Alaska and northwestern Canada (Morlan 1970). These sites are older in the Old World than in the New World, and a "genetic" connection between the industries of western and eastern Beringia seems clear. Conceivably, these sites may represent a separate wave of population movement from the Old World to the New.

Denali and Nenana

Sites exhibiting tools of the locally designated **Denali Complex** of wedge-shaped cores, microblades, bifacial knives, and **burins** have been excavated in the Nenana Valley, about 100 km (62.5 mi) southwest of Fairbanks, in east-central Alaska (Figure 9.10; Powers and Hoffecker 1989). Sites such as Dry Creek (Component II), Panguingue Creek (Component II), Usibelli, and Slate

Creek in the Nenana Valley are assigned to the Denali Complex; Dry Creek has produced a radiocarbon date of about 10,700 B.P. (Powers and Hamilton 1978). Denali Complex sites outside of the Nenana Valley include Donnelly Ridge in central Alaska, the Campus Site near Fairbanks, the Teklanika River sites in Mt. McKinley National Park, and Healy Lake (West 1967). These all date to around 10,000 years ago (West 1975). A very different-looking industry of microblades and cores has been found in the earliest levels at the Onion Portage site (Akmak) in western Alaska, also dating to around 10,000 B.P. (Anderson 1968, 1970).

All this seems to provide a very neat and simple answer to questions surrounding the first human settlement of the Americas: Beginning some 18,000 years ago, microblade-making northeast Asians slowly made their way across Beringia, ending up in Alaska by about 10,700 years ago or a few hundred years earlier. The problem is that Denali Complex sites are not the oldest in the New World; they're not even the oldest in Alaska. There is a cultural level at Dry Creek (Component I) earlier than the Denali level at the same site, and the Moose Creek and Walker Road sites have produced radiocarbon dates ranging between 11,000 B.P. and 11,800 B.P. in their lowest levels. The stone-tool assemblages at these sites—classified as the **Nenana Complex**—show no evidence of Denali Complex wedge-shaped cores and look very little like the stone-tool assemblage at Dyuktai. Instead, these assemblages include bifacially flaked spearpoints (Figure 9.11). Interestingly, an assemblage consisting of a broad array of bifacial spearpoints has been identified at a series of sites around Ushki Lake in the central Kamchatka peninsula in eastern Russia. Ushki is dated to about 14,000 years ago (Dikov 1978; Dikov and Titov 1984).

The Nenana Complex may be derived from the industry seen at Ushki in Kamchatka, representing an early movement of Asians (about 12,000 B.P.) across the Bering Land Bridge into the New World. Following the hypothesis of West (1981), Powers and Hoffecker (1989) suggest that the Siberian microblade industry seen at sites like Dyuktai may be at least indirectly ancestral to the later Denali Complex (dated to about 11,000 B.P.) and other early New World microblade industries. Denali, in this view, represents a migration subsequent to an earlier movement of Siberians with a bifacial industry like that seen at the Ushki and Nenana Complex sites.

As Powers and Hoffecker see it, the Denali Complex was restricted to the far north. However, in their view, possessors of the earlier Nenana stone-tool tradition were able to expand to the south. Archaeologists Ted Goebel, Roger Powers, and Nancy Bigelow (1991) point out that, with the exception of fluted spearpoints (to be discussed shortly), the Nenana stone-tool assemblage is virtually identical to that seen to the south and associated with these points. Descendants of these people, Powers and Hoffecker argue, made a small technological step in spearpoint form—the so-called **fluted point**—that allowed for an enormous adaptive leap and the successful occupation of two continents.

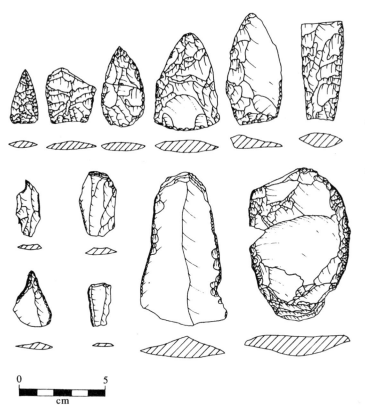

FIGURE 9.11

In these stone tools from the Nenana Complex of Alaska, dating to 11,800 B.P., the lack of wedge-shaped cores, the presence of bifacially flaked tools, and dates that are older than those associated with the Denali Complex suggest a different and older migration of northeast Asians into the New World. (Courtesy of William Powers)

CLOVIS

As already stated, in Powers and Hoffecker's view, the Nenana Complex, which derived from industries originating in Siberia and included a heavy component of bifacially flaked spearpoints, is the ultimate source for the most widespread and successful of the late Pleistocene cultures of the New World. Sometimes called **Clovis,** for the site in New Mexico where the distinctive spearpoints that characterize the tool assemblage were first recognized, these **Paleoindian** sites number in the hundreds and are found throughout the continental United States. Where dates have been derived through ¹⁴C, almost all Clovis sites fit into a narrow range, between 11,200 B.P. and 10,500 B.P., appearing virtually simultaneously across much of the New World (Haynes 1982, 1987, 1992). The actual "calendar" ages of these sites may be even a bit greater. Variations in some of the conditions affecting radiocarbon dating (for example, the amount of ¹⁴C in the atmosphere) during the late Pleistocene suggest that these sites (and all other sites worldwide dated by radiocarbon to the same time period) are actually about 2,000 years older than their radiocarbon dates; in other words, the oldest Paleoindian sites are actually 13,200 years old (Fiedel 1999). For the sake of consistency and to avoid additional confusion,

FIGURE 9.12

The flutes, or channels, on both faces of this Paleo-indian Clovis projectile point from the Lamb site in western New York State extend less than halfway up the point. Clovis dates to between 11,200 and 10,500 B.P. (Courtesy of Michael Gramly, Great Lakes Artifact Repository; drawn by Val Waldorf)

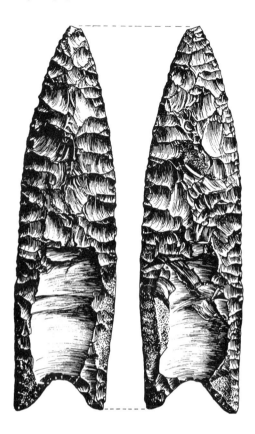

we will continue to refer to the radiocarbon ages of sites; you simply need to keep in mind that these radiocarbon ages do not necessarily translate directly into actual calendar dates.

The oldest human skeletons yet found in the New World date to approximately this same Paleoindian period. The Arlington bones from Santa Rosa Island in California (Owen 1984) have recently produced a date of 13,000 B.P., making them the oldest human remains in the New World. The female skeleton from Midland, Texas (originally called "Midland Man" but now known to have been a female) has been dated by uranium series to 11,600 years ago (Hoppe 1992). A small number of other human remains have been dated, with varying degrees of certainty, to the period between about 11,500 and 10,500 years ago: the Tepexpán skeleton from Mexico; the Pelican Rapids find (known as "Minnesota Man," another misidentified female); the Marmes skull from Washington state; and Wilsall (Anzick) in Montana.

Clovis Technology

Clovis spearpoints are distinctive in having a channel, or flute, on both faces (Figure 9.12; see Color Plate 8). The channel, made by removing (usually) a single broad flake from both faces of the point, originating at the base and ordinarily extending one-quarter to one-third of the way toward the tip, is assumed to have been an aid in hafting the stone point onto a wooden shaft. As mentioned previously, this small technological step seems to have resulted in an adaptive leap that allowed for the rapid expansion of human groups across the New World. This great leap forward is strictly an American invention. It was not part of any western Beringian technology, nor is it present in the Nenana Complex in Alaska. With one very uncertain possible exception (King and Slobodin 1996), fluted points are unknown in northeast Asia and are, in fact, older in the American Southwest than in Alaska. The recently excavated Mesa site in northern Alaska has produced about 50 bifacially flaked spearpoints, none of which possesses a channel. The Mesa site's 13 radiocarbon dates range from 9700 B.P. to 11,700 B.P. (Bower 1993a) and may be contemporary with fluted points farther south. Michael Kunz, the excavator of the Mesa site, maintains that the points there are not directly related to fluted points and represent yet another separate and distinct early stone-tool industry in northwestern North America (Bower 1993a, 215).

The rapid, almost simultaneous appearance of fluted points throughout much of the New World is striking. Whereas there are either no sites or, at best, very few sites in America dated to before 12,000 years ago (see "Issues and Debates"), there is a virtual explosion of Clovis sites in the American Southwest and beyond, dating to after 11,200 B.P. (Haynes 1992). Stratified sites such as Clovis, Lehner, Murray Springs, Dent, Colby, and Domebo, all in the Southwest, produced fluted spearpoints and dates in that time range (Haynes 1982).

But Clovis points are also found throughout Canada, the continental United States, and Mexico. In the Northwest, the spectacular Richey Clovis Cache in central Washington State (see Color Plate 8), an apparent ceremonial interment of huge fluted points as much as 23.25 cm (a bit more than 9 in.) in length, has been dated at 11,200 B.P. (Gramly 1993; Mehringer and Foit 1990). In the American Northeast and Southeast, thousands of fluted points have been recovered from hundreds of sites (Anderson 1990). Sites may be younger in the East—but not much: The Vail site in Maine has produced radiocarbon dates of 10,300 B.P. and 11,120 B.P. (Gramly 1982); the mean radiocarbon age of the Debert fluted-point site in Nova Scotia is 10,600 B.P. (MacDonald 1985); and Templeton (6LF21) in Connecticut has been dated to 10,190 B.P. (Moeller 1980).

Even at the most distant New World spot imaginable from Beringia, Fell's Cave at the southern tip of South America (Tierra del Fuego), a fluted point in association with the bones of extinct horse and sloth has been recovered from a site dated to 10,000 years ago (Bruhns 1994). Nonfluted fishtail points were also found in Fell's Cave and in other sites dating to this time in South America at sites such as Palli Aike, also in Tierra del Fuego, Los Toldos in Patagonia, and El Inga in northern Ecuador. Long, leaf-shaped El Jobo points were found at Taima Taima in Venezuela, also dating to the late Pleistocene.

The Clovis Advantage

It is not entirely clear what it was about the Clovis adaptation that allowed its bearers to spread so quickly across two continents. The Americas south of the ice sheets must have been a treasure trove for a people whose subsistence depended, at least in part, on hunting (Haynes 1964, 1980b). Ecologist Paul S. Martin (1987) has jokingly referred to the New World, with its abundant big-game resources, as "Clovisia, the Beautiful." Imagine a continent teeming with animals—animals that had never seen a human hunter, with no fear of this puny, two-legged beast. There were mammoths, mastodons, bison, horse, caribou, musk ox, ground sloths, giant beavers, tapirs, and more, all ripe for the taking by efficient hunters who had very little competition (Martin and Guilday 1967). A new hunting technology such as the fluted spear may have been a key factor in the success of the culture. Even a small initial population, given a reasonably high birth rate, could have moved out in a rapid wave of population expansion, resulting in the narrow range of the Clovis radiocarbon dates (Martin 1973; Mosimann and Martin 1975).

Clovis Subsistence

The megafauna (big-game) hunting component of Paleoindian subsistence has been exaggerated in the past. Kill sites tend to be highly visible archaeologically, with their large complement of bones, broken weapons, and butchering equipment (see the "Case Study Close-Up"). Though the image of Paleoindians risking life and limb to track down and kill a two-ton, hairy elephant is more romantic, they most probably relied on root grubbing, seed gathering, and small-mammal trapping, at least some of the time (Meltzer 1993a; Johnson 1991). Still, some Paleoindians, like the Inuit people (Eskimos), must have relied on hunting, since little else was available in their territories. During some parts of the year, most Paleoindian groups relied on hunting for survival. But once past the glacial and periglacial north and onto the American plains, they could find and exploit many other foods, including seeds, nuts, berries, fish, and small mammals. Away from the glacial front, where animals may have been the only consistent source of food—for example, in the woodlands of eastern North America—Paleoindians were probably "generalist foragers" who not only took big game when the opportunity presented itself but also exploited smaller game and plant foods in their territories (Dincauze 1993).

Nonetheless, large game animals played a part in their economy. C. Vance Haynes points out that the remains of the extinct North American elephants, woolly mammoth or mastodon, have been recovered from the majority of Clovis sites in the American West, where animal bones have been preserved (1982, 390). When these elephants became extinct around 11,000 years ago, the Paleoindians in the western United States shifted their hunting focus to bison. The technology changed, producing shorter spearpoints, but with channels extending almost to the tip. These so-called **Folsom** points (Figure 9.13) are of the culture that bears the same name and includes sites such

FIGURE 9.13

Folsom points are younger and generally smaller than Clovis points, and the flute extends nearly the entire length of the point. This is a Paleoindian fluted Folsom point from the Johnson site, Colorado. (Courtesy of Michael Gramly, Great Lakes Artifact Repository; drawn by Val Waldorf)

as Lindenmeier in Colorado (Wilmsen 1974), Olsen-Chubbuck in Colorado (Wheat 1972), and Casper in Wyoming (see the "Case Study Close-Up"; Frison 1974a,b).

Though the makers of the fluted points may have been the bearers of the first widely successful New World culture, it would be a mistake to consider all of the earliest inhabitants of the Americas as Clovis hunters. Paleoindians lived and thrived in diverse habitats, including the tropical rain forest to the south. One site in South America displaying the great range of Paleoindian adaptation has been excavated by a team of researchers led by archaeologist Anna C. Roosevelt (Roosevelt et al. 1996). The Caverna da Pedra Pintada site is located in the Amazon basin in Brazil. The researchers recovered more than 30,000 stone flakes and 24 formal tools, including triangular, stemmed bifacial points from a layer in the cave that has been radiocarbon-dated to between 10,000 and 11,200 years ago. Paleoenvironmental evidence recovered at the cave—in particular, preserved remains of plants and animals used by the inhabitants—shows quite clearly that when the site was occupied, the area was, as it is today, a tropical rain forest. Big game was only a part of the diet; abundant remnants of tree fruits, fish, mollusks, and birds, as well as small game, attest to the broad food base of the cave's occupants.

In the same layer as the Paleoindian artifacts, hundreds of lumps and drops of red pigment and two spalls of painted cave wall were found. The chemistry of the drops of red pigment match that of painted images found on the cave wall, implying a similar age for the paintings. The Pedra Pintada paintings, therefore, may be the oldest known examples of cave art in the New World.

INTO THE PACIFIC

The Pacific Ocean, the last great frontier on the planet that humans have explored and settled (with the exception of the modern investigation of Antarctica), covers one-third of the earth's surface. It stretches 15,500 km (9,600 mi) from north to south and 20,000 km (more than 12,000 mi) from east to west. Its total area is about 180 million km^2 (70 million mi^2).

Europeans, considered relative latecomers, did not cross the Pacific until Ferdinand Magellan's circumnavigation of the globe in A.D. 1519–22. Close to a thousand of the 25,000 islands scattered across the ocean were already inhabited—and had been for a few thousand years—by the time of Magellan's voyage.

A Pacific Islander "Age of Exploration"

The fascinating story of the initial exploration and settlement of the Pacific belies the cultural conceit that the "age of exploration" began and ended in the European Renaissance. The successful exploration and colonization of

Pacific islands by a people without some of the technological advantages of European explorers (such as quadrants, sextants, compasses) is all the more remarkable when you consider the following: The total landmass of the 25,000 Pacific islands represents only 0.7% of the total area of the ocean, and average island size is only about 10 km by 6 km (6 mi by 4 mi) (Terrell 1986, 14). Some of the inhabited islands are far smaller. Though many of these islands are geographically clustered and "intervisible" (visible one from the other), the individual clusters are often separated by hundreds, even thousands, of kilometers. Simply finding such island clusters while sailing a small canoe required great skill and not just a little luck. Finding one's way home and then returning to settle the newly discovered island was nothing short of miraculous.

Yet, discover, explore, and colonize many of those islands is precisely what settlers from southeast Asia and New Guinea did. And they accomplished this largely as the result of intentional geographic expansion. Certainly serendipity played a role in the peopling of the Pacific. Though countless sailors must have been blown off course and died before making it to safe haven, some lucky ones may have made accidental landfall on uninhabited islands and become their permanent settlers. But this cannot be the primary way in which Pacific islands were colonized. Just as Europeans in the fifteenth century began deliberately to explore the oceans, the southeast Asians and New Guineans must have been doing the same many years before. As archaeologist Geoffrey Irwin (1993, 7) points out, "We know colonisation was deliberate, because explorers took with them the plants and animals, women and men necessary to establish viable settlements." In other words, colonization of the Pacific was largely planned, and colonists brought with them the people and things necessary for the successful establishment of new communities (Figure 9.14).

Geoffrey Irwin (1993) has, with his colleagues S. H. Bickler and P. Quirke (1990), conducted computer simulations of exploration and colonization strategies in the Pacific. They have shown that, under the right conditions and when the right search strategies are applied, even Pacific islands at great distance from each other can be safely and successfully explored and colonized, with return trips possible to the original homes of the migrants. They have shown graphically and mathematically that, as archaeologist John Terrell (1986, 72) has suggested, to the highly skilled navigators and sailors of ancient Polynesia, "the sea must have been more an enticing highway than an encompassing barrier."

Pacific Geography

The Pacific islands are usually divided into three groupings: **Melanesia**—the so-called black islands of New Guinea and smaller islands to the east, including the Solomon Islands, the Bismarck Archipelago, Santa Cruz, New Caledonia, Vanuatu, and Fiji; **Micronesia**—the "small islands" north of Melanesia; and **Polynesia**—"many islands," including a broad triangle of islands

FIGURE 9.14

Modern Polynesians use traditional navigational techniques to travel hundreds of miles across the open ocean, much as their ancestors did when they initially explored and settled the Pacific islands. (Transparency K6306, courtesy of Department of Library Services, American Museum of Natural History)

demarcated at its points by Hawaii to the north, Easter Island to the southeast, and New Zealand to the southwest.

Pacific Archaeology

Some of the larger islands of Melanesia, including New Britain and New Ireland in the Bismarck Archipelago, were settled by seafaring explorers from Australia by at least 35,000 years ago, not that long after the initial settlement of the island continent (O'Connell and Allen 1998). Even farther to the east, Buka, in the Solomon Island chain, was discovered and settled no less than 28,000 years ago. At a distance of 180 km (110 mi) from the Bismarck Archipelago, the initial settlement of the Solomons is proof of sophisticated navigational skills on the part of the settlers. The Melanesian islands farther to the east and in deeper water, as well as all the islands of Micronesia and Polynesia, were settled much later in a second wave of exploration and migration beginning probably little more than 3,500 years ago (Irwin 1993).

We know from the ethnographic record that the native peoples of the Pacific were brilliant navigators. They built up a substantial reservoir of knowledge about currents and wind patterns. Even without navigational devices, the native navigators of the Pacific could reckon by the stars, were familiar with cloud patterns indicating that land was nearby, possessed a detailed knowledge of bird flight paths from island to island, and constructed seaworthy ships capable of journeys across wide stretches of open ocean.

The spread of people through east Melanesia and Polynesia was accompanied by a common culture. Because they were a maritime people, fishing played a significant role in their food quest. They also were food producers, who brought non-native agricultural staples with them as they colonized

FIGURE 9.15

Lapita pottery is found virtually everywhere Polynesians explored and settled after 3500 B.P. (Courtesy of Dr. Richard Shutler, Jr., and Dr. Mary Elizabeth Shutler)

islands; these staples included pig, as a major source of animal protein, and domesticated root crops, especially yams. They also brought a common pottery style, called **Lapita** (Figure 9.15). In fact, the earliest occurrence of a human population on the inhabited islands of Polynesia is invariably marked by the appearance of Lapita pottery. The Lapita designation is now applied to the entire cultural complex of Polynesia and includes a maritime adaptation, the raising of pigs, the growing of certain root crops and fruit trees, the use of shell in producing tools and ornaments, and the manufacture of Lapita pottery.

The Lapita complex is absent from Australia or the islands of Micronesia. It appears first in the archaeological record of the Bismarck Archipelago and, perhaps, Fiji a little more than 3,500 years ago (Irwin 1993, 39). Expansion proceeded eastward, with large island groups like Samoa, the Cook Islands, and the Society Islands being settled in turn, after about 2,500 years ago. The Hawaiian Islands, far to the north, were settled by about 1600 B.P. (about A.D. 400); Easter Island, at the eastern limit of Polynesia, was settled at about the same time. New Zealand, though much closer to the Australian coast, was

FIGURE 9.16

Altogether there are more than 800 of these stone sculptures in various conditions and positions on Easter Island. (Courtesy of Sonja Gray)

settled not by natives of that continent, but by Polynesians. The earliest evidence for a human presence on New Zealand dates to about A.D. 1000.

Why the Pacific Islands Were Settled

Irwin (1993, 211–12) lists some of the possible motives for the expansion into the vast and previously uncharted Pacific: curiosity about what lay beyond the horizon, a desire to find areas suitable for habitation and rich in resources, and the need to find new land as a result of overpopulation or warfare. As Irwin points out, motives are not testable archaeologically. And, as Terrell (1986) indicates, the motives to move out into the Pacific were likely as mixed and as varied as those of Europeans in their own age of exploration.

Whatever the reasons, the many inhabited islands of the Pacific, populated initially by people possessing very few, rather homogenous cultures, produced a wide array of adaptations once they were settled. Settlers exploited the most valuable resources, developing their own unique adaptations to each island or island chain. On New Zealand, the moa—a large flightless bird unique to that nation—became a major component in the diet of a hunting society. Powerful and complex agricultural societies arose on Hawaii and Tonga (Kirch 1984). The fascinating people of Easter Island developed great skills at organizing their own labor, which enabled the quarrying, carving, transportation, and erection of the hundreds of enormous sculpted stone heads that have generated such interest and speculation (Figure 9.16). All of today's enormous diversity developed from those first courageous voyages across the vast Pacific Ocean a few thousand years ago.

WHO WERE THE FIRST AMERICANS AND WHEN DID THEY GET HERE?

Linguistic Diversity

Were the coastal-living ancestors of Monte Verde's inhabitants the first Americans? How about the ancestors of Meadowcroft Rockshelter's interior-dwelling residents? Did the first northeast Asians cross through the interior of the Bering Land Bridge or along its coast? Did the initial migration occur about 20,000 years ago or even earlier? Or are the dates from Monte Verde and Meadowcroft somehow incorrect? Did the first people to populate the New World enter at about 13,000 or even only 12,000 years ago and soon thereafter develop the fluted Clovis spearpoint? Unfortunately, at this point in time, the archaeological record is unclear on all of these questions.

The "Clovis first" hypothesis has been supported for some time by the linguistic analysis of Joseph Greenberg (Greenberg, Turner, and Zegura 1986). Greenberg's linguistic analysis suggested that there are three distinct language groupings among modern Native Americans and, therefore, that there had been three distinct waves of population movement into the New World from northeast Asia: the ancestors of most American Indians beginning at about 12,000 years ago, then a second wave of migration of Na-Dene speakers (Indians living along the northwest coast of North America), and most recently speakers of Eskimo and Aleut.

Recently, however, a consensus has been growing among linguists that the number and diversity of Native American languages would have required far more than 12,000 years to develop. Linguists have devised a number of crude methods for measuring change in languages—how long it takes for languages to diverge, first becoming different dialects and then becoming mutually unintelligible languages. No one believes these linguistic clocks are entirely accurate; but assuming they are in the right ballpark, linguists such as Johanna Nichols (1990) maintain that 22,000 years is the minimum amount of time it would have taken for a small initial group of migrants to spread throughout North and South America and develop the astonishing array of languages spoken by native people here. In fact, 30,000 or even 40,000 years are reasonable estimates of the time depth implied by the degree of diversity present in American Indian languages (Gibbons 1998).

Genetic Diversity

When the mitochondrial DNA (mtDNA) of Native Americans was analyzed, four distinctly different DNA clusters were discovered (Gibbons 1993, 1996b; Stone and Stoneking 1993). All Native Americans exhibit one of the clusters, and all four are found in each of the three linguistic groups defined by Greenberg (Greenberg, Turner, and Zegura 1986). These four DNA clusters are also found among northeast Asians, but none of them are ever found in Africans, Europeans, or Australians.

This evidence certainly supports the notion that Native Americans are transplanted Asians. More recent genetic research goes beyond merely associating the native peoples of the New World with Asians; it also seeks to measure how long ago the American natives became separate from their source population or populations in the Old World. A European team of geneticists has looked at the mtDNA data and has suggested that the amount of genetic variation in Native Americans, when compared to native northeast Asians, suggests a separation of 20,000 to 25,000 years (Gibbons 1996b).

Unfortunately, linguistic and genetic clocks cannot yet be precisely calibrated. They provide us with some tantalizing clues about the timing of the first migration into the New World, but they cannot prove when it occurred—at least not yet. The most reliable clock we now have for dating the earliest migration of people into the New World is that of radiocarbon-dated material in precise stratigraphic context at undisturbed archaeological sites left behind by those first Americans. Archaeologists will, of necessity, continue to search for the material remains of those people—and they will almost certainly succeed.

WHO IS KENNEWICK MAN AND WHAT DOES HE HAVE TO DO WITH THE SETTLING OF THE AMERICAS?

The so-called Kennewick Man is a 9,300-year-old skeleton found in Washington State in July 1996. It is among the older—though not among the very oldest—human skeletons found in the New World. The controversy that has erupted around this particular find is twofold: A local Indian tribe has claimed ownership of the remains and wants to rebury the individual with no further analysis, while, at the same time, some research indicates that the skeleton exhibits non-Asian, distinctly European, characteristics (Morell 1998).

Some have jumped to the conclusion that if Kennewick possesses some "Caucasian" skeletal features and does not possess the stereotypical suite of Asian, or "Mongoloid," features, then he must be a representative of an unsuspected, very early colonization of the New World by Europeans—a possibility for which no evidence has been presented in this book simply because no such evidence exists.

Most skeletal features used to distinguish one population from another appear in statistically measured frequencies. Many or perhaps most members of a group may possess a certain skeletal morphology; but in most cases, not all members of the group possess each of these features. Kennewick Man's lack of certain features that are typical of Native Americans proves very little about where he came from and what his genetic heritage is.

We can only hope that when controversy over the skeleton subsides, DNA analysis will clear up lingering questions about the origin of Kennewick Man. No one should be surprised if, though lacking in some of the more typical skeletal features of Asians or American natives, he exhibits one of the four mtDNA haplogroups restricted to these very groups.

WHAT—OR WHO—KILLED THE AMERICAN MEGAFAUNA?

Ecologist Paul S. Martin's "Pleistocene overkill" hypothesis (Martin 1967; and see Martin and Wright 1967) involves a compelling scenario: The first human migrants to the American heartland find a flourishing bestiary that would put any modern African game park to shame. The seemingly limitless food source allows these paleohunters to expand their population at a rapid rate, ultimately filling two continents. Yet the seeds of their destruction are planted in the magnitude of their success. Large game animals, their populations already stressed by the changing climate at the end of the Pleistocene, are overhunted and ultimately suffer extinction. The human hunters at the root cause of this disaster go on to shift their adaptive strategies to other resources, having little choice but to drastically restructure their subsistence and their culture.

This scenario would be remarkable if it were true. We in the late twentieth century are well aware of our role in the destruction of habitat and the endangering of species—all wrought by our technologically sophisticated hand. Could ancient people with little more than stone spears similarly have caused the extinction of numerous species of animals? Thirty-five genera (and many species) suffered extinction in North America around 11,000 B.P., soon after the appearance and expansion of Paleoindians throughout the Americas (27 genera disappeared completely, and another 8 became locally extinct, surviving only outside of North America; Grayson 1987, 8).

Although climate changed at the end of the Pleistocene, warming trends had happened before (see Figure 5.9). A period of massive extinction of large mammals like that seen about 11,000 years ago had not occurred during the previous 400,000 years, despite those changes (Guthrie 1990). The only apparently significant difference in the Americas 11,000 years ago was the presence of human hunters of these large mammals. Was this coincidence or cause-and-effect?

We do not know. Ecologist Paul S. Martin has championed the model that associates the extinction of large mammals at the end of the Pleistocene with human predation. He has co-authored a work (Mosimann and Martin 1975) in which a computer simulation showed that in around 300 years, given the right conditions, a small influx of hunters into eastern Beringia 12,000 years ago could have spread across the New World in a wave and wiped out game animals in a "blitzkrieg" (their term) to feed their burgeoning population.

The researchers ran the simulation several ways, always beginning with a population of 100 humans in Edmonton, Alberta, Canada, at 11,500 years ago. Assuming different initial North American big-game-animal populations

(75–150 million animals) and different population growth rates for the human settlers (0.65%–3.5%), and varying kill rates, Mosimann and Martin (1975, 314) derived figures of between 279 and 1,157 years from initial contact to big-game extinction.

Many scholars continue to support this scenario. For example, geologist Larry Agenbroad (1988) has mapped the locations of dated Clovis sites alongside the distribution of dated sites where the remains of woolly mammoth have been found (in both archaeological and purely paleontological contexts). These distributions show remarkable synchronicity (Agenbroad 1988, 71).

There are, however, many problems with this model. Significantly, though a few sites are quite impressive (see the "Case Study Close-Up"), there really is very little archaeological evidence to support it. Writing in 1982, Martin himself admitted to the paucity of evidence; for example, at that point, the butchered remains of only 38 individual mammoths had been found at Clovis sites (Martin 1982, 403). In the years since, few additional mammoths have been added to the list; there still are fewer than 20 Clovis sites where the remains of one or more butchered mammoths have been recovered (Agenbroad 1988, 66), a miniscule proportion of the millions that necessarily would have had to have been slaughtered within the overkill scenario.

Though Martin claims the lack of evidence actually supports his model (the evidence is sparse because the spread of humans and extinction of animals occurred so quickly), this argument seems weak. And how could we ever disprove it? As archaeologist Donald Grayson (1987) points out, in other cases where extinction resulted from the quick spread of human hunters—for example, the extinction of the moa, the large flightless bird of New Zealand mentioned earlier—archaeological evidence in the form of butchered remains is abundant. Grayson (1991) has also shown that the evidence is not so clear that all or even most of the large herbivores in late Pleistocene America became extinct after the appearance of Clovis. Of the 35 extinct genera, only 8 can be confidently assigned an extinction date of between 12,000 and 10,000 years ago (Grayson 1991, 209). Many of the other genera, Grayson argues, may have succumbed before 12,000 B.P., at least half a century *before* Clovis showed up in the American West.

Ultimately, environmental change at the end of the Pleistocene may have played a more significant role in the widespread extinctions that occurred at this time among large game animals. Biologist R. Dale Guthrie (1990) suggests that the Pleistocene–Holocene boundary was unlike previous periods of warming and resulted in far more drastic consequences for large herbivores hunted by humans and also for small rodents and other species not part of Clovis subsistence. Geologist Ernest Lundelius (1988) proposes that the end of the Pleistocene produced climates that displayed greater seasonality—more seasonal differences in temperature and precipitation. As climate became more seasonal, biotic diversity decreased because extreme seasonal conditions made large areas uninhabitable for many species. This, Lundelius maintains, was the primary cause of late Pleistocene extinction.

As of this moment, which factors were key and which were incidental in the extinction of large American mammals at the end of the Pleistocene is unclear. As most researchers admit, it will take years of research to solve this puzzle.

CASE STUDY CLOSE-UP

At the Naco site in Arizona, a single mammoth was slaughtered by Paleoindian hunters more than 11,000 years ago. Eight large fluted points were found resting in the skeleton of the dead prehistoric elephant.

At the Lehner site, also in Arizona, 13 elephants were killed by Clovis hunters brandishing spears tipped with fluted points (Haury, Sales, and Wasley 1959). The age profile of the Lehner mammoths is catastrophic. In other words, the age spread of the mammoths killed at the site (from 2 to 30 years) is similar to the age spread in a living group of elephants. This suggests to archaeologist J. Saunders (1977) that the Lehner mammoths do not represent 13 individual, random kills of elephants in nearly the same spot over an extended period. Instead, it suggests that an entire small family group of adult, adolescent, and juvenile elephants was killed at the same time. Though some have questioned whether Clovis hunters equipped with only stone-tipped spears could have killed so many elephants at one time (Haynes 1982), the age profile is significant.

The hunting skills of the Paleoindian hunters at the Casper site in Wyoming have been questioned by no one (Frison 1974a,b). Though they ordinarily lived in small hunting bands for much of the year, several bands coalesced in a larger encampment during the late summer and fall, when the bison were traveling in larger groups and were relatively easy to herd. The bringing together of small bands for communal hunts also allowed for the reinforcement of social connections and trade and gave young people an opportunity to find suitable mates in other bands.

A bit more than 10,000 years ago, a small group of bison approached the dune field at what is today the Casper archaeological site. Using whatever natural cover was available, perhaps camouflaging themselves with brush and even smearing themselves with bison dung to mask their human smell, the hunters quietly surrounded the beasts—members of an extinct subspecies (*Bison bison antiquus*) of today's American buffalo (*Bison bison bison*). As the bison approached the edge of the sand dune, the hunters burst from their hiding places, creating an enormous amount of noise and commotion.

Heeding their instinct to flee when threatened, the beasts rushed headlong into what appeared to be the only safe avenue, where no hunters were in their way. But instead of escape, the bison found a natural trap as they stampeded into the sandy hollow on the leeward side of the parabolic dune, precisely where the hunters had intended them to go. The animals quickly became mired in the soft sand. They panicked as they dimly perceived their predicament and then quickly exhausted themselves, trying helplessly to extricate their huge bulks on hooves intended for long treks across the hard ground of the plains, not the soft footing of sand. They became easy targets

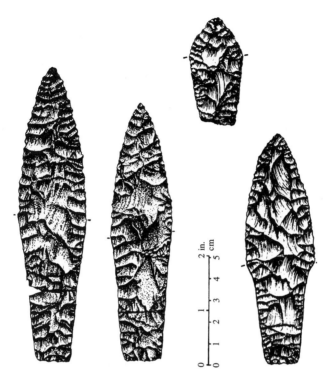

FIGURE 9.17
These projectile points from the Casper site in Wyoming were probably used to kill bison who were stampeded into the leeward side of a parabolic sand dune about 10,000 years ago. (Courtesy of George Frison)

for human hunters wielding stone-tipped spears (both fluted Folsom points and an unfluted variety called "Hell Gap"; Figure 9.17). Nearly 80 bison were caught, killed, butchered, and eaten by the Paleoindians at Casper (Figure 9.18, p. 270). After eating their fill and then drying and preserving the huge quantity of meat left over, the various bands went their separate ways, perhaps to meet again in another year and another place where the bison could be hunted yet again.

Most larger natural history and university museums in the United States have displays on the earliest human settlement of the New World and information regarding Paleoindians. For example, the Denver Museum of Natural History devotes space to the Dent site Paleoindian mammoth kill as well as the Folsom site, showing the original points in situ, between the ribs of an ancient bison. The University of Colorado Museum has an informative display on the Olsen-Chubbuck Paleoindian bison kill site. In the East, the Thunderbird Museum and Archaeological Park in Front Royal, Virginia, has displays on the Thunderbird Paleoindian site. Excavations conducted by the museum in the Shenandoah Valley are open to visitors interested in witnessing archaeological excavation. In the Southwest, the Blackwater Draw Museum, located between Clovis and Portales, New Mexico, devotes part of its display to the nearby Blackwater Draw Paleoindian site.

VISITING THE PAST

FIGURE 9.18

This is part of the bison bone bed at the 10,000-year-old Casper site in Wyoming. The animals were trapped in the sand by the ancient hunters and then killed with projectile points like those shown in Figure 9.17. (Courtesy of George Frison)

SUMMARY

In the late Pleistocene, expanding human populations intruded into new territories and, ultimately, migrated into three previously uninhabited continents: Australia, North America, and South America. Australia was populated by coastally adapted southeast Asians. Using watercraft, by accident and perhaps through intentional exploration, they moved out into the western Pacific, inhabited the oceanic islands of Borneo, Sulawesi, and Timor, and eventually made landfall on Greater Australia: New Guinea, Tasmania, and Australia proper. Archaeological evidence offers a date for this habitation of 40,000 years ago—possibly more—during a period of lowered sea level, when the trip by watercraft would have been easier than it is today. The first settlers maintained a tropical/coastal orientation to their economy, initially turning inland only along major rivers. The dry interior of the continent was settled about 20,000 years later.

During the Pleistocene, the New World was intermittently connected to the Old World by a vast land bridge, making it possible for interior-dwelling people in northeast Asia to travel through the interior of the land bridge into the interior of northwest America and for coastal people in northeast Asia to travel along the southern Beringian coast onto the coast of northwestern North America and from there south.

Sites as distant from the land bridge as Monte Verde in Chile (dated to 12,500 B.P.) and Meadowcroft Rockshelter in western Pennsylvania (dated to 12,800 B.P.) imply a much earlier time of entry onto the land bridge—20,000 years ago or possibly more—but no definitive archaeological evidence of sites this old in the New World has yet been found. Many sites that would have been evidence of migrants taking a coastal route to the south were long ago inundated by rising sea level at the end of the Pleistocene. Interior sites may be so ephemeral that finding them could be almost impossible.

Several early sites in Alaska and the Canadian Yukon date to the period immediately after 12,000 years ago and bear lithic industries analogous to those in Siberia. Some of the early settlers moved south, perhaps through an ice-free corridor, into the American West, where they invented a new projectile-point technology. The projectile's fluted points allowed these settlers to expand across two continents. These Clovis people may not have been the first arrivals; some sites in both North and South America may be older. But Clovis represents the first broadly successful occupation of the New World.

TO LEARN MORE

Technical Summaries

Though by archaeological standards an old book, J. Peter White and James F. O'Connell's *A Prehistory of Australia, New Guinea, and Sahul* (1982) is still the best synthesis of the archaeology of Greater Australia. For the best recent summary of the controversy over the timing of the earliest settlement of Australia, see James F. O'Connell and Jim Allen's 1998 piece, "When Did Humans First Arrive in Greater Australia and Why Is It Important to Know?" in the journal *Evolutionary Anthropology* (volume 6, issue 4).

Frederick Hadleigh West's *The Archaeology of Beringia* (1981) is still a useful source on the connection between Siberia and the first settlement of the New World. A newer book on Beringia edited by West is *American Beginnings: The Prehistory and Paleoecology of Beringia* (1996). For an evenhanded treatment of the controversy over the earliest settlement of the Americas, read David Meltzer's 1993 article, "Pleistocene Peopling of the Americas" in the journal *Evolutionary Anthropology.* For a personal perspective on the controversies concerning the acceptance of the early date for the Monte Verde site in Chile, see "The Battle of Monte Verde," by that site's principal researcher, Tom Dillehay, in the journal *The Sciences* (January–February 1997).

For detailed information about the Paleoindian adaptation to the Americas, see the numerous articles in *Clovis: Origins and Adaptations,* edited by Rob Bonnichsen and K. L. Turnmire (1991). Two excellent sources on the colonization of the Pacific are John Terrell's *Prehistory in the Pacific Islands* (1986) and Geoffrey Irwin's *The Prehistoric Exploration and Colonisation of the Pacific* (1993).

Popular Summaries

For a nontechnical discussion of the archaeology of the first Australians, see Josephine Flood's *Archaeology of the Dreamtime* (1990).

David Meltzer's book, *Search for the First Americans* (1993), in the Smithsonian's series Exploring the Ancient World, remains one of the most thorough and best-written examinations of who the first Americans were and when they got here. Meltzer's short article in the weekly magazine *Science,* "Monte Verde and the Pleistocene Peopling of America" (1997), provides the current archaeological consensus on the significance of that site. Take a look at E. James Dixon's *Quest for the Origins of the First Americans* (1993) for useful discussions about the archaeology of northeast Asia, the early American Arctic, and Paleoindians. For a very well written account of one of the oldest archaeological sites in the American Arctic—Bluefish Caves—see *In Search of Ancient North America,* by science writer Heather Pringle (1996).

On the Web

An excellent Internet resource on the topic of the initial human migration into the New World has been provided by The Center for the Study of the First Americans. The information on this organization's Web site is absolutely up-to-date and allows you to see the various controversies about the timing and geography of the first human settlement of the Americas unfold on the homepage. This homepage can be found at http://www.peak.org/csfa/csfa.html. Electronic versions of the Center's newsletter, *The Mammoth Trumpet,* can be found at http://www.peak.org/csfa/mthome.html. Concerning the archaeology of the Pacific islands, visit the University of Otago (New Zealand) Web site at http://www.otago.ac.nz/Anthropology/Pacific/research.html.

KEY TERMS

Sunda (or Sundaland)	wedge-shaped core	Nenana Complex
Sahul	microblade	fluted point
Wallace Trench	Paleo-Arctic tradition	Clovis
Wallacea	Laurentide	Paleoindian
fire-cracked rock	Cordilleran	Folsom
gracile	ice-free corridor (or	Melanesia
robust	McKenzie corridor)	Micronesia
Beringia (or Bering Land	Denali Complex	Polynesia
Bridge)	burin	Lapita

10

After the Ice

CULTURAL CHANGE IN THE POST-PLEISTOCENE

CHAPTER OVERVIEW

The end of the Pleistocene was marked by massive, long-term climate change. Human beings throughout the world faced the challenge of adapting to the new environments being established in the early Holocene.

Different societies responded in different ways. In many areas subsistence shifted as plant and animal species became locally extinct. Small mammals and plant foods increased in importance in some regions. Some groups intensified the subsistence quest, focusing on particularly rich resources. As a result, some societies became more sedentary. Most areas were marked by increasing cultural diversity.

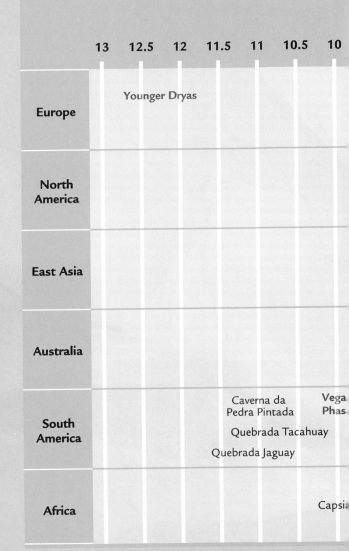

	13	12.5	12	11.5	11	10.5	10
Europe		Younger Dryas					
North America							
East Asia							
Australia							
South America				Caverna da Pedra Pintada Quebrada Tacahuay Quebrada Jaguay			Vega Phas
Africa							Capsia

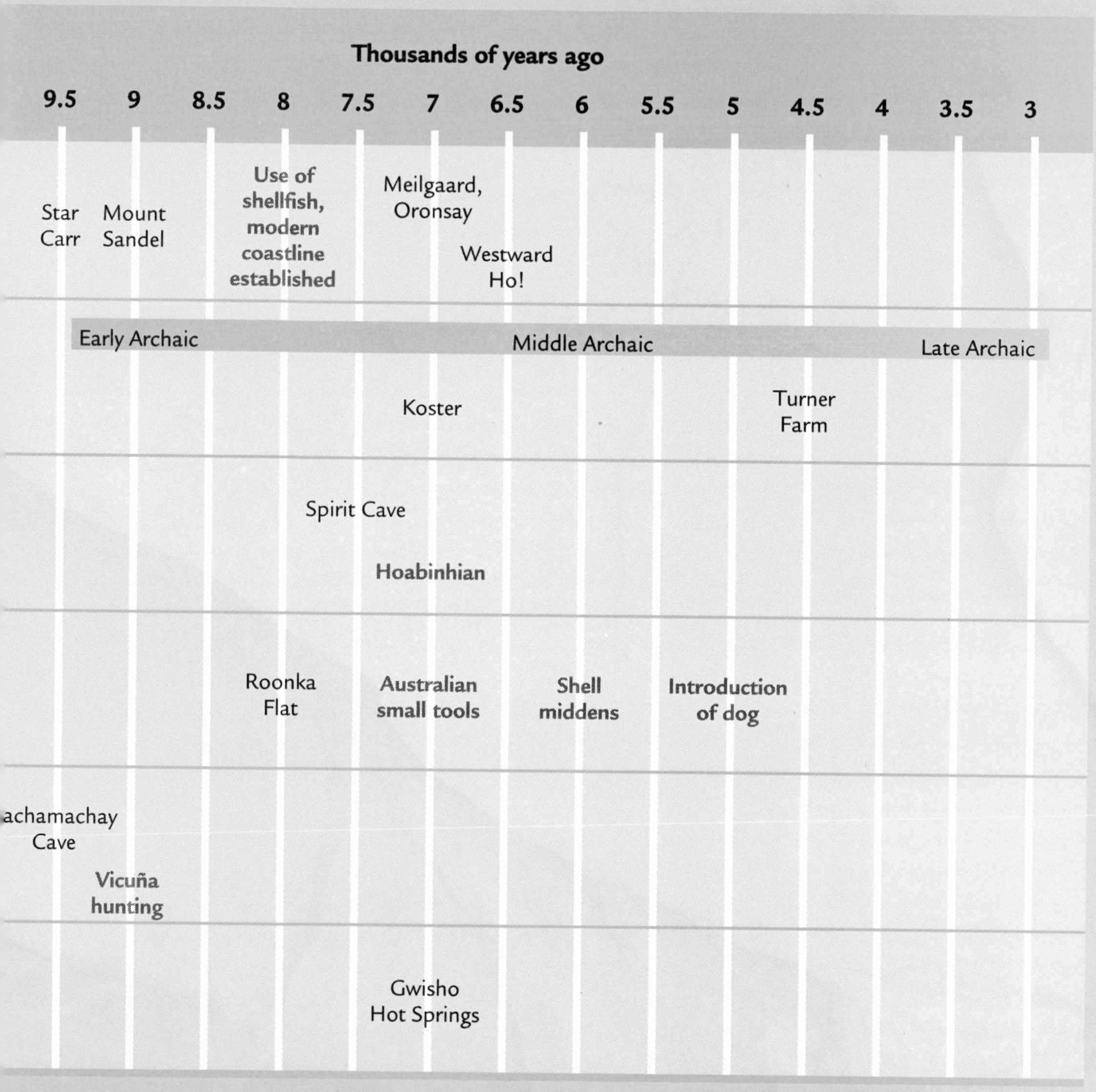

Thousands of years ago

9.5	9	8.5	8	7.5	7	6.5	6	5.5	5	4.5	4	3.5	3

Star Carr

Mount Sandel

Use of shellfish, modern coastline established

Meilgaard, Oronsay

Westward Ho!

Early Archaic   Middle Archaic   Late Archaic

Koster

Turner Farm

Spirit Cave

Hoabinhian

Roonka Flat

Australian small tools

Shell middens

Introduction of dog

achamachay Cave

Vicuña hunting

Gwisho Hot Springs

PRELUDE

We tend to think of the Pleistocene as enormously distant in time from us. The Ice Age isn't *our* age; it's a time when conditions were much colder and glaciers covered large portions of the earth that today are home to tens of millions of people. We blithely refer to the period after 10,000 years ago as the Holocene (recent) epoch, as if giving it a separate name ensures that our time is different and our climate more pleasant and constant than that of times past.

But this pleasant view is almost certainly false. In Figure 5.9 we saw variations in the ^{18}O content of seawater and, by inference, the amount of glacial coverage on land. That figure shows a series of other breaks from cold climate—long **interglacials** and shorter **interstadials**—other remissions from glaciation during the Pleistocene. The current, relatively ice-free period most likely is simply another break in Arctic-like conditions over much of the higher elevations and higher latitudes, an interglacial inevitably to be followed by another descent into glacial conditions.

Deep cores taken in the Greenland ice cap, where ice formed in strata that can be analyzed for air temperature during each period of formation, indicate that we are in the most recent of a series of relatively warm periods punctuating the last 90,000 years (Monastersky 1994a). The previous interglacial lasted about 20,000 years (from 135,000 to 115,000 years ago), and at least one of the ice cores taken in Greenland indicates wild swings of climate even within that relatively warmer period (Monastersky 1994b). With that as our guide, then, perhaps we are only about halfway into an interglacial, and glacial conditions are poised to return in 10,000 years.

Even when we look back into the recent past, we see relatively short-lived, minor "blips" in the warm trend that has characterized the earth's climate for the last 10,000 years. In fact, the climate from the mid-twelfth to the mid-nineteenth centuries has been characterized as a "Little Ice Age." Historical records make it clear that this short relapse into glacial conditions had a significant impact on the agricultural patterns and lives of millions of Europeans and Americans (Grove 1988).

For example, historical records as well as paleoclimatological data indicate a significant, though brief, cooling trend between A.D. 1150 and 1400. The Vikings were forced to abandon their western Greenland colony by A.D. 1345 as expanding pack ice and a sharp increase in the number of North Atlantic icebergs made the voyage between the colony and Scandinavia treacherous and as life on Greenland became increasingly harsh.

Things warmed up between A.D. 1400 and 1550, but then cooled off again for another three centuries. In the mid-nineteenth century, when another warming trend commenced—a trend we probably are still in (but for how long?)—people were once again forced to respond and readapt to the new climatic conditions.

But any adaptations developed in response to such short-term, small-scale environmental changes pale in comparison to what it must have been like between 12,000 and 10,000 years ago, when enormous, fundamental, and sometimes quite abrupt changes in climate occurred, changes so vast that they often rendered previous human subsistence systems untenable. Certainly, human groups were faced with environmental changes at the end of the Pleistocene, and they needed to adjust their way of life in response to those changes if they were to survive. But the end of the Pleistocene cannot be described as just an overall, measured, steady warming trend that human groups might readily adjust to. Conditions were in a far more severe state of flux, with the climate oscillating between the new warmer temperatures and previous colder temperatures. This set of circumstances was far less stable and, in fact, more difficult for human groups to adapt to, especially when we consider that these changes were taking place on a time scale of a few or even, in some cases, a single human generation (Stager and Mayewski 1997).

From the cave painters of Upper Paleolithic Europe to the mammoth hunters of central Asia, from the Paleoindian hunters of Pleistocene megafauna in the New World to the reindeer hunters of northern Europe, from the lakeside dwellers of southeast Australia to the lake dwellers of central Africa—people were faced with massive and rapid changes in their accustomed environments. Temperatures rose, ice sheets melted, coastlines were inundated and reconfigured, large herbivores became extinct, new game and unfamiliar plant life invaded home territories, lakes dried up, and weather patterns changed. The old ways of living no longer meshed with changed climates, altered habitats, and different floral and faunal populations.

Human beings had little choice but to adapt, move, or die. Where they could, some groups shifted territories, trying to follow conditions with which they were most familiar. Others may have seen their cultures wither and die as conditions changed more rapidly than they could or were willing to respond to. Many groups, however, changed their ways of life by adapting to the new conditions of the Holocene. Their cultural response to the changes wrought by the end of the Pleistocene is the focus of this chapter.

The key characteristic of the cultures of the early Holocene is adaptive change, reflected in the following features:

CHRONICLE

- In most places the archaeological record shows that human groups quickly shifted their subsistence focus as the animals and plants on which they previously had relied became extinct or unavailable in their home regions.
- In some regions the post-Pleistocene subsistence base changed from megafauna to smaller animals, fish, shellfish, and birds and included a greater reliance on plant foods previously absent or rare during glacial conditions.
- In other regions, rather than a broadening, the subsistence shift involved more intensive exploitation of some uniquely productive elements in

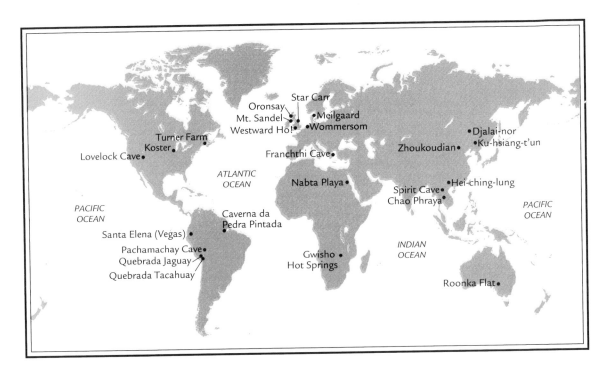

FIGURE 10.1

Sites of the early post-Pleistocene.

the food quest. More intense exploitation means there was a focus on a small number of highly productive resources in those areas where such resources existed—for example, wild cereal grasses in the Middle East.

- In some areas, the focus on certain abundant resources encouraged a shift from a nomadic existence to a more sedentary one.
- Various groups responded in unique ways to their newly established, heterogeneous conditions, producing far more cultural diversity, even within relatively circumscribed regions, than seen across vast geographical expanses during the Pleistocene.

The discussion will now turn to how various world regions reflected these cultural changes. Unfortunately, while vast regions during the Paleolithic can be readily characterized in terms of cultural adaptations, that cannot be done for the cultures of the Holocene. After the Pleistocene, the cultural situation becomes far more complicated, and an increasing number of distinct adaptations evolved in many different regions. The picture is so complex that only a brief description of some of the best-known adaptations to life "after the ice" will be presented (Figure 10.1).

EUROPE

A warming trend can be deduced from the pollen record of Europe for the period after 16,000 B.P. This trend was sufficient to render even Scandinavia

FIGURE 10.2

As this map of the coastline of Europe during the early Holocene shows, broad areas that were dry land 9,500 years ago are today under the sea. (Courtesy of T. Douglas Price)

ice-free just 3,000 years later, by about 13,000 B.P. This warming was interrupted at least once by a rapid and severe shift back to glacial conditions. This so-called **Younger Dryas** interval began soon after 13,000 years ago and appears to have lasted for about 1,300 years, until about 11,600 years ago (Severinghaus et al. 1998). Paleoclimatologists studying air trapped in bubbles in Greenland's ancient ice have estimated that at the peak of the return to glacial conditions during the Younger Dryas, mean air temperature at the summit of Greenland may have been as much as 15°C (27°F) cooler than it is today—and that huge drop in mean temperature occurred during the course of only about a decade (Severinghaus et al. 1998). Mean air temperature in Europe would have been similarly depressed when compared to modern, interglacial conditions.

The Younger Dryas was, nevertheless, a relatively minor deviation from a trend that would result in near-modern conditions across much of Europe by 8500 B.P. (Gamble 1986; Price 1991; C. Smith 1992). Sea level was rising, too, breaking the connection between Great Britain and the continent by 8,000 years ago and establishing modern coastlines relatively soon thereafter (Figure 10.2; Megaw and Simpson 1979; C. Smith 1992).

Though the northernmost reaches of the continent retained their Arctic-like characteristics, the Pleistocene tundra and its suite of large game animals, including woolly mammoth and rhinoceros, wild cattle, horse, and reindeer, was gone throughout most of Europe after 9000 B.P. The cold-loving grasses and sedges of the tundra on which those large herbivores subsisted were replaced first by birch and pine trees and later by elm and oak to the south. The gregarious megafauna whose huge migratory herds were accommodated by the treeless expanse of the tundra could not exist in or migrate through the expanding, dense woodlands. These large animals were replaced by smaller, less mobile, forest-dwelling animal species, including red deer, roe deer, and wild pig, along with even smaller fur-bearing animals such as marten, beaver, otter, and wolf (Price 1991). As archaeologist T. Douglas Price (1991, 190) points out, the key characteristic of the environment of Holocene Europe when compared to that of the Pleistocene was the vast array of plants and animals available for exploitation. Thus, the most salient feature of the food resource base of post-Pleistocene Europe was its diversity.

It was to the extremely diverse mixture of plants and animals establishing themselves in post-Pleistocene Europe that human groups adjusted themselves. This diversity, both within and between regions, helps to explain the cultural record of Europe after the ice. The European **Mesolithic**—the cultural period that follows the Paleolithic in Europe and precedes the appearance of farming cultures—was marked by many of the features of post-Pleistocene cultures (see earlier list).

Mesolithic Subsistence Patterns

Archaeologist Christopher Meiklejohn (1978) points out the greater diversity of species exploited by Mesolithic Europeans than by their Paleolithic forebears. In a survey of seven Mesolithic sites in Great Britain and France, 11 different large-animal species were reported, with an average of 4 different species at each site (Meiklejohn 1978, 67). Upper Paleolithic sites in northern Europe commonly have only a single large mammal species represented.

Sites of the **Maglemosian** culture of the Mesolithic exemplify the broadening of the subsistence quest as well as the spread of a sedentary way of life made possible by the establishment of productive Holocene habitats. Maglemosian people built sizable semipermanent villages on the margins of large, post-Pleistocene lakes in northern Europe (see the "Case Study Close-Up").

The Irish site of Mount Sandel shows evidence of the use of seasonally available resources that together span the entire year, beginning 9,000 years ago (Price 1987, 250). This, along with the size of the substantial residential structures—circular buildings about 6 m (20 ft) in diameter—argues for a degree of permanence of occupation not seen previously.

In the cold climate of post-Pleistocene northern Europe, hunting was a significant element in the subsistence quest. Mesolithic sites ordinarily produce a wide array of animal food species, including red deer, roe deer, elk, wild ox, wild sheep, goat, pig, and rabbit. Small fur-bearing mammals such as wolf, fox, badger, beaver, marten, squirrel, and hare were used by these Mesolithic people, almost certainly for their warm pelts.

Charred seeds provide evidence for the significance of plant foods in the Mesolithic diet. Hazelnut shells are commonly found in Mesolithic sites in northern Europe, and the hazelnut and other nut foods, along with water lily and wild apple, probably made a significant seasonal contribution to the diet (Price 1987). At Mesolithic sites in southern France, a wider array of plant-food remains have been recovered, including vetch, lentils, and chickpeas (Price 1987).

Although rising post-Pleistocene sea levels have inundated most Mesolithic coastal sites and many ancient lakes have become dry land (see Figure 10.2), there still is evidence of the extensive use of lake and coastal resources during the Mesolithic. Modern dredging in the English Channel and the North Sea to facilitate ship traffic has brought up Mesolithic bone and antler artifacts from sites now located many meters underwater (Price 1987). Where local topography has preserved the ancient coast, Mesolithic sites are numerous. Excavation of such sites has shown an extensive reliance on coastal resources. Of greatest significance was the pike, a saltwater fish that enters inland channels and inlets to spawn. But the bones of cod, ling, perch, bream, eel, and haddock have also been recovered (Clark 1980). Marine mammals are also found in Mesolithic contexts. Species that were hunted include ringed, harp, and gray seals. The remains of hunted or beached whales and porpoises are also found. Fifty-five different bird species have been found in Mesolithic sites. For example, at Mount Sandel in Ireland, the remains of duck, pigeon, dove, grouse, goshawk, and capercaillie were excavated (Price 1987, 248).

Shellfish also made an important contribution to the diet in coastal localities. For example, at the Danish site of Meilgaard, a shell **midden** with a volume of 2,000 m³ (21,000 ft³) was made up of millions of mollusk shells (Bailey 1978). In Portugal, coastal middens consisting primarily of mollusk shell are common for the period after 7400 B.P. Mesolithic shell middens dot the island of Oronsay, 30 km (20 mi) off the west coast of Scotland (Mellars 1978). Crab and limpet shells, along with the bones of seal, fish, and 30 species of birds, were found among the food remains (Price 1987). At Westward Ho! in north Devon, England, Mesolithic kitchen middens of oyster, winkle, mussel, and limpet shells have been dated to more than 6,500 years ago (Price 1987).

Diversity and Regionalization

Regionalization is another process seen clearly in European Mesolithic sites. While a single lithic tradition characterized the Middle Paleolithic across much of Europe and while only a few geographically demarcated, different, but related traditions were present there in the Upper Paleolithic, the Mesolithic period in Europe was marked by a far more diverse cultural pattern.

For example, the **Hamburgian** cultural tradition of the northern European Upper Paleolithic was quite homogenous throughout northern Europe. Whereas at most 3 geographically separate and distinct stone-tool traditions within the Hamburgian have been recognized, archaeologist T. Douglas Price (1991, 199) counts at least 15 different regional stone-toolmaking patterns by the end of the Mesolithic.

Cultural regions of the European Upper Paleolithic—as determined by the geographical extent of archaeological sites where similar tool styles and types are found—have been estimated to encompass as much as 100,000 km² (42,250 mi²). During the Mesolithic, defining cultural regions or territories the same way results in a far greater number of much smaller territories, more on the order of 1,000 km² (422.5 mi²) each (Price 1991, 200).

It seems clear that various groups settled into their own distinct regions in Europe after the Pleistocene, evolved their own adaptations to their unique set of local postglacial environmental conditions, and developed their own tool assemblages and their own distinctive patterns of subsistence and settlement.

Trade in the European Mesolithic

Mesolithic trade networks expanded, but in a pattern different from that established during the Upper Paleolithic (Price 1987). While trading networks actually extended over longer distances in the Upper Paleolithic (see Chapter 8), trade during the Mesolithic was more intraregional. Lithic raw materials were exchanged in greater amounts, but trading was generally restricted to within smaller cultural regions. In other words, materials didn't move as far, but more of them were moving through the more geographically restricted regional systems.

For example, obsidian from the Mediterranean island of Melos is found abundantly in Mesolithic levels of Franchthi Cave on the Greek mainland. English Portland chert was traded, but only within England and not more than 240 km (160 mi) from its source. Brown quartzite from Wommersom in Belgium and the southern Netherlands has been found spread across a restricted area in northern Europe, at Mesolithic sites no more than 120 km (78 mi) from the source (Clark 1980) and almost always within an area about 250 km by 200 km (160 mi by 130 mi; Figure 10.3; Price 1991, 200).

Innovation in the Mesolithic

The European Mesolithic was also a time of great innovation. Early evidence of the manufacture of canoes is dated to the Mesolithic. The use of bow and arrow may predate the Mesolithic, going back perhaps more than 15,000 years to the Upper Paleolithic. The earliest evidence for the use of the bow in Europe, however, dates to between 8000 B.P. and 9000 B.P. in northern Europe. In addition, the bones of wolflike animals have been found at Star Carr (see the "Case Study Close-Up"), dating to before 9000 B.P. These animals had not been used for food; and based on their relatively small size and the crowded

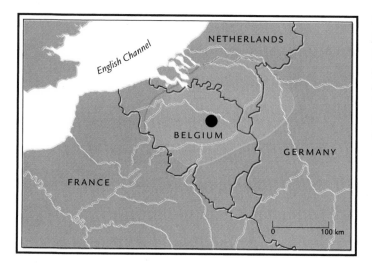

FIGURE 10.3

Map showing the distribution of Wommersom quartzite (lighter area) during the Mesolithic. The black circle marks the source of the stone.
(Courtesy of T. Douglas Price)

nature of their teeth, they seem to have been removed from a purely wild state. In fact, the wolflike bones at Star Carr and many other Mesolithic sites are examples of domesticated wolves—that is, dogs (Clark 1980).

NORTH AMERICA

Though the post-Pleistocene prehistory of the New World is distinct from that of the Old World, parallel patterns are apparent in the human response to the end of the Ice Age in both hemispheres. As in Europe, with deglaciation and the extinction of large herbivores that accompanied the end of the Pleistocene, the archaeological record bears witness to a dramatic shift in culture in North America after 10,000 B.P. Whether purely a result of climate change, overhunting, or some combination of the two (see Chapter 9), the massive disappearance of large game animals necessitated dramatic changes in the cultures of the Native Americans of the early post-Pleistocene.

New World prehistorians have recognized the great cultural changes that accompanied the end of the Pleistocene by bestowing a different name on the cultures of this period. In Europe, the Upper Paleolithic is followed by the Mesolithic; in America the Paleoindian period is followed by the **Archaic,** lasting from about 9,000 to 3,000 years ago. The Archaic represents a complex era when specific adaptations to the different climatic and environmental regimes became established across North America.

Regionalism in the New World Archaic

Archaic cultures of North America traditionally have been divided geographically, as adaptations to the post-Pleistocene Arctic, the Desert Archaic of the

FIGURE 10.4

Lake Forest Archaic people exploited the shores of the Great Lakes and other large inland bodies of water. Chipped-stone spearpoints are typical artifacts of this culture. (Artifact drawings from *A Typology and Nomenclature for New York State Projectile Points,* by William A. Ritchie, 1971, reprinted with the permission of the New York State Museum and Science Service; photo by K. L. Feder)

Great Basin, the Southwestern Archaic, the Eastern Archaic, Central Archaic, and Western Archaic (Willey 1966). In other words, various prehistoric people in North America began following their own adaptive pathways in the face of the new conditions being established at the end of the Pleistocene.

Even this geographic breakdown masks the diversity within these regions. As in Europe, regionalization is the hallmark of the post-Pleistocene of North America. For example, archaeologist Dean Snow (1980), in his synthesis work on the archaeology of New England and New York State, further breaks down the Archaic cultures based on region, subsistence focus, and other behavioral characteristics. Snow describes a **Lake Forest Archaic** tradition (northern New England west of Maine and western New York), which apparently developed as a response to the unique conditions of the areas adjacent to the Great Lakes and the lake region of western New England. The material culture shows a heavy reliance on **lacustrine** (lake) resources, with a settlement pattern of home bases on lake shores occupied in the spring and seasonal winter and summer hunting in the uplands surrounding the lakes (Figure 10.4).

Snow's **Maritime Archaic** is situated on New England's north Atlantic coast—primarily in Maine but also extending north into New Brunswick. Sites such as Turner Farm in Maine, dating to 4,600 years ago, show a clear subsistence focus on sea resources. Bone fishhooks, net weights and plummets, and faunal remains indicate that fish was a major component of the diet; even **pelagic** (open ocean as opposed to coastal) creatures like swordfish were hunted from open boats in the deep sea. Human burials were filled with finely crafted objects such as long slate knives and carvings of whales and dolphins (Figure 10.5). The human remains were powdered with red ochre (a

FIGURE 10.5

The Maritime Archaic people developed an adaptation that focused on resources of the Atlantic coast (the southern coast of Maine is shown here). Ground-stone artifacts are typical of this culture. (Artifact drawing from C. C. Willoughby's *Antiquities of the New England Indians,* 1935; photo by K. L. Feder)

mineral), giving the name "the Red Paint People" to these Archaic inhabitants of coastal Maine. The rich maritime resources allowed for sedentary coastal home bases.

Snow also defines a **Mast Forest Archaic** for most of southern New England. The term "mast" refers to the acorns and other nut foods from trees (hickory, beechnut, chestnut, walnut) that accumulate on the ground of the forest and serve as food for animals. These Mast Forest Indians focused on the rich resources of the river-drained woodlands of New England. They hunted deer and trapped small animals, fished in the rivers using nets and weirs as well as hooks and lines, collected acorn, hickory, walnut, and chestnut in the fall and the seeds, leaves, and roots of wild plants in the spring (Figure 10.6).

While deep-sea fishing and marine mammal hunting in New England seem to have been the exclusive province of the Maritime Archaic tradition, the use of shore resources was not confined to them. The Mast Forest Archaic also has a coastal component, with a heavy reliance on shellfish such as oyster, scallop, soft-shell clam, and quahog. Before development in shoreline communities destroyed them, large shellfish middens were common in Mast Forest Archaic coastal sites in Connecticut and Massachusetts.

The same pattern of cultural regionalization in the Archaic is repeated elsewhere in North America. Piñon nuts were a major component of the diet throughout much of the desert West. The Archaic occupation of the desert shows a subsistence focus on desert lakes that are now dry, low-lying areas called sinks. For example, at Lovelock Cave, in Nevada, paleofeces provide direct evidence for the diet of its Archaic inhabitants. The cave was located

FIGURE 10.6

The Mast Forest Archaic cultural pattern is centered in the thickly wooded valleys of southern New England (a Connecticut woodland is shown here). Chipped-stone spearpoints are typical of Mast Forest Archaic artifacts. (Artifact drawings from *A Typology and Nomenclature for New York State Projectile Points,* by William A. Ritchie, 1971, reprinted with the permission of the New York State Museum and Science Service; photo by K. L. Feder)

near a desert lake (now the dry Humboldt Sink). Virtually all of the food remains retrieved from the preserved human feces in the cave came from the lake and its immediate environs (Heizer and Napton 1970) and included duck, mudhen, chub fish, and plant foods like cattail and wetland grasses.

In the Arctic, the resources of the coast were heavily exploited by the Holocene inhabitants, with evidence of seal, sea lion, walrus, and puffin as major elements in the diet. In the far West, nut foods became key elements in the diet, establishing a subsistence pattern that would continue into the historic period.

Koster: Emblem of the Archaic

Perhaps no site in the American Midwest exemplifies better the Archaic period than the Koster site in Illinois (Struever and Holton 1979). Adjacent to the Illinois River, the site is the location of a series of villages dated from soon after the end of the Pleistocene. The inhabitants of all periods exploited the rich and seasonally varied habitat. In fact, the environs of the site were so economically rich from the standpoint of subsistence that as early as 7,000 years ago the inhabitants were cutting down sizable trees and constructing permanent houses. This was far earlier than for the permanent villages that appeared in most of ancient North America, usually only after the introduction of an agricultural way of life.

The Archaic people of Koster hunted deer, small mammals, and migratory fowl, including ducks and geese. The carbonized seeds of wild smartweed, sunflower, goosefoot, pigweed, and marsh elder were found at the site and were major contributors to the diet (see the discussion of the domestication of these crops in Chapter 11). Fish and freshwater shellfish were collected in the river, and nut foods such as hickory, hazelnut, and acorn were harvested seasonally in the uplands around the river valley. Ground nuts, wild duck potatoes, cattail shoots, pecans, pawpaws, persimmons, and sassafras root rounded out the broad subsistence base at Koster.

A Diverse Set of Adaptations

The focus on locally available foods and the development of highly specialized and localized economies is the most characteristic feature of the Archaic in North America. Evidence is provided by the foods eaten, the types of settlements people lived in, and the material culture seen in archaeological excavations. No longer is a single artifact style with a small number of regional and temporal variants the rule, as it was with the fluted-point tradition during Paleoindian times. We now see a complex, diverse pattern of stone-tool technologies spread across North America, much as was seen in the European Mesolithic, a pattern discernible across virtually all of the inhabited world in the post-Pleistocene.

ASIA

The Asian Mesolithic is less well known than that of Europe, but what is known follows the pattern established there. Kwang-Chih Chang's (1986) synthesis work on the archaeology of China describes different Mesolithic adaptations to China's distinct post-Pleistocene habitats. He begins by dividing the country geographically and culturally into north and south. In the north, Chang recognizes two major Mesolithic groupings on the basis of stone tools: a blade-and-flake industry in the forests of Manchuria and a microblade industry in the riverine and lake habitats that constituted oases in the deserts of Mongolia (Figure 10.7).

The regions of Mongolia inhabited by the microblade manufacturers are analogous to the region inhabited by the Desert Archaic culture of North America: Their sites are on the margins of dry, shallow depressions that were small lakes during early post-Pleistocene times. Spears and arrow points are few at these sites, probably indicating the marginality of hunting in the north. The most common faunal remain is ostrich shell fragments, and people almost certainly relied on the fish available in the lakes around which they settled.

Evidence at sites like Djalai-nor and Ku-hsiang-t'un, in the woodlands of Manchuria, indicates that hunting was more important than in the lakeside habitations. Spearpoints are more common, as are bone and antler tools. At sites like the Upper Cave at Zhoukoudian, a Mesolithic occupation of north China near where *Homo erectus* remains were discovered (see Chapter 5), the faunal remains of wapiti (elk) and ostrich have been found. While these were hunted for food, smaller mammals such as badger, fox, wildcat, and tiger were hunted for their thick, warm fur and their teeth, which the Mesolithic

FIGURE 10.7

Artifacts from the post-Pleistocene culture in Manchuria, northern China. (From *The Archaeology of Ancient China*, by K. C. Chang, Yale University Press, with permission)

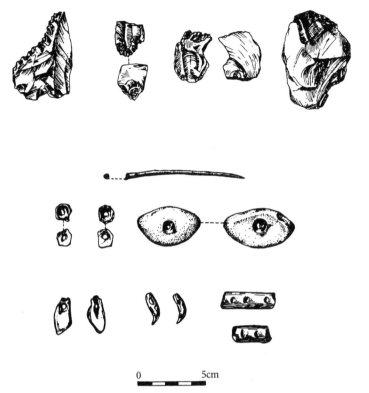

0   5cm

occupants of the Upper Cave site perforated to make items of personal adornment. Zhoukoudian is located some distance from the Chinese coast, yet also found in abundance in the Upper Cave Mesolithic deposits were the remains of marine shellfish, which were traded for and then used to manufacture beads and other nonutilitarian items found at the site.

In southern China, another distinct set of Mesolithic adaptations evolved in response to the end-of-Pleistocene conditions. Environmental change was not as dramatic here, and there is great continuity with the Upper Paleolithic cultures of the region. The tradition of making stone tools from chipped pebbles is called **Hoabinhian** and marks the southern Chinese Mesolithic. Sites such as Hei-ching-lung imply a subsistence base that included wapiti, wild cattle, other small game, mollusks, and wild plant foods.

A similar pattern of regionalization can be seen farther south in mainland southeast Asia (Higham 1989). Along with a great diversity of archaeological cultures dated to the Mesolithic, an increasingly sedentary way of life is also seen in some particularly rich areas. The broad range of foods available in Thailand at the Spirit Cave site, occupied more than 7,500 years ago, apparently allowed for a settling into and focusing on the territory immediately surrounding the cave. The Khong stream at the base of the cliff face where the cave was located provided fish and freshwater crab. The surrounding forest provided otter, several monkey species (including langur and macaque), bamboo rat, badger, porcupine, and the sambar and pig deer, the bones of which have all been found in the Spirit Cave excavations (Gorman 1972). Along with animal foods, the remains of 22 genera of plants have been recovered in the cave, including bamboo, betel nut (a stimulant), butternut, and assorted tropical fruits (Higham 1989, 53).

Spirit Cave and other upland sites in north Thailand not only share their own unique set of adaptations, but also exhibit the same pattern seen in many other ecologically distinct regions of southeast Asia: the Red River Delta region of northern Vietnam, the Vietnamese coast, the Chao Phraya plains of southern Thailand, and the Gulf of Siam coast. Each region has produced vastly different yet contemporaneous archaeological cultures dating to the Mesolithic. In each case, local people developed distinctive adaptations to their own rather narrowly circumscribed regions. In this way, the Asian cultures of the Mesolithic exhibit the same pattern seen in Europe and North America: cultural diversity evolving as a result of the developing ecological diversity of the post-Pleistocene.

In western Asia, hunter-gatherers also were adapting to the changing environment that characterized the end of the Pleistocene. Their adaptation would include a new and innovative approach to subsistence—the cultivation of plants and the domestication of animals—an adaptation that ultimately was to make the modern world possible. We will pick up their story in the next chapter.

AUSTRALIA

As a result of its geography, Australia experienced no drastic environmental changes at the end of the Pleistocene. This is not to say that there were no impacts. A drying in the southeast of the country resulted in the disappearance of most inland lakes by 16,000 B.P. The northern coast, on the other hand, saw an increase in rainfall as storm tracks changed. But because there had been no extensive glaciation in Australia during the Pleistocene, we find no deglaciation and attendant warming like that seen in northern Europe and North America.

Perhaps most significantly, worldwide rising sea level at the end of the Pleistocene reconfigured the Australian coastline. By 12,000 B.P., the land connection between Australia and Tasmania was breached; by 8000 B.P., the bridge between New Guinea and Australia was inundated; and by 6,000 years ago, modern sea levels were reached and the modern configuration of the coast largely was achieved (see Figure 9.1; J. White and O'Connell 1982).

Without seeing the kinds of major environmental changes in Europe and North America at the end of the Pleistocene, we also fail to see in Australia the kinds of major cultural changes that characterized the Holocene on those

FIGURE 10.8

Stone hatchets and flaked adzes from the post-Pleistocene culture of Australia. (From *A Prehistory of Australia, New Guinea, and Sahul,* by J. Peter White and James F. O'Connell, Academic Press, with permission)

cm

continents. Again, however, things don't remain static. For example, ground stone hatchets and flaked stone adzes make their appearance about this time (Figure 10.8). The Australian "small-tool tradition," with its blades, burins, and bifacial projectile points, dated to a bit before 5,000 years ago and as much as 7,000 years ago, represents another addition to the Holocene archaeological record. These small tools are often made of nonlocal raw materials and may indicate an increase in trade between groups living great distances from one another.

The inhabitants of Australia seem to have maintained a relatively stable subsistence adaptation through the late Pleistocene and Holocene and even into the modern era. While shellfish were collected as much as 30,000 years ago at Lake Mungo (see Chapter 9), marine shellfish became a major component of the diet of Australia's coastal people only after 8,000 years ago, around the time that the modern coastal configuration was established. Large shell middens dating especially to after 6000 B.P. are common along the temperate southeast coast and to a lesser degree on the tropical north coast. Shellfish seems not to have been a significant food source along the southwest coast at any time in Australia's history; there are no shell middens, and ethnographic groups in the area were not reported to have been much interested in shellfish (J. White and O'Connell 1982).

The major period of cultural change in Holocene Australia dates to the period beginning about 5,000 years ago. In their synthesis of Australian prehistory, J. Peter White and James F. O'Connell (1982, 104–5) point out that at about this time the dingo, a wild dog (a nonmarsupial introduced to Australia by human settlers) tamed for hunting, is seen in archaeological contexts for the first time. Also, macrozamia, an otherwise poisonous plant whose underground stem, when properly prepared, produces an edible starch, becomes an important food source. There is also a substantial increase in site density in the eastern Australian highlands, made possible by the broadening of the subsistence quest to include new food sources and the development of new cooking techniques in southeast Australia (marked by the appearance after 4500 B.P. of a new style of hearth made from pieces of termite nest).

A few sites, Roonka Flat being the most impressive, exhibit evidence of an elaboration of burial ritual in the Holocene. Of the 82 burials located at this site, most date to recent times, but 12 can be assigned to the period between 4,000 and 7,000 years ago. A few of these were shaft tombs, vertical interments of the deceased. Most of the Roonka Flat burials contained grave goods, including the lower jaws of animals (with drilled holes for suspension), drilled shells, and bone pins. A few adults were buried with the bones of human infants.

Australia is huge and has been occupied for 40,000 years. On the one hand, its material culture is easier to analyze than that of Europe, Asia, or North America because it is both more homogenous and stable through time. On the other hand, there is a level of diversity apparent in subsistence data that more clearly follows the post-Pleistocene pattern seen in the rest of the world. As J. White and O'Connell (1982) maintain, the post-Pleistocene archaeological record of Australia reflects the significance of highly localized environmental factors in molding a settlement/subsistence pattern. Coastal, upland, desert, lake, and riverine foci all became established in different parts of the country. In that sense, Australia after the Pleistocene exhibits a pattern common to the one seen in the rest of the world.

SOUTH AMERICA

We saw in the last chapter that great diversity characterized the subsistence patterns of the late Pleistocene inhabitants of South America. Certainly, as archaeologist Karen Olsen Bruhns (1994) states, some societies were largely dependent on big-game hunting. At the same time, the newly discovered sites of Quebrada Jaguay (Sandweiss et al. 1998) and Quebrada Tacahuay (Keefer et al. 1998; see Chapter 9) show that some South Americans had a maritime-based economy before 10,000 B.P. Also mentioned in Chapter 9, Anna C. Roosevelt's work (Roosevelt et al. 1996) at the Caverna da Pedra Pintada site in the Amazon basin in Brazil indicates that by about 11,000 years ago, in the late Pleistocene, some groups in South America had already developed an adaptation to the tropical rain-forest habitat. A rich array of food remains at the site indicates a broad reliance by the inhabitants on tropical fruit and nut trees as well as on the animal life that abounds in the tropics, including freshwater fish and mollusks, tortoises, turtles, snakes, birds, and small game.

The end of the Pleistocene wrought changes of climate in South America and attendant changes in the subsistence focus of the people living there. In some areas with a restricted community of edible plants and animals, human goups became highly specialized in exploiting individual species or a small number of species. For example, with the extinction of mastodon, horse, glyptodont (giant armadillo), megatherium (giant ground sloth), and many other Pleistocene species, some human groups who previously had at least partially relied on the hunting of these animals shifted focus to the single set of large game animals remaining after the Pleistocene—**camelids.** The South American camels included the wild guanaco and vicuña (llamas and alpacas are the domesticated versions of South American camels). For example, at Pachamachay Cave in the Peruvian Andes, a subsistence focus on vicuña hunting developed after 9000 B.P. (Bruhns 1994).

Elsewhere, a broadening of the subsistence quest is apparent. The Vegas complex, located in the Santa Elena Peninsula of Ecuador, shows an early (late Paleoindian) evolution of a maritime subsistence focus. This shift is ultimately seen in the coastal desert from northern Peru to southern Chile, where archaeological evidence shows early post-Pleistocene groups heavily exploiting resources like mollusks. This maritime, or **littoral,** tradition is seen, if a bit later, in coastal Colombia and Venezuela and also along the Caribbean Atlantic coasts of South America. Hunting remained important in some areas; some of the coastal sites are located near tar pits, natural traps where animals could have been killed once mired in the thick natural petroleum deposits. But maritime resources seem to have become most important to those living near the coast in post-Pleistocene South America. Some places even show signs of a population movement away from the interior and toward the coast. These post-Pleistocene coastal sites tend to be larger than earlier sites, more permanent, and with more elaborate burials. A sedentary way of life on the coast, made possible by the rich and reliable resources of the sea, seems to have set the stage, at least in part, for the great cultural changes that were to occur in South America (see Chapters 11 and 15).

AFRICA

Like Australia, the African continent was not affected as severely by climate change at the end of the Pleistocene as were Europe, Asia, and the Americas. Africa was not glaciated and suffered much less extinction of large mammals. And the kind of regionalization seen on the other continents in the early post-Pleistocene is seen in Africa in an earlier period. As indicated by archaeologist David W. Phillipson in his synthesis of African prehistory, the period of 100,000–8,000 years ago is characterized by the movement away from "broad cultural uniformity" and "towards the establishment of distinct regional traditions" (1993, 60).

Typical among the regional cultures was that of the **Iberomaurusians** of northwest Africa (Klein 1993). At about 16,000 B.P. they inhabited the coastal plain and interior of what is today Tunisia and Morocco. They made small stone blade artifacts used as scraping and piercing tools—the former for scraping animal hides in clothing manufacture and the latter as arrow points or spearpoints for hunting. The animals that were the core of their subsistence strategy included wild cattle, gazelle, hartebeest, and Barbary sheep. Also important in their coastal habitat were marine mollusks, including snails. Though no plant food remains have been found in Iberomaurusian sites, grinding stones and digging stick weights indicate some reliance on seeds, nuts, and roots.

Change accompanies the end of the Pleistocene, but there is no great cultural upheaval in Africa. After 10,000 B.P. in northwest Africa, the Iberomaurusian culture is replaced by another, called **Capsian;** as Richard Klein (1993) points out, this may have involved an actual migration of new people into the area, where they replaced the older inhabitants. Capsian subsistence is not very different from that of the preceding Iberomaurusians. The inhabitants continued to hunt wild sheep, collect shellfish and snails, dig for roots, and grind seeds and nuts. The Capsians set very small **microlith** blades into

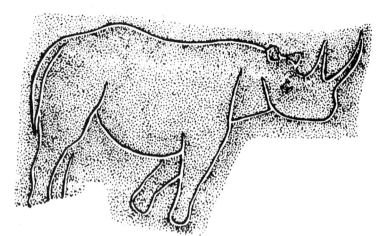

FIGURE 10.9

Naturalistic engraving of a rhinoceros found in southern Africa and dating to the post-Pleistocene. (From *African Archaeology,* by David W. Phillipson, p. 76, Fig. 4.8, Cambridge University Press, with permission)

wooden or bone handles. These tools appear to have been used to harvest wild stands of grains; the microliths themselves exhibit a diagnostic kind of wear, or polish, called "sickle sheen" from repeated use in cutting the stalks of tall, grasslike plants.

The use of microlithic **backed blades** is all but ubiquitous in Holocene Africa. During the early post-Pleistocene of southern Africa, microlithic industries predominate at coastal locales where preservation is high—in dry caves and waterlogged sites such as Gwisho Hot Springs in Zambia, a broad array of artifacts was recovered, including bows and arrows, digging sticks, bark trays, and bags and clothing of leather. Plant foods were important in the diet within a seasonal round that saw winter settlement of the coast and summers spent inland.

South Africa also saw a proliferation of artwork, with an abundance of naturalistic rock paintings depicting animals and people (Figure 10.9). As Phillipson (1993, 77) points out, the paintings almost certainly had a ritual significance. The eland—a large antelope—is depicted most frequently, but it is not the animal most commonly represented in the faunal assemblage at archaeological sites dated to the same period. Historically, however, the eland played an important role in the religions of some southern African people, and its abundance in ancient rock paintings may indicate that the ritual importance of the eland has a long history. Also, some of the paintings show people in positions and contexts that were common in historical times and related to trance. Again, as Phillipson (1993, 77) points out, early Holocene rock paintings of people bent over or in a crouched position, often with blood apparently flowing from their noses, match the descriptions of trance experience of the San people living in southern Africa (Figure 10.10). The San describe their trances as riding on the backs of snakes, and people riding on the backs of enormous serpents or snakes are also found in the rock paintings.

FIGURE 10.10

Rock paintings from southern Africa interpreted as representing two shamans in a trance. (From *African Archaeology,* by David W. Phillipson, p. 77, Fig. 4.10, Cambridge University Press, with permission)

Central, eastern, and western Africa also have produced archaeological evidence of microlithic tool industries as well as diversity and regionalization of subsistence and settlement. In East Africa, on the shores of Lake Turkana, where so many key finds have been made related to human physical evolution (see Chapters 4 and 5), evidence of a specialized fishing adaptation has been recovered. In the dense forests of West Africa, a culture with a nonmicrolithic tool assemblage has been identified. Large stone hoes and axes predominate, with little evidence of hunting equipment. Subsistence may have been based on the abundant plant foods of the forest.

Africa too is marked by an explosion of cultural diversity as people became more specifically adapted to their own particular regions in the early Holocene. The stage is now set, here as elsewhere, for a revolution in human subsistence.

ISSUES AND DEBATES

WAS THE MESOLITHIC ONLY A "PRELUDE"?

For many scholars, the period immediately following the Pleistocene is not as intriguing as the periods before or a few thousand years after. It has not commanded as much attention in publications, for instance. Graham Clark's classic work on the European Mesolithic, *Mesolithic Prelude* (1980), implies, by its very title, that the significance of this period rests not so much in what transpired, but in what it led to: the Neolithic (see Chapter 11). Archaeologist T. Douglas Price (1987, 227) points out that for many scientists, at least until fairly recently, the Mesolithic was marked by cultural "impoverishment." Remains were sparse, the artwork was unimpressive, and the period seemed less interesting than the more romantic Upper Paleolithic (with its images of bands of big-game-hunting artists) and less important than the Neolithic, with the inception of a sedentary, "civilized," farming way of life.

As Price points out, this view is no longer tenable. The Mesolithic in Europe—in fact, the early post-Pleistocene of much of the world—was a vital period during which human groups responded to one of the greatest environmental challenges humanity had yet faced. The evidence indicates that environmental changes at the end of the Pleistocene were substantial, rapid, and unpredictable. Mean temperature fluctuated widely over relatively short spans of time, and this had an enormous effect on human groups as well as the plant and animal species on which they relied for their subsistence. It took some time for conditions to become relatively stable and predictable, and this instability and unpredictability must have presented extraordinary challenges to human beings attempting to adjust their lifeways to the new circumstances.

Yet humanity thrived by fairly quickly developing many varied cultural adaptations to the changing conditions. While food resources, including shellfish, small mammals, and wild grains, were available to many groups in the Pleistocene, those who relied on big game had little reason to exploit these other possibilities. The end of the Pleistocene and the scaling back and even extinction of many of these big-game resources brought major change for these groups.

Wherever we look in the Old and New Worlds, human groups rose to the challenge of drastically changing environmental conditions, each in its own way. The ability of culture, with its enormous flexibility, to respond to such changes is the hallmark of our species and a reason for its great success—both then and now. Being able to invent, virtually instantly, new strategies for survival rather than having to wait for nature somehow to "come up with" a new adaptation, and being able to adjust quickly to rapidly changing environmental conditions puts humanity at a tremendous advantage relative to other animal species. For human groups at the end of the Pleistocene, the only limitations were those of the imagination. And based on the diversity of the responses, this was hardly any limitation at all.

The post-Pleistocene also was the crucible in which was forged the adaptations that would lead to subsistence strategies that make modern life possible. It is hard to argue now with the characterization of the Mesolithic—and it could be applied to post-Pleistocene cultures the world over—by Russian archaeologist G. I. Mathyushin (Clark 1980, 6; Price 1987, 229) as "the most important epoch in history."

CASE STUDY CLOSE-UP

The site of Star Carr is perhaps the best known of the Maglemosian Mesolithic sites because of its fine state of preservation and its exemplary excavation by British archaeologist J. G. D. Clark (1971). The site has been reinterpreted since the publication of Clark's research, and many of his specific conclusions have been questioned (Price 1982, 1987; Price and Feinman 1993). Nevertheless, all agree that Star Carr provides a richly detailed image of life in the Mesolithic of western Europe.

This 9,500-year-old settlement most likely occupied a high, dry area on a peninsula extending into a now dry lake—in an area probably destroyed before the site was excavated. Luckily, an extensive array of artifacts was lost in or discarded into the lake by the site's inhabitants. First encased in mud and later covered with peat, many organic artifacts at the site—including bone, antler, and even wood—preserved remarkably well, and Clark's meticulous excavation resulted in their recovery. Some 17,000 flint artifacts were found,

FIGURE 10.11

Sample of barbed antler harpoons from the Mesolithic site of Star Carr in England. (From *The Excavation at Star Carr*, by J. G. D. Clark, p. 139, Fig. 49, Cambridge University Press, with permission)

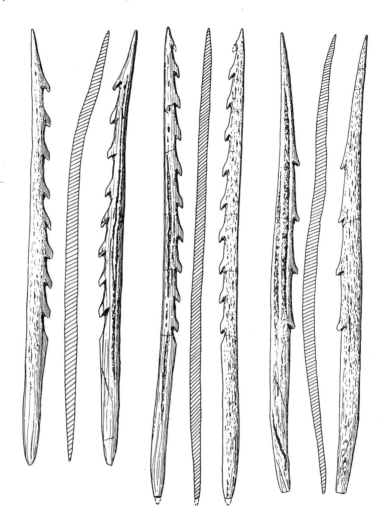

along with an array of antler spearpoints, animal bones, a wooden paddle, and birch bark, in an excavation that covered 350 m^2 (3,780 ft^2).

The faunal assemblage at the site indicates that the inhabitants hunted red deer, roe deer, elk, ox, and pig. Since deer shed and grow their antlers at fixed intervals during the year, the presence or absence of antlers on the skulls of hunted animals, as well as the stage of antler development, can inform us about the season or seasons during which the site was inhabited. An analysis of the antlers and skulls showed that Star Carr was occupied most intensively in the summer, though evidence exists for a year-round human presence (Price and Feinman 1993, 171).

Smaller mammals also were used by the inhabitants: The bones of fur-bearing animals such as fox, wolf, badger, beaver, and hare were found at the site. The inhabitants also ate birds: The bones of duck, mergansers, grebes, and cranes were recovered. Surprisingly, despite the excellent level of preser-

FIGURE 10.12

Artist's conception of life at Star Carr, 9,500 years ago. (From *Ancient Britain*, by James Dyer, B. T. Batsford Limited, with permission. Tracey Croft, artist)

vation, no fish bones were found, perhaps indicating the inhabitants' lack of interest in that particular lake resource. Also, though the lakeside was home to a wide variety of plants, no direct evidence was collected at the site for the use of plant foods.

One category of tools found at the site could have been used for digging for roots—the elk antler **mattocks.** Flat sections of connected skull and antler were used as the digging blade, and a large hole was drilled through the base of the blade, into which a wooden handle was fastened. One of the mattocks found had a charred remnant of the wooden handle in place.

At Star Carr, the evidence points to the reliance on hunting for subsistence. Along with the faunal remains is substantial artifactual evidence. Most of the stone artifacts were manufactured on flakes removed from cores. Functionally, they constitute a hunter's tool kit with various cutting and scraping tools used in butchering and hide preparation. Though there are no stone spearpoints as such, an extensive assemblage of finely made antler and bone barbed points exists: The stone burins were used to craft the antler and bone into tools. These antler and bone points are vicious-looking weapons, each with many sharp, down-pointing barbs (Figure 10.11). Once in an animal, they could not fall out or be pulled out without serious damage to the creature. These were highly effective hunting tools.

Star Carr provides a rich picture of life in the Mesolithic (Figure 10.12). The preservation of so much organic material allows for a detailed look at the subsistence of this group of post-Pleistocene people. Though it is difficult to generalize about Mesolithic culture precisely because it represents a period of such great diversity, one impression left by Star Carr probably can be widely applied: The inhabitants exploited a broad range of resources in their subsistence quest. In this sense, the people of Star Carr are models of the Mesolithic adaptation.

VISITING THE PAST

As a result of the common assumption that the early post-Pleistocene is a culturally uninteresting period, there are fewer places to visit that relate directly to this time in human antiquity. It is true that post-Pleistocene, pre-Neolithic sites produce less visually exciting artifacts and, therefore, are of less interest to casual tourists. You will find information on the pre-Neolithic in any museum that presents material on the origins of agriculture, at least as context for a display on the revolution in food production.

Perhaps one of the most impressive sites you can visit is that of Koster in Kampsville, Illinois. The Kampsville complex of research buildings is at the hub of an ambitious archaeology project that has identified thousands of sites in the area. The Koster site is the centerpiece of the work that has been conducted there. Though the Koster excavation itself has long been filled in, you'll find an on-site museum with displays focusing on the site.

SUMMARY

The common thread running through this chapter has been post-Pleistocene adaptation. Wherever we have looked in Europe, Asia, North and South America, Australia, or Africa we have seen the same trend. After about 12,000 B.P., human beings were faced with fundamental changes in the Pleistocene environments to which they had become adapted. Land covered in ice became exposed, temperatures rose, and some areas became drier, others wetter. Land connections were breached, and coastal configurations rapidly changed. Animals on which some humans subsisted became extinct, and new, different animals took their place. Plants became available that were useful for food, in the form of nuts, seeds, fruits, leaves, or roots.

People were faced with many options in the rapidly changing post-Pleistocene world. Some broadened the subsistence quest to include a wide variety of plant and animal resources. Some intensified the subsistence quest, focusing on a single resource or very few particularly productive resources. Some human groups became increasingly sedentary as they adapted to rich Holocene environments. As a result of the diversity of the post-Pleistocene resource base, cultural diversity increased exponentially, with myriad cultures proliferating, each thriving in its own territory.

Some settlements became more permanent, and population grew. In a number of cases, the food quest was intensified further still as groups attempted to increase the productivity of the resources on which they depended.

This intensification set the stage for what will be discussed in Chapter 11: the revolution in food production.

TO LEARN MORE

Technical Summaries

There are some excellent technical sources on regional post-Pleistocene adaptations. For Europe, Grahame Clark's classic book, *Mesolithic Prelude* (1980), is a good place to start. For a more up-to-date summary of the European Mesolithic, T. Douglas Price's 1987 article titled "The Mesolithic of Western Europe" in the *Journal of World Prehistory* is a good source. For North America, see Brian Fagan's *Ancient North America* (1991) for a detailed textbook treatment of post-Pleistocene adaptations. For an excellent source on this and other periods of South America's prehistory, see Karen Olsen Bruhns's *Ancient South America* (1994). For the post-Pleistocene cultures of Australia, as for the rest of Australian prehistory, there is the venerable *A Prehistory of Australia, New Guinea, and Sahul,* by J. Peter White and James F. O'Connell (1982). For Asia, the general works by Kwang-Chih Chang—including *The Archaeology of Ancient China* (1986)—as well as Charles Higham's *The Archaeology of Mainland Southeast Asia* (1989) include considerable discussions of the post-Pleistocene. For Africa, see David W. Phillipson's *African Archaeology* (1993).

Popular Summaries

A terrific popular book focusing on one of the best-known post-Pleistocene sites in North America is Stuart Struever and Felicia Holton's *Koster: Americans in Search of Their Prehistoric Past* (1979). The book is aimed at a popular audience; see especially the chapter titled "A Day at Koster in 3500 B.C."

On the Web

It cannot be said that the Internet is bristling with sites dedicated to the Mesolithic or Archaic period in the Old and New Worlds. You can retrieve detailed information about the Archaic period in Oregon at http://www.ncn.com/~gilsen/webdoc7.htm. You can download a series of photographs of stone tools recovered by archaeologists at the Skyrocket site at http://users.ap.net/~bpacs/skyintro.html. You can visit the homepage of the Center for American Archaeology at http://www.caa-archeology.org. The CAA has been investigating the Koster site and its surroundings for more than 25 years.

KEY TERMS

interglacial	Archaic	camelid
interstadial	Lake Forest Archaic	littoral
Younger Dryas	lacustrine	Iberomaurusian
Mesolithic	Maritime Archaic	Capsian
Maglemosian	pelagic	microlith
midden	Mast Forest Archaic	backed blade
Hamburgian	Hoabinhian	mattock

11

The Neolithic

ROOTS OF A REVOLUTION IN SUBSISTENCE AND SOCIETY

CHAPTER OVERVIEW

Beginning about 12,000 years ago, some human groups began not just foraging for food, but actually producing it. Various groups began tending plants and taming animals, allowing only those with characteristics desirable from a human subsistence standpoint to survive and propagate. This shift to food production occurred independently in several places in the New and Old Worlds. Each "agricultural revolution" involved the manipulation of local wild plants and/or animals. The vast majority of the foods we rely on today were domesticated by ancient people many millennia ago.

Chronology of domestication				
	12	11	10	9
Southwest Asia		sheep, barley, dog	wheat, lentils	goat, dog, cattle
Meso-america				squash
Africa				
East Asia		rice	pig	
Europe				cattle
North America				
Sourth America				

Thousands of years ago

8	7	6	5	4	3	2	1
			camel				
			maize	beans, chili peppers			
sorghum	millet		yams				
	chickpea, barley, lentil, wheat, sheep, goat, cattle						
chicken, dog							
millet, pig							
wheat, barley, legumes, sheep, goat, dog		millet, lentils					
				sumpweed	smartweed, knotweed, maygrass, little barley, goosefoot	maize	
				squash			
				sunflower			
	llama, alpaca		beans, chili peppers, ulluco, potato, manioc, cotton, quinoa	oca, maca, yacon, jícama, arracacha, maize			

Twentieth-century anthropologists are not the first to ponder the human past and to imagine how humanity has changed and evolved over the millennia. Many people, often through myth or legend, have tried to explain their own past and to chronicle major changes they realize must have occurred in their societies over time.

Consider, for example, the ancient Chinese legend of Shen Nung, first written down close to 3,000 years ago (Chang 1968). According to this legend, Shen Nung was a great hero who gave the people of China the tools necessary for the development of their civilization, including the knowledge of plant cultivation: "The ancient people ate meat of animals and birds. At the time of Shen Nung, there were so many people that the animals and birds became inadequate for people's wants, and therefore Shen Nung taught the people how to cultivate.... At the time of Shen Nung, millet rained down from Heaven. Shen Nung collected the grains and cultivated them" (Chang 1968, 79).

The legend of Shen Nung represents a self-conscious attempt by the Chinese to explain what they understood as a fundamental change in their culture in past times—a shift from hunting and gathering to the cultivation of crops. Shen Nung gave the people the knowledge to plant, tend, and harvest crops, which, in turn, provided additional food. This rationale for the origins of agriculture actually sounds quite modern: the growth of human population beyond what hunting and gathering can support. We will see in this chapter's "Issues and Debates" that some twentieth-century anthropologists have suggested much the same cause.

Like the Chinese of 2,500 years ago, twentieth-century anthropologists also recognize the significance of agriculture in making modern life possible, and realize that humanity has not always had the knowledge of cultivation and animal husbandry. Like them, we seek to understand how and why we became agricultural. Our explanations do not rely on myth, but on scientific investigation of a period after the Pleistocene in many parts of the world when human groups began to change their relationship with their resource base. At that time a revolutionary change occurred. We call that revolution the **Neolithic.**

CHRONICLE

For most of human history, people have relied for their subsistence on **foraging**—hunting, fishing, and collecting wild plant foods. Myriad combinations of hunting; trapping; line and net fishing; collecting shellfish; digging for roots; harvesting wild grains; collecting seeds, nuts, and fruits, and so on have served to provide human groups with food for subsistence. Some groups had a broad resource base; others focused on a few highly productive resources. Some human groups were nomadic, continually traveling to wherever food could be found; others were more sedentary, staying in one place where a particularly abundant and constant food source was available. Some groups in some regions adhered to a schedule of movement that coincided with seasonal changes in resource availability; other groups in other regions followed a less varied schedule, doing much the same work and relying on the same set of food sources year round.

What all these groups had in common, regardless of the particular plants or animals they relied on for food, was that those food sources were wild. For more than 99% of human prehistory, people have relied exclusively on the wild foods that nature provides (Figure 11.1). Only very recently have human groups begun actively to encourage the survival of certain wild plants or animals and to manipulate them so as to alter them from their ancestral state.

HUMANS TAKING THE PLACE OF NATURE: ARTIFICIAL SELECTION

Though we refer to the shift from foraging to farming as a revolution, that term may be misleading. In fact, settled agricultural life represents not so much a rapid revolution as a point along a lengthy continuum of change. The transition from food gathering to a total reliance on agriculture took thousands of years. As archaeologist Bruce Smith (1998, 1651) points out, in the Middle East as much as 3,000 years separates the earliest domestication of plants and animals and the first full-blown agricultural societies. In eastern North America it took as much as 4,000 years for the shift to an agricultural way of life to take place, and in Mexico as much as 5,000 or even 6,000 years passed between the first steps in plant domestication and the evolution of a fully agricultural people.

As archaeologist Naomi Miller (1992) lays out the continuum from foraging to farming, it begins with collecting wild foods and continues through a lengthy period of tending and encouraging plants or animals that are genetically identical to their wild relatives. In some instances, this may lead to manipulation of the reproduction of economically important plants or animals through **artificial selection**—that is, the directed evolution of new species possessing characteristics deemed beneficial to human beings. At this stage, human beings (in a manner analogous to natural selection as defined by Charles Darwin—see Chapter 2) select for propagation only those individuals within a plant or animal species that possess some natural endowments useful to people. In describing the "art" of artificial selection, Darwin pointed out: "One of the most remarkable features in our domesticated races is that we see in them adaptations, not indeed to the animal's or plant's own good, but to man's use or fancy" (1859, 47).

So, both at the origins of agriculture and in our modern systems, humans protect and encourage only those individual plants that produce more or larger seeds, only those animals that exhibit less aggression and produce the most meat, milk, or wool, or only those trees that bear larger fruits. Selected individual animals in a wild species may be corralled and protected from

CHAPTER SITES

MESOAMERICA
Guilá Naquitz Cave
Juanaqueña
Tamaulipas
Tehuacán

NORTH AMERICA
Bat Cave
Cloudsplitter
    Rockshelter
Hayes
Holding
Icehouse Bottom
Jemez Cave
Milagro
Napoleon Hollow
Newt Kash Hollow
Phillips Spring
Salts Cave
Tornillo Rockshelter
Tumamoc Hill

SOUTH AMERICA
Ayacucho Cave
Chilca Caves
El Paraíso
Guitarrero Cave
Lauricocha
Pachamachay
Panaulauca
Tres Ventanas Cave
Vegas

FIGURE 11.1

The San people of the Kalahari are one of the very few foraging groups that survived into the twentieth century. (Copyright © R. Lee/ Anthro-Photo)

predators. Certain individual plants within a wild species may be watered or weeded or planted near the village and then fenced in to prevent animals from eating them.

After many generations of such treatment, and as people have an increased opportunity to even more carefully select for propagation plants or animals with desirable characteristics, the cultivated plants and animals no longer resemble their wild ancestors or neighbors. They have been so altered through artificial selection that, again in a manner analogous to natural selection, they can no longer be considered the same species. They have, in essence, coevolved with their human overseers, no longer changing under entirely natural conditions, but under the conditions established by people (Rindos 1984). Such plants and animals are said to be domesticated. Under extreme conditions of domestication, they cannot survive without human beings to attend to their needs and to propagate them. They are no longer adapted to a natural world but, rather, to a culturally constructed world of agriculture and animal husbandry. And in every case, the prehistoric record is clear: Wherever such a "revolution" occurred, it transpired over thousands of years. This chapter documents such a process for the Near East, Mesoamerica, Asia, Africa, Europe, North America, and South America.

THE DOMESTICATION OF PLANTS AND ANIMALS

The **domestication** of plants and animals occurred in several world areas beginning after the end of the Pleistocene. There were two distinct contexts in which domestication occurred: "pristine" (or "primary") and "secondary"

(Cowan and Watson 1992b). As defined by C. Wesley Cowan and Patty Jo Watson in their edited volume *The Origins of Agriculture,* pristine situations are those in which the ancient culture engaged independently in a process that led to the domestication of locally available plants or animals. In a pristine situation, domesticated crops and animals are slowly added to a broader foraging subsistence base. Domesticates at first are a minor, supplementary component of the diet and become increasingly important as continuing refinements in the selected characteristics improve the quality of the food source for human exploitation. We will see that this process of independent, pristine agricultural development occurred in the Near East, Mexico, eastern North America, South America, Africa south of the Sahara, and east Asia.

Secondary conditions are those in which a local group adopts the already domesticated plants and/or animals of another group. In some cases, the indigenous local adaptation was that of foraging for wild plants and animals, and a set of foreign domesticates supplemented and then ultimately replaced the local wild plant foods. This is the pattern seen in the archaeological record of Neolithic Europe and in the American Southwest. In other instances, the local economy was already using indigenous domesticates, which were then replaced by a set of superior (in yield, nutrition, and other features) plant and/or animal foods introduced from the outside. In both eastern North America and parts of Africa, an indigenous, initially independent agricultural revolution was supplanted by a foreign, more productive agricultural system.

WHY AGRICULTURE?

Many hypotheses have been put forth to explain why, more or less simultaneously, people the world over adopted an agricultural subsistence system. As archaeologist Mark Cohen (1977) has pointed out, under different environmental conditions and focusing on many kinds of plant and animal resources, most of the world's people, between 11,000 and 2,000 years ago, either developed a domesticated food base independently or adopted the agricultural pattern of their neighbors. In other words, a revolution occurred over 9,000 years and supplanted a pattern of foraging that had been successful for the hominid family for 4 million years.

That such a revolution took place is obvious. That there must have been some compelling human need behind it seems reasonable. What is not obvious, however, is *why* this shift took place at all.

Environmental Change

An environmental cause has often been suggested for this shift: The extinction at the end of the Pleistocene of plant and animal species on which some human groups depended for subsistence stimulated the development of agriculture to replace these extinct food sources. Environmental change is also at the root of British prehistorian V. Gordon Childe's (1942, 1951, 1953) "oasis hypothesis": Increasing post-Pleistocene aridity in the Near East forced surviving plants, animals, and people to congregate around permanent water sources. People became more knowledgeable about the wild species now in close proximity to them and slowly tamed and molded the species to fill their needs.

Cultural Evolution

Other researchers have proposed that agriculture developed as the result of cultural evolution. This "readiness hypothesis," championed by archaeologist Robert Braidwood (1960, 1975), assumes that human groups accumulated knowledge about the wild plants and animals on which they depended and then discovered ways to increase the reliability, productivity, and usefulness of those species through selective breeding.

Population Growth

Some researchers have suggested that domestication resulted from the need to increase productivity to feed a growing population. In his provocative book, *The Food Crisis in Prehistory,* archaeologist Mark Cohen (1977) argues that only an overriding necessity could have induced human groups to shift to a subsistence pattern that involved fundamentally altering their way of life and adopting a far more labor-intensive pattern. Hunter-gatherers are known to work relatively short hours for their subsistence, especially compared to agriculturalists. The !Kung San people living in the Kalahari Desert in southern Africa, one of the least hospitable places on earth, work just 20 hours a week in subsistence activities (see Figure 11.1; Lee 1979). In Cohen's view, only the pressing need to feed an increasing number of mouths could compel people to abandon a more leisurely mode of life.

An Accident

Others maintain that the domestication of plants and animals was not accomplished through conscious choice to improve the subsistence base, but instead because human beings naturally alter the habitats they exploit. Humans change natural conditions simply by returning to the same place to collect foods seasonally, by killing or weeding out economically useless species, by disturbing the soil, by concentrating garbage, by moving plants or animals into areas outside of natural habitats, and by clearing out vegetation for villages (Anderson 1956). In this way people unintentionally create better conditions for individual members of species that fortuitously thrive in a human-dominated and culturally altered and manipulated habitat. Species adapt to these new conditions, while humans, in turn, culturally adapt to take full advantage of these species, all in a process that archaeologist David Rindos (1984) calls "co-evolution."

A Multitude of Reasons

There probably was no single "prime cause" for the development of agriculture in all the places that it occurred. Perhaps there was no one "Neolithic revolution," but many, each with its own explanation. As archaeologist Donald O. Henry (1989, 236) points out, "given the complex ecological relationships that governed the transition from forager to food-producer," complexity and diversity in explaining these transitions is to be expected. And as archaeologist Ofer Bar-Yosef (1998) has pointed out, if there was a single, universal cause for the origins of plant and animal domestication, then nearly all foragers would have developed a subsistence system based on agriculture or animal husbandry when faced with the same or similar climatic or demographic conditions. That this universal adaptation did not occur is a clear indication that different cultural groups can and did respond differently to changes in the environment or in their population. It can be said no more clearly: Though several different groups at different times and places developed it, "there is no need to seek one single model to explain the origins of agriculture" (Bar-Yosef 1998, 173).

However, significant patterns do exist in the record. A sedentary settlement pattern (evidenced by substantial and permanent architectural forms) *preceded* the appearance of domesticated foods. In other words, in the late Pleistocene/early Holocene, some human groups began to settle into regions so plentiful in food resources that people could stay in one place for much of the year and collect enough food to survive and even thrive. Population might have grown exponentially as the sedentary life may have lowered infant mortality and extended the length of life. During a long period of population growth, the food quest would have been intensified to feed the growing number of mouths. One step in this intensification would have been to artificially raise the productivity of the nearby wild plants by creating conditions that increased the yield of food: clearing forest, planting seedbeds, weeding, fencing in. At this point, the plant selection process changed: Whereas before plants were adapting to natural conditions, now they were adapting to artificial conditions produced by the cultural manipulation of the environment. This was the first step toward domestication and, ultimately, a way of life dependent entirely on food production.

THE NEAR EAST

Late Pleistocene people in the Near East, in the area that now makes up parts of Iran, Iraq, Israel, Jordan, Lebanon, Syria, and Turkey, exhibited a long period

FIGURE 11.2

Archaeological sites in the Middle East where evidence of early food production has been found.

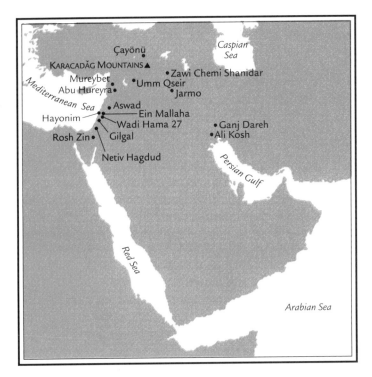

FIGURE 11.3

The Fertile Crescent in the Near East provided rich habitats for late Pleistocene and early Holocene hunter-gatherers where the wild ancestors of some of the earliest domesticated crops grew.

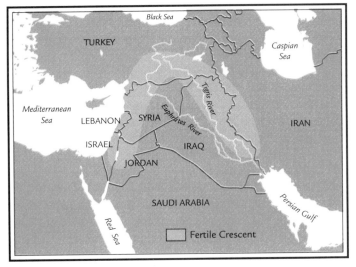

of intensive use of wild **cereal** grasses, especially wheat and barley (Figure 11.2; Bar-Yosef 1998; Henry 1989; Maisels 1990; Miller 1992). Beginning along the Mediterranean and arcing first to the northeast and then down to the southeast, this area, today marked by highly productive agricultural lands, is referred to as the **Fertile Crescent** (Figure 11.3).

Paleoclimatological data indicate that the Middle East was cold and dry during the late Pleistocene, but the hilly Mediterranean coast was wetter and thickly forested. People living in the Middle East relied on hunting for part of their subsistence; the bones of wild boar, fallow deer, gazelle, and ibex have been found in sites dating to the period 20,000–14,500 B.P. (Bar-Yosef 1998). During this same period, wild plant foods were a significant part of the diet. At the 19,000-year-old Ohalo II site, a large number of the seeds and fruits of several different plant species have been found (Kislev and Carmi 1992).

The period from 14,500 to 11,000 years ago is marked by increasing precipitation in the Middle East, and a number of cultures have been defined for this period of climatic improvement. For example, the **Geometric Kebaran,** beginning at about 14,500 B.P. and lasting until 12,500 B.P., is located in the moist Mediterranean woodlands of the central **Levant,** southward into the margins of the Negev and Sinai Deserts, and across southern Jordan (Henry 1989). The contemporary late Pleistocene **Mushabian** culture is located to the south in the steppe and arid zones of what today are the cores of the Negev and Sinai Deserts. The later **Natufian,** dating from about 13,000 to 9800 B.P., is located in the Mediterranean woodland zone, part of the same area occupied by the Kebaran from which it almost certainly developed. Farther north, in the foothills of the Zagros Mountains in Turkey, are the pre-Neolithic cultures of the **Zarzian** and **Karim Shahirian.**

As archaeologist Donald O. Henry (1989) indicates, the Mushabian sites seem to reflect the remains of small groups of highly mobile **simple foragers** with no particular focus on or commitment to any one food resource. Sites are small and impermanent, with direct evidence of the hunting of wild goats and gazelle. Dating to the same period as the Mushabian sites to the south, Kebaran sites vary more in size and complexity, indicating a pattern of population aggregation to take advantage of rich and seasonally available resources, particularly the wild cereal and nut foods available in the lowlands during spring and summer.

The Origins of a Sedentary Life: The Natufian

It is during the Natufian, at about 13,000 years ago, that we see a dramatic shift in subsistence from simple to **complex foraging** based on plant foods. In complex foraging, subsistence is focused on a few rich resources. These are collected intensively and stored, both requiring and allowing for more sedentary, denser human populations. This pattern is reflected in the archaeological record of the Natufian by the appearance of grinding stones, large bedrock mortars and smaller, more portable mortars and pestles, food storage pits, pits for roasting plant foods, and microblades of flint exhibiting sickle polish. The stone blades exhibit a sheen or polish that has been shown through replicative experiment to be the result of their use in cutting cereal plant stalks such as those of wheat, barley, millet, and sorghum (Unger-Hamilton 1989; Figure 11.4).

FIGURE 11.4

In Kenya, this traditional harvest, in which women use sickles, is probably quite similar to how wheat was harvested thousands of years ago in the Near East, where it was first domesticated. (Food and Agriculture Organization, United Nations; photo by Peyton Johnson)

The Natufian culture homeland was located in the belt of woodland in the Levant. Here, wild cereal grasses offering human foragers protein and carbohydrate-rich seeds would have grown abundantly in open areas and as forest underbrush (Bar-Yosef 1998). Kernels and stalks of wild wheat and barley have been found at several Natufian sites. For example, at Mureybet and Abu Hureyra, in Syria, wild einkorn wheat and vetch (a **legume**—a plant that produces pods with seeds) have been found in roasting pits dated to more than 11,000 years ago and as much as 13,000 years ago. These sites are located about 100 km (65 mi) from where wheat grows wild today. This may be an indication of intentional movement of the wild plant into a new territory by people consciously attempting to increase its geographical range. Carbonized kernels of wild barley, lentils, chickpeas, and field peas have been recovered at Wadi Hama 27 in Jordan, dated to 12,000 B.P.

Indirect evidence of the use of wild cereals by late Pleistocene people in the Near East includes heavy wear on human teeth (P. Smith 1972). This probably resulted from the ingestion of stone particles that became mixed into the meal or flour when wild cereals were processed with stone grinding tools. An increase in the strontium level of human bones seen at these sites may be the result of an increase in the use of cereal grains at this time; high levels of strontium are found in these cereals (Smith, Bar-Yosef, and Sillen 1985).

The intensive collection and storage of wild cereals necessitates a more sedentary way of life because the food source stays put and needs to be monitored regularly for the best time to harvest. At the same time, the abundant and dependable wild cereals, legumes, and nut foods allow for a sedentary life. As a result, Natufian sites exhibit a far more complex and sophisticated architectural pattern than do the Mushabian or Kebaran. Whereas Mushabian and Geometric Kebaran sites generally are small and impermanent, preagricultural Natufian sites show the distinctive architecture of permanent villages. At Ein Mallaha, Hayonim Cave, and Rosh Zin in Israel, the remains of substantial houses with stone foundations ranging in diameter from 2 to 9 m (about 6 to 29 ft) have been found (Henry 1989, 211–12). Similarly substantial and permanent structures are known from Mureybet in Syria, where the preferred building materials were clay and wood, and Abu Hureyra, also in Syria, where the houses were built down into the earth. The amount of labor needed to build such domiciles is a clear indication that they were intended for long-term use.

Material culture, too, is far more complex and sophisticated at Natufian sites than at Mushabian or Kebaran sites. Bone, tooth, and shell beads and pendants are commonly found in burials. Dentalium shells, which were a favorite raw material, were available—often at great distances from the Natufian sites where they were found. Along with such items of personal adornment, other works of art have been recovered from Natufian sites, primarily carved stone statuettes of animals and people (Figure 11.5).

The First Agriculturalists

A return to colder and drier conditions in the Middle East between 11,000 and 10,000 years ago in all likelihood resulted in a decrease in the abundance of wild cereal crops there. Many of these cereals, especially barley and wheat, were the crops on which the Natufians had come to rely for their subsistence. Archaeologist Ofer Bar-Yosef (1998) suggests that it is during this period that Natufians initiated an attempt to artificially increase the abundance of these cereals, perhaps by planting and then tending the wild crops. In this scenario, as people gained some measure of control over these wild plants, selection shifted from natural to artificial. As people began imposing their will by encouraging those individual plants that possessed useful characteristics (they had larger seeds and were hardier), the population of tended plants changed from a wild pattern to a pattern determined by human selection.

Late Natufian and Karim Shahirian sites provide evidence of very early steps down the pathway of domestication, sometime around 11,000 years ago. At Netiv Hagdud and Gilgal in Israel and at Ganj Dareh in Iran, recovered barley kernels have been identified as an early domesticated version of that cereal. The size and morphology of the kernels distinguish them from wild barley, and they show features present in the domesticated grain. At Aswad in Syria and Çayönü in Turkey, domesticated wheats known as **emmer** and **einkorn** have been dated to more than 10,000 B.P. At both sites, lentils may also have been cultivated: At Aswad, 55% of the seeds of food plants recovered were from cultivated peas and lentils (Miller 1992, 48).

The evolution of dependence on domesticated plants can be traced at the site of Ali Kosh in southwestern Iran: More than 29,000 seeds from the Bus Mordeh phase at Ali Kosh, dated to earlier than 10,000 B.P., were recovered.

FIGURE 11.5

Natufian artwork: a carved animal (top) *and two carved sickle hafts.* (From *From Foraging to Agriculture: The Levant at the End of the Ice Age,* by Donald O. Henry, University of Pennsylvania Press, with permission)

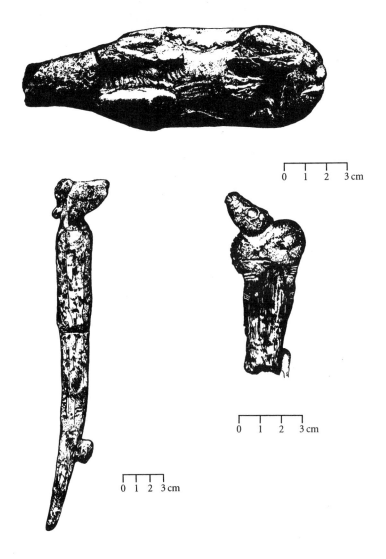

The vast majority were from wild legumes and grasses, and only 10% were from domesticated emmer wheat and barley (Hole, Flannery, and Neely 1969, 343). Forty percent of the seeds from the later Ali Kosh phase were from domesticated emmer wheat; in the subsequent Mohammed Jaffar phase, the seeds of legumes rose to prominence.

In the Zagros Mountains, the site of Zawi Chemi Shanidar has produced a substantial faunal assemblage of sheep bones dated to 10,600 B.P. (Wright 1971). The population structure of the archaeological sample of the sheep is unlike what would be derived from a group of hunted animals. Almost all were slaughtered when young. This kind of consistency in the population profile of an animal species implies a level of control over the animals usually possible only under conditions of corralling. The animals, though genetically the same as those roaming wild, were kept, controlled, and tended by people. This incipient stage in domestication enabled the human overseers to dispose of (and eat) those animals with undesirable characteristics and to allow only those with attractive features to survive and reproduce more generations like them. This practice led to intensive and rapid selection that soon altered the captive animal population, creating a group so different from the wild population that it no longer was of the same species. This process can be seen in changes in the bones of now domesticated sheep and goats in the Near East after 10,000 B.P. (Gilbert 1989).

A Model of the Shift to a Food-Producing Way of Life in Southwest Asia

Archaeologist Donald O. Henry (1989) has proposed an explanation for what happened in the Natufian period in the Near East that led to the origins of agriculture: When Natufians abandoned a mobile pattern of simple foraging and adopted a complex foraging strategy, they produced an inherently unstable subsistence system. Whereas simple foragers faced with a food shortage can move to where food is more abundant, complex foragers (who have adopted a sedentary mode to exploit locally abundant wild plant foods) can, under the right circumstances with the right kinds of plants, artificially raise the "resource ceiling" (Henry 1989, 4) of their territory by tending and encouraging economically important wild crops. In other words, complex foragers respond to a food shortage by beginning artificial selection.

In Henry's model, the Natufian pattern of complex foraging that focused on wild cereals and nuts expanded geographically when the Mediterranean woodlands, where wild cereals were particularly abundant, expanded as the Pleistocene waned and as conditions became wetter. But by the onset of the Younger Dryas glacial re-advance in the north, 13,000 years ago, conditions had changed for the worse: By 10,500 B.P. the Mediterranean woodlands that had sustained an increasing Natufian population had shrunk to half the size they were at the beginning of the Natufian. Having committed their subsistence energies to wild cereals whose abundance was declining, the Natufians responded by more actively encouraging those plants. This response included tending the plants as well as artificially selecting those that had beneficial characteristics. These were the first shots fired in the Neolithic revolution.

MESOAMERICA

Mesoamerica includes most of the modern nations located south of the United States and north of South America (including Mexico, Guatemala, Belize, El Salvador, the western regions of Honduras and Nicaragua, and northwestern Costa Rica). This area contributed many valuable agricultural crops to the world, none more important than maize (corn), beans, and squash, the triumvirate of plants that provided the subsistence base for indigenous

FIGURE 11.6

Archaeological sites in Mesoamerica where evidence of early food production has been found.

New World civilizations (see Chapter 15). The shift to an agricultural mode of subsistence has been documented in only a few sites: Guilá Naquitz Cave (Flannery 1986), Tamaulipas, and Tehuacán (MacNeish 1964, 1967). The Western Hemisphere's earliest evidence for the domestication of plants has been found in Mesoamerica (Figure 11.6).

The First Agriculturalists in the New World

Though maize (corn) is probably the first crop most people think of when asked to name the key agricultural crops domesticated by Native Americans, it was not the first wild plant they domesticated. The oldest evidence for domestication in the New World comes from Guilá Naquitz cave in Oaxaca, Mexico, where squash seeds, rind fragments, and stems that are demonstrably different from those of wild squash have been recovered and dated to the period between 10,000 and 8,000 years ago (B. Smith 1997).

The seeds of the Guilá Naquitz squash are larger, the rinds thicker, and the stems bigger (likely implying larger fruits) than in wild specimens. Archaeologist Bruce Smith maintains that such increases result automatically when people plant and tend initially wild crops as they thin out later-germinating, slower-growing individual sprouts in a process called **seedbed selection.**

Like all people who rely on wild plants, the ancient inhabitants of Guilá Naquitz Cave had a detailed knowledge of the characteristics of plants on which they depended and knew full well that seeds produce plants. They also were aware of the conditions necessary for the plants to flourish in seedbeds. Just like modern gardeners tending domesticated crops, ancient people would have tended these spring seedbeds carefully. There would have been a high level of unintentional artificial selection for plants that produced larger seeds: Where the endosperm is larger, food reserves for growth are greater and the plant grows faster. Slower-growing plants are normally weeded out of a patch to provide room for the larger and faster-growing varieties. In the same way,

FIGURE 11.7

View of the Tehuacán Valley in central Mexico, where the earliest evidence of domestication in the New World has been recovered, dating to after 5000 B.P. (Copyright © Robert S. Peabody Museum of Archaeology, Phillips Academy, Andover, Mass. All rights reserved. Photo by R. S. MacNeish and Paul Manglesdorf)

seeds with thinner seed coats sprout more quickly, again giving the young plants a jump on the competition in the seedbed. Later-germinating (thicker seed coats), slower-growing (smaller seeds) plants are at a distinct selective disadvantage under the culturally controlled conditions of a seedbed. After generations of encouraging the growth of those plants that produced larger seeds with thinner seed coats because they grew more quickly, plants were created that produced bigger seeds, which, in turn, produced larger squashes with larger stems. This process resulted in plants that had been so intensively manipulated by human action that they no longer resembled their wild antecedents. They had been, in fact, domesticated.

The Tehuacán Valley

Though found at archaeological sites much later than squash is, maize is the most important crop domesticated in the New World. The **Tehuacán** Valley project, conducted in 1961–64 in Mexico by archaeologist Richard MacNeish and an international team of 50 scholars from many disciplines (MacNeish 1964, 1967), provided archaeologists with a detailed picture of the process of maize domestication (Figure 11.7). The project also resulted in a sequence of archaeological cultures spanning the period from 12,000 to 500 years ago, from the late Pleistocene to the period of initial European contact (De Tapia 1992).

The Cultural Sequence at Tehuacán

MacNeish defined a series of stages, or periods, in the valley based on evidence gathered from a series of occupied caves. He began the sequence with the

Ajuereado phase, dated from 12,000 to 9,000 years ago. Recovered food remains indicate that hunting was of primary significance in the seasons when the caves were occupied. Sites were small and impermanent, leading MacNeish to suggest that small family groups—**microbands** of fewer than 10 people each—wandered the valley, primarily hunting antelope and jackrabbit. Other, smaller fauna, such as turtles, rodents, gophers, and birds, were utilized, as were wild plant foods, including avocado, foxtail grass, and amaranth, a grain (see Figure 11.9).

Toward the end of the Ajuereado phase, in the waning years of the Pleistocene, the Tehuacán valley experienced a period of drying that eliminated some of the resources on which local groups depended. In MacNeish's view, the increased aridity led to a decrease in the importance of hunting and an increased reliance on wild plant foods. This can clearly be seen in the subsequent **El Riego phase,** dated from 9,000 to 7,000 years ago. Strong evidence for an increasing focus on wild plants at this time can be seen in the preserved remains of wild squash, beans, chili peppers, amaranth, and avocado. In MacNeish's construct, the previous pattern of year-round nomadic microbands was replaced during El Riego times with a more complex settlement system that included dry season fall/winter microbands but added larger macrobands during the wetter spring and summer months.

The settlement pattern of seasonal shifting from micro- to macrobands is continued in the **Coxcatlán phase,** dated from 7000 to 5400 B.P. The reliance on wild plant foods continued among those living in the caves. Later, in the **Abejas phase** (5400–4300 B.P.), an increasingly sedentary pattern of central-based bands was established. Larger, semipermanent villages or home bases were settled, though a geographically broad strategy of wild-food collection continued. During this phase domesticated plants first contributed to the diet; squash and maize date to this period in the valley.

Much less is known about the **Purrón phase** (4300–3500 B.P.) than about previous or subsequent phases. Pottery was used for the first time by the inhabitants of the valley, but little else is known. In the following **Ajalpán phase,** dating from 3,500 to 2,850 years ago, diet was based on foraging for wild foods as well as on domesticated maize, beans, and squash. Ajalpán settlements continued to grow, and the degree of sedentism (remaining in one place) increased from the previous phase. Simple irrigation canals were built to water crops, a clear indication of the importance placed on agriculture and further confirmation of the abandonment of a nomadic way of life (construction of canals represents a long-term commitment to stay in one place).

Dating the Shift to Agriculture at Tehuacán

In MacNeish's original analysis of the Tehuacán materials, the maize remains (Figure 11.8) were dated indirectly. Carbon dating is a destructive process, and the world's oldest maize specimens were deemed too valuable to sacrifice

FIGURE 11.8
Some of the prehistoric maize cobs recovered in excavations in the Tehuacán Valley. The chronology proceeds from left to right: The tiny cob on the far left is the oldest maize, now AMS-dated to after 5000 B.P.; the modern variety is on the right. (Copyright © Robert S. Peabody Museum of Archaeology, Phillips Academy, Andover, Mass. All rights reserved)

for dating purposes. Of necessity, MacNeish derived dates from more abundant (and less precious) additional organic remains and then associated those radiocarbon dates with maize remains found in the same layers. By this method MacNeish concluded that the oldest domesticated maize was about 7,000 years old, originating in the beginning of the Coxcatlán phase in the valley.

Unfortunately, caves like the ones MacNeish excavated can present the archaeologist with stratigraphy that is notoriously difficult to interpret. Especially in caves that have been used repeatedly over long periods, it is always possible that younger materials have moved down into deeper, older soil layers (for example, by burrowing animals or by people digging into the soil). So the validity of the dates derived for the maize has been a problem. Luckily, the recent introduction of **accelerator mass spectrometry** (**AMS**) dating (a form of radiocarbon dating) allows for the use (and destruction) of miniscule samples. As a result, 12 of the Tehuacán maize samples have now been dated directly. These direct dates, universally more recent than MacNeish's original determinations (Long et al. 1989; Fritz 1994), place the oldest maize at about 4700 B.P., though some of the material may be a bit older (Fritz 1994).

Though quite different from modern corn, the Tehuacán maize cannot have been the first domesticated version of that plant. The oldest examples from Tehuacán are only an inch or two long, with eight rows of six to nine kernels each. But even these oldest, tiny cobs from Tehuacán exhibit a morphology that is entirely inappropriate for life in the wild. The kernels of this maize were held tightly in place by long **glumes** (the casings in which individual kernels are enclosed). It took a human hand to remove the kernels from the glumes for eating or planting; the kernels would not have fallen out on their own, and so the crop could no longer have survived in the wild. Human beings must have already selected for this characteristic before the date of the Tehuacán corn, perhaps because it made the early maize easier to harvest and to process without losing kernels. Older, even more primitive maize almost certainly will be discovered, bringing us back further toward the origin of its domestication in Mesoamerica.

The Shift to Domesticated Foods Among the People of Tehuacán

The original analysis of dietary change through time at Tehuacán was based in part on the analysis of food remains in preserved fecal specimens recovered in archaeological strata in the excavated caves. A total of 116 preserved human fecal deposits were recovered in the valley. E. O. Callen (1967) was able to derive dietary percentages from the Tehuacán deposits. Unfortunately, those percentages necessarily reflect just a few meals of individual people, so Callen's statistics cannot be assumed to represent their diets over the long term. Moreover, if the caves were occupied only part of the year, then paleofeces and food remains recovered in middens or hearths reflect only those foods eaten when the caves were occupied. Since the caves were occupied during those seasons when wild plants were the subsistence focus, it stands to reason that the remains of wild plants would predominate in the archaeological record (Farnsworth et al. 1985, 110), even if during the rest of the year other foods made significant contributions to the diet.

There is a way around this problem. An analysis of carbon isotopes has been successfully conducted on bones from 12 of the human skeletons recovered at Tehuacán, allowing for the reconstruction of the general diet of the inhabitants (Farnsworth et al. 1985). As discussed in Chapter 4, uptake of the ^{13}C isotope differs among plant groups. Those following the C4 photosynthesis pathway—chiefly grasses and sedges—use proportionally more ^{13}C than those following the C3 pathway—most trees, herbs, and shrubs. Animals (this includes people) incorporate into their bones proportions of ^{13}C that reflect the proportions in the plant foods they eat (or the proportions in the animals they eat, which reflect the proportions in the plant foods the animals eat). Because the carbon isotopes present in an individual's bones are the product of a lifetime's diet, seasonal changes or recent meals have little effect.

The isotope analysis of the Tehuacán material shows a clear jump in the reliance on C4 plants early in the Tehuacán sequence and then little change thereafter. Therefore, tropical grasses must have been mainstays of the diet of the people who produced the archaeological sites in the Tehuacán Valley. Based on the isotope analysis, their overall diet (meaning their reliance on C4 plants) did not change much for several millennia.

Combining MacNeish's reconstruction with the isotope data, it appears that the inhabitants of the valley went through a long period of increasing sedentism before adopting an agricultural way of life. This lengthy period of dietary reliance on C4-pathway tropical grasses—including, perhaps, the wild progenitor of maize, **teosinte** (see Figure 11.26)—is similar to the situation seen in the Near East. Farnsworth and colleagues (1985, 112) suggest that an extended period of reliance on wild plants and increasing sedentism in Tehuacán was "a Mesoamerican equivalent of the Natufian."

A Model of the Shift to a Food-Producing Way of Life in Mesoamerica

Kent Flannery (1968) has proposed a detailed explanation for the shift to an agricultural mode in Mesoamerica: The subsistence systems of late Pleistocene Mesoamerica were inherently stable. The seasonally restricted availability of certain resources and scheduling preferences for some resources over others available at the same time of year maintained a stable system in which no one resource was so intensively exploited that its abundance was threatened. Such a system can be said to be in "equilibrium."

In Flannery's view, however stable such a system might have been, it was susceptible to even a minor change in general conditions. For example, a mutation in teosinte that produced more easily harvested plants (see this chapter's "Issues and Debates") might have rendered this previously minor wild food more attractive. To take advantage of this more desirable form of teosinte, other elements in the intricately balanced system may have been shifted. To encourage the growth of the new teosinte/wild maize, the settlement pattern may have changed to allow more time in those places where teosinte grew, to encourage the new form. But this could only have been accomplished by changing the entire system of seasonal movement and scheduling. A pattern of larger and more sedentary groups may have developed to take advantage of the new teosinte. Overall population would have increased, necessitating a continual refinement through artificial selection of the new crop, to feed more mouths. Microbands would have become macrobands, seasonal encampments semipermanent and then permanent villages.

In this way, the initial, casual, and almost accidental step of intensifying the exploitation of a crop could have thrown the entire system out of balance. The initial minor deviation from the established equilibrium would have become amplified as the culture tried to reestablish a new status quo. Other resources would have had to be granted less attention, resulting in the need to intensify further the use of the new crop. But intensification would have required a greater degree of sedentism, which would have meant even less time or opportunity for other resources. In Flannery's view, the intensification of the use of a particular food species can be the first step toward the inevitable destruction of a foraging subsistence system and the establishment of an entirely new equilibrium based on agriculture (Figure 11.9).

FIGURE 11.9

Agriculture established a new equilibrium for subsistence systems in Mesoamerica. Left: *In this traditional agricultural field in modern Mexico, the farmer is harvesting amaranth that is growing among the corn plants.* Right: *The same process is seen in an image from a Spanish source dating to the sixteenth century.*
(*Left:* Courtesy of Dan Early; right: *Florentine Codice*)

AFRICA

It cannot be said that there was a single agricultural revolution in Africa or even that there was a single point of origin for the African shift to a domesticated food base. Africa is enormous and has a broad range of climates and environments and a wide range of plant and animal communities. Myriad hunting-and-gathering cultures developed in Africa during postglacial times, each adapting in its own way to its region. And many different food-producing cultures developed in the African Neolithic, each devising its own adaptation through food production of the available plants and animals (Figure 11.10).

Neolithic Culture Complexes in Africa

Jack Harlan (1992) defines three distinct archaeological culture "complexes" of the African Neolithic: Savanna, Forest Margin, and Ethiopian. Savanna complex sites, located in the dry interior of central Africa, exhibit a reliance on pearl millet, a grain crop known for its resistance to drought. Watermelon was another important crop, not so much for its nutritive value, but for its ability to store water and therefore to serve as a source of liquid. In the wetter, broad-leaved savanna, sorghum and African rice played major roles in subsistence. Other savanna plants contributing to the food quest were fonio (a cereal), Bambara groundnut, and kenaf, roselle, and tossa jute, all used as herbs in cooking.

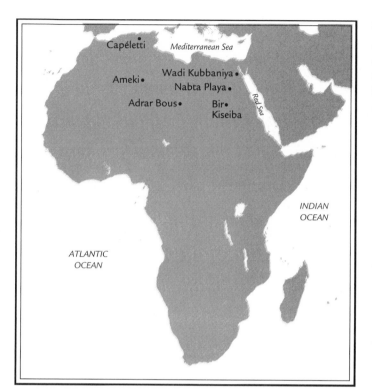

FIGURE 11.10

Archaeological sites in Africa where evidence of early food production has been found.

In Harlan's Forest Margin complex, the focus is on forest resources combined with reliance on products of the savanna. Akee apples, Guinea millet, and kolas formed a part of the subsistence base. Oil palm and cowpea also were important. Historically, the cultivation of yams, which grew wild on the forest edge, was one of the most important contributors to subsistence. Finally, in Harlan's Ethiopian complex, finger millet, teff (a cereal), enset (a relative of the banana), and noog (which produces an edible oil) were significant.

A Chronology of Food Production

The African reliance on wild plants extends well back into the late Pleistocene. At the Egyptian site of Wadi Kubbaniya, charred tubers of wild nutgrass have been dated to the period 18,000–17,000 years ago (Wendorf, Schild, and Close 1989; Wendorf et al. 1979). Heavily worn grindstones at the site were probably used to process the fat, starchy roots into flour. Stone blades inset into wooden or bone handles that served as sickles used in harvesting wild grains and the grinding stones necessary to process the grains into flour are both dated to 15,000–11,000 years ago in southern Egypt in a culture called the Qadan (Phillipson 1993).

FIGURE 11.11

Sorghum, used in the United States primarily to produce animal feed, has been an important food crop historically, particularly in Africa, where it was domesticated as early as 8,000 years ago. (Food and Agriculture Organization, United Nations; photo by J. Chevalier)

An 8,000-year-old site in the Sahara Desert of southern Egypt, Nabta Playa, supplies further evidence of early Holocene subsistence in Africa. Researchers excavated 1 storage pit, 14 hearths, and 122 cooking features (Wendorf et al. 1992). They recovered thousands of seeds, representing 40 different species of wild plants. Among the plants represented in the archaeological sample were sorghum and a number of varieties of millet. There are hundreds of varieties of sorghum; many produce edible grains, and others produce a sweet molasses or syrup. Millet and sorghum are commonly grown in modern, indigenous African agricultural systems (Figure 11.11). In fact, though not well known outside the semiarid tropics, millet and sorghum are the primary sources of protein in certain regions of the world.

Also found in the storage and cooking features at Nabta Playa were the remains of various legumes, fruits, tubers, and nut foods. There is even some suggestion that the sorghum at least was in an incipient stage of domestication at this site (Figure 11.12). To the eye, the sorghum looks like the wild plant, but the chemistry of the fats within the seeds is more like that of the modern domesticate. The identification of the sorghum from the site as a domesticate on this basis, however, is still far from clear. Nevertheless, as the site researchers point out, it is a "short step" (Wendorf et al. 1992, 724) from the intensive use of sorghum and other wild plants to their domestication.

The earliest clear evidence of a shift from foraging to food production in Africa dates to about 7,000 years ago, in an area that today is the Sahara Desert. A wet period, or **pluvial,** began about 8000 B.P., and lakes dotted areas that today are desert. Faunal evidence indicates that **pastoralists** raising sheep,

FIGURE 11.12

Charred seeds recovered from Nabta Playa. Among the 40 or so plants identified in the archaeological sample were those of sorghum, in what has been identified chemically as an incipient stage of domestication. (Courtesy of Krystyna Wasylikowa)

goats, and cattle proliferated throughout the Sahara during this wet period. A thousand years later, by 7000 B.P., early agriculturalists were living along the Nile River in Egypt, raising sheep, goats, and cattle and planting barley, emmer, lentil, and chickpea for food and flax for linen. The wild ancestors of domesticated sheep and goats are not native to Africa. These animals can be traced to the Middle East and Europe, where they lived in the wild and where domesticated versions appeared earlier than in Africa. Some of the crops were likewise introduced from the outside, but some may have been the result of indigenous experimentation. An analysis of the mitochondrial DNA of modern domesticated cattle in India, Africa, and Europe indicates that their initial domestication occurred separately and independently, involving two separate species, in southern Asia and Africa. The wild, native African species, *Bos taurus* (distinguished from *Bos indicus* in Asia), was the ancestor of domesticated cattle in Africa (Bradley et al. 1998).

Archaeological evidence allows us to trace back this domestication to at least about 6,500 years ago. The bones of fully domesticated cattle were found at the Capéletti site in Algeria that dates to this time. Some cattle bones were also found at the Nabta Playa site just discussed and at Bir Kiseiba, with dating at both places close to 9,000 years ago. Though the bones themselves cannot be shown to be those of domesticated animals, the sites were occupied at a time when the local climate would not have been suitable for wild cattle. Their existence and survival in the environment surrounding these sites 9,000 years ago may imply at least that they were being tended and cared for by the people who lived there.

Neolithic Cultures South of the Sahara

In Africa south of the Sahara, another set of largely independent agricultural revolutions took place, focusing on entirely indigenous tropical crops. Various millets (pearl, foxtail, finger, bullrush, broomcorn) were domesticated in

FIGURE 11.13

Though a mainstay of agriculture in modern Asia, rice was not the first crop domesticated on that continent. (Top: Preparation of the seedbed for rice sowing.*) Even long after its domestication about 11,500 years ago, rice remained a minor component of the diet. Today, along with wheat and corn, it is one of humanity's primary foods. (Bottom: a modern rice paddy.)* (Both photographs, Food and Agriculture Organization, United Nations; *top:* photo by F. Botts, *bottom:* photo by Banoun/ Caracciolo)

tropical Africa. Domesticated pearl millet has been found dating to as early as 6,500 years ago—for example, at the Ameki site (Harlan 1992). Early sorghum domestication is seen at the Adrar Bous site dating to 4000 B.P. Yams, African rice, teff, fonio, groundnuts, enset, and noog are among other, entirely indigenous crops that were domesticated in sub-Saharan Africa in antiquity—all of which are unknown in the rest of the Neolithic world.

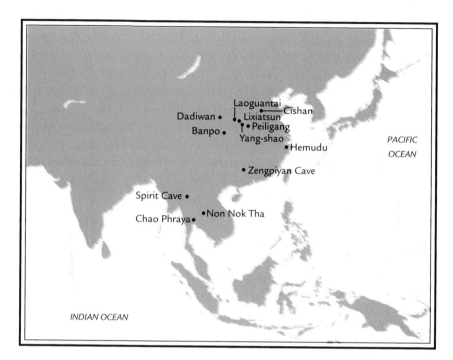

FIGURE 11.14

Archaeological sites in East Asia where evidence of early food production has been found.

EAST ASIA

Most of us in the Western world think of rice as the agricultural food base of Asian peoples (Figure 11.13). As pointed out by archaeologist Gary Crawford (1992, 8), however, there actually are 284 separate taxa of domesticated plants and animals known to have been used in east Asia.

Chronology of Food Production in China

The earliest evidence of plant or animal domestication in China from the Zengpiyan Cave site in Guilan dates to the period after 10,300 B.P. (Figure 11.14). A large proportion (85%) of the animal bones are those of young pigs, less than two years of age (Chang 1986, 102–3). As was the case at Zawi Chemi Shanidar in Iraq, this may indicate that the animals were not being hunted in the wild, but were kept and tended. That the canine teeth are smaller than in a wild pig population may be explained by the artificial selection for the propagation of less dangerous animals with smaller teeth.

An analysis of a spate of new radiocarbon dates associated with the remains of rice grains, husks, and other rice-plant remains, as well as the impressions of rice grains on ceramics, shows that domesticated rice dates back to as much as 11,500 years ago along the middle Yangtze River in central

China (Normille 1997). Ancient sites where early rice has been found both upstream and downstream of the middle Yangtze are younger, indicating that researcher Syuichi Toyama may have identified an early hearth for rice domestication in east Asia.

In northern China, the earliest Neolithic culture currently recognized is the **Peiligang,** as represented by sites such as Cishan, Peiligang, Laoguantai, Dadiwan, and Lixiatsun (Chang 1986). Dating to between 8,500 and 7,000 years ago, the Peiligang culture is centered in the deciduous forest zone of northern China. The evidence shows clearly that Peiligang sites do not represent the first steps toward settled life based on agriculture; Peiligang sites are already well-established farming villages, with hunting, fishing, and the gathering of wild plants also contributing to the food quest. Cultigens include foxtail millet, broomcorn millet, and Chinese cabbage. Domesticated animals include pig, dog, and chicken.

The better-known, later Neolithic culture of China is called the **Yang-shao.** Typified by the Banpo site near Xian, Yang-shao sites are five times larger than Peiligang sites, and the villages are not arranged as haphazardly; they appear to have been planned out before construction. Crops of the Yang-shao include foxtail millet, Chinese cabbage, and rice, though it was a relatively minor component of the diet. Domesticated rice has been identified at the Hemudu site on the Yangtze River just south of Shanghai, with a radiocarbon date of 7000 B.P. (Crawford 1992, 25).

The proportion of carbon isotopes in the human bones recovered at Yang-shao sites has been interpreted as indicating that nearly three-fifths of the diet was supplied by millet (An 1989). The various millets are grasses producing a large quantity of small seeds in long spikes. The seeds are ground into a flour and used in porridge and bread.

Food Production in Southeast and Northeast Asia

The situation is not as clear in the rest of east Asia. Spirit Cave in northeast Thailand (mentioned in Chapter 10) shows a clear reliance by about 12,000 B.P. on foods that were to become an integral part of the agricultural economies of later Neolithic peoples, including soybean, almond, cucumber, and water chestnut (Gorman 1972). A possibly early form of domesticated rice—at least rice that has been altered only slightly from its wild form—has been identified at Non Nok Tha in Thailand, dating to 5500 B.P. (Chang 1986). Indisputable evidence for domesticates in southeast Asia comes from excavations in the Chao Phraya valley in northeast Thailand at sites dated to about 5,000 years ago (Higham 1989, 80). The hunting and gathering of wild foods, along with the cultivation of rice, was the basis of this economy.

Data for Korea are sparse. Soils are very acidic, and few organic remains have been recovered in early archaeological contexts. We do know that by 3000 B.P., domesticated millet was used in a mixed economy that included hunting, fishing, gathering, and agriculture (Nelson 1993). Some archaeolog-

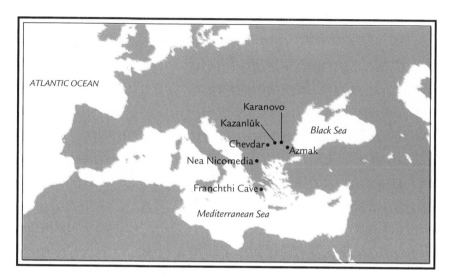

FIGURE 11.15

Archaeological sites in Europe where evidence of early food production has been found.

ical evidence, in the form of increased sedentism, suggests that farming may have begun a couple of thousand years earlier.

There is far more information for Japan, but the sequence is not clear. The late Pleistocene/early Holocene Jomon culture had a foraging subsistence base, with an emphasis on resources of the sea. This productive resource base allowed for a sedentary settlement pattern, with dense populations, elaborate material culture, and some large, semipermanent villages at more than 10,000 years ago. Evidence of domesticates, including rice, soybean, adzuki bean, buckwheat, and pear, does not appear at Jomon sites but appears in the later Yayoi culture, dated to about 2400 B.P.

EUROPE

Europe is a diverse continent with a complex prehistory. Regarding the shift to an agricultural mode of subsistence, it can be argued that, as for Africa, there was not one revolution but several (Whittle 1985). Archaeologist Robin Dennell (1992) indicates that a series of parallel shifts to domesticated plants and animals occurred in southeast Europe, in central Europe, along the northern margin of the Mediterranean, in the Alps, along the Atlantic coast, and in eastern and northeastern Europe. These agricultural revolutions, though not entirely independent of one another, occurred at different times, involved different crop and animal species, and had varying degrees of success (Figure 11.15).

The Shift to Agriculture in Southeast Europe

The earliest evidence of a shift toward agricultural life comes from southeast Europe. As seen elsewhere in the world, this shift is prefaced by an extended

FIGURE 11.16

At Franchthi Cave in Greece wild oats, barley, peas, and lentils were eaten by the inhabitants 13,000 years ago. (Courtesy Thomas W. Jacobsen)

period during which the subsistence focus was on the wild ancestors of crops that would later become important domesticates. For example, Franchthi Cave in Greece (Figure 11.16) contains evidence of the exploitation of wild oats, barley, peas, and lentils by 13,000 years ago (Hansen 1981). Pear and pistachio also appear to have been used during the early occupation of the cave.

By about 7,500 years ago, the focus on wild plants seems to have evolved into at least a partial reliance on domesticated crops. At Nea Nicomedia, also in Greece, levels dated to this time produced evidence of domesticated varieties of wheat, barley, and legumes (Whittle 1985). Similar evidence was found at the sites of Azmak, Karanovo I, Chevdar, and Kazanlŭk in Bulgaria, where wheat, lentils, and grass-pea seem to have been the most important food crops (Dennell 1992, 77).

The Shift to Agriculture in Western Europe

Throughout the rest of Europe, the shift to agriculture seems to have taken place later than in the southeast. For example, sites in the Swiss Alps exhibiting a reliance on domesticated crops, including emmer and bread wheat, lentils, peas, and millet, date to after 5500 B.P. In the central European, early Neolithic culture called **Linienbandkeramik** (**LBK**), a subsistence base that included emmer, barley, and pulses (grainlike legumes) has been traced back to about 6500 B.P. Along the Atlantic coast, in Great Britain, France, and Spain, evidence of the use of domesticates (a similar mixture of cereals and legumes) dates to no more than about 6,000 years ago.

British archaeologists Ian Simmons and John Innes have investigated the shift to an agricultural economy by the ancient inhabitants of northern Britain (Moore 1996). In an extremely detailed analysis of pollen found in stratigraphic layers in a peat deposit, these researchers were able to accurately reconstruct alterations in plant communities in the North York moors caused by changes in human adaptive strategies. Simmons and Innes discovered a dramatic drop in tree pollen, especially elm, probably indicating forest clearing by the human inhabitants of North York, sometime before 5400 B.P. There is no direct evidence for cultivation at this time, and Simmons and Innes suggest that the clearing was being done by hunters hoping to produce a habitat that would attract red deer, which had been an important food species to people in northern Europe since the Mesolithic. Following this time, an increasing proportion of weed pollen is evident, indicating the existence of cleared areas; and then, for the first time in the pollen sequence, there is evidence for the pollen of cereal plants, notably wheat, showing that agriculture had penetrated the northern half of Great Britain. For Simmons and Innes, the introduction of domesticated cereals in northern Britain was almost an afterthought, an add-on to an economic pattern that focused on producing a better hunting habitat.

For the most part, the Neolithic of Europe appears to have been imported from the south and east. Virtually all of the crops important in the European Neolithic, including einkorn, barley, bean, vetch, and lentils, are demonstrably Near Eastern in origin; there is little or no evidence for the existence of wild forms in Europe. The first appearance of these crops is in their domesticated form in the cultural contexts of archaeological sites dating to after 8000 B.P. Often, these domesticated food sources seem to have been superimposed on an earlier, indigenous Mesolithic subsistence pattern (see Chapter 10) based on hunting animals and gathering acorns and hazelnuts (Dennell 1992). Certain crops—oats and some legumes—were probably domesticated independently by Europeans, but evidence so far indicates that the domestication occurred rather late in the Neolithic, after Near Eastern domesticates had already entered (via migrating farmers) and become important parts of the food base.

NORTH AMERICA

One of the most enduring images of the Indians of eastern North America is that of the natives helping the Pilgrims of seventeenth-century Plymouth, in Massachusetts, to survive their first winter in the New World. They brought the European settlers corn, beans, and squash and taught them how to plant and prepare these native agricultural foods.

Indeed, most historical native cultures in North America that were agricultural were dependent on these three crops. As we have seen earlier in this chapter, however, the wild ancestors of two of these crops—maize and beans— were tropically adapted plants, certainly not native to New England or the rest of North America. These crops were introduced into those areas north of Mexico in some unknown way—trade, migration, indirect contact?

It is clear, however, that when maize penetrated the eastern woodlands of native America sometime after 1800 B.P., it did not replace an indigenous system of foraging for wild foods. Instead, maize initially supplemented an aboriginal pattern of hunting, collecting wild plants, and cultivating native squash and locally available seed plants. An independent, "pristine" pattern of indigenous domestication was established at about 4000 B.P., more than 2,000 years *before* the initial appearance of maize in the East (B. D. Smith 1989, 1992, 1995).

Indigenous Domestication North of Mexico

The primary native crops domesticated by the Indians of the eastern woodlands were sunflower, marsh elder, goosefoot, and lamb's-quarter (pigweed)—all producers of starchy or oil-rich seeds (Figures 11.17 and 11.18). At Napoleon Hollow in Illinois, for example, charred marsh elder seeds retrieved from a 4,000-year-old archaeological deposit are uniformly larger (by almost a third) than the seeds of wild marsh elder (Ford 1985). The oldest evidence of domesticated sunflower has been dated to 4265 B.P., at the Hayes site in central Tennessee, where the seeds are substantially larger than those of wild varieties (B. D. Smith 1995, 191). Goosefoot seeds from Newt Kash Hollow and Cloudsplitter Rockshelter in Kentucky, though not larger, do have significantly thinner seed coats than do wild plants. These thinner coats are most likely the result of intentional human selection for plants that produced seeds with inedible coverings that were thinner and therefore easier to penetrate and remove. Both sites have been dated to about 3400 B.P.

Squash was domesticated in Mesoamerica as part of a triad of agricultural crops that also included maize and beans. Though squash was long thought to have moved into North America from Mexico, archaeological evidence now indicates that it was domesticated independently in eastern North America as well. Squash seeds recovered at the Phillips Spring site in Missouri, dating to 4500–4300 B.P., are significantly larger than their modern wild counterparts (B. D. Smith 1995). The date for the site places squash domestication in eastern North America at about the time of the domestication of some of the seed crops mentioned earlier, further supporting a picture of a broad indigenous agricultural revolution in the East two millennia before the introduction of maize.

The degree of reliance on these native domesticates is difficult to determine. One important source of quantitative information comes from Salts Cave in Kentucky, dated to between 2600 and 2200 B.P. In the 119 paleofeces found in the cave, domesticated goosefoot, sunflower, and marsh elder seeds make up nearly two-thirds of the undigested food remains recovered (goosefoot 25%, sunflower 25%, marsh elder 14%; Yarnell 1974, 1977).

Farming communities based on these native domesticates proliferated in the eastern woodlands, specifically in the American Midwest and Midsouth, between 3,000 and 1,700 years ago. Along with goosefoot, pigweed, marsh elder, and sunflower, other crops that were used included knotweed, maygrass, squash, and a little barley. As B. D. Smith (1992a) indicates, the representation of the remains of these plants varies across the Midwest and Midsouth

FIGURE 11.17

A modern, many-headed form of sunflower. The sunflower was domesticated by the native inhabitants of eastern North America by about 4,200 years ago, at least 2,400 years before the introduction of Mesoamerican cultigens. (K. L. Feder)

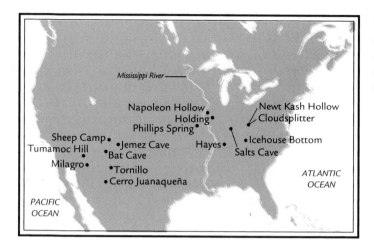

FIGURE 11.18

Archaeological sites in North America where evidence of early food production has been found.

during this period. Their overall significance varied in different times and places as these domesticates became incorporated into a "mosaic of regionally variable . . . food production systems" (B. D. Smith 1992a, 109).

The Appearance of Maize in the Eastern Woodlands

Maize begins to turn up in the archaeological record by about 1800 B.P.; some of the earliest evidence in North America for use of this most significant New World domesticate has been found at the Icehouse Bottom site in eastern Tennessee, with a radiocarbon date of 1775 B.P. (Chapman and Crites 1987). The Holding site, east of St. Louis, also has produced maize and may be slightly older (B. D. Smith 1995, 191). For close to 1,000 years, however, maize continued to be a minor component of a broad subsistence system that still included hunting, fishing, collecting wild plants, and cultivating native seed crops.

All of the indigenously domesticated crops of eastern North America are C3 plants; maize, however, is a C4-pathway plant. Analysis of the carbon-isotope chemistry of human bones recovered at archaeological sites in this region shows a shift away from C3- and toward C4-pathway plants just before A.D. 1000, preserving a chronicle in bone of the adoption of maize-based agriculture by the native peoples of eastern North America (Figure 11.19). This shift to maize enabled the evolution of the most complex archaeological culture north of Mexico, the Mississippian temple mound builders of the Midwest and Southeast (see Chapter 14).

The American Southwest

Unlike the situation in eastern North America, there is little evidence in the Southwest for the development of agricultural economies before the introduction of the Mesoamerican domesticates of maize, beans, and squash. These

FIGURE 11.19

The dramatic jump in the level of ¹³C *concentration in the bones of prehistoric Native Americans around* A.D. *1000 is taken to indicate an increase in the reliance on maize agriculture in eastern North America.* (From *The Emergence of Agriculture,* by Bruce Smith. Copyright © 1995 by Scientific American Library. Used with the permission of W. H. Freeman and Company)

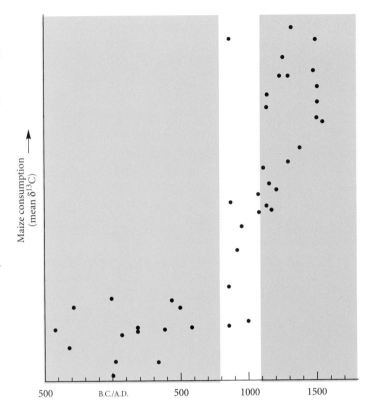

crops moved in and became part of the subsistence base of people who had not practiced agriculture previously.

The route taken by maize agriculture as it expanded north from its Mexican source can, in some measure, be traced archaeologically. For example, maize has been found at the Cerro Juanaqueña site in northern Mexico, very close to the border with New Mexico. The site is large, with a substantial commitment to agriculture; it dates to sometime soon after 3500 B.P. (Hard and Roney 1998).

On the U.S. side of the border, AMS dates on maize from Bat Cave in western New Mexico and Tornillo Rockshelter in the southern part of that state show the crop to have been present by about 3200 B.P. (B. D. Smith 1995, 202–3). A growing list of other sites shows the appearance of maize by 3,000 years ago or soon thereafter—for example, Milagro in Arizona and Tumamoc Hill and Jemez Cave in New Mexico (Minnis 1992). As Bruce Smith (1995) points out, it was during the four-century span between 3200 and 2800 B.P. that maize fully penetrated the American Southwest. Domesticated squash has been dated to about the same period at Sheep Camp Shelter (Simmons 1986), and beans appear to have come in 200 or 300 years later.

Though maize, squash, and beans originated as Mesoamerican crops, there was no movement of Mexican farmers northward, just the movement of the idea of domestication and the crops themselves, perhaps through trade. Most everything else in Southwest culture—tools, pots, habitations—remained more or less the same. Mesoamerican crops simply were grafted onto already existing lifeways. These new foods required only minor cultural adjustments, and the native people continued to exploit the wild plants and animals they always had.

Archaeologist Alan Simmons (1986, 83–84) suggests that maize was initially a secondary and supplemental resource for otherwise nonagricultural people in the Southwest. Maize would have been planted in late spring and early summer and harvested in the late fall for use as a "survival food" in the leaner winter months. A little bit of extra work in preparing the soil and planting the crops provided extra food and perhaps greater subsistence stability. Archaeologist Paul Minnis (1992, 122) calls it "casual agriculture."

This pattern was successful, continuing essentially unchanged for more than a thousand years. It was only around 2000 B.P. that southwestern cultures began to shift their subsistence drastically, relying ever more completely on domesticated crops.

SOUTH AMERICA

South America, like Africa, is enormous and contains a broad range of habitats with their attendant diverse plant and animal communities. As in Africa, this geographic expanse and biological diversity mean human groups evolved many different regional cultural adaptations. And again, there was not just a single agricultural revolution in South America, but several (Figure 11.20).

Three Regional Neolithics

Archaeologist Deborah Pearsall (1992) divides the South American Neolithic into three physiographic areas: low altitude, mid-altitude, and high altitude. Different plants growing wild in each of these divisions became the basis for distinct agricultural revolutions, with some crops from individual areas expanding into the others.

After about 10,000 B.P. in South America, the system of foraging for wild foods developed by Paleoindians was replaced by a more diverse and regionally specialized series of subsistence systems. In the Andes, hunters shifted from megafauna to small post-Pleistocene game such as deer and camelids (guanaco and vicuña). Elsewhere, subsistence shifted to a reliance on the abundant root crops of both the lowlands and the highlands; there is evidence in Chile for the use of a wild species of potato at Monte Verde by about 10,000 years ago (see Chapter 9 for a discussion of the earliest occupation of that site).

FIGURE 11.20

Archaeological sites in South America where evidence of early food production has been found.

The timing of the appearance of domesticates in South America is still unclear, and AMS dating has not yet been widely applied, so the plant remains themselves have not been dated directly. Some researchers argue for an early agricultural revolution dating back to close to 10,000 years ago, but the evidence so far presented has been equivocal.

There is evidence of the domestication of common beans and chili peppers by 5,000 years ago at Guitarrero Cave in highland Peru, located in Pearsall's mid-altitude division (Kaplan, Lynch, and Smith 1973; Lynch et al. 1985). Also interpreted as an early domesticate at this site is the root crop ulluco, a source of brightly colored, carbohydrate-rich **tubers.** Ulluco is still popular as a delicacy in parts of South America. Dating to about the same time, in Holocene South America, is Tres Ventanas Cave. The inhabitants were eating domesticated potato, manioc (the root crop from which tapioca is made), and other root crops.

FIGURE 11.21

A stand of quinoa, a significant food crop in ancient South America that, in higher altitudes, surpassed maize as a staple in the native diet. (Courtesy of John F. McCamant)

Domesticated squash and gourds were recovered at Ayacucho Cave. Also at this site is some of the earliest evidence for the domestication of an extremely important crop in the agriculture of South America: quinoa (Figure 11.21). Quinoa is a species of the genus *Chenopodium*. North American goosefoot is another species in this genus. The earliest evidence of domesticated quinoa comes from Panaulauca Cave in Peru. Quinoa seeds with thinner seed coats than in wild specimens have been dated there to between 4000 and 5000 B.P. (B. D. Smith 1995, 173). Quinoa plants produce particularly nutritious seeds, with a mix of amino acids superior to that of the better-known grains (see "Issues and Debates"). In some areas of South America, particularly the higher altitudes, quinoa exceeded maize in agricultural importance (McCamant 1992). Only the potato was more important in the diet of the inhabitants of high-altitude South America.

Cold-loving, high-altitude-adapted domesticated root crops, especially the potato, were the staples of much of upland South America. The potato, today a major component of European cuisine, was certainly South America's most significant agricultural contribution to Europe. Other important root crops, today unknown to most North Americans, also played important roles in the diet of ancient South America (Vietmeyer 1992). Oca, second in importance only to the potato, produced nutritious tubers at altitudes of up to 4,100 m (13,500 ft). The turniplike maca was cultivated at elevations of 4,300 m (14,000 ft), making it the only domesticated food crop able to be grown at that altitude. Other high-altitude roots domesticated and relied on as sources of food in the South American uplands were yacon, the legume jícama, ulluco, and arracacha. The 500-year-old Inka culture (to be discussed in Chapter 15), which occupied large portions of the western highlands of South America, relied more heavily on root crops than did any other of the world's ancient civilizations.

In lowland South America, domestication followed its own, largely separate, path. At Chilca Caves, evidence has been recovered of domesticated manioc and sweet potato. Also at Chilca Caves are domesticated jícama, beans, and bottle gourds.

Though maize became a significant element of South American subsistence, it appears late in the sequence, probably after 4000 B.P.; B. D. Smith (1995, 159) suggests a date of 3200 B.P. The first evidence of maize in South America was found at the Vegas site on the Ecuadorian coast. Though most archaeologists believe that maize was domesticated in Mesoamerica and diffused from there into South America, where it was adopted by cultures already practicing agriculture with their own native crops, that conclusion is not unanimous. As Karen Bruhns (1994) points out, we simply do not know the ancient geographical extent of teosinte. This wild ancestor of maize may have grown in South America, where local people could have carried out the same selective process as their northern neighbors. In any event, maize did not become an essential part of the diet in South America until well after 4000 B.P.

Animal Domestication in South America

Unlike in the Old World, where domesticated animals were a major part of human diets, animal husbandry played a relatively minor role in the New World. Among the few New World species that were successfully domesticated were the guinea pig (used as a food), the turkey, the dog, and the Muscovy duck. By far the most significant animal domestication in the New World was in South America (Kent 1987).

As mentioned earlier, the wild camelid species, the guanaco and vicuña, were exploited by post-Pleistocene hunters in western South America. In the central Andes, camelids became increasingly important in the diet, replacing deer as the subsistence focus sometime after 8000 B.P. Though why this shift occurred remains unclear, the ratio of camelid to deer bones at archaeological sites increases dramatically as wild camels were exploited more intensively.

Vicuñas and guanacos are herd animals, with rigid dominance hierarchies. Their pattern of living in social groups and adhering to social hierarchies, along with their territoriality, rendered them attractive candidates for herding, controlling, taming, and then domesticating. Humans, placing themselves in the position of the most dominant members of the herd, could have exerted control over herds of wild camelids within their defined territory. Through artificial selection for animals more amenable to carrying heavy burdens and for animals that produced more meat and thicker wool, ancient South Americans produced domesticated llamas (as beasts of burden and for meat) and alpacas (for their wool and meat; Figure 11.22). Earliest evidence for this domestication has been found at Pachamachay and Lauricocha Caves in Peru, dating to as early as 6500 B.P. (Wing 1977).

FIGURE 11.22

Llamas and alpacas were the only large animal species domesticated in the New World. Llamas like this one were used as beasts of burden and for food. (Food and Agriculture Organization, United Nations; photo by F. Mattioli)

Cotton

As was the case in the Near East, where flax was domesticated for use as a fiber at about 7000 B.P., a nonfood domesticate became an important element in the agricultural complex of South America. Domesticated cotton has been recovered at Ayacucho Cave dating to just after 5000 B.P.

Cotton has also been recovered at the El Paraíso site on the Peruvian coast, a large and permanent settlement that has been dated to between 3800 and 3500 B.P. (Quilter et al. 1991). Eight or nine large complexes of rooms, covering a broad area, demarcate the site. Evidence found there suggests a mixed and broad subsistence base. Remains of domesticated food crops were recovered, including squash, chili pepper, common and lima bean, jícama root, and fruits, especially guava. At least of equal importance in the food quest were the rich natural resources of the coast, including anchovies, mussels, and clams. Wild plant foods also contributed to the subsistence base.

Remains of domesticated cotton were far more abundant at the site than any of the domesticated foods. Cotton fiber was a major raw material for the production of fishing nets and lines as well as cloth. The authors of the El Paraíso report maintain that the growth of this site is attributable to its location, perfect for the growing of cotton. Later, cotton became a major fiber for use in textiles of many cultures in South America.

FIGURE 11.23

Seed heads of wild and domesticated varieties of einkorn and emmer wheat.

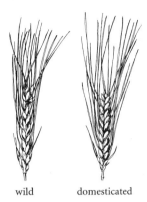

wild   domesticated   wild   domesticated

ISSUES AND DEBATES

HOW WAS DOMESTICATION ACCOMPLISHED?

In the domestication of plants and animals, human beings take the place of nature in the selection process. We can examine how this may have occurred for a number of different crops: wheat, maize, and beans.

The Domestication of Wheat

The **rachis** of wild wheat—the area of attachment of the individual kernels of wheat—becomes quite brittle when the wheat ripens. A brittle rachis is a distinct advantage in nature. It promotes seed dispersal, which, in turn, promotes the growth of more wheat plants in the following growing season. When the kernels are ripe, a brittle rachis can be shattered by the wind, a rain storm, or even an animal walking through a field (Figure 11.23).

Within any community of wild wheat plants today are individual plants that possess a combination of mutant genes for rachis form that results in a tougher, less brittle seed spike. Under conditions of natural selection, such forms are always in the minority, and they are at a clear disadvantage in terms of propagation: Their seeds are far less likely to disperse into the surrounding soil.

When humans enter the picture, however, the nature of selection changes drastically. Though preferred under wild conditions, a brittle rachis is *disadvantageous* for humans harvesting a wild crop, especially for those using a sickle to cut the plants off at the base. The impact of the tool is likely to shatter a brittle rachis, widely disperse the seeds, and make harvesting quite time-consuming.

Either by accident or by design—and likely a combination of the two—when humans harvested wild wheat, a greater proportion of the mutant plants with a tough rachis were brought back to the village. Most of the seeds of the more abundant plants with brittle connections simply fell off and did not make it back to the settlement. Again either by accident or by design, more of the seeds of tough-rachis plants carrying the genetic instructions for that tough rachis became planted near human habitations. In this way, human beings fundamentally changed the process of selection, replacing a natural context with a human context to which the plants adapted (Figure 11.24).

Genetic evidence indicates that this process may first have occurred in southeast Turkey in the area of the Karacadağ Mountains. Researchers examined the DNA of 261 lines of wild wheat (einkorn), including 11 lines that grow abundantly in the Karacadağ Mountain region (Heun et al. 1997). Next, they compared the DNA of these strands of wild wheat to that of 68 lines of modern, domesticated einkorn wheat. They found that not only were the 11 lines of wheat from the Karacadağ Mountains the most genetically distinct of all the wild wheats, but of all the wild varieties sampled, the Karacadağ wheat was also the most genetically similar to the modern domesticated varieties examined. The presence of archaeological sites in the same region with evidence of the very early domestication of einkorn (for example, Abu Hureyra and Çayönü mentioned earlier in this chapter) lends further support to the hypothesis that the Karacadağ wild wheat was the ultimate source for the einkorn domesticated more than 10,000 years ago in southwest Asia.

FIGURE 11.24

One of the many modern forms of wheat. (Food and Agriculture Organization, United Nations; photo by the Kenya Information Office)

From Teosinte to Maize

Wild maize, or teosinte, in some respects resembles the corn plant with which we are familiar. In fact, primitive varieties of maize are nearly identical to teosinte in cell form and genetic structure (Galinat 1992). However, teosinte produces not large cobs with rows of plump kernels, but small seed spikes, each with a brittle rachis and tiny, thickly encased seeds (Figure 11.25). Teosinte seeds are nutritious and were exploited by ancient Mesoamericans. With their brittle rachis, however, they must have been difficult to harvest effectively; and with their thick glumes, or seed cases, they were equally difficult to process into an edible form.

Luckily, just a few genes control those features. Recent genetic analysis has shown that probably only about five genetic loci control the physical characteristics that distinguish maize from teosinte (Raloff 1993; Doebley, Stec, and Hubbard 1997), and maizelike teosinte mutants are produced in wild populations (Beadle 1977). These mutants yield naked seeds and possess a tougher rachis than regular teosinte, features that are not advantageous in the wild but are preferred by humans. We also know that a single mutation on one teosinte chromosome doubles the number of rows of kernels, and another alters the standard pattern of single spikelets to paired, again greatly increasing seed yield (Galinat 1992). Still another mutation enlarges the individual kernels.

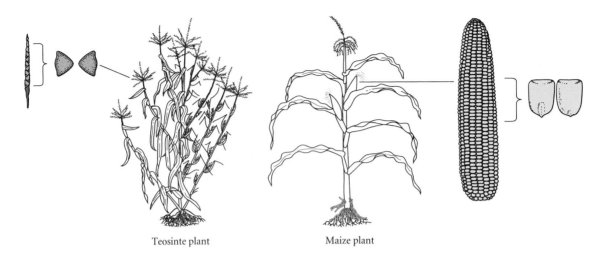

Teosinte plant   Maize plant

FIGURE 11.25

Teosinte plant, spike, and seeds and maize plant, cob, and kernels.

As maize researcher Walton C. Galinat (1992) points out, ancient users of teosinte would have recognized the desirable characteristics of some of the mutant forms of that plant. In the wild, these rare forms would remain rare, since cross-pollination would be occurring with the overwhelming abundance of nonmutant forms. By isolating the mutants, however, ancient Mesoamericans could have ensured that plants with rare features, maladaptive in nature but desirable for humans, cross-bred only with mutants with the same or other desirable characteristics. As Galinat indicates, though ancient people lacked our knowledge of genetics, their powers of observation of the world around them were probably far better than our own—including, perhaps especially, their observation of the plant life on which they depended for survival. Applying the knowledge derived from such observation, they could have domesticated maize rather quickly. Genetic analysis of the hundreds of varieties of maize and the many different kinds of wild teosinte has been conducted by plant biologist John Doebley. He has identified one particular teosinte subgroup that, based on its genetic makeup, could be the common ancestor of the many varieties of the domesticated crop: a race of teosinte that grows along the Balsas River in Mexico (Raloff 1993; Figure 11.26).

Beans

Wild beans grow in twisted pods that become brittle when ripe, and the beans themselves are rather impermeable. People selected for mutant beans with straight, limp, nonshattering pods for easier harvesting, and for more permeable varieties, which reduced the time needed for soaking in water before they could be cooked (Kaplan 1981; Kaplan and Kaplan 1992; De Tapia 1992). This process may have been repeated several times in Mesoamerica and South America, ultimately providing the world with four separate domesticated bean species: common, lima and sievas, scarlet runner, and tepary beans, and the many varieties of these various species, including kidney, lima, pinto, wax, and navy (Kaplan and Kaplan 1992, 61; another commonly eaten bean, fava, is an Old World domesticate).

The Nature of Artificial Selection

Charles Darwin, who used artificial selection in agriculture as an analogy for natural selection in the wild, phrased it appropriately when, referring to horticulturists' ability to produce a spectacular array of plants and animals for human use, he stated: "The art is simple, and as far as the final result is concerned, has been followed almost unconsciously. It has consisted in always cultivating the best-known variety, sowing its seeds, and, when a slightly better variety chanced to appear, selecting it, and so onwards" (Diamond 1994, 106). Much the same was true during the early post-Pleistocene.

THE REMARKABLY MODERN CUISINE OF THE ANCIENT WORLD

You have probably tried and perhaps eat often the "ethnic" foods of different cultures that are widely available in the modern world. Virtually every city in North America has restaurants specializing in many kinds of foods: Chinese and Japanese food with their rice-based dishes, Mexican cuisine with its corn flour tortillas and tacos and beans, Middle Eastern food with wheat flour pita bread, Greek food with lamb, German food with beef and pork, the Native American turkey we eat on Thanksgiving, and so on—all part of our modern diet.

All of these foods—rice, wheat, potato, corn, beef, chicken, pork, turkey—form the basis for the diet of the world's burgeoning human population at the turn of the twenty-first century. And all were domesticated in antiquity. In fact, it is difficult to come up with any economically significant modern food sources that were not part of the food base thousands of years ago, during the Neolithic. Two exceptions are strawberries, which were not domesticated until the Middle Ages, and pecans, which were not domesticated until 1846 (Diamond 1994).

So, although we may think of ancient people as primitive, we have them to thank for virtually all the foods we rely on today. We have refined the work of the ancients by improving yield, increasing drought resistance, and accelerating ripening. But we have not added significantly to the inventory of domesticates. Statistics on 1986 worldwide yields of modern agriculture show this to be the case (Table 11.1). Most of the crops in Table 11.1 were discussed in this chapter. Wheat, corn, rice, potato, barley, manioc, sweet potato, soybean, and sorghum are among the top modern crops, and all are ancient in origin (Heiser 1990, 63). Sugarcane surpasses their yields, but this is misleading because its weight is exaggerated as a result of water content.

FIGURE 11.26

Teosinte is the wild ancestor of maize. This is a modern variety (Zea mays parviglumis), *from the Rio Balsas in Mexico, which may be the form from which domesticated maize is descended.*
(Courtesy of Dolores Piperno, Smithsonian Tropical Research Institute)

TABLE 11.1

Agricultural Yields Worldwide, 1986

CROP	MILLION METRIC TONS	CROP	MILLION METRIC TONS
Sugarcane	932	Apple	40
Wheat	536	Coconut	39
Corn	481	Cabbage	38
Rice	476	Rye	32
Potato	309	Millet	31
Sugar beet	286	Watermelon	28
Barley	180	Yam	27
Manioc	137	Onion	25
Sweet potato	110	Sunflower	21
Soybean	95	Rape	20
Sorghum	71	Bean (dry)	15
Banana and plantain	68	Pea (dry)	14
Grape	67	Mango	14
Tomato	60	Avocado	10
Oat	48	Pineapple	10
Orange	41	Olive	9

From Heiser (1990, 63).

NEOLITHIC NUTRITION

Some of the plant foods domesticated by Neolithic people are high in protein. For example, on a scale comparing relative protein content of various foods (Table 11.2), where eggs represent a perfect score of 100 for their rich and complete complement of amino acids, wheat rates a 44, rice a 57, and corn a 41. Compare this to 69 for beef, 64 for chicken, and 70 for fish.

There is a serious problem, however, with relying on the cereals for protein: As Table 11.2 also shows, neither wheat, rice, nor maize provides complete proteins, for each lacks at least one of the eight essential amino acids necessary to sustain human life (isoleucine, leucine, lysine, methionine, phenylalanine, threonine, tryptophan, and valine). Wheat, rice, and maize, though high in protein, are each deficient in lysine. Quinoa, a significant South American domesticate, offers a more complete complement of amino acids, including lysine.

Remarkably, in the Near East, the Far East, and Mesoamerica, where wheat, rice, and maize, respectively, became the basis for a way of life, people also domesticated other wild crops that, though even less complete than wheat, rice, or maize in the amino acids they contain, are rich in lysine (Heiser

TABLE 11.2

Amino Acid Content of Various Foods

FOOD	AMINO ACID[a]								PROTEIN SCORE[b]
	ISO-LEUCINE	LEUCINE	LYSINE	METHI-ONINE	PHENYL-ALANINE	THREO-NINE	TRYPTO-PHAN	VALINE	
Hen's egg	393	551	436	210	358	320	93	428	100
Beef	301	507	556	169	275	287	70	313	69
Cow's milk	295	596	487	157	336	278	88	362	60
Chicken	334	460	497	157	250	248	64	318	64
Fish	299	480	569	179	245	286	70	382	70
Corn	230	783	167	120	305	225	44	303	41
Wheat	204	417	179	94	282	183	68	276	44
Rice	238	514	237	145	322	244	78	344	57
Bean	262	476	450	66	326	248	63	287	34
Soybean	284	486	399	79	309	241	80	300	47
Potato	236	377	299	81	251	235	103	292	34
Manioc	175	247	259	83	156	165	72	204	41
Coconut	244	419	220	120	283	212	68	339	55

From Heiser (1990, 31).
[a]*Measured in milligrams per gram of nitrogen.*
[b]*Each food's protein content is scored relative to that of the hen's egg, which, as the highest in protein, is given a score of 100.*

1990). In the Near East it was a suite of legumes—including lentil, chickpea, and peas—that provided the amino acid missing in wheat. In the Far East, lentils provided the lysine missing in rice. In Mesoamerica, beans supplied the missing protein component.

So, without any knowledge of nutrition or biochemistry, prehistoric people in different parts of the world domesticated a range of plants that together provided the essential amino acids needed for them to survive and prosper.

WAS AGRICULTURE THE "WORST MISTAKE IN THE HISTORY OF THE HUMAN RACE"?

Scientist Jared Diamond (1987b) labeled agriculture the "worst mistake in the history of the human race" in the title of a provocative essay. His interesting idea is backed up by some impressive archaeological evidence. Clearly, agriculture can provide more food than can most foraging systems and can do so in a wide variety of habitats. In terms of caloric output, when agriculture works, it wins, hands down. At the same time we have just seen that many of the world's ancient agricultural systems produced crops that complemented each other in amino acid content. So theoretically, not only can agriculture produce lots of food for lots of mouths, but it also can give a mixture of foods that together provide a healthy diet. Unfortunately, the evidence shows that this system often did not work in this way.

Mark Cohen and George Armelagos (1984) have summarized the evidence for the prevalence of paleopathology—ancient disease—coincident with the origins of agriculture in North, Central, and South America, the eastern Mediterranean, western Europe, the Middle East, southern Asia, and Nubia. When comparing parameters of health as revealed by prehistoric skeletons, in most instances older hunter-gatherer groups exhibited higher levels of health and nutrition than did the farmers who succeeded them. Specifically, there were higher levels of infection in farmers than in previous foragers in the same regions. Some early farming populations show increases in tubercular infections (Buikstra 1984); others show higher levels of gastrointestinal infections (seen in a survey of mummified humans in South America; Allison 1984). Many more farming groups show higher rates of infections of uncertain origin. Of course, agriculture itself doesn't cause disease; it merely establishes the conditions conducive for disease to spread: large, dense, sedentary populations.

Ironically, chronic malnutrition seems to be another major problem that accompanied the shift to an agricultural way of life. While many people may stereotype hunter-gatherers as living hand-to-mouth, where every meal might be their last for some time, in most of the studies Cohen and Armelagos summarize, farmers show more evidence of malnutrition than do their foraging forebears. Nutritionally based anemia (as evidenced by porosity of the skull) was found to be severe in a number of farming groups in the American Midwest. Other evidence for poorer nutrition among some farming groups included an overall decline in stature. Episodes of severe malnutrition among farmers was further indicated by more incidences of enamel hypoplasia (see the discussion in Chapter 6 regarding the Neandertals and this condition).

Perhaps most remarkable of all, for the majority of cases reported in a symposium Cohen and Armelagos organized on this issue, where age at death was calculated for the archaeological samples, hunter-gatherers lived longer than did the farmers in the same regions. They conclude: "Taken as a whole, these indicators fairly clearly suggest an overall decline in the quality—and probably in the length—of human life associated with the adoption of agriculture" (1984, 594).

Another rather nasty result of a shift to an agricultural way of life seems to have been the institutionalization of warfare and violence. Direct evidence of personal violence is rare in Pleistocene archaeological contexts. Few skeletons exhibit traumatic wounds that might have resulted from interpersonal violence. In the Neolithic, however, such evidence becomes far more common within a context not of just one person killing another, but of whole groups taking up arms against their neighbors. Perhaps the problems inherent in an agricultural way of life and the always present potential for a collapse of the subsistence base are at the heart of this phenomenon. Agriculture, though potentially of enormous benefit, is a fragile basis for subsistence. It allows for the existence of large and dense populations as long as it works; but when it doesn't work, there are a lot of hungry people. And when the neighbors of starving people have food, the hungry may become violent.

Maybe agriculture wasn't a mistake, but it had a fundamental drawback: Though it allowed more people to live, many did not live as well as their hunter-gatherer ancestors.

IMPLICATIONS OF THE NEOLITHIC: THE ROOTS OF SOCIAL COMPLEXITY

For most of human history, we have foraged for food. Small nomadic groups could easily supply the necessities for their families. No one needed more, and providing for more than one's needs made little sense. The organization of such societies could be rather simple, revolving around age and sex categories. Such societies likely were largely **egalitarian;** beyond the usual distinctions based on age and sex, virtually all people had equivalent rights, status, and access to resources.

Archaeologist Donald Henry (1989) suggests that the combination of a rich habitat and sedentism led to a dramatic increase in human population. In his view, nomadic, simple foragers have a relatively low level of fertility. Their high-protein, low-carbohydrate diets produce low proportions of body fat, and these low proportions are commonly associated with low fertility in women. High physical activity and long periods of nursing common among recent simple foragers also probably contributed to low levels of female fertility.

In Henry's view, the shift to complex foraging and a more sedentary existence would have contributed to higher fertility levels. A diet higher in wild cereals produces proportionally more body fat, leading to higher fertility among women. Cereals produce easily digested foods that would have supplemented and then replaced mother's milk as a primary food for older infants. Since lactation is a natural dampener of fertility, earlier weaning would have resulted in closer spacing of births and the potential for a greater number of live births for each woman. A more sedentary existence may also have lowered infant mortality and perhaps increased longevity among the aged. These more vulnerable members of society could safely stay in a fixed village rather than be forced regularly to move great distances as part of a nomadic existence with its greater risk of accident and trauma.

All of these factors may have resulted in a trend of increasing size among some local human populations in the Holocene. Given sufficient time, even in very rich habitats, human population size can reach **carrying capacity:** the maximum population an area can sustain within the context of a given subsistence system. And human population growth is like a runaway train: Once it picks up speed, it is difficult to control. So even after reaching an area's carrying capacity, Holocene human populations probably continued to grow in food-rich regions, overshooting the ability of the territory to feed the population, again within the context of the same subsistence strategy. In some areas, small changes in climate or minor changes in plant characteristics may have further destabilized local economies.

One possible response to surpassing the carrying capacity of a region is for a group to exploit adjoining land. However, good land may itself be limited—for example, to within the confines of a river valley. Where neighbors are in the same position, having filled up all the available desirable habitat in their home territories, expansion also is problematic. Impinging on the neighbors' territory can lead to conflict, especially when they too are up against the capacity of the land to provide enough food.

Another option is to stay put but shift and intensify the food quest in the same territory. The impulse to produce more food to feed a growing population was satisfied in some areas by the development of more complex subsistence strategies involving intensive labor and requiring more cooperation and greater coordination of increasing numbers of people. This development resulted in a change in the social and economic equations that defined those societies. Hierarchies that did not exist in earlier foraging groups but that were helpful in structuring cooperative labor and in organizing more complex technologies probably became entrenched, even before domestication and agriculture, as pre-Neolithic societies reacted to population increase.

The results of this strategy of intensification of the exploitation of wild foods were, at least in some regions, even better than the participants could have anticipated. Not only were people able to increase their wild food base enough to feed a larger population, but they actually were also able to produce a food surplus by artificially selecting for propagation the most productive individuals in their wild food species. This food surplus changed the social and economic equations yet again, setting the stage for a dramatic increase in complexity in some human societies. The results of this increase are the focus of the next chapter.

CASE STUDY CLOSE-UP

The revolution that is the focus of this chapter was not an event, but a slow process that only gradually changed the fundamental way people made a living. Analysis of this shift in the Khabur Basin in northeastern Syria is a perfect example (Zeder 1994a,b).

The area had been only sparsely occupied before 12,000 B.P. Beginning about 10,000 years ago, villages began turning up in the archaeological record with a subsistence base that included a variety of early domesticates, including wheat, lentils, peas, and beans. The bones of domesticated sheep and goats were found in early levels of these settlements, with pig and cattle remains showing up later.

A detailed analysis of one site in the Khabur Basin, Umm Qseir, clearly shows the evolutionary nature of the shift from foraging to farming. For example, after 8000 B.P., domesticated sheep, goat, and pig contributed to the diet in the settlement. But the Neolithic residents of Umm Qseir had not abandoned their earlier pattern of hunting and gathering. More than half the animal remains recovered at the site were of wild animals—gazelle, deer, wild cattle, hare, turtles, wild ass, birds, and freshwater clams (Zeder 1994b, 5).

The use of both wild and domesticated sources of food seems to reflect a seasonal rhythm at Umm Qseir. Most animal species have a particular mating season and a fairly consistent gestational period for each species, so most of the offspring are born within a narrow period of time during the year. Since the age of death of a juvenile animal can be estimated based on tooth eruption and bone development, archaeologists can often determine the time of year an animal was killed. In other words, if the young of a particular species tend to be born in the early spring, and many of the younger animals at a site were slaughtered in their 15th month of life, just count 15 months from early spring to determine when they were slaughtered. In this hypothetical example, they were killed in the summer.

Pigs were slaughtered most commonly at Umm Qseir between August and October. The ages of sheep and goats killed at the site correspond to this same period, which actually extended until January. This is the arid summer and early rainy season, precisely when wild resources would have been at their leanest. So domestication did not supplant foraging in the subsistence system at Umm Qseir. Instead, domestication allowed for the permanent occupation of an area rich with seasonally available wild foods, even during seasons when those wild foods were not plentiful.

As archaeologist Melinda Zeder (1994b) points out, here and elsewhere the Neolithic was not a period during which all people marched down the path to a purely agricultural mode of subsistence. For a long time, domestication complemented foraging but did not replace it. Only much later did agriculture and animal husbandry become the primary sources of food for most of the world's people, setting the stage for the period of time to be described in Chapters 12–15.

VISITING THE PAST

The Chinese site of Banpo is highlighted in an exhibit built at the site in Shaanxi. Many artifacts unearthed at the site are on display, including tools for tilling the soil (stone spades and hoes) and ceramic jars for storing food. Particularly informative is the array of recovered food remains on display. Clearly the people of Banpo had a diverse economy; on display are the remains of chestnuts, hazelnuts, hackberries, pine nuts, snails, antelopes, pigs, foxes, cattle, and many species of fish that have been found. Domesticated millet, Chinese cabbage, and leaf mustard were also found. Part of the excavated site has been preserved at the museum, and visitors can also see reconstructed houses, or "cottages."

Many other sites dating to after the food-producing revolution do not contain any direct evidence of the dramatic shift in human subsistence. But each such site is an object lesson in the enormous impacts of that revolution:

the degree of sedentism implied, the size of the resident population, the specialization of labor, social stratification, the construction of monuments.

SUMMARY

Beginning sometime after 12,000 B.P., and in a number of world areas, the archaeological record shows a subtle, barely perceptible shift in how people supplied their subsistence needs. Whereas humans previously had fed themselves, like all other animals, by foraging for wild foods, some groups began intentionally encouraging the growth of particular plants (by turning over soil, planting seeds, weeding, thinning out, and in other ways tending them) and herding and selectively culling herds of animals. Human beings replaced nature as the selective force operating on certain species. This "artificial selection" encouraged the growth of those individuals within plant and animal species that were not necessarily well adapted to a life in the wild but that had characteristics advantageous to their human caretakers. Over many generations of selection, human beings in the Near East, Europe, eastern Asia, Africa, and North and South America developed new species that were the product not of natural processes, but of cultural requirements. This was the Neolithic Revolution, which, while slow, would revolutionize the way people made a living and how they lived—and how we live in the modern world.

TO LEARN MORE

Technical Summaries

A very useful volume with a series of articles on each of the major centers of plant and animal domestication in antiquity is *The Origins of Agriculture: An International Perspective*, edited by archaeologists C. Wesley Cowan and Patty Jo Watson (1992). For coverage of Old World domestication from a geneticist's point of view, see Daniel Zohary and Maria Hopf's *Domestication of Plants in the Old World* (1994). Theirs is a virtual encyclopedia featuring a detailed crop-by-crop discussion of all of the important Old World domesticates. For a very up-to-date summary of the Neolithic of southwest Asia and the probable first plant and animal domestication in the world, see Ofer Bar-Yosef's 1998 article in *Evolutionary Anthropology* focusing on the Natufian culture of the Levant. An extremely detailed treatment of the origins of agriculture in the Near East is Donald O. Henry's *From Foraging to Agriculture: The Levant at the End of the Ice Age* (1989). See the volume edited by Bruce Smith, *Rivers of Change* (1992), for a series of discussions on the patterns and sequences of domestication in North America.

Popular Summaries

Archaeologist Bruce Smith's excellent synthesis titled *The Emergence of Agriculture* (1995) presents a broad, comparative survey of the origins of food production. His is the best detailed discussion of domestication written not just for other scientists, but also for everybody interested in the topic. For a series of useful summaries of New World domestication, read the papers in *Chilies to Chocolate: Food the Americas Gave the World,* edited by Nelson Foster and Linda S. Cordell (1992). For a concise piece on the process of domestication, read Jared Diamond's "How to Tame a Wild Plant," in the September 1994 issue of *Discover* magazine. For a discussion of the health impacts of the agricultural revolution, see the article "Disease and Death at Dr. Dickson's Mound" (1985) by A. H. Goodman and George Armelagos in *Natural History* magazine.

On the Web

A terrific Internet site on the general topic of the agricultural revolution can be found at http://www.mc.maricopa.edu/anthro/lost_tribes/hg_ag/where.html. There are links to online articles discussing the implications of domestication and a very useful map with links to lists of plants and animals domesticated in each of the active locations on the map. I really enjoyed this site. For the domestication of animals, visit the Agripedia site at http://frost.ca.uky.edu/agripedia/asc106/HISDOMES.HTM, with links to several domesticated species. For more information on animal domestication, with a useful chart presenting the timing of the earliest domestication for a number of species, visit http://asci.uvm.edu/bramley/DOMESTIC.html.

KEY TERMS

Neolithic	legume	glume
foraging	emmer	teosinte
artificial selection	einkorn	pluvial
domestication	seedbed selection	pastoralist
cereal	Tehuacán	Peiligang
Fertile Crescent	Ajuereado phase	Yang-shao
Geometric Kebaran	microband	Linienbandkeramik
Levant	El Riego phase	(LBK)
Mushabian	Coxcatlán phase	tuber
Natufian	Abejas phase	rachis
Zarzian	Purrón phase	egalitarian
Karim Shahirian	Ajalpán phase	carrying capacity
simple forager	accelerator mass	
complex foraging	spectrometry (AMS)	

12

The Roots of Complexity

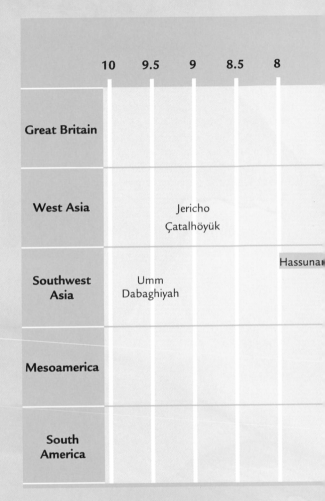

	10	9.5	9	8.5	8
Great Britain					
West Asia			Jericho Çatalhöyük		
Southwest Asia		Umm Dabaghiyah			Hassuna
Mesoamerica					
South America					

CHAPTER OVERVIEW

For nearly all of the human past, societies were largely egalitarian. Populations were small and dispersed, and family relationships determined how decisions were made. Following the shift to food producing, however, some societies in the Old and New Worlds became socially, politically, and economically more complex. Authority, work, and decision making were organized on the basis of a larger social group, not just the household or family. People most likely developed complex social and political systems in situations where the coordinated labor of a large group of people was needed to meet some immediate challenge or to exploit a unique opportunity. The great monuments that now dominate the archaeological record of some ancient cultures and, therefore, occupy the time of so many archaeologists are one result of the evolution of complex social, political, and economic systems.

350

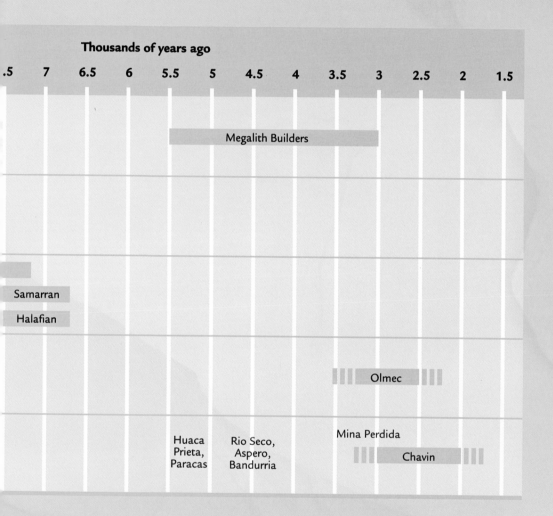

Thousands of years ago

| .5 | 7 | 6.5 | 6 | 5.5 | 5 | 4.5 | 4 | 3.5 | 3 | 2.5 | 2 | 1.5 |

Megalith Builders

Samarran

Halafian

Olmec

Mina Perdida

Huaca Prieta, Paracas

Rio Seco, Aspero, Bandurria

Chavin

Everyone reacts differently upon seeing Stonehenge for the first time (Figures 12.1 and 12.2; Color Plates 9 and 10). Surprisingly, for some the initial reaction is one of disappointment. The major highway that today transects the site certainly detracts from one's first impression of this 5,000-year-old monument. And because visitors are often familiar with artists' conceptions of the site at its peak, the current ruin, with most of its component stones either missing or lying recumbent and sometimes in pieces, simply does not live up to their expectations. Anticipating an intact monument, instead they are confronted by a ruin.

For others, however, even in ruin, Stonehenge is an ancient monument of uncommon beauty, majesty, and even mystery (Chippindale 1983). Though the pyramids of ancient Egypt were built on a far grander scale (see Chapter 13), though the stone blocks that make up the city walls of the Inka were cut with much greater precision (Chapter 15), though the painted murals of the Maya may be more visually arresting (Chapter 15), and though the tombs of the ancient rulers of Mesopotamia may reflect greater wealth, the Stonehenge ruin that can be seen today is every bit as compelling and impressive as these other works of the ancient world (Ruggles 1996).

FIGURE 12.1

The location of Stonehenge, which was an early chiefdom-level society in England.

ATLANTIC OCEAN

Stonehenge

THE CONSTRUCTION OF STONEHENGE

Stonehenge was an awe-inspiring construction project, accomplished not by a sophisticated nation-state, but by a people who otherwise appear to have been simple farmers (Figure 12.3; Castleden 1987). About 5,000 years ago, people living in the south of England in an area of low, undulating hills called the Salisbury Plain, began construction of Stonehenge by excavating a ditch, nearly perfectly circular and about 100 m (300 ft) in diameter. At first, this ditch was all that constituted Stonehenge. Then, by about 4,500 years ago, the people who built the monument began transporting dozens of volcanic stones (called bluestones for their slightly blue hue) from the Preseli Mountains in southwest Wales, a distance of about 200 km (125 mi) from the Salisbury Plain. The Stonehenge bluestones are a heavy, dense rock, each one weighing as much as 4,000 kg (more than 4 tons). They were arranged in a double half-circle located in the center of the area circumscribed by the circular ditch. Transporting stones weighing more than 8,000 lb more than 100 miles and then erecting them was no mean feat for an otherwise technologically unremarkable farming people with no machines or even draft animals. But even this impressive, early version of Stonehenge was a pale harbinger of what it was to become.

Barely a hundred years after erecting the bluestone semicircle, major construction commenced on the monumental Stonehenge we are familiar with today. Beginning around 4,400 years ago, the builders of Stonehenge began shaping and transporting 30 upright stones called **sarsens** from the area

FIGURE 12.2

Stonehenge is both massive and marvelous—a remarkable monument made possible by the development of a society in which the labor of many could be commanded by the few. (K. L. Feder)

FIGURE 12.3

The small village of Skara Brae in the Orkney Islands, Scotland, was occupied at about the time Stonehenge was being built. Though the inhabitants of this village did not play a role in the construction of Stonehenge— they simply were too far away—it is likely that the populations of a large number of small villages like Skara Brae provided the labor that made Stonehenge possible. (K. L. Feder)

around the village of Avebury to the north, which is a distance of about 30 km (18 mi). The sarsens dwarf the bluestones and are hard as iron; each sarsen is over 3 m (10 ft) tall and weighs 25,000 kg (55,000 lb). The 30 sarsens were erected in a circle 30 m (100 ft) across, within and concentric with the older circular ditch.

The tops of each of the 30 roughly rectangular sarsens were precisely carved to produce two knobs, or tenons. Next, the builders of Stonehenge shaped 30 stone cap pieces, or **lintels,** of about 5,500 kg (12,000 lb) each, sculpting two hollows, or mortises, on the bottom of each. Then, in an absolutely remarkable feat, they lifted up these lintels and perched them on top of the sarsens, fitting the mortises on each lintel onto the tenons of two adjacent uprights (Figure 12.4). Each lintel had to be shaped precisely, curved on the exterior and interior surfaces to match the arc of the circle of the sarsens. Even a slight deviation in shape and size of any of the 30 lintels and any slight misalignment of the tenons on the sarsens or of the mortises on the lintels would have made completion of the monument impossible. What resulted was a smooth circle of stones, precisely positioned and joined together (Figure 12.5, p. 356).

And there is more. Within the sarsen circle are five sets of three stones each—two uprights and one lintel. Arranged in a giant horseshoe shape, these **trilithon** uprights were the largest stones erected by the builders of Stonehenge. Each trilithon upright stands about 8 m (24 ft) above the surface, with an additional 2 m (6 ft) of stone nestled in the chalky ground underlying the monument. The largest of the trilithon uprights weighs 45,000 kg (50 tons), and the associated lintel weighs 9,000 kg (10 tons); and, remember—this 10-ton block had to be raised up to and perched precisely on the top of its 24-ft-high trilithon upright pair.

IMAGINING STONEHENGE

In a project replicating ancient technology sponsored by the PBS science series *Nova* (Page and Cort 1997), a series of experiments were conducted in an attempt to determine how Stonehenge and other ancient monuments could have been built. Two parallel sets of squared-off log beams were placed in the ground, producing a wooden trackway, and a cement trilithon upright weighing 50 tons was attached to a wooden sled that fit onto the trackway. After a bit of trial and error, a crew of about 200 volunteers was able to move the enormously heavy replica. With the help of some fundamental engineering principles reasonably within the capability of ancient people, the volunteers were able to erect the trilithon upright, setting it into a 6-ft-deep socket they had excavated in the chalky subsoil. Then, using staging, levers, counterweights, and human muscle power, they raised the 10-ton trilithon lintel up above a trilithon upright pair and positioned it firmly on top of them, attaching it by using the same mortise and tenon joinery employed by the builders of Stonehenge. Many mistakes were made along the way, but the participants in this experiment showed that a group of people willing to work hard, a sensible division of labor, and an effective organization of that labor force could produce truly remarkable results in a relatively short period of time. It could have been no different for the builders of Stonehenge and the hundreds of other stone monuments that can be found across much of Europe (Burl 1995), monuments whose primary features—being built of stone and tending to be massive—provide the name we apply to them: the **megaliths** (Figure 12.6).

The builders of Stonehenge are emblematic of a pattern we see throughout much of the world at various times after the beginning of the Neolithic. The roots of this new revolution in economic, social, and political complexity, evidenced in the archaeological record as monumental works, is the focus of this chapter.

FIGURE 12.4

Artist's conception of the raising of the stone lintels that topped the sarsens and trilithons of Stonehenge by using wooden platforms.
(From C. Chippindale. 1983. *Stonehenge Complete.* London: Routledge)

Earlier in this book, archaeology was defined as the study of the material remains of human behavior. Most archaeol-

CHRONICLE

ogists focus on the material record—the stuff that people made and used—because these material remains are the only direct evidence we have of how people lived and what they accomplished during their lifetimes in the time before the invention of writing and the keeping of historical records. Ancient monuments such as Stonehenge engage the archaeologist, at least in part, in the same way they engage everybody else: Very simply, they are beautiful and fascinating. Beyond this, however, anthropologists are drawn to ancient monuments not just because of their visual magnificence or enchantment, but also for what they imply about the abilities of past peoples to conscript and organize the labor necessary to produce them.

FIGURE 12.5

Depiction of an intact Stonehenge upon completion 4,000 years ago. Note the precision with which the enormous sarsens and trilithon uprights were connected to each other by their associated lintels.

SIMPLICITY AND COMPLEXITY

Most hunting-and-gathering societies organize their social, political, and economic lives at the level of the household or the family. Populations tend to be small and dispersed. Decisions are made; labor is divided, distributed, and organized; and wealth is apportioned on the basis of family relationships.

Many of you probably have been involved in a family or local community project. Perhaps you helped your parents build a storage shed for gardening tools, or maybe it was a deck added on to the back of your house; some of you may have helped set up a community garden in your neighborhood, or you assisted in cleaning up and renovating an abandoned house. The number of people involved in the project likely was small, the number of distinctly different chores or jobs in the overall project relatively few, and the task of coordinating the labor fairly straightforward. After all, organizing a labor party can be pretty simple when all the folks involved in the project are related to one another; it's usually pretty clear who the head or heads of a family are, and the task of organizing and overseeing the project usually falls to them.

The project becomes a little more complicated when the labor party consists of a small number of friends, acquaintances, close neighbors, or merely people who happen to live in the same community. Obviously, what's needed is some consensus about who will direct the project and which jobs will be done by whom and when. But consensus can be reached relatively easily when the group is small, the abilities of each individual are readily apparent, and there is a direct benefit for each person involved.

The project becomes far more complicated, however, when the group is large and there is no overall family or accepted community structure on which to base the coordination of a task. Remember the group of 200 volunteers who moved the single Stonehenge trilithon replica and who then raised the one lintel? They were not members of the same family or community. Of necessity, for the short period of time they participated, they had to accept the dictates of the people who organized the project. Now imagine the hundreds and even thousands of ancient farmers who built the real Stonehenge in fits

FIGURE 12.6

Stonehenge may be the best known, but it is only one of literally thousands of Megalithic monuments located in western Europe. Three of the better preserved are shown here: Swinside and Castlerigg, stone circles in the west of England, and Avebury, an enormous stone circle located near Stonehenge in the south of England. (K. L. Feder)

and starts over the course of hundreds of years. In all likelihood, at any one time, many of the builders did not even know one another. There could have been no agreed-upon family head to coordinate the project, no clear sense of obligation based on kinship that convinced people to participate or follow the dictates of the family head; and there probably was not even an expectation of reciprocity, no prospect that one would get something tangible in return for participating in the project. For the decision to be made to build the monument in the first place and to conscript the labor force, to delegate tasks and coordinate all of the many jobs that needed doing, there had to have been someone or, perhaps, a small group in charge. At the same time, there had to have been a social and political structure of command and an attendant process of decision making that transcended the individual household, family, or local community and that applied to the larger social group needed to accomplish the monumental task. Without such a structure, there likely would have been chaos. Chaos is the last thing needed when a large number of people are involved in a difficult and dangerous task requiring a great deal of precision.

The Origins of Complexity

In some instances, the food-producing revolution led to societies arranged in just such a way, where social, political, and economic systems were organized in a complex fashion. In these **complex societies,** authority, work, and decision making were organized not simply on a household or family basis, but on the basis of a larger social group.

This shift to social, political, and economic complexity was not inevitable or universal; the archaeological record of Neolithic food producers does not reflect a pattern where all peoples marched in lockstep toward such complexity. Instead, the ability to produce and control the production of a surplus of food, with few exceptions made possible exclusively by agriculture, made such complexity not certain, but possible. In other words, where agricultural efficiency allowed just a few people to produce enough food to feed entire communities—and where these communities could greatly increase in size and density because agriculture allowed for the production of great amounts of food in a relatively small area—an enormous labor potential was released to accomplish other things, among them, construction of impressive monuments like Stonehenge. A recent television commercial for the agribusiness Archer Daniels Midland claims that each American farmer in the 1990s produces enough food to feed 130 people, the vast majority of whom are free, therefore, to engage in other pursuits. On a smaller scale, some farmers of the ancient Neolithic, as a result of the agricultural richness of their region and the sophistication of their agricultural technology, similarly could feed masses of people whose labor, once appropriated and organized, could be directed to other tasks.

Why Complexity?

Why might a group of people take the road toward complexity? Why might individuals surrender some of their social, political, and economic independence and volunteer their labor to participate in a community project like the construction of a Stonehenge? In all likelihood, these monuments were *not* the cause of such complexity, but an effect. Complex social, political, and economic structures did not develop explicitly so that people could build great and impressive monuments. It is far more probable that Neolithic people developed complex social and political structures to respond to more practical challenges where individuals gave up some of their independence and donated their labor, at least initially, to reap individual and practical benefits. For example, large-scale labor projects requiring coordination of the work of many people may have been made necessary by the need to increase agricultural output. The production of seedbeds or the construction of water-control structures (dams, canals, reservoirs) may have required complex social, political, and economic organization. An external military threat may have required the organization of an army or of a construction gang to build defensive works—for example, a wall around a settlement. Even the discovery of an abundant source of an important raw material—for example, clay, stone, or metal—may have been seen as an opportunity to generate wealth or concentrate power if people organized their labor to quarry the raw material or devise ways of monopolizing it.

The notion here is that once a complex social or political structure develops to meet an immediate and practical need, that structure might not simply disappear once the threat is eliminated, the challenge answered, or the opportunity exploited. Such a structure might find other projects, not always practical ones, to devote its time to. The great monuments that dominate the archaeological record of some ancient cultures and, therefore, occupy the time of so many archaeologists are, in this interpretation, merely the incidental effects of the evolution of complex social, political, and economic structures that developed in response to more concrete challenges, threats, or opportunities.

A REVOLUTION IN SUBSISTENCE, A REVOLUTION IN SOCIETY

Society may become more complex when the labor of many must be organized—to prepare seedbeds, to clear forests, to control water, to build animal corrals—to meet the requirements of a growing population. Certain individuals, as a result of their competence or charisma, are given the authority to organize these group or communal activities. These individuals are able to organize the labor, assign tasks, divide responsibilities, direct actions, and oversee duties. Through their skills to persuade, bargain, marshall group opinion, and cajole, and even simply by the force of their will, they can get things done. They are invested not so much with power—there are no laws, police force, or army to coerce others to heed their directions—but with authority. They are good at organizing labor, keeping people happy, and successfully conducting projects that people recognize are for the good of the group. In Melanesia, such individuals are called "Big Men"; in anthropology that term is applied to individuals in any culture who perform such functions (Service

1975). When there are Big Men and some others below them who fill a limited number of specific roles in the society—in essence, people of higher status with differential access to resources—such a group is no longer egalitarian. Anthropologist Morton Fried (1967) labels these groups **rank societies.** Rather than everyone being more or less equal, a few sociopolitical "ranks" are filled by a relatively small number of people.

A Neolithic Base for Big Men

In some post-Pleistocene settings, the extra work involved in applying new, more intensive subsistence strategies, as organized by these newly developed leaders, substantially increased the food base. The additional labor invested in planting seedbeds, tending wild plants, or corralling wild animals created a new cultural environment in which natural selection was supplanted by artificial selection. The result was domesticated plants and animals that eventually produced far more food than was actually needed to feed even the growing Holocene human population in some areas.

Those who could control the new food surplus—redistribute it, save it for times of need, or even own it—possessed, for perhaps the first time in human history, wealth and power. To be able to redistribute excess food, reward some and punish others, accumulate precious materials in trade, and distribute other resources—or withhold them—during lean times is to have power.

A food surplus poses the challenge of what to do with it all. To begin with, it needs to be stored. Village granaries are one solution, and their construction requires more communal labor. Once granaries are built and the grain is stored, the surplus must be protected from hungry animals, insects, and rot—not to mention greedy humans. So more communal projects are needed, more jobs are created for leaders to oversee, and there is more reinforcement for their position as leaders, as long as they are successful.

It is expensive to build storage facilities and to protect the food. So why bother? The most obvious reason is that a surplus can help tide people over during lean times—during nongrowing seasons or during slim harvests. Plus, a food surplus can be distributed to individuals or families who have contributed significantly to the group, as a reward for hard work. Also, a food surplus can be used as wealth to obtain other valuable goods; the surplus can be traded with the inhabitants of other regions for stone, metal, or other resources not locally available or accessible.

From Big Men to Chiefs

As long as such societies remain small, with Big Men managing only individual villages, the potential for complexity ordinarily is limited. As population grows, however, and as more importance is vested in the Big Man, that role may change. Anthropologist Elman Service (1975, 71) refers to this as "the institutionalization of power": As the system expands geographically, group labor projects and the broader redistribution of food and other goods has a

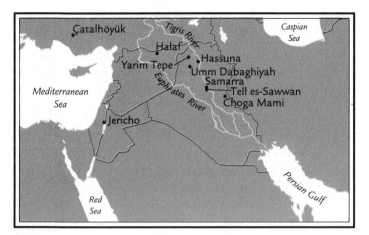

FIGURE 12.7

Archaeological sites in western Asia where evidence of the evolution of chiefdom and early state-level societies has been found.

"politically integrative effect" (Service 1975, 94). Social strata may develop, with the leader, or chief, and the chief's family at the top of the social pyramid. Chieftainship may be handed down from parent to child, further solidifying the position of the chief's family in the upper echelon of a stratified social system. A cadre of subordinate regional chiefs may also develop, each responsible for a local area, and all reporting to the head chief. Most everyone else makes up the broad base of the social pyramid of these **chiefdoms,** giving at least some of the surplus they produce to the chiefs.

COMPLEXITY'S EARLIEST TRACES IN THE OLD WORLD

Though certainly a dramatic indicator of the capacity of chiefs to mobilize labor, Stonehenge and the other stone monuments of the European Neolithic are not the earliest archaeological evidence for the kind of complexity found in chiefdom societies; some archaeological evidence for nonegalitarian societies turns up early in the Neolithic.

Jericho

Some of the earliest evidence of large-scale communal construction and social stratification in the world can be seen deep in the sequence at a few sites in western Asia (Figure 12.7). For example, the archaeological site of Jericho, in Israel, was a village with a number of distinct features that imply a movement away from the egalitarian pattern seen at other Neolithic sites (see Chapter 11). More than 9,000 years ago, the inhabitants of Jericho—later memorialized in the Old Testament of the Bible—built a massive stone wall around their community (Kenyon 1954). Made of dry-laid stone, the wall was 2 m (6½ ft) thick at the base and nearly 7 m (22 ft) high in places, with ramparts

FIGURE 12.8

The wall at Jericho, probably built by members of an ancient chiefdom society beginning some 9,000 years ago, is among the earliest archaeological evidence in the world for construction on a monumental scale.
(M. H. Feder)

up to 9 m (30 ft) high (Figure 12.8). The construction of this wall required a level of coordination of labor not previously seen in the world.

Trade was an important element in the economy of early Jericho. Exotic raw materials, including Turkish obsidian, turquoise from the Sinai Peninsula, and cowrie shells from the Red Sea, are found at early levels of the site. The distribution of some of these exotic materials in human interments indicates a certain degree of social differentiation at Jericho: Whereas most burials were rather plain and undistinguished, one group of interments was set apart—the skulls were coated with a mask of clay, and the exotic cowrie shells were set into the eye sockets.

Çatalhöyük

The 9,000-year-old site of Çatalhöyük is located in central Turkey near the town of Çumra (Mellaart 1965; Todd 1976). The site covers an area about three times as large as Jericho's and consists of about a thousand interconnected rooms (Figure 12.9). Initially excavated in the 1960s, the site immediately drew worldwide attention. Çatalhöyük clearly was far different from other settlements of the same time period; it was much larger, and the standardized size and configuration of its architecture implied a far greater degree of organization. It seems to represent the community of an ancient society organized at a level that allowed for the construction of a massive complex of residences and that was capable of organizing and controlling a resident population estimated in the thousands.

Archaeology at Çatalhöyük began again in 1993, led by British archaeologist Ian Hodder. The mission of these more recent excavations includes placing the site in a regional context, examining the changes in the natural environment and the domestication of plants and animals during the period

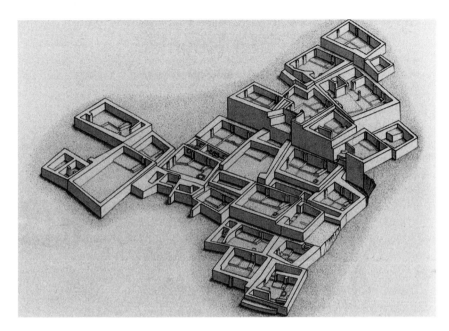

FIGURE 12.9
Çatalhöyük was a large, complex settlement of more than 5,000 people by about 8,000 years ago. Its location near an important obsidian source may explain the size and complexity of the community at this early date.
(Drawing by Eliza McFadden, from *Plato Prehistorian*, by Mary Settegast, published by the Rotenberg Press, 1986. Permission to reprint, courtesy of Rotenberg Press)

between 13,000 and 7,000 years ago, investigating the ceremonial nature of the so-called shrines, and explaining the reasons why an early Neolithic complex culture developed here in the shadow of the Konya Mountains. It is hoped that this planned 25-year project will shed light on the origins of cultural complexity in southwest Asia.

The new research at Çatalhöyük is proceeding at a painstaking pace (Balter 1998). It is becoming increasingly clear from this research that the settlement was not a true city. For example, there is no public architecture, no evidence of municipal buildings, palaces, temples, or government structures; at least, none have been found in the 4% sample of the site excavated so far. In fact, all of the rooms excavated to date at Çatalhöyük are very similar living quarters and associated shrines.

Most of the rooms at the site are of a standard size: about 25 m² (264 ft²). Archaeologist Ian Hodder suggests that the social unit at Çatalhöyük was the extended family living in four or five clusters of these rooms (Balter 1998, 1443). The residents of the community relied on a mixed economy of which agriculture was only one component. They planted wheat and barley; but they also harvested wild plants, including lentils, acorns, hackberries, pistachios, and wild grasses and tubers. They raised domesticated animals, primarily sheep but cattle as well.

There is little evidence of labor specialization at the site. For example, a detailed analysis by Wendy Matthews of the mud bricks that make up the primary construction material of the community as well as the plaster used to coat the bricks shows tremendous variation (Balter 1998, 1443). In other words, the evidence seems to indicate that family groups made these materials on their own; there were no specialist brick or plaster makers following standard recipes. Also, the newest analysis of the obsidian tools found in the excavated residences indicates that there were no specialist toolmakers at the site. It is more likely that each family produced its own obsidian tools in its own residential compounds.

Around 40 of the excavated rooms produced no archaeological evidence of habitation, but appear instead to have been used for ceremonial purposes. These rooms have been labeled as shrines since they contain what seem to be images of fertility goddesses (some depicted as giving birth) as well as stylized bull heads carved into the walls. There also are painted depictions of leopards with women riding on their backs, birds, and headless human beings.

The site's population has been estimated at about 10,000. The large size and apparent complexity of Çatalhöyük at this early date is probably related to its location adjacent to a major source of obsidian (volcanic glass) in the Konya Mountains. Konya obsidian is found widely distributed throughout southeastern Europe and western Asia via ancient trade networks; perhaps Big Men or chiefs managed or controlled the obsidian trade.

Çatalhöyük clearly was different from contemporary sites, but explaining that difference remains problematic. The size and complexity of its architecture offer evidence of a degree of social and political complexity. On the other hand, research indicates that Çatalhöyük, as large and integrated as it appears as a structure, was rather decentralized as a community. Only further research will help us better understand how Çatalhöyük was organized and why so many people chose to congregate at the foot of the Konya Mountains 9,000 years ago.

Mesopotamia: Land Between the Rivers

The waters of the Tigris and Euphrates Rivers begin their journey to the Persian Gulf as a series of small streams in the modern nations of Turkey, Syria, Iraq, and Iran. Flowing southeast, the twin rivers are separated across their lengths by no more than about 200 km (130 mi) and commonly by less than 100 km (65 mi) until they meet and jointly flow into the Persian Gulf. Together their valleys demarcate the boundaries of the region called **Mesopotamia**—Greek for "the land between the rivers" (see Figure 12.7). These rivers played a fundamental role in producing the flat expanse of fertile soil in which the seeds of the world's first civilization were planted (see Chapter 13).

The Roots of Complexity in Southwest Asia

To the north, in the eastern horn of the Fertile Crescent, Neolithic villages had evolved in the early post-Pleistocene, where subsistence was based on wheat, barley, lentils, sheep, and goats (see Chapter 11). In northern Mesopotamia, this period is symbolized by the **Umm Dabaghiyah** culture. Villages were small, and the subsistence economy was mixed; some wheat and barley was planted, and sheep, goats, pigs, and cattle were raised (Lamberg-Karlovsky and Sabloff 1995). Of at least equal importance was the hunting of onager (wild ass); the bones of this animal made up more than two-thirds of the faunal assemblage at the site.

Beginning from this simple Neolithic base, by about 8,000 years ago, a subtle transformation toward social, political, and economic complexity is evident in the archaeological record. The sites of Hassuna, Samarra, and Halaf, each exhibiting distinctive pottery and architecture, lend their names to a chronological succession of three distinctive farming cultures (with substantial temporal overlap): **Hassunan, Samarran,** and **Halafian.**

Dating from 8000 to 7200 B.P., Hassunan sites are small, typically about 100 m in diameter, with populations estimated at a few hundred (Lamberg-Karlovsky and Sabloff 1995, 96). These sites show clear evidence of the primacy of agriculture in the subsistence base. At the Hassunan site of Yarim Tepe, for example, there is evidence of the planting of einkorn, emmer, bread, and club wheat as well as barley, peas, and lentils (Merpert and Munchaev 1987). While the hunting of wild animals persisted at Yarim Tepe, as evidenced by the appearance of the remains of fallow deer, gazelle, and onager, some 82% of the bones recovered archaeologically were from domesticated animals, including sheep, goat, pig, and especially cattle (Maisels 1990, 112).

Though in most ways unremarkable Neolithic villages, Hassunan sites do exhibit just a few hints of what was to come in Mesopotamia in the form of architectural sophistication. There are multiroomed houses with courtyards, for example, at Yarim Tepe. But, as archaeologists C. C. Lamberg-Karlovsky and Jeremy Sabloff (1995, 97–98) point out, overall, Hassunan sites reflect a pattern of "rustic simplicity"; architecture was simple and homogeneous, there is no evidence of temples or palaces, few precious or luxurious items have been found, and there is no evidence of high-status burials reflective of status differentiation.

The site of Samarra and others included in the Samarran culture are located farther south, deep into the floodplain of the Tigris. These sites date to after 7500 B.P. The diets of the inhabitants of Samarran sites included the resources offered by the river, with archaeological evidence for the heavy use of fish and mussels. The inhabitants of the Samarran site of Tell es-Sawwan supplemented their diets by hunting gazelle and fallow deer, while they planted emmer and bread wheat, barley, and caper (a fruit-producing shrub; Helbaek 1965).

That agriculture was a significant part of the subsistence system at Samarra and related sites is itself informative. As pointed out by archaeologist Joan Oates (1973), here, in the central section of Mesopotamia, rainfall is meager, and an agricultural way of life would have been generally difficult and in some places impossible without the construction of irrigation canals. Direct evidence of this canal building has been found at the Samarran site of Choga Mami. Remember, when we discussed the reasons for the evolution of social, political, and economic complexity, one factor cited was the need, under certain conditions, to develop an organizational structure to conscript and coordinate labor at a level above the household, family, or local community. Control of water resources needed to expand agricultural production can be a powerful incentive for such an organizational structure to develop and an important factor in its perpetuation.

There is evidence for developing complexity in Samarran sites, including nonsubsistence-related large-scale works that would have required a level of cooperation and coordination of labor not previously seen. Tell es-Sawwan, for example, was surrounded by an enormous wall and a ditch that would have required the pooled labor of a large number of workers. Samarra has a large, buttressed fortification wall that similarly would have required a large regulated workforce.

At the same time, there is telling archaeological evidence at Samarran sites that differences in status between leaders and followers, between those giving the orders in large-scale construction projects and those following the orders, were being ritually legitimized. Some of the graves at Tell es-Sawwan are far more elaborate than those at Hassunan sites, and the differences among the burials are much greater. While most Samarran burials are rather plain, some are filled with luxurious goods made of alabaster, turquoise, copper, green-stone, obsidian, carnelian (a lustrous, reddish-brown stone), and shell-bead necklaces and bracelets. Differences in grave wealth imply an increasing economic and social gulf among members of the society (Lamberg-Karlovsky and Sabloff 1995). Some of these raw materials must have been valuable because they were rare; required a great amount of work to locate, quarry, or work; or were available only at a great distance. Turquoise, carnelian, and obsidian, for example, are not locally available in the Samarran territory and must have been traded for by the inhabitants of Tell es-Sawwan.

It may be suggested that these more elaborate burials are the graves of a developing elite or chief class whose special treatment in death was made possible—or, perhaps, necessary—by their differentiation in life. These individuals may have been singled out to organize, coordinate, and lead large-scale construction projects such as the canals at Choga Mami or the walls at Samarra and Tell es-Sawwan. Socially, politically, and, perhaps, economically elevated in life because of the special and powerful role they played in the society, these people seem to have then been exalted in death as well through the elaboration of their graves.

A new architectural feature is also seen at Samarran sites. After about 7400 B.P., the inhabitants constructed T-shaped buildings that were used to house the community's grain. As Lamberg-Karlovsky and Sabloff (1995, 100–1) point out, the communal storage of grain suggests a pooling of labor in both farming and the construction of the building where the grain was stored. Again, to accomplish the construction of communal granaries and to ensure the maintenance of the stored grain at the scale suggested by the archaeological data for Samarran sites, people needed to be organized beyond the level of the household or family, and a more complex social and political structure evolved to accomplish these tasks. This process portends what will happen a few centuries later, farther south into Mesopotamia.

Halafian sites, dating from 7500 to 6700 B.P., are not as well known as those of Hassuna or Samarra. Almost certainly the inhabitants were farmers. The residential architecture was simple, but in Halafian villages, a new architectural form is seen in nonresidential, round buildings (sometimes called **tholoi**). They seem initially to have served as communal storage buildings, like the T-shaped buildings of the Samarran culture. The round buildings at some sites contained human burials along with ceremonial objects, leading some to suggest that these structures also served as burial places for important people.

These archaeological discoveries dated to the Mesopotamian Neolithic show a clearly evolutionary pattern of increasing sophistication and complexity in architecture and material culture. Communal projects and high-status burials imply the existence of chiefdoms at this point in the development of these societies. The existence of communal storage/ceremonial structures by the middle of the eighth millennium B.P. is intriguing, perhaps foreshadowing the key role of the temple in the first true civilization, the Sumerian city-states (see Chapter 13).

COMPLEXITY'S EARLIEST TRACES IN THE NEW WORLD

A pattern of increasing social, political, and economic complexity can also be seen in the New World after the development of agricultural economies. These more complex societies developed, almost certainly, completely independently from the sequence in the Old World, albeit at a substantially later date (see "Issues and Debates" in this chapter). An agricultural economy that was based on the cultivation of corn, beans, and squash and that included a host of other domesticates was the key to the social, political, and economic complexity that developed in the New World as seen in Mesoamerica and South America (Figures 12.10 and 12.11).

The Olmec

Small agricultural communities had been developing in Mesoamerica since about 5000 B.P. (see Chapter 11). It seems as though a geographically expansive pattern of small, egalitarian, and independent farming villages located along the Gulf Coast tropical lowlands, particularly in the Mexican states of Tabasco and Veracruz, evolved into a pattern of more closely interconnected and complexly structured communities sometime after 3,250 years ago (Diehl 1989).

The complexity of the social, political, and economic order, as well as a pattern of unity seen across a fairly broad geographic expanse, is reflected in the archaeological record by a constellation of common art motifs and

FIGURE 12.10

Archaeological sites in Mesoamerica where evidence of the development of complexity has been found.

monumental architectural patterns not previously seen in the New World. The motifs and patterns constitute what archaeologists label **Olmec** (Sharer and Grove 1989). The Olmec pattern includes several elements: depictions of a half-human, half-jaguar god; the production of jade sculptures (see Color Plates 11 and 12); iron-ore mirrors; the construction of large earthen platforms; the construction of earthen pyramids; and the carving of huge basalt boulders into the form of human heads—perhaps actual depictions of some of the regional chiefs.

The Evolution of Complexity   The Olmec heartland, located between the Tuxtla Mountains to the west and the tropical lowlands of the Chontalpa to the east, is a vast and richly varied region of uplands, estuaries, and floodplains. Population growth facilitated by the abundant and diverse habitats of the Olmec region may be part of the explanation for how and why complex societies developed here. Some places in the lowlands offered particularly rich farmland. In the tropical lowlands of the Mexican Gulf Coast, the richest agricultural lands can be found along the natural levees produced by rivers that flow through it. These rich regions attracted a relatively larger portion of the growing population. Archaeologist Michael Coe (1968) has suggested that those families who controlled the most productive lands along the Gulf Coast could have produced agricultural surpluses, allowing them to amass wealth and ultimately power. These developing elites—perhaps initially Big Men and

FIGURE 12.11

Archaeological sites in South America where evidence of the development of complexity has been found.

then chiefs—could mobilize the large regional populations to produce monumental works that might further legitimize their elevated social and economic status (Lowe 1989). At the same time, the patchiness of resource distribution rendered other areas of the Olmec heartland uniquely attractive and valuable as well. The estuarine region provided rich coastal resources, while the mountains provided a valuable source of volcanic rock for toolmaking and monument construction (Grove 1996). People living in proximity to these resource-privileged areas may have been able to monopolize important resources and elevate their own status relative to the people who had to come to them for their supply of those valuable commodities.

Olmec Capitals   Those initially small farming villages that were located on the best farmlands or in those areas most accessible to valuable resources became regionally significant as the residences of a developing elite class of people. Two such communities, La Venta in Tabasco and San Lorenzo in

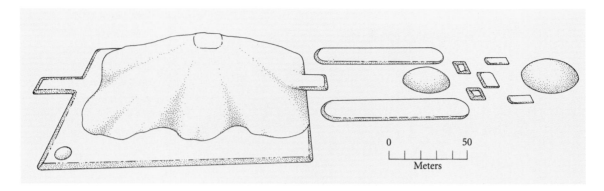

FIGURE 12.12

Layout of the Olmec capital of San Lorenzo with its major earthen mound and associated earthworks.

Veracruz, were settled initially nearly 3,650 years ago. A third, Laguna de los Cerros, also in Veracruz, was settled soon thereafter. These three villages became more than just farming settlements. Beginning first at San Lorenzo at about 3,100 years ago and a little later at La Venta and Laguna de los Cerros, they became political, economic, social, and religious focal points and, in turn, the most powerful settlements in the realm of the Olmec.

Archaeologist David Grove points out that each of the three primary Olmec centers was uniquely positioned to exploit a particular set of natural resources and to, in turn, provide them to the rest of the Olmec domain (Grove 1996). At the western edge of the Olmec heartland, Laguna de los Cerros is located next to the Tuxtla Mountains with their rich supply of the volcanic rock basalt at the Cerro Cintepec outcrop. In the center of the Olmec territory was San Lorenzo, located in a broad topographic basin with extraordinarily rich alluvial soil, crossed by the Coatzacoalcos River, through which raw materials and finished goods were traded across the Olmec realm. The residents of San Lorenzo, therefore, were geographically positioned to control the flow of these materials through the Olmec heartland. La Venta, at the eastern margin, was located closest to the rich estuary habitat and its resources of rubber, salt, and cacao—the source for chocolate (Grove 1996).

The ability of the Olmec rulers to conscript and control the labor of a large population is evident in the archaeological record. For example, the Olmec moved enormous amounts of earth to construct platforms and pyramids and even to modify the landscape of their settlements. San Lorenzo is situated on a natural topographic eminence that had been added to and flattened by the inhabitants. It is estimated that the top 9 m (10 ft) of the plateau on which the community is located is artificial (Figure 12.12).

Perhaps the most striking of the Olmec sculpted works are the colossal boulders of basalt they carved into the representations of the heads of their rulers (Figure 12.13). Several of these sculptures have been found at San Lorenzo: The largest is over 3 m (9 ft) tall and weighs nearly 40,000 kg (44 tons). As archaeologist David Grove indicates, these individualized depic-

FIGURE 12.13

This visage of an ancient Olmec chief was carved from an enormous solid block of basalt. (Courtesy of Michael Coe)

tions "glorified the rulers while they were alive, and commemorated them as revered ancestors after their death" (1996).

Monumental undertakings reflect the Olmec's growing ability to command and organize the labor of a large number of people, a characteristic typical of chiefdom societies. The artificial platform constructed at La Venta, for example, contained more than 2 million m³ (75 million ft³) of earth and is more than 32 m (105 ft) high. Many tons of basalt slabs were used to construct an elaborate water-supply system, now shown by recent excavations at San Lorenzo to have served as part of an aqueduct, providing drinking water to residents (Grove 1996). As indicated, the volcanic rock used to build the aqueduct as well as the raw material for the carved heads was obtained from the Tuxtla Mountains. A large quarry found at Llano del Jicaro, only about 7 km (4 mi) from Laguna de los Cerros, almost certainly was controlled by the elite at this Olmec center. This quarry is more than 80 km (50 mi) from San Lorenzo, yet large amounts of basalt were transported there, much of it by river. The movement of large quantities of this stone—and the enormous size of the boulders intended for the stone head sculptures—over such a great distance is another indicator of the ability of the Olmec chiefs to mobilize and manage the labor of a great mass of people.

As seen with the evolution of complex societies in Mesopotamia, the growing authority of leaders in Olmec society is reflected in the archaeological record of their burials. At La Venta, for example, one ruler or chief was buried in a sandstone sarcophagus carved into an elaborate depiction of a caiman (a Central and South American crocodile). Most Olmec rulers were similarly interred, with many beautifully rendered artworks, including jewelry, sculptures, and celts, many of them carved of highly polished jade or greenstone (see Color Plates 11 and 12).

In addition to the three major Olmec ceremonial centers, San Lorenzo, Laguna de los Cerros, and La Venta, a number of smaller centers, including the very impressive site of Tres Zapotes in Veracruz, provide material evidence of the ability to harness a large pool of labor and to expend surplus wealth. None of these communities were urban, but they hardly were sparsely inhabited. There are over 200 individual house mounds at San Lorenzo, and population estimates for the largest Olmec sites are generally about 1,000 people. This figure includes the small elite class that inhabited residences placed on top of the raised earthen platforms and the larger population of individuals who served the needs of each center's elite, including artisans and farmers. These centers likely relied on the labor of tens of thousands of people living in small farming villages and regional centers in the area surrounding each ceremonial center (Adams 1991, 59).

What Was Olmec?   Olmec can be interpreted as a common religious iconography—a standardized set of visual images—that provided ideological and symbolic support for the sociopolitical system. The shared elements of Olmec religious iconography may have served to unify the large populations living around the ceremonial centers into politically unified chiefdoms.

The spread of Olmec influence across a wide swath of Mesoamerica can be seen between 3,000 and 2,800 years ago. At this time, Olmec-like imagery appeared in El Salvador, Honduras, Costa Rica, and Guatemala, as well as the highlands of Mexico (the Valley of Mexico and Oaxaca).

The Olmec were responsible for one more significant innovation: They produced the earliest writing in the New World. A carved monument called a **stela** bearing a hieroglyphic inscription was found more than 50 years ago at Tres Zapotes. The writing on the stela can be read since the symbolic system used was the same as the writing system used later by the Maya (Harris and Stearns 1992; and see the discussion that follows). Stela C at Tres Zapotes bears the date corresponding to our year 31 B.C.

South America

As early as 8,000 years ago, the inhabitants of the Peruvian coast practiced a sedentary way of life. Though they still relied on foraging for their subsistence, the incredibly rich resources of the coast combined with productive inlands allowed for a settled way of life.

Neolithic Roots and Accelerating Complexity   Between 5500 and 5000 B.P., coastal villages increased in size and subsistence expanded to include domesticates such as gourds, squash, and kidney and lima beans (Pineda 1988). At this time at sites like Huaca Prieta and Paracas, there is some evidence of increasing social complexity. While most residential buildings at these sites are quite similar in size and form, other structures are a bit larger and more ambitious. Small pyramids and platforms are included in this category.

After 5000 B.P., these specialized structures became increasingly large and sophisticated. Large pyramids were built, dominating the sites of Bandurria, Rio Seco, and Aspero (Pineda 1988, 76). At these sites there also is evidence of a developing pattern of social stratification in the form of differing house sizes. Aspero, for example, is a large site, covering 12 hectares (30 acres). There are seven large and six smaller ceremonial mounds at Aspero, on top of which were constructed small temples that contained human burials. Around the mounds were open plazas and artificial terraces. A large resident population exploited the rich resources of the coast.

By about 4500 B.P., population growth in these coastal communities forced expansion 10 or 20 km into the interior, where agriculture would have been possible only with the construction of irrigation canals. This period was also marked by a dramatic increase in the significance of cultigens in the diet of the inhabitants. Maize, beans, gourds, squash, peanuts, avocado, and guava were all important food sources.

The first evidence of the use of metals in South America dates to about 3100 B.P. Among a series of six early ceremonial centers with earthen pyramids and mounds located in Peru's Lurin Valley, Mina Perdida has produced gold and copper artifacts (Burger and Gordon 1998). No smelting or casting was done at this early date. Both the gold and copper had been found by the natives in a natural, nearly pure or "native" state and then hammered into thin foils. The existence of substantial earthworks along with fine metal work at Mina Perdida is clear evidence of increasing complexity in the Andean region at this time. There is no obvious archaeological evidence before 3000 B.P. at these Lurin Valley sites for social stratification or wealth differentiation. The construction of large earthworks implies the existence of chiefs, but these chiefs were treated no differently—their residences were no larger and their graves no more elaborate—than those who followed them.

Though the precise process is not at all clear, it seems that the development of irrigation technology, population growth, and movement into the interior was accompanied by social differentiation. Some villages like Kotosh and Chavín de Huántar were strategically located along natural trade routes between the coast to the west and the uplands to the east, and trade seems to have played an important role in the developing social complexity at these sites. The focus on monumental architecture associated with ceremonial structures like pyramids is a good indication that the newly evolved social and economic power, perhaps as a result of trade, was focused on a religious elite class who could control the increasingly complex economy.

As long as this pattern of development was restricted to the rather small, individual river valley systems that cross Peru, sociopolitical differentiation could not become too marked. There simply were not enough resources and wealth for the developing elites to monopolize to enable them to attain the status of Egyptian pharaohs or Mesopotamian city-state kings (see Chapter 13). But sometime after 3000 B.P., populations started growing, and their needs expanded beyond the narrow confines of their own particular river valleys. In the view of archaeologist Tom Patterson (1993), contact and competition among the political entities within individual valleys was a significant factor in the development of Andean civilization.

Cultural Convergence: Chavin   About 3,000 years ago, an apparently unifying religion with a distinct and striking art style began to spread across the previously highly regionalized valleys. Called **Chavin** and initially centered at the site of Chavín de Huántar, like Olmec it seems to have served to bring together a large and geographically broad population under the banner of a single religious, if not political, entity. Archaeologist Richard Burger (1988, 111) calls Chavin an empire, but a "religious," not a political, one. The Chavin art style that accompanied the religion included the depiction of felines (possibly jaguars), raptorial birds, snakes, the caiman (a South American crocodile), and the so-called Staff God—a presumed deity holding two rods or staffs (Figure 12.14). Accompanying Chavin artistic and religious expression were several technological innovations that further served as unifying elements during this period of Peruvian prehistory. Beautiful and intricately woven textiles displaying common Chavin motifs were woven with the hairs of domesticated camelids. Across the broad and expanding region where Chavin motifs spread, hammered gold objects and three-dimensional objects made from joined sheets of gold are also found. Metallurgists producing Chavin motifs also used such production techniques as soldering and sweat welding as well as the decoration technique of repoussé. Silver-gold alloys, a hallmark of South American metallurgy, are first seen in Chavin artifacts.

Chavín de Huántar itself was strategically placed along a natural route of trade and transportation between the highland valleys, the Peruvian coast, and the interior tropical forest (Burger 1995). As a result, it likely was a magnet for excess wealth generated by trade. A unifying art-religion would certainly have served to encourage this trade among previously very diverse groups. As archaeologist Karen Olsen Bruhns (1994) indicates, the site began about 3,000 years ago as a ceremonial center with a small population of residents, serving at least in part to facilitate trade between disparate groups living in different habitats, newly combined through a common mode of religious expression. By a little after 2500 B.P., however, this ceremonial center had grown to become one of the earliest urban centers in South America: a bustling town, with a large, dense population spread out across about 40 hectares (400,000 m², or about 100 acres). Houses and neighborhoods were constructed

FIGURE 12.14

Some of the distinctive iconography of the Chavin art style is shown in this depiction of the staff god.
(Gordon Willey)

according to a plan, a drainage system was in place, and temples and huge food-storage facilities served the residents.

Perhaps as river valleys filled up with population, the need to obtain resources from outside of these valleys increased. Places like Chavín de Huántar that were propitiously placed took advantage of this increased need by regulating the trade that had to pass through their territories. The Chavin art style spreading a common and unifying religion initially simply served to facilitate trade among various groups, but it ultimately brought people closer together in all spheres, spreading technological innovations as well as new social patterns. Those in a position to control trade and information as it flowed through this coalescing system became the first members of a differentiated class of people who lived in larger houses, spent their time propitiating the Chavin gods, and monopolized certain key symbols of power in the developing civilization.

ISSUES AND DEBATES

IS COMPLEXITY INEVITABLE?

This chapter has focused on the development of social, political, and economic complexity in the Neolithic. Remember that the evolution of complex societies, though certainly facilitated by the development of food-producing economies, was not the inevitable outcome of this shift in subsistence. The capacity to produce a surplus of food and the attendant ability to free a proportion of the population from subsistence activities in no way guarantees that a society will elect to do so. Food production and the surplus it makes possible merely open a door; other factors come into play in a society's determination whether or not to pass through that portal and follow a pathway that leads to a fundamental change in how the society is organized. In some cases the decision to do so may be borne of necessity. The need to produce more food to feed a burgeoning population or to respond to an external military threat may require the development of a new kind of societal structure in response. In other instances, the opportunity offered by a locally available resource may provide a source of wealth that can be more efficiently exploited by a complex social and political structure. The point is, the shift to complexity was neither universal nor inevitable. Archaeologists tend to focus on such complexity for the simple reason that the large-scale projects— Australian archaeologist Rowland Fletcher calls them MVSs, or Monstrous Visual Symbols—are extremely visible in the archaeological record.

IS COMPLEXITY RESTRICTED TO FOOD PRODUCERS?

Though an agricultural economy ordinarily has a far greater potential for producing a food surplus, it is not universally the case that only such a mode of subsistence can do so. Anthropologists have discovered hunter-gatherer people living in environments where the wild foods provided by nature were so rich and predictable that the production of a food surplus also was possible. Native Americans living along the northwest coast of the United States and Canada, for example, found themselves in such a situation; in their case, the yearly run of salmon produced an emormous amount of storable food in a relatively short period of time, allowing for the production of a food surplus that, in turn, freed people to engage in activities outside of subsistence when the salmon were not abundant.

Complexity in a foraging economy can be seen at the Ozette site, located on the Olympic Peninsula of Washington State. The Pacific migration routes of a number of whale species passed close by the peninsula on which Ozette— occupied 500 years ago—was located. Other marine resources and a rich forest habitat inland allowed for the production of an enormous food surplus by the inhabitants, with no contribution from agricultural products. The Ozette village was, in part, destroyed by a mudslide between A.D. 1400 and 1500. The wet mud, in essence, froze a moment in Ozette's time and preserved even the organic material that it encapsulated.

Ozette village was large and complex, stretching for nearly a mile along the coast. The five houses preserved under the mud and clay are large and reflect a degree of permanence usually associated only with agricultural people. The material culture preserved in the mud provides evidence for the sophisticated technology of Ozette's people. Basketry, mats, and wooden bowls all reflect the great time, effort, and care that Ozette's artisans applied to their work. Ozette was not a city, nor is there any compelling evidence of social stratification. Nevertheless, the material record at Ozette shows that under certain circumstances, hunter-gatherers can produce large, dense, permanent settlements that imply a degree of social and political complexity.

Rich and predictable natural habitats such as those in which Ozette was located are the exception, however, Ordinarily, it is only with the adoption of agriculture that a small proportion of the populace can regularly produce enough food to adequately feed all of the other members of the group, who then can devote all or part of their time to nonsubsistence pursuits. When these groups grow in size, the labor released from food production also grows. Where a social or political organization develops to direct that labor, complex societies evolve that often are then reflected in the archaeological record by the monumental works produced.

CASE STUDY CLOSE-UP

It must have been an imposing site for pilgrims visiting Chavín de Huántar—and that almost certainly was the intention. The two major trails that led to the site along the Huachecsa and Mosna Rivers led not to the front entrance of the Old Temple, but to the back sides of the monumental, U-shaped structure. At the end of either trail, visitors found themselves at the base of a massive, towering four-story wall of stone. Its setting and appearance were almost certainly intended as a message

FIGURE 12.15

A ghoulish figure set into the wall of the Old Temple at the site of Chavín de Huántar is one of several that gaze down upon visitors to the site. To the rear of the heads were carved tenons that fit into sockets in the wall of the temple.
(Copyright © Ric Ergenbright/ Corbis)

to all who saw it: Here is the seat of our power, the center of our might (Burger 1995).

The Old Temple was a mammoth construction project, with thousands upon thousands of granite, sandstone, and limestone blocks laid upon each other in thin courses. The temple spread out across a broad area, covering more than 7,100 m² (nearly 77,000 ft²; more than 1.75 acres). Different segments of the temple differed somewhat in height; the top platform stood between 14 and 16 m (about 46 and 53 ft) above the surface. At about 10 m (33 ft) above the ground, at 3-m (39-in.) intervals, the builders of the Old Temple had inserted a series of striking, carved anthropomorphic (human-like) and zoomorphic (animal-like) stone heads (Figure 12.15). At the back of each of the heads, carvers had made tenons that fit into sockets made in the wall behind them. Twice the size of actual human heads, snarling, with exposed fangs and contorted faces, these stone heads seem to float in the air, gazing down upon visitors, expressing the power and authority of the Chavin gods.

At the center of the Old Temple, ensconced in a tall chamber at the end of a dark corridor, stands a 4.5-m (almost 15-ft) tall upright monolith of granite today called the Lanzón. Onto the shaft of granite has been carved the shape of an anthropomorphc deity (Figure 12.16). The size and setting of the Lanzón have led scholars to the conclusion that this is the chief god in the Chavin pantheon of powerful supernatural beings, the god that the pilgrims may have come to worship.

The precise meaning of the Old Temple has been lost to us. Perhaps its alignment has astronomical significance, the open section of the U facing the rising or setting of an important set of stars. Maybe the shape and setting of

FIGURE 12.16

Deep within the Old Temple at the site of Chavín de Huántar is the famous Lanzón carving, a fantastic creature—perhaps the chief god of the Chavin pantheon—carved from a single piece of granite. (From G. Willey. 1971. *Introduction to American Archaeology: South America.* Englewood Cliffs, N.J.: Prentice Hall. Reprinted with permission of the author) the building conveyed some symbolic message to those who followed the Chavín religion, a message we may never be able to comprehend. But this much is clear: The Old Temple was made possible by the social and political structures that characterize complex societies; and, at the same time, it communicated to all who saw it the power of the Chavín gods as well as those upon whom they looked down with favor. It must have been a powerful message indeed.

 **VISITING THE PAST**

Precisely because one of the material correlates of complexity so often is monumental construction, some of the sites discussed in this chapter are, millennia after they were built, still impressive places to visit and investigate. There is no better example of this than the stone monuments of western Europe. Although Stonehenge is, in some ways, the most impressive of these, it is but one of literally hundreds of stone henges, circles, uprights, and dolmens (large stones raised up and balanced on three or more uprights) that can be seen throughout western Europe. To find them in westernmost Europe, one needs little more than some sturdy hiking boots and Aubrey Burl's (1995) *A Guide to the Stone Circles of Britain, Ireland, and Brittany,* with its photographs and detailed directions and even reviews of the various monuments and their settings.

In the massiveness of the component stones of Stonehenge and the other megalithic monuments and in the precision with which their stones were quarried, transported, erected, and, in some cases, conjoined, these monument engage us in the present on an emotional level and convey in a visceral way a feeling for the kind of society that must have evolved to produce it.

SUMMARY

Beginning after the Neolithic, in several regions in both the Old and New Worlds, some societies began to shift from a simple social and political organization based on the household or family to a more complex framework. In some cases the shift to complexity was fueled by the need to organize the labor of a large group of people to increase food production—for instance, to construct water-control facilities. In other instances, the development of a social and political structure to organize and coordinate monumental projects was necessitated by some external threat—for example, the construction of a defensive wall around a community. In still other cases, the evolution of an organizational framework beyond the household or family may have come about as the result of the unique opportunities offered by a particularly rich habitat or proximity to and monopolization of a valued resource.

Whatever the particular case, the results of this shift to more complex social, political, and economic life and the shift to rank societies and chiefdoms are evidenced in the archaeological record by the monumental works made possible by large groups of organized people—Stonehenge is but one example. In some cases, the shift to complexity and the creation of ranks or classes are also evidenced in the archaeological record by the appearance of burials differentiated by the inclusion of precious raw materials and finely made works of art.

The earliest examples of the development of complexity in the Old World are seen at Jericho in Israel and Çatalhöyük in Turkey. Soon thereafter, this complexity can be seen developing in Mesopotamia. The earliest examples in the New World are seen along the Mexican Gulf Coast among the people called Olmec and in South America at the site called Chavín de Huántar.

TO LEARN MORE

Technical Summaries

Evidence for the development of cultural complexity as exemplified at Jericho, the earliest site exhibiting material evidence for this shift, can be found in Kathleen Kenyon's 1954 article in *Scientific American*. The best summary of the archaeological work conducted at Çatalhöyük in the 1960s is James Mellaart's book *Earliest Civilizations of the Near East* (1965). For the shift from the early Neolithic to complex farming communities in Mesopotamia, see Charles Maisels's *The Emergence of Civilization: From Hunting and Gathering to Agriculture, Cities, and the State in the Near East* (1990). To learn more about the Olmec, see Robert Sharer and David Grove's *Regional Perspectives on the Olmec* (1989). For information about Chavin and its significance in the development of civilization in pre-Hispanic South America, see Richard Burger's book *Chavin and the Origins of Andean Civilization* (1995).

Popular Summaries

For an inclusive summary of how people through the centuries have viewed Stonehenge—and how they have been confused by the obvious sophistication exhibited by the monument in the context of an otherwise seemingly simple farming society—there is no better source than Christopher Chippindale's *Stonehenge Complete* (1983). A wonderful new book on Stonehenge aimed at a popular audience is David Souden's *Stonehenge Revealed* (1997).

On the Web

The Web is the best place to read about the original work and to get recent updates on the new research now being conducted at Çatalhöyük. Log on to http://www.smm.org/catal/findings for an extremely intimate view of the archaeology being conducted at the site, with lots of explanatory text and photographs of the site, artifacts, and human skeletal remains recovered. You can even click on an audio button to hear how the site name is actually pronounced.

Stonehenge and associated megalithic monuments are well represented on the Web. Some of the Web sites espouse unscientific New Age nonsense about Stonehenge. Among the terrific sites, however, are these two online atlases of megalithic sites:

http://www.stonepages.com/utenti/dmeozzi/HomEng.html
http://easyweb.easynet.co.uk/~aburnham/stones.htm

For information on the Olmec, see http://udgftp.cencar.udg.mx/ingles/Precolombina/
Olmecas/docs/olmin.html.

KEY TERMS

sarsen	chiefdom	Halafian
lintel	Mesopotamia	tholoi
trilithon	Umm Dabaghiyah	Olmec
megalith	Hassunan	stela
complex society	Samarran	Chavin
rank society		

13

An Explosion of Complexity

THE FLOWERING OF CIVILIZATION IN THE OLD WORLD

CHAPTER OVERVIEW

"Civilization," including a formal government, social stratification, large and dense settlements, monumental edifices, elaborate burials, large armies, full-time artisans, and a system of record keeping, developed in some parts of the Old World as fewer people were needed in the subsistence quest and as rulers attempted to legitimize and reinforce their position of power. Mesopotamia, Egypt, the Indus Valley, Chinese Shang, and Minoan Crete are examples of the first civilizations in the Old World. The Khmer in southeast Asia represent a more recent Old World civilization.

		9	8	7.5	7
West Asia		Çatalhöyük Jericho			
Egypt					
Sudan					
South Asia				Mehrgarh	Kili Ghul Muhammad
China					
Crete			First settlement		
Khmer					

Thousands of years ago

6.5	6	5.5	5	4.5	4	3.5	3	2.5	2	1.5	1	.5

Ubaid   Uruk

Eridu

Ur

Khufu

Hierakonpolis,   Narmer   Tutankhamun
Nagada

Djoser

Kerma

Napata

Meroë

Mundigak

Kot Diji   Harappa,
Mohenjo-daro

Ch'eng tzu-yai   Erh-li-t'ou   An-yang

Knossos   Knossos
temple

Thera
eruption

Angkor
Thom

Angkor
Wat

By the summer of 1922, the earl of Carnarvon had all but run out of patience. For 15 years, he had provided financial support for the work of archaeologist Howard Carter, who was digging in Egypt in the Valley of the Kings—the royal burial ground, or "necropolis," outside of the ancient Egyptian capital of Thebes. In all that time, Carter had found little to interest Carnarvon or to enhance his benefactor's reputation as a sponsor of significant Egyptian archaeology.

In the peculiar practice of archaeological colonialism rampant throughout the eighteenth, nineteenth, and early twentieth centuries, wealthy Europeans purchased excavation "concessions" from foreign governments and then paid archaeologists to conduct investigations. Such excavation concessions, put bluntly, were the equivalent of mining permits. The objects recovered by foreign archaeologists in places such as Egypt, Iraq, and Syria in the Old World and Mexico and Peru in the New World were considered to belong not to the nation in which the materials were found, but to the individual who had purchased the right to dig and who had funded the excavations. In most cases, these benefactors had contracts with their archaeologists detailing how artifacts were to be distributed on their recovery. Sponsors commonly dispersed their portion to other wealthy friends and to museums, enhancing their reputations as supporters of important research; at the same time they were divesting nations of their cultural heritage and rendering analysis of significant archaeological sites all but impossible.

In the summer of 1922 Carter returned to England to see Carnarvon. Without any significant discoveries after 15 years, without any glory to bask in, without any archaeological treasures to distribute, Carnarvon had decided to cut off Carter's support, and he informed Carter that this would be the final season he would fund archaeological research in the valley. Dejected, Carter returned to Egypt and commenced what he presumed would be his last digging for Carnarvon.

Carter knew there was not much time. His fieldwork season began in early November and he would be forced to quit by mid-December, when the tourist season began. Excavation in the tiny piece of ground still unexamined by Carter—the only such piece left in the excavation concession purchased by Carnarvon from the Egyptian government—would block the entrance to the tomb of Pharaoh Rameses VI, the valley's most popular visitor destination.

Carter began work on November 1, 1922, and within three days his Egyptian workers had discovered the beginning of a staircase leading down into the ground. The staircase was slowly cleared of rock; at the bottom was a sealed door bearing the official symbol of the royal burial ground: jackals, symbolically protecting the king's tomb. It seemed possible that Carter at last had found a sealed tomb of an Egyptian king.

Carter was cautiously optimistic, but there had been false starts and false hopes before. Believing that this was his last chance, Carter took a gamble and telegrammed Carnarvon in England: "At last have made wonderful discovery in the Valley. A magnificent tomb with seals intact. Recovered same for your arrival: congratulations" (Fagan 1994, 205). Carter suggested that the earl travel to Egypt to witness the opening of what Carter fervently hoped was an unplundered tomb.

After a difficult trip, Carnarvon arrived, with his daughter. Carter provided a viewing area for Carnarvon and his daughter where, protected from the relentless Egyptian sun by an umbrella, they watched while workers opened the door at the bottom of the staircase. But instead of the hoped-for tomb, beyond the door was a rubble-filled corridor carved in the rock. Disappointed but intrigued, the workers began the laborious process of removing the rock and debris from the corridor, which extended an excruciating 25 feet. At the end lay yet another door.

The cleared second doorway stood before Carter and Carnarvon on November 26, a little more than two weeks before Carnarvon's patience and money—and Carter's time—were to run out. Carter drilled a hole through the door. Beyond was clearly an open space, a subterranean room. Carter widened the drilled hole just enough so he could put his head, one arm, and a candle through. Carter's own words to describe what he saw are some of the most famous in all archaeology:

> At first I could see nothing, the hot air escaping from the chamber causing the candle flame to flicker. But presently, as my eyes grew accustomed to the light, details of the room within emerged slowly from the mist, strange animals, statues, and gold—everywhere the glint of gold. For the moment—an eternity it must have seemed to the others standing by—I was struck dumb with amazement, and when Lord Carnarvon, unable to stand the suspense any longer, inquired anxiously, "Can you see anything?" it was all I could do to get out the words, "Yes, wonderful things!" (Buckley 1976, 13).

Thus began the excavation of the fabulous tomb of the Egyptian "boy king," Tutankhamun (Figure 13.1). Though a relatively minor figure in Egyptian history, having served as pharaoh as a child from 1334 B.C. to 1325 B.C., Tutankhamun was to become the most famous of all ancient Egypt's rulers. His tomb had gone largely untouched since his death, and the spectacular array of burial goods in the tomb were to excite people everywhere (see Color Plate 15).

We saw in Chapter 12 how, in both the Old and New Worlds, some food-producing societies followed a pathway that led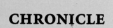

CHRONICLE

them to organize their social, political, and economic lives in ways that were more complex than in other Neolithic and most hunter-gatherer societies. The resulting cultures—called rank societies or chiefdoms—provide material evidence for the elevation of a proportion of a population to higher social, political, and often economic status. These elevated individuals achieved authority

FIGURE 13.1

The gold mask that covered the face of the boy king Tutankhamun as it was found by Howard Carter.
(Photography by Egyptian Expedition, The Metropolitan Museum of Art)

and accumulated wealth by becoming the heads of new social and political structures that developed out of a need to organize labor at a level beyond the household or the family. We see in the archaeological record the material manifestation of the end products of that organized labor—Jericho's wall, Çatalhöyük's architecture, megalithic monuments like Stonehenge—and in the ritual sanctification of the higher status of the leaders by their elevated treatment in death—in other words, their entombment in elaborate burials with precious grave goods.

In a few areas, the elaboration of social, political, and economic systems did not end with these developments, but continued to intensify, producing societies where the authority of a chief to *convince* others to follow his lead became the power of a pharaoh or king to *demand* obedience. With an exponentially greater degree of control combined with improved technology and a larger population, we see the development of a new kind of social order: the **state.**

The far greater concentration of power and control that characterizes and even defines the state allowed for the production of far larger and more impressive monuments and artwork, albeit made possible by the subjugation of a large class of people whose labor was devoted to the dictates of the ruler or rulers. Perhaps because in the present only the admittedly impressive material manifestations of these early state societies are immediately apparent—and the toil and servitude of the workers and peasants whose backbreaking work produced them is hidden from our view—we refer to the evolution of state societies as the development of "civilization." The material achievements of these societies are impressive indeed, and we will devote much of this chapter to discussing them. As we do so, however, we need to remind ourselves that great pyramids, ziggurats, temples, and palaces come at a human price. For every King Tut buried in great splendor, there must have been hundreds and even thousands of peasants whose labor made possible the life the Boy King lived and whose toil provided Tut and his cohorts with an eternity surrounded by grandeur.

THE EVOLUTION OF THE STATE

Civilization is easier to recognize than to define. Certainly, when we visit or see images of Egyptian pyramids or Mesopotamian temples (in this chapter) or ancient Maya cities or the palaces of the Inka (in Chapter 15), we know we are in the presence of the complex phenomenon called "civilization." But how can we formally define what we recognize intuitively?

A state is both quantitatively and qualitatively different from a chiefdom. States ordinarily are bigger and their material accomplishments more impressive. But they are more than simply big, impressive chiefdoms; states are true class societies, often rigidly stratified into social levels. The ruling class controls the populace not by consensus, but by coercion and force. A state possesses a true government, and the ruling class in a state society runs the government. "Civilization" is most often used to characterize the recognizable material results of the development of state societies. Since archaeologists deal most directly with such material consequences, this discussion will use the terms "state" and "civilization" interchangeably.

THE CHARACTER OF CIVILIZATION

The most obvious material symbols of state societies are **monumental works.** The ruins of huge public buildings, tombs, temples, palaces, pyramids, and such are all the spoor of ancient civilizations. Works such as the Egyptian

Sphinx, the Pyramid of the Sun at Teotihuacán in Mexico, the Citadel at Mohenjo-daro in Pakistan, and the great ziggurat at Ur in Iraq are the features by which we recognize ancient civilizations.

Food Surplus

Certainly, there can be no monumental works without an available labor force and there can be no available labor force without a food surplus. Like the chiefdoms and rank societies discussed in Chapter 12, but on a far larger scale, state societies engage in monumental construction projects; and such projects require a large number of workers. A large workforce can be made available only where a sizable proportion of the populace is freed from the day-to-day necessities of subsistence. As mentioned previously, the modern American farmer is said to produce enough food to feed 130 people, most of whose labor is, therefore, freed to engage in nonsubsistence pursuits. The large labor force needed to build the pyramids, temples, and palaces that symbolize the early states was made possible by the production of a large food surplus on the part of those engaged in farming.

Large, Dense Populations

Since without a sizable labor pool great monuments could never be built, a large population is a requirement of such societies, again supported by the evolving ability of farmers to produce increasing amounts of food. Increasingly efficient agricultural systems allow for increasingly large and dense communities, sometimes culminating in the development of urban centers—in other words, the city.

As a local population increases in size and density—in other words, as a growing population becomes packed into a relatively restricted area in the process of urbanization—a host of challenges are presented: How is order to be maintained among the many people now living virtually next door to each other? How are disputes among neighbors to be resolved? How are necessities—including food—produced outside of the urban area to be distributed among the populace? Issues of property ownership, transportation, and even practical concerns such as the disposal of human waste become greatly magnified when a large number of people are living in close proximity to one another. Social and political structures need to be developed to deal with these and other problems. These structures fundamentally change the social and political lives of people living in urban centers by restricting behaviors that might be detrimental to the larger group.

Social Stratification

Monumental works and the fine art of ancient civilizations do not define those civilizations; they merely reflect their more fundamental elements. Great pyramids, walls, palaces, irrigation networks, temples, and roads, as well as beautiful paintings, exquisite ceramics, gold statues, and fine linen—the "wonderful things" that Howard Carter saw in Tut's tomb—are the result of a socioeconomic system. **Social stratification** in a complex civilization is a division of society into levels, or strata, that one does not achieve, but into which one is born. One's social level defines one's role in life, one's status, one's power (or degree of powerlessness)—in essence, one's destiny. Monuments and great art are only the material symbols of the power of members of the elite social strata in these societies.

A Formal Government

Along with social stratification, a state possesses a true "government," defined by archaeologist Joseph Tainter (1988, 26) as a "specialized decision-making organization with a monopoly of force, and with the power to draft for work, levy and collect taxes, and decree and enforce laws." The power of the state provided by its formal government is wielded by members of the upper social classes. Pharaohs, emperors, and kings, along with the nobles serving under them, are members of a permanently circumscribed social class of people ruling the great masses of people who make up a state society.

As shown in Chapter 12, complex societies are defined, in part, by the organization of society beyond the level of the household or family. Leadership accrues to those who are good at organizing the projects that need to be accomplished by a large labor force. Leaders in non-state complex societies achieve their status by their ability to convince other people to follow their commands and to marshal the opinion of the group. Chiefs and Big Men don't have laws, a police force, or an army to compel people to comply with their wishes. Chiefs do not have absolute power. They do, however, have authority—they are good at organizing labor, keeping people happy, and undertaking projects that people recognize are for the good of the group. Their leadership usually comes about as a result of their accomplishments and abilities. It is this earned respect that convinces people to listen and follow.

The kings, pharaohs, or emperors of state societies have much more than authority; they rule by more than simply the consensus of the populace. Instead, they have true power: the ability to make decisions, give commands, and then make sure those commands are carried out. Jail, enforced labor, and the gallows await those who fail to heed the dictates of the ruler of a state society. The rulers of state societies sit atop a formal government with fixed laws. Leaders in such societies possess the ability to enforce those laws.

Labor Specialization

With the **specialization of labor,** certain individuals can devote all their time to perfecting skills in sophisticated and time-consuming specialties, such as technology, engineering, the arts, and crafts. Without the devotion of a lifetime's work, the level of skill exhibited in the great works associated with early civilizations, like the "wonderful things" in King Tut's tomb, could not have been achieved. Specialists can exist only in a society where enough food can be produced to feed all those people engaged in full-time specialist pursuits and where the social system provides a rationale for their existence. Such specialists are needed only in a society that demands their work by and for certain powerful people of an even higher class.

Record Keeping

Without some **system of record keeping** by which the elite could keep track of food surpluses and labor and, in essence, control history by recording it in a manner beneficial to them, it is unlikely that the entire system supporting the civilization could ever have developed. In modern America, for instance, how well would the Internal Revenue Service function—and how well would the country work—if there were no way to record individual income and yearly tax contribution? On the other hand, a system of keeping records that can reinforce the legitimacy of the rule of the king—for instance, by demonstrating descent from previous rulers or even from the gods—is another important way the system justifies and maintains itself. As a result of the record keeping of civilizations, in this chapter and Chapter 15 we begin to breach the edge of history, reaching the end of the human story that is the focus of this book—that part of the human saga from the period before history.

Monumental Works

Finally, let us return to the most obvious symbols of civilizations, the monumental works by which we recognize them in the archaeological record. Those monuments are made possible by the characteristics of the state just enumerated. A food surplus freeing the labor of a large labor force; a large, dense population; a stratified social system in which the many serve the dictates of the few; a formal government that enforces that social inequality; specialization; and a system of record keeping together make possible the production of the monumental works and great art that first command our attention when we are confronted by the remains of an ancient civilization.

Great monuments and art, therefore, are enabled by the social and political system of the state. The rulers in state societies have the power to cause the construction of fabulous tombs filled with splendid works of art. They can conscript armies, collect taxes, and call up workforces. Without some degree of social stratification, these large-scale construction projects and other activities, requiring the ability of the few to command the labor of the many, as well as associated complex patterns of coordination of such labor, would have been impossible to organize and carry out.

In a feedback process, such power, at the same time, adds compelling support for the existence of the state. In complex civilizations, the great mass of people must believe that there are individuals who can rightfully require their labor, time, and wealth. As archaeologist Joseph Tainter (1988) puts it, the early elites had to convince the great mass of society that their rule was legitimate—in other words, "proper and valid"—and that the political world with a powerful elite commanding from on high and accumulating great wealth was "as it should be" (Tainter 1988, 27). And, as the old saying goes, "nothing succeeds like success"; an awe-inspiring pyramid or temple goes a long way toward convincing the populace that the ruler who commanded that such a thing be built actually is as powerful as he is purported to be and that allegiance is due him.

Pyramids, great tombs, huge palaces, and the like become the material symbols of the power of the state, both for those living within such systems and for those of us in the modern world who study them. In addition to being literal monuments to kings, gods, or generals, they also stand as symbolic monuments to the power of the state. They serve the role of providing, as archaeologist Tainter characterizes it (1988, 28), "sacred legitimization" for the power of the elite, and they reflect "the need to establish and constantly reinforce legitimacy" (Tainter 1988, 27).

THE GEOGRAPHY OF CIVILIZATIONS

Perhaps most remarkably, these features of the world's first civilizations evolved from an earlier Neolithic base not once, but several times, in both the Old and New Worlds: in at least southwest Asia, Egypt, the Indus Valley of Pakistan, and eastern China and on the island of Crete (all discussed in this chapter), and in Mesoamerica and Peru (discussed in Chapter 15). These primary civilizations developed more or less independently, each following its own path. The next sections will present brief synopses of the evolution of each of the centers of early civilization in the Old World.

MESOPOTAMIA

In Chapter 12, we discussed the origins of one of the world's earliest complex societies in the land between the Tigris and Euphrates Rivers. We saw the evidence for complexity reflected in large-scale communal works such as granaries and defensive walls that surrounded entire villages. Southern Mesopotamia is also the place where archaeological evidence indicates that the world's first civilization developed.

Accelerating Change: The Ubaid

Not until after about 6300 B.P. did the area of southern Mesopotamia show a great change toward what we call civilization. The culture of southern

FIGURE 13.2

Archaeological sites in western Asia where evidence of the evolution of chiefdom and early state-level societies has been found.

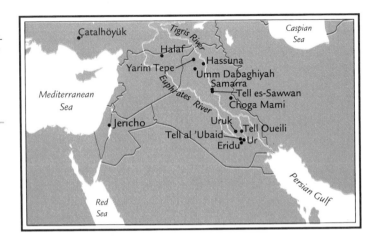

Mesopotamia during this period is called **Ubaid** and is reflected at the sites of Tell al 'Ubaid, Tell Oueili, Eridu, 'Usaila, and Ur (Figure 13.2).

Southern Mesopotamia is not an area in which the world's first civilization might be expected. It is a land of sand dunes and marshes, a semiarid plain surrounded by a double river system prone to unpredictable, ferocious flooding. Agriculture based on rainfall is impossible outside the marsh edges—the region receives as little as 15 cm (6 in.) of rain per year (Crawford 1991, 8). The construction of irrigation canals is an absolute necessity for farmers in southern Mesopotamia.

Beyond its rich floodplain soil, Mesopotamia proper has few other resources. As archaeologist Harriet Crawford (1991) points out, there are no sources for stone or metal in Mesopotamia and few areas with enough trees to provide wood for construction. It is not surprising, therefore, that Ubaid sites appear rather suddenly in this area, with no evidence of previous development. Much of the area simply was not immediately attractive to Neolithic farmers in the Middle East. Southern Mesopotamia was populated only after 6,300 years ago, when population growth, made possible by the settled life of the Neolithic, forced people to expand out onto the floodplain and away from the areas immediately adjacent to watercourses. Similarly, this area was populated only when the construction of a system of water control became technologically—and socially—feasible.

The Role of Irrigation

As archaeologist Charles Maisels (1990) points out, while the floodplain of the Tigris-Euphrates system is not an easy habitat to exploit, with the construction of irrigation canals to bring water to fields in the summer and to drain them after the spring floods, it becomes enormously productive farmland. Canal construction requires a large population whose labor can be organized. At the same time, an effective irrigation system allows for the production of even

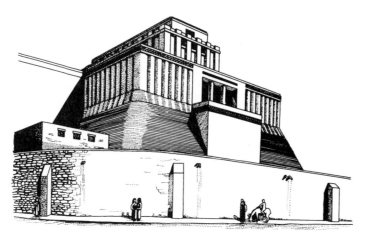

FIGURE 13.3
Artist's conception of the temple at the early Mesopotamian city of Eridu at around 5000 B.P. (From *Art of the Ancient Near East* by Seton Lloyd, copyright © 1961, Thames and Hudson, page 259, Praeger Publishers, an imprint of Greenwood Publishing Group, Inc., Westport, CT. Reprinted with permission)

more food to support a larger and denser population. Maisels proposes that the deciding factors in the development of Mesopotamia's complex societies were (1) the need to concentrate population along the arable lands near the rivers, thereby increasing population locally, (2) the need to develop a complex social system that would allow the construction of canals, and (3) the ability of irrigation to produce a food surplus. In other words, the development of civilization was the result of dynamic feedback among population growth, the development of complex irrigation systems, and the attendant new social order necessary to organize and ultimately command the labor of the growing population.

Power Invested in the Temple

In Mesopotamia, as elsewhere, no political or military structure was in place that could provide designers, builders, supervisors, maintainers, and controllers of the irrigation networks. Early Neolithic cultures were likely largely egalitarian or rank societies. But in Mesopotamia, again as elsewhere, one institution in society was set apart, and there extraordinary powers resided even before social complexity increased. That institution was the temple (Figure 13.3). As seen in Chapter 12, religious shrines or temples date back to well before the Ubaid period in Mesopotamia. The familiar T-shaped northern Mesopotamian temple can be seen in prototype at Samarran sites and, perhaps, in the sense of a functional prototype, in the Halafian round storage buildings, which seem to have served as communal granaries and, at the same time, places of religious significance. In the view of archaeologists C. C. Lamberg-Karlovsky and Jeremy Sabloff (1995), when population grew and expanded onto the floodplain and when irrigation works became a necessity, a need developed for the evolution of an institution that could organize the labor necessary to build and maintain these works. In their view, the religious elite quickly filled the power vacuum and became the dominant political and social as well as religious force in Mesopotamian society. In other words, priests became chiefs. Control of the irrigation networks led to power and with power came the ability to control the enormous food surplus that the evolving system produced.

Mesopotamia's First Cities: The Uruk Period

With the large and complex settlements of the Ubaid as a base, after 6000 B.P., dramatic changes occurred in southern Mesopotamia, and a number of communities became much larger. Between 5500 and 5000 B.P., the settlement at Uruk (also called Warka) became so large, with a population estimated to be more than 10,000, that we can reasonably call it a city—in fact, the world's first. Uruk's population continued to grow; and by 4,700 years ago, it may have had as many as 50,000 residents.

The growth of Uruk occurred, at least in part, through a process of population implosion. Archaeological evidence indicates that many of the smaller farming communities around Uruk were abandoned, with their populations congregating in the growing urban center after 5000 B.P. That this movement of population may have resulted from widespread warfare is supported by evidence at Uruk itself, where defensive fortifications were built at this time.

Another site, Eridu, became an urban center soon after Uruk, with an estimated population of 5,000; a large, finely built temple; and a neighborhood of larger houses with more impressive material culture, belonging to the newly evolved elite. By the Early Dynastic Period of the Sumerian civilization, dated from 4850 to 4600 B.P., there were more than 20 urban centers, or **city-states**—each with its own temple and territory consisting of a four-tiered hierarchy of settlement types, including the city and its associated towns, villages, and hamlets (Adams and Nissen 1972; see Color Plate 13).

Along with monumental works such as great temples, palaces, and pyramids, state societies express in symbolic ways the social and political stratification that defines them. There is no more obvious example of this than in how the rulers of these societies are treated in death. The elite classes in state society are buried in a splendor that symbolizes their superior economic, social, and political positions in life.

Consider, for example, the cemetery at the Mesopotamian city of Ur; it contains more than 2,000 graves, only 16 of which were the interments of members of the elite class. Most of the graves are simple, the final resting places of ordinary people. They are little more than holes in the ground with a few personal effects placed in the graves. The burials of the elite are far different, placed in stone chambers with vaulted roofs—one even possessed a dome. One of the tombs, that of a queen called Pu-abi, is typical of the royal interments at Ur.

A headdress of gold, festooned with semiprecious stones, was placed on Pu-abi's head. Around her were gold and silver containers, an intricately designed harp, a gaming table, and another 250 or so objects (see Color Plate

FIGURE 13.4

These clay tokens with impressed or incised symbols from the Middle East may represent the first evidence for a system of record keeping anywhere in the world. (Courtesy of Département des Antiquités Orientales, Musée du Louvre, Paris. Photograph courtesy of Denise Schmandt-Besserat)

14). Following a pattern seen among the elite of other early civilizations, humans and animals were sacrificed as part of the royal burial ceremony; in Pu-abi's burial chamber were two female attendants. Just outside the royal chamber were 10 more women (one with a harp—musical accompaniment for the journey), 5 soldiers, and 2 oxen. Beneath Queen Pu-abi's chamber was another tomb—a man's, possibly her husband's. This king was accompanied by 6 soldiers, 19 females wearing gold headpieces, 6 oxen, 2 chariots, a lyre, a gaming table, and an exquisite silver model of a boat. Such were the death settings of Ur nobility. Pu-abi's interment is emblematic of the wealth, power, and social position of the nobility of ancient Mesopotamia and, in fact, all of the other civilizations discussed in this text.

The Beginnings of the Written Record

Discussion of Mesopotamian civilization brings us to a description of the origins of a written language. The first literate civilizations represent the beginning of history and, hence, the end of the period this book focuses on. Nevertheless, it is important to touch upon the origins of record keeping.

Denise Schmandt-Besserat, whose 1992 book is one of the most important works on the origins of writing in the Middle East, where writing first appeared, suggests that small baked clay counters found in archaeological sites in the Middle East represent elements in an early system of record keeping for goods such as bushels of wheat, sheep and goats, and jars of oil.

These counters—called **tokens**—were made in 16 basic shapes, mostly simple geometric forms but also stylized animals and jars (Figure 13.4). Schmandt-Besserat examined more than 8,000 of these tokens. The oldest date back to early Neolithic cultures of the Middle East; they are perhaps as much as 10,000 years old. Tokens have been found at Hassuna, Samarra, and Halaf, all sites mentioned in Chapter 12 as part of our discussion of early evidence for an agricultural way of life.

Schmandt-Besserat (1992, 163) describes the tokens as a method of "communication and data storage." In other words, the token form (and, later, markings incised in the tokens) represents a code, the first step in a record-keeping system that allowed Neolithic inhabitants of the Middle East to keep track of valuable commodities such as food, oil, and animals. Tokens have been found primarily in public buildings rather than individual houses. Their presence in temples suggests their public function as well as the early connection

FIGURE 13.5

The cuneiform writing of Mesopotamia was the world's first written language. (Copyright © Lee Boltin/Boltin Picture Library)

between religion, the religious elite, and control of a food surplus. It would seem, therefore, that the tokens were used to keep track of food flowing into communal grain storage facilities or surplus food provided to the temple, perhaps as part of a tax or tithe.

Between 10,000 and 6,000 years ago, the tokens were plain, but after 6000 B.P., tokens became increasingly more complex, with standardized designs incised into the clay. Furthermore, tokens were stored in hollow clay balls called "envelopes," which also bore incised designs. Though initially used only to complement the information on the tokens themselves, the incised markings on the envelopes became the preferred medium of communication. It became simpler and more efficient to dispose of the tokens entirely and record information by making standardized impressions on clay tablets. These standardized impressions represented another code, **cuneiform,** which is in essence the first written language (Figure 13.5).

Schmandt-Besserat's view of the origins of a system of record keeping and, ultimately, record keeping through writing, meshes quite well with the reason why such a system was required by civilized societies. Knowledge is power, and the ability to control knowledge through a system of coded, permanent records gave those who knew the code and kept the records an enormous advantage in their ability to control first the economic system, but ultimately the political and social systems. Such a system allows those who keep the records to know precisely which individuals have contributed in the form of food or wealth to the temple or the king—and to know how much more is owed. Originating as a method for keeping track of mundane information, record keeping became a powerful tool for those who controlled it, a way of solidifying the power of the state. A system of record keeping, usually but not universally through writing (see the discussion of the Inka in Chap-

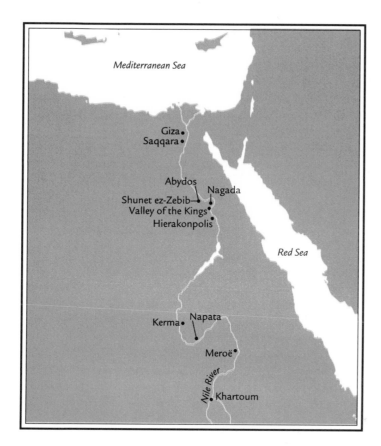

FIGURE 13.6

Archaeological sites in northern Africa where evidence of the evolution of chiefdom and early state-level societies has been found.

ter 15), played a major role in Mesopotamia and elsewhere in allowing the state to maintain its level of control.

EGYPT OF THE PHARAOHS

Ancient Egypt is, for most people, uniquely illustrative of the mystery and essence of ancient civilization: the great pyramids at Giza, the enigmatic half-human, half-lion that is the Sphinx (see Color Plate 16), and fabulous tombs filled with remarkable treasure. These monuments are all emblematic of the Egypt of the pharaohs and symbolic of the remarkable achievements of ancient Egyptian civilization at its peak. The roots of Egyptian civilization lie in the earliest Neolithic cultures that developed in the Nile Valley (Figure 13.6).

The Egyptian Neolithic

The Egyptian Neolithic appears to be culturally derivative. Most crops and domesticated animals on which the Neolithic inhabitants subsisted were all used in southwest Asia at an earlier date (see Chapter 11). Between 7,000 and 5,000 years ago, a gradual shift to a Neolithic economy occurred along the Nile, the only region where agriculture not based on irrigation is possible in Egypt. At the sites of Merimde, Tasa, and Badari, wheat and barley appear to have been the most significant plant foods; domesticated flax provided fibers; and sheep, goats, cattle, and pigs were the primary sources of animal protein (Trigger 1983).

Sometime after 6500 B.P. and at an accelerating rate after 5500 B.P., a process of political coalescence began among some of the early farming villages along the Nile. As mentioned, the floodplain of the Nile rigidly demarcates the viable farmland in Egypt before the development of a sophisticated system of irrigation. The Nile runs its course through a virtual desert, and small Neolithic villages developed along the river like a series of pearls on a necklace.

Foundations of Complexity Along the Nile

Perhaps as a result of increasing competition for the primary resource of good agricultural land, some well-positioned towns seem to have become what geographers call **central places**—sites viewed by the local populace as locations of great spiritual and social power. We know of at least two of these incipient "states," by their "capitals": Nagada and Hierakonpolis.

Nagada predates Hierakonpolis, though the latter ultimately far exceeds the former in terms of historical significance. At Nagada we see early evidence for the kind of social differentiation that is a defining element of civilization. That evidence occurs in the form of sumptuous burials afforded to a very small proportion of the population. It seems that Nagada controlled a large surrounding territory by 5500 B.P., and the power needed for that control was vested in a small group of people, a developing social elite whose status was symbolized—then and now—by their placement in elaborate tombs.

Hierakonpolis

The evidence for the evolution of an increasingly complex society is far clearer at Hierakonpolis, largely due to the diligent efforts of archaeologist Michael Hoffman (1979, 1983). Hierakonpolis began its history nearly 6,000 years ago as a small Neolithic village on the west bank of the Nile. This is now called the Nagada I, or Amratian, period of Egyptian prehistory. Pottery manufacture became a booming business at Hierakonpolis, and ceramics manufactured in that town's kilns are found up and down the Nile. While pottery likely originated as a small-scale, family-run affair, here it developed into a specialized craft, and a class of "pottery barons" developed. The burials of these people were larger and far more elaborate than were the interments of the rest of society. Brick-lined tombs cut into the bedrock mark the final resting places of the growing class of pottery makers.

After 5500 B.P., during Nagada II, or Gerzean, times, irrigation canals were constructed, likely in response to a change in the local climate. A dry period that began at this time possibly resulted from local deforestation, which, in turn, resulted from the need to fuel the pottery kilns. The tombs of a developing elite became larger; some include a square stone building called a **mastaba** built on top of a subterranean, brick-lined or rock-cut tomb.

As population along the Nile grew and as competition for resources increased, previously small arguments or perceived injustices among and between neighboring towns grew into full-scale battles for control of the precious land base. Interestingly, the period after 5100 B.P. was marked by the abandonment of small villages located around the central places of Nagada and Hierakonpolis. The populations of the small towns seem to have moved into the larger settlements, making them substantially larger and more complex. Fortifications around Nagada and Hierakonpolis were built and expanded at this time, and the burials of the growing elite became increasingly elaborate (Kemp 1977). At Hierakonpolis, for example, Tomb 100 is brick-lined, is much larger than previous tombs, and has various wall paintings that depict the deceased as a ruler.

First Pharaoh

Archaeologists have recovered a king list, now called the Royal Canon of Turin for the Italian museum where the list is housed, from the New Kingdom (the period 1540–1070 B.C.); it contains the names of about 300 pharaohs (Kemp 1991, 23). The list apparently was a virtually complete enumeration of Egyptian rulers to that point in time, providing the duration of their reigns, sometimes to the exact numbers of years, months, and even days. This list traces Egyptian kingship back 958 years, to the rule of the first historically known pharaoh, Menes, who united Lower (northern) and Upper (southern) Egypt (because the Nile runs from south to north, the upper region of the river—its source—lies to the south, while its lower section—the delta—is in the north). Menes created a single political entity that was to become one of the most remarkable of the early civilizations.

A plaque celebrating the unification of Egypt and the ascension of the first pharaoh was discovered at Hierakonpolis. One side depicts a man with a mace or baton raised as if about to strike a kneeling enemy soldier (Figure 13.7). The standing man is wearing a crown that we know from later writing is the symbol of leadership of Upper Egypt. On the obverse of the plaque, the same man is depicted wearing a crown that includes the symbol of kingship of Lower Egypt. We can read his name on the object; it is Narmer. In all likelihood, Narmer is another name for Menes (who is also called the Scorpion), positioned in the king list mentioned earlier as the first pharaoh of a unified Egyptian state. Narmer's ascension to the throne of Egypt occurred around 5100 B.P.

FIGURE 13.7

The Narmer Palette of Hierakonpolis depicts symbolically the unification of Upper and Lower Egypt under the leadership of Narmer, the first pharaoh, in about 5100 B.P. (Copyright © Giraudon/Art Resource, N.Y.)

This all sets the stage for developments in Egypt that again cross over the boundary between prehistory and history and pass beyond the scope of this book. Suffice it to say that when we cross this threshold and examine the royal cemetery at Abydos, we encounter royal tombs far beyond anything seen at Hierakonpolis. For example, built almost 5,000 years ago, the Shunet ez-Zebib is an enormous burial enclosure, surrounded by a monumental wall measuring about 125 m (404 ft) in length and 65 m (210 ft) in width, with the walls measuring more than 5 m (16 ft) thick and reaching a height of more than 11 m (36 ft) (Kemp 1991, 53). The exterior of the wall is decorated in a way that provides a paneled effect. Soon after the Shunet ez-Zebib was built, the burial tomb of the pharaoh Djoser was constructed at Saqqara (Figure 13.8). Built about 4,600 years ago, Djoser's tomb is a stepped pyramid, a stone construction on a scale much larger than anything built previously in ancient Egypt. Ultimately, pharaohs commanded the labor of hundreds of thousands

FIGURE 13.8

The form of the stepped pyramid at Saqqara, built to memorialize the Egyptian pharaoh Djoser in about 4600 B.P., was based on earlier mastaba tombs of Egypt's elite. (M. H. Feder)

of workers and were buried in spectacular fashion, though only a fraction were buried in the pyramid tombs that today are emblematic of ancient Egypt.

After the period of pyramid construction had long passed, a young boy ascended to the throne during a period of great turbulence. He ruled for approximately 10 years; he became pharaoh at the age of 9 and died when he was only 19. His name was Tutankhamun, and his splendid burial, which served as a metaphor for ancient civilization in the "Prelude" of this chapter, will likely forever stand as a symbol of ancient Egypt (see Color Plate 15).

OTHER AFRICAN CIVILIZATIONS

Ancient Egypt's influence reached far from its center in northeasternmost Africa. To the south, the ancient civilizations of **Nubia,** initially inspired by the colossus to the north, developed their own uniquely African early civilization.

The Egyptians called the land to the south **Kush.** If you travel south past the so-called first cataract near Aswan in modern Egypt (the first extensive rapids encountered moving along the Nile from north to south) into the modern nation of Sudan, continuing to the sixth cataract, north of the Sudanese city of Khartoum, you have traversed the territory of ancient Nubia (O'Connor 1993).

To be sure, ancient Nubian civilization developed, at least initially, in response to the impact of having one of the world's first great civilizations literally just downstream. But, it must be understood that ancient Egyptian civilization was not merely imported upstream, nor do we see Egyptian culture grafted wholesale onto an indigenous population's culture. Rather, developments to the north seem to have inspired the evolution of what was not a pale reflection of ancient Egyptian civilization, but, as archaeologist David

O'Connor (1993) characterizes it in the subtitle of his book, a distinct civilization that was "Egypt's rival" in ancient Africa.

Dating to more than 3,500 years ago, the civilization of Kerma represents the first indigenous complex civilization in Africa south of the ancient Egyptian nation (Connah 1987). The site of Kerma itself is located on the east bank of the Nile, south of the third cataract in Sudan. The site has been called "the earliest city in Africa outside of Egypt" (O'Connor 1993, 50). The center of Kerma covered 15–25 acres and was surrounded by a huge wall about 10 m (33 ft) high. Its fortifications included monumental towers called **deffufa,** constructed of mud-brick; the Western Deffufa is an enormous, solid mass of brick some 52 m (170 ft) long and 27 m (88 ft) wide. Today it still stands more than 19 m (57 ft) high, and it was even taller in antiquity.

To the east of the city was a large cemetery, marked by enormous tumuli—earth mounds marking the graves of the elite—averaging 88 m (288 ft) in diameter (O'Connor 1993, 54). These graves bear witness to the degree of social stratification present in that society. The elite were placed on finely made wooden beds, some encased in gold; and well-crafted items were entombed with them for their enjoyment in the afterlife: bronze swords, bronze razors, fine clothing of leather, fans made of ostrich feathers, and large quantities of pottery. The most impressive grave in the cemetery, Tumulus X, represents the final resting place of an obviously important ruler of Kerma, surrounded by the remains of close to 400 sacrificed retainers (322 actual remains were found, but the burial was disturbed, and there likely were more burials interred with the primary grave).

After 2800 B.P., the influence of Kerma faded, and another Nubian kingdom rose to take its place. Called Napata, it was centered just downstream of the fourth cataract. It likely developed when Egypt's long reach to the south weakened. Social stratification is evident at the cemeteries of El Kurru, Jebel Barkal, and Nuri, where the elite were buried in tombs topped with small pyramids reminiscent of those in ancient Egypt, yet clearly of local construction. The main population center of the Napata polity was the very large town of Sanam.

Perhaps the best known of the ancient Nubian cultures is that of Meroë. The Meroitic civilization dates from about 2500 to 2200 B.P. and is clearly the most complex and the most urban of the ancient civilizations south of Egypt (Connah 1987). The city of Meroë was a large settlement covering an area of about 0.75 km^2 (0.3 mi^2). The center of the settlement consisted of a maze of monumental structures made of mud-brick and faced with fired brick. These buildings appear to have been palaces, meeting halls, temples, and residences for nobility and their workers. The central area of Meroë was surrounded by a monumental wall of mud-brick.

In an enormous graveyard excavated to the east of the city were about 600 simple interments of common people. Even farther to the east, in a graveyard called North Cemetery, the tombs of Meroitic nobility were found with small, stone pyramids built on top (Figure 13.9).

FIGURE 13.9

The pyramids of the rulers of Meroë, an African civilization, are located to the south of pharaonic Egypt and date to between 2500 and 2200 B.P. (Copyright © Marc and Evelyne Bernheim 1980, all rights reserved, Woodfin Camp and Associates)

Clearly the civilizations of Nubia were at least partially indigenous developments with a heavy dose of influence from the north. Contact with Egypt may have been the catalyst that set local people on the road to great social complexity and technological sophistication. Once the process was initiated, however, Nubians evolved their own, distinct version of civilization.

THE INDUS VALLEY CIVILIZATION

Though it has generated less interest as well as less archaeology than either Mesopotamia or ancient Egypt, the Indus Valley civilization reflected in the enormous cities of Harappa and Mohenjo-daro deserves recognition for being another primary Old World civilization (Allchin and Allchin 1982; Fairservis 1975; Kenoyer 1998; Possehl 1980).

The Indus civilization has been known to scholars in the West only since its two largest cities were first excavated in the early 1920s. The roots of the culture are barely known, with only a small handful of pre-Indus sites excavated. In addition, although like Mesopotamia and ancient Egypt, the Indus culture did possess a written language, its writing as yet remains largely undeciphered. There are close to four thousand preserved samples of Indus writing, but only a few of the individual signs have as yet been interpreted (Parpola 1993). So, while we can examine self-conscious attempts by the

FIGURE 13.10

Archaeological sites in India, Pakistan, and Afghanistan where evidence of the evolution of chiefdom and early state-level societies has been found.

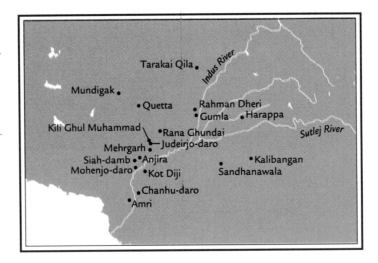

people within Mesopotamian and Egyptian civilizations to explain or chronicle the origins of their world, this avenue is as yet closed to us in our investigation of the Indus Valley. Unless and until that script is deciphered, the people of the Indus cannot speak directly to us in the way that ancient Mesopotamians and Egyptians can.

Neolithic Cultures

With this lack of evidence serving as a disclaimer, current data indicate that Neolithic roots for the Indus civilization can be traced to the hills of Baluchistan (in modern Pakistan; Figure 13.10). One site excavated in the uplands is that of Kili Ghul Muhammad, a small site covering an area of about 90 m (292 ft) by 55 m (178 ft). The structures at the site were mud-brick, and subsistence included the raising of sheep, goats, and oxen (Allchin and Allchin 1982). The only radiocarbon dates for Kili Ghul Muhammad are between 6400 and 6100 B.P., but these were not derived from the earliest levels at the site. Those levels likely date to a thousand or more years earlier. Another site in the Baluchistan Hills is Rana Ghundai. The houses, again, were of mudbrick and here, too, sheep and goats were important for subsistence, along with cattle and wild ass.

Moving out of the uplands and east, closer to the Indus River, we find the site of Mehrgarh, first occupied by about 8500 B.P. At this time the inhabitants had no pottery or metal tools. They subsisted primarily on hunting and gathering.

Mehrgarh's location at the zone of transition between the uplands to the west and the floodplain to the east is important in our investigation of the Indus Valley civilization. The Indus is a treacherous river characterized by devastating and unpredictable flooding. Unlike the situation seen in Egypt or

Mesopotamia, early Neolithic sites are not found along the river. As archaeologists Bridget and Raymond Allchin (1982, 105) point out, local inhabitants' realization that the Indus system offered incredibly rich agricultural soil, coupled with their development of flood control and protection technology, allowed for the evolution of "an entirely new way of life."

Mehrgarh marks a place and time of transition from small, simple farming villages (such as Kili Ghul Muhammad, Rana Ghundai, Anjira, and Siah-damb) to the urban civilization (such as that at Mohenjo-daro and Harappa). By 7100 B.P. the inhabitants of Mehrgarh were practicing a mixed farming economy—the earliest evidence for a sedentary, agricultural way of life on the Indian subcontinent. The inhabitants planted wheat, barley, and dates; and they raised domesticated cattle, water buffalo, sheep, and goats. Mehrgarh also has produced the earliest evidence in Asia of the domestication of cotton.

By a little before 7000 B.P., Merhgarh was no longer a simple Neolithic village. It boasted a rather sophisticated architecture that included the use of mud-brick to produce a substantial and permanent settlement. The village included a number of domestic units—probably the homes of individual families—containing six and sometimes nine rooms. Some separate structures appear to have been public granaries.

Exotic materials found in burials at the site include conch shell from the Arabian Sea, lapis lazuli from Badakhshan, and turquoise from Turkmenia; these source areas are located as much as 500 km (325 mi) from the settlement.

Trade and competition—perhaps with attendant warfare—appear to have been important factors in the growth of increasingly complex and larger sites in Baluchistan after 6000 B.P. One site, Mundigak, is located on a well-known historical trade route between the Near East and south Asia that apparently was first established at this time. Mundigak was surrounded by enormous defensive walls interrupted with bastions. These walls had a practical purpose; the village was twice destroyed and twice rebuilt during its occupation.

All these Neolithic sites west of the Indus provide us with a glimpse of the earliest stages of development of the Indus Valley civilization. They all exhibit a reliance on a diverse agricultural base of crops and animals. They show a notable dependence on trade with points as distant as the Arabian Sea and central Asia. They share an architectural form of substantial and planned-out mud-brick houses. And they show a shift through time from the uplands of Baluchistan to the floodplain of the Indus itself. This shift is clearly seen in the archaeological record by about 5500 B.P.

Flood Control and Civilization in the Indus Valley

This shift to the floodplain was the key to the development of civilization in this part of the world. It was made possible by the development of technology for flood control and protection, including the construction of artificial

FIGURE 13.11

Kot Diji, located on an ancient flood channel of the Indus River in Pakistan, was surrounded by a monumental wall whose purpose probably was to keep residents secure from human enemies as well as the floodwaters of the Indus.
(Department of Archaeology and Museums, Karachi)

mounds, on which at least a portion of the settlements were built, as well as monumental walls around entire villages for protection from enemies and floodwaters. In this way, villages were protected from the periodic rampages of the Indus by being built, in part, above the floodwaters and by being surrounded by walls higher than those same floodwaters.

The site of Kot Diji is located on the incredibly rich floodplain about 32 km (20 mi) east of the Indus River, immediately adjacent to one of its ancient flood channels (Figure 13.11). The village is surrounded by a huge wall with a limestone rubble foundation and a mud-brick superstructure with bastions upwards of 5 m (more than 16 ft) high. This wall almost certainly served as defense against human enemies but also against a natural enemy—the floodwaters of the Indus. To the northeast is another large village called Kalibangan. Here, too, a massive mud-brick wall surrounds the settlement. Other substantial walled villages on the Indus floodplain, dating to the period after 5500 B.P., include the sites of Amri, Gumla, Rahman Dheri, and Tarakai Qila.

Cultural Convergence

An interesting feature of these settlements is the degree of what the Allchins refer to as "cultural convergence" (1982, 163). Where previous Neolithic sites in Baluchistan all exhibit their own artifact styles in pottery and items of adornment, as people began moving out onto the floodplain of the Indus, a certain degree of uniformity appears, indicating a greater level of cultural and perhaps political unification. Most significantly, a common image of a horned water buffalo head begins appearing on pottery throughout the area at many of the sites mentioned. Also, terra-cotta statues of women, following a standardized style, appear at many of the sites dating to this period; some archaeologists have dubbed these "mother goddesses," implying a degree of religious unification as well (Allchin and Allchin 1982, 163).

A few of these floodplain settlements began undergoing an exponential increase in size sometime after 4500 B.P., culminating in their crossing the

FIGURE 13.12

The citadel of Mohenjo-daro (background) looms over the remnants of a neatly gridded layout of streets lined with the houses of the Indus Valley civilization's elite social class.

(Copyright © P. Agee/Anthro-Photo)

boundary between town and true city. Though several Indus Valley settlements certainly qualify to be called "cities" in size and complexity—among them the sites of Kalibangan, Chanhu-daro, Judeirjo-daro, Sandhanawala, and Dhoraji—two settlements stand out far above the others as representing the pinnacle of urban development: the ancient cities of Mohenjo-daro in the southern reaches of the Indus and Harappa, to the north, located on the now dry channel of the Ravi River, tributary to the Indus.

Cities of the Indus

During what specialists refer to as the "Mature Harappan period," lasting for five hundred years, from 4500 to 4000 B.P. (Possehl 1980, 5), Mohenjo-daro and Harappa developed into complex urban centers, with planned neighborhoods following a rectangular grid pattern, a sophisticated drainage system (most individual homes in Mohenjo-daro and Harappa had indoor bathrooms connected by drains to a citywide sewage system), communal granaries, bathhouses, "citadels" consisting of great structures (palaces, temples, or even granaries; their function is not clearly known) built atop artificial mounds, and populations estimated to have been in excess of 35,000 people in each community (Figure 13.12). Literally hundreds of smaller farming villages were aligned with these two great cities, which together were the central places of a cultural entity that encompassed more than 775,000 km² (300,000 mi²) of territory (Possehl 1980, 2). Even beyond the Indus Valley itself, large frontier settlements show the same material culture and written language. For example, the site of Lothal, located to the east of the Indus, still exhibits many of the architectural characteristics as well as the spatial layout of Mohenjo-daro and Harappa, if on a smaller scale.

The degree of planning that went into Indus Valley urban sites is unmatched among the earliest civilizations. Mohenjo-daro, Harappa, and Kalibangan follow virtually identical plans (Figure 13.13). In these three cases, a citadel was built up on a platform of mud-brick on the western margin of the city. The citadel was surrounded by large public buildings, including bathhouses and granaries, and this "upper city" was encompassed by a monumental wall. In each of these three cases, the vast expanse of the city—the residential area where tens of thousands of people lived—was spread out to the east of the citadel. The lower city likewise was surrounded by a great wall. In all three cases it is clear that the cities did not grow simply by accretion, blocks of residences added haphazardly as they were needed in response to population growth. Instead, these cities reflect a pattern of forethought in their construction, with broad main thoroughfares separated by secondary streets, which were, in turn, separated by narrow passageways leading to individual residences. Most of the roads were laid out in an often precise grid of parallel and perpendicular pathways. The alignment of the roads is precisely along the cardinal directions, which likely were determined astronomically (Kenoyer 1998, 52). And the houses themselves were constructed with mud-bricks that are so regular, it is clear that their makers, much in the way of modern brickyards, adhered to established size and form standards.

The dwellings in the lower cities of Indus urban centers exhibit a wide range in size, from single-room apartments to mansions with dozens of rooms and enclosed courtyards. The size and elaborateness of some residences almost certainly reflect vast differences in the wealth and status of the individuals who lived in them (see Color Plate 17). Neighborhoods of craft specialists have been identified at Mohenjo-daro and Harappa. Certain sections of the city clearly were blocked out for metal workers, potters, clothmakers, bakers, stone workers, and bead makers and can be defined archaeologically; the tools of their various trades have been found restricted to their respective neighborhoods. Other areas of the cities appear to have been the residences of scribes, priests, administrators, and traders (Allchin and Allchin 1982, 185).

Indus Valley cities were also trading centers into which exotic and undoubtedly expensive raw materials flowed and in which finely finished goods were produced. Gold, copper, lead, lapis lazuli, turquoise, alabaster, amethyst, agate, chalcedony, and carnelian were brought into the city, although they often originated at sources many hundreds of kilometers distant (Allchin and Allchin 1982, 186). Also, some trade was carried out between these Indus Valley cities and the city-states of ancient Mesopotamia. Harappan **seals** have been found in Mesopotamia, and a small number of Mesopotamian **cylinder seals** have been found in Indus Valley sites. The island of Bahrain, located in the Persian Gulf, served as a central point in this intercivilization trade network. In other words, more than 4,000 years ago, Mesopotamia and the Indus Valley were part of an international trading system.

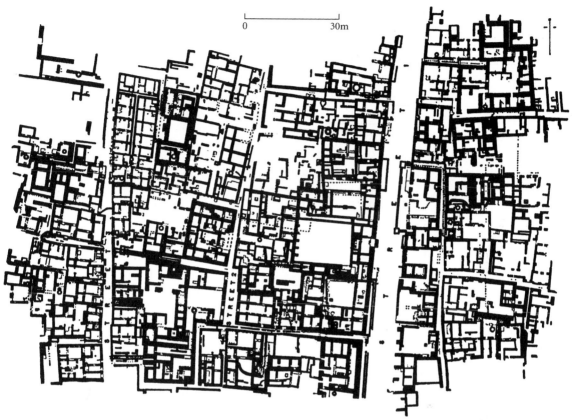

0   30m

THE CIVILIZATION OF ANCIENT CHINA

FIGURE 13.13

This map of Mohenjo-daro exhibits the planned nature of the city, with its major avenues, parallel and perpendicular streets, and regularly sized buildings and rooms. (From M. Wheeler 1968. The Indus Civilization. New York: Cambridge University Press. Reprinted with permission of the publisher)

THE CIVILIZATION OF ANCIENT CHINA

The roots of Chinese civilization can be traced back to the Yang-shao culture discussed in Chapter 11. Yang-shao sites are small, and subsistence was based on the cultivation of millet and, only later, rice (Figure 13.14).

The Lung-shan Culture

Chinese archaeologists perceive a change in Yang-shao sometime after 5000 B.P. and define a new culture, the **Lung-shan,** as replacing Yang-shao. A number of new features distinguish Lung-shan sites from earlier Yang-shao sites and presage the development of early Chinese complex civilizations. Rice became the dominant cultigen, and sites are larger and more permanent. For example, at the Lung-shan site of Ch'eng tzu-yai, the village was enclosed by a monumental wall of stamped earth. The Chinese term for the stamped or pounded earth technique used in construction is **hang-t'u.** The hang-t'u technique was used frequently in later periods of Chinese history in making house walls as well as in defensive structures.

FIGURE 13.14

Archaeological sites in China where evidence of the evolution of chiefdom and early state-level societies has been found.

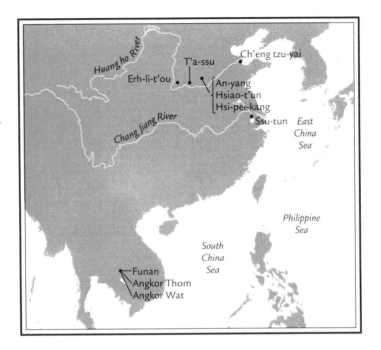

The wall at Ch'eng tzu-yai is enormous and far beyond the abilities—and needs—of earlier people to muster the labor of a large population. The wall is measured at 390 m (nearly 1,300 ft) by 450 m (nearly 1,500 ft), is 9 m (29 ft) wide at the top, and is 6 m (more than 19 ft) high (Chang 1986, 248).

The cemetery at the site reflects another significant element of civilization: status differentiation as reflected in highly differentiated burials. Chinese American archaeologist Kwang-chih Chang (1986) notes the existence of a four-tiered burial hierarchy. There are large elaborate graves at the site—high-status tombs where the deceased was interred in a wooden casket and accompanied by fine ceramics. In the same cemetery there are narrow burial pits barely large enough to hold a human body, with no casket or grave goods. In the typical pattern of a stratified society, there were far fewer members of the elite than of the peasant classes, again as reflected in the burial statistics. From most to least elaborate interments, at Ch'eng tzu-yai there were 5 upper-class burials, 11 second-class, 17 third-class, and 54 fourth-class, or low-class, burials (Chang 1986, 249). This ratio compares to socioeconomic class structure as evidenced at the enormous later Neolithic cemetery at T'a-ssu. Of the excavated graves there, 9 were judged to be of the upper class, 80 belonged to a middle tier, and 610 were plain, lower-class interments (Chang 1986, 277). Some of the upper-class burials dating to this same period contained an incredible array of rare items that exhibited a high level of artistic sophistication. For example, a young man buried at the site of Ssu-tun was interred with 57 finely carved, intricate jade rings and jade tubes (called *ts'ung*).

Along with monumental village walls, which later became a common feature of Chinese civilization, and status-differentiated burials, the period from 5,000 to 4,000 years ago in China is marked by the appearance of a number of other features that represent key elements in the earliest Chinese civilization. The increasing use of metal, especially copper, and the earliest use of bronze is evidenced during this time. Historian Jacques Gernet (1987) suggests that the sophisticated kilns—capable of producing very high, constant temperatures—used in the Chinese Neolithic to produce the fine ceramics that mark even the early years of that period were an enabling factor in the rapid advancement in metallurgy that marks Chinese civilization. In Gernet's view, the ability to manufacture bronze weapons was a key element in the evolution of Chinese civilization; the development of bronze metallurgy and the rise of China's first civilization do indeed overlap temporally. Gernet proposes that power was invested in those who controlled bronze production, and walled cities evolved as a result of competition and warfare.

A number of other identifiable hallmarks of later Chinese civilization appear at this time, between 5,000 and 4,000 years ago. The jade ts'ung tubes and the practice of **scapulimancy**—divining by interpreting the patterns produced by heating animal shoulder blades in a fire—become geographically widespread, indicating a spatially broad sphere of interaction and the initial unification of people into first a religiously defined and ultimately a politically drawn entity. This pattern is highly reminiscent of the "cultural convergence" seen in the Indus Valley immediately prior to the development of civilization there. We will see much the same process at work again in Mesoamerica and South America (see Chapter 15).

In this period we can also perceive evidence of violence on a scale not previously seen in Chinese prehistory. Monumental village walls with ramparts, as well as the skeletal evidence of trauma, imply that institutional violence with armies clashing had already established itself during Lung-shan times.

Acceleration Toward Civilization

The culmination of these early developments can be seen at the site of Erh-li-t'ou, dated to about 3800 B.P. The site itself is an order of magnitude bigger than anything seen previously, covering an area of 2.5 km (1.6 mi) by 1.5 km (a little less than 1 mi). Bronze artifacts are common at the site, as are jade ts'ung tubes. Some of the bronzes were utilitarian tools, including knives, chisels, axes, adzes, and arrowheads and other weapons. Many of the bronze artifacts at the site, including disks, fancy drinking vessels, and musical instruments, were ceremonial or ornamental.

There are large, impressive burials at Erh-li-t'ou, and some members of what we can confidently call the wealthy, elite class were buried in lacquered coffins. A unique feature at Erh-li-t'ou is the remains of two palaces. These structures are far larger than any of the residences located at the site. One

FIGURE 13.15

The burial remains of beheaded people who were sacrificed in ceremonies surrounding the death of a member of the royal class of the Shang civilization in China. (Courtesy of the Institute of History and Philology, Academia Sinica, Taiwan)

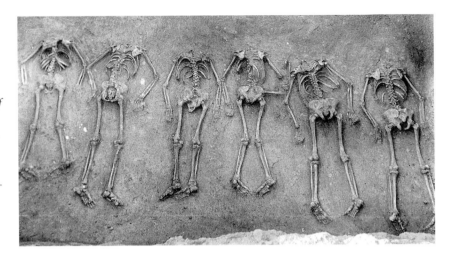

palace was about 100 m (325 ft) on a side; the second was somewhat smaller. The walls of both palaces consisted of thick berms of stamped earth.

The Shang Civilization

The site of Erh-li-t'ou was a precursor to the early florescence of Chinese civilization as represented by the Shang Dynasty. The Shang was China's first true urban civilization. For example, the modern city of An-yang is the site of the ancient city of Yin, a Shang capital city ruled by a succession of 12 kings beginning about 2,400 years ago. Great tombs of the rulers residing at Yin have been found at the sites of Hsiao-t'un and Hsi-pei-kang. These royal interments are enormous and must have taken the labor of thousands of peasants. The royal graves are cruciform—in the shape of a giant cross. The king or emperor was buried in the center of the cross, with long, broad access ramps leading to the burial itself. The deceased noble was placed in an elaborate wooden coffin, surrounded by the symbols of rank and wealth that differentiated him or her from the rest of society: jade, bronze, and ceramic artifacts and even chariots and sacrificed horses (see Color Plate 18). Along the access ramps to the royal gravesite were found the remains of dozens of humans sacrificed to accompany their leader into the afterlife, decapitated and laid out neatly in rows along the rampways (Figure 13.15).

It is with the Shang that we enter into the historical period of China's past. A written language containing more than 5,000 characters, only a fraction of which have been translated, has been found at Shang sites. Shang set the stage for all subsequent Chinese civilization. In at least a symbolic sense, the Chinese emperors who ruled well into the twentieth century were the inheritors of a culture that can be traced back to the time of the first dynasty of the Shang civilization.

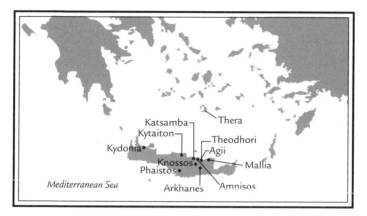

FIGURE 13.16

Archaeological sites in Crete where evidence of the evolution of chiefdom and early state-level societies has been found.

MINOAN CRETE

The island of Crete is a tiny jewel in the eastern Mediterranean (Figure 13.16). It is long and narrow, less than 250 km (152 mi) from east to west and not more than 56 km (35 mi) from north to south. Its entire area is barely 8,260 km² (3,189 mi²), equaling, approximately, the combined area of the two smallest states in the United States: Rhode Island and Delaware. Along with being small, since it is an island located at a great distance from the mainland, it was occupied relatively late in prehistory. It was reachable only when the people of the Mediterranean developed seaworthy boats and navigational skills. The oldest occupation of the island dates only to around 8000 B.P.; it was uninhabited by human beings before this time. Yet on this small island, occupied only relatively recently, Europe's first civilization was to develop.

The Rediscovery of Minoan Crete

In the 1890s, archaeologist Sir Arthur Evans discovered the remains of what he labeled the **Minoan** civilization on Crete (Evans 1921–1936). Evans had been inspired in his search by the Greek myth of King Minos of Crete, who kept a terrible half-human, half-bull monster called the Minotaur deep in the recesses of a tortuous labyrinth. Until the twentieth century, King Minos and his civilization were assumed by many to be mythological, entirely the product of the imaginations of the myth- and legend-makers of ancient Greece. But some thinkers felt that the Greek myths reflected, in at least some of their particulars, historical truths. In perhaps the best-known example, archaeologist Heinrich Schliemann found the real Troy—assumed by many to be the product of the ancient Greek poet Homer's imagination—by taking Homer literally in his description of that ancient city and its location. In turn, Evans took seriously the core of the story of King Minos and a great civilization on Crete contemporary with or even older than that of ancient Greece.

FIGURE 13.17

The temple at Knossos on Crete is the most impressive, though by no means the only, material evidence of the monumental architecture of the ancient Minoan civilization. (Copyright © Fritz Henle 1974/Photo Researchers, Inc.)

Evans first visited Crete in 1894, and almost immediately recognized the great archaeological potential of a hillside at **Knossos** on the north-central part of the island. Eventually, Evans was able to purchase the site. In 1900 he initiated excavations and quickly discovered the spectacular remains of a great palace or temple (Figure 13.17; see the chapter titled "Arthur Evans and the Minoans" in Brian Fagan's 1994 book *Quest for the Past: Great Discoveries in Archaeology*). This seemed to be the remains of King Minos's city, as described by the ancient Greeks. The temple was built up on an artificial mound some 7 m (almost 22 ft) high, composed of the piled-up remains of 10 successive building levels of Neolithic housing dating back to 8000 B.P. (J. D. Evans 1968).

Who Were the Minoans?

The settlers of Crete were people from the mainland of southeastern Europe and southwestern Asia, likely from Greece and Anatolia (Renfrew 1972, 1979). Though probably initially discovered by chance, Crete soon was intentionally settled, in the ninth millennium B.P., by people who brought their Neolithic food base with them. Archaeological excavation of Neolithic Crete reveals the presence of emmer and bread wheat, along with sheep, goats, pigs, and cattle, none of which are native to the island (Warren 1987). The Neolithic population grew, and a number of farming villages dotted the island in the millennia following its initial settlement.

Crete was fortuitously positioned geographically, at a crossroads for people sailing between southeastern Europe and the ancient civilizations of the Middle East and ancient Egypt. An influx of wealth from ancient trade between the peoples of three continents seems to have spurred a period of increasing complexity on Crete. The island itself provided perfect conditions for growing olives, and the olive oil produced on Crete and traded throughout the Mediterranean provided even more wealth to the island. A burst of development, centered on the site of Knossos, occurred at about 5000 B.P., beginning with the importation of bronze from the mainland. By about 3880 B.P., the first monumental edifice, the temple discovered and initially excavated by Evans, was constructed at the site of Knossos. The building consisted of a mazelike jumble of rooms, chambers, halls, and corridors. This main temple at Knossos is sometimes called, in fact, the "Labyrinth," a reference to the myth of King Minos's labyrinth with the Minotaur at its core (Castleden 1990a).

Though fueled by trade and contact with older, established civilizations in Africa and the Middle East, civilization on Minoan Crete does not represent the transplantation of an alien culture. Crete benefited from its location, and the ideas and wealth that passed through the island certainly acted as a catalyst in the development of Minoan civilization. But, as archaeologist Colin Renfrew (1979) points out, Minoan Crete by and large reflects an indigenous European development of civilized life, traceable to evolving complexity that had been going on in the Aegean for a thousand years.

The Temple at Knossos

The temple at Knossos would at its peak ultimately cover an area of some 20,000 m² (more than 210,000 ft², or about 5 acres) and would contain about 1,000 separate rooms. The temple included a central courtyard with a pillar-lined hallway, a huge number of storage rooms, a ceremonial bath, and grand staircases leading to upper levels—some parts of the temple possessed three or even four stories. The walls of some of the living quarters and large halls were covered with magnificent fresco paintings of dolphins and especially bulls. The artistic depiction of bulls in ceremonial settings may be connected to the Greek story of the Minotaur, which is half-human, half-bull. Where the Minoans depicted themselves in these paintings, we see a graceful and athletic people (Figure 13.18).

One set of rooms has been interpreted as being the living quarters of the nobility of Knossos, replete with thrones, bathrooms, and a sophisticated drainage system for wastewater. The monumental proportions and complexity of the temple at Knossos are a clear indication of developing complexity in social, political, and economic spheres of the community. Further evidence of Minoan civilization is seen in the form of writing—so-called Linear A, as yet undeciphered.

Developments on Crete were halted, if only temporarily, by a catastrophic earthquake that all but destroyed the temple at Knossos in 3650 B.P. Another impressive temple on Crete at the site of Phaistos was also damaged at this time. That temple later was destroyed utterly in a fire. Remarkably, however, this catastrophe served only to spur further subsequent development on Crete in what is called the **New Temple Period.** Apparently, the wealth still pouring into the island was sufficient to overcome the impact of this natural disaster.

This peak in Minoan civilization occurred during the period 3650 to 3420 B.P. The temple of Knossos was rebuilt and became even larger and more

FIGURE 13.18

One of the many frescoes depicting everyday life among the Minoans, as reconstructed by the excavator of Knossos, Sir Arthur Evans. (M. H. Feder)

impressive. Paintings and statuettes indicate a developing religion focused on goddesses and priestesses. There is little evidence of the kind of conspicuous consumption that marks ancient Egypt or Mesopotamia; there are no overwhelmingly ornate burials of an elite at Knossos or elsewhere on Crete. Small rural farming villages continued to supply their food surplus to support the temples located at Knossos and elsewhere. Large towns developed, each with its own temple and residential areas; Knossos was the largest and most impressive of these, but it was not the only one. At its peak, the population of Knossos and its surrounding "suburbs" may have been close to 100,000 people (Marinatos 1972, 709), making it the largest concentration of people anywhere in the ancient world to that point in time.

The Eruption on Thera

This pattern of evolving complexity was brought to a halt by another, even more devastating natural catastrophe. Sometime around 3420 B.P. (perhaps a bit earlier) there was a cataclysmic volcanic eruption on the island today called Santorini (the ancient Greeks called it Thera, and before that it was Kalliste), 120 km (72 mi) north of Crete. Though it cannot be said that the explosion on Thera immediately destroyed Minoan civilization, it certainly had a major impact on the island nation (Marinatos 1972). The eruption itself, accompanied by severe earthquakes, badly damaged many settlements on Crete. The explosive force of the eruption of Thera has been judged to have been some four times as powerful as the volcanic conflagration of Krakatoa, a historically witnessed eruption in the Dutch East Indies in 1883 (Marinatos 1972, 718). That catastrophe killed 36,000 people.

Even more devastating were the great waves, or tsunamis, produced by the eruption of Thera, nearly 100 m (300 ft) in height, traveling at the remarkable speed of 320 km (200 mi) an hour. These waves wiped out Minoan port settlements on the north coast of Crete, including those at Katsamba, Amnisos, Agii, and Theodhori and inflicted enormous damage on the ports of Kytaiton, Kydonia, and Mallia (Castleden 1990b, 33).

Certainly the damage to Knossos and other communities and the destruction of so many ports were devastating blows to the Minoan polity. The Minoan civilization developed and flourished, at least in part, as a result of trade; the loss of ports through which trade items passed and the probable destruction of the Minoan fleet of trading vessels must have had a tremendous impact on the Minoan economy. But ports can be rebuilt, ships replaced, and damaged temples repaired. Perhaps of even greater significance, however, for the Minoans over the long term was the deposit of poisonous white ash some 20–30 cm (8–12 in.) thick that fell from the sky following the explosive eruption on Thera. This rain of volcanic ash all but destroyed the agricultural economy on Crete for a time. To be sure, Crete was not damaged as badly as Thera, itself home to a Minoan outpost that was utterly destroyed in the eruption. The effects of the volcanic eruption on Thera were so widespread and catastrophic that it may have become the stuff of legend later on in the Mediterranean world; some have argued that Thera was the model for Plato's description of the Lost Continent of Atlantis (see Feder 1999a and Stiebing 1984).

Clearly the Minoans were able to survive after Thera's eruption. As historian William Stiebing (1984) points out, there is plenty of evidence of destruction on Crete coinciding with the eruption of Thera, but equally plentiful evidence of repair work afterward. There is new evidence that Minoan structures were constructed on top of the volcanic deposit soon after the eruption (Bower 1990). But it also seems clear that the Minoans never fully recovered from the devastation delivered up by the eruption on Thera. It weakened them sufficiently so that, soon after, they were conquered by a developing civilization on mainland Greece, the **Mycenaeans,** the precursors to the ancient, historical Greeks. From there the Minoans passed into the stuff of myth and legend until Sir Arthur Evans conducted his archaeological investigation at Knossos at the outset of the twentieth century.

Many issues and debates concerning the evolution of the world's earliest civilizations revolve around two broad questions: (1) Why did state societies develop? and (2) Why do civilized societies collapse? An attempt to answer the first question will be made here, though the discussion applies also to the New World civilizations described in Chapter 15. The second question is dealt with in Chapter 15, though that discussion, too, applies equally to the Old World civilizations described in this chapter.

ISSUES AND DEBATES

WHY DID STATE SOCIETIES DEVELOP?

Living as we do in the modern version of a civilized, complex state society, we may take it for granted that such a condition is intrinsically superior to other, perhaps simpler lifeways. After all, our complex civilization affords us our materially rich lives and provides us with opportunities to follow our own paths—including the pursuit of education.

But there is another perspective to consider, especially when dealing with early civilizations. Complex state societies offer to only a very small proportion of the population the "perks" so many of us expect. In discussing the development of civilization in ancient China, historian Jacques Gernet points out that the archaeological evidence for most of the people whose work propped up the state organization shows "the existence of a peasantry whose culture and tools (stone knives and wooden spades with curved handles) do not seem to have been very different from those of the Neolithic Age" (1987, 44). Such was the case for all of the early civilizations discussed.

Especially in these older civilizations, most people worked harder than did people who lived in simpler Neolithic villages, and they gave up much of the control they had over their lives. Most people were needed to produce a surplus, part of which they turned over to the temple or the army or the state bureaucracy. The peasants, who made up the greatest proportion of the population in such societies, also provided labor for the state and often sons for military service—and possible death in foreign wars. Finally, as mentioned earlier in this chapter, simpler Neolithic societies probably were largely egalitarian, and most people had the same amount of wealth and about as much control over their lives as everyone else. With social stratification and the attendant evolution of an elite class or classes of kings, nobles, generals, and specialists, most people became second- or third-class citizens of a much larger political entity; archaeologist Thomas Patterson (1993, ix) characterizes the rulers of state societies as "bullies." Considering these factors, asking why civilization developed seems reasonable.

Conflict Models

Archaeologist Jonathan Haas (1982) divides explanations for the evolution of the complex civilization into the categories "conflict" and "integration." Conflict-based explanations, which Joseph Tainter (1988) calls "internal conflict" models, propose that complex civilizations evolved as a way to reduce, control, and mediate conflict among people living in a society. The conflict theorists include Lewis Henry Morgan (1877) and Friedrich Engels (1891), archaeologist V. Gordon Childe (1951), and anthropologists Leslie White (1959) and Morton Fried (1967).

Conflict theories, though diverse, have a number of fundamental propositions in common: Civilization is viewed as the outcome of a series of steps that began with the development of an agricultural economy by Neolithic people. In certain areas during the Neolithic, a substantial food surplus was possible. The production of a surplus by an individual or family resulted in surplus, privately owned wealth. Some people got richer than others as a result of their larger surpluses. This, in turn, led to differences in status and ultimately to conflict between developing social classes. According to Joseph Tainter (1988, 33), conflict theorists view the evolution of civilization and the state as the result of "divided interests" leading to domination and exploitation. An organizational solution to these conflicts arose in the form of a bureaucracy that served to validate the existence of social classes and at the same time served to mediate conflicts that arose between them.

Thus, according to the various conflict theories, agriculture led to surplus, which led to wealth, which produced different socioeconomic classes within Neolithic societies. With socioeconomic differentiation came the need to develop institutions that suppressed or mediated conflict between the newborn socioeconomic classes, often by sanctifying the newly evolved nonegalitarian social system. Symbols were needed to justify this new system ritually, and great works of art and architecture were produced. Thus do the social and material trappings of the state appear in the cultural evolutionary record.

Archaeologist V. Gordon Childe (1951) provides an even more explicit conflict-based explanation for the development of early civilizations. Childe also viewed the food surplus made possible by agriculture as central to the evolution of these civilizations. In his view, such a surplus was used by the inhabitants of agriculturally rich but otherwise resource-poor regions to trade for needed raw materials like metal, wood, and stone. To carry out such widescale trade most efficiently, some people would abandon the subsistence focus of the majority and become full-time specialist traders or administrators of that trade. From Childe's perspective, the need to produce ever larger surpluses to obtain more trade goods encouraged the use of more intensive agricultural technologies, especially the construction of irrigation canals. The existence of these canals put more and more power in the hands of those who controlled them; the water supply was turned off to those who were not sufficiently cooperative or compliant to the will of the developing administrative elite. Ultimately, between increasing trade and increasingly complex and labor-intensive irrigation projects, a centralized bureaucracy developed. Though such a "class" may have developed initially only to give everyone the needed raw materials unavailable locally, it ultimately changed dramatically, monopolizing this excess wealth for its own use and aggrandizement.

Integration Models

Theories of state development that rely on models of integration rather than conflict have been proposed by thinkers as diverse as sociologist Herbert Spencer (1967), anthropologists Elman Service (1975) and Robert Carniero (1970), and historian Karl Wittfogel (1957). Integration theories, also, have a set of core propositions: Integration theories, which Joseph Tainter (1988, 32) divides into "managerial" and "external conflict" models, see civilization as evolving from the need for increasingly complex integrative mechanisms in increasingly complex situations (Haas 1982, 73). As Tainter (1988) points out, from the integrationist perspective, as the need developed to mobilize large and diverse populations to work together for the good of society, social institutions developed to expedite and at the same time justify, rationalize, codify, legitimize, and sanctify these activities.

From the integrationist perspective, most members of civilizations benefit both directly and indirectly from the complex, stratified social system. To be sure, a few people benefit much more than the masses. The benefits that accrue to the few—great palaces, spectacular tombs, luxurious lifestyles—are viewed as the price paid by society as a whole for the benefits that accrue to everyone as a result of the key social roles played by the elite.

For example, in the view of historian Karl Wittfogel (1957) in his "hydraulic hypothesis," irrigation works played a pivotal role in the development of civilization. The sedentary and secure lifeway made possible by agriculture fostered the growth of human population, and the size of some local populations increased significantly. With growth came the need to produce greater amounts of food to feed an increasing number of mouths. This need then stimulated the need to increase the productivity of existing farmland and to expand the acreage under cultivation. Along the floodplains of large rivers, this expansion was made possible by the construction of sometimes enormous, complex, and costly (in labor investment) irrigation networks. Such waterworks required not just new technology, but also new social and political institutions to organize and coordinate the labor necessary for their construction and maintenance. Consider, for example, the amount of labor, as well as the level of coordination, necessitated by the construction of Mesopotamian canals, some of which were up to 40 km (26 mi) long. Of necessity, power was vested in a class of managers who could call up and oversee the labor. Specialist groups who could design irrigation systems were needed. The same social and political apparatus used to organize labor to build canals could also help build defensive works around settlements as competition for land increased. Surplus labor could also be used to construct great homes and tombs for the members of the developing elite class; these material trappings of power were powerful symbols that served to legitimize the role of the elite class, further increasing the ability of these people to control the peasants.

Anthropologist Robert Carniero (1970) has suggested another avenue by which Neolithic societies may have crossed the threshold to civilization. Carniero cites the apparent ubiquity of evidence for warfare in the world's early civilizations (many of the examples in this chapter show archaeological evidence of the construction of defensive walls and other fortifications). He views this common thread as significant in the development of complex societies.

Though Carniero's use of warfare might seem to imply that his is a conflict-based model for the evolution of the state, in fact his model fits under the integrative approach, Tainter's (1988, 32) "external conflict" subset of the integrative model. In Carniero's view, in certain areas agricultural communities developed where their territories were inherently "circumscribed"—that is, geographically or socially restricted, surrounded either by unproductive farmland or productive land already inhabited by another group or groups of people. In such a scenario, once a group's home territory is filled up with a growing population, a rational option is to expand into the surrounding viable farmland or into the next group's territory by taking over their land through wars of conquest. The conquered group then becomes integrated into a larger political entity as second-class citizens. In this way, a system of social stratification develops. Social and political institutions develop to incorporate these people into a growing political unit; symbols of power evolve, legitimizing the control of the victors over the vanquished; and the seeds of civilized life are sown.

Many Paths to Civilization

None of the hypotheses proposed to explain the evolution of the world's first civilizations can be applied universally. There was no unilinear sequence of development reflected in all the cases discussed in this chapter. Not all civilizations responded to the same pressures, not all societies passed through the same sequence of steps.

In some cases (Egypt and the Indus Valley here, and lowland Mesoamerica in Chapter 12), rich farmland coupled with the lack of other important resources was key to the evolution of civilization. Social complexity developed in these regions partly because society could produce a food surplus and because they needed to create an effective system of trade. In other regions (early developments at Çatalhöyük and Chavín de Huántar, discussed in Chapter 12, and places like Cerros in the Yucatán, discussed in Chapter 15), a rich resource base may have produced nodes of great surplus wealth and a developing social complexity. In some regions, the need to create enormous irrigation networks may have stimulated the growth of social institutions that led to social stratification. In some cases, social stratification and early state institutions may have already existed, but a quantum leap in their power may have occurred with the kind of social control made possible by the reliance on irrigation technology. In other regions, the need for large-scale defensive works may have resulted in the same kinds of changes in society (for example, in Mesopotamia, China, and the Indus Valley).

It seems there were many different pathways leading to societies we today recognize archaeologically as possessing the requisite features of what we have defined as civilization. Many cultural evolutionary roads have led to essentially the same place, and it is likely that not one, but some—possibly all—of the explanations offered here can help us understand the process in each of the areas discussed. It also is likely that quite different combinations of these explanations can be differentially useful in explaining what transpired in the world's first civilizations. As Egyptologist Barry Kemp has put it: "It is as justifiable to look for 'causes' which slowed down the process in some parts of the world as it is to search for those which allowed its rapid passage in others" (1991, 32).

Ultimately, the Neolithic shift to a settled way of life based on food production may have, under certain circumstances, not only fostered the development of civilization, but also rendered it inevitable.

CASE STUDY CLOSE-UP

THE KHMER KINGDOM

Henri Mahout had heard the stories of great temples in the jungle— great palaces "built by the gods," local people had told him—and was determined to find out if they were true. Exploring in the dense jungle near the town of Siam Reap in Cambodia in the 1860s, Mahout came upon the spectacular ruins of the ancient **Khmer** culture and those of its immediate predecessors. His discovery brought to light the remains of what had been a remarkable world previously unknown to Western historians and archaeologists.

Mahout was to die in the jungle before he could announce his remarkable discovery to the world. He kept a detailed diary, however, and the precise records he maintained of his historical research were sent back to his family in France after his death. Among scholars, Mahout's account sparked a flurry of interest and research on the Khmer culture that has continued to this day, interrupted intermittently, most recently by the tragedy of the Cambodian civil war (see Figure 13.14).

Funan

The Khmer were a local people, but the development of their complex society was inspired by contact with the outside world—in particular India and later China. During the first century A.D., merchants from India established a mercantile community in what is today southern Cambodia. These merchants brought their customs with them, and local people adopted the Hindu religion of the Indian settlers. According to legend, the first settler of this community was a mythical Indian Brahmin (wise man) called Kambu, and the town he founded was called "Kambuja" (the basis for the modern name "Cambodia"). Later records of the Chinese court that conducted trade with these merchants refer to this community as **Funan.** Funan is at the root of the complex society today called the Khmer.

The development of the Khmer is "secondary" in the sense that it evolved in response to outside influences. Nevertheless, it repeats the same pattern in the development of complexity that occurred in the other examples discussed in this book. Just as was the case for the Olmec in lowland Mesoamerica (Chapter 12) as well as for the Indus Valley and China (this chapter) and for South America (Chapter 15), a common religious belief, reflected in a shared iconography that modern archaeologists can readily recognize, seems to have served to bring disparate groups under the umbrella of a common polity in southeast Asia. Here, the Hindu religion brought in by the Indian traders provided a common bond that served to fuse a large number of people across a broad geographic expanse. This common religion formed the basis of Khmer civilization.

Funan had evolved from a merchant outpost community to a complex society by A.D. 500. Chinese texts that date to this period describe a rich country with a wealthy nobility living in ornate wooden palaces, slaves serving the needs of the noble class, and a powerful ruler at the top of this social pyramid. These same texts detail a complex history of growth, of forming alliances, of decay and revitalization. They also speak of a royal marriage, combining the nation of Funan with one called "Chenla" to the north. After this alliance was sealed in marriage, ties to India were broken, and a period of destruction ensued, with the area coming under the control of a kingdom centered on the island of Java.

The Khmer

Rapid changes were in the offing, however, after a new ruler ascended to the throne of Funan. This ruler, Jayavarman II, ruled between A.D. 800 and 850. He took a decaying society and initiated a period of expansion and construction that would lead to the monuments which today spark the imagination of modern scholars. With his appearance on history's stage, Funan is no longer known by the name given it by its Chinese neighbors. With his rule, we use the local name Khmer, to label the culture.

Through the efforts of Jayavarman II, the Khmer polity became increasingly powerful again. He oversaw the construction of great canals and sandstone, brick, and laterite palaces, or "pyramid-temples" (laterite is a hard, red soil). These temples, built as homes of the gods, were conscious symbols of the power of the king. The great temples housed not only statues of the various Hindu gods, but also thousands of priests who attended to the needs of the gods in their palaces. The temples themselves were built on a plan that reflected Hindu beliefs. In Hinduism, the gods reside on the mythical Mount Meru. Khmer temples were built up on artificial platforms and had five towers; this construction was meant both to symbolize the location of Mount Meru and to represent its five peaks.

After the death of Jayavarman II, his programs of expansion and growth were continued. His successors built larger and increasingly spectacular pyramid-temples. By A.D. 944, the capital of the kingdom was moved to Angkor by King Yasovarman I. At that time Angkor was largely a ceremonial center, where only the king, his noblemen and noblewomen, and the temple priests resided. By A.D. 980, however, Angkor had begun a period of rapid population growth, and a full-fledged, walled city called Angkor Thom was built there, covering 15 km^2 (6 mi^2) and surrounded by a moat (Ciochon and James 1994). The city itself was accessible by any one of five huge bridges crossing the waters of the moat. At the center of the city was an incredible, otherworldly

FIGURE 13.19

The Bayon temple at Angkor Thom, built more than 1,000 years ago, is covered with sculpted images of Hindu gods, bas-reliefs, columns, and colonnades.
(Copyright © Christophe Loviny/Corbis)

temple called the **Bayon,** covered with sculpted images of Hindu gods, bas-reliefs, columns, and colonnades (Figure 13.19). Most of the buildings in the city were made of sandstone. An incredible amount of this relatively soft rock—estimated in the millions of tons (Ciochon and James 1994, 40)—was obtained from a huge quarry at Phnom Kulen, located 40 km (25 mi) to the northeast; from there it was floated on rafts or barges down the river to Angkor. Angkor Thom remained the capital of the Khmer kingdom until the thirteenth century (P. White 1986). Today, the ruins of the city mark the center of a 317-km^2 (124-mi^2) archaeological district, littered with several hundred temples, palaces, and other monuments of the Khmer civilization.

Angkor Wat

Angkor Wat, the most impressive and best-known Khmer temple, was constructed beginning in A.D. 1113 (Figure 13.20). It has been called the single largest religious structure ever built (Royal Geographical Society 1993a). The temple, with its towers, courtyards, plazas, and intricately carved walls, covers an area of about 2.5 km^2 (almost 1 mi^2). The tallest of its five intricately carved towers rises gracefully to a height of nearly 62 m (more than 200 ft). In the center of the temple complex is a tiny shrine housing the image of Vishnu, the Hindu god to whom Angkor Wat is dedicated (Ciochon and James 1994). An outer gallery of Angkor Wat consists of eight enormous sculpted panels, together more than 800 m (nearly half a mile) long. Sculpted in bas-relief are hundreds of figures related to Hindu mythology, including the Hindu creation myth.

FIGURE 13.20
The temple/palace of Angkor Wat represents the culmination of architectural complexity of the ancient Khmer civilization of southeast Asia. (Copyright © Alison Wright/Corbis)

Along with the great temples, Khmer cities are marked by huge artificial reservoirs called **barrays.** The so-called Western Barray at Angkor Wat is 8 km (5 mi) long and 2.25 km (1.25 mi) wide. It was carved out of the laterite that underlies the site. This quarried laterite may have been used in constructing the foundations of the monuments at Angkor. Allowed to fill with water after quarrying, these barrays then served as reservoirs for storing impounded rainwater to be used in rice cultivation (Engelhardt, as cited in Ciochon and James 1994, 47–48).

The Khmer civilization came to an end in the fifteenth century A.D. Alien invaders regularly attacked Angkor, and it was abandoned in A.D. 1431. It experienced a renaissance of a sort late in the sixteenth century, only to be abandoned once again. Slowly the magnificent temples were swallowed by the jungle, where they lay buried in the rich flora of the tropical forest until their rediscovery in the nineteenth century. They have inspired wonder and fascination ever since.

Because civilizations produced great works of art as well as monumental and durable works of architecture, many sites have been made readily accessible for tourism, and myriad opportunities exist for you to visit the past of these societies. Most standard tour guides will include information about visiting such sites.

Unfortunately, modern political uncertainties and conflicts make visiting some of the most important and impressive sites of ancient civilizations problematical or even downright dangerous. As with all foreign travel, it is wise

VISITING THE PAST

for U.S. citizens to contact the State Department for information on travel advisories.

Currently, Mesopotamia, located in southern Iraq, is not available for visitation by American citizens and terrorism in Egypt has been directed toward tourists. On the other hand, problems are not all that common, and thousands of tourists safely flock to the pyramids, King Tut's tomb, the Sphinx, and other sites in Egypt. Though attacks on tourists get quite a bit of publicity, some of our own urban areas are probably at least as dangerous as many foreign destinations. Harappa and Mohenjo-daro are open for tourist inspection, though it is probably wise to visit them with a group. While Shang material is somewhat limited, later periods in Chinese history are well documented by museums and sites. The most impressive of these sites almost certainly is Xian, where a virtual army of more than 8,000 life-size clay sculptures of soldiers that are part of an elite burial can be seen in their original place of burial.

The temple at Knossos on Crete is today a major tourist destination for Mediterranean cruise ships. Earlier in this century, Sir Arthur Evans reconstructed part of the temple, repairing and replacing columns and restoring some of the beautiful frescoes. Though such work is often controversial, some of Evans's reconstructions are probably fairly accurate and afford the casual visitor the unique opportunity to view at least some of the rooms in the temple as they appeared to the inhabitants more than 3,600 years ago. The museum at Herakleion, Crete, houses most of the impressive artifacts recovered at Knossos and other Minoan sites. In the United States, the University of Pennsylvania Museum in Philadelphia has an extensive collection of Minoan objects.

In the past 20 years, the nation of Cambodia (sometimes called Kampuchea) has been the scene of some of the most terrible genocidal insanity that our species is capable of. For quite some time, the Khmer temples discussed in this chapter were largely ignored by Cambodians, whose collective agony did not afford them the luxury of reflection on their distant past, and foreign scientists were not welcome or safe there. Anthropologist Russell Ciochon (Ciochon and James 1994) reports that when he visited Angkor Wat in 1989 (under the watchful eye of a heavily armed contingent of government soldiers), the place was all but deserted. His more recent visit in 1993 shows that a more stable political situation has brought tourists back to the area. Nevertheless, the U.S. State Department should be consulted before travel to Cambodia.

Computer technology provides another avenue for visiting the past. Though not a substitute for a real visit, perhaps a "virtual visit" can suffice until time, finances, and circumstance allow you to see the real thing. There currently are a number of fine CD-ROMs focusing on ancient cities and civilizations. These discs include detailed text, maps, narrated color slide shows, movies, and animations. The Royal Geographical Society has produced a helpful electronic guide called *The Egyptian Pyramids.* Sumeria Publishing and *Scientific American* have produced a disc entitled *Exploring Ancient Cities* that includes a section on Minoan Crete. Microsoft has released a CD-ROM, called *Ancient Lands,* focusing on ancient civilizations. Interlaced with 1,000 color and black-and-white images, animations, videos, a detailed text, and haunting music, *Voyage in Egypt: A Virtual Journey Through Ancient Egypt* is another entertaining and informative CD-ROM. A "virtual visit" to the Khmer kingdom is possible through the CD-ROM titled *Angkor Wat,* produced by the Royal Geographical Society (1993). The number of these CD-ROMs is increasing rapidly; by the time you read this, many more will be available.

Though they currently do not come close to providing the emotional impact of an actual visit, multimedia CD-ROMs and Web sites put the archaeological world at your fingertips. Virtual visits are an inexpensive and convenient way to expand your archaeological horizons.

SUMMARY

The Neolithic set the stage for the development of sedentary farming villages in various places in the Old World. In a select few regions, an acceleration of cultural complexity led to the development of a stratified social system that controlled the excess wealth made possible through the ability to produce an agricultural food surplus. Social elites developed as part of a reorganization of society that allowed for orderly and systematic trade, the construction of irrigation canals to increase the food base, and the construction of monumental defensive fortifications. In these same regions, the new way of organizing and controlling human labor was utilized by the developing elite to construct less practical monumental works—temples, palaces, and mortuary features such as pyramids. This kind of monumental construction, today diagnostic of ancient civilizations, was both cause and effect of the new social dynamic of the world's first civilizations. Large, impressive monuments served as dramatic evidence of the power of the elite and symbolized and reified this power at the same time that it magnified it.

In the Old World, the processes that led to the kinds of societies we are calling civilization occurred in Mesopotamia in the Middle East, in the Nile Valley of Egypt and the Sudan, in the Indus Valley of Pakistan, in eastern China, in southeastern Europe on Crete, and, later, in southeast Asia.

TO LEARN MORE

Technical Summaries

Ancient Civilizations, by C. C. Lamberg-Karlovsky and Jeremy Sabloff (1995), is an extremely thorough investigation of the origins of civilization in the Middle East and the Indus Valley (and Mesoamerica as well). Thomas C. Patterson's *Archaeology: The Historical Development of Civilizations* (1993) is another terrific source. For a theoretical discussion of the origins of civilization, see Jonathan Haas's *The Evolution of the*

Prehistoric State (1982). Joseph Tainter's book, *The Collapse of Complex Societies* (1988), contains a brief and useful discussion of the origins of civilization.

To learn more about the florescence of any of the early civilizations mentioned in this chapter, see the sources cited in each discussion. In particular, for Mesopotamia, see Harriet Crawford's (1991) *Sumer and the Sumerians* (1991) and J. N. Postgate's *Early Mesopotamia: Society and Economy at the Dawn of History* (1992). For a detailed chronology of the reigns of each of the pharaohs, see Peter A. Clayton's *Chronicle of the Pharaohs* (1994). You can explore Indus Valley civilization in Jonathan Kenoyer's *Ancient Cities of the Indus Valley Civilization* (1998). K. C. Chang's synthesis work, *The Archaeology of Ancient China* (1986), is the best source on the Shang. Geographer Rodney Castleden's *Minoans: Life in Bronze Age Crete* (1990) is a well-written, non-technical presentation of the prehistory and history of the Minoan civilization. The CD-ROMs mentioned in "Visiting the Past" are filled with information in the form of text and visuals and provide an interesting and often entertaining way to obtain more information about some of the early civilizations discussed in this chapter.

Popular Summaries

To learn more about the discovery of King Tut's tomb, see Brian Fagan's chapter on Howard Carter and Tutankhamun in his book, *Quest for the Past: Great Discoveries in Archaeology* (1994). If you are interested in the civilization of Egypt, see Barry Kemp's *Ancient Egypt* (1991). John Romer's *Ancient Lives: Daily Life in Egypt of the Pharaohs* (1984) presents a fascinating account of ordinary occurrences in the lives of ancient Egyptians. For a wonderful chronological treatment of ancient Egypt, see Mark Lehner's *The Complete Pyramids* (1997). A useful work that focuses on the Sphinx but that also covers much of Egyptian civilization is Paul Jordan's *Riddles of the Sphinx* (1998).

Popular and useful sources on the ancient Khmer culture, with many photographs, include Peter White's 1986 *National Geographic* article, "The Temples of Angkor: Ancient Glory in Stone," and Russell Ciochon and Jamie James's "The Glory That Was Angkor" in *Archaeology* (1994).

On the Web

Many Internet sites deal with the civilizations discussed in this chapter. Obviously, searching under the names of these societies will bring up a large number of sites of varying quality. The following sites are good places to start, and most have links to a wide variety of other pages dedicated to the Old World's earliest civilizations.

For ancient Mesopotamia, visit
http://www.wsu.edu:8080/~dee/MESO/CONTENT1.HTM

For ancient Egypt, visit
http://guardians.net/egypt

For the Indus Valley, visit
http://www.harappa.com/har/har1.html

For ancient China, visit
http://www.wsu.edu:8080/~dee/ANCCHINA/SHANG.HTM

For Minoan Crete, visit
http://195.170.12.01/DAEI/THEME/Knossos.htm

For a sample of photographs of the ancient Khmer temples that were the focus of the "Case Study Close-Up," visit the Southeast Asian Monuments Web site at http://

www.leidenuniv.nl/pun/ubhtm/mjk/angkorwa.htm. To learn how photographs taken by space shuttle astronauts have aided in archaeological research in the area around Angkor Wat and Angkor Thom, visit NASA's site at http://lightsar.jpl.nasa.gov/lightsar/arch.htm.

KEY TERMS

state	central place	Minoan
civilization	mastaba	Knossos
monumental work	Nubia	New Temple Period
social stratification	Kush	Mycenaean
specialization of labor	deffufa	Khmer
system of record keeping	seal	Funan
Ubaid	cylinder seal	Bayon
city-state	Lung-shan	barray
token	hang-t'u	
cuneiform	scapulimancy	

14

An Explosion of Complexity

RANKED SOCIETIES IN THE OLD AND NEW WORLDS

CHAPTER OVERVIEW

The Native American moundbuilders were part of a socially, politically, and economically complex society whose great rulers could command the labor of thousands and were, in turn, buried in splendor. In the American Southwest, an entirely different pathway led also to complexity, with clear archaeological evidence for the coordination of large groups of people to construct great edifices of adobe brick, clay, and stone. In southern Africa at Great Zimbabwe, native people constructed an enormous complex of monumental, granite brick buildings and walls. The mound-building societies of the American Midwest and Southeast, along with the pueblo-dwelling people of the American Southwest and the builders of Great Zimbabwe, are examples of ancient, complex non-state societies.

	5,500		3,250	3,000	2,
Mound builders	Watson Brake		Poverty Point		
American Southwest					
Zimbabwe					

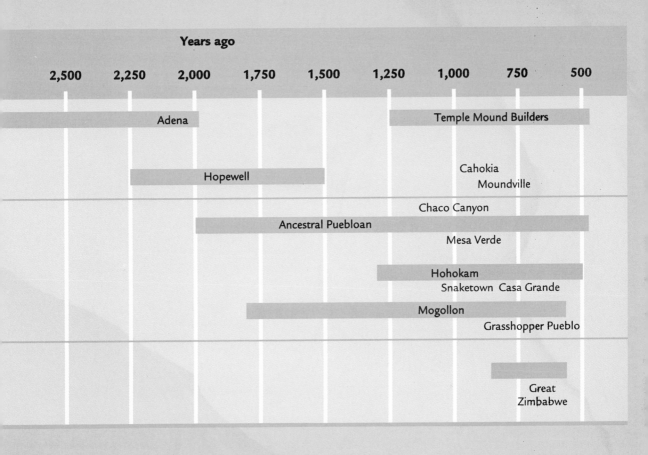

Years ago

| 2,500 | 2,250 | 2,000 | 1,750 | 1,500 | 1,250 | 1,000 | 750 | 500 |

Adena

Temple Mound Builders

Hopewell

Cahokia
Moundville

Chaco Canyon

Ancestral Puebloan

Mesa Verde

Hohokam

Snaketown Casa Grande

Mogollon

Grasshopper Pueblo

Great
Zimbabwe

PRELUDE

For most of us, the word "pyramid" conjures up images of the ancient Egyptian culture discussed in Chapter 13. Few of us would immediately think of Native Americans living in a place just east of the modern city of St. Louis. Yet there and at dozens of other impressive sites, beginning more than a thousand years ago, a complex society built great truncated, or flat-topped, pyramids—not of stone, but of earth. In the ceremonial centers of the ancient Midwest and Southeast, we are confronted with a Native American chiefdom that produced some of the most impressive monumental works and finest art seen in prehistoric North America.

CAHOKIA

If you stand at the top of the Monks Mound pyramid, thousands of acres of floodplain lie at your feet. The soil is rich and dark, the surrounding foliage thick and lush. (The name "Monks Mound" comes from much later, historical inhabitants of a small monastery built on an adjacent earthwork.) Construction of this huge flat-topped pyramid in the settlement called Cahokia was begun more than 1,000 years ago by the native inhabitants of what is today East St. Louis, Illinois (Figure 14.1).

Monks Mound is impressive, representing a substantial investment of time and energy on the part of the settlement's inhabitants (Figure 14.2). The pyramidal mound of earth covers more than 94,000 m², or some 16 acres. Its volume of earth totals 640,000 m³ (22 million ft³)—moved basketful by basketful by a people who had no animal power or mechanical contrivances. At its summit, the mound stands more than 30 m (100 ft) above the floodplain (all figures for Monks Mound are taken from Fowler 1989 and Silverberg 1989). The huge pile of earth served as the platform for the palace or temple that symbolized the power of the political entity that was Cahokia.

FIGURE 14.1

Archaeological sites in North America where evidence of the evolution of chiefdom-level societies has been found.

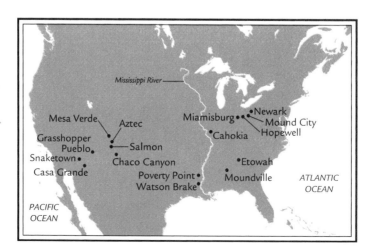

434

From the summit you can try to look past the modern suburban sprawl and cut grass, the paved roads, highways, and commercial structures and imagine what the ancient town of Cahokia with Monks Mound as its focal point must have looked like at its peak more than 700 years ago (Figure 14.3). In the year A.D. 1200, from your vantage point atop the great pyramid, you would have gazed down upon a dense settlement of 5,000 and perhaps as many as 10,000 people, buzzing with activity (Figure 14.4); the most extreme estimates place Cahokia's population at closer to 30,000 (Fowler 1989, 191), though most today agree with a smaller estimate of about 5,000. In front of the great pyramid were smaller but only slightly less impressive earthworks, demarcating an expansive plaza teeming with people. Scattered across the settlement were dozens of other pyramidal and conical mounds of earth, probably more than 100 in total. To the west was an enormous circle of towering logs, the largest located in the precise center of the monument. To

CHAPTER SITES

AFRICA
Danamombe
Great Zimbabwe
Khami
Manekweni
Thulamela

FIGURE 14.2
Monks Mound at Cahokia in East St. Louis served as the platform on which a chief's house or a temple was built. (K. L. Feder)

FIGURE 14.3
Aerial photograph of Monks Mound at Cahokia. (Courtesy of Cahokia Mounds State Historic Site)

FIGURE 14.4

Artist's conception of Cahokia at its peak, around A.D. *1150. The dense, near-urban character of the settlement is clearly evident.* (Courtesy of Cahokia Mounds State Historic Site. William R. Iseminger, artist. Reprinted with permission)

the south was the burial of a great chief, laid to rest wearing a cape of 20,000 finely made mother-of-pearl beads, marked now by only a small earthen mound (Mound 72 in Cahokia's official enumeration). In his tomb were more than 1,000 finely made arrowpoints, a copper tube, sheets of mica, and shaped stones (called chunky stones), as well as the remains of people sacrificed as part of the ceremony surrounding his interment (Figure 14.5).

Surrounding the main part of the settlement was a log fence or palisade with bastions and watchtowers. The wall of logs enclosed an area of more than 800,000 m^2 (200 acres) and within it were 18 separate earthen mounds, including Monks Mound. Consisting of an estimated 20,000 logs (and it was rebuilt three times), the huge stockade fence was as monumental a feat as Monks Mound itself, enclosing the central part of the settlement, protecting the homes of Cahokia's elite.

Occupation debris from the sprawl of Cahokia's neighborhoods, suburbs, and satellite communities has been found by archaeologists across an area of about 14 km^2 (more than 5 mi^2). As archaeologist Melvin Fowler (1989, 207) points out, "Cahokia is unique. There is nothing else like it, either in size or complexity, representing Native American achievements within the boundaries of the United States."

Today, from the top of the impressive monument that stood at the center of the settlement, you might wonder why people would have devoted their lives to the construction of this impressive, but otherwise apparently useless, monument. Today, from the top of that same, still impressive structure, you can also look to the west and see the imposing Gateway Arch in downtown St. Louis, its polished steel surface shimmering in the distance. At 630 feet tall, the arch weighs nearly 17,000 tons and is a remarkable feat of engineering. Built between 1961 and 1966, the arch and its associated below-ground mu-

FIGURE 14.5

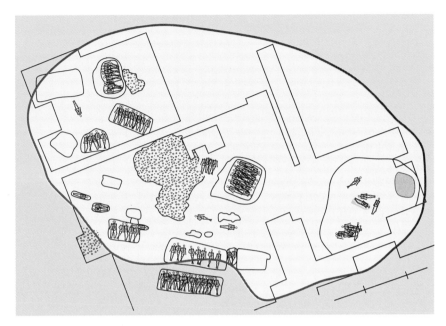

Layout of burials in Mound 72, Cahokia. The primary burial in Mound 72 is that of a young man, laid out on a bed of more than 20,000 mother-of-pearl shell beads. In a practice reminiscent of ancient Egypt, the other interments in Mound 72 are the burials of more than 50 other people, mostly young women, who had been killed, apparently to accompany the primary individual to his afterlife. See Figure 3.7 for a reconstruction of the Mound 72 primary burial. (Courtesy of William Fowler)

seum cost more than $11,000,000 (all figures on the arch are taken from Arteaga 1991).

In all fairness, we can ask the same question about the arch that we posed for Monks Mound; indeed, why would a people devote so much of their energy and wealth to the construction of such an impressive, but again merely symbolic, monument? As we saw in Chapters 12 and 13, such works are diagnostic of complex chiefdoms and state societies alike—both ancient and modern. The monumental proportions of Monks Mound and many other earthen structures produced by the mound builders provide clear evidence of the power invested in the elite of an emerging, indigenous, complex North American society.

A Word About Organization of Human Societies—And This Book

In this chapter we focus on the development of complex, ranked, but non-state societies—some of which are, in fact, more recent than the societies to be discussed in Chapter 15. We do so because the growth of complexity, rather than chronology, is our organizing theme. Ancient societies did not march in lockstep from simple to complex to state societies. The world's ancient cultures did not follow a single, inevitable trajectory of cultural evolution with a universal chronology that we can neatly follow. The chapters of this book follow the development and flowering of complexity, which did not rigidly follow a single chronology.

CHRONICLE

The Mound Builders of North America:
Earliest Manifestations

The so-called temple mound builders of Cahokia and elsewhere were not the first Native Americans to produce monuments by mounding up earth. Using great quantities to demarcate ceremonial spaces, to cover the remains of the dead, to produce monumentally scaled images of animals or humanlike creatures, and to produce artificial mountains on top of which temples or the homes of the elite were placed has a very long history among the complex societies of America north of Mexico.

To date, the oldest example of mound building can be seen at the Watson Brake site in Louisiana (Saunders et al. 1997). Beginning between 5,400 and 5,300 years ago, the inhabitants of the site constructed 11 distinct earthen mounds and connecting ridges that together form an oval enclosure of mounded soil about 280 m (more than 900 ft) along its long axis. The tallest of the mounds at Watson Brake is about 7.5 m (about 25 ft) high.

Clearly, moving the amount of earth necessary to produce the monuments at Watson Brake required the kind of large, coordinated labor force that is a hallmark of cultural complexity. It is interesting to point out that, in this instance, the requisite complexity evolved without agriculture. Fish played the dominant role in subsistence at the site; 175,000 animal bones were found there, the majority representing various species of freshwater fish. Also found in the trash midden were the bones of deer, raccoon, opossum, squirrel, rabbit, and dog (Saunders et al. 1997, 1798). Also key to the subsistence base at Watson Brake were two of the wild plant species that were to become key components in the independent Neolithic Revolution seen among the native people of the American Mid-South and Southeast (see Chapter 11); the charred seeds of goosefoot and knotweed were recovered in excavation of the site. The rich food base of local, wild seed plants, medium and large mammals, and, especially, abundant aquatic resources made the area of Watson Brake so economically rich that the social and political complexity needed to construct the earthworks seen there developed in the absence of an agricultural food base.

The much larger and more impressive mound complex at the Poverty Point site, also in Louisiana, dates to before 3200 B.P. Located adjacent to the Macon Bayou and the broad, rich floodplain of the Mississippi River, the Poverty Point earthworks are truly monumental in scale (Figure 14.6). The site consists of a series of six segmented, concentric earth ridges, enclosing a rough semicircle with a radius of 0.65 km (0.4 mi; the distance from its center to the edge of the outermost ridge). The ridge tops were living surfaces; archaeologists have found evidence of construction along their tops, along with hearths and trash pits. Each of the six segmented ridges is about 24 m (80 ft) wide, 3.5 m (10 ft) tall, and separated from adjacent ridges by about 45 m (150 ft).

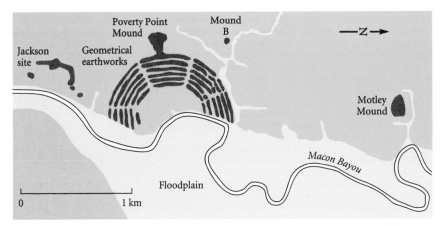

FIGURE 14.6

Depiction of the massive, semicircular earthworks at Poverty Point, Louisiana. An enormous amount of labor, perhaps coordinated by some central authority, was needed for the construction of this earthwork. (From *Images of the Past*, Second Edition, by T. Douglas Price and Gary M. Feinman. Mayfield Publishing Company, 1997, p. 238)

The outermost ridge is about 2 km (1.25 mi) long; altogether there are 6 miles of these ridges in the Poverty Point earthwork surrounding a flat central plaza of 37 acres. If the soil to produce Poverty Point had been mounded up in 50-lb basket loads, it would have taken 30 million such loads to complete the monument (Kopper 1986). Also part of the complex, outside of the ridge enclosure was another monumental earthwork, a bird-shaped mound of dirt about 70 ft high, covering an area of nearly 13 acres.

Just as at Watson Brake, but on a substantially larger scale, the construction of the Poverty Point earthworks implies the existence of a large labor force coordinated through a complex social and political structure. The inhabitants of Poverty Point also were engaged in a broad trading network that enabled them to obtain raw materials, including hematite, slate, and lead ore, as well as good stone for making sharp-edged tools. The presence of these materials also implies that some people were freed from subsistence pursuits to obtain these precious resources not available in their local territory.

Once again, as at Watson Brake, the natural abundance of the surrounding territory seems to have been the key to subsistence at Poverty Point and the factor that allowed for the production of a food surplus, freeing the labor of hundreds of people for the construction of the earthworks. At Poverty Point there is evidence of domesticated squash; but wild foods, especially fish and other aquatic resources, again seem to have been the mainstays of the Poverty Point diet. Watson Brake and Poverty Point are clear indicators that while the rich and abundant surplus made possible by an agricultural way of life may be the more likely precursor to cultural complexity, it is not the only pathway to such complexity.

Intensification of Complexity: Adena and Hopewell

Beginning about 2,800 years ago and centered in the Ohio River valley, people bearing a culture today called **Adena** began constructing conical mounds of

FIGURE 14.7

This enormous Adena burial mound in Miamisburg, Ohio, is the largest in that state, standing 21 m (68 ft) high. (K. L. Feder)

earth in which a religious and perhaps economic and social elite were buried. Somewhat later, about 2200 B.P., a different burial-mound-building group, the **Hopewell,** appeared with its own unique set of artifacts (Lepper 1995a; see Color Plate 19). The two traditions can be said to have overlapped for about two hundred years and are differentiated on the basis of certain artifact types. Over that 200-year period of overlap, the Hopewell pattern gradually replaced Adena in the Ohio Valley and then spread far more widely throughout the American Midwest.

There were no great urban centers in Adena/Hopewell society. The residential settlements of both Adena and Hopewell people generally were small, consisting of tiny hamlets located across much of southern and central Ohio and surrounding states to the south and west. Unlike the mound builders at Watson Brake or Poverty Point, the Hopewell depended on agriculture for a significant part of their subsistence. Hopewell farmers planted many of the crops independently domesticated by Indians north of Mexico, including sunflower, squash, maygrass, knotweed, and goosefoot (Lepper 1995a; see Chapter 11). On the other hand, the major crop that characterized later Indian agricultural societies was not an important component of Hopewell subsistence; evidence for maize agriculture is scanty.

Some of the burial mounds are quite impressive, covering as much as 8,300 m² (2 acres, or more than 1½ football fields) and stretching up to heights of 21 m (68 ft). For example, Mound 25 at the Hopewell site is 150 m (500 ft) long, 55 m (180 ft) wide, and 9 m (30 ft) high. The volume of earth moved and piled to produce such a monument is enormous and again reflects one of the defining elements of a complex society: its ability to mobilize a large labor force to produce a monumental structure (Figure 14.7).

The conical mounds were constructed over the remains of either individuals or groups of people. Finely crafted goods, including many made from exotic raw materials not native to the core of the Hopewell region, are found in the mound burials. A widespread trade network brought these natural resources to the Hopewell from all over the United States. Copper and silver were brought in from the Great Lakes region. Turtle shells, pearls, fossil shark teeth, alligator teeth, and conch shells from the Gulf of Mexico traveled up the major river systems of eastern North America also to be included in the burials of the Adena and Hopewell. Obsidian from the Rocky Mountains and quartz crystals and mica from the Appalachian Mountains also made long journeys into the hands of the elite of Adena/Hopewell society, often being placed in their tombs. Objects made from local materials were also found in these burials, and they are often finely made. For example, beautifully made ceramics, intricately flaked lithics far too delicate to have been used as tools, and whimsically carved stone pipes in the form of animals or even people were also included in the burials (see Color Plate 19). In the enormity of the work necessary to build the actual mounds and in the effort expended to obtain raw materials from distant sources, as well as in the care taken in the manufacture of grave goods, Adena and, especially, Hopewell mound interments represent clear archaeological evidence for the existence of an elite or chieftain class of people in burial-mound society.

Some Hopewell earthworks are not mounds, but earth-wall-enclosed spaces of unknown purpose. For example, in Newark, Ohio, a series of long, narrow, earthen walls about 1.5 m (5 ft) high enclose an octagonal plot of more than 160,000 m² (40 acres), which is, in turn, connected by two parallel earthen walls to an enormous circular area of more than 80,000 m² (20 acres), also enclosed with an earth wall more than a meter in height (Figure 14.8). This large earthwork is located at the end point of what appears to have been a ceremonial road, 90 km (60 mi) long, demarcated again by two earth walls approximately 60 m (200 ft) apart and several feet—perhaps as much as 2.5–3 m (8–10 ft)—in height (Lepper 1995b). The "Great Hopewell Road" is absolutely straight and seems—geographically and, perhaps, ritually—to connect the earthworks at Newark with a Hopewell necropolis, or "city of the dead," today called Mound City, located in Chillicothe, Ohio (Lepper 1998). Mound City is a square area of about 120,000 m² (30 acres) enclosed by an earth wall, containing 23 burial mounds (Figure 14.9). Connecting these sacred or ceremonial mound sites and enclosures, the Great Hopewell Road may have been used by pilgrims visiting these sites for religious observances—perhaps burial ceremonies or worship services. They are yet another example of the ability of the Hopewell to organize a large labor force and produce works of monumental proportions.

As archaeologist Bradley Lepper (1996) suggests, the Great Hopewell Road may have served to formalize connections between groups living along it and practicing what we today identify as Hopewell. Hopewell people lacked the formal government or military apparatus of a true state society (see Chapters 13 and 15), so symbolic activities like building the road and using it for pilgrimages may have served to make connections between people living at great distances more concrete.

FIGURE 14.8

Nineteenth-century map of the extensive prehistoric earthworks seen in Licking County, Ohio, in the vicinity of Newark. The largest of the areas enclosed by the mounded earth in this map is 40 acres, an enormous expanse surrounded by a vaguely square configuration of linear mounds in the upper left of the map.
(From *Ancient Monuments of the Mississippi Valley*, AMS Press and Peabody Museum of Archaeology and Ethnology, Harvard University)

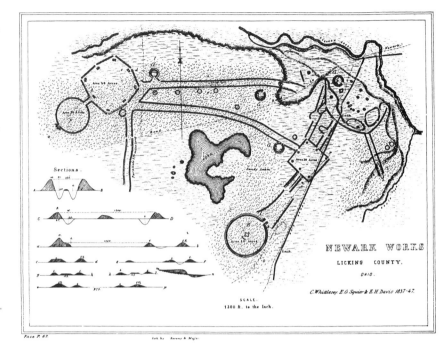

FIGURE 14.9

Mound City in Chillicothe, Ohio, is a virtual necropolis, or city of the dead. The site consists of 23 burial mounds, a few of which can be seen here, within a 13-acre area enclosed by an earth embankment.
(K. L. Feder)

Hopewell culture and its construction of enclosures and burial mounds ceased by about 1,500 years ago. Among the numerous possible reasons for Hopewell's decline (Lepper 1995a) are population growth and warfare: Perhaps the largely informal organization of Hopewell society was not up to the task of coordinating the activities of an expanding population, or growing competition among various groups for good farmland may have led to warfare and the subsequent concentration of the previously dispersed Hopewell farmers in dense settlements for protection.

FIGURE 14.10
The flat-topped temple mounds of Moundville served as the platforms on top of which temples or the houses of elite members of society were constructed. Though smaller than Cahokia, Moundville nevertheless was the central place of mound-building, chiefdom-level society in west-central Alabama. (K. L. Feder)

The Mississippian Temple Mound Builders

With the decline in Hopewell, another culture, more formally structured and even more materially impressive, arose in the Mississippi River valley and the American Southeast. This development led to a qualitatively different pattern of social, political, and economic organization, one more complex and more formally and rigidly structured than Hopewell. In fact, it now appears that the Mississippi Valley and Southeast were the centers of an emerging Native American civilization—how far along that path they were is still a matter of some debate, but certainly these new, major mound-builder sites were the central places of complex chiefdoms.

A cultural pattern evolved in the American Midwest and Southeast that included the construction of large ceremonial and population centers where the pooled labor of a sizable surrounding population was called upon by a religious elite to construct large truncated (cut off at the top) pyramids of earth. Cahokia was the largest and most impressive of these—and the only one with a resident population of a size and density that approaches an urban character (see Figures 14.3 and 14.4). But many others, such as Etowah in Georgia and Moundville in Alabama, while smaller in size and complexity, with fewer and smaller monumental earthworks, nevertheless present a fascinating picture of developing complexity and emerging civilization in the period after A.D. 1000 (Figure 14.10).

These temple mound builders were able to maintain their society with a subsistence base primarily of maize and squash agriculture; the use of domesticated beans began relatively later, at about A.D. 1200. Rivers provided fish, and the forests surrounding their habitations provided wild game as well as wild plant foods such as acorn and hickory. Many of the larger, impressive sites—Cahokia in particular—were located on the richest farmland. The enormous food surplus made possible by the agricultural use of these naturally rich "bottom lands" enabled the evolution of a class of priests and an

FIGURE 14.11

A sample of the more than 1,000 finely made stone arrowpoints recovered in the primary burial in Mound 72 at Cahokia (see Figure 14.5). The amount of labor invested in this enormous assemblage of stone points is an indication of the importance of the young man with whom they were buried. (Courtesy of Cahokia Mounds State Historic Site)

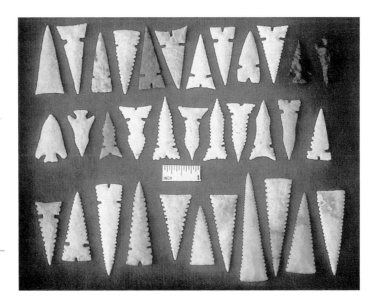

attendant nobility and artisans. As we have seen again and again (in Chapters 12, 13, and now 14—and as we will see again in Chapter 15), the ability to produce a food surplus surely was at the heart of the development of stratified, complex societies. The ability of a chief or king to control that surplus is the enabling factor in that leader's amassing of the wealth and power that allow or demand the other characteristics of complex societies.

Cahokia

Archaeologist Timothy Pauketat (1994) has examined the evolution of Cahokia as a ceremonial and population center. In his detailed analysis, he shows that Cahokia was a central place in a three-tiered hierarchy of communities. Cahokia was at the apex of the sociopolitical pyramid, "a paramount center, a qualitatively different place" (Pauketat 1994, 73). Beneath Cahokia was a second level of communities with a few small mounds, perhaps the villages of secondary chiefs. Pauketat (1994, 76) counts as many as 25 mound sites in the area around Cahokia, at least some of which may have been part of the Cahokia polity. The bottom tier of sites includes numerous farmsteads in the surrounding hinterlands, inhabited by communities of people who likely supplied most of the food and labor needed to keep the chiefdom running.

The archaeological record at Cahokia shows that craft production was centralized at the site; specialist artisans filled the demands of a powerful elite class for shell and bead pendant necklaces, copper ornaments, fire clay figurines, fine ceramics and lithics, and other items made from exotic raw materials (Figure 14.11; Pauketat 1994, 106). The exotic materials from distant sources that made their way into the hands of Cahokia's artisans included copper from Illinois or possibly from as far away as Michigan, shell from the Gulf Coast, and galena (a lead mineral) from the eastern Ozarks (Pauketat 1994). The works of craft and art were produced for the elite class of Cahokians who lived safely within the walls of the palisade and who were buried in the elaborate interments found at the site.

When the Spanish explorer Hernando de Soto and his contingent of more than 600 men traversed much of the American Southeast in the years 1539–43, they encountered the direct descendants of the builders of the prehistoric temple-mound ceremonial centers (de la Vega 1988; Elvas 1611). They may actually have visited the site of Etowah during a late stage of its occupation. De Soto's chroniclers described a number of large settlements they visited as having populations numbered in the thousands. They also described agricultural fields stretching for miles. They even described the native practice of constructing earthen mounds, upon which the chief's house sat.

Ironically, de Soto may have brought more than curiosity and greed with him on his trip. It has been suggested that he and his men unintentionally brought with them infectious diseases (perhaps including smallpox) that the natives had not previously encountered and, as a result, for which they possessed no immunity (Brain 1979; Dobyns 1983; Ramenofsky 1987). Though some of the ceremonial centers had already been abandoned—Cahokia among them—as a result of internal collapse, it is not certain that mound-builder society was destined for disintegration. It may have continued to develop, becoming increasingly complex and more recognizably a civilization. As Timothy Pauketat (1994, 6) puts it when assessing the significance of the kind of social stratification and political power evidenced in the archaeological record at Cahokia: "In other regions around the world similar conditions may have been necessary precursors to the rise of early states." But the accidental spread of lethal microbes may have diverted the trajectory of mound-builder culture, and we will never know what might have been.

The American Southwest

As mentioned in Chapter 11, the Mesoamerican domesticates maize and squash appear in the archaeological record of the American Southwest beginning about 3,200 years ago, and beans show up a bit later (Wills 1988). These domesticates initially served to complement and supplement a highly productive indigenous foraging economy based on local wild crops.

Not until over a thousand years later, at approximately 2000 B.P., did maize-based agriculture replace the traditional foraging subsistence system. A number of different cultural traditions based on agriculture then evolved in the prehistoric Southwest with the development of a new variety of maize, Maize de Ocho, that was better suited to the dry conditions and short growing season of this region. The best known of these cultures were the **Ancestral Puebloan,** or **Anasazi,** in the Four Corners region (the broad area around the intersection of Arizona, New Mexico, Utah, and Colorado), the **Mogollon** in the uplands of New Mexico and northeastern Mexico, the **Hohokam** in southern Arizona, and the **Sinagua** in central Arizona (Cordell 1984; Willey 1966). These cultures vary in pottery styles, geography, and settlement patterns; but all relied to varying degrees on a subsistence base of maize, beans, and squash, and all eventually lived a sedentary lifeway before the coming of the Spanish. One more pattern shared by these cultures is social and political complexity, manifested in the archaeological record by the construction of monumental buildings.

Hohokam

Some nineteenth-century cultural geographers thought that the natural surroundings of each culture determined the degree of complexity and the level of civilization that the culture could achieve. "Environmental determinists" believed that a challenging—but not too demanding—environment produced civilization, while other habitats—rain forests and deserts, for example—limited absolutely the level of complexity and cultural achievement that cultures in those environments could attain. The environmental determinists were Europeans who believed, not coincidentally, that the continental climate of Europe provided the perfect context for the evolution of the most "advanced" and civilized nations.

The Sonoran Desert home of the Hohokam (as well as the rain-forest home of the Maya; see Chapter 15) belies this outdated notion that any one type of environment spawns complexity while others uniformly produce simple societies. The Sonoran Desert is one rather extreme example of the environmental diversity reflected in the myriad settings of the world's ancient complex societies. In contradiction to the assertions of the environmental determinists, from A.D. 700 to close to A.D. 1000, the dry Sonoran Desert of southern Arizona served as a backdrop for the flowering of a complex society capable of building huge structures and a complex system of irrigation (Reid and Whittlesey 1997).

The settlement pattern of the Hohokam (literally, "those who have gone" in the Pima Indian language) focused on the major river systems of southern Arizona: the Gila, the Salt, and the Santa Cruz. The reason is obvious. The territory of the Hohokam averages less than 30 cm (12 in.) of rain each year. Though the Hohokam included game (deer, bighorn sheep, antelope, and cottontail and jackrabbits) and wild plant foods (mesquite beans and cactus) in their diet, growing corn, beans, and squash was of primary importance and was made possible in this dry environment only by the construction of extensive irrigation networks. The Hohokam irrigated thousands of acres of otherwise dry land through a hierarchical series of canals whose combined length is measured in many kilometers. For example, the Hohokam irrigation network north of the Salt River near modern Phoenix consists of 50 large, primary artificial water channels, hundreds of secondary arteries, and an even greater number of smaller irrigation ditches feeding individual fields (Reid

FIGURE 14.12

Casa Grande, a large Hohokam community in southern Arizona. The Great House, shown here, is partially protected from the elements by a large metal superstructure built in the 1930s. (K. L. Feder)

and Whittlesey 1997, 76). The labor needed to construct this one irrigation network—and then to maintain it, keeping it clear of clogging silt—must have been enormous and is clear evidence of the Hohokam ability to conscript and organize a substantial workforce far beyond the level of an individual household or family. This, in turn, is a hallmark of social and political complexity.

Hohokam material culture provides additional evidence of the complexity that bloomed in the desert. The Hohokam maintained a trading system that brought in exotic raw materials such as marine shell from the Gulf of California. Hohokam craftspeople produced beautiful and intricate works in carved stone. They also fashioned shell-bead necklaces, shell bracelets, and shell pendants carved into the shapes of animals. They also worked in turquoise and produced an array of finely made ceramics, including red-on-buff painted household wares—a style of pottery that is a defining attribute of Hohokam culture—and whimsical pots in humanlike shapes.

Most individual Hohokam villages consisted of multiple sets of separate residential structure clusters called **courtyard groups.** Each courtyard group consisted of from 2 to 10 family residences surrounding a common area or courtyard.

The Hohokam also constructed residential compounds called "Great Houses," large apartment buildings that housed most residents of a village. The best example of a Hohokam Great House can be found at the Casa Grande site, located midway between Tucson and Phoenix. Built around A.D. 1350 the main structure at the site is a multistoried, 60-room building surrounded by several smaller adobe structures (Figure 14.12). Casa Grande was built of bricks made of caliche, a desert soil that becomes extremely hard

FIGURE 14.13

Aerial photograph of the partially excavated ruins of Snaketown; approximately 60 individual house floors can be seen. (Copyright © Arizona State Museum, University of Arizona; photo by Helga Teiwes)

when it dries out. For added strength and stability, the walls of the Great House were massive, about 4 ft thick at their base, and set into deep trenches dug into the desert soil. Approximately 600 logs were used in its construction, serving as roof beams and ceilings. An adobe wall more than 2 m (6½ ft) high surrounded the entire complex, enclosing a space of more than 8,000 m^2 (2 acres). Obviously, a large, well-organized labor force was necessary to construct and maintain Casa Grande; it is likely that a few hundred people lived there.

The largest discovered Hohokam village is Snaketown, located on the Gila River; it was the focus of intensive archaeological excavation in the 1930s and then again in the 1960s (Figure 14.13). The ruins at Snaketown cover more than 2.5 km^2 (1 mi^2), and more than 200 family residences have been excavated in this elaborate town. There is a significant irrigation network at the site. Snaketown has also produced evidence of a ceremonial ballgame that also was played by the native people of Mesoamerica (Figure 14.14; see Chapter 15). Hohokam ballcourts like the one at Snaketown may have been places where disputes between families or villages were worked out on a ritually sanctified stage.

Clearly, irrigation initially allowed for the development of the agriculture-based Hohokam society in the Sonoran Desert. Intensification of this irrigation technology—building longer and deeper canals that extended the range of arable land ever greater distances from the permanent water courses—allowed for population growth and the production of a larger food surplus. Elaboration of Hohokam material culture coincided with a probable attendant increase in social and political differentiation among different classes of

FIGURE 14.14
Enclosed ballcourts like this one at the Wupatki ruin in north-central Arizona indicate that some groups of ancient inhabitants of the Southwest played a ceremonial ballgame similar to one played by the Maya (Chapter 15) to the south. (K. L. Feder)

people as excess wealth became concentrated in the hands of those who controlled, at least to a degree, the irrigation system.

Mogollon

Where the Hohokam were dwellers of the desert, the Mogollon were mountain people, living in the highlands of eastern Arizona and New Mexico—and south into Mexico. Long dependent on hunting and gathering and well adapted to life in the mountains, their shift to agriculture, a sedentary lifestyle, and some degree of social and political complexity occurred rather late in prehistory.

Traced by the diagnostic styles of their artifacts, the Mogollon appear in the archaeological record by about A.D. 200. At this time, they lived in small nomadic groups, hunted deer and turkey, gathered the wild plants that grew abundantly in the mountains, and lived in impermanent villages characterized by small **pit-houses**—semi-subterranean structures covered with a thatched roof. Sometime after A.D. 650, the Mogollon began to supplement their diet by farming small garden plots, raising corn, beans, and squash. Not until after A.D. 1150, however, did the Mogollon, probably in contact with the more complex Ancestral Puebloan culture to the north (discussed later in this chapter) and as the result of a significant drought in about A.D. 1300, give up their nomadic, foraging existence, settle down into permanent habitations, and adopt an agricultural mode of subsistence.

The need to increase the agricultural portion of their diet also caused a shift in settlement patterns among the Mogollon. Although before the drought it had made sense for the Mogollon to spread themselves out across the mountains, after A.D. 1300, it made more sense to settle in at those places that

FIGURE 14.15

Map of room distribution at Grasshopper Pueblo, a Mogollon culture site in Arizona.

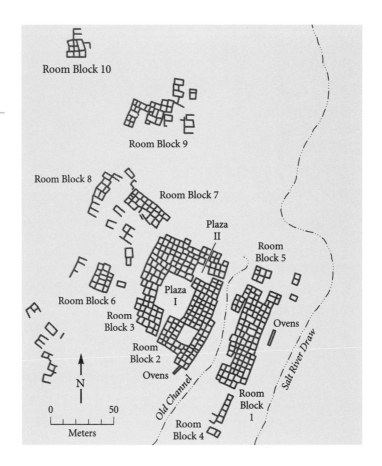

Room Block 10

Room Block 9

Room Block 8

Room Block 7

Plaza II

Room Block 5

Room Block 6

Plaza I

Room Block 3

Room Block 2

Ovens

Ovens

Salt River Draw

Old Channel

Room Block 1

Room Block 4

N

0   50

Meters

offered good agricultural land. These areas experienced a population explosion or, more precisely, an implosion, as the Mogollon began to concentrate their settlements on arable land.

Grasshopper Pueblo, for example, is a large Mogollon settlement dating to this period, located on the best and most extensive agricultural lands in Mogollon territory (Figure 14.15; Reid 1989). Archaeology around the region of Grasshopper shows that before A.D. 1300 there were a total of only about 200 Mogollon dwellings, located in a series of scattered, impermanent communities. After A.D. 1300 in the same region there were 10 times that number, as the scattered Mogollon began concentrating their population on good farmland (Reid and Whittlesey 1997, 156). Grasshopper itself consists of 500 rooms arranged in three distinct clusters. Each block possessed its own common area, or plaza.

Great care was taken by the residents of Grasshopper Pueblo in the construction of buildings intended for ceremony and ritual. One of the large plazas at Grasshopper was roofed over at about A.D. 1330, producing an enclosed ritual space called a **kiva** by the historical and modern Hopi. Kivas were places where the community met to engage in and observe important rituals; they were, essentially, churches. The "Great Kiva" at Grasshopper is, as its name implies, an enormous gathering place some 25 m (82 ft) long, with its roof supported by nine huge juniper posts. As archaeologists Jefferson Reid and Stephanie Whittlesey (1997) suggest, the Great Kiva at Grasshopper played an integrative role in Mogollon society. Because large Mogollon communities such as Grasshopper represent the aggregation of previously separate, smaller communities, it is likely that a shared ritual space and communal ceremonies served to bring people together into a more integrated and complex social and political system. A decrease in rainfall after A.D. 1335 made untenable the agricultural way of life to which the Mogollon had become committed. By A.D. 1400, they had left their mountain homeland, lost their separate identity, and merged with other farmers in the Southwest.

Ancestral Puebloan

The Ancestral Puebloans of the Four Corners region, where the modern states of Arizona, New Mexico, Utah, and Colorado meet at right angles, produced the most spectacular masonry architecture in indigenous North America. The largest prehistoric **pueblos** and incredible settings characterize the Ancestral Puebloans. (You will find these people most commonly referred to as the Anasazi. This term means, literally, "ancient enemies" in the language of another group of Native Americans living in the Southwest, the Navajo, many of whom call themselves the Dineh. Many descendants of the people who built the pueblos object to having their ancestors named by another group, especially a group that they have historically been at odds with. It is with that in mind that we will call their predecessors the Ancestral Puebloans.)

Very early in their sequence, beginning about 2,000 years ago, the Ancestral Puebloans developed a subsistence system that, while including a broad array of wild plants and animals, depended quite heavily on maize agriculture. The most diagnostic elements of their culture at this point were baskets, textiles, and nets used in hunting. In fact, the early years of Ancestral Puebloan development are divided into periods called Basketmaker I and II (500 B.C. to A.D. 600) and III (A.D. 600–800).

The florescence of Ancestral Puebloan culture occurred after A.D. 1000. A burst of social and political complexity is demonstrated by the construction of monumental residential structures, including Great Houses exponentially larger than the Great Houses of the Hohokam, remarkable and beautiful cliff dwellings, and enormous ceremonial buildings in the form of Great Kivas. Chaco Canyon is the most obvious manifestation of such complexity; nine Great Houses were built at the base of the cliffs demarcating the margins of the arable land along the Chaco River (Figure 14.16). The largest of these, Pueblo Bonito, was a single immense structure made from millions of quarried sandstone blocks. Altogether Pueblo Bonito consisted of about

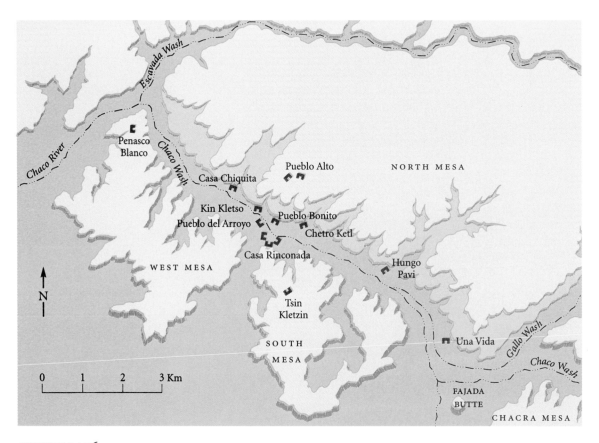

FIGURE 14.16

Locations of the Great Houses of Chaco Canyon, in New Mexico.

800 rooms in its five stories (Figure 14.17). Roofs and ceilings were constructed from thousands of trees cut down and transported from forested areas as much as 80 km (50 mi) distant. The Great Houses at Chaco are monumental structures but likely were not the residences of huge numbers of people. Rather, the Great Houses may have been a kind of public architecture intended by the Ancestral Puebloans, on the practical side, for storage (see the "Case Study Close-Up" in this chapter) and also, in a metaphorical sense, as symbols of the power of their societies.

In all, about 75 substantial settlements and more than 300 smaller communities have been found that were part of the Chaco Ancestral Puebloan culture, most of them outside of the canyon itself. The major towns were connected to Chaco by a series of roads 9 m (30 ft) wide that together measured more than 650 km (about 400 mi) in length. The longest single Chaco road traversed approximately 68 km (42 mi), linking Chaco Canyon with the Great Houses to the north at the Salmon and Aztec ruins. These roads were not simply timeworn trails; they were carefully engineered and constructed and traveled in quite straight lines. Chaco roads never avoided steep slopes but simply climbed them. Where the roads traveled over bare rock, walls were built to demarcate them.

FIGURE 14.17

A small section of Pueblo Bonito, the largest of the Ancestral Puebloan Great Houses. Casa Grande is one of more than a dozen Great Houses built at Chaco Canyon. (K. L. Feder)

The Chaco road system may have served an economic purpose, allowing for the transportation of precious raw materials and finely made art objects within the Chaco sphere; but, as archaeologist John Kantner (1996) points out, a detailed analysis of the paths taken by the roads shows that most were not even close to providing the most efficient or fastest travel between Chaco villages. He feels that the roads played a far more important role in ritually and symbolically uniting the far-flung communities in the Chaco universe. Whatever the case, there is little doubt that economically, politically, and ritually, as more than one writer has put it, "all roads led to Chaco."

Chaco Great Houses and Great Kivas are enormously impressive, the product of a large, coordinated labor force (see the "Case Study Close-Up" in this chapter). If cultural complexity can be assumed to be directly proportional to the massiveness of construction projects as manifested in the archaeological record, then the inhabitants of Chaco represent the most complex of the indigenous people of the American Southwest.

FIGURE 14.18

Mesa Verde contains some of the most spectacular and monumental of the cliff dwellings. Cliff Palace is a remarkable town built into the side of a mountain.
(K. L. Feder)

Though smaller than Chaco's Great Houses, the cliff dwellings of Mesa Verde in southeastern Colorado, built during a hundred-year period beginning at the tail end of the twelfth century A.D., are even more striking. These houses look like fairy castles, set into natural depressions in the cliffs that characterize the region (Figure 14.18). There are more than 600 such cliff dwellings at Mesa Verde. Most are quite small, but some consist of a series of residences and storage rooms constructed with stone blocks and stretching across cliff faces more than 100 m (330 ft) in length, with delicate four-story square bastions and graceful round towers (see Color Plate 20). It is not clear why the residents of Mesa Verde built their homes in such difficult, inaccessible, though visually striking, locations. Perhaps defense from marauding outsiders explains their location, or perhaps it was protection from the elements or ease of access to fresh water seeping through the cliff face. Whatever the case, it is clear that their construction required careful planning and the communal effort of a large force of people. Though there is little evidence at Mesa Verde for the presence of an elite class, certainly the size of their dwellings and the difficulty posed by their construction are material evidence of the complexity of their society. A combination of factors may have precipitated abandonment of the majestic cliff homes by the later thirteenth century, soon after Mesa Verde's population peaked. The population of Mesa Verde may have outstripped the environment's ability to support it, especially during the great drought that afflicted the area in the last quarter of the thirteenth century. Shortages of wood for fuel and construction may have played a role. It is also possible that a new religion may have attracted the Mesa Verdeans to the south. The inhabitants of Mesa Verde did not become extinct. They merely moved and today live in modern Hopi villages in New Mexico.

FIGURE 14.19

Made of thousands of precisely cut granite bricks, the monumental stonework at Great Zimbabwe reflects a level of labor organization and coordination that is the hallmark of a complex society. (Copyright © Robert Holmes/Corbis)

GREAT ZIMBABWE

For the Europeans who first encountered its ruins in southern Africa in the late nineteenth century, Great Zimbabwe was an enigma. Its name was taken from the local Shona people who called the ruin, appropriately, *dzimbabwe*, "houses of stone." Indeed, these first European visitors were impressed by the immensity of its stone construction—the huge number of carefully shaped granite bricks used to build the walls that enclosed parts of the site and the majestic beauty of its dry-laid masonry (Figure 14.19). Clearly, the people who had built the great walls and enclosures of Zimbabwe had been a technologically

FIGURE 14.20

Site map of Great Zimbabwe.

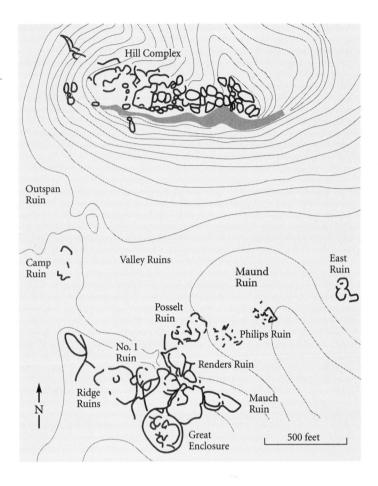

and architecturally sophisticated people. Equally clearly, a complex social system must have been necessary to organize and oversee the labor needed to construct the very impressive remains.

The first Europeans to investigate Zimbabwe found it inconceivable that local Africans had been responsible for building the site. Their racist assumption was that sub-Saharan Africans were incapable of such a complex undertaking. As archaeologist Graham Connah (1987, 183) points out, the European colonizers of Africa sought to deny the indigenous people of that continent their rightful cultural heritage. Some went so far as to suggest that Zimbabwe was associated with Solomon's Temple in Jerusalem, implying that Zimbabwe had been built not by native Africans, but by interlopers from the Middle East.

Such nonsense persisted for more than a century. Even into the 1960s and 1970s, attempts were made to disassociate ancient Zimbabwe from the modern inhabitants of sub-Saharan Africa (see the discussion in Garlake 1973).

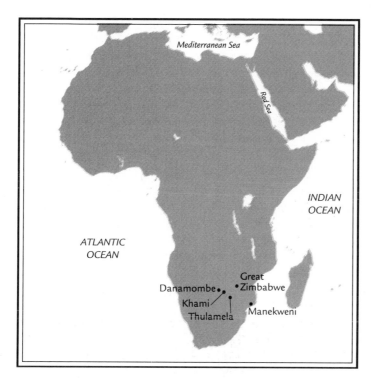

FIGURE 14.21

Archaeological sites in southern Africa associated with Great Zimbabwe.

But the archaeological record is quite clear on this point; the builders of Great Zimbabwe and a large number of smaller sites of the same cultural tradition were the ancestors of the contemporary people of south-central Africa. More than 700 years ago, the people of Great Zimbabwe had produced their own indigenous complex society, inspired primarily by their own ability.

The Glory of Zimbabwe

Great Zimbabwe itself consists of an impressive set of stone-brick structures demarcating the central or elite precinct of a large town that likely also served as a ceremonial center for a widespread rural population, a residence for their gods as well as their chiefs. Massive and impressive, Great Zimbabwe grew by accretion as its population expanded and as its role as the central place of a developing complex society changed through time (Figure 14.20; Ndoro 1997).

Great Zimbabwe is the largest of close to 200 settlements built in the same style in an area known geologically as the Zimbabwe Plateau. A greater number of smaller sites in Botswana and South Africa without impressive stonework—for example, Danamombe, Khami, Manekweni, and Thulamela—likely represent the remains of villages that were part of a large and impressive chiefdom with Great Zimbabwe as its focal point, dating to the period A.D. 1100–1600 (Figure 14.21; Ndoro 1997). While these secondary sites cover tens or even

FIGURE 14.22

This stone tower, an example of the beautiful masonry used in Zimbabwe construction, is located within one of the enormous granite brick enclosures at the site. (Copyright © J. Laure 1991/Woodfin Camp and Associates)

hundreds of acres, Zimbabwe is larger by at least an order of magnitude, with its stone structures spread out over more than 7 km² (close to 3 mi², or nearly 1,800 acres).

Zimbabwe-style architecture includes large, dry-laid stone walls made of rectangular granite "bricks." Zimbabwe-style walls are massive and broad, with bastions, stepped platforms, towers, and large monoliths (massive, upright, single stones) incorporated into their construction (Figure 14.22). Some wall sections are ornately designed with the granite bricks laid in chevron and herringbone patterns. The monumental granite brick walls served as enclosures for a small part of the population, likely the elite of Zimbabwe society. Their homes were constructed of an extremely high quality clay locally called *dagga*.

The two main structures at Great Zimbabwe—the "Hill Ruin" and the "Great Enclosure"—are the most imposing of the monuments built by these people (Figure 14.23). The Hill Ruin is the smaller of the two, yet its walls

FIGURE 14.23

The so-called Great Enclosure, one of the stone enclosures at Great Zimbabwe, consists of an imposing elliptical wall. (Copyright © MIT Collection/Corbis)

stand some 11 m (nearly 37 ft) high. The Hill Ruin actually consists of two separate enclosures connected by a narrow passageway walled in with granite bricks. Altogether, the long axis of the Hill Ruin is more than the length of a football field, about 100 m (328 ft) long and 45 m (148 ft) wide.

The Great Enclosure is larger still, an elliptical wall some 244 m (nearly 800 ft) in circumference, 5 m (16 ft) thick, and 10 m (33 ft) tall, enclosing a space with a maximum diameter of nearly 90 m (almost 300 ft). This truly monumental construction project required nearly 1 million granite bricks for its completion. More than simply massive, the masonry of the Great Enclosure is the finest in ancient Africa outside of Egypt. The bricks fit together virtually seamlessly; the walls are imposing, yet, in places, delicately graceful. Interior walls demarcate space within the Great Enclosure, and there is, again, extensive evidence of dagga huts throughout. It has been suggested by some that the Great Enclosure housed the elite of Zimbabwe society and that it was, in fact, a palace (Ndoro 1997).

Early archaeology at Great Zimbabwe centered on the great enclosures. Only recently have archaeologists turned their attention to the zone surrounding the enclosures. There they have found the remains of extensive settlements of dagga huts, likely the houses of people of lower status than those residing within the walled compounds. The community had a dense, near-urban character; even the most conservative estimate puts Zimbabwe's population at its peak at about 2,000 adults (Ndoro 1997). Some have gauged the total population of Great Zimbabwe to have been as high as 18,000 at its peak (Connah 1987, 184).

By one interpretation, Great Zimbabwe was the capital of a far-reaching chiefdom, sitting atop a hierarchy that included a middle level of smaller towns; there, secondary, regional elites lived within stone enclosures. A third level included small peasant villages without monumental stonework. Those living outside of the enclosures and those living in smaller villages provided the necessary economic support for the sociopolitical system by growing surpluses of sorghum and millet and by raising sheep, goats, and cattle.

The peasants provided food for the elite living in the enclosures. Archaeological faunal evidence implies that the elite had a diet different from that of the masses. For example, at the Zimbabwe site of Manekweni, it is apparent that those living outside of the enclosure were limited in their diet, with sheep and goat providing the bulk of their meat, while those living inside the enclosure, though they produced no food, were provided with beef for their subsistence (Barker 1978).

Zimbabwe's location may have been the key to its growth and complexity. Its location took strategic advantage of a number of trade routes, including those along which valuable ivory moved during the occupation of the site. Also, like the inhabitants of Çatalhöyük (Chapter 12), who were located near a precious and valuable resource (obsidian) and who could amass wealth as a result of controlling that resource, Great Zimbabwe was located near a significant natural source of gold and likely came to dominate in its trade. The Zimbabwe elite may have derived and maintained their position as a class above the masses on the basis of the wealth they were able to accumulate through all manner of trade but, perhaps, especially this gold. That trade was widespread is evidenced in the archaeological record. Glass from Syria, faience (tin-glazed earthenware) bowls from Persia, and even Chinese celadon dishes (finely made ceramics with an olive, gray, or blue glazing) have been found at Zimbabwe (Ndoro 1997).

The walls of Great Zimbabwe and related settlements today are the most conspicuous evidence of the power of the elite in that society. It is likely that as trade in gold and other commodities served to enrich some families on the Zimbabwe Plateau, these families became economically and socially distinguished from everybody else. These elites were able to have the enclosures constructed, setting them physically apart from the great mass of people and reinforcing the fact that they were economically and socially apart from these people as well. Today the silent walls speak volumes to the archaeologist and historian, telling us that enormous power was invested in the elite of this chiefdom society to direct and control the labor of the great mass of people.

IS THE STATE INEVITABLE?

As we saw in Chapter 12, social and political complexity was not inevitable. Some societies, primarily hunter-gatherers, maintained a relatively simple form of social and political organization virtually up to the **ethnographic present.** For example, though their societies certainly did not remain static, the residents of the Kalahari Desert in South Africa, the people who lived in the heart of the Australian desert, and the Inuit people of the Arctic maintained much of their traditional social and political organization for thousands of years, right up to and past their contact with societies having a more complex form of organization, such as the Europeans who first came into contact with them. Their social structures remained largely egalitarian: Virtually all individuals within the same age/sex category had equal wealth and a fair degree of control over their own lives. Authority was vested in families, not in a political structure imposed from above. There were no social classes and no all-powerful chiefs or kings, and no one was buried in sumptuous style.

Just as social and political complexity itself was not an inevitable development in the historical trajectories of all people, rank societies or chiefdoms did not lead inevitably to state societies. In fact, some complexly organized people remained as rank societies or chiefdoms for millennia. For example, the megalith builders of western Europe discussed in Chapter 12, though clearly a complex culture capable of marshaling the forces and coordinating the work of a large group of laborers to construct the monuments that give the society their modern name, never developed some of the diagnostic characteristics of state societies. There apparently was no formal government, no highly and formally organized political bureaucracy, and no hierarchy separating rigidly defined social classes.

The cultures discussed in this chapter similarly may best be characterized as complex, non-state societies. Such societies do not necessarily represent a step on some cultural evolutionary ladder to an inevitable state level of organization. Instead, they reflect a different way in which people constructed and organized their societies.

THE MYTH OF THE MOUND BUILDERS

As we have just seen, the first Europeans to encounter the impressive ruins at Great Zimbabwe presumed that indigenous Africans were not capable of producing such sophisticated and complex architecture. Zimbabwe certainly was not the only instance in which Europeans were confronted by archaeological evidence that the ancestors of people they wished desperately to believe were inferior had produced a sophisticated culture. Actually, the European response to Zimbabwe is part of a general pattern whereby Europeans denied civilized status to many of the non-European people they encountered in their exploration of the world in the fifteenth through nineteenth centuries. The story of the European reaction to the mound builders of North America is an example of this form of racism in its extreme.

Robert Silverberg's book *The Mound Builders* (1989) is a wonderful treatment of this sorry saga in American history (also see chapters in Feder 1999a and Williams 1991 for summaries of this issue). In the eighteenth and nineteenth centuries, European settlers of the North American continent were confronted with clear evidence, in the form of monumental works (the mounds themselves) and sophisticated artifacts found in and around the mounds, of the previous existence of an advanced, "civilized" culture in the heartland of the continent. Rather than conclude from this that the ancient native people of North America, the descendants of whom those European settlers were displacing and whose cultures they were destroying, had been responsible for the clearly impressive achievements of the mound builders, instead a myth of a "vanished race" was concocted. This vanished race, many believed, *not* the Indians, had built the mounds and manufactured the beautiful artifacts found in association with them. This myth took hold, despite the complete lack of evidence for the existence of anyone but the Indians and their ancestors on this continent. And it took hold even though historical records clearly described mound-building Indians living in dense settlements in the sixteenth century, before their populations were decimated by diseases introduced by European explorers and colonists (de la Vega 1988; Elvas 1611).

The controversy concerning the source of mound-builder culture was a vigorous one until relatively recently. It was an issue of great concern to the Smithsonian Institution, which funded a number of major investigations into the mound-builder question in the nineteenth century. More than 100 years ago a federal agency, the Bureau of American Ethnology, published Cyrus Thomas's (1894) voluminous work on the topic. During the course of his study, Thomas and his assistants examined 2,000 mound sites, collected over 40,000 artifacts, and examined countless historical documents and accounts. Not a shred of the evidence they examined supported the hypothesis of some vanished race of mound builders. Everything showed conclusively that the people who had built the mounds, the people who had produced the sophisticated material culture, the people who had developed the complex society that left these things behind had been none other than the American Indian. Stereotypes of primitive, nomadic tribes of Native Americans were hard to break, but break them Cyrus Thomas did. It is remarkable to think that this issue was resolved barely 100 years ago. Today, Cahokia is included on the World Heritage Site list, an honor roll kept by the United Nations of significant archaeological sites worldwide. Its inclusion on this list memorializes the marvelous cultural achievements of the Native Americans who built it.

**CASE STUDY
CLOSE-UP**

Chaco in particular, but other areas of the prehistoric Southwest as well, shows extensive evidence of monumental architecture and social stratification, implying a level of organization beyond that of simple, egalitarian societies. Archaeologist Lynne Sebastian (1992) suggests an explanation for the development of this complexity, at least as it relates to the Chaco Anasazi. (This term is so ingrained that we will continue to use it here, with no disrespect intended to the Pueblo people.) She sees a shift in the settlement pattern in the area occurring between A.D. 700 and 900 from small, largely undifferentiated settlements to larger, more monumental construction. Sebastian feels that the excess labor available for these large construction projects resulted from a shift in subsistence strategies.

The Southwest is an arid climate prone to prolonged periods of dought. Agriculture is an iffy proposition under such conditions, and years of low agricultural yields are always a possibility. This situation may explain why for such a long time farming merely supplemented the subsistence system in this region. As population increased, however, there was a shift toward agriculture and greater sedentism. But herein a problem arose. Certainly in good years, more mouths could be fed through agriculture, but a greater reliance on farming brought with it the potential for greater possible disaster from a bad year with little rainfall and low crop yields.

In Sebastian's (1992, 100) opinion, the strategy at Chaco to cope with just such a problem was the *overproduction* of food—the intentional production of a surplus through intensification of the agricultural system—in good years. The surplus could then be stored for distribution in bad crop years. Indeed, there is a marked increase in storage areas in villages during the period A.D. 700–900. There is also evidence of the construction of water-management facilities, providing for the capture and distribution of rainwater—in other words, irrigation technology. In Sebastian's view, groups living in hydraulically privileged areas, such as Chaco Canyon, were able to produce food surpluses through water management. In her model, large construction projects resulting in some of the impressive structures at Chaco had the goal of producing large storage areas for the food surplus.

The distribution of that surplus in bad years resulted in a large population being obliged to the people at Chaco who produced, stored, maintained, and then distributed the food. In Sebastian's (1992, 123) words, it is possible that "the great house residents were able to convert long-term patterns of power and obligation into permanent status and roles of leadership." She further suggests that they cemented and rationalized this power through Ancestral Puebloan religion. People able to produce a large food surplus and then distribute it during lean times may have been thought to have supernatural connections. Sebastian relates this religious link to the mid-eleventh-century construction of Great Kivas at Chaco, structures of great religious significance in Ancestral Puebloan and later cultures (Figure 14.24).

Roads were built connecting the main settlements in Chaco; an extensive trading network is evidenced by the use of exotic raw materials; and some of the material culture, especially the pottery, was quite elaborate and sophisticated. This exotic material was used in religious ceremonies, and some of it ended up in the burials of powerful people, likely providing further legitimacy for their privileged position. When the overall climate improved between A.D.

FIGURE 14.24

Casa Rinconada, associated with the settlement of Pueblo Bonito, is one of the Great Kivas in Chaco Canyon, New Mexico.
(K. L. Feder)

1050 and 1130, the capacity for the production of a food surplus increased, and the power of those who produce and controlled food became even greater.

 **VISITING THE PAST**

I first visited Cahokia in 1976 while I was in nearby St. Louis for an archaeology conference. I had great trouble getting to the site at the time; nobody in the hotel had even heard of the place, much less knew how I might get there. Through sheer perseverance I made it to the site, where I found what was essentially an empty state park with a tiny, cinder-block museum. When I next visited, in 1991, there was a splendid, multimillion-dollar museum that receives tens of thousands of visitors each year. Cahokia is a place of wonder; the mounds are impressive, as are the artifacts housed in the museum, and the audiovisual presentation in the museum is informative and extremely beautiful. If you are in the area don't miss it! Etowah in Georgia and Moundville in Alabama are just two of the many additional fascinating mound-builder sites open to visitors. The Ohio Historical Society's museum in Columbus has an extensive display on Adena and Hopewell cultures.

Many of the most spectacular of the complex sites in the American Southwest are on federal land or Indian reservations. Many of the most impressive are readily accessible to even the casual tourist. Mesa Verde in southwestern Colorado offers probably the best views and walk-throughs of cliff dwellings. Chaco Canyon is accessible only via a dirt road, but it is well worth the bumpy trip; a series of pueblo structures, including the most monumental of the Ancestral Puebloan buildings, are located within a short drive of each other. See David Grant Noble's (1991) book, *Ancient Ruins of the Southwest: An Archaeological Guide,* for maps, descriptions of many of the most important sites in the Southwest, and a practical guide for visiting them.

The political situation in southern Africa since the dissolution of the apartheid governments of Rhodesia and South Africa has improved greatly. The modern nation of Zimbabwe (formerly Rhodesia) was named for the African civilization discussed here. Great Zimbabwe is protected and administered by a government agency, the National Museums and Monuments of Zimbabwe. The site has been designated a World Heritage Site, one site on a worldwide honor roll of significant historical sites. Tourist visits to Great Zimbabwe are possible; there is even a hotel within walking distance of the ruins.

By visiting any one of the cultural sites discussed in this chapter, you can achieve a visceral appreciation for the power of rank and chiefdom societies to mobilize great numbers of people for communal projects and to produce social systems in which some are afforded an opportunity to devote their lives to the perfection of an artistic or scientific specialty.

SUMMARY

Processes set in motion by the food-producing revolution led to the development of the world's first complex societies, as discussed in Chapters 12 and 13. We have seen in this chapter that many of these same processes continued to produce complex societies throughout the world. The burial and temple mound builders of the American Midwest and Southeast, the pueblo builders of the American Southwest, and the builders of Great Zimbabwe in Africa constitute but a small sample of the various expressions of cultural complexity exemplified in the ancient world.

TO LEARN MORE

Technical Summaries

For details on Cahokia archaeology, see Melvin Fowler's *Cahokia Atlas: A Historical Atlas of Cahokia Archaeology* (1989). An extremely valuable book is Timothy Pauketat's *The Ascent of Chiefs* (1994), a theoretical look at the evolution of a stratified social system at Cahokia. Jefferson Reid and Stephanie Whittlesey have written a broad overview of the American Southwest titled *The Archaeology of Ancient Arizona* (1997). Lynne Sebastian's highly readable, theoretical look at the origins and evolution of Ancestral Puebloan society at Chaco Canyon is titled *The Chaco Anasazi: Sociopolitical Evolution in the Prehistoric Southwest* (1992). On Great Zimbabwe and its place in the development of complex societies in Africa, see Graham Connah's book *African Civilization: Precolonial Cities and States in Tropical Africa, an Archaeological Perspective* (1987).

Popular Summaries

For the mound builders at Cahokia and the history of their acceptance as an indigenous American civilization, see Robert Silverberg's wonderful historical summary, *The Mound Builders* (1989). David Roberts's book, *In Search of the Old Ones: Exploring the Anasazi World of the Southwest* (1997) provides a detailed look at this region. In the Smithsonian Institution's series, Exploring the Ancient World, Linda S. Cordell's

Ancient Pueblo Peoples (1994) is an overview of prehistory in the Southwest. Webber Ndoro's *Scientific American* article, "Great Zimbabwe" (1997), is a terrific place to start learning more about this complex society in southern Africa.

On the Web

The Cahokia site has its own homepage located at http://medicine.wustl.edu/~mckinney/cahokia/cahokia.html. Along with photographs, maps of the mounds, and lots of text, this site lists the various activities conducted at the site, including excavations, lectures, hands-on programs, powwows, and so forth.

For an overview of the various cliff dwellings at Mesa Verde, visit the National Park Service's page devoted to this national monument at http://www.desertusa.com/ver/du_ver_desc.html. For an excellent and very thorough site covering many issues related to the ancient inhabitants of Chaco Canyon, there is no better place on the Internet than another National Park Service site, located at http://www.nps.gov/chcu/home.htm. For a detailed description and analysis of Chaco's road system, see http://sipapu.ucsb.edu/roads/full.html.

A worthwhile Internet site focusing on Great Zimbabwe, with some very nice photographs, can be found at http://www.stg.brown.edu/projects/hypertext/landow/post/zimbabwe/art/gz1.html. For more photographs and a helpful bibliography a useful site is located at http://www.mediazw.com/natparks/g_zim.htm.

KEY TERMS

Adena	Mogollon	pit-house
Hopewell	Hohokam	kiva
Ancestral Puebloan	Sinagua	pueblo
(or Anasazi)	courtyard group	ethnographic present

15

An Explosion of Complexity

THE FLOWERING
OF CIVILIZATION
IN THE NEW WORLD

CHAPTER OVERVIEW

"Civilization," including monumental edifices, elaborate burials, large armies, and full-time artisans, developed in some parts of the New World as fewer people were needed in the subsistence quest and as rulers attempted to legitimize and reinforce their position of power and wealth. Highland and lowland Meso-america and western South America saw the development of the first state-level societies—the first civilizations—in the New World.

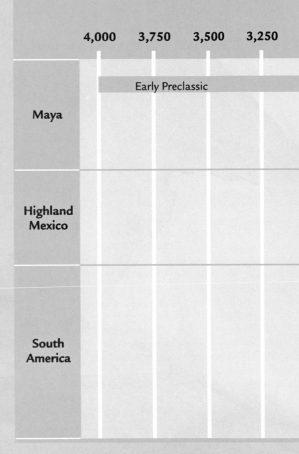

	4,000	3,750	3,500	3,250
Maya	Early Preclassic			
Highland Mexico				
South America				

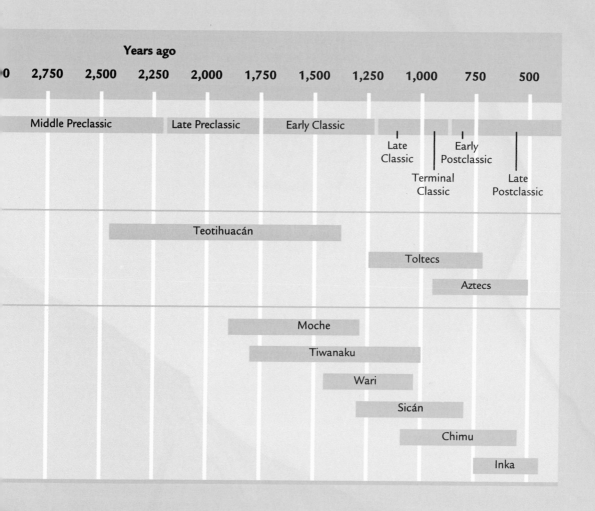

Years ago

| 0 | 2,750 | 2,500 | 2,250 | 2,000 | 1,750 | 1,500 | 1,250 | 1,000 | 750 | 500 |

Middle Preclassic   Late Preclassic   Early Classic

Late Classic

Terminal Classic

Early Postclassic

Late Postclassic

Teotihuacán

Toltecs

Aztecs

Moche

Tiwanaku

Wari

Sicán

Chimu

Inka

PRELUDE

Pacal the Great was 12, only three years older than Tutankhamun (Chapter 13) when he too ascended to the throne of a great nation. His reign, however, was to last far longer than the Egyptian boy-king's, and he would have a far greater impact on the history of his people. Pacal's story as related here is taken largely from *A Forest of Kings: The Untold Story of the Ancient Maya,* by Linda Schele and David Freidel (1990).

Pacal became the ruler of a Maya state centered in the city of Palenque in Chiapas, Mexico, on July 29 in the year A.D. 615 (using our modern calendar). Though from a noble clan, Pacal the Great's father had not been king. Pacal's mother, however, Lady Zac-Kuk, was from a family of kings and had served for three years as the ruler of Palenque, inheriting the throne from her uncle, who likely had no offspring of his own.

Because Maya descent was figured in the male line, it was unusual, but not unheard of, that Pacal became king. That he did so is largely a testament to the strength and power of his mother, who likely continued to wield great power during the early years of her son's reign. It seems that it was not until after her death in A.D. 640 that the now 37-year-old Pacal fully became king in deed as well as in law. After his mother's death, he initiated a vigorous campaign of construction that saw the completion of some of the most impressive temples and palaces built by an ancient civilization. The marvelous site of Palenque, visited by thousands of tourists each year, is largely the result of Pacal's leadership and that of his two sons (Figure 15.1).

Perhaps the greatest architectural achievement of Pacal's reign was the temple that would serve as his burial place (Figure 15.2). Not just a tomb, the Temple of the Inscriptions was intended to legitimize Pacal's kingship, even though his father had not been king, and to sanctify and confirm the legitimacy of the ascendance of his son, Kan-Xul II, to the kingship after Pacal's death. In an attempt to solidify his claim to the throne, as well as that of his son and his grandsons and great-grandsons yet to be, Pacal had a detailed king list inscribed in the halls of the temple located atop his imposing burial pyramid. This king list elevated Pacal's mother to the status of a virtual goddess, comparable to the mother of the gods in Maya mythology. Just as the three central gods of Maya religion legitimately ascended to their "godship" through the divinity of their heavenly mother, the Temple of the Inscriptions seems to be asserting that so too had Pacal legitimately ascended to his kingship through his earthly mother.

Pacal died on August 31, A.D. 683, at the age of 80, following a 67-year reign. In the ceremonies that marked the king's journey from this life into the next, his body was first brought up the steeply inclined stairway of the pyramid and then into the temple at its apex. Next, the body of the king was carried down into the pyramid itself; the pyramid had actually been constructed around and over Pacal's burial chamber, located down a vaulted, internal stairway leading to the base of the pyramid.

At last, the lord and king of Palenque, Pacal the Great, was laid to rest in a sarcophagus carved out of a solid block of limestone. On his face was placed a mask made of obsidian, shell, and jade, bearing a mosaic of Pacal himself.

FIGURE 15.1

Pacal the Great ruled over the Maya city of Palenque between A.D. 615 and A.D. 683. He oversaw the construction of many of the splendid temples that define this center of Maya civilization. His burial pyramid can be seen in the rear center of this photograph. (Copyright © Danny Lehman/Corbis)

Pieces of jade, a precious stone of enormous significance to the Maya, were placed around the body. The coffin lid is itself an exquisite work of art, depicting Pacal in his journey from life to death. Around the side of the coffin were carved the names of the kings that had preceded Pacal, further emphasizing the legitimacy of his lineage's claim to the kingship of Palenque.

There Pacal rested until 1952, when his burial was discovered and the coffin lid raised. That we can tell his story today, more than 1,300 years after Pacal last looked out upon his city in the jungle, is a testament to the ancient Maya. Though perhaps not in the way they intended, in building the Temple of the Inscriptions to house their king for eternity, in placing the king list inscriptions on the temple walls, and in sealing him in his limestone coffin, they assured Pacal a measure of immortality.

As was the case for Tutankhamun, with the burial pyramid of Pacal, we are faced with the enormous material and social consequences of the evolution of state societies. The description of Pacal's tomb shows quite clearly that complex, stratified societies such as those discussed in Chapter 13 evolved in the New World as well as the Old. This chapter focuses on the ancient civilizations of Mesoamerica and South America.

MESOAMERICA

CHRONICLE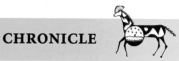

When Hernán Cortés entered the Aztec capital city of Tenochtitlán in central Mexico in A.D. 1519, he and his soldiers were astonished by what they saw. Laid out before them was a huge urban sprawl, centered on two islands in the middle of an enormous lake. The islands were connected by

FIGURE 15.2

The Temple of the Inscriptions, at the Maya site of Palenque, is where Pacal the Great was buried.
(Copyright © Barry D. Kass/ Anthro-Photo)

numerous bridges and artificial causeways. The city these Spaniards saw and described was a teeming hub of people; modern estimates place the sixteenth-century population of Tenochtitlán at about 200,000 (Adams 1991; Sabloff 1989). Tenochtitlán was a planned urban center with precisely laid out streets demarcating neighborhoods and plazas. Enormous pyramids and temples defined the architectural style of the city, which was, in turn, surrounded by a huge expanse of raised agricultural fields called **chinampas.** Tenochtitlán obviously was the capital of a New World civilization. The Aztec civilization encountered by the Spanish conquistadors was the product of a lengthy process of cultural evolution: The Aztecs clearly were not the first such society in the New World (Figure 15.3).

The Maya

Perhaps the best-known and most interesting aboriginal culture in the New World evolved to the south and east of Tenochtitlán, as much as 3,200 years before Cortés described the Aztecs, in the tropical lowlands adjacent to those where the Olmec originated (Chapter 12; Coe 1993). Archaeologist Jeremy Sabloff (1994) summarizes the evidence for the evolution of Maya civilization in this way:

In a region today encompassed by the modern national borders of Guatemala, Belize, Honduras, and Mexico, originating perhaps in a small number of minor agricultural hamlets more than 2,800 and as much as 3,200 years ago, the Maya began their historical journey. By 2300 B.P., villages such as Nakbe, El Mirador, Lamanai, Cerros, and Tikal in the south and Dzibilchaltún and Komchén in the north had become local central places where the earliest evidence of public architecture has been found in the form of large stone platforms (Figure 15.4). Such structures likely were related to Maya religion,

FIGURE 15.3

Archaeological sites in Mesoamerica where evidence of the evolution of chiefdom and early state-level societies has been found.

FIGURE 15.4

This platform structure, probably used for ceremonial or religious purposes, is in Dzibilchaltún, in the north Yucatán. Dzibilchaltún is an early example of a complex Maya settlement and ceremonial center.
(K. L. Feder)

and these villages, like the ceremonial centers of the Olmec, probably housed members of a religious elite and their attendants. Some geographically advantaged settlements such as Cerros—located on a bay by the mouth of a river—became trading centers where raw obsidian and jade, finely crafted goods from these raw materials, agricultural products like cotton and cacao, and perhaps fine ceramics were distributed, adding to the power of the developing religious elite (Sabloff 1994, 115).

A highly productive agricultural system focusing on maize provided food for a growing population. Village population grew, and new villages were established during the period from 2600 to 2300 B.P. As a result of this growth as well as an apparent movement of people from the countryside to the population centers, at this time some of the Maya villages evolved into true urban settlements with large, dense populations.

As population grows, the amount of surplus that can be produced and concentrated in the hands of the elite also grows, as does their ability to solidify, sanctify, and symbolize that power. Monumental, communal construction projects here, as in other early states, were both a cause and an effect of this process. The elite had the power to command the construction of monuments; and the construction of monuments, in turn, served to further integrate people into the political entity of the emerging state. At the same time, monuments provided tangible evidence of the power of the elite, further legitimizing their position of power and enabling them to command the construction of ever more impressive pyramids and temples.

The amount of energy and resources needed to support the large urban centers and their substantial elite population grew, resulting in increased competition for resources and competition for people among the urban centers. Competition almost certainly led to serious conflicts and even warfare. Evidence of extensive defensive earth embankments can be found at some Maya sites, and Maya art includes numerous depictions of military conflicts.

Agriculture probably intensified at this time. Of necessity, the Maya employed a number of methods, both extensive and intensive, to feed the large and dense populations in their cities. In some regions the Maya practiced slash-and-burn agriculture, where forest land is cut and burned to produce fields that are abandoned after only a short period of use and allowed to grow over, to be used again after a period of agricultural dormancy. In some regions, however, a more energy-intensive agriculture was practiced with the construction of extensive ridged fields. Here, ridges of land were built up in the rich and fertile floodplains of rivers. The artificial high ground remained dry even when the river flooded. Some Maya sites dating to this period show evidence of canals and even swamp-reclamation projects. The Maya also employed a number of other intensive agricultural techniques, including terracing of hill slopes, planting kitchen gardens, and tree-cropping—the specialized use of tree crops in rain forests and within settlements (McKillop 1994).

The need for increasing control of information in an increasingly complex cultural system may explain the development of a sophisticated system of writing and mathematics that the Maya derived from the Olmec (Coe 1992; Harris and Stearns 1992). In this civilization, the information deemed worthy of recording related not to accounting or economics, as was the case, for example, in Mesopotamia. Maya writing focused on the culture's history, often emphasizing kingly succession (Schele and Freidel 1990). The desirability of keeping accurate records of time and the Maya ability to do so led to their development of a highly accurate calendar that was based on sophisticated astronomical observations, particularly of the movements of other planets visible in the night sky (Aveni 1977).

All this coalesced by about A.D. 300 into what is called the Classic Maya civilization, with spectacular sites such as Palenque, Tikal, and Uaxactún and their temples, pyramids, and palaces (Sabloff 1994). Maya cities continued to grow (see Color Plate 21). For example, by about 1,350 years ago, Tikal, in Guatemala, had a resident population of at least 40,000 people and perhaps thousands more in the surrounding countryside. Tikal also has produced

FIGURE 15.5

The pyramid known as El Castillo, or the Temple of the Feathered Serpent, is from the site of Chichén Itzá in the northern Yucatán.
(K. L. Feder)

archaeological evidence of neighborhoods where particular craftspeople lived and produced their goods: stone tools, ceramics, and wooden implements. Maya burials, such as Pacal's at Palenque, reflect the high status and great wealth of the upper classes.

Maya urban centers vied for scarce resources, and bloody wars were waged for control of trade and agricultural land as well as for control of the large populations living in the hinterlands. Here, the Maya enter into history—one that they told themselves in their hieroglyphic written language—with their stories of great hereditary rulers whose names are highly evocative: Flint-Sky-God, Great-Jaguar-Paw, Stormy-Sky, and Lord Water, as well as Pacal and his mother Lady Zac-Kuk (Schele and Freidel 1990). Later, after about A.D. 800, the great cities in the southern portion of the Maya realm stopped building great temples and pyramids, and their populations declined dramatically. The geographical focus of the Maya shifted to the north at this time, where the great cities of Chichén Itzá and Uxmal developed, thrived, engaged in struggles for dominance, and also ultimately collapsed (Figure 15.5; see Color Plate 22). Between A.D. 1250 and 1450, the Maya city of Mayapán was the dominant political entity in the Yucatán, though a number of independent Maya states continued to thrive, outside of Mayapán's political reach. Warfare and politics led to the decline of Mayapán, and no single polity took its place. When the Spanish invaded the Yucatán in the sixteenth century A.D., the much-changed Maya society was decentralized and its population was scattered. The construction of great monuments had all but ceased. There is no way of knowing what might have developed next had the Spanish not invaded.

Teotihuacán

Teotihuacán was Mesoamerica's first urban civilization. The valley in which the city was located is a part of the Basin of Mexico. Though the area presented its inhabitants with rich agricultural soil, timber, obsidian, and other valuable lithic resources, rainfall is unpredictable and its high elevation (over 2,200 m, or 7,000 ft) produces a short growing season for agricultural plants.

A detailed and thorough archaeological survey of the Basin of Mexico directed by archaeologist William Sanders (Sanders, Parsons, and Santley 1979) provides us with a chronology of settlement leading up to the dominance of the Teotihuacán urban center. Between 3500 and 2600 B.P., the basin was lightly occupied by a people increasingly dependent on agriculture for their subsistence. Population increased dramatically after 2600 B.P., and local villages began to be drawn into broader polities, owing their allegiance and labor to developing urban centers: The site of Cuicuilco had a population of a few thousand at this time.

Contemporary with Cuicuilco, Teotihuacán began its history as a small farming village, part of the developing settlement system of the Basin of Mexico. Its location afforded its inhabitants decided advantages over their neighbors. The village was located adjacent to a significant source of obsidian, and the site straddles a major trade route to the south and east. The site is also well suited to irrigation-aided agriculture, and so it was well positioned when overall population growth in the Basin of Mexico strained the ability of simple agriculture to feed the increasing number of people living there.

By 2100 B.P. there were a number of growing population centers, but these were all secondary to Cuicuilco until a series of devastating volcanic eruptions effectively destroyed that site. In the ensuing struggle for dominance in the basin, Teotihuacán was victorious. The key to its success may have been a combination of its location, its resources, the great potential of irrigation, and the evolution of an elite able to take advantage of this constellation of factors. As Lamberg-Karlovsky and Sabloff (1995) suggest, the growth of Teotihuacán may have been the result of all of these factors, with each enhancing the other. To take advantage of its obsidian resource, miners of the stone, makers of tools, and full-time traders were needed. A greater emphasis on irrigation developed to produce more food, which, in turn, allowed a greater proportion of the population to engage in specialties related to the obsidian trade. Enormous responsibility and attendant power and wealth rested in the hands of the elite who controlled both trade and irrigation.

By 2000 B.P. the city had a population of more than 60,000, and its urban character was fully established in its broad avenues, huge residential complexes, expansive plazas, and impressive pyramids (Figure 15.6). The Pyramid of the Sun, the centerpiece of the city, is a huge edifice with a volume of more than 1 million m^3 (more than 10 million ft^3). Teotihuacán's population ultimately exceeded 125,000, and by its peak at A.D. 600 the city had become a political capital for an empire of more than 500,000 people (Millon 1967, 1981).

The Aztecs

As mentioned previously, the Aztecs were the reigning civilization encountered by the Spanish conquistadors when they entered the Valley of Mexico in

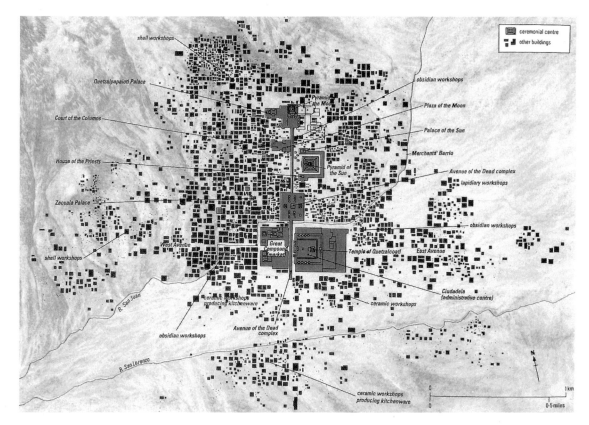

ceremonial centre
other buildings

shell workshops
Quetzalpapalotl Palace
Court of the Columns
House of the Priests
Zacuala Palace
West Avenue
shell workshops
R. San Juan
obsidian workshops
R. San Lorenzo
ceramic workshops producing kitchenware
Avenue of the Dead complex
Pyramid of the Moon
Great Compound (market)
ceramic workshops producing kitchenware
obsidian workshops
Plaza of the Moon
Palace of the Sun
Merchants' Barrio
Pyramid of the Sun
Avenue of the Dead complex
lapidary workshops
Temple of Quetzalcoatl
East Avenue
obsidian workshops
ceramic workshops
Ciudadela (administrative centre)

0   1 km
0   0·5 miles

FIGURE 15.6

Compare this site map of the ancient Mexican city of Teotihuacán with that of the Indus Valley city of Mohenjo-daro in Pakistan (Figure 13.13). One city was in the Old World, one in the New World, but both were planned settlements and the capitals of vast ancient states. (Reproduced from *Past Worlds: The Times Atlas of Archaeology* by kind permission of Times Books, Ltd., London)

1519 (see Color Plate 23). These Spanish invaders wrote detailed historical accounts of sixteenth-century Aztec culture (Soustelle 1964) that have given us the name of the supreme ruler of the Aztec polity: Motecuhzoma (or Montezuma). We also know that he sat atop a multitiered sociopolitical system that included the rulers of city-states that had been incorporated into the Aztec realm; in turn, these leaders ruled over local nobles. As always, at the base of the social, political, and economic pyramid in complex state societies was the vast majority of the population, made up of the commoners whose labor provided the resources that supported the entire system. Motecuhzoma's domain was vast; the Valley of Mexico over which he ruled directly had a population of close to one million people in the period A.D. 1350–1519. The population of the surrounding territories that can still be considered part of his empire numbered in the millions (M. E. Smith 1997, 78). This large population was made possible by an intensive and sophisticated agricultural technology that included substantial irrigation works such as dams and canals. The Aztecs also built walls on hillsides and flattened out slopes naturally too steep for agriculture to produce cultivable terraces. Swamps were drained and artificially raised, and fertilized fields—the *chinampas* mentioned earlier in this

FIGURE 15.7

The Aztec capital city, Tenochtitlán, is largely gone; the modern capital of Mexico, Mexico City, stands in its place. Here, an image of the great pyramid that dominated the skyline of Tenochtitlán more than 500 years ago has been superimposed over the Mexico City neighborhood where the pyramid once stood.
(Copyright © Ned M. Seidler/ National Geographic Society Image Collection)

chapter—were produced, resulting in one of the most productive farming patterns seen anywhere before the development of modern agricultural techniques.

The ample historical documentation of the Aztec civilization focuses on the final chapter of that culture. Archaeology has given us an appreciation for how Aztec society evolved.

Archaeologist Michael Smith (1997) points out that much of the archaeology conducted in the Aztec realm has focused on the remains discovered at the Aztec capital, Tenochtitlán (Figure 15.7; see Color Plate 23). The capital of the modern nation of Mexico, Mexico City, was built over the remains of the Aztec capital; and, indeed, it seems that in every construction project in the modern nation's city, ancient remains from the previous inhabitants are brought to light. Archaeologists, naturally enough, are drawn to these spectac-

FIGURE 15.8

The so-called Aztec Calendar Stone is not a calendar for keeping track of time in the modern sense. Instead, it depicts the Aztec notion of the cyclical nature of time on a universal scale. The central face on the 23,000-kg (25-ton), painted block of basalt (a hard volcanic rock), 4 m (13.5 ft) in diameter, represents the sun and is surrounded by four other suns that shone in four previous eras of Aztec time. (Negative no. 315090, courtesy of Department of Library Services, American Museum of Natural History)

ular artifacts, palaces, and pyramids that reflect the great architectural and artistic achievements of the Aztecs (Figure 15.8). On the other hand, archaeologists realize that an ancient civilization cannot truly be understood without an examination of the lives of the common people who made up the majority population of the society and whose labor made the civilization possible. As a result, Smith has focused his research not on the compounds of the great ruler or the great works of art and architecture, but on the settlements of the common people living in the hinterlands.

Michael Smith (1997) has excavated at two rural villages: Capilco, with a population of about 135, and Cuexcomate, with about 800 people. Agriculture was intense at both villages; terraced slopes allowed for the increased production of corn, beans, and cotton. This agricultural intensity provided the food surplus that passed into the hands of local nobles and from there to the kings of local city-states and ultimately up the line to support the rulers at Tenochtitlán.

The commoners lived in small houses (only about 15 m² —about 160 ft², or a room a little more than 12½ ft on a side). The inhabitants of these houses were, however, part of a complex and interconnected economic system. They produced goods for sale or trade and obtained desired material in exchange. For example, each household grew cotton, and Smith found artifacts used in cotton production (spindle whorls and small bowls used in spinning the cotton) in every excavated house. Cotton textiles were a major product of Aztec peasants and served, for peasants anyway, as the coin of the realm.

Most of the pottery found at Capilco and Cuexcomate had been produced locally, but even the poorest of peasants possessed imported ceramics. Residents also used thousands of obsidian blades, but there is no local source for volcanic glass. It is available 100 km (62 mi) away. Also, though there is no evidence for metallurgy at either site, residents were able to obtain bronze sewing needles, most likely manufactured in western Mexico.

As Smith points out, at least in the outlying sites he excavated, there does not appear to be the kind of grinding poverty that characterizes our modern state societies. In fact, the archaeological record indicates that Aztec commoners did fairly well for themselves. We know from historical records that the Aztecs did not rule with an iron fist; their rule was mostly indirect. As long as each successive rung up the sociopolitical hierarchy received its portion of tribute from those below, people were left alone. In return, they were protected from external threats posed by competitor states, and the goods that people wanted and needed were supplied to the markets.

SOUTH AMERICA

Moche

If asked to enumerate the ancient civilizations of pre-Hispanic South America, most of us would be at a loss once we named the Inka. But this largest and best-known South American state society, encountered by the Spanish in 1532, was only one in a long sequence of impressively powerful civilizations that characterize the history of western South America (Figure 15.9).

For example, about 1,700 years ago, on Peru's northern coast, a culture called Moche developed, with stepped pyramids, hilltop forts, unique pottery styles, and fabulous burials. There are continuities in iconography between Chavín de Huántar (Chapter 12) and Moche, as there are, in fact, between South America's earliest, unifying religious art style and all of the later state societies to be discussed in this chapter.

Beginning construction at their capital in about A.D. 100 and reaching their zenith at about A.D. 400, the Moche produced one of the earliest kingdoms in South America. With a degree of control across an extent of nearly 600 km (370 mi) of coastline, the Moche state constructed enormous monumental works at its primary city, oversaw an extensive trading network that brought in precious raw materials from all over western South America, and ran a large-scale irrigation system of canals and aqueducts.

At its central urban center in the Trujillo Valley, the Moche built the so-called Pyramid of the Sun (Huaca del Sol). Construction commenced on this monumental project at about A.D. 100; the pyramid was built in eight distinct phases and ultimately was more than 40 m (130 ft) high. Though not espe-

FIGURE 15.9

Archaeological sites in western South America where evidence of the evolution of chiefdom and early state-level societies has been found.

cially tall when compared to the largest Egyptian pyramids—for example, the pharaoh Khufu's burial pyramid is close to 150 m (500 ft) high—the Moche Pyramid of the Sun covers a vast area; along its longer axis it is 342 m (1,122 ft) in length (that's about 3½ football fields) and nearly 160 m wide. In other words, this one monument covers an area of more than 54,000 m² (13.5 acres, or the area covered by more than 12 football fields). Its enormous volume contains 143,000,000 mold-made, sun-dried adobe bricks (Figure 15.10). Its accompanying, smaller Pyramid of the Moon (Huaca de la Luna) is made of 50,000,000 adobe bricks and rises to a height of 20 m (66 ft).

In the interior of the Egyptian pharaoh Khufu's pyramid, work gangs left graffiti, often referring proudly to their role in building the great burial monument to the absolute leader of their society. Archaeologists Charles Hastings and Michael Mosely have examined the construction of the Moche pyramids and have found a similar phenomenon. Though none of the pre-Columbian civilizations in South America, including the Moche, possessed a written language, Hastings and Mosely (1975) found more than 100 different kinds of markings on the adobe bricks in the Pyramid of the Sun. They suggest that such

FIGURE 15.10

The Moche culture Pyramid of the Sun stood over 40 m (135 ft) in height. Begun in about A.D. *100, it consists of more than 143 million adobe bricks.* (Negative no. 334912, courtesy of Department of Library Services, American Museum of Natural History)

markings may have served to record the material contributions of local groups of people to Moche's great leaders for construction of the pyramid. This record keeping, as Hastings and Mosely suggest, implies a complex, hierarchical political organization in which local people were expected to contribute to the needs of the elite—including the monumental construction projects they ordered.

Moche society manifested status differentiation in a definitive way by interring its leaders in a sumptuous splendor that is breathtaking even to our jaded turn-of-the-century sensibilities (see Color Plate 24). See the "Case Study Close-Up" in this chapter for a detailed discussion of one remarkable set of Moche elite burials, those of the "Lords of Sipán."

South American Empires: Tiwanaku

At an elevation of 3,870 m (12,690 ft), the capital of the Tiwanaku civilization, located in Bolivia, just southeast of the enormous and economically productive Lake Titicaca, was one of the highest cities of the ancient world. Beginning in about A.D. 200 and reaching a zenith by about A.D. 400, the builders and sculptors of Tiwanaku constructed a remarkable city encompassing an area of some 4.5 km² (1.74 mi²), filled with a series of palaces, temples, platforms, and massive monoliths, enormous works crafted from single pieces of stone (Figure 15.11).

The stone used by the builders of Tiwanaku included the hard and dense volcanic rock andesite and the softer sandstone; both were abundant in the Tiwanaku region. Quarrying and transporting this stone, often in enormous blocks—one sandstone monolith moved to the capital weighed 118,000 kg (130 tons)—was a truly monumental undertaking. Andesite was quarried at a site located across the lake from Tiwanaku; it was, in all likelihood, floated over to the city on reed boats. Some of the large sandstone blocks were transported 10 km (6 mi) over land.

The intricately carved Gateway of the Sun, the Ponce Monolith of an enormous Tiwanaku deity, and the Bennett Monolith, a huge sandstone depiction of a Tiwanaku god, are but a small part of the legacy of this civilization (Morris and von Hagen 1993). The amount of labor and the degree of spe-

FIGURE 15.11

The great gateway at Tiwanaku is an enormous monolith. It was formed by expert carvers from a single slab of extremely hard and dense volcanic rock. (Copyright © Kevin Shafer/Corbis)

cialization needed to produce these monuments, as well as the impressive architecture of the city of Tiwanaku itself, show just how powerful ancient civilizations can become.

Like all complex state societies, Tiwanaku thrived as the result of a highly productive agricultural system. Though the surrounding territory today seems barren, the farmers of Tiwanaku developed an efficient pattern of raised fields. Through communal labor, they constructed huge platforms of rich soil surrounded by lower swales. The largest of the platforms were 200 m (about 650 ft, or more than two football fields) long and 15 m (50 ft) wide (Morris and von Hagen 1993, 105). Excavation of these platforms indicates that they were not simply mounds of earth, but carefully engineered agricultural facilities. At one site, Pampa Koani, the platforms were shown to have been built in stages (Kolata 1986). First, a layer of stone cobbles was laid down as a base. The cobbles were covered with a layer of clay, which was, in turn, covered with three separate sheets of gravel. The productive topsoil was placed on top. The low-lying areas between the raised fields allowed the waters of Lake Titicaca to flow between the plantings. The complex design of these engineered fields ensured that brackish lake water would not percolate up through the mound to damage plants and that the entire facility would be well drained. As with raised fields elsewhere in the New World, the standing water between the platforms produced a rich organic soup that would then be scooped up and laid over the fields to fertilize the soil. This highly productive agricultural system was at the core of Tiwanaku wealth and power.

As in all ancient civilizations, this wealth and power were invested in an elite class who lived in the palaces of Tiwanaku and who ruled over a vast area

FIGURE 15.12

Located on the southern frontier of Wari territory, the community of Pikillacta was part of the Wari polity and consists of a large number of walled compounds. (Negative no. 334818, courtesy of Department of Library Services, American Museum of Natural History)

of hamlets populated by the commoners of Tiwanaku society—the people whose labor made it all possible. And, as in all ancient—and modern—civilizations, there had to be a way to legitimize the rule, wealth, power, and comfort of the few over the many. As Morris and von Hagen (1993) point out, legitimization at Tiwanaku was accomplished through religion. The position of the elite class was seen as part of the natural order of things. A complex social and political order was necessary to produce, maintain, and expand the culture's highly engineered agricultural system. That social and political order was reinforced by religious symbolism and monumental construction of palaces, temples, and monoliths.

The influence of Tiwanaku extended across an enormous expanse of South America. Up to 1 million people living in what is now Peru, Bolivia, Ecuador, and Chile were followers of the Tiwanaku state religion.

South American Empires: Wari

Other civilizations also evolved in highland South America. For example, the Wari developed near the modern Peruvian city of Ayacucho. The Wari partly overlapped with Tiwanaku, but peaked later, after A.D. 600. The capital of Wari was an enormous enclosure whose walled neighborhoods covered about 2 km² (about three-quarters of a square mile, or nearly 500 acres). The construction is truly monumental; some of the walls are 12 m (40 ft) high and several meters thick and extend for hundreds of meters. Much of the city seems to have been multistoried (Figure 15.12; Morris and von Hagen 1993).

FIGURE 15.13

Ears of corn and the heads of snakes sprout from the head of the Wari sun god, who, in turn, grasps two serpents. (From *The Inca Empire and Its Andean Origins* by Craig Morris and Adriana von Hagen. American Museum of Natural History and Abbeville Press)

Unlike Tiwanaku or the Aztecs, the Wari were not located on the shores of a lake and did not practice raised-field agriculture. They, nevertheless, practiced a labor-intensive and highly productive, engineered agricultural system that involved the construction of terraced fields, similar to those seen in Mexico at Teotihuacán. Agriculture also depended on an extensive system of irrigation works, including long canals that brought water from the uplands and distributed it across a complex network of branching secondary canals that led to the terraced fields.

Religious iconography centered at Wari is found represented in textiles and pottery across a broad swath of western South America (Figure 15.13). That the Wari gods appear to have been worshipped in a broad area is an indication of the power and influence of the Wari elite who were identified with those gods. As Morris and von Hagen (1993) point out, one of the most fascinating aspects of Wari is the way in which the leaders maintained their far-flung, religion-based empire. In a pattern that was to be followed again by the Inka, the Wari elite controlled outlying regions, funneling surplus labor and wealth to their capital, by the construction of regional administrative centers across Wari territory. For example, Azángaro, located 15 km northwest of Wari itself, was a walled enclosure built as a smaller version of Wari. Wari pottery is found at Azángaro, and the religious iconography is typically Wari. Other large regional centers scattered throughout Wari territory include Pikillacta and Jincamocco. These regional centers likely served as local offices of the elite, perhaps staffed by Wari nobility, making sure that local populations were participating fully in the Wari state by sending their surplus food to the capital and providing labor for the monumental works required by the elite.

South American Empires: Sicán and Chimu

The Andean region was fertile ground for the development of New World civilizations. After the Moche culture faded along the north coast of Peru after

FIGURE 15.14

Aerial view of one of the approximately ten walled palace compounds of the Chimu capital of Chan Chan. Enclosed within its walls were storage areas, government buildings, and burial platforms. (Negative no. 334900, courtesy of Department of Library Services, American Museum of Natural History)

A.D. 700, it was replaced by the culture known as Sicán, which peaked between A.D. 900 and 1100. The Sicán capital city, Batán Grande, also exhibits monumental pyramids and a cemetery for the elite. Everywhere in the iconography seen in textiles and ceramics and on the finely crafted solid gold and gilded objects that typify Sicán, one sees the image of the so-called Sicán lord, presumably the religion's most important god, who ruled a pantheon of other spirit beings. Once again, the Sicán empire had, at its core, a complex agricultural system with enormous irrigation works that allowed production of a food surplus. This surplus supported an economic system with an elite class; a class of artisans who spent their time manufacturing the ceramic, cloth, and gold artworks that ended up in the hands of the elite; and a large class of commoners whose labor built the monuments and whose sons staffed the military.

Sicán was a significant state society, but it pales in comparison to one of the largest empires ever seen in the ancient New World. The empire of Chimor, or the Chimu, extended across more than 1,300 km (800 mi) of the western coast of South America, essentially the entire northern coast of Peru.

Built beginning sometime before A.D. 900 and expanding at around 1200, the Chimu capital at Chan Chan was one of the most impressive urban centers constructed in the ancient world. From the air it is absolutely remarkable (Figure 15.14). Where Tiwanaku covers an area of 4.5 km², Chan Chan's remnants reflect a city some 20 km² (almost 8 mi²) in extent. It is a true city, with neighborhoods divided, in part, according to which crafts were produced by the inhabitants (Topic 1990).

Irrigation was crucial in the development of the Chimu state and was, perhaps, along with the desire of the elite to incorporate surrounding territories into its polity, the reason for its expansion across a huge territory. A sophisticated and monumental complex of irrigation canals produced a rich harvest for the inhabitants of Chan Chan. However, local irrigation in the Moche valley may not have been enough to satisfy the growing population. In addition, as archaeologist Michael Mosely (cited in Morris and von Hagen 1993) points out, irrigated lands build up a concentration of salt, which diminishes harvests and necessitates the incorporation of additional, new lands into the system. Also, as Mosely suggests, the western coast of South America is geologically active. Earthquakes were more than merely a frightening nuisance to the ancient inhabitants of South America, seriously damaging and even destroying irrigation works. Mosely suggests that the Chimu elite found it easier and likely more productive to abandon fields fed by canals if they were destroyed by earthquakes and to annex new territories into their state. This approach would have served the dual purpose of providing more farmland and also new workers—the inhabitants of the annexed territories—for the state.

South American Empires: The Inka

As seen in the context of this chapter, the Inka civilization that most people have at least heard of did not arise without antecedents in South America. In fact, the Inka were merely the latest in a series of empires that had achieved prominence and hegemony over the Andean region of South America when the Spanish conquistadors, led by Francisco Pizarro, entered their territory in A.D. 1532.

The Inka began their historical journey as a small tribe of people living in the region of the modern city of Cuzco in Peru. Cuzco, in fact, became their capital city when their military expansion began in the middle of the fifteenth century A.D. By A.D. 1500 the Inka, who called their nation Twantinsuyu, controlled a broad empire of close to 1 million km² (380,000 mi²), extending across 4,000 km (2,500 mi) of South America's Pacific coast (Figure 15.15).

Their capital at Cuzco was typical of the capitals of older Andean states, only bigger. It was filled with palaces, temples, and plazas. The impressive masonry seen at older sites was raised to a level of perfection at Cuzco. Enormous stone blocks, often weighing several tons, were carved into various polygonal shapes and then fitted precisely together, much like a jigsaw puzzle.

Many people in Cuzco's population were the elite of Inka society, though there were substantial clusters of non-Inka people living there. The powerful Inka army subdued thousands of people spread across a broad territory and incorporated them all into the Inka state. In a clever political strategy, representatives of these subdued people were ordered to live in Cuzco as well. Many of those removed to Cuzco had been the rulers (and their heirs) of territories

FIGURE 15.15

*Extent of the Inka empire
at its peak.*

the Inka had defeated in battle. These foreign leaders likely played a role in administering their home territories for the Inka; but, also, as Morris and von Hagen (1993) maintain, they likely served as de facto hostages, ensuring the obedience of their homelands to Inka rule.

Like the other Andean states, Inka subsistence was provided by a sophisticated farming technology. Maize and other crops were grown on spectacularly terraced fields that were linked together by massive irrigation works (Figure 15.16).

Among the ways the Inka state grew was military conquest, but it also grew by the peaceable incorporation of other, smaller, existing Andean states. For example, we know that the Chincha state on Peru's southern coast joined the Twantinsuyu empire, ostensibly of its own free will. In all likelihood, the ruler of Chincha recognized the military superiority of the Inka and the inevitability of their control over his territory. His agreement to join the empire spared his society a war it was bound to lose and likely ensured some level of local control over his nation. The Inka built administrative centers in the

FIGURE 15.16

Aerial view of a system of concentric terracing, an intensive method of farming by which the Inka increased the productivity of their farmland. (Negative no. 334812, courtesy of Department of Library Services, American Museum of Natural History)

capitals of the states they subdued and continued to maintain their control over these incorporated territories by a system of roads that stretched for thousands of miles, connecting Cuzco to the most outlying Inka outpost. Though the Inka military possessed no special technology for moving along these roads—no llama-drawn wheeled vehicles, for example—the roads ensured that they could move relatively quickly in response to any threat or rebellion that faced their empire.

As with all ancient state societies, the monumental works and beautifully crafted objects made of precious raw materials that legitimized the power of the elite were made possible by the labor of the many (see Color Plate 25). States become more powerful as more people are incorporated into them, increasing the size of the labor force available to be exploited by the elite. The Inka are a perfect example of this. From historical records, we know that able-bodied men had to pay a "labor tax" to the state. This labor was ritually sanctified; those who worked for the Inka elite were considered to be working for the gods.

Alone among the ancient world's civilizations, the Inka did not possess a written language, but they did develop a recording system that used knotted string called **quipu.** The pattern of individual knots and their placement in a series of knotted strings could, in essence, be read by people who had been taught the code (Figure 15.17).

The story of the Inka brings us to the very edge of prehistory. In a sense, the rigidly hierarchical political and social system that had been the source of their success was turned against them by the Spanish conquistadors when they invaded Inka territory in 1532. Though armed with guns and having the advantage of being on horseback, the Spanish arrived in small numbers—there were only about 180 of them—and could easily have been defeated by the powerful Inka army, an army that had played a major role in constructing the largest empire seen in the New World. In August 1533, when Pizarro captured the Inka ruler Atawalpa, who, in Inka political culture, was the source of all decisions, the Inka were paralyzed. Though nearly 4,000 Inka soldiers were present when Atawalpa was taken, they were unable to attack the much smaller Spanish force because that would have risked the life of their ruler.

Though the Inka paid a huge ransom to effect Atawalpa's release, Pizarro realized that in freeing the Inka ruler, he likely would be sealing his own doom. After accepting the ransom, Pizarro killed Atawalpa anyway, throwing the Inka political system into disarray. The empire fell apart as its component parts, always resentful of Inka control, broke away, ending the reign of the most powerful indigenous civilization in the New World.

ISSUES AND DEBATES

The world's first civilizations had many features in common. They all were remarkable cultures, spectacularly successful and complex adaptations to their environments. Yet, as successful as they were, all of these early civilizations shared another element that may reflect a fundamental instability in their adaptation; all of these civilizations collapsed.

WHY DO CIVILIZATIONS COLLAPSE?

Perhaps "collapsed" is not the best word to describe what happened to these first civilizations. Archaeologist George Cowgill (1988) points out that virtually all "collapsed" civilizations continued on in an attenuated form. In fact, many regained strength and power, only to "collapse" again in a number of cycles. Cowgill (1988, 256) feels that "political fragmentation" is a better term to describe what happened to these early state societies—and, perhaps, eventually to all state societies. They don't really collapse, dry up, and blow away. They merely break up into smaller, often less centrally organized, politically simpler, autonomous entities. We will continue to use the term "collapse" here because it is so ingrained in both the archaeological literature and pop-

FIGURE 15.17
The Inka had no system of writing, but they did have quipu, a system of knotted strings by which they kept the records of their empire.
(Courtesy of Peabody Museum, Harvard University, Photo #N21754)

ular parlance, but we will use it to signify Cowgill's concept of political fragmentation.

The Causes of Collapse

Anthropologists, archaeologists, and historians have long wondered why civilized societies consistently and ultimately collapse. What are the causes of such collapses, and is collapse inevitable?

George Cowgill (1988) suggests that state societies historically run into trouble for a number of reasons. These societies depend on tax revenues, and through time an increasing number of organizations obtain legal exemptions from taxation, while increasing numbers of citizens may avoid taxes illegally. Expensive bureaucracies proliferate, marked by "increasing corruption, rigidity, incompetence, extravagance, and (perhaps) inefficiency" (Cowgill 1988, 263). At the same time, citizens of complex state societies have increasing expectations of services the state should be providing them. All of this sounds depressingly familiar and does not bode well for our own complex civilization.

Archaeologist Joseph Tainter (1988, 89–90) has summarized the causes proposed for the collapse of civilizations in this way:

1. *Resource depletion*—The large, dense populations associated with civilizations and their intensive exploitation of the environment lead to the depletion of key resources and the ultimate collapse of the society.

2. *New resources*—The discovery of new resources eliminates the need for the more complex and stratified social hierarchy of civilizations, and this decentralization leads to the dissolution of the society.
3. *Catastrophes*—Natural catastrophes such as hurricanes, earthquakes, and volcanic eruptions are the root cause of the collapse of civilizations.
4. *Insufficient response to circumstances*—As a result of their inherent complexity, civilizations become rigid in their adaptation, and their own inertia makes it difficult, if not impossible, for them to change quickly enough to respond to changes in external or internal conditions.
5. *Other complex societies*—Competition or conflict with other civilizations can lead to the collapse of a civilized society.
6. *Intruders*—Attacks by a more mobile, more aggressive group of intruders can lead to collapse.
7. *Mismanagement*—The elite in a civilization may so abuse their power and direct so much of the surplus wealth and labor of their society to their own benefit that not enough is left for the maintenance of the economic and political system, leading to collapse.
8. *Economic explanations*—Civilizations are expensive to keep going and require increasing amounts of labor and wealth to maintain themselves. As civilizations grow, the upper classes grow—and so does their need for surplus wealth. The overall costs of supporting the system with specialists, servants, slaves, soldiers, police, and so on grow at an increasing rate. Eventually, civilizations simply become top-heavy and economically nonviable. The increasing effort to maintain them produces diminishing returns and leads to their collapse.

Just as there was no single explanation, no "prime mover," in the explanation of the initial development of civilizations, there can be no single explanation for their collapse. For example, the extensive use of irrigation and the resultant salinization of previously rich farmland in southern Mesopotamia (see Chapter 13) may have led to decreasing yields, which may have contributed to collapse (Crawford 1991); but this theory has been sharply questioned by some researchers. M. A. Powell (1985) interprets the written record of the Sumerian civilization as showing that, though salinization presented a challenge to the farmers of Sumer, it was recognized and routinely dealt with.

As Tainter indicates, most of the explanations for why civilizations ultimately collapse beg the question. Explanations of environmental catastrophe, the presence of intruders, competition with other civilizations, or resource depletion still leave open the fundamental question: "Why can't civilization adequately deal with or respond to such challenges?"

Tainter prefers his final explanation of fundamental economic causes for civilization collapse. It is, after all, the broadest and most all-encompassing. Such an explanation can be interpreted as covering virtually all of the others. Civilizations can and do respond to resource depletion, external threats, class warfare, mismanagement, and the like, but at an increasingly high price. Eventually, even in the most complex and sophisticated of civilizations—and this would certainly include our own Western culture—when the cost of complexity exceeds the ability of the society to bear it, the society collapses under its own weight. From our perspective this may seem like an awful prospect but Tainter's (1988, 198) outlook is useful here: "Collapse then is not intrinsically a catastrophe. It is a rational, economizing process that may well benefit much of the population."

CASE STUDY CLOSE-UP

In the village of Sípan, located about 150 km (95 mi) north of the Pyramid of the Sun, are the royal cemeteries of the Moche elite. Initially discovered and looted in 1986–87, the cemeteries caught the attention of the world when the thieves were caught by the police. The violated tomb led archaeologists to excavate in the cemetery, and, remarkably, several other spectacular, unlooted tombs were found and excavated by archaeologists Walter Alva and Christopher Donnan (1993, 1994; Figure 15.18).

The first excavated tomb, dating to about 1,660 years ago, was of a man in his late 30s or early 40s (Alva and Donnan 1994, 29). In death he wore an elaborate feathered headdress, nose ornaments, and beaded pectoral ornaments (a chest covering). The tomb was filled with turquoise, copper, silver, and gold jewelry. At his right side lay a gold and silver scepter, and on his left was another scepter of cast silver. Also accompanying this lord of the Moche were hundreds of pottery vessels, some quite elaborate and displaying human shapes; a number were in the form of warriors vanquishing their enemies. The chief resident of the grave did not make his voyage to the Moche version of heaven alone; he was buried with llamas, a dog, two men, three women, and a child. The additional males appear to have been sacrificed as part of the burial ceremony.

It is rare for archaeologists to encounter one such spectacular tomb in a lifetime. Walter Alva and Christopher Donnan were to find two more at the Moche royal cemetery at Sípan. Another royal was found in a plank coffin wearing a headdress of gilded copper. The headdress was in the shape of an owl, with long hanging bands representing the bird's feathered wings. A final burial was also richly appointed with marvelous gold, silver, and turquoise artifacts.

The royalty buried at Sípan appear to represent a class of warrior-priests. Their clothing, ornamentation, and headdresses match quite closely artistic depictions of great warriors from other Moche sites. In those depictions, victorious warriors are presented with the hands and feet of their enemies as trophies. Alva and Donnan discovered the remains of human hands and feet associated with the major burials at Sípan.

These royal Moche burials are emblematic of civilization. The ability to unify a large population, to control their behavior, and to exploit their labor and wealth were the factors that made possible such sumptuous splendor in death for the Moche lords.

FIGURE 15.18

View of one of the spectacular burials of a Moche warrior-priest, filled with artifacts of gold and jade.
(Copyright © Kevin Shafer/ Corbis)

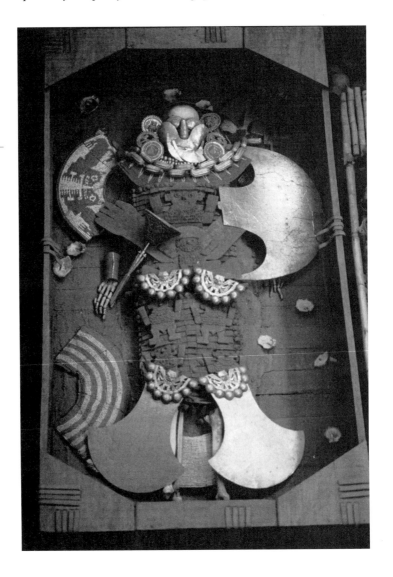

 **VISITING THE PAST**

Founded about A.D. 500, Uxmal is located in the northern lowlands of the Yucatán in what is known as the Puuc region. The Maya accomplished a series of truly stunning architectural achievements at Uxmal. The site is dominated by the Pyramid of the Magician, a steep-sided, elliptical structure devoid of right angles; the corners of the pyramid are rounded. A staircase brings the visitor to the top of the pyramid, where, as in most Maya pyramids, a magnificent and intricately designed ceremonial structure was built.

The sound-and-light show at the site is surprisingly well done. But the artificial light show at Uxmal, painting the ruins in shades of blue and red, could not compare with the light show nature had in store during my visit.

Standing at the ruin called the "Palace of the Governors," which looks remarkably like a government office building with a broad staircase and imposing façade, one can look down across the main section of the site into the building called the "Nunnery"—four long structures surrounding a massive courtyard—into the ceremonial ballcourt and, to the right, the wonderful Pyramid of the Magician.

As my family and I stood there, literally in awe of the alien beauty of the city, an intensely dark set of rain clouds moved in from the north. Behind us the sun blazed brightly, illuminating the southern face of the pyramid with an eerie glow, while to the north, behind it, the sky turned frighteningly dark. Lightning sparked in the distance. It seemed as if the Mayan rain god Chaac were putting on a spectacular light show for those of us visiting the ancient city.

The great Maya sites of Chichén Itzá, Uxmal, Tikal, and Palenque are relatively accessible and absolutely marvelous places, cities literally carved out of the jungle by the ancient Maya. Political unrest notwithstanding, Machu Picchu still is a popular tourist destination in Peru.

Virtual visits via computer technology are available for New World civilizations, just as they are for ancient state societies of the Old World. Sumeria Publishing and *Scientific American* have produced a CD-ROM titled *Exploring Ancient Cities,* which includes a section on Teotihuacán. The Royal Geographical Society has produced a detailed electronic guide called *Inca Ruins* loaded with photographs, maps, time lines, and detailed text.

SUMMARY

In the New World, just as in the Old, some farming societies eventually developed the ability to produce a food surplus. This surplus enabled the development of social complexity and inequality. Eventually, some of these complex societies developed into true states with a formal government and true power invested in an elite class. The Maya and the complex pre-Aztec cultures of central Mexico, as well as the pre-Inka states of western South America developed independently of Old World civilizations.

TO LEARN MORE

Technical Summaries

Once again, *Ancient Civilizations,* by C. C. Lamberg-Karlovsky and Jeremy Sabloff (1995), presents an extremely thorough investigation of the origins of civilization in Mesoamerica (and the Middle East and Indus Valley as well). Thomas C. Patterson's *Archaeology: The Historical Development of Civilizations* (1993) is as valuable for its discussion of New World civilization as it is for the Old World.

For Teotihuacán and the civilizations of highland Mexico, see Richard Adams's *Prehistoric Mesoamerica* (1991).

Joseph Tainter's book *The Collapse of Complex Societies* (1988) contains a very detailed presentation on the collapse of such societies. The volume edited by Norman

Yoffee and George Cowgill, *The Collapse of Ancient States and Civilizations* (1988), presents papers on the collapse of Mesopotamia, the Maya, Teotihuacán, Rome, and Chinese civilizations.

Popular Summaries

There is a wealth of good material aimed at a general readership on the Maya of Mesoamerica—in particular, Michael Coe's *The Maya* (1993), Jeremy Sabloff's *The New Archaeology and the Ancient Maya* (1994), T. Patrick Culbert's *The Maya Civilization* (1993), and the wonderfully written *A Forest of Kings,* by Linda Schele and David Freidel (1990). Focusing on seven Maya sites, *The Code of Kings,* by Linda Schele and Peter Mathews (1998) provides the most up-to-date information about the history of the ancient Maya kingdoms. Though its spectacular photographs might give you the impression it is a coffee-table book, Craig Morris and Adriana von Hagen's *The Inka Empire and its Andean Origins* (1993) offers detailed information about the evolution of civilization in South America presented in a nontechnical manner. James B. Richardson's *The People of the Andes* (1994) provides a useful summary of the evolution and flowering of state societies in western South America. The Royal Geographic Society's *Inca Ruins,* mentioned in "Visiting the Past," is a very good, accessible source on the Inka.

On the Web

There are far too many Web sites devoted to the ancient civilizations of the Americas to provide an inclusive list here. Good places to begin for the cultures discussed in this chapter are, for the Maya, http://www.halfmoon.org/; for Teotihuacán, http://archaeology.la.asu.edu/teo/; for the Aztecs, http://northcoast.com/~spdtom/aztec.html; and for the Inka, http://www.incaproject.com/incas.html. These sites are excellent entry points on the Web for information about these ancient societies. Follow the links they all provide for more information, photographs, and maps.

KEY TERMS

chinampas   quipu

16

Evolutionary Epilogue

CHAPTER OVERVIEW

Our story began with the birth of the universe, the origin of life, the evolution of the primates, and the florescence of the apes. We saw one ape species pushed out onto the savanna at the end of the Miocene—able to survive as a result of its unique ability to walk on two legs. We witnessed the enormous success of this species' descendants as their brains expanded and as they relied increasingly on the intellectual power of those big brains to invent tools, tame fire, domesticate plants and animals, and develop complex societies.

We have reached a milepost in our investigation of the human past, where we literally have caught up with ourselves on the human evolutionary pathway. We can gaze back, as we have in this book, along its winding and serendipitous route, and in the distance we can see, if only dimly, our ancient evolutionary ancestors. Ahead, we can imagine our species racing forward to some unknown and unfathomable point on the horizon of our own future.

498

This book has chronicled our species' long and exciting journey as revealed through the scientific investigation of the period of time literally before history. Together we have traveled a pathway paved with the material remains of those who have passed here before us. Littering the trail have been their bones and their trash, their tools and their monuments. These are the things that have informed us of their story. And *their* story has been *our* story, the physical and cultural evolutionary history of all humankind. It is a tale yet unfolding and of which we are all a part.

The Human Adaptation

As we have seen, 2.5 million years ago our human ancestors crossed an intellectual threshold that would forever determine the focus of the human adaptation. In our species' African nursery was born our unique reliance on *culture*—our ability to conceive strategies for survival intellectually, to implement those plans, and to teach our children, who, in turn, teach theirs. Using the intellectual potential conferred on us by our expanding brains, our *Homo habilis* ancestors initiated a pattern that has defined the hominid line. Though nature has not endowed us with great strength or speed, though we lack wings to fly and powerful jaws to bite, though our senses are muted in comparison with those of other animals, we nevertheless have become a hugely successful species. What makes us unique and constitutes the foundation of our success is our intellectual capacity and the manifold cultural adaptations we have invented out of our creative imaginations. Our intelligence enables us to define our evolutionary destinies. We needn't wait for natural selection to slowly shift our adaptations to match our environments. We change ourselves and simultaneously construct our environments, all in the time it takes to formulate a thought or to express an idea.

This process began when *Homo habilis* first visualized a sharp, durable edge within a dull, round rock. A few carefully placed, sharp blows with another stone, and the visualized edge became an actual one, capable of cutting, slicing, or chopping more effectively than any of the bodily "tools" nature had given us. In that instant our ancestors had evolved the equivalent of more powerful, piercing canine teeth, razor-sharp slicing claws, and rock-solid fists.

In a sense, all human history is based on the Oldowan stone-tool industry, and all human achievement has been but a series of variations on the theme established 2.5 million years ago on the African savanna. The Acheulean hand-axe of *Homo erectus,* the Levallois and Mousterian industries associated with anatomically archaic varieties of our own species, *Homo sapiens,* and even cave paintings and barbed harpoons, domesticated plants and animals, socially stratified societies and walled cities—in fact, civilization itself—all these things are mere variations on the theme established in the Oldowan tools of the Lower Paleolithic. Throughout our stay on earth, human beings have per-

FIGURE 16.1

The space shuttle Columbia *blasts off on its maiden voyage, April 12, 1981.*
(Courtesy of NASA)

ceived the need and possessed the intellectual capacity to develop new ways of gathering resources, manipulating the environment, recording and transmitting information, organizing labor—in essence, of living our lives. And cultural adaptation continues today to distinguish us from all other life on the planet.

From Stone Tools to Star Trek

Consider this example. On April 12, 1981, at 7:00 A.M., the first space shuttle, the *Columbia,* was successfully launched from pad 39A at the Kennedy Space Center, Cape Canaveral, Florida (Figure 16.1). It is probably not an exaggeration when writers describe this piece of U.S. space exploration hardware, this "artifact" of the late twentieth century, as the "single most complex machine ever built by man" (Melvyn Smith 1985, 120). The shuttle orbiter weighed 75,000 kg (165,000 lb), had 49 rocket engines, 4 on-line computers and 1 backup, 23 antennas, sophisticated fuel cells to provide electrical energy for all the machinery onboard, and millions of interworking, individual parts (all statistics from Gurney and Forte 1988). The entire shuttle, consisting of the delta-wing orbiter plus booster rockets, weighed 2 million kg (4.5 million lb).

At launch, the booster rocket engines developed 3 million kg (6.5 million lb) of thrust. In an achingly slow upward push against the powerful pull of the earth, the shuttle slipped through gravity's grasp and cleared the height of the 92-m (300-ft) launch tower in 6 seconds. At 12 minutes into its maiden

FIGURE 16.2

Space exploration, one of the truly monumental undertakings of twentieth-century civilization, has provided a unique perspective for all of us inhabitants of the earth. (Courtesy of NASA)

voyage, the spacecraft was orbiting the earth. This first shuttle reached an altitude of 280 km (175 mi), compared to the standard altitude of commercial jets of 9.6 km (6 mi), traveling at 28,000 km per hour (17,500 mph), compared to the standard commercial jet speed of under 960 km per hour (600 mph).

Though the *Columbia* carried no payload and circled the earth only 36 times in a little more than 2 days, its successful flight ushered in a new era of space exploration that included the deployment of satellites for investigating the earth, its weather patterns, its resource concentrations, and even the effects of our own civilization on the ecological balance of the planet. The shuttle also enabled the launch of the defective Hubble space telescope—and its later in-space repair—which is adding immeasurably to our understanding of the universe. Recently, the shuttle carried into orbit a large section of a planned, multinational space station that will allow human beings to live and work together in space over extended periods, providing all of humanity with the ultimate "bird's-eye" view of our home planet and a small window into the infinite universe.

The shuttle paved the way for regular and almost routine return to space. Shuttle launches and safe returns are front-page news today only when their missions are largely nostalgic, carrying aging astronauts like Senator John Glenn for just one more great ride. And although tragedies like the *Challenger* disaster have occurred, the shuttle program has also led to triumphs both small and large—of the human will to expand beyond our own planet. The space program represents some of the first faltering steps our species has taken to become not just inhabitants of the small planet that gave us life, but citizens of the universe.

In all of our achievements in space, we have evolved literally beyond gravity. We have escaped the confines of our own planet, taking our environment with us. We have even walked on the surface of another world, to look back at our planet and recognize, perhaps for the first time in the history of our species, the fragility and the unity of our home (Figure 16.2).

All of these space accomplishments have taken place in little more than 50 years. Humans did not evolve an ability to live in the cold, dark airless vacuum of space in that short period of time. This accomplishment is entirely a result of our ability to think. Given a few more generations, perhaps our children's children will be exploring farther into our universe and actually fulfilling the fictional promise of Captain James T. Kirk and Captain Jean-Luc Picard of the Starship(s) *Enterprise:* "to boldly go where no one has gone before."

Many Pathways

The heaviest Oldowan tools weigh little more than half a kilogram and took just a few blows with another rock to create. The space shuttle orbiter weighs 75,000 kg and took years to create from its millions of constituent parts. But the shuttle, as complex as it is, is simply a tool, a point along a continuum of complexity that began with Oldowan. The simple stone tool took our hominid ancestors where they had not gone before as surely as has the space shuttle, our computers, and all the other tools we have invented to allow us more effectively to feed ourselves, provide for our physical necessities, and explore the world and ourselves.

I am comparing Oldowan tools and the space shuttle because, though incredibly different in scale, they bespeak a common bond between our modern civilization and our ancient hominid forebears. But this implies no inevitable sequence of change, no inexorable "march of progress" from ancient hominids to Western society. When in this book we have looked back along our evolutionary pathway, we have seen that the pathway is, in actuality, made up of many intersecting and diverging avenues. There is no single highway of change leading inevitably to Western civilization, no necessary trail from stone tools to spacecraft. Our society represents merely one point along one of many possible pathways, one of many possible modes of adaptation, not better or more "evolved" than any others, and in no way an inevitable outcome of cultural evolution.

This is a difficult, but crucial, point to make. Many of us in the West view history as an endless upward spiral of material progress, an inevitable pathway of "improvement" of the human condition leading necessarily to us, to Western civilization. We also often view history as teaching moral lessons—history as a tale of good guys versus bad guys, with the good guys (that would be us) always coming out on top and their destiny being realized.

The belief that all of human prehistory and history followed a single, inevitable pathway—the perspective of **orthogenesis**—provides the philosophical underpinning for a hypothesis of **unilineal evolution** (see the discussion of cultural evolutionist Lewis Henry Morgan in Chapter 2). The view of the universality of cultural evolutionary sequences may be a popular one, but it is not the only view. The ancient Egyptians discussed in Chapter 13, for example, perceived history quite differently. As Egyptologist Barry Kemp

(1991) points out, the Egyptians saw history not as a trajectory leading somewhere, but as a constant, ordered, linear series of transitions from pharaoh to pharaoh. History, for the ancient Egyptians, leads nowhere in particular, but proceeds along a constant line of kingship. When Egyptians wrote their own history, there was no search for meaning or pattern, no saga of a destiny fulfilled. For them, history simply was a list of kings, a succession of rulers.

Anthropologists view history differently. History for us is played out on an evolutionary stage where the only direction is that of change and adaptation. We view the ancient past neither as a continual parade of divine and semidivine leaders nor as a parable of the inevitability of material progress. We see a unique series of winding cultural pathways reflecting the myriad ways by which people adapted to their environment and constructed a way of life.

If a pattern leading to increasing technological complexity has been one of the cultural evolutionary pathways followed by our species and navigated in this book, it must be remembered that this has been neither the only nor the inevitable avenue traced by human beings. The trajectories seen in this book exhibit tremendous cultural diversity. Such diversity in the evolutionary pathways followed by human beings may be a key to our species' survival.

"Diversity" has become an American buzzword nowadays in an ongoing argument about what our nation has become and what it should be. Often, it refers to so-called racial diversity in neighborhoods, schools, and businesses. But I mean the term to signify variation on a broader geographic and temporal scale, a worldwide and "timewide" diversity of human cultural adaptation, from Arctic hunters to tropical rain-forest horticulturists, from desert wanderers to seafaring islanders, from megalith-building farmers to grassland hunters, from urban nation-states to tribal societies. It may take the collective wisdom of the cultures of all these people to ensure the survival of the species, ironically at the very time when cultural homogenization—the Westernization of the world—seems to be overtaking us.

I began this epilogue by likening the human story to a lengthy journey. Now, at last, in this book we have reached a milepost in our investigation. We have literally caught up with ourselves on the human evolutionary pathway; we have reached our present location on the trail. We can gaze back, as we have in this book, along the tortuous, serendipitous route and in the distance see, if only dimly, our ancient evolutionary ancestors. Ahead, we can imagine our species racing forward to some unknown, unfathomable point on the horizon of our future. Though the twists and turns will almost certainly bring us to a point that anthropologists have never even considered, we can all be certain of one thing: The journey will take us where no one has gone before.

KEY TERMS

orthogenesis   unilineal evolution

Glossary

Abejas phase The period of time in the **Tehuacán** Valley in highland Mexico from 5400 to 4300 B.P. Characterized by increased sedentism and the first appearance of domesticated maize, beans, and squash.

absolute date Any date where a year or range of years can be applied to a site or artifact, as opposed to a **relative date,** where only a chronological order can be established.

accelerator mass spectrometry (AMS) A technique in radiocarbon dating in which the actual number of ^{14}C atoms (or a proportion of them) is counted, as opposed to the traditional method, which measures the amount of radioactivity given off by the sample.

Acheulean handaxe Symmetrical stone tool of the later **Lower Paleolithic.** The bifacially flaked, teardrop-shaped, all-purpose handaxe dates to as early as 1.4 million years ago in Africa. There, and after about 1.0 million B.P. in Europe, the handaxe was manufactured by members of the species *Homo erectus.*

adaptation A mode or strategy for survival. An adaptation can be a physical characteristic; for example, the thick fur of a polar bear is a physical adaptation for life in the Arctic. Adaptation can also be a cultural behavior; for instance, the material culture of the Inuit people (Eskimos), including harpoons, igloos, parkas, and dog sleds, are their invented, cultural adaptations to life under very cold environmental conditions.

adapted The state of being biologically designed or culturally prepared to survive in a given environment.

Adena A burial-mound-building culture centered in the Ohio River valley. Beginning about 3,000 years ago, this culture developed at the **chiefdom** level of sociopolitical integration, often building impressive tombs for its chiefs.

Ajalpán phase The period of time in the **Tehuacán** Valley in highland Mexico from 3500 to 2850 B.P. Characterized by increased sedentism and increasing reliance on domesticated maize, beans, and squash, though still more than half of the diet consisted of wild foods.

Ajuerdo phase The period of time in the **Tehuacán** Valley in highland Mexico from 12,000 to 9000 B.P. Human groups in the valley lived in small, nomadic microbands of fewer than 10 people, subsisting on wild plant and animal foods.

altricial The condition of being born at an immature stage of development. The term originated in ornithology to describe bird species in which hatchlings are entirely dependent on one or both parents for all of their needs for an extended period. Used here to describe a similar circumstance in hominid species, both ancient and modern.

anatomically modern *Homo sapiens* Human beings anatomically indistinguishable from those living today. They are found in the paleoanthropological record dating to about 100,000 years ago.

Ancestral Puebloan A prehistoric culture centered in the Four Corners region of the American Southwest. The Anasazi sometimes constructed large and impressive structures that housed the population of the village. Formerly called Anasazi.

anthropological linguistics The subfield of anthropology that studies language.

anthropology The study of humanity. A broad social science with varied foci on human biological and cultural adaptations, human origins, biological and cultural evolution, and modern cultures.

arboreal Life in the trees. Primates, for the most part (our species is a notable exception), possess an arboreal adaptation.

archaeologist A scientist who studies human beings through the analysis of the material remains of their behavior—that is, the artifacts they made and used and that have been preserved. Archaeologists often focus on human cultural evolution.

Archaic The chronological period in the New World that follows the **Paleoindian** period, begins at the end of the Pleistocene, and represents a period of cultural adaptation to the new, postglacial environment by Native Americans.

archaic *Homo sapiens* Extinct varieties of humanity that share much in common with modern *Homo sapiens* or **anatomically modern *Homo sapiens*** but that commonly retain primitive skeletal features and possess a somewhat smaller mean cranial capacity than do modern people. The Neandertals are the best-known archaic variety of the human race. Also called **premodern *Homo sapiens.***

artifact Anything manufactured by a human being or human ancestor, but usually a portable object like a stone spearpoint or a clay pot, as distinguished from larger, more complex archaeological **features.**

artificial selection   The process used in the **domestication** and refinement of plants and animals by which human beings select which members of a species will live and produce offspring. Humans make such decisions on the basis of their needs or desires concerning the form or behavior of the species—for example, plants that produce larger seeds, animals that produce woollier coats, or animals that produce more milk.

association   The spatial relationships among archaeological **artifacts, ecofacts,** and **features.** Objects found in proximity to each other are said to be in association.

Aurignacian   A lithic tool technology associated with anatomically modern human beings in Europe dating from 34,000 to 27,000 years ago. Includes long, narrow blade tools.

australopithecine   Any member of the genus *Australopithecus,* including several species: *anamensis, afarensis, garhi, africanus, robustus, boisei,* and *aethiopicus.* The oldest members of the genus date back to at least 4.2 million years ago. The genus became extinct by 1 million years ago and was characterized by an ape-sized brain but also by the modern human behavioral trait of bipedal locomotion.

backed blade   A stone blade tool in which one edge has been dulled, or "backed," so it can more readily be held in the hand during use.

barray   Large reservoir constructed by the ancient Khmer people in their elaborate ceremonial centers such as Angkor Wat and Angkor Thom. Initially resulting from sandstone quarrying for the construction materials for Khmer temples, these large depressions filled with water and probably served as reservoirs.

basicranium   The bones of the base of the cranium. Because the soft parts of hominid anatomy involved in the production of sound are connected to the base of the skull, the basicranium is a crucial part of the anatomy when assessing the ability of human ancestors to produce human speech.

Bayon   The spectacular temple complex in the center of the ancient Khmer city of Angkor Thom that is covered with images of Hindu gods, bas-reliefs, columns, and colonnades.

Beringia, or **Bering Land Bridge**   A broad piece of land, more than 1,500 km (1,000 mi) across, that connected northeastern Asia with northwestern North America during periods of sea-level depression in the Pleistocene. People living in Asia walked east across the land bridge into the lands of the Western Hemisphere at least 15,000 years ago and possibly earlier.

bipedal locomotion   The ability to walk on two feet. With a few notable exceptions (such as some dinosaurs and birds), the hominids are the only creatures who habitually and efficiently walk on two feet.

blade   A long, thin stone flake, commonly twice as long as it is wide, that represents an efficient use of stone, producing a high proportion of edge for the amount (weight) of stone used.

brachiating   Moving through the trees by swinging, arm over arm. Many primates are expert brachiators.

burin   A sharp and durable stone tool used in engraving to etch out thin slivers of antler or bone, which then were modified to make awls and needles.

C3 pathway   The photosynthetic process employed by most trees, whereby a radioactive isotope of carbon—^{13}C—is differentially filtered out.

C4 pathway   The photosynthetic process employed by most grasses and sedges, whereby a radioactive isotope of carbon—^{13}C—is more readily used than in plants that follow the **C3 pathway.**

calibration curve   Curve resulting from the graphing of dendrochronologically derived dates for an extensive series of tree rings and the carbon dates determined for each of those same rings.

calvarium   The top part of a skull minus the lower jaw (mandible) and facial bones.

camelid   A large, ruminant animal, including bachtrian and dromedary camels in the Old World and llamas, alpacas, guanacos, and vicuñas in the New World.

Capsian   A culture in northwestern Africa dating to after 10,000 B.P. and characterized by hunting of wild sheep, collecting of shellfish and snails, and harvesting of wild grains.

carbon dating   See **radiocarbon dating.**

carrying capacity   The number of organisms a given region or habitat can support without degrading the environment.

catastrophist   A person who believes that the current appearance of the earth can be explained best as having resulted from a series of natural catastrophes—for example, floods and volcanoes. Catastrophism was quite popular prior to the nineteenth century and lent support to the claim of a recent age for the earth.

central place   As used in the field of cultural geography, the geographic focal point of a political entity. A large city or ceremonial center with religious structures often are central places for **states** or **chiefdoms.**

cereals Plants, especially grasses, that produce starchy grains. These were among the first domesticated foods produced during the **Neolithic.**

Châtelperronian A lithic technology that includes the use of blades and appears to be intermediate in form and time between **Mousterian** and **Aurignacian.** Associated with some late populations of Neandertals following contact with modern *Homo sapiens.*

Chavin A distinctive art style that developed in western South America beginning about 3,000 years ago. The religious iconography of Chavin seems to have served as a unifying influence, setting the stage for the later development of geographically broad empires.

chiefdom A level of sociopolitical integration more complex than the tribe but less complex than the **state.** The social system is ranked, not **egalitarian.** Individuals are placed in a hierarchy of power and prestige. Chiefdoms are less rigidly structured than state societies, and a chief's power is less than that of a king or a pharaoh.

chinampas Artificial islands in lakes and swamps produced by the Aztecs of central Mexico for intensive farming.

city-state A political entity characteristic of some early civilizations, especially in **Mesopotamia.** A central population center dominates the surrounding hinterlands. The wealth of the countryside flows into the city, where it is concentrated in the hands of the elite classes.

civilization As used here, cultures exhibiting social stratification, a formal government, labor and craft specialization, a food surplus that supports a political and/or religious elite, monumental construction, and a system of record keeping.

Clovis A **fluted point** type of the Paleoindians. Large, laurel-leaf-shaped stone blades exhibiting a channel, or "flute" (as in a fluted column), on both faces to aid in hafting the stone point onto a wooden shaft. The channel begins at the base and generally extends from one-third to no more than one-half the length of the point. Clovis points date from about 11,500 to 10,000 B.P. (Compare to **Folsom.**)

complex foraging A system of hunting animals and gathering wild plants in which subsistence is focused on a few highly productive resources. These foods are collected and stored, allowing for a more sedentary settlement system. (Compare to **simple foragers.**)

complex societies Societies organized beyond the level of the household, family, or local community. Complex societies exhibit differences in social status, political power, and wealth.

Cordilleran The Pleistocene ice mass in North America centered in the Rocky Mountains.

core In stone-tool manufacturing, the nucleus from which flakes or blades are removed. In manufacturing a core tool like an **Acheulean handaxe,** the stone nucleus becomes the tool. In a core-and-blade or core-and-flake technology, the core is merely the source for numerous sharp flakes or blades that are then used as is or modified into tools.

cortex The exterior surface or rind of a **core,** usually removed in the process of stone-tool manufacturing.

courtyard groups Clusters of separate residential structures in **Hohokam** villages surrounding a common area or courtyard. Most individual villages consisted of multiple courtyard groups. Each courtyard group consisted of from 2 to 10 family residences.

Coxcatlán phase The period of time in the **Tehuacán** Valley in highland Mexico from 7000 to 5400 B.P. that is characterized by a reliance on wild foods.

cranial suture The lines of connection between cranial bones, which appear as a squiggly line on both the interior and the exterior surfaces of the skull. Sutures progressively disappear with age and can be used to provide a general estimate for age at death.

cranium The bones of the head and face (excluding the lower jaw).

creationist One who believes that the universe, the earth, life, and humanity are the creation of an all-powerful god.

culture The invented, taught, and learned patterns of behavior of human groups. The extrasomatic (beyond the body or beyond the biological) means of adaptation of a human group.

cuneiform An early form of written records in Mesopotamia, involving the impression of standardized symbols on wet clay. Dating to close to 6,000 years ago, cuneiform is the earliest writing in the world.

cylinder seal Mesopotamian system of impressing symbolic notation onto wet clay with a marked cylinder.

deciduous dentition   The baby teeth.

deffufa   Monumental mud-brick towers built by the inhabitants of the ancient Nubian civilization of Kerma located south of the third cataract of the Nile in modern Sudan. Kerma dates to more than 3,500 years ago.

Denali Complex   A lithic technology seen in the Arctic and consisting of wedge-shaped cores, microblades, bifacial knives, and burins. Dating to about 10,000 years ago, several features of the Denali Complex are reminiscent of elements of older complexes in northeastern Asia, particularly that of Dyuktai Cave.

dendrochronology   Tree-ring dating. By placing a tree section found at an archaeological site within a **master sequence** of tree-ring widths through time, the year when the tree died or was cut down can be determined and associated with the site.

descent with modification   The notion that each successive generation can be modified slightly through evolutionary processes; a fundamental feature of biological evolution.

diaphysis   The shaft of a long bone. On either end of the diaphysis is an **epiphysis.**

diastema   A gap between the teeth of both the mandible (lower jaw) and the maxilla (upper jaw). The large canine teeth of apes fit into the diastemas of their opposing jaws when those jaws are closed.

DNA (deoxyribonucleic acid)   The genetic code; the genetic instructions for each life-form on the planet.

domestication   Through **artificial selection,** the production of new species of plants and animals that owe their existence to human intervention. Some domesticated species become so highly specialized to the demands of human beings that they can no longer survive and propagate without human assistance.

ecofact   An element found in an archaeological context that exhibits human activity but that was not made by people and so is not, strictly speaking, an **artifact.** Burned wood in a fireplace, butchered animal bone in a trash pit, and charred seeds or nuts in a midden are all ecofacts.

egalitarian   Social systems in which all members of the same age/sex category are equal in the sense that they all possess the same wealth, social standing, and political influence.

einkorn   A variety of wheat, *Tripsicum monococcum,* that possesses hulled grains and was an important domesticate in the Neolithic. Today it is not a significant agricultural crop. (Compare to **emmer.**)

electron spin resonance dating (ESR)   A radiation-damage dating technique based on measurement of the buildup of electrons in crystalline materials. It can be applied to sites more than a few thousand years old. The upper limit of the technique is estimated to be more than 10 million years.

El Riego phase   The period of time in the **Tehuacán** Valley in highland Mexico from 9000 to 7000 B.P., which was characterized by a subsistence focus on wild plants, including squash, beans, chili peppers, amaranth, and avocado. During this period, people traveled in microbands for part of the year but gathered in macrobands in the spring and summer months.

emmer   A variety of wheat, *Tripsicum turgidum,* that became the primary stock of early agricultural wheat. It is the source of cultivated wheat in the modern world. (Compare to **einkorn.**)

enamel hypoplasia   A medical condition affecting the outside layers of teeth. Horizontal imperfections develop on the enamel in individuals who have experienced malnutrition during their early years.

endocast   A mold of the brain produced naturally when sediment enters the skull and then mineralizes. Also produced artificially by coating the inside of the skull with a latex-based material. Endocasts can exhibit features of the exterior surface of the brain.

epiphyseal fusion   The **epiphyses** of each long bone join to the **diaphysis** during physical maturation. The age of death of a juvenile individual can be assessed by reference to the degree of epiphyseal fusion exhibited.

epiphysis (pl., *epiphyses*)   The long-bone endcap. The epiphyses join at the ends of the **diaphysis** of each long bone.

epistemology   The study of knowledge; how you know what you know.

erosion   The disintegration and transportation of geological material by wind, water, or ice.

ethnoarchaeology   The archaeological study of a living group of people that often focuses on the processes by which human behavior becomes translated into the archaeological record.

ethnographer   A cultural anthropologist who lives among a group of people or a cultural group and interacts with them daily, often for an extended period of time, observing their behavior.

ethnographic present   The ethnographic present includes that period of time when Western people have been in contact with, studying, and writing about traditional cultures.

ethnology   The comparative study of culture. Ethnologists study human behavior cross-culturally, looking for similarities and differences in how people behave: how they raise their children, how they treat elders, how they organize their labor, and so forth.

evolution   The systematic change through time of biological organisms or human cultural systems.

experimental replication   The reproduction, under laboratory conditions, of facsimiles of archaeological artifacts. A process employed to analyze ancient technology.

faunal assemblage   The animal bones found at a site and the species represented by those bones.

feature   The combination of artifacts and/or ecofacts at a site, reflecting a location where some human activity took place. Features include fireplaces, middens, burials, cooking hearths, activity areas, and buildings. Also defined as nonportable, complex artifacts.

femur   The upper leg bone.

Fertile Crescent   A crescent-shaped region extending from the Mediterranean coast of modern Israel, Lebanon, and Syria, north into the Zagros Mountains and then south toward the Persian Gulf (see Figure 11.3), marked by an abundance of wild cereal grain at the beginning of the **Holocene Epoch.** Not coincidentally, this region is where some of the world's first domestication of plants took place.

fire-cracked rock   Rock that has been heated to a high temperature in, for example, a fireplace or hearth, and that has fractured as a result. Large quantities of fire-cracked rock in a given location are often diagnostic of an archaeological site.

fission-track dating   A radiation-damage dating technique that measures the age of an artifact as a function of the amount of physical damage in the form of damage tracks left in a material by radioactive decay.

flake   A stone fragment removed from a **core** by the blow of a **hammerstone,** antler baton, or pressure flaker. The flake can be discarded, used as is, or further modified for use as a specific tool.

fluted point   Projectile point made by Paleoindians in the New World between 11,500 and 10,000 B.P. Exhibits a distinctive channel, or "flute" (as in a fluted column), on both faces. These channels aided in hafting the spearpoint onto its wooden shaft. The two major forms of fluted point are **Clovis** and **Folsom.**

Folsom   A **fluted point** type of the Paleoindians. Generally smaller than **Clovis** points, Folsom points are also later in time, dating to after 11,000 B.P. Clovis points have been found in association with the bones of extinct elephants, whereas Folsom points have been found in association with the bones of bison. Folsom points are fluted, with the channels commonly extending nearly the entire length of the point.

foraging   A subsistence system based on the collection of wild foods, including any combination of hunting wild game, gathering wild plants, fishing, and shellfish collecting.

foramen magnum   Large hole at the base or back of the skull through which veins, arteries, and nerves pass. The location of the foramen magnum in a fossil skull is an indicator of how the skull was attached to the vertebral column and, by inference, the form of locomotion employed by the creature.

foraminifera   Microorganisms used in the study of ancient environments. By measuring the ratio of ^{16}O to ^{18}O in foraminifera fossils, the amount of the earth's surface covered in ice at any given point in time can be indirectly determined.

Funan   The name given to the earliest civilization in southeast Asia, established in Cambodia during the first century A.D. by merchants from India.

gene flow   The movement and exchange of genetic material among populations of a species through interbreeding.

genetic replacement model   The view that anatomically modern *Homo sapiens* evolved from premodern humans in one place at one time (usually Africa between 100,000 and 200,000 years ago) and that by interbreeding with already existing premodern humans, especially in Asia and Europe, modern genes spread through populations of premoderns, ultimately causing them to become anatomically modern as well.

Geometric Kebaran   Pre-**Neolithic** culture in the Middle East, dating to the period 14,500–12,500 B.P. Located in the moist Mediterranean woodlands of the central **Levant** and extending into the margins of the Negev and Sinai Deserts and across southern Jordan, subsistence was based on **foraging.**

glacial   Period of ice advance during the **Pleistocene epoch.** Glacials generally last many thousands of years. Cold glacials were interrupted by equally long warmer periods called **interglacials.**

glacier   A massive body of ice that, through a number of processes, can expand and move.

glume   The case in which an individual cereal grain is enclosed.

gracile   Lightly constructed, as referring to the overall appearance of a hominid skeleton. Modern humans are gracile, and when the term is applied to the fossils of extinct hominids it is in reference to their appearance relative to anatomically modern human beings. Bones that are more massive than those of modern humans are said to be **robust.**

grave goods   Cultural materials placed into a grave, sometimes in a conscious attempt to provide the deceased with items it is believed are needed in the afterlife.

Gravettian   Toolmaking tradition of the **Upper Paleolithic,** characterized by the production of small **blades** and denticulate knives. Dated from 27,000 to 21,000 B.P.

Halafian   A culture in Mesopotamia dating from 7500 to 6700 B.P. Halafian sites generally are small farming villages.

half-life   The amount of time it takes for half of the radioactive **isotope** in a given sample to decay into a stable form. The half-life of radiocarbon, for example, is 5,730 years and that of radioactive potassium is 1.3 billion years.

Hamburgian   A culture of the northern European **Upper Paleolithic.**

hammerstone   In stone toolmaking, the lithic tool used in percussion flaking to remove flakes or blades from a core or to detach additional flakes from flakes or blades.

hang-t'u   The Chinese term for stamped or pounded and compacted earth used to make structures.

Harris lines   Longitudinal cracks located at the ends of long bones; indicative of dietary stress during physical development.

Hassunan   A culture in **Mesopotamia** dating from 8000 to 7200 B.P. that was characterized by small farming villages where subsistence was based on the growing of wheat, barley, peas, and lentils. Hunting supplemented the diet.

Hoabinhian   Southeast Asian **mesolithic** stone-tool tradition based on the manufacture of tools from chipped pebbles.

Hohokam   A culture in the American Southwest centered in southern Arizona. The Hohokam people constructed irrigation canals to water the fields in which they grew maize, beans, and squash.

Holocene epoch   The recent and current geological epoch. The Holocene followed the Pleistocene and represents a break with glacial climates.

hominid   Any creature believed to be in the direct human line, a member of the taxonomic family Hominidae. **Bipedal locomotion** is the single most salient characteristic of the hominids.

Hopewell   Burial-mound-building culture centered in the Ohio River valley. Beginning about 2,400 years ago, this culture developed at the **chiefdom** level of sociopolitical integration, sometimes building impressive tombs for their chiefs. Hopewell is generally later than **Adena.**

humerus   The upper arm bone.

hypothesis   A proposed explanation for some phenomenon that may be derived initially from empirical observation of the phenomenon by the process called induction. A hypothesis must be tested; predictions are deduced about what new data must be found if the hypothesis is to be supported. When data are found that contradict these predictions, the hypothesis is rejected or modified.

Iberomaurusians   A culture in northwestern Africa dating to after 16,000 B.P. that inhabited the coastal plain and interior of modern Tunisia and Morocco. Subsistence was based on hunting wild cattle, gazelle, hartebeest, and Barbary sheep and collecting marine mollusks.

ice-free corridor (or **McKenzie corridor**)   A proposed route of safe passage between the farthest-west extent of the **Laurentide** ice field and the farthest-east extent of the **Cordilleran** glacier. Paleoindians may have traveled down this corridor from the western Arctic into the heartland of America.

ilium   The upper blade of the pelvis.

impact wear   Distinctive damage scars on stone tools that can be experimentally shown to have resulted from the tool's use as a projectile.

innominate   The left or right side of the pelvis that consists of the **ilium,** the **ischium,** and the pubis.

interglacial   A period during the **Pleistocene** when glacial ice melted and temperature ameliorated. Interglacials lasted for thousands of years and were preceded and followed by **glacials.**

interstadial   A short period during a glacial when glacial ice melted and temperature increased.

ischium The bottom rear portion of the **innominate** bone of the pelvis.

isotope A variety of an element's atomic form. Isotopes are distinguished by the number of neutrons in their atomic nuclei. Some isotopes are unstable and decay into other forms; these are said to be radioactive. Some radioactive isotopes can be used in dating paleontological or archaeological material.

Kabuh Formation A geological formation in Java dating to after 800,000 years ago that has been the source of several hominid fossils belonging to the species *Homo erectus.*

K/Ar dating Potassium/argon dating. The **half-life** of radioactive potassium has been measured as 1.3 billion years. Since potassium is an abundant element in the earth's crust and since argon collects in rock solely as a result of the decay of radioactive potassium, this technique is widely applicable.

Karim Shahirian Pre-**Neolithic** culture located in the foothills of the Zagros Mountains in modern Turkey.

Khmer Local name given to the civilization of Southeast Asia dating to after A.D. 800. The great temple cities of Angkor Thom and Angkor Wat represent the culmination of this civilization at around A.D. 1000.

kiva A structure, usually round, used in religious ceremonies by Native American societies in the Southwest. Most kivas are relatively small, but so-called Great Kivas are enormous. Casa Rinconada in Chaco Canyon, for example, is nearly 20 m (63.5 ft) across.

knapper One who makes stone tools. To *knapp* is to make stone tools through the application of percussion and pressure.

Knossos An enormous and impressive site representing the culmination of Minoan civilization. The temple at Knossos was built beginning in 3880 B.P. and at its height covered an area of about 20,000 m² and had 1,000 rooms built up to three stories and, in some sections, four stories high.

Kush The Egyptian name for the land south of their territory. Kush began at the first cataract of the Nile in southern Egypt and extended to the sixth cataract, near the modern Sudanese city of Khartoum.

lacustrine Having to do with lakes.

Lake Forest Archaic An **Archaic** culture of eastern North America centered in, though not restricted to, the region of the Great Lakes. Lake Forest people exploited the food resources of the large lakes of eastern North America.

Lapita A pottery style known from the inhabited Pacific Islands. The movement of people from the western to the eastern Pacific can be traced by the presence and spread of Lapita pottery.

Laurentide The massive continental ice sheet of **Pleistocene** North America, centered in central northeastern Canada.

legume A large family of flowering plants, all of which produce fruits that grow in the form of a pod that splits along its seams when mature and opens to reveal the seeds. Garden peas, snap beans, lima beans, lentils, and chickpeas are all legumes domesticated during the **Neolithic.**

Levallois Stone tool technology involving the production of consistently shaped flakes from carefully prepared **cores.** Levallois technology is associated with archaic forms of *Homo sapiens.*

Levant The name applied to the areas along the eastern shore of the Mediterranean, including present-day Greece, Turkey, Syria, Lebanon, Israel, and Egypt.

Linienbandkeramik (LBK) An early **Neolithic** culture of central Europe dating to about 6500 B.P. The subsistence base was domesticated **emmer** wheat, barley, and pulses.

lintels Horizontal cross-members of the Stonehenge monument. The 30 lintels at Stonehenge rest on top of and connect the 30 upright **sarsens.**

littoral Related to the seashore.

logistical collecting A settlement-subsistence strategy that involves the movement of a group in a fixed seasonal round. The food collectors know when resources are available and where during the course of a year. They plan the movements of their settlements to coincide with the availability of food resources in their territory.

Lower Paleolithic Period from 2.5 million years ago to 250,000 years ago that encompasses the stone tool industries of *Homo habilis* and *Homo erectus.*

luminescence dating Determining the age of an object by releasing as light the energy it has accumulated since a fixed point in time. The amount of light it emits in this process is directly proportional to its age. Light (**optically stimulated luminescence**) or heat (**thermoluminescence**) can be used to release this energy.

Lung-shan A Chinese culture that followed the **Neolithic Yang-shao.** Dated to 5000 B.P., Lung-shan sites are larger, with evidence of substantial **hang-t'u** construction. Lung-shan cemeteries have produced clear evidence of a socioeconomically stratified society. Lung-shan laid the foundation for China's first complex state, the Shang.

Magdelanian **Upper Paleolithic** culture in Europe dating from 16,000 to 11,000 B.P. Known from sites primarily in France and Spain, Magdelanian material culture included finely made barbed harpoons, carved decorative objects, and cave paintings.

Maglemosian An early **Mesolithic** culture of Europe adapted to a forest and lakeside environment. The famous site of Star Carr is a Maglemosian site.

mandible The lower jaw. (Compare to **maxilla.**)

Maritime Archaic An Archaic-period culture of northeastern North America centered along the coast of northern New England and the Canadian Maritime provinces. The subsistence focus was on the sea, fishing and hunting sea mammals. Burials with elaborate grave goods mark the Maritime Archaic.

mastaba Mud-brick structures built over the tombs of a developing elite in Egypt before the pharaohs. They became larger through time, were stacked on top of each other, and ultimately evolved into the pyramid tomb emblematic of ancient Egyptian civilization.

master sequence The regional pattern of yearly variation in tree-ring width. The master sequence for the American West extends back close to 11,000 years ago. When an archaeological tree-ring section can be placed within the master sequence, it can be dated directly, and this date can be associated with the archaeological site at which it was found.

Mast Forest Archaic An Archaic-period culture of northeastern North America centered in central and southern New England. Subsistence focus was on the interior forest of New England, especially on the resources of the mast forest: nut foods such as acorn, hickory, chestnut, and walnut, and animals, especially deer.

mattock A digging tool with a working blade set at right angles to the handle. Antler mattocks have been found in European **Mesolithic** sites such as Star Carr.

maxilla The upper jaw. (Compare to **mandible.**)

McKenzie corridor See **ice-free corridor.**

megafauna Very large animals; commonly used to describe the large, now-extinct herbivores of the Pleistocene world.

megaliths Large stone monuments. The Megalithic culture erected thousands of these monuments beginning more than 5,000 years ago. Stonehenge is the most famous of the Megalithic monuments.

Melanesia Islands located north of New Guinea in the western Pacific.

Mesolithic The culture period after the Paleolithic and before the **Neolithic;** a period of the proliferation of many regional adaptations and an explosion of local cultural diversity.

Mesopotamia The land between the Tigris and Euphrates Rivers in modern Iraq. The world's first cities and complex civilization developed in Mesopotamia.

microbands Small cohabiting groups, commonly 10 to 15 people, who move together seasonally and nomadically.

microblade A very small stone blade, often with very sharp cutting edges. Groups of microblades often were set into wooden, bone, or antler handles.

microlith A very small stone tool.

Micronesia Small islands in the western Pacific, east of New Guinea.

midden An archaeological **feature** that consists of a refuse heap. A preserved pile of trash, often food remains.

Middle Paleolithic The Middle Stone Age, the period after the **Lower Paleolithic** and before the **Upper Paleolithic.** Covers the span from 250,000 to 40,000 years ago and includes the cultures of archaic and modern varieties of human beings.

Minoan The name given by Sir Arthur Evans to the early European civilization that evolved on the island of Crete. The temple at **Knossos** is the best-known manifestation of this culture.

Miocene epoch The period of time from 25 million years ago to 5 million years ago. Forests were more extensive during the Miocene than they are today. A broad array of **arboreally** adapted ape species thrived during this epoch; most became extinct at the end of the Miocene, when the forests diminished in geographical extent.

mitochondrial DNA (mtDNA) Genetic material located in the mitochondria of cells. Analysis of mtDNA has proven useful in assessing evolutionary relationships among existing species.

mobiliary art Art that is portable. Mobiliary art made during the **Upper Paleolithic** includes **Venus figurines,** animal carvings, and geometrically incised bone and antler.

Mogollon A prehistoric culture located in the American Southwest, centered in the uplands of New Mexico and northeastern Mexico. The Mogollon people grew maize, beans, and squash, relying mostly on rainfall agriculture.

monumental works Large-scale communal construction projects characteristic of complex societies.

morphology Literally, the study of form. An analysis of the shape and form of skeletons or artifacts.

mosaic Environments characterized by patches of different habitats rather than a single, homogeneous habitat. It is believed that the first hominids lived in a mosaic environment characterized by a mixture of woodlands and savannas.

Mousterian The stone-tool tradition of the Neandertals and early anatomically modern human beings. A core-and-flake technology in which a series of different, standardized tool types were produced from stone flakes struck from cores.

Movius Line Geographic division, running through central India, that marks the break between the manufacture of handaxes by *Homo erectus* populations to the west and less symmetrical chopping tools to the east.

multiregional (or **regional continuity**) **model** The view that anatomically modern *Homo sapiens* evolved from premodern humans in several regions simultaneously.

musculoskeletal hypertrophy Great size and associated strength in the muscles and bones of a species or individual. Among recent human ancestors, the Neandertals exhibit an extreme level of musculoskeletal hypertrophy.

Mushabian Pre-**Neolithic** culture located in the steppe and arid zones of the Negev and Sinai Deserts in modern Israel and Egypt. Contemporary with the **Geometric Kebaran,** dating from 14,500 to 12,500 B.P.

Mycenaeans A southern European civilization that followed the **Minoans** and preceded the Greeks.

Natufian A Middle Eastern culture dated from 13,000 to 9000 B.P., located in the Mediterranean woodland zone. The Natufian reliance on wild wheat and barley set the stage for the **Neolithic.**

natural selection The process proposed by Charles Darwin for how species evolve: Those individuals in a species that possess advantageous characteristics are more likely to survive and pass on those characteristics than are individuals that do not possess them.

Nenana Complex Perhaps the oldest stone tool complex identified in Alaska dating from 11,800 to 11,000 B.P. Predating the **Denali Complex,** Nenana includes bifacially flaked, unfluted spearpoints. Nenana bifaces are similar and perhaps related to tools made in eastern Russia about 14,000 years ago.

Neolithic The "New Stone Age." In the past, Neolithic was defined on the basis of the appearance of ground-stone tools as opposed to chipped-stone tools. Today, Neolithic refers to the period after 12,000 years ago when food producing through the domestication of plants and animals replaced foraging as the dominant mode of subsistence.

neoteny The apparent retention, in adults of one species, of juvenile physical characteristics of an evolutionarily related species. For example, physical features of adult human beings are similar to those of juvenile chimpanzees, which is an indication of our species neoteny.

neutron activation analysis Form of **trace element analysis.** The precise and unique chemical make-up of numerous raw material sources have been determined through neutron activation analysis. Archaeological **artifacts** can be analyzed for their chemical make-up as well. When the artifact's chemistry matches that of a source area, it is concluded that the ancient people obtained the material from the chemically matching source.

New Temple Period The culture period for **Minoan** Crete dating from 3650 to 3420 B.P. It followed a catastrophic earthquake that badly damaged the temple at **Knossos** and marks a florescence of Minoan culture.

niche The actual physical area occupied by an organism as well as its functional role in a community of organisms. Sometimes referred to as an organism's ecological address.

Nubia The territory south of the ancient Egyptian nation, primarily between the first and sixth cataracts of the Nile, from southern Egypt to Sudan. The ancient Egyptians called this area **Kush.**

nuclear DNA The genetic instructions contained in the nucleus of the cell that determine the biological makeup of the organism.

object piece In the manufacturing of stone tools, the stone that is being worked through the application of either percussion or pressure.

obsidian hydration A dating method based on the rate at which a freshly exposed surface of obsidian begins to alter physically by chemically combining with water in the air or soil. The thickness of the hydration layer that develops in a given environment is a factor of time.

occipital The area at the rear of the skull. In ancient hominids, the occipital area tends to be massive and **robust.** In anatomically modern human beings, the occipital tends to be smooth and **gracile.**

Oldowan The earliest stone tools, simple chopping tools and sharp flakes, dated to 2.4 million years ago, that were probably made by *Homo habilis.* Some evidence suggests they may also have been produced by *Australopithecus garhi* and, possibly, *robustus.*

Olmec An ancient culture of lowland Mesoamerica dating to 3,200 years ago. The Olmec produced a number of large ceremonial centers where they created great earthworks, finely carved jade sculptures, and massive basalt carvings of human heads. The religious iconography of Olmec art seems to have served as a unifying element in ancient Mesoamerica.

opportunistic foragers Groups that follow a subsistence pattern in which they take advantage of whatever resources become available without much patterning or planning in advance.

optically stimulated luminescence Method of **luminescence dating** in which the time-dependent energy stored in an archaeological specimen is released by the application of laser light.

orthogenesis The invalid notion of a predestined and progressive pattern of evolutionary change.

osteological Related to bones.

osteological comparative collection A bone library; a collection of bones used as models to aid in identifying the bones (species, sex, anatomical part) recovered in a paleontological or archaeological excavation.

paleoanthropologist An anthropologist who focuses on the physical evolution of our species, studying the skeletal remains and cultures of ancient hominids.

Paleo-Arctic tradition Stone-tool tradition in the Arctic dating to the period before 9,000 years ago. The technology involved the production of **microblades** detached from **wedge-shaped cores.**

Paleoindian The period and culture in the New World dating from about 11,500 B.P. to about 10,000 B.P. **Fluted points** are the most distinctive element in the Paleoindian stone **tool kit.** Paleoindians hunted the late Pleistocene megafauna of the New World. The Paleoindians are no longer believed to have been the first human settlers of the New World.

paleomagnetic dating A dating method based on the movement of the earth's magnetic poles.

paleopathology The study of ancient disease, trauma, or dietary deficiency, of which hominid skeletons often bear evidence.

parietal art Art on the walls of a cave, like the cave paintings of the **Upper Paleolithic.**

pastoralists People who raise and tend livestock, such as sheep or cattle, as the focus of their subsistence.

Peiligang Earliest **Neolithic** culture in northern China, with well-established farming villages dating to 8,500–7,000 years ago.

pelagic Anything related to or that lives in the open sea, far from shore.

petroglyph A design etched into a rock face. Darker, weathered rock surface is removed, creating a design or pattern by exposing lighter-colored rock beneath.

pit-houses Semi-subterranean houses constructed by the ancient inhabitants of the American Southwest. Pit-houses commonly were circular pole-and-mud-covered residences.

Pleistocene epoch The geological epoch beginning about 1.6 million years ago and ending about 10,000 years ago. It was marked by a succession of colder periods, or **glacials,** interrupted by warmer periods, or **interglacials.**

pluvial A period of increased rainfall in areas far south of large glacial masses during the **Pleistocene.**

Polynesia Islands of the central and eastern Pacific; they are volcanic in origin.

pongid A member of the taxonomic family Pongidae; an ape.

population replacement model The view that anatomically modern *Homo sapiens* evolved from premodern humans in one place at one time (usually Africa between 200,000 and 100,000 years ago) and spread out from that point of origin, replacing populations of premodern human beings as they encountered them, especially in Asia and Europe.

postcranial Referring to the skeleton, all of the bones below the cranium.

preform A partially worked **core, flake,** or **blade.** In a preform, the first general steps have been made in producing a tool.

premodern *Homo sapiens* Extinct varieties of humanity that share much in common with modern *Homo sapiens* or **anatomically modern *Homo sapiens*** but that commonly retain primitive skeletal features and possess a smaller mean cranial capacity than modern people. The Neandertals are the best-known archaic variety or subspecies of the human race. Also called **archaic *Homo sapiens.***

primary refuse   Archaeological artifacts and ecofacts left at the place they were used or produced.

primate   A member of the taxonomic order Primates: prosimians, monkeys, and apes. An animal with grasping hands and feet, stereoscopic vision, and a relatively large brain (in proportion to body size). Most, but not all, primates have nails instead of claws, tails, and an **arboreal** adaptation.

primatologist   A person who studies primates.

prognathous   Having a forward-thrusting lower face. Apes are prognathous, as are extinct hominids. Anatomically modern human beings tend to have flat, nonprognathous faces.

pubic symphysis   The point of articulation between the two pubic bones of the pelvis. Changes in the appearance of the pubic symphysis occur fairly regularly during an individual's life and so can be used to determine the age of death.

pueblo   Apartment-house-type structure of the ancient, and some modern, inhabitants of the American Southwest that were constructed of adobe brick, rubble, and shaped stone.

punctuated equilibrium   A mode of evolution in which long periods of stasis or equilibrium in a species are interrupted by short, relatively rapid bursts (punctuations) of great change, producing a new species.

Purron phase   The period of time in the **Tehuacán** Valley in highland Mexico from 4300 to 3500 B.P. Little is known about this period in terms of subsistence. Pottery was used for the first time by valley inhabitants.

quipu   A record-keeping system of the Inka in which a series of knotted strings were used as mnemonic devices to help record keepers keep track of information.

rachis   The area of attachment between seeds and other seeds or between seeds and other parts of the plant. A brittle rachis is an adaptive feature under natural conditions, but, since it makes harvesting more difficult, it is selected against by humans through **artificial selection.**

radiocarbon dating   **Radiometric** dating technique based on the decay of a radioactive isotope of carbon: ^{14}C, or radiocarbon. Carbon dating can be applied to virtually anything that was once part of a living organism, within a range from about 300 to 40,000 years ago. Also called **carbon dating.**

radiometric   Referring to any dating technique based on the measurement of radioactive decay.

rank societies   Societies characterized by a few sociopolitical levels filled by a relatively small number of people.

relative date   A date that places a fossil or an archaeological site or artifact in a sequence with other specimens but does not allow for the assignment of an age in terms of years or even a range of years. (Compare to **absolute date.**)

remote sensing   A procedure that allows for the discovery of archaeological sites or artifacts without digging and that may include aerial photography and a number of technologies that allow for scanning below ground without disturbing the soil (proton magnetometry, electrical resistivity survey).

robust   A term applied to skeletal features that are heavily built.

sagittal crest   A ridge of bone that runs along the top of the skull from front to back and that provides added surface area for the attachment of powerful temporalis muscles that attach to the jaws. Male gorillas and some ancient hominid fossils possess a sagittal crest.

Sahul   The land mass of "Greater Australia," including Australia proper, New Guinea, and Tasmania. During periods of **glacial** maxima in the **Pleistocene,** these three islands were combined in the single land mass of Sahul.

Samarran   **Neolithic** culture of southern **Mesopotamia** dating to after 7500 B.P. Samarran sites are located on the floodplain of the Tigris and Euphrates Rivers. There is evidence of communal works, including the construction of irrigation canals, fortification walls, and communal grain storage structures.

sarsen   The 30 upright stones at Stonehenge are called the sarsens. Each sarsen is over 3 m (10 ft) tall and weighs 25,000 kg (55,000 lb).

savanna   Grasslands. The replacement of the Miocene forests of Africa with savannas set the stage for the evolution of an upright primate adapted for life under conditions of flat, open expanses and few trees.

scapulimancy   A process of divining the future, popular in ancient China, in which the scapulae (shoulder blades) of animals are burned and the pattern of burning and breakage is "read" by a diviner.

seal   A carved or molded symbol (on a ring, stamp, or cylinder) that was impressed into soft clay to leave one's official mark. Used in early **Mesopotamia** as a system of record keeping. (See also **cylinder seal**.)

secondarily altricial Human infants are born at an advanced—precocial—state in terms of sensory and brain development, but at an immature and dependent—**altricial**—state physically. This combined condition is labeled secondarily altricial.

secondary refuse Archaeological artifacts and ecofacts that were removed by the people who made, used, or produced them from the place where they were made, used, or produced to a designated refuse area or areas—for example, a trash pile or pit.

seedbed selection Process wherein the seeds of wild plants are tended in planted seedbeds. As later-germinating and slower-growing plants are weeded out of the seedbed, plants that sprout and grow quickly because they have larger seeds and thinner seed coats are selected for unintentionally. This can be a first step in the domestication of plants.

settlement pattern The location, size, function, and seasonality of the various communities or activity areas within a given cultural system. The pattern of land use.

sexual dimorphism Differences in the form and size of the two sexes. Among most primates, the male tends to be larger and physically more powerful than the female.

simple foragers Hunters and gatherers with no particular focus on or commitment to any one food source.

Sinagua Literally "without water," refers to a prehistoric culture group in the American Southwest, especially in central Arizona.

site A place where people lived and/or worked and where the physical evidence of their existence, in the form of **artifacts, ecofacts,** and **features,** can be or has been recovered.

social stratification A pattern of social integration in which individuals are placed into a hierarchy of social levels. The presence of a hierarchy of differences in status and wealth in a society.

social system A system coordinating activities and interrelationships among individuals living in a group. Includes rules of kinship, descent, marriage, division of labor, and the definition of the roles, rights, and responsibilities of members of the group.

Solutrean The stone-toolmaking tradition of the European **Upper Paleolithic** dating from 21,000 to 16,000 B.P. Solutrean bifaces include exquisitely made, symmetrical, leaf-shaped projectile points.

spear-thrower A tool used to increase the range and accuracy of the hand-thrown spear. It is a straight rod or board with a hook at one end that articulates with the end of the spear and effectively increases the length of the arm of the individual throwing the spear.

specialization of labor A cultural pattern in which some individuals can focus all or most of their labors on some specialty: metal working, pottery manufacturing, stone working, weaving, architectural design, and so on. By specializing, these individuals can become quite proficient at their craft, art, or science. The specialization of labor is characteristic of complex civilizations.

stadial A short period of increased glaciation. Stadials can occur during either **glacials** or **interglacials** and are separated by **interstadials.**

state A class society, often rigidly stratified into social levels. The ruling class controls the populace not by consensus but by coercion and force. The rulers in a state society have the powers to levy and collect taxes, to establish and enforce laws, and to conscript people to do the work of the state.

stela (pl., *stelae*) A column on which images or written messages have been inscribed. The Maya of Mesoamerica, for example, left a large number of stelae.

stratigraphic (stratigraphy) Related to the geological or cultural layer in which something has been found. Stratigraphic layering represents a relative sequence of geological time and/or cultural chronology.

striking platform Part of a stone **core** or worked **flake** that presents an area where the desired flake can be removed when struck with a **hammerstone** or antler hammer.

subsistence The material necessary to sustain life: water, food, clothing, shelter. Here it usually refers to the quest for food.

Sunda (or **Sundaland**) The combined land mass of the modern islands of Java, Sumatra, Bali, and Borneo. These islands became a single, continuous land mass during periods of glaciation and attendant lowered sea level during the **Pleistocene.**

supraorbital torus A continuous, projecting ridge of bone above and across the eye orbits. Commonly seen in modern apes and in ancient hominids, it is lacking in anatomically modern human beings, though less conspicuous brow ridges are present in some individuals.

system of record keeping Any symbolic system that usually, but not always, involves some form of writing for keeping track of economic transactions, historical events, religious rules, and the like. A fundamental need in complex civilizations.

taphonomic Referring to how materials become part of the paleontological or archaeological record.

taphonomy The study of how materials become part of the paleontological or archaeological record.

taxonomy A systematic classification based on similarities and differences among the items being classified. Organisms, artifacts, or even whole cultures can be classified in this way.

Tehuacán A valley in central highland Mexico that was the focus of a multidisciplinary research project that produced important archaeological data concerning the domestication of plants in the New World, particularly the **domestication** of maize and squash.

teosinte The wild ancestor of domesticated maize; grew and grows wild throughout the American tropics. The mutation of a very few teosinte genes changes the spikey stem, with its small, encased seeds, into a cob with a larger number of bigger, naked kernels.

test pit A hole or boring into soil in the search for archaeological evidence. In some parts of the world, a pattern of test pits spread out across an area is a primary method by which archaeological sites are searched for and by which the spatial distribution of buried materials at a site is first identified.

thermoluminescence (TL) A trapped-charge, radiation-damage technique for dating archaeological objects. Energy produced by natural radiation in soil becomes stored in nearby objects. The amount of stored energy is a function of the background radiation level (which can be measured) and time. Once the level of background radiation at a particular place is known, how much has accumulated in an archaeological object can be measured, and from that the age of the object (how long it has been accumulating the energy) can be determined.

tholoi A new architectural form seen at **Halafian** sites in **Mesopotamia** dating to after 7500 B.P. Tholoi appear to have been communal storage facilities for **Neolithic** people and may also have served as burial chambers for a growing class of socioeconomically important individuals.

three-age system The chronological breakdown of the history of human culture into a Stone Age, a Bronze Age, and an Iron Age, developed in 1836 by J. C. Thomsen as part of a guidebook for the archaeological collections at the Danish National Museum.

tibia The larger of the two long bones making up the lower leg; the shin bone.

tokens Small geometric shapes of clay, some bearing impressed symbols, dating back to 10,000 years ago in the Middle East that appear to represent an early system of record keeping that led ultimately to a system of writing.

tool kit A set of tools used together in performing a single task (for example, a butchering tool kit for dismembering an animal carcass). A tool kit can also refer to the entire range of tools used at a particular site or during a given time period or produced by a particular group of hominids.

trace element analysis Determining the geographic source of the materials used by an ancient people through the analysis of small, or trace, concentrations of elements or chemicals in those raw materials. The levels measured in archaeological artifacts are compared to the levels present in various possible sources. Where the concentrations in an artifact and a source closely match, it is suggested that the prehistoric people obtained the raw material from that source.

trilithon Set of three stones, two uprights and one lintel, at Stonehenge. There are five trilithons at Stonehenge. The largest of the trilithon uprights stand about 8 m (24 ft) above the surface, with an additional 2 m (6 ft) of stone nestled in the ground. The largest of the trilithon uprights weighs 45,000 kg (50 tons) and the associated lintel weighs 9,000 kg (10 tons).

tuber A relatively short, fleshy, usually underground stem of a plant, often rich in starch and carbohydrates. Tubers have long contributed to the human food quest.

turnover-pulse A term coined by Elisabeth Vrba to refer to periods of significant environmental change that produce rapid and significant change in plant and animal species leading either to extinction or rapid evolution.

Ubaid The name given to the culture of southern **Mesopotamia** at 6300 B.P. Irrigation canals constructed by the Ubaidic people made agriculture possible, and larger settlements grew up in the Mesopotamian floodplain at this time. Evidence of the growing power of the religious elite is seen at Ubaidic sites, with wealth becoming concentrated in the temples.

ulna   One of the bones of the forearm. The ulna is the more interior bone, closer to the body, while the radius is the more exterior bone (on the thumb side).

Umm Dabaghiyah   A **Neolithic** culture in northern **Mesopotamia** dating to more than 8,000 years ago and characterized by a subsistence base of wheat, barley, sheep, and goats. Hunting was still important, and their settlements were small.

uniformitarianism   The belief that the appearance of the earth could be understood as resulting from the slow action of known processes over a very long period of time. This belief, first championed in the late eighteenth and early nineteenth centuries, allowed for a great age of the earth.

unilineal evolution   All cultures pass through the same stages of development. It is usually asserted that some cultures may become stuck at a given stage. This concept is no longer widely accepted.

Upper Paleolithic   The final phase of the Paleolithic, dating to after 40,000 years ago and associated with anatomically modern human beings in Europe.

Venus figurines   **Upper Paleolithic** sculptures of females, often, but not always, with exaggerated secondary sexual characteristics. They have been found in geographic clusters in western, central, and eastern Europe, usually dated to the narrow time span between 25,000 and 23,000 years ago.

Wallacea   The name given to the sea over the **Wallace Trench.**

Wallace Trench   An undersea chasm located between New Guinea/Australia and Java/Borneo and nearly 7,500 m (25,000 ft) deep. It was not breached during periods of lowered Pleistocene sea levels, so population movement from southeast Asia to **Sahul** was accomplished, of necessity, via water.

wear patterns   Characteristic and diagnostic traces of damage or polish left on stone tools as a result of their use. Analysis of wear patterns can often tell the researcher how a tool was used and on what material.

weathering   The decomposition and disintegration of rock, usually at or near the earth's surface.

wedge-shaped cores   **Cores** shaped like wedges from which blades are struck; found as part of the **Paleo-Arctic tradition** in northeastern Asia and also found as part of the **Denali Complex** in the American Arctic.

Yang-shao   An early **Neolithic** culture of China, dating to about 7000 B.P. Yang-shao settlements appear to have been planned out. Subsistence was based on the cultivation of foxtail millet. Domesticated rice, initially a minor dietary component, becomes an important part of the diet at this time.

Younger Dryas   The name given in Europe to a cold period that lasted from 12,600 years ago to 11,450 years ago. Though a relatively short interlude of renewed glacial expansion during a general warming trend at the end of the **Pleistocene,** the Younger Dryas may have been severe enough to have caused the temporary abandonment by humans of much of northwest Europe.

Zarzian   A pre-**Neolithic** culture identified in the foothills of the Zagros Mountains in Turkey.

References

Abbate, E., and et al. 1998. One-million-year-old *Homo* cranium from the Danakil (Afar) Depression of Eritrea. *Nature* 393:458–60.

Adams, Richard E. W. 1991. *Prehistoric Mesoamerica.* Norman: University of Oklahoma Press.

Adams, R. McC., and H. J. Nissen. 1972. *The Uruk Countryside.* Chicago: University of Chicago Press.

Adovasio, J. M., J. Donahue, and R. Stuckenrath. 1990. The Meadowcroft Rockshelter radiocarbon chronology—1975–1990. *American Antiquity* 55:348–53.

———. 1992. Never say never again: Some thoughts on could haves and might have beens. *American Antiquity* 57:527–30.

Adovasio, J., O. Soffer, and B. Klíma. 1996. Upper Paleolithic fibre technology: Interlaced woven finds from Pavlov I, Czech Republic, c. 26,000 years ago. *Antiquity* 70(269).

Adovasio, J. M., et al. 1979–80a. Meadowcroft Rockshelter—Retrospect 1977: Part 1. *North American Archaeologist* 1(1):3–44.

———. 1979–80b. Meadowcroft Rockshelter—Retrospect 1977: Part 2. *North American Archaeologist* 1(2):99–138.

Agenbroad, Larry D. 1988. Clovis people: The human factor in the Pleistocene megafauna extinction question. In *Americans Before Columbus: Ice-Age Origins,* edited by R. C. Carlisle. 63–74. Vol. 12 of Ethnology Monographs. Pittsburgh: University of Pittsburgh.

Agnew, N., and M. Demas. 1998. Preserving the Laetoli footprints. *Scientific American* 279(3):44–55.

Aiello, Leslie C. 1993. The fossil evidence for modern human origins in Africa: A Revised view. *American Anthropologist* 95:73–96.

———. 1994. Variable but singular. *Nature* 368:399–400.

Allchin, Bridget, and Raymond Allchin. 1982. *The Rise of Civilization in India and Pakistan.* Cambridge: Cambridge University Press.

Allison, Marvin J. 1984. Paleopathology in Peruvian and Chilean populations. In *Paleopathology at the Origins of Agriculture,* edited by M. N. Cohen and G. J. Armelagos. 515–29. New York: Academic Press.

Allsworth-Jones, P. 1990. The Szeletian and the stratigraphic succession in central Europe and adjacent areas: Main trends, recent results, and problems for resolution. In *The Emergence of Modern Humans: An Archaeological Perspective,* edited by P. Mellars. 160–242. Ithaca: Cornell University Press.

Alva, Walter, and Christopher B. Donnan. 1993. *Royal Tombs of Sípan.* Los Angeles: Fowler Museum of Culture History.

———. 1994. Tales from a Peruvian crypt. *Natural History* 103:26–34.

An, Zhimin. 1989. Prehistoric agriculture in China. In *Foraging and Farming,* edited by D. R. Harris and G. C. Hillman. 643–49. London: Unwin Hyman.

Anderson, David. 1990. The Paleoindian colonization of eastern North America. *Research in Economic Anthropology* Supplement 5:163–216.

Anderson, Douglas D. 1968. A stone age campsite at the gateway to America. *Scientific American* 218(6):24–33.

———. 1970. Microblade traditions in northwestern Alaska. *Arctic Anthropology* 7(2):2–16.

Anderson, Edgar. 1956. Man as a maker of new plants and new plant communities. In *Man's Role in Changing the Face of the Earth,* Vol. 2, edited by W. L. Thomas. 767–77. Chicago: University of Chicago Press.

Andrews, Peter. 1985. Species diversity and diet in monkeys and apes during the Miocene. In *Primate Evolution and Human Origins,* edited by R. Ciochon and J. Fleagle. 194–204. Menlo Park, Calif.: Benjamin/Cummings.

Andrews, Peter, and Chris Stringer. 1989. *Human Evolution: An Illustrated Guide.* Cambridge: Cambridge University Press.

Ardrey, Robert. 1961. *African Genesis: A Personal Investigation into the Animal Origins and Nature of Man.* New York: Dell.

Arensburg, Bernard, L. A. Schepartz, A. M. Tillier, B. Vandermeersch, and Yoel Rak. 1990. A reappraisal of the anatomical basis for speech in Middle Paleolithic hominids. *American Journal of Physical Anthropology* 83:137–46.

Arnheim, R. 1956. *Art and Visual Perception: A Psychology of the Creative Eye.* London: Faber and Faber.

Arsuaga, Juan-Luis, Ignacio Martinez, Ana Garcia, José-Miguel Carretero, and Eudald Carbonell. 1993. Three new human skulls from the Sima de los Huesos Middle Pleistocene site in Sierra de Atapuerca, Spain. *Nature* 362:534–37.

Arteaga, Robert F. 1991. *Building of the Arch.* St. Louis: Jefferson National Expansion Historical Association.

Asfaw, Berhane, Yonas Beyene, Gen Suwa, Robert Walter, Tim White, Giday WoldeGabriel, and Tesfaye Yemane. 1992. The earliest Acheulean from Konso-Gardula. *Nature* 360:732–35.

Asfaw, Berhane, T. White, O. Lovejoy, B. Latimer, S. Simpson, and G. Suwa. 1999. *Australopithecus garhi:* A new species of early hominid from Ethiopia. *Science* 284:629–34.

Ashmore, Wendy, and Robert J. Sharer. 1995. *Discovering Our Past: A Brief Introduction to Archaeology.* Mountain View, Calif.: Mayfield.

Aveni, Anthony, ed. 1977. *Native American Astronomy.* Austin: University of Texas Press.

Bahn, Paul G. 1994. *Homo erectus* in Europe. *Archaeology* 47:25.

———. 1996. Further back down under. *Nature* 383:577–88.

———. 1998. Neanderthals emancipated. *Nature* 394:719–21.

Bailey, G. N. 1978. Shell middens as indicators of postglacial economies: A territorial perspective. In *The Early*

Postglacial Settlement of Northern Europe: An Ecological Perspective, edited by P. Mellars. 37–63. Pittsburgh: University of Pittsburgh Press.

Balter M. 1998. Why settle down? The mystery of communities. *Science* 282:1442–45.

Barbetti, M., and H. Allen. 1972. Prehistoric man at Lake Mungo, Australia, by 32,000 years B.P. *Nature* 240:46–48.

Barker G. 1978. Economic models for the Manekweni Zimbabwe, Mozambique. *Azania* 13:71–100.

Barlow, Nora, ed. 1958. *The Autobiography of Charles Darwin.* London: Collins.

Bartstra, G. J., S. Soegondho, and A. V. D. Wijk. 1988. Ngandong Man: Age and artifacts. *Journal of Human Evolution* 17:325–37.

Bar-Yosef, Ofer. 1998. The Natufian culture of the Levant, threshold to the origins of agriculture. *Evolutionary Anthropology* 6(5):159–77.

Bar-Yosef, Ofer, B. Vandermeersch, B. Arensburg, A. Belfer-Cohen, P. Goldberg, H. Laville, L. Meignen, Y. Rak, J. D. Speth, E. Tchernov, A-M. Tillier, and S. Weiner. 1992. The excavations in Kebara Cave, Mt. Carmel. *Current Anthropology* 33:497–534.

Beadle, G. 1977. The origin of *Zea mays.* In *The Origins of Agriculture,* edited by C. A. Reed. 615–35. The Hague: Mouton.

Beaumont, Peter, H. de Villiers, and J. C. Vogel. 1978. Modern man in sub-Saharan Africa prior to 49,000 B.P.: A review and evaluation with particular reference to Border Cave. *South African Journal of Science* 74:409–19.

Bednarik, Robert G. 1993. Oldest dated rock art in the world. *International Newsletter on Rock Art* (4):5–6.

Begun, David R. 1992. Miocene fossil hominids and the chimp-human clade. *Science* 257:1929–33.

Begun, David R., and Alan Walker. 1993. The endocast. In *The Nariokotome* Homo erectus *Skeleton,* edited by A. Walker and R. Leakey. 326–58. Cambridge: Harvard University Press.

Behrensmeyer, A. K., N. E. Todd, R. Potts, and G. E. McBrinn. 1997. Late Pliocene faunal turnover in the Turkana Basin, Kenya and Ethiopia. *Science* 278:1589–94.

Belfer-Cohen, Anna, and N. Goren-Inbar. 1994. Cognition and communication in the Levantine Lower Paleolithic. *World Archaeology* 26:144.

Belfer-Cohen, Anna, and Erella Hovers. 1992. In the eye of the beholder: Mousterian and Natufian burials in the Levant. *Current Anthropology* 33:463–71.

Ben-Itzhak, S., P. Smith, and R. A. Bloom. 1988. Radiographic study of the humerus in Neandertals and *Homo sapiens sapiens. American Journal of Physical Anthropology* 77:231–42.

Bermúdez de Castro, J. M., J. L. Arsuaga, E. Carbonell, A. Rosas, I. Martinez, and M. Mosquera. 1997. A hominid from the lower Pleistocene of Atapuerca, Spain: Possible ancestor to Neandertals and modern humans. *Science* 276:1392–95.

Binford, Lewis. 1978. *Nunamiut Ethnoarchaeology.* New York: Academic Press.

———. 1984. *Faunal Remains from Klasies River Mouth.* Orlando: Academic Press.

———. 1987a. *Bones: Ancient Men and Modern Myths.* New York: Academic Press.

———. 1987b. Were there elephant hunters at Torralba? In *The Evolution of Human Hunting,* edited by M. H. Nitecki and D. V. Nitecki. 47–105. New York: Plenum Press.

Binford, Lewis, and Sally Binford. 1966. A preliminary analysis of functional variability in the Mousterian of Levallois facies. *American Anthropologist* 68:239–95.

Binford, Lewis, and Chuan Kun Ho. 1985. Taphonomy at a distance: Zhoukoudian, "The Cave Home of Beijing Man." *Current Anthropology* 26:413–43.

Binford, Lewis, and Nancy M. Stone. 1986. Zhoukoudian: A closer look. *Current Anthropology* 27:453–76.

Binford, Sally. 1968. Variability and change in the Near Eastern Mousterian of Levallois facies. In *New Perspectives in Archaeology,* edited by L. Binford and S. Binford. 49–60. Chicago: Aldine.

Birdsell, Joseph H. 1977. The recalibration of a paradigm for the first peopling of Greater Australia. In *Sunda and Sahul: Prehistoric Studies in Southeast Asia, Melanesia, and Australia,* edited by J. Allen, J. Golson, and R. Jones. 113–67. New York: Academic Press.

Bischoff, James L., Narcis Soler, Julià Maroto, and Ramon Julià. 1989. Abrupt Mousterian/Aurignacian boundary at c. 40 ka bp: Accelerator ¹⁴C dates from l'Arbreda Cave (Catalunya, Spain). *Journal of Archaeological Science* 16:563–76.

Blumenschine, Robert J. 1987. Characteristics of an early hominid scavenging niche. *Current Anthropology* 28:383–407.

———. 1989. A landscape taphonomic model of the scale of prehistoric scavenging opportunities. *Journal of Human Evolution* 18:345–71.

Blumenschine, Robert J., and Fidelis T. Masao. 1991. Living sites at Olduvai Gorge, Tanzania? Preliminary landscape archaeology results in the basal Bed II lake margin zone. *Journal of Human Evolution* 21:451–62.

Boaz, Noel. 1992. First steps into the human dawn. *Earth* (March): 38–43.

Bonnichsen, Rob, and K. L. Turnmire, eds. 1991. *Clovis: Origins and Adaptations.* Corvallis, Ore.: Center for the Study of the First Americans.

Bordaz, J. 1970. *Tools of the Old and New Stone Age.* New York: Natural History Press.

Bordes, François. 1961. Mousterian cultures in France. *Science* 134:803–10.

———. 1972. *A Tale of Two Caves.* New York: Harper and Row.

Bordes, François, and J. Labrot. 1967. La stratigraphie du gisement de Roc de Combe et ses implications. *Bulletin de la Société Préhistorique Française* 64:15–28.

Borziyak, Ilia A. 1993. Subsistence practices of Late Paleolithic groups along the Dnestr River and its tributaries.

In *From Kostenki to Clovis: Upper Paleolithic-Paleoindian Adaptations,* edited by O. Soffer and N. Preslov. 67–84. New York: Plenum.

Boule, Marcellin, and H. V. Vallois. 1923. *Fossil Men.* New York: Dryden Press.

Bowdler, Sandra. 1974. Pleistocene date for man in Tasmania. *Nature* 252:697–98.

———. 1977. The coastal colonisation of Australia. In *Sunda and Sahul: Prehistoric Studies in Southeast Asia, Melanesia, and Australia,* edited by J. Allen, J. Golson, and R. Jones. 205–46. New York: Academic Press.

———. 1990. Peopling Australasia: The "Coastal Colonization" hypothesis re-examined. In *The Emergence of Modern Humans: An Archaeological Perspective,* edited by P. Mellars. 327–43. Ithaca: Cornell University Press.

Bower, Bruce. 1990. Minoan culture survived volcanic eruption. *Science News* 137:22.

———. 1992a. Early hominid's diet expands. *Science News* 141:253.

———. 1992b. *Erectus* unhinged. *Science News* 141:408–409, 411.

———. 1993a. Ancient American site identified in Alaska. *Science News* 143:215.

———. 1993b. Fossil jaw offers clue to human ancestry. *Science News* 144:277.

———. 1993c. Fossil may extend antiquity of human line. *Science News* 141:134.

———. 1993d. Lucy's new kin take a powerful stand. *Science News* 144:324.

———. 1994a. Asian hominids make a much earlier entrance. *Science News* 145:150.

———. 1994b. Neandertal tot enters human-origins debate. *Science News* 145:5.

———. 1994c. Siberian site cedes stone-age surprise. *Science News* 145:84.

———. 1994d. Savannas leave signs of slow takeover. *Science News* 145:38.

———. 1995. Fossil hints at hominids' European stall. *Science News* 147:85.

———. 1996. Visions on the rocks. *Science News* 150:216–17.

———. 1997a. Ancient human saunters into limelight. *Science News* 152:117.

———. 1997b. Ancient roads to Europe. *Science News* 151:12–13.

———. 1997c. Early humans make their marks as hunters. *Science News* 151:222.

Bowlby, John. 1990. *Charles Darwin: A New Life.* New York: Norton.

Bowler, J. M., Rhys Jones, Harry Allen, and A. G. Thorne. 1970. Pleistocene human remains from Australia: A living site and human cremation from Lake Mungo, western New South Wales. *World Archaeology* 2:39–60.

Bowler, J. M., A. G. Thorne, and H. A. Polach. 1972. Pleistocene man in Australia: Age and significance of the Lake Mungo skeleton. *Nature* 240:48–50.

Bradley, D. G., R. T. Loftus, P. Cunningham, and D. E. MacHugh. 1998. Genetics and domestic cattle origins. *Evolutionary Anthropology* 6(3):79–86.

Braidwood, Robert. 1960. The agricultural revolution. *Science* 203:130–48.

———. 1975. *Prehistoric Men.* Glenview, Ill.: Scott, Foresman.

Brain, J. P. 1979. *Tunica Treasure.* Cambridge, Mass.: Peabody Museum of Archaeology and Ethnology Papers 71.

Bräuer, Günter. 1984. A craniological approach to the origin of anatomically modern *Homo sapiens.* In *The Origins of Modern Humans: A World Survey of the Fossil Evidence,* edited by F. H. Smith and F. Spencer. 327–410. New York: Liss.

———. 1992. Africa's place in the evolution of *homo sapiens.* In *Continuity or Replacement: Controversies in Homo sapiens Evolution,* edited by G. Bräuer and F. Smith. 83–98. Rotterdam: Balkema.

Bräuer, Günter, Hilary J. Deacon, and Friedrich Zipfel. 1992. Comments on the new maxillary finds from Klasies River Mouth, South Africa. *Journal of Human Evolution* 23:419–22.

Bräuer, Günter, and Emma Mbua. 1992. *Homo erectus* features used in cladistics and their variability in Asian and African hominids. *Journal of Human Evolution* 22:79–108.

Bräuer, Günter, and Klaus W. Rimbach. 1990. Late archaic and modern *Homo sapiens* from Europe, Africa, and Southwest Asia: Craniometric comparisons and phylogenetic implications. *Journal of Human Evolution* 19: 789–807.

Bräuer, G., Y. Yokoyama, C. Falguères, and E. Mbua. 1997. Modern human origins backdated. *Nature* 386:337.

Brennan, Louis A. 1982. A compilation of fluted points of eastern North America by count and distribution: An AENA project. *Archaeology of Eastern North America* 10:27–45.

Brennan, M. U. 1991. *Health and Disease in the Middle and Upper Paleolithic of Southwestern France: A Bioarchaeological Study.* Ph.D. diss., New York University.

Brice, William R. 1982. Bishop Ussher, John Lightfoot, and the age of creation. *Journal of Geological Education* 30: 18–24.

Brooks, Alison S., and Bernard Wood. 1990. The Chinese side of the story. *Nature* 344:288–89.

Brown, Frank, John Harris, Richard Leakey, and Alan Walker. 1985. Early *Homo erectus* skeleton from west Lake Turkana, Kenya. *Nature* 316:788–92.

Brown, Michael. 1990. *The Search for Eve.* New York: Harper and Row.

Bruhns, Karen Olsen. 1994. *Ancient South America.* Cambridge World Archaeology. Cambridge: Cambridge University Press.

Buckley, Tom. 1976. The discovery of Tutankhamun's tomb. In *The Treasures of Tutankhamun,* edited by K. S. Gilbert, J. K. Holt, and S. Hudson. 9–18. New York: Metropolitan Museum of Art.

Buikstra, Jane E. 1984. The lower Illinois River region: A prehistoric context for the study of ancient diet and health. In *Paleopathology at the Origins of Agriculture,* edited by M. N. Cohen and G. J. Armelagos. 215–34. New York: Academic Press.

Bunn, Henry, and Ellen Kroll. 1986. Systematic butchery by Plio-Pleistocene hominids at Olduvai Gorge, Tanzania. *Current Anthropology* 27:431–52.

Burger, Richard L. 1988. Unity and heterogeneity within the Chavin horizon. In *Peruvian Prehistory,* edited by R. W. Keatinge. 99–144. Cambridge: Cambridge University Press.

———. 1995. *Chavin and the Origins of Andean Civilization.* London: Thames and Hudson.

Burger, Richard L., and R. B. Gordon. 1998. Early central Andean metalworking from Mina Perdida, Peru. *Science* 282:1108–11.

Burl, Aubrey. 1995. *A Guide to the Stone Circles of Britain, Ireland, and Brittany.* New Haven: Yale University Press.

Burnet, Reverend Thomas. 1680. *Sacred Theory of the Earth.* London.

Burns, James A. 1990. Paleontological perspectives on the ice-free corridor. In *Megafauna and Man: Discovery of America's Heartland,* edited by L. D. Agenbroad, J. I. Mead, and L. W. Nelson. 61–66. Hot Springs, S.D.: The Mammoth Site of Hot Springs and Northern Arizona University.

Butzer, Karl. 1991. An Old World perspective on potential mid-Wisconsin settlement of the Americas. In *The First Americans: Search and Research,* edited by T. Dillehay and D. Meltzer. 137–56. Boca Raton: CRC Press.

Callen, E. O. 1967. Analysis of the Tehuacan coprolites. In *Prehistory of the Tehuacan Valley,* Vol. 1—*Environment and Subsistence,* edited by D. Byers. 261–89. Austin: University of Texas Press.

Cann, Rebecca L. 1992. A mitochondrial perspective on replacement or continuity in human evolution. In *Continuity or Replacement: Controversies in* Homo sapiens *Evolution,* edited by G. Bräuer and F. Smith. 65–73. Rotterdam: Balkema.

Cann, Rebecca, Olga Richards, and J. Koji Lum. 1994. Mitochondrial DNA and human evolution: Our one lucky mother. In *Origins of Anatomically Modern Humans,* edited by M. H. Nitecki and D. V. Nitecki. 135–48. New York: Plenum.

Cann, Rebecca, Marc Stoneking, and Allan Wilson. 1987. Mitochondrial DNA and evolution. *Nature* 325:31–36.

Carbonell, E., J. M. Bermúdez de Castro, J. L. Arsuaga, J. C. Diez, A. Rosas, G. Cuenca-Bescós, R. Sala, M. Mosquera, and X. P. Rodriguez. 1995. Lower Pleistocene hominids and artifacts from Atapuerca–TD 6 (Spain). *Science* 269: 826–30.

Carlisle, R. C., and J. M. Adovasio, eds. 1984. *Meadowcroft: Collected Papers on the Archaeology of Meadowcroft Rockshelter and the Cross Creek Drainage.* Pittsburgh: University of Pittsburgh, Department of Anthropology.

Carniero, Robert. 1970. A theory of the origin of the state. *Science* 169:733–38.

Castleden, Rodney. 1987. *The Stonehenge People: An Exploration of Life in Neolithic Britain 4700–2000 B.C.* London: Routledge.

———. 1990a. *The Knossos Labyrinth.* London: Routledge.

———. 1990b. *Minoans: Life in Bronze Age Crete.* London: Routledge.

Catto, Norm, and Carole Mandryk. 1990. Geology of the postulated ice-free corridor. In *Megafauna and Man: Discovery of America's Heartland,* edited by L. D. Agenbroad, J. I. Mead, and L. W. Nelson. 80–85. Hot Springs, S.D.: The Mammoth Site of Hot Springs and Northern Arizona University.

Cerling, Thure, Yang Wang, and Jay Quade. 1993. Expansion of C4 ecosystems as an indicator of global ecological change in the late Miocene. *Nature* 361:344–45.

Cerling, T. E., et al. 1997. Global vegetation change through the Miocene/Pliocene boundary. *Nature* 389:153–58.

Chang Kwang-chih. 1968. *The Archaeology of Ancient China.* 2nd ed. New Haven: Yale University Press.

———. 1986. *The Archaeology of Ancient China.* 4th ed. New Haven: Yale University Press.

Chapman, Jefferson, and Gary D. Crites. 1987. Evidence for early maize (Zea mays) from Icehouse Bottom Site, Tennessee. *American Antiquity* 52:318–29.

Chard, Chester. 1974. *Northeast Asia in Prehistory.* Madison: University of Wisconsin Press.

Charteris, J., J. C. Wall, and J. W. Nottrodt. 1981. Functional reconstruction of gait from the Pliocene hominid footprints at Laetoli, northern Tanzania *Nature* 290: 496–98.

Chase, Philip G. 1991. Symbols and Paleolithic artifacts: Style, standardization, and the imposition of arbitrary form. *Journal of Anthropological Archaeology* 10:193–214.

Chase, Philip G., and Harrold L. Dibble. 1987. Middle Paleolithic symbolism: A review of current evidence and interpretations. *Journal of Anthropological Archaeology* 6: 263–96.

Chauvet, J.-M., Éliette Deschamps, and Christian Hillaire. 1996. *Dawn of Art: The Chauvet Cave.* New York: Abrams.

Chen Tiemei, Yang Quan, and Wu En. 1994. Antiquity of *Homo sapiens* in China. *Nature* 368:55–56.

Chen Tiemei and Zhang Yinyun. 1991. Paleolithic chronology and possible coexistence of *Homo erectus* and *Homo sapiens* in China. *World Archaeology* 23(2):147–54.

Childe, V. Gordon. 1942. *What Happened in History.* Baltimore: Pelican Books.

———. 1951. *Man Makes Himself.* New York: Mentor Books.

———. 1953. *New Light on the Most Ancient East.* New York: Norton.

Chippindale, Christopher. 1983. *Stonehenge Complete.* Ithaca: Cornell University Press.

Churchill, Steven E., and Erik Trinkaus. 1990. Neandertal scapular glenoid morphology. *American Journal of Physical Anthropology* 83:147–60.

Cinque-Mars, J. 1978. Bluefish Cave I: A late Pleistocene eastern Beringian cave deposit in the northern Yukon. *Canadian Journal of Anthropology* 3:1–32.

Ciochon, Russell, and Jamie James. 1994. The glory that was Angkor. *Archaeology* 47(2):38–49.

Clark, Grahame. 1980. *Mesolithic Prelude*. Edinburgh: University of Edinburgh Press.

Clark, J. G. D. 1971. *Excavation at Star Carr*. Cambridge: Cambridge University Press.

Clarke, R. J. 1990. The Ndutu cranium and the origin of *Homo sapiens*. *Journal of Human Evolution* 19:699–736.

Clayton, Peter A. 1994. *Chronicle of the Pharaohs: The Reign-by-Reign Record of the Rulers and Dynasties of Ancient Egypt*. London: Thames and Hudson.

Clottes, J., J. Courtin, and M. Garner. 1996. *The Cave Beneath the Sea: Paleolithic Images at Cosquer*. New York: Abrams.

Coe, Michael. 1968. *America's First Civilization*. New York: Van Nostrand.

———. 1992. *Breaking the Maya Code*. New York: Thames and Hudson.

———. 1993. *The Maya*. New York: Thames and Hudson.

Cohen, Mark. 1977. *The Food Crisis in Prehistory*. New Haven: Yale University Press.

Cohen, Mark Nathan, and George J. Armelagos. 1984. Paleopathology at the origins of agriculture: Editors' summation. In *Paleopathology at the Origins of Agriculture*, edited by M. N. Cohen and G. J. Armelagos. 585–601. New York: Academic Press.

Coltorti, M., M. Cremaschi, M. C. Delitala, D. Esu, M. Fornaseri, A. McPherron, M. Nicoletti, R. van Otterloo, C. Peretto, B. Sala, V. Schmidt, and J. Sevink. 1982. Reversed magnetic polarity in an early Paleolithic site in central Italy. *Nature* 300:173–76.

Conkey, Margaret. 1978. Style and information in cultural evolution: Towards a predictive model for the Paleolithic. In *Social Archaeology: Beyond Subsistence and Dating*, edited by C. Redman, M. J. Berman, E. V. Curtin, W. T. Langhorne, N. M. Versaggi, and J. C. Wanser. 61–85. New York: Academic Press.

———. 1980. The identification of prehistoric hunter-gatherer aggregation sites: The case of Altamira. *Current Anthropology* 21:609–30.

———. 1981. A century of Paleolithic cave art. *Archaeology* 34(4):20–28.

Connah, Graham. 1987. *African Civilization: Precolonial Cities and States in Tropical Africa; An Archaeological Perspective*. Cambridge: Cambridge University Press.

Connolly, Bob, and Robin Anderson. 1987. *First Contact: New Guinea's Highlander Encounter with the Outside World*. New York: Viking.

Conroy, G. C., G. W. Weber, H. Seidler, P. V. Tobias, A. Kane, and B. Brunsden. 1998. Endocranial capacity in an early hominid cranium from Sterkfontein, South Africa. *Science* 280:1730–31.

Constable, George, and the Editors of Time-Life Books. 1973. *The Neanderthals*. New York: Time-Life.

Cook, J., C. B. Stringer, A. P. Currant, H. P. Schwarz, and A. G. Wintle. 1982. A review of the chronology of the European Middle Pleistocene hominid record. *Yearbook of Physical Anthropology* 25:19–65.

Cordell, Linda. 1984. *The Archaeology of the Southwest*. New York: Academic Press.

———. 1994. *Ancient Pueblo Peoples*. Exploring the Ancient World series. Washington, D.C.: Smithsonian Books.

Cosgrove, Richard, Jim Allen, and Brendan Marshall. 1990. Paleo-ecology and Pleistocene human occupation in south-central Tasmania. *Antiquity* 64:59–78.

Cowan, C. Wesley, and Patty Jo Watson, eds. 1992a. *The Origins of Agriculture: An International Perspective*. Washington, D.C.: Smithsonian Institution Press.

———. 1992b. Some concluding remarks. In *The Origins of Agriculture: An International Perspective*, edited by C. Wesley Cowan and Patty Jo Watson. 207–12. Washington, D.C.: Smithsonian Institution Press.

Cowgill, George L. 1988. Onward and upward with collapse. In *The Collapse of Ancient States and Civilizations*, edited by N. Yoffe and G. L. Cowgill. 244–76. Tucson: University of Arizona Press.

Crawford, Gary W. 1992. Prehistoric plant domestication in East Asia. In *The Origins of Agriculture: An International Perspective*, edited by C. W. Cowan and P. J. Watson. 7–38. Washington, D.C.: Smithsonian Institution Press.

Crawford, Harriet. 1991. *Sumer and the Sumerians*. New York: Cambridge University Press.

Crelin, Edmund S. 1987. *The Human Vocal Tract: Anatomy, Function, Development, and Evolution*. New York: Vantage.

Crompton, Robin H., Li Yu Wang Weijie, Michael Günther, and Russell Savage. 1998. The mechanical effectiveness of erect and "bent-hip, bent-knee" bipedal walking in *Australopithecus afarensis*. *Journal of Human Evolution* 35(1): 55–74.

Culbert, P. 1993. *Maya Civilization*. Exploring the Ancient World series. Washington, D.C.: Smithsonian Books.

Cummins, John, ed. 1992. *The Voyage of Christopher Columbus: Columbus' Own Journal of Discovery*. New York: St. Martin's Press.

Dalrymple, G. Brent, and Marvin A. Lanphere. 1969. *Potassium-Argon Dating: Principles, Techniques, and Applications to Geochronology*. San Francisco: W. H. Freeman.

Daniel, Glyn, and Colin Renfrew. 1988. *The Idea of Prehistory*. Edinburgh: Edinburgh University Press.

Darwin, Charles. 1845. *Journal of Researches into the Natural History and Geology of the Countries Visited During the Voyage of H.M.S. Beagle Round the World*. 2nd ed. London: John Murray.

———. 1859. *The Origin of Species by Means of Natural Selection*. 1952 ed. Chicago: Encyclopaedia Britannica.

Day, Michael H. 1986. *Guide to Fossil Man*. Chicago: University of Chicago Press.

Day, Michael, and E. H. Wickens. 1980. Laetoli Pliocene hominid footprints and bipedalism. *Nature* 286:385–87.

Deacon, Hilary J., and Ria Shuurman. 1992. The origins of modern people: The evidence from Klasies River. In *Continuity or Replacement: Controversies in* Homo sapiens *Evolution,* edited by G. Bräuer and F. Smith. 121–30. Rotterdam: Balkema.

Dean, M. C., C. B. Stringer, and T. G. Bromage. 1986. Age at death of the Neandertal child from Devil's Tower, Gibraltar, and the implications for students of general growth and development in Neandertals. *American Journal of Physical Anthropology* 70:301–9.

Deino, A., P. R. Renne, and C. C. Swisher III. 1998. ^{40}Ar/^{39}Ar dating in paleoanthropology and archaeology. *Evolutionary Anthropology* 6(2):63–75.

de la Vega, Garcilaso. 1605. *The Florida of the Inca.* 1988 ed. Translated by John Varner and Jeannette Varner. Austin: University of Texas Press.

Dennell, Robin. 1986. Needles and spear-throwers. *Natural History* 95(10):70–78.

———. 1992. The origins of crop agriculture in Europe. In *The Origins of Agriculture: An International Perspective,* edited by C. W. Cowan and P. J. Watson. 71–100. Washington, D.C.: Smithsonian Institution Press.

De Tapia, Emily McClung. 1992. The origins of agriculture in Mesoamerica and South America. In *The Origins of Agriculture: An International Perspective,* edited by C. W. Cowan and P. J. Watson. 143–71. Washington, D.C.: Smithsonian Institution Press.

Dettwyler, K. A. 1991. Can paleopathology provide evidence for "compassion"? *American Journal of Physical Anthropology* 84:375–84.

Diamond, Jared. 1987a. How do flightless mammals colonize oceanic islands? *Nature* 327:324.

———. 1987b. The worst mistake in the history of the human race. *Discover* 8:50–60.

———. 1994. How to tame a wild plant. *Discover* 15: 100–106.

Dibble, Harold. 1987. The interpretation of Middle Paleolithic scraper morphology. *American Antiquity* 52:108–18.

Dickson, D. Bruce. 1990. *The Dawn of Belief: Religion in the Upper Paleolithic of Southwestern Europe.* Tucson: University of Arizona Press.

Diehl, Richard A. 1989. Olmec archaeology: What we know and what we wish we knew. In *Regional Perspectives on the Olmec,* edited by R. J. Sharer and D. C. Grove. 17–32. New York: Cambridge University Press.

Dikov, N. N. 1978. Ancestors of Paleoindians and proto-Eskimo-Aleuts in the Paleolithic of Kamchatka. In *Early Man in America from a Circum-Pacific Perspective,* edited by A. L. Bryan. 68–69. Edmonton, Canada: Archaeological Researches International.

Dikov, N. N., and E. E. Titov. 1984. Problems of the stratification and periodization of the Ushki sites. *Arctic Anthropology* 21(2):69–80.

DiLeo, Joseph H. 1970. *Young Children and Their Drawings.* New York: Brunner/Mazel.

Dillehay, Tom D. 1987. By the banks of the Chinchihuapi. *Natural History* 96(4):8–12.

———. 1989. *Monte Verde: A Late Pleistocene Settlement in Chile.* Vol. 1—*Paleoenvironment and Site Context.* Washington, D.C.: Smithsonian Institution Press.

———. 1997a. The battle of Monte Verde. *The Sciences* (January/February):28–33.

———. 1997b. *Monte Verde: A Late Pleistocene Settlement in Chile.* Vol. 2—*The Archaeological Context and Interpretation.* Washington, D.C.: Smithsonian Institution Press.

Dillehay, Tom D., and Michael B. Collins. 1988. Early cultural evidence from Monte Verde in Chile. *Nature* 332:150–52.

Dincauze, Dena. 1993. Fluted points in the eastern forests. In *Fron Kostenki to Clovis: Upper Paleolithic-Paleoindian Adaptations,* edited by O. Soffer and N. Preslov. 279–92. New York: Plenum.

Dixon, E. J. 1993. *Quest for the Origins of the First Americans.* Albuquerque: University of New Mexico Press.

Dobyns, H. 1983. *Their Numbers Became Thinned.* Knoxville: University of Tennessee Press.

Doebley, J., A. Stec, and L. Hubbard. 1997. The evolution of apical dominance in maize. *Nature* 386:485–88.

Dubois, Eugene. 1894. *Pithecanthropus erectus.* Eine Menschenähnliche Übergangsform Aus Java. Batavia: Landersdruckerei.

Duhard, Jean-Pierre. 1993. Upper Paleolithic figures as a reflection of human morphology and social organization. *Antiquity* 67:83–91.

Dyer, James. 1990. *Ancient Britain.* Philadelphia: University of Pennsylvania Press.

Eldredge, Niles, and Stephen Jay Gould. 1972. Punctuated equilibrium: An alternative to phyletic gradualism. In *Models in Paleobiology,* edited by T. S. Schopf. 82–115. San Francisco: Freeman, Cooper.

Elias, S. A., S. K. Short, C. H. Nelson, and H. H. Birks. 1996. Life and times of the Bering Land Bridge. *Nature* 382: 60–63.

Elvas, Gentleman of. 1611. *The Discovery and Conquest of Tierra Florida by Don Ferdinando de Soto and Six Hundred Spaniards, His Followers.* New York: Burt Franklin.

Engels, Friedrich. 1891. *The Origins of the Family, Private Property, and the State.* 1972 ed. Chicago: Kerr.

Evans, Arthur. 1921–1936. *Palace of Minos.* 4 vols. Oxford: Oxford University Press.

Evans, J. D. 1968. Neolithic Knossos: The Growth of a Settlement. *Proceedings of the Prehistoric Society* 37(2):95–117.

Excoffier, Laurent, and André Langaney. 1989. Origin and differentiation of human mitochondrial DNA. *American Journal of Human Genetics* 44:73–85.

Fagan, Brian M. 1991. *Ancient North America: The Archaeology of a Continent.* London: Thames and Hudson.

———. 1994. *Quest for the Past: Great Discoveries in Archaeology.* Prospect Heights, Ill.: Waveland Press.

———. 1997a. *Archaeology: A Brief Introduction.* 6th ed. New York: Longman.

————. 1997b. *In the Beginning: An Introduction to Archaeology.* 9th ed. New York: Longman.

————. 1998. *Eyewitness to Discovery.* New York: Oxford University Press.

Fairservis, William. 1975. *The Roots of India.* Chicago: University of Chicago Press.

Falk, Dean. 1984. The petrified brain. *Natural History* 93(9): 36–39.

Farnsworth, Paul, James E. Brady, Michael J. DeNiro, and Richard S. MacNeish. 1985. A re-evaluation of the isotopic and archaeological reconstruction of diet in the Tehuacán Valley. *American Antiquity* 50:102–16.

Feder, Kenneth L. 1999a. *Frauds, Myths, and Mysteries: Science and Pseudoscience in Archaeology.* Mountain View, Calif.: Mayfield.

————, ed. 1999b. *Lessons from the Past: A Reader in Introductory Archaeology.* Mountain View, Calif.: Mayfield.

Feibel, C. S., F. H. Brown, and I. McDougal. 1989. Stratigraphic context of fossil hominids from the Omo Group deposits: Northern Turkana Basin, Kenya, and Ethiopia. *American Journal of Physical Anthropology* 78:595–622.

Fiedel, S. J. 1999. Older than we thought: Implications of corrected dates for Paleoindians. *American Antiquity* 64: 95–115.

Fischman, Joshua. 1992. Hard evidence. *Discover* 13:44–51.

Flannery, Kent V. 1968. Archaeological systems theory and early Mesoamerica. In *Anthropological Archaeology in the Americas,* edited by B. Meggars. 67–87. Washington, D.C.: Anthropological Society of Washington.

————, ed. 1986. *Guilá Naquitz: Archaic Foraging and Early Agriculture in Oaxaca, Mexico.* New York: Academic Press.

Fleagle, John. 1988. *Primate Adaptation and Evolution.* New York: Academic Press.

Flint, Richard Foster. 1971. *Glacial and Quarternary Geology.* New York: Wiley.

Flood, Josephine. 1990. *Archaeology of the Dreamtime: The Story of Prehistoric Australia and Its People.* New Haven: Yale University Press.

Foley, R. A., and P. C. Lee. 1989. Finite social space, evolutionary pathways, and reconstructing hominid behavior. *Science* 243:901–6.

Folger, T., and S. Menon. 1997. Or much like us? *Discover* 18(1):33.

Ford, R. 1985. Patterns of prehistoric food production in North America. In *Prehistoric Food Production in North America,* edited by R. Ford. 341–64. Vol. 75 of Anthropological Papers. Ann Arbor: University of Michigan, Museum of Anthropology.

Foster, Nelson, and Linda S. Cordell, eds. 1992. *Chilies to Chocolate: Food the Americans Gave the World.* Tucson: University of Arizona Press.

Fowler, Melvin. 1989. *The Cahokia Atlas: A Historical Atlas of Cahokia Archaeology.* Studies in Illinois Archaeology 6. Springfield: Illinois Historic Preservation Agency.

Franciscus, R. G., and Eric Trinkaus. 1988. Nasal morphology and the emergence of *Homo erectus. American Journal of Physical Anthropology* 75:517–27.

Frayer, David W. 1992. Neanderthal features in post-Neanderthal Europeans. In *Continuity or Replacement: Controversies in* Homo sapiens *Evolution,* edited by G. Bräuer and F. Smith. 179–88. Rotterdam: Balkema.

Frayer, David W., Milford H. Wolpoff, Alan G. Thorne, Fred H. Smith, and Geoffrey G. Pope. 1993. Theories of modern human origins: The paleontological test. *American Anthropologist* 95:14–50.

Freeman, Leslie. 1973. The significance of mammalian faunas from Paleolithic occupations of Cantabrian Spain. *American Antiquity* 38:3–44.

Frere, John. 1800. Account of flint weapons discovered in Hoxne in Suffolk. *Archaeologia* 13:204–5.

Freud, Sigmund. 1976. *Introductory Lectures on Psychology.* Translated by J. Strachey. Harmondsworth, England: Penguin.

Fried, Morton H. 1967. *The Evolution of Political Society: An Essay in Political Anthropology.* New York: Random House.

Frison, George C. 1974a. Archaeology of the Casper site. In *The Casper Site: A Hell Gap Bison Kill on the High Plains,* edited by G. C. Frison. 1–112. New York: Academic Press.

————, ed. 1974b. *The Casper Site: A Hell Gap Bison Kill on the High Plains.* New York: Academic Press.

Fritz, Gayle. 1994. Are the first American farmers getting younger? *Current Anthropology* 35(3):305–9.

Galinat, Walton C. 1992. Maize: Gift from America's first people. In *Chilies to Chocolate: Food the Americas Gave the World,* edited by N. Foster and L. S. Cordell. 47–60. Tucson: University of Arizona Press.

Gamble, Clive. 1982. Interaction and alliance in Paleolithic society. *Man* 17:92–107.

————. 1986. *The Paleolithic settlement of Europe.* Cambridge, Mass.: Cambridge University Press.

Gardner, Howard. 1980. *Artful Scribbles: The Significance of Children's Drawings.* New York: Basic Books.

Gargett, Robert H. 1989. The evidence for Neandertal burial. *Current Anthropology* 30:157–77.

Garlake, P. S. 1973. *Great Zimbabwe.* London: Thames and Hudson.

Garn, S. M., A. B. Lewis, K. Koski, and D. Polachesk. 1958. The sex difference in tooth calcification. *Journal of Dentistry Research* 37:561–67.

Gernet, Jacques. 1987. *A History of Chinese Civilization.* Cambridge: Cambridge University Press.

Gero, J., and M. Conkey, eds. 1990. *Engendering Archaeology.* Cambridge: Basil Blackwell.

Gibbons, A. 1993. Geneticists trace the DNA trail of the first Americans. *Science* 259:312–13.

————. 1996a. Did Neandertals lose an evolutionary "arms" race? *Science* 272:1586–87.

————. 1996b. The peopling of the Americas. *Science* (274): 31–33.

————. 1997. Y chromosome shows that Adam was an African. *Science* 278:804–5.

————. 1998. Mother tongues trace steps of earliest Americans. *Science* 279:1306–7.

Gifford-Gonzalez, Diane. 1993. You can hide, but you can't run: Representation of women's work in illustrations of Paleolithic life. *Visual Anthropology Review* 9(1): 23–41.

Gilbert, Allan S. 1989. Microscopic bone structure in wild and domestic animals: A reappraisal. In *Early Animal Domestication and Its Cultural Context,* edited by P. J. Crabtree, D. Campana, and K. Ryan. 46–86. Philadelphia: University of Pennsylvania. Museum Applied Science Center.

Gingerich, P. D. 1986. *Plesiadapis* and the delineation of the order Primates. In *Major Topics in Primate and Human Evolution,* edited by B. Wood, L. Martin, and P. Andrews. 32–46. Cambridge: Cambridge University Press.

Gish, Duane. 1972. *Evolution: The Fossils Say No.* San Diego: Creation Life Publishers.

Glob, P. V. 1969. *The Bog People.* New York: Ballantine.

Glover, Ian C. 1993. Tools and cultures in Late Paleolithic southeast Asia. In *The First Humans: Human Origins and History to 10,000 B.C.,* edited by G. Burenhult. 128–30. San Francisco: HarperSanFrancisco.

Goebel, Ted, Roger Powers, and Nancy Bigelow. 1991. The Nenana Complex of Alaska and Clovis origins. In *Clovis: Origins and Adaptations,* edited by R. Bonnichsen and K. L. Turnmire. 49–79. Peopling of the Americas. Corvallis, Ore.: Center for the Study of the First Americans.

Goodall, Jane. 1986. *The Chimpanzees of Gombe: Patterns of Behavior.* Cambridge, Mass.: Belknap Press.

Goodman, A. H., and George Armelagos. 1985. Disease and death at Dr. Dickson's mound. *Natural History* 94(9): 12–18.

Gorman, Charles, 1972. Excavations at Spirit Cave, North Thailand: Some interim impressions. *Asian Perspectives* 13:79–107.

Gould, Stephen Jay. 1977. Human babies as embryos. In *Ever Since Darwin.* 70–75. New York: Norton.

————. 1988. A novel notion of Neanderthal. *Natural History* 97(6):16–21.

————. 1991. Fall in the house of Ussher. *Natural History* 100(11):12, 14–16, 18–21.

————. 1994. Lucy on the earth in stasis. *Natural History* 103(9):12, 14, 16, 18–20.

Gowlett, John. 1984. Mental abilities of early man. In *Hominid Evolution and Community Ecology,* edited by G. N. Bailey and P. Callow. 169–92. London: Academic Press.

————. 1986. Culture and conceptualisation: The Oldowan-Acheulian gradient. In *Stone Age Prehistory: Studies in Memory of Charles McBurney,* edited by G. N. Bailey and P. Callow. 243–60. Cambridge: Cambridge University Press.

Gramly, Richard Michael. 1982. *The Vail Site: A Palaeo-Indian Encampment in Maine.* Bulletin of the Buffalo Society of Natural Sciences 30. Buffalo, N.Y.: Buffalo Society of Natural Sciences.

————. 1993. *The Richey Clovis Cache.* Buffalo: Persimmon Press.

Gray, D. 1996. Champion of Aboriginal art. *Archaeology* 46(4):44–47.

Grayson, Donald K. 1983. *The Establishment of Human Antiquity.* New York: Academic Press.

————. 1987. Death by natural causes. *Natural History* 96(5): 8, 10, 12–13.

————. 1991. Late Pleistocene mammalian extinction in North America: Taxonomy, chronology, and explanations. *Journal of World Prehistory* 5(3):193–231.

Greenberg, Joseph, Christy G. Turner II, and Stephen L. Zegura. 1986. The settlement of the Americas: A comparison of linguistic, dental, and genetic evidence. *Current Anthropology* 27(5):477–94.

Greene, J. C. 1959. *The Death of Adam: Evolution and Its Impact on Western Thought.* Ames: Iowa State University Press.

Grimaldi, David. 1993. Forever in amber. *Natural History* 102(6):59–61.

Grine, F. E. 1987. The diet of South African australopithecines based on a study of dental microwear. *L'Anthropologie* 91:467–82.

————. 1993. Australopithecine taxonomy and phylogeny: Historical background and recent interpretation. In *The Human Evolution Sourcebook,* edited by R. L. Ciochon and J. G. Fleagle. 198–210. Englewood Cliffs, N.J.: Prentice-Hall.

Groube, Les, John Chappell, John Muke, and David Price. 1986. A 40,000-year-old human occupation site at Huon Peninsula, Papua New Guinea. *Nature* 324:453–55.

Grove, D. 1996. The Olmec. Available at http://www.stevensonpress.com/Maya/Olmec.html

Grove, Jean. 1988. *The Little Ice Age.* London: Methuen.

Groves, Colin P. 1989. A regional approach to the problem of the origin of modern humans in Australasia. In *The Human Revolution: Behavioural and Biological Perspectives in the Origins of Modern Humans,* edited by P. Mellars and C. Stringer. 274–85. Princeton, N.J.: Princeton University Press.

Grün, Ranier. 1989. Electron spin resonance (ESR) dating. *Quaternary International* 1:65–109.

————. 1993. Electron spin resonance dating in paleoanthropology. *Evolutionary Anthropology* 2(5):172–81.

Grün, Ranier, Peter B. Beaumont, and Christopher B. Stringer. 1990. ESR dating evidence for early modern humans at Border Cave in South Africa. *Nature* 344:537–39.

Grün, R., J. S. Brink, N. A. Spooner, L. Taylor, C. B. Stringer, R. G. Franciscus, and A. S. Murray. 1996. Direct dating of Florisbad hominid. *Nature* 382:500–501.

Grün, Ranier, Nicholas J. Shackleton, and Hilary J. Deacon. 1990. Electron-spin-resonance dating of tooth enamel from Klasies River Mouth cave. *Current Anthropology* 31(4):427–32.

Grün, Ranier, and Christopher B. Stringer. 1991. Electron spin resonance dating and the evolution of modern humans. *Archaeometry* 33:153–99.

Gurney, Gene, and Jeff Forte. 1988. *Space Shuttle Log: The First 25 Flights.* Blue Ridge Summit, Penn.: Aero.

Guthrie, R. Dale. 1990. Late Pleistocene faunal revolution—New perspective on the extinction debate. In *Megafauna and Man: Discovery of America's Heartland,* edited by L. D. Agenbroad, J. I. Mead, and L. W. Nelson. 42–53. Hot Springs, S.D.: The Mammoth Site of Hot Springs and Northern Arizona University.

Haas, Jonathan. 1982. *The Evolution of the Prehistoric State.* New York: Columbia University Press.

Habgood, Phillip J. 1992. The origin of anatomically modern humans in east Asia. In *Continuity or Replacement: Controversies in* Homo sapiens *Evolution,* edited by G. Bräuer and F. Smith. 273–87. Rotterdam: Balkema.

Hager, Lori D. 1994. Fashioning the primitive: 100 years of looking at Neandertals, looking at us. Paper presented at the Annual meeting of the Society for American Archaeology, Anaheim, California.

Halvorson, John. 1987. Art for art's sake in the Paleolithic. *Current Anthropology* 28:63–71.

Hansen, J. M. 1981. *The Paleoethnobotany of Franchthi Cave, Greece.* Bloomington: Indiana University Press.

Hard, Robert J., and John R. Roney. 1998. A massive terraced village complex in Chihuahua, Mexico, 3,000 years before present. *Science* 279:1661–64.

Harlan, Jack. 1992. Indigenous African agriculture. In *The Origins of Agriculture: An International Perspective,* edited by C. W. Cowan and P. J. Watson. 59–70. Washington, D.C.: Smithsonian Institution Press.

Harmon, R., J. Glaze, and K. Nowak. 1980. 230 Th/234 U dating of travertines from the Bilzingsleben archaeological site. *Nature* 284:132–35.

Harris, John F., and Stephen K. Stearns. 1992. *Understanding Maya Inscriptions.* Philadelphia: University of Pennsylvania, the University Museum.

Harrold, Francis B. 1980. A comparative analysis of Eurasian Palaeolithic burials. *World Archaeology* 12:195–211.

———. 1989. Mousterian, Châtelperronian, and Early Aurignacian in western Europe: Continuity or discontinuity? In *The Human Revolution: Behavioural and Biological Perspectives in the Origins of Modern Humans,* edited by P. Mellars and C. Stringer. 677–713. Princeton, N.J.: Princeton University Press.

———. 1992. Paleolithic archaeology, ancient behavior, and the transition to modern *Homo.* In *Continuity or Replacement: Controversies in* Homo sapiens *Evolution,* edited by G. Bräuer and F. Smith. 219–30. Rotterdam: Balkema.

Hasten, L., ed. 1998. *Annual Editions: Archaeology.* Guilford, Conn.: Dushkin/McGraw-Hill.

Hastings, M. C., and M. Mosely. 1975. The adobes of Huaca del Sol and Huaca de la Luna. *American Antiquity* 40:196–203.

Haury, Emil W., E. B. Sayles, and William W. Wasley. 1959. The Lehner Mammoth site, southeastern Arizona. *American Antiquity* 25:2–30.

Hay, R. L., and Mary Leakey. 1982. The fossil footprints of Laetoli. *Scientific American* 246:50–57.

Haynes, C. Vance. 1964. Fluted projectile points: Their age and dispersion. *Science* 145:1408–13.

———. 1980a. Paleoindian charcoal from Meadowcroft Rockshelter: Is contamination a problem? *American Antiquity* 45:582–87.

———. 1980b. The Clovis culture. *Canadian Journal of Anthropology* 1:115–21.

———. 1982. Were Clovis progenitors in Beringia? In *Paleoecology of Beringia,* edited by D. M. Hopkins, J. V. Matthews, Jr., C. E. Schweger, and S. B. Young. 383–98. New York: Academic Press.

———. 1987. Clovis origins update. *The Kiva* 52(2):83–93.

———. 1992. Contributions of radiocarbon dating to the geochronology of the peopling of the New World. In *Radiocarbon Dating After Four Decades: An Interdisciplinary Perspective,* edited by R. R. Taylor, A. Long, and R. S. Kra. 355–374. New York: Springer-Verlag.

Hedges, S. B., S. Kumar, K. Tamura, and Marc Stoneking. 1992. Human origins and analysis of mitochondrial DNA sequences. *Science* 255:737–39.

Heinzelin, Jean de, J. D. Clark, T. White, W. Hart, P. Renne, G. WoldeGabriel, Y. Beyenne, and E. Vrba. 1999. Environment and the behavior of 2.5-million-year-old Bouri hominids. *Science* 284:625–29.

Heiser, Charles B., Jr. 1990. *Seed to Civilization: The Story of Food.* Cambridge, Mass.: Harvard University Press.

Heizer, R. F., and L. K. Napton. 1970. Archaeology as seen from Lovelock Cave, Nevada. *University of California Research Facility Contributions* 10(1).

Helbaek, Hans. 1965. Early Hassunan vegetable food at Tell es-Sawwan near Samarra. *Sumer* 20:45–48.

Henning, G. J., W. Herr, E. Weber, and N. I. Xirotiris. 1981. ESR-dating of the fossil hominid cranium from Petralona Cave, Greece. *Nature* 292:533–36.

Henry, Donald O. 1989. *From Foraging to Agriculture: The Levant at the End of the Ice Age.* Philadelphia: University of Pennsylvania Press.

Heun, M., R. Schäfer-Pregl, D. Klawan, R. Castagna, M. Accerbi, B. Borghi, and F. Salamini. 1997. Site of einkorn wheat domestication identified by genetic fingerprinting. *Science* 278:1312–13.

Higham, Charles. 1989. *The Archaeology of Mainland Southeast Asia.* Cambridge: Cambridge University Press.

Higuchi, Russell, B. Bowman, M. Freiberger, O. A. Ryder, and A. C. Wilson. 1984. DNA sequences from the quagga, an extinct member of the horse family. *Nature* 312:282–84.

Hill, Andrew, Steven Ward, Alan Deino, Garniss Curtis, and Robert Drake. 1992. Earliest *Homo. Nature* 355:719–22.

Hoffman, Michael A. 1979. *Egypt Before the Pharaohs: The Prehistoric Foundations of Egyptian Civilization.* New York: Knopf.

————. 1983. Where nations began. *Science '83* 4(8):42–51.

Holden, C. 1999. Making Neandertals part of the human family. *Science* 284:737.

Hole, Frank, Kent Flannery, and James A. Neely. 1969. *Prehistory and Human Ecology of the Deh Luran Plain: An Early Village Sequence from Khuzistan, Iran.* Ann Arbor: University of Michigan Press.

Holloway, Ralph. 1980. Indonesian "Solo" (Ngandong) endocranial reconstructions: Preliminary observations and comparisons with Neandertal and *Homo erectus* groups. *American Journal of Physical Anthropology* 53: 285–95.

————. 1981. The Indonesian *Homo erectus* brain endocasts revisited. *American Journal of Physical Anthropology* 55: 503–21.

Hoppe, Kathryn. 1992. Antiquity of oldest American confirmed. *Science News* 142:334.

Howell, F. C. 1960. European and northwest African Middle Pleistocene hominids. *Current Anthropology* 1:195–232.

Hublin, J.-J., F. Spoor, M. Braun, F. Zonneveld, and S. Condemi. 1996. A late Neanderthal associated with Upper Paleolithic artefacts. *Nature* 381:224–26.

Huddleston, Lee. 1967. *Origins of the American Indians: European Concepts 1492–1729.* Austin: University of Texas Press.

Hughes, Robert. 1995. Behold the Stone Age. *Time* 145:52–57, 60, 62.

Hutton, James. 1795. *Theory of the Earth: With Proofs and Illustrations.* 2 vols. 1959 ed. Weinheim, Germany: H. R. Engelmann (J. Cramer) and Wheldon & Wesley.

Ikeya, M. 1982. Petralona Cave dating controversy: Response to Henning et al. *Nature* 299:281.

Irwin, Geoffrey. 1993. *The Prehistoric Exploration and Colonisation of the Pacific.* Cambridge: Cambridge University Press.

Irwin, Geoffrey, S. H. Bickler, and P. Quirke. 1990. Voyaging by canoe and computer experiments in the settlement of the Pacific. *Antiquity* 64:34–50.

Isaac, Glynn. 1977. *Olorgesailie: Archaeological Studies of a Middle Pleistocene Lake Basin in Kenya.* Chicago: University of Chicago Press.

James, Steven R. 1989. Hominid use of fire in the lower and middle Pleistocene. *Current Anthropology* 30(1):1–26.

Janus, Christopher, and William Brashler. 1975. *The Search for Peking Man.* New York: Macmillan.

Jelinek, Arthur J. 1992. Perspectives from the Old World on the habitation of the New. *American Antiquity* 57: 345–47.

————. 1994. Hominids, energy, environment, and behavior in the late Pleistocene. In *Origins of Anatomically Modern Humans,* edited by M. Nitecki and D. Nitecki. 67–92. New York: Plenum.

Jia Lanpo and Huang Weiwen. 1990. *The Story of Peking Man.* New York: Oxford University Press.

Jian Guan and J. A. Rice. 1990. The dragon bones of Tongxin. *Natural History* 99(9):60–67.

Jochim, Michael. 1983. Paleolithic cave art in ecological perspective. In *Hunter-Gatherer Economy in Prehistory: A European Perspective,* edited by G. Bailey. 212–19. Cambridge: Cambridge University Press.

Johanson, Donald. 1993. A skull to chew on. *Natural History* 102(5): 52–53.

Johanson, Donald, and Maitland Edey. 1981. *Lucy: The Beginnings of Humankind.* New York: Warner Books.

Johanson, Donald, and B. Edgar. 1996. *From Lucy to Language.* New York: Simon and Schuster.

Johanson, Donald, Lenora Johanson, and Blake Edgar. 1994. *Ancestors: In Search of Human Origins.* New York: Villard.

Johanson, Donald, and James Shreeve. 1989. *Lucy's Child: The Discovery of a Human Ancestor.* New York: Morrow.

Johanson, D. C., F. T. Masao, G. G. Eck, T. D. White, R. C. Walter, W. H. Kinbel, B. Asfaw, P. Manega, P. Ndessokia, and G. Suwa. 1987. New partial skeleton of *Homo habilis* from Olduvai Gorge, Tanzania. *Nature* 327:205–9.

Johnson, E. 1991. Late Pleistocene cultural occupation on the southern Plains. In *Clovis: Origins and Adaptations,* edited by R. Bonnichsen and K. L. Turnmire. 215–36. Corvallis, Ore.: Center for the Study of the First Americans.

Jones, Rhys. 1987. Pleistocene life in the dead heart of Australia. *Nature* 328:666.

————. 1989. East of Wallace's Line: Issues and problems in the colonisation of the Australian continent. In *The Human Revolution: Behavioural and Biological Perspectives in the Origins of Modern Humans,* edited by P. Mellars and C. Stringer. 741–82. Princeton, N.J.: Princeton University Press.

————. 1992. The human colonisation of the Australian continent. In *Continuity or Replacement: Controversies in* Homo sapiens *Evolution,* edited by G. Bräuer and F. Smith. 289–301. Rotterdam: Balkema.

Jordaan, H. V. F. 1976. Newborn:adult brain ratios in hominid evolution. *American Journal of Physical Anthropology* 44:271–78.

Jordan, P. 1998. *Riddles of the Sphinx.* New York: New York University Press.

Kantner, J. 1996. An evaluation of Chaco Anasazi roadways. Available at http://sipapu.ucsb.edu/roads/.

Kaplan, Lawrence. 1981. What is the origin of the common bean? *Economic Botany* 35:241–54.

Kaplan, Lawrence, and Lucille N. Kaplan. 1992. Beans of the Americas. In *Chilies to Chocolate: Food the Americas Gave the World,* edited by N. Foster and L. S. Cordell. 61–79. Tucson: University of Arizona Press.

Kaplan, Lawrence, Thomas F. Lynch, and C. E. S. Smith, Jr. 1973. Early cultivated beans (*Phaseolus vulgaris*) from an intermontaine Peruvian valley. *Science* 179:76–77.

Kappelman, John. 1993. The attraction of paleomagnetism. *Evolutionary Anthropology* 2(3):89–99.

Karl, W., and Lorenz Bruchert. 1997. Spearthrower performance: Ethnographic and experimental research. *Antiquity* 71:890–97.

Keefer, D. K., S. D. deFrance, M. E. Moseley, J. B. Richardson III, D. R. Satterlee, and A. Day-Lewis. 1998. Early maritime economy and El Niño events at Quebrada Tacahuay, Peru. *Science* 281:1833–35.

Keeley, Lawrence. 1980. *Experimental Determination of Stone Tool Use: A Microwear Analysis.* Chicago: University of Chicago Press.

Keeley, Lawrence, and Nicholas Toth. 1981. Microwear polishes on early stone tools from Koobi Fora, Kenya. *Nature* 293:464–65.

Kemp, Barry J. 1977. The early development of towns in Egypt. *Antiquity* 51:185–99.

———. 1991. *Ancient Egypt.* New York: Routledge.

Kennedy, Kenneth A. R., Arun Sonakia, John Chiment, and K. K. Verma. 1991. Is the Narmada hominid an Indian *Homo erectus*? *American Journal of Physical Anthropology* 86:475–96.

Kenoyer, J. M. 1998. *Ancient Cities of the Indus Valley Civilization.* Oxford: Oxford University Press.

Kent, J. 1987. The most ancient south: A review of the domestication of the South American camelids. In *Studies in the Neolithic and Urban Revolutions,* edited by L. Manzanilla. 169–84. Vol. 349 of BAR International Series. Oxford: British Archaeological Review.

Kenyon, Kathleen. 1954. Ancient Jericho. *Scientific American* 190:76–82.

Kiernan, Kevin, Rhys Jones, and Don Ranson. 1983. New evidence from Fraser Cave for glacial age man in southwest Tasmania. *Nature* 301:28–32.

Kimbel, William H., Donald C. Johanson, and Yoel Rak. 1994. The first skull and other new discoveries of *Australopithecus afarensis* at Hadar, Ethiopia. *Nature* 368:449–51.

King, M. L., and S. B. Slobodin. 1996. A fluted point from the Uptar site, northeastern Siberia. *Science* 273:634–36.

Kirch, Patrick Vinton. 1984. *The Evolution of Polynesian Chiefdoms.* Cambridge: Cambridge University Press.

Kislev, M. E., and N. D. Carmi. 1992. Epi-Paleolithic (19,000 B.P.) cereal and fruit diet at Ohalo II, Sea of Galilee, Israel. *Review of Paleoethnobotany and Palynology* 71:161–66.

Klein, Richard G. 1969. *Man and Culture in the Late Pleistocene: A Case Study.* San Francisco: Chandler.

———. 1977. The ecology of early man in Southern Africa. *Science* 197:115–26.

———. 1983. The stone age prehistory of southern Africa. *Annual Review of Anthropology* 12:25–48.

———. 1989. *The Human Career: Human Biological and Cultural Origins.* Chicago: University of Chicago Press.

———. 1992. The archaeology of modern human origins. *Evolutionary Anthropology* 1(1):5–14.

———. 1993. Hunter-gatherers and farmers in Africa: The transformation of a continent. In *People of the Stone Age: Hunter-Gatherers and Early Farmers,* edited by G. Burenhult. 39–47, 50–55. San Francisco: HarperSanFrancisco.

———. 1994. The problem of modern human origins. In *Origins of Anatomically Modern Humans,* edited by M. Nitecki and D. Nitecki. 3–17. New York: Plenum.

Knecht, Heidi, Anne Pike-Tay, and Randall White. 1993. Introduction. In *Before Lascaux: The Complex Record of the Early Upper Paleolithic,* edited by H. Knecht, A. Pike-Tay, and R. White. 1–4. Boca Raton: CRC Press.

Kolata, A. 1986. The agricultural foundations of the Tiwanaku state: A view from the heartland. *American Antiquity* 51: 748–62.

Kopper, P. 1986. *The Smithsonian Book of North American Indians Before the Coming of the Europeans.* Washington, D.C.: Smithsonian Books.

Kramer, Andrew. 1991. Modern human origins in Australasia: Replacement or evolution? *American Journal of Physical Anthropology* 86:455–73.

Krings, Matthias, A. Stone, R. W. Schmitz, H. Krainitzki, M. Stoneking, and S. Pääbo. 1997. Neandertal DNA sequences and the origin of modern humans. *Cell* 90(1): 19–30.

Krogman, Wilton Marion. 1973. *The Human Skeleton in Forensic Medicine.* Springfield, Ill.: Thomas.

Krotova, Aleksandra A., and Natalia G. Belan. 1993. Amvrosievka: A unique Upper Paleolithic site in eastern Europe. In *From Kostenki to Clovis: Upper Paleolithic-Paleoindian Adaptations,* edited by O. Soffer and N. Preslov. 125–42. New York: Plenum.

Kunzig, R. 1997. Atapuerca: The face of an ancestral child. *Discover* 18(12):88–101.

Kurtén, Björn. 1976. *The Cave Bear Story: Life and Death of a Vanished Animal.* New York: Columbia University Press.

———. 1980. *Dance of the Tiger.* New York: Pantheon.

Lahr, M. M., and R. A. Foley. 1992. Discriminant analysis of five traits used in the multiregional model of modern human origins. *American Journal of Physical Anthropology* Supplement 14:104.

Lamberg-Karlovsky, C. C., and Jeremy A. Sabloff. 1995. *Ancient Civilizations: The Near East and Mesoamerica.* 2d ed. Prospect Heights, Ill.: Waveland Press.

Leakey, L. S. B., P. V. Tobias, and J. R. Napier. 1964. A new species of the genus *Homo* from Olduvai Gorge. *Nature* 202:7–9.

Leakey, Mary. 1971. *Olduvai Gorge 3.* Cambridge: Cambridge University Press.

Leakey, Mary, and Alan Walker. 1997. Early hominid fossils from Africa. *Scientific American* 276(6):74–79.

Leakey, M. D., and R. L. Hay. 1979. Pliocene footprints in the Laetoli Beds at Laetoli, northern Tanzania. *Nature* 278: 317–23.

Leakey, M. G., C. S. Feibel, I. McDougall, and A. Walker. 1995. New four-million-year-old hominid species from Kanapoi and Allia Bay, Kenya. *Nature* 376:565–71.

Leakey, M. G., C. S. Feibel, I. McDougall, C. Ward, and A. Walker. 1998. New specimens and confirmation of an early age for *Australopithecus anamensis*. *Nature* 393: 62–65.

Leakey, Richard, and Roger Lewin. 1992. *Origins Reconsidered: In Search of What Makes Us Human.* New York: Doubleday.

Leakey, Richard, and Alan Walker. 1985a. A fossil skeleton 1,600,000 years old: *Homo erectus* unearthed. *National Geographic* 168(5):624–29.

———. 1985b. Further hominids from the Plio-Pleistocene of Koobi Fora, Kenya. *American Journal of Physical Anthropology* 64:135–63.

Lee, Richard. 1979. *The !Kung San: Men, Women, and Work in a Foraging Society.* Cambridge: Cambridge University Press.

Lehner, M. 1997. *The Complete Pyramids.* New York: Thames and Hudson.

Leigh, Steven R. 1992. Cranial capacity evolution in *Homo erectus* and early *Homo sapiens. American Journal of Physical Anthropology* 87:1–13.

Lepper, Bradley T. 1995a. *People of the Mounds: Ohio's Hopewell Culture.* Hopewell, Ohio: Hopewell Culture National Historical Park.

———. 1995b. Tracking Ohio's Great Hopewell Road. *Archaeology* 48(6):52–56.

———. 1996. The Newark earthworks and the geometric enclosures of the Scioto Valley: Connections and conjectures. In *A View from the Core: A Synthesis of Ohio Hopewell Archaeology,* edited by P. Pacheco. 226–41. Columbus: Ohio Archaeological Council.

———. 1998. The archaeology of the Newark Earthworks. In *Ancient Earthen Enclosures of the Eastern Woodlands,* edited by R. C. Mainfort, Jr., and L. P. Sullivan. 114–34. Gainesville: University Press of Florida.

Leroi-Gourhan, André. 1968. The evolution of Paleolithic art. *Scientific American* 218(2):58–70.

———. 1982. *The Dawn of European Art: An Introduction to Paleolithic Cave Painting.* Cambridge: Cambridge University Press.

Lewin, Roger. 1987. *Bones of Contention: Controversies in the Search for Human Origins.* New York: Simon and Schuster.

Lewis-Williams, J. D., and T. A. Dowson. 1988. The signs of all times. *Current Anthropology* 29(2):201–17.

Lieberman, Philip. 1984. *The Biology and Evolution of Language.* Cambridge: Harvard University Press.

———. 1992. On Neanderthal speech and Neanderthal extinction. *Current Anthropology* 33:409–10.

Lieberman, Philip, Edmund Crelin, and D. H. Klatt. 1972. Phonetic ability and related anatomy of the newborn and adult human, Neanderthal Man, and the chimpanzee. *American Anthropologist* 74:287–307.

Lieberman, Philip, Jeffrey T. Laitman, J. S. Reidenberg, and P. J. Gannon. 1992. The anatomy, physiology, acoustics, and perception of speech: Essential elements in analysis of the evolution of human speech. *Journal of Human Evolution* 23:447–67.

Li Tianyuan and D. A. Etler. 1992. New Middle Pleistocene hominid crania from Yunxian in China. *Nature* 357:404–7.

Lloyd, Seton. 1961. *Art of the Ancient Near East.* New York: Praeger.

Long, A., B. Benz, J. Donahue, A. Jull, and L. Toolin. 1989. First direct AMS dates on early maize from Tehuacán, Mexico. *Radiocarbon* 31:1035–40.

Long, Jeffrey C., Aravinda Chakravarti, Corinne D. Boehm, Stylianos Antonarakis, and Haig H. Kazazian. 1990. Phylogeny of human b-globin haplotypes and its implications for recent human evolution. *American Journal of Physical Anthropology* 81:113–30.

Lovejoy, Owen C. 1981. The origin of man. *Science* 211:341–50.

———. 1984. The natural detective. *Natural History* 93(10):24–28.

———. 1988. Evolution of human walking. *Scientific American* 259(5):118–25.

Lovejoy, Owen C., K. G. Heiple, and Albert Burnstein. 1973. The gait of *Australopithecus. American Journal of Physical Anthropology* 38:757–80.

Lowe, Gareth W. 1989. The heartland Olmec: Evolution of material culture. In *Regional Perspectives on the Olmec,* edited by R. J. Sharer and D. C. Grove. 33–67. New York: Cambridge University Press.

Lundelius, Ernest L., Jr. 1988. What happened to the mammoth? The climatic model. In *Americans Before Columbus: Ice-Age Origins,* edited by R. C. Carlisle. 75–82. Vol. 12 of Ethnology Monographs. Pittsburgh: University of Pittsburgh.

Lu Zun'e. 1987. Cracking the evolutionary puzzle: Jinniushan Man. *China Pictorial* 4:34–35.

Lyell, Charles. 1830. *Principles of Geology; Being an Attempt to Explain the Former Changes of the Earth's Surface, by Reference to Causes Now in Operation.* 1990 ed. 2 vols. Chicago: University of Chicago Press.

———. 1863. *The Geological Evidences of the Antiquity of Man.* London: Murray.

Lynch, Thomas F. 1990. Glacial-age man in South America? A critical review. *American Antiquity* 55:12–36.

Lynch, Thomas F., R. Gillespie, John A. J. Gowlett, and R. E. M. Hedges. 1985. Chronology of Guitarrero Cave, Peru. *Science* 229:864–67.

MacDonald, G. F. 1985. *Debert: A Paleo-Indian Site in Central Nova Scotia.* Buffalo: Persimmon Press.

MacNeish, Richard S. 1964. Ancient Mesoamerican civilization. *Science* 143:531–37.

———. 1967. An interdisciplinary approach to an archaeological problem. In *Prehistory of the Tehuacan Valley:* Vol. 1—*Environment and Subsistence,* edited by D. Beyers. 14–23. Austin: University of Texas Press.

Magnusson, M., and H. Paulsson. 1965. *The Vinland Sagas.* New York: Penguin.

Maisels, Charles Kenneth. 1990. *The Emergence of Civilization: From Hunting and Gathering to Agriculture, Cities, and the State in the Near East.* New York: Routledge.

Malthus, Thomas. 1798. *Essay on the Principle of Population.* London: J. Murray.

Mandryk, Carole A. 1990. Could humans survive the ice-free corridor? Late-glacial vegetation and climate in west-central Alberta. In *Megafauna and Man: Discovery of America's Heartland,* edited by L. D. Agenbroad, J. I. Mead, and L. W. Nelson. 67–79. Hot Springs, S.D.: The Mammoth Site of Hot Springs and Northern Arizona University.

Marean, C. W., and S. Y. Kim. 1998. Mousterian large-mammal remains from Kobeh Cave: Behavioral implications for Neanderthals and early modern humans. *Current Anthropology* 39:S79–113.

Marinatos, Spyridon. 1972. Thera: Key to the riddle of Minos. *National Geographic* 141(5):702–26.

Marks, Anthony E. 1990. The Middle and Upper Paleolithic of the Near East and the Nile Valley: The problem of cultural transformations. In *The Emergence of Modern Humans: An Archaeological Perspective,* edited by P. Mellars. 56–80. Ithaca: Cornell University Press.

———. 1993. The early Upper Paleolithic: The view from the Levant. In *Before Lascaux: The Complex Record of the Early Upper Paleolithic,* edited by H. Knecht, A. Pike-Tay, and R. White. 5–21. Boca Raton: CRC Press.

Marshack, Alexander. 1972. Upper Paleolithic notation and symbol. *Science* 178:817–28.

———. 1976. Some implications of the Paleolithic symbolic evidence for the origin of language. *Current Anthropology* 17:274–82.

Martin, Paul S. 1967. Prehistoric overkill. In *Pleistocene Extinctions: The Search for a Cause,* edited by P. S. Martin and H. E. Wright. 75–120. New Haven: Yale University Press.

———. 1973. The discovery of America. *Science* 179:969–74.

———. 1982. The pattern and meaning of holarctic mammoth extinction. In *Paleoecology of Beringia,* edited by D. M. Hopkins, J. V. Matthews, Jr., C. E. Schweger, and S. B. Young. 399–408. New York: Academic Press.

———. 1987. Clovisia the beautiful. *Natural History* 96:10–13.

Martin, Paul S., and John E. Guilday. 1967. A bestiary for Pleistocene biologists. In *Pleistocene Extinctions: The Search for a Cause,* edited by S. Martin and H. E. Wright. 1–62. New Haven: Yale University Press.

Martin, P. S., and H. E. Wright, eds. 1967. *Pleistocene Extinctions: The Search for a Cause.* New Haven: Yale University Press.

Martin, Robert D. 1989. Evolution of the brain in early hominids. *Ossa* 14:49–62.

McCamant, John F. 1992. Quinoa's roundabout journey to world use. In *Chilies to Chocolate: Food the Americas Gave the World,* edited by N. Foster and L. S. Cordell. 123–41. Tucson: University of Arizona Press.

McDermott, F., R. Grün, C. B. Stringer, and C. J. Hawkesworth. 1993. Mass-spectrometric U-series dates for Israeli Neanderthal/early modern hominid sites. *Nature* 363:252–55.

McHenry, Henry M. 1991. Sexual dimorphism in *Australopithecus afarensis. Journal of Human Evolution* 20:21–32.

McKillop, H. 1994. Ancient Maya tree-cropping. *Ancient Mesoamerica* 5:129–40.

Megaw, J. V. S., and D. D. A. Simpson, eds. 1979. *Introduction to British Prehistory.* Leicester: Leicester University Press.

Mehringer, Peter J., and Franklin F. Foit, Jr. 1990. Volcanic ash dating of the Clovis cache at East Wenatchee, Washington. *National Geographic Research* 6(4):495–503.

Meiklejohn, Christopher. 1978. Ecological aspects of population size and growth in late-glacial and early postglacial northwestern Europe. In *The Early Postglacial Settlement of Northern Europe: An Ecological Perspective,* edited by P. Mellars. 65–79. Pittsburgh: University of Pittsburgh Press.

Mellaart, James. 1965. *Earliest Civilizations of the Near East.* London: Thames and Hudson.

Mellars, Paul. 1978. Excavation and economic analysis of Mesolithic shell middens on the Island of Oronsay (Inner Hebrides). In *The Early Postglacial Settlement of Northern Europe: An Ecological Perspective,* edited by P. Mellars. 371–96. Pittsburgh: University of Pittsburgh Press.

———, ed. 1990. *The Emergence of Modern Humans: An Archaeological Perspective.* Ithaca: Cornell University Press.

———. 1996. *The Neanderthal Legacy: An Archaeological Perspective from Western Europe.* Princeton, N.J.: Princeton University Press.

Meltzer, David J. 1989. Why don't we know when the first people came to North America? *American Antiquity* 54:471–90.

———. 1993a. Is there a Clovis adaptation? In *From Kostenki to Clovis: Upper Paleolithic-Paleoindian Adaptations,* edited by O. Soffer and N. Preslov. 293–310. New York: Plenum.

———. 1993b. Pleistocene peopling of the Americas. *Evolutionary Anthropology* 1(5):157–69.

———. 1993c. *Search for the First Americans.* Smithsonian: Exploring the Ancient World series. Washington, D.C.: Smithsonian Books.

———. 1997. Monte Verde and the Pleistocene peopling of America. *Science* 276:754–55.

Menon, S. 1997. Neanderthal noses. *Discover* 18(3):30.

Mercier, N., H. Valladas, J.-L. Joron, J.-L. Reyss, F. Léveque, and B. Vandermeersch. 1991. Thermoluminescence dating of the late Neanderthal remains from Saint-Césaire. *Nature* 351:737–39.

Merpert, N. Y., and R. M. Munchaev. 1987. The earliest levels at Yarim Tepe I and Yarim Tepe II in northern Iraq. *Iraq* 49:1–36.

Michael, Gramly Richard. 1993. *The Richey Clovis Cache.* Buffalo: Persimmon Press.

Miller, Joseph A. 1991. Does brain size variability provide evidence of multiple species in *Homo habilis? American Journal of Physical Anthropology* 84:385–98.

Miller, Naomi. 1992. The origins of plant cultivation in the Near East. In *The Origins of Agriculture: An International Perspective,* edited by C. W. Cowan and P. J. Watson. 39–58. Washington, D.C.: Smithsonian Institution Press.

Millon, René. 1967. Teotihuacán. *Scientific American* 216:38–49.

————. 1981. Teotihuacán: City, state, and civilization. In *Supplement to the Handbook of Middle American Indians*. Vol. 1, edited by J. Sabloff. 198–243. Austin: University of Texas Press.

Minnis, Paul E. 1992. Earliest plant cultivation in the desert borderlands of North America. In *The Origins of Agriculture: An International Perspective*, edited by C. W. Cowan and P. J. Watson. 121–41. Washington, D.C.: Smithsonian Institution Press.

Moeller, Roger. 1980. *6LF21: A Paleo-Indian Site in Western Connecticut*. Washington, Conn.: American Indian Archaeological Institute.

Molnar, Stephen, and I. M. Molnar. 1985. The incidence of enamel hypoplasia among the Krapina Neandertals. *American Anthropologist* 87:536–49.

Monastersky, Richard. 1994a. Staggering through the ice ages. *Science News* 146:74–75.

————. 1994b. How stable is the current climate? *Science News* 146:75.

————. 1998. Children of the C4 world. *Science News* 153: 14–15.

Moore, P. D. 1996. Hunting ground for farmers. *Nature* 382: 675–76.

Moorrees, M. A., E. A. Fanning, and E. E. Hunt. 1963. Age variation of formation stages for the permanent teeth. *Journal of Dental Research* 42:1490–1502.

Morell, Virginia. 1998. Kennewick Man's trials continue. *Science* 280:190–92.

Morgan, Lewis Henry. 1877. *Ancient Society*. 1964 ed. Cambridge, Mass.: Belknap Press.

Morgan, Michèle, John Kingston, and Bruno Marino. 1994. Carbon isotope evidence for the emergence of C4 plants in the Neogene from Pakistan and Kenya. *Nature* 367: 162–65.

Morlan, Richard E. 1970. Wedge-shaped core technology in northern North America. *Arctic Anthropology* 7(2):17–37.

Morris, Craig, and Adriana von Hagen. 1993. *The Inka Empire and Its Andean Origins*. New York: American Museum of Natural History.

Morris, Henry. 1974. *The Troubled Waters of Evolution*. San Diego: Creation Life Publishers.

Morwood, M. J., P. B. O'Sullivan, F. Aziz, and A. Raza. 1998. Fission-track ages of stone tools and fossils on the east Indonesian island of Flores. *Nature* 392:173–76.

Moser, Stephanie. 1992. The visual language of archaeology: A case study of the Neanderthals. *Antiquity* 66:831–44.

Mosimann, James E., and Paul S. Martin. 1975. Simulating overkill by Paleoindians. *American Scientist* 63:305–15.

Mowat, Farley. 1987. *Woman in the Mists*. New York: Warner Books.

Müller-Beck, Hansjürgen. 1967. On migrations of hunters across the Bering Land Bridge in the upper Pleistocene. In *The Bering Land Bridge*, edited by D. M. Hopkins. 373–408. Stanford: Stanford University Press.

Napier, J. 1967. The antiquity of human walking. *Scientific American* 216:56–66.

Napier, J. R., and P. H. Napier. 1967. *A Handbook of Living Primates*. New York: Academic Press.

Ndoro, W. 1997. Great Zimbabwe. *Scientific American* 277(5): 94–99.

Nelson, Sarah Milledge. 1993. *The Archaeology of Korea*. Cambridge: Cambridge University Press.

Newcomer, Mark. 1971. Some quantitative experiments in handaxe manufacture. *World Archaeology* 3:85–94.

Nichols, J. 1990. Linguistic diversity and the first settlement of the New World. *Language* 66:475–521.

Noble, David Grant. 1991. *Ancient Ruins of the Southwest*. Flagstaff: Northland.

Normille, D. 1997. Yangtze seen as earliest rice site. *Science* 275:309.

Oates, Joan. 1973. The background and development of early farming communities in Mesopotamia and the Zagros. *Proceedings of the Prehistoric Society (London)* 39:147–81.

O'Brien, Patricia. 1984. What was the Acheulean hand ax? *Natural History* 93(7):20–23.

O'Connell, J. F., and J. Allen. 1998. When did humans first arrive in Greater Australia and why is it important to know? *Evolutionary Anthropology* 6(4):132–46.

O'Connor, David. 1993. *Ancient Nubia: Egypt's Rival in Africa*. Philadelphia: University of Pennsylvania, University Museum.

Oglivie, Marsha D., Bryan K. Curran, and Erik Trinkaus. 1989. Incidence and patterning of dental enamel hypoplasia among the Neandertals. *American Journal of Physical Anthropology* 79:25–41.

Ohnuma, K., and C. A. Bergman. 1990. A technological analysis of the Upper Paleolithic levels (XXV–VI) of Ksar Akil. In *The Emergence of Modern Humans: An Archaeological Perspective*, edited by P. Mellars. 91–138. Ithaca: Cornell University Press.

Oliva, Martin. 1993. The Aurignacian in Moravia. In *Before Lascaux: The Complex Record of the Early Upper Paleolithic*, edited by H. Knecht, A. Pike-Tay, and R. White. 37–55. Boca Raton: CRC Press.

Ovey, C., ed. 1964. *The Swanscombe Skull: A Survey of Research on a Pleistocene Site*. Occasional Paper 20. London: Royal Anthropological Institute of Great Britain and Ireland.

Owen, Roger C. 1984. The Americas: The case against an Ice-Age human population. In *The Origins of Modern Humans: World Survey of the Fossil Evidence*, edited by F. H. Smith and F. Spencer. 517–64. New York: Liss.

Pääbo, Svante. 1985. Molecular cloning of ancient Egyptian mummy DNA. *Nature* 314:644–45.

Pääbo, Svante, J. A. Gifford, and Allan C. Wilson. 1988. Mitochondrial sequences from a 7,000-year-old brain. *Nucleic Acids Res.* 16:9775–87.

Pääbo, Svante, Russell G. Higuchi, and Alan C. Wilson. 1989. Ancient DNA and the polymerase chain reaction. *The Journal of Biological Chemistry* 264(17):9709–12.

Page, Cynthia, and Julia Cort. 1997. Secrets of lost empires: Stonehenge. *Nova*. Television documentary. Boston: WGBH.

Parés, J. M., and A. Pérez-González. 1995. Paleomagnetic age for hominid fossils at Atapuerca archaeological site, Spain. *Science* 269:830–32.

Parpola, Asko. 1993. *Deciphering the Indus Script.* Cambridge: Cambridge University Press.

Patterson, Thomas C. 1993. *Archaeology: The Historical Development of Civilizations.* Englewood Cliffs, N.J.: Prentice-Hall.

Pauketat, Timothy R. 1994. *The Ascent of Chiefs: Cahokia and Mississippian Politics in Native America.* Tuscaloosa: University of Alabama Press.

PBS. 1980. Other people's garbage. *Odyssey.* Television documentary, Public Broadcasting Service.

Pearsall, Deborah. 1992. The origins of plant cultivation in South America. In *The Origins of Agriculture: An International Perspective,* edited by C. W. Cowan and P. J. Watson. 173–205. Washington, D.C.: Smithsonian Institution Press.

Pfeiffer, John E. 1982. *The Creative Explosion: An Inquiry into the Origins of Art and Religion.* New York: Harper and Row.

Philip, Lieberman, Edmund Crelin, and D. H. Klatt. 1972. Phonetic ability and related anatomy of the newborn and adult human, Neanderthal man, and the chimpanzee. *American Anthropologist* 74:287–307.

Phillipson, David W. 1993. *African Archaeology.* 2nd ed. Cambridge: Cambridge University Press.

Piaget, Jean, and B. Inhelder. 1969. *The Psychology of the Child.* London: Routledge and Kegan Paul.

Pickford, M. 1983. Sequence and environments of the lower and middle Miocene hominoids of western Kenya. In *New Interpretations of Ape and Human Ancestry,* edited by R. L. Ciochon and R. S. Corruccini. 421–38. New York: Plenum.

Pineda, Rosa Fung. 1988. The late Preceramic and Initial Period. In *Peruvian Prehistory,* edited by R. W. Keatinge. 67–96. Cambridge: Cambridge University Press.

Pope, Geoffrey G. 1992. Craniofacial evidence for the origin of modern humans in China. *Yearbook of Physical Anthropology* 35:243–98.

Possehl, Gregory L. 1980. *Indus Civilization in Saurashtra.* Delhi: B. R. Publishing.

Postgate, J. N. 1992. *Early Mesopotamia: Society and Economy at the Dawn of History.* New York: Routledge.

Potts, R. 1996. Evolution and climate variability. *Science* 273: 922.

Potts, Richard, and Pat Shipman. 1981. Cutmarks made by stone tools on bones from Olduvai Gorge, Tanzania. *Nature* 291:577–80.

Poulianos, A. N. 1971–72. Petralona: A Middle Pleistocene cave in Greece. *Archaeology* 24/25:6–11.

Powell, M. A. 1985. Salt, seed, and yields in Sumerian agriculture: A critique of the theory of progressive salinisation. *Zeitschrift für Assyriologie* 75(1):7–38.

Powers, William Roger, and Thomas D. Hamilton. 1978. Dry Creek: A late Pleistocene human occupation in central

Alaska. In *Early Man in America from Circum-Pacific Perspective,* edited by A. L. Bryan. 72–77. Edmonton, Canada: Archaeological Researches International.

Powers, William R., and John F. Hoffecker. 1989. Late Pleistocene settlement in the Nenana Valley, central Alaska. *American Antiquity* 54:263–87.

Price, A. Grenfell, ed. 1971. *The Explorations of Captain James Cook in the Pacific: As Told by Selections of His Own Journals 1768–1779.* New York: Dover Publications.

Price, T. Douglas. 1982. Willow tales and dog smoke. *Quarterly Review of Archaeology* 3(1):4–8.

———. 1987. The Mesolithic of western Europe. *Journal of World Prehistory* 1:225–305.

———. 1991. The view from Europe: Concepts and questions about terminal Pleistocene societies. In *The First Americans: Search and Research,* edited by T. D. Dillehay and D. J. Meltzer. 185–210. Boca Raton: CRC Press.

Price, T. Douglas, and Gary M. Feinman. 1993. *Images of the Past.* Mountain View, Calif.: Mayfield.

Pringle, Heather. 1996. *In Search of Ancient North America.* New York: Wiley.

———. 1997. Ice Age communities may be earliest known net hunters. *Science* 277:1203–4.

———. 1998a. New women of the Ice Age. *Discover* 19(4): 62–69.

———. 1998b. Traces of ancient mariners found in Peru. *Science* 281:1775–77.

Quilter, Jeffrey, Bernardino Ojeda E., Deborah M. Pearsall, Daniel H. Sandweiss, John G. Jones, and Elizabeth S. Wing. 1991. Subsistence economy of El Paraíso, an early Peruvian site. *Science* 251:277–83.

Rak, Yoel. 1990. On the differences between two pelvises of Mousterian context from the Qafzeh and Kebara Caves, Israel. *American Journal of Physical Anthropology* 81:323–32.

Raloff, Janet. 1993. Corn's slow path to stardom. *Science News* 143:248–50.

Ramenofsky, Ann F. 1987. *Vectors of Death.* Albuquerque: University of New Mexico Press.

Raven, C. E. 1950. *John Ray, Naturalist: His Life and Works.* London: Cambridge University Press.

Ray, John. 1691. *The Wisdom of God Manifested in the Works of the Creation.* 1974 ed. New York: Verlag.

Reid, J. 1989. A Grasshopper perspective on the Mogollon of the Arizona Mountains. In *Dynamics of Southwest Prehistory,* edited by L. S. Cordell and G. J. Gummerman. 65–97. Washington, D.C.: Smithsonian Institution Press.

Reid, J., and S. Whittlesey. 1997. *The Archaeology of Ancient Arizona.* Tucson: University of Arizona Press.

Renfrew, Colin. 1972. *The Emergence of Civilization.* London: Methuen.

———. 1979. *Before Civilization: The Radiocarbon Revolution and Prehistoric Europe.* Cambridge: Cambridge University Press.

Renfrew, Colin, and Paul Bahn. 1996. *Archaeology: Theories, Methods, and Practice.* New York: Thames and Hudson.

Rice, Patricia. 1981. Prehistoric Venuses: Symbols of motherhood or womanhood. *Journal of Anthropological Research* 37:402–14.

Rice, Patricia, and Ann Paterson. 1985. Cave art and bones: Exploring the interrelationships. *American Anthropologist* 87:94–100.

———. 1986. Validating the cave art-archaeofaunal relationship in Cantabrian Spain. *American Anthropologist* 88:658–67.

———. 1988. Anthropomorphs in cave art: An empirical assessment. *American Anthropologist* 90:664–774.

Richardson, J. B. III. 1994. *People of the Andes.* Exploring the Ancient World series. Washington, D.C.: Smithsonian Books.

Rightmire, G. Philip. 1979a. Cranial remains of *Homo erectus* from Beds II and IV, Olduvai Gorge, Tanzania. *American Journal of Physical Anthropology* 51:99–116.

———. 1979b. Implications of Border Cave skeletal remains for later Pleistocene evolution. *Current Anthropology* 20: 23–35.

———. 1981. Patterns in the evolution of *Homo erectus. Paleobiology* 7(2):241–46.

———. 1984. *Homo sapiens* in sub-Saharan Africa. In *The Origins of Modern Humans: A World Survey of the Fossil Evidence,* edited by F. H. Smith and F. Spencer. 295–326. New York: Liss.

———. 1985. The tempo of change in the evolution of mid-Pleistocene *Homo.* In *Ancestors: The Hard Evidence,* edited by E. Delson. 255–264. New York: Liss.

———. 1990. *The Evolution of* Homo erectus: *Comparative Anatomical Studies of an Extinct Human Species.* New York: Cambridge University Press.

———. 1991a. Comparative studies of late Pleistocene human remains from Klasies River Mouth, South Africa. *Journal of Human Evolution* 20:131–56.

———. 1991b. The dispersal of *Homo erectus* from Africa and the emergence of more modern humans. *Journal of Anthropological Research* 47:177–91.

Rindos, David. 1984. *The Origins of Agriculture: An Evolutionary Perspective.* New York: Academic Press.

Ritchie, William A. 1971. *A Typology and Nomenclature for New York State Projectile Points.* Albany: University of the State of New York, New York State Museum, Bulletin 384.

Roach, Mary. 1998. Ancient altered states. *Discover* 19(6): 52–58.

Roberts, David. 1993. The Ice Man: Voyager from the Copper Age. In *National Geographic* 183(6):36–67.

———. 1997. *In Search of the Old Ones: Exploring the Anasazi World of the Southwest.* New York: Simon and Schuster.

Roberts, R., et al. 1998. Optical and radiocarbon dating at Jinmium Rockshelter in northern Australia. *Nature* 393: 358–62.

Roberts, Richard G., Rhys Jones, and M. A. Smith. 1990. Thermoluminescence dating of a 50,000-year-old human occupation site in northern Australia. *Nature* 345:153–56.

Rogan, P. K., and J. J. Salvo. 1990. Molecular genetics of pre-Columbian South American mummies. *UCLA Symposium in Molecular Evolution* 122:223–34.

Romer, John. 1984. *Ancient Lives: Daily Life in Egypt of the Pharaohs.* New York: Holt, Rinehart and Winston.

Roosevelt, A. C., et al. 1996. Paleoindian cave dwellers in the Amazon: The peopling of the Americas. *Science* 272: 373–84.

Rose, Mark. 1993. Early skull found in Java. *Archaeology* 46(5):18.

———. 1995. The last Neandertals. *Archaeology* 48(5): 12–13.

Rosenberg, Karen R. 1992. The evolution of modern human childbirth. *Yearbook of Physical Anthropology* 35: 89–124.

Ross, Anne, and Don Robins. 1989. *The Life and Death of a Druid Prince: The Story of Lindow Man, An Archaeological Sensation.* New York: Summit Books.

Ross, Philip E. 1991. Mutt and Jeff: Did Cro-Magnons and Neanderthals co-exist? *Scientific American* 265(3):40–48.

Royal Geographical Society. 1993a. *Angkor Wat.* San Francisco: InterOptica. CD-ROM.

———. 1993b. *The Egyptian Pyramids.* San Francisco: InterOptica. CD-ROM.

———. 1993c. *Inca Ruins.* San Francisco: InterOptica. CD-ROM.

Ruff, Christopher B. 1993. Climatic adaptation and hominid evolution: The thermoregulatory imperative. *Evolutionary Anthropology* 2(2):53–60.

Ruff, Christopher B., Erik Trinkaus, Alan Walker, and Clark Spencer Larsen. 1993. Postcranial robusticity in *Homo.* I: Temporal trends and mechanical interpretation. *American Journal of Physical Anthropology* 91:21–53.

Ruggles, Clive. 1996. Stonehenge for the 1990s. *Nature* 381: 278–79.

Ruspoli, Mario. 1986. *The Cave of Lascaux: The Final Photographs.* New York: Abrams.

Sabloff, Jeremy A. 1989. *The Cities of Ancient Mexico: Reconstructing a Lost World.* New York: Thames and Hudson.

———. 1994. *The New Archaeology and the Ancient Maya.* New York: Scientific American Library.

Sakellarakis, Yannis, and Efi Sapouna-Sakellaraki. 1981. Drama of death in a Minoan temple. *National Geographic* 159(2):205–22.

Sanders, William, J. R. Parsons, and R. Santley. 1979. *The Basin of Mexico: The Cultural Ecology of a Civilization.* New York: Academic Press.

Sandweiss, D. H., H. McInnis, R. L. Burger, A. Cano, B. Ojeda, R. Paredes, M. Sandweiss, and M. D. Glasscock. 1998. Quebrada Jaguay: Early South American maritime adaptations. *Science* 281:1830–32.

Santa Luca, A. P. 1980. The Ngandong fossil hominids: A comparative study of a Far Eastern *Homo erectus* group. *Yale University Publications in Anthropology* 78:1–175.

Saunders, J. J. 1977. Lehner Ranch revisited. *The Museum Journal* 17:48–64.

Saunders, J. W., et al. 1997. A mound complex in Louisiana at 5,400–5,000 years before the present. *Science* 277: 1796–99.

Savage, Donald E., and Donald E. Russell. 1983. *Mammalian Paleofaunas of the World*. Reading, Mass.: Addison-Wesley.

Scala Archives. 1994. Voyage in Egypt: A Virtual Journey Through Ancient Egypt. Acta-Emme. CD-ROM.

Schele, Linda, and David Freidel. 1990. *A Forest of Kings: The Untold Story of the Ancient Maya*. New York: Morrow.

Schele, Linda, and Peter Mathews. 1998. *The Code of Kings: The Language of Seven Sacred Maya Temples and Tombs*. New York: Scribner.

Schick, Kathy D., and Nicholas Toth. 1993. *Making Silent Stones Speak: Human Evolution and the Dawn of Technology*. New York: Simon and Schuster.

Schmandt-Besserat, Denise. 1992. *Before Writing: From Counting to Cuneiform*. 2 vols. Austin: University of Texas Press.

Schrenk, F., Timothy Bromage, Christian Betzler, Uwe Ring, and Yusuf Juwayayi. 1993. Oldest *Homo* and Pliocene biogeography of the Malawi Rift. *Nature* 365:833–36.

Sebastian, Lynne. 1992. *The Chaco Anasazi: Sociopolitical evolution in the prehistoric Southwest*. Cambridge: Cambridge University Press.

Semaw, S., P. Renne, J. W. K. Harris, C. S. Feibel, R. L. Bernor, N. Fesseha, and K. Mowbray. 1997. 2.5-million-year-old stone tools from Gona, Ethiopia. *Nature* 385:333–36.

Service, Elman. 1975. *The Origins of the State and Civilization: The Process of Cultural Evolution*. New York: Norton.

Settegast, Mary. 1987. *Plato Prehistorian: 10,000 to 5000 B.C. in Myth and Archaeology*. Cambridge, Mass.: Rotenberg Press.

Severinghaus, J. P., T. Sowers, E. J. Brook, R. B. Alley, and M. L. Bender. 1998. Timing of the abrupt climate change at the end of the Younger Dryas interval from thermally fractionated gases in polar ice. *Nature* 391:141–46.

Shackleton, Nicholas, and Neil Opdyke. 1973. Oxygen isotope and paleomagnetic stratigraphy of equatorial Pacific core V28-238: Oxygen isotope temperatures and ice volumes on a 10^5 and 10^6 year scale. *Quaternary Research* 3: 39–55.

———. 1976. Oxygen-isotope and paleomagnetic stratigraphy of Pacific core V28–239 late Pliocene and latest Pleistocene. In *Investigation of Late Quaternary Paleoceanography and Paleoclimatology*, edited by R. M. Cline and J. Hays. 449–64. Vol. 145. New York: Geological Society of America.

Shackleton, Nicholas, J. Backman, H. Zimmerman, D. V. Dent, M. A. Hall, D. G. Roberts, D. Schnitker, J. G. Baldauf, A. Despraires, R. Homrighausen, P. Huddleston, J. B. Keene, A. J. Kaltenback, K. A. O. Krumsiek, A. C. Morton, J. W. Murray, and J. Westberg-Smith. 1984. Oxygen isotope calibration of the onset of ice-rafting and history of glaciation in the North Atlantic region. *Nature* 307:620–23.

Shapiro, Harry L. 1974. *Peking Man*. New York: Simon and Schuster.

Sharer, Robert, and D. Grove. 1989. *Regional Perspectives on the Olmec*. New York: Cambridge University Press.

Sharer, Robert J., and Wendy Ashmore. 1993. *Archaeology: Discovering Our Past*. 2nd ed. Mountain View, Calif.: Mayfield.

Shea, John J. 1988. Spear points from the Middle Paleolithic of the Levant. *Journal of Field Archaeology* 15:441–50.

———. 1989. A functional study of the lithic industries associated with hominid fossils in Kebara and Qafzeh Caves, Israel. In *The Human Revolution: Behavioural and Biological Perspectives in the Origins of Modern Humans*, edited by P. Mellars and C. Stringer. 611–25. Princeton, N.J.: Princeton University Press.

———. 1990. A further note on Mousterian spear points. *Journal of Field Archaeology* 17:111–14.

———. 1992. Lithic microwear analysis in archaeology. *Evolutionary Anthropology* 1(4):143–50.

———. 1993. Lithic use-wear evidence for hunting by Neandertals and early modern humans from the Levantine Mousterian. In *Hunting and Animal Exploitation in the Later Palaeolithic and Mesolithic of Eurasia*, edited by G. L. Peterkin, H. M. Bricker, and P. Mellars. 189–97. Vol. 4 of Archaeological Papers. Washington, D.C.: American Anthropological Association.

———. 1994. Hunting technology in the Middle Paleolithic/Middle Stone Age: An interregional perspective. Paper presented at the Society for American Archaeology, Anaheim, California.

———. 1998. Neandertal and early modern human behavioral variability: A regional-scale approach to lithic evidence for hunting in the Levantine Mousterian. *Current Anthropology* 39:S45–61.

Shipman, Pat. 1983. Early hominid lifestyle: Hunting and gathering or foraging and scavenging? In *Animals and Archaeology*, edited by J. Clutton-Brock and C. Grigson. 31–49. Vol. 1 of International Series 163. London: British Archaeological Association.

———. 1984. Scavenger hunt. *Natural History* 93(4):20–27.

———. 1986. Scavenging or hunting in early hominids: Theoretical framework and tests. *American Anthropologist* 88:27–43.

———. 1990. Old masters. *Discover* 11(7):60–65.

Shipman, Pat, and Jennie Rose. 1983. Evidence of butchery and hominid activities at Torralba and Ambrona; An evaluation using microscopic techniques. *Journal of Archaeological Science* 10:465–74.

Shreeve, James. 1993. As the old world turns. *Discover* 14(1): 24–28.

———. 1996. New skeleton gives path from trees to ground an odd turn. *Science* 272:654.

Sillen, Andrew, and C. K. Brain. 1990. Old flame. *Natural History* 99(4):6–10.

Silverberg, Robert. 1989. *The Mound Builders*. Athens: Ohio University Press.

Simek, Jan F. 1992. Neanderthal cognition and the Middle to Upper Paleolithic transition. In *Continuity or Replacement: Controversies in* Homo sapiens *Evolution,* edited by G. Bräuer and F. Smith. 231–46. Rotterdam: Balkema.

Simmons, Alan H. 1986. New evidence for the early use of cultigens in the American Southwest. *American Antiquity* 51:73–89.

Singer, Ronald, and John Wymer. 1982. *The Middle Stone Age at Klasies River Mouth in South Africa.* Chicago: University of Chicago Press.

Sjøvold, Torstein. 1992. The Stone Age Iceman from the Alps: The find and the current status of investigation. *Evolutionary Anthropology* 1(4):117–24.

Skelton, Randall R., and Henry M. McHenry. 1992. Evolutionary relationships among early hominids. *Journal of Human Evolution* 23:309–49.

Smith, B. Holly. 1993. The physiological age of KNM-WT 15000. In *The Nariokotome* Homo erectus *skeleton,* edited by A. Walker and R. Leakey. 195–220. Cambridge, Mass.: Harvard University Press.

Smith, Bruce. 1989. Origins of agriculture in eastern North America. *Science* 246:1566–70.

———. 1992a. Prehistoric plant husbandry in eastern North America. In *The Origins of Agriculture: An International Perspective,* edited by C. W. Cowan and P. J. Watson. 101–19. Washington, D.C.: Smithsonian Institution Press.

———. 1992b, ed. *Rivers of Change.* Washington, D.C.: Smithsonian Institution Press.

———. 1995. *The Emergence of Agriculture.* New York: Scientific American Library.

———. 1997. The initial domestication of Cucurbita pepo in the Americas 10,000 years ago. *Science* 276:932–34.

———. 1998. Between foraging and farming. *Science* 279: 1651–52.

Smith, Christopher. 1992. *Late stone age hunters of the British Isles.* London: Routledge.

Smith, Fred H. 1991. The Neandertals: Evolutionary dead ends or ancestors of modern people? *Journal of Anthropological Research* 47(2):219–38.

———. 1992. The role of continuity in modern human origins. In *Continuity or Replacement: Controversies in* Homo sapiens *Evolution,* edited by G. Bräuer and F. Smith. 145–58. Rotterdam: Balkema.

———. 1994. Samples, species, and speculations in the study of modern human origins. In *Origins of Anatomically Modern Humans,* edited by M. Nitecki and D. Nitecki. 227–52. New York: Plenum.

Smith, Fred H., Anthony B. Falsetti, and Steven M. Donnelly. 1989. Modern human origins. *Yearbook of Physical Anthropology* 32:35–68.

Smith, Grafton Elliot. 1927. *Essays on the Evolution of Man.* London: Oxford University Press.

Smith, Melvyn. 1985. *An Illustrated History of the Space Shuttle.* Newbury Park, Calif.: Haynes.

Smith, M. A. 1987. Pleistocene occupation in arid Central Australia. *Nature* 328:710–11.

Smith, Michael E. 1997. Life in the provinces of the Aztec Empire. *Scientific American* 277(3):76–83.

Smith, Pat. 1972. Diet and nutrition in the Natufians. *American Journal of Physical Anthropology* 37:233–38.

Smith, Pat, Ofer Bar-Yosef, and A. Sillen. 1985. Archaeological and skeletal evidence for dietary change during the late Pleistocene/early Holocene in the Levant. In *Paleopathology at the Origin of Agriculture,* edited by M. N. Cohen and G. J. Armelagos. 101–30. New York: Academic Press.

Snow, Dean. 1980. *The Archaeology of New England.* New York: Academic Press.

Soffer, Olga. 1992. Social transformations at the Middle to Upper Paleolithic transition. In *Continuity or Replacement: Controversies in* Homo sapiens *Evolution,* edited by G. Bräuer and F. Smith. 249–59. Rotterdam: Balkema.

———. 1993. Upper-Paleolithic adaptations in central and eastern Europe and man-mammoth interactions. In *From Kostenki to Clovis: Upper Paleolithic-Paleoindian Adaptations,* edited by O. Soffer and N. Preslov. 31–50. New York: Plenum.

———. 1994. Ancestral lifeways in Eurasia: The Middle and Upper Paleolithic record. In *Origins of Anatomically Modern Humans,* edited by M. Nitecki and D. Nitecki. 101–19. New York: Plenum.

Solecki, Ralph. 1971. *Shanidar: The First Flower People.* New York: Knopf.

Souden, D. 1997. *Stonehenge Revealed.* New York: Facts on File.

Soustelle, J. 1964. *The Daily Life of the Aztecs.* London: Pelican.

Spencer, Herbert. 1967. *The Evolution of Society* [selections from *Principles of Sociology:* Vol. 1, 1876; Vol. 2, 1882; Vol. 3, 1896]. Chicago: University of Chicago Press.

Spencer-Wood, S. 1991. Toward an archaeology of materialistic domestic reform. In *The Archaeology of Inequality,* edited by R. H. McGuire and R. Paynter. 231–86. Cambridge, Mass.: Basil Blackwell.

Spindler, Konrad. 1994. *The Man in the Ice.* New York: Harmony Books.

Stager, J. C., and P. A. Mayewski. 1997. Abrupt early to mid-Holocene climatic transition registered at the equator and the poles. *Science* 276:1834–36.

Stern, Jack T., and Randall L. Susman. 1983. The locomotor anatomy of *Australopithecus afarensis. American Journal of Physical Anthropology* 60:279–317.

Stiebing, William H., Jr. 1984. *Ancient Astronauts, Cosmic Collisions, and Other Popular Theories About Man's Past.* Buffalo: Prometheus Press.

———. 1993. *Uncovering the Past: A History of Archaeology.* New York: Oxford University Press.

Stiles, Daniel. 1991. Early hominid behaviour and culture tradition: Raw material studies in Bed II, Olduvai Gorge. *The African Archaeological Review* 9:1–19.

Stiner, M. 1994. *Honor Among Thieves: A Zooarchaeological Study of Neandertal Ecology.* Princeton, N.J.: Princeton University Press.

Stipp, J. J., J. H. A. Chappell, and I. McDougall. 1967. K/Ar age estimate of the Pliocene-Pleistocene boundary in New Zealand. *American Journal of Science* 265:462–74.

Stone, Anne C., and Mark Stoneking. 1993. Ancient DNA from a pre-Columbian Amerindian population. *American Journal of Physical Anthropology* 92:463–71.

Stoneking, Mark. 1993. DNA and recent human evolution. *Evolutionary Anthropology* 2(2):60–73.

Straus, Lawrence Guy. 1989. Age of the modern Europeans. *Nature* 342:476–77.

Stringer, Christopher B. 1988. The dates of Eden. *Nature* 331: 565–66.

———. 1990. The emergence of modern humans. *Scientific American* 263:1263–68.

———. 1992a. Reconstructing recent human evolution. *Philosophical Transactions of the Royal Society of London (B)* 337:217–24.

———. 1992b. Replacement, continuity, and the origin of *Homo sapiens.* In *Continuity or Replacement: Controversies in* Homo sapiens *Evolution,* edited by G. Bräuer and F. Smith. 9–24. Rotterdam: Balkema.

———. 1993. Secrets of the pit of the bones. *Nature* 362:501–2.

———. 1994. Out of Africa: A personal history. In *Origins of Anatomically Modern Humans,* edited by M. Nitecki and D. Nitecki. 149–74. New York: Plenum.

Stringer, Christopher B., and Philip Andrews. 1988. Genetic and fossil evidence for the origin of modern humans. *Science* 239:1263–68.

Stringer, Christopher, and Clive Gamble. 1993. *In Search of the Neanderthals.* New York: Thames and Hudson.

Stringer, Chris B., and Ranier Grün. 1991. Time for the last Neandertals. *Nature* 351:701–2.

Stringer, Christopher B., R. Grün, H. P. Schwarcz, and P. Goldberg. 1989. ESR dates for the hominid burial site of Es Skhul in Israel. *Nature* 338:756–58.

Stringer, Christopher, and R. McKie. 1996. *African Exodus.* New York: Henry Holt.

Struever, Stuart, and Felicia Antonelli Holton. 1979. *Koster: Americans in Search of Their Prehistoric Past.* Garden City, N.Y.: Anchor.

Susman, Randall L. 1994. Fossil evidence for early hominid tool use. *Science* 265:1570–73.

Susman, Randall L., Jack T. Stern, and William L. Jungers. 1984. Arboreality and bipedality in the Hadar hominids. *Folia Primatologica* 43:113–56.

Suwa, G., B. Asfaw, Y. Beyene, T. D. White, S. Katoh, S. Nagaoka, H. Nakaya, K. Uzawa, P. Renne, and G. Wolde-Gabriel. 1997. The first skull of *Australopithecus boisei. Nature* 389:489–92.

Svoboda, Jirí. 1993. The complex origin of the Upper Paleolithic in the Czech and Slovak Republics. In *Before Lascaux: The Complex Record of the early Upper Paleolithic,* edited by H. Knecht, A. Pike-Tay, and R. White. 23–36. Boca Raton: CRC Press.

Swisher, C. C., G. H. Curtis, T. Jacob, A. G. Getty, A. Suprijo, and Widiasmoro. 1994. Age of the earliest known hominids in Java, Indonesia. *Science* 263:1118–21.

Swisher, C. C., W. J. Rink, S. C. Antón, H. P. Schwarcz, G. H. Curtis, A. Suprijo, and Widiasmoro. 1996. Latest *Homo erectus* of Java: Potential contemporaneity with *Homo sapiens* in Southeast Asia. *Science* 274:1870–74.

Szabo, B., and D. Collins. 1975. Ages of fossil bones from British interglacial sites. *Nature* 254:680–82.

Szalay, F., and Eric Delson. 1979. *Evolutionary History of the Primates.* New York: Academic Press.

Tague, Robert G. 1992. Sexual dimorphism in the human bony pelvis, with a consideration of the Neandertal pelvis from Kebara Cave, Israel. *American Journal of Physical Anthropology* 88:1–21.

Tague, Robert G., and C. Owen Lovejoy. 1986. The obstetric pelvis of A. L. 288-1 (Lucy). *Journal of Human Evolution* 15:237–55.

Tainter, Joseph. 1988. *The Collapse of Complex Societies.* New York: Cambridge University Press.

Tankersley, Kenneth B. and Cheryl Ann Munson. 1992. Comments on the Meadowcroft Rockshelter radiocarbon chronology and the recognition of coal contaminants. *American Antiquity* 57:321–26.

Tanner, Nancy. 1981. *On Becoming Human.* Cambridge: Cambridge University Press.

Tattersall, Ian. 1995a. *The Last Neanderthal: The Rise, Success, and Mysterious Extinction of Our Closest Human Relatives.* New York: Macmillan.

———. 1995b. *The Fossil Trail: How Do We Know What We Know About Human Evolution?* New York: Oxford University Press.

———. 1998. Neanderthal genes: What do they mean? *Evolutionary Anthropology* 6(5):157–58.

Taylor, R. E. 1991. Frameworks for dating the Late Pleistocene peopling of the Americas. In *The First Americans: Search and Research,* edited by T. D. Dillehay and D. J. Meltzer. 77–111. Boca Raton: CRC Press.

Templeton, Alan. 1992. Human origins and analysis of mitochondrial DNA sequences. *Science* 255:737.

———. 1993. The "Eve" hypothesis: A genetic critique and reanalysis. *American Anthropologist* 95:51–72.

Terrell, John. 1986. *Prehistory in the Pacific Islands.* Cambridge: Cambridge University Press.

Thieme, H. 1997. Lower Paleolithic hunting spears from Germany. *Nature* 385:807–10.

Thomas, Cyrus. 1894. *Report on the Mound Explorations of the Bureau of American Ethnology.* 1985 ed. Washington, D.C.: Smithsonian Institution Press.

Thomas, David Hurst. 1998. *Archaeology.* 3rd ed. New York: Harcourt Brace.

———. 1999. *Archaeology: Down to Earth.* 2nd ed. New York: Harcourt Brace.

Thomas, Glyn V., and Angèle M. J. Silk. 1990. *An Introduction to the Psychology of Children's Drawings.* New York: New York University Press.

Thorne, Alan G. 1977. Separation or reconciliation? Biological clues to the development of Australian society. In *Sunda and Sahul: Prehistoric Studies in Southeast Asia, Melanesia, and Australia,* edited by J. Allen, J. Golson, and P. Jones. 187–204. New York: Academic Press.

Thorne, Alan G., and Milford H. Wolpoff. 1992. The multiregional evolution of humans. *Scientific American* 264(4): 76–83.

Tianyuan, Li and Dennis A. Etler. 1992. New Middle Pleistocene hominid crania from Yunxian in China. *Nature* 357:404–7.

Tiemei Chen and Zhang Yinyun. 1991. Paleolithic chronology and possible coexistence of *Homo erectus* and *Homo sapiens* in China. *World Archaeology* 23(2):147–54.

Tierney, John, Lynda Wright, and Karen Springer. 1988. The search for Adam and Eve. *Newsweek* (Jan. 11):46–52.

Tobias, Philip V. 1991. *Olduvai Gorge IV: The Skulls, Endocasts, and Teeth of* Homo habilis. Cambridge: Cambridge University Press.

Todd, I. A. 1976. *Çatal Hüyük in Perspective.* Menlo Park: Benjamin/Cummings.

Topic, J. 1990. Craft production in the kingdom of Chimor. In *The Northern Dynasties: Kingship and Statecraft in Chimor,* edited by M. Moseley and A. Cordy-Collins. 145–76. Washington, D.C.: Dumbarton Oaks.

Toth, Nicholas. 1985. The Oldowan reassessed: A close look at early stone artifacts. *Journal of Archaeological Science* 2: 101–20.

———. 1987. The first technology. *Scientific American* 256: 112–21.

Trigger, B. G. 1983. The rise of Egyptian civilization. In *Ancient Egypt: A Social History,* edited by B. G. Trigger, B. J. Kemp, D. O'Connor, and A. B. Lloyd. 1–70. New York: Cambridge University Press.

Trinkaus, Erik. 1983a. Neandertal postcrania and the adaptive shift to modern humans. In *The Mousterian Legacy.* 165–200. Vol. 164 of British Archaeological Reports, International Series. Oxford.

———. 1983b. *The Shanidar Neandertals.* New York: Academic Press.

———. 1984. Neandertal pubic morphology and gestation length. *Current Anthropology* 25:509–14.

———. 1985. Pathology and the posture of the La Chapelle-aux-Saints Neandertal. *American Journal of Physical Anthropology* 15:193–218.

———. 1986. The Neandertals and modern human origins. *Annual Review of Anthropology* 15:193–218.

———. 1989. The upper Pleistocene transition. In *The Emergence of Modern Humans: Biocultural Adaptations in the Later Pleistocene,* edited by E. Trinkaus. 42–46. Cambridge: Cambridge University Press.

Trinkaus, Erik, and Pat Shipman. 1993. *The Neandertals: Changing the Image of Mankind.* New York: Knopf.

Trinkaus, Erik, and D. D. Thompson. 1987. Femoral diaphyseal histophometric age determinators for the Shanidar 3, 4, 5, and 6 Neandertals and Neandertal longevity. *American Journal of Physical Anthropology* 72:123–29.

Trinkaus, Erik, and Isabelle Villemeur. 1991. Mechanical advantages of the Neandertal thumb in flexion: A test of an hypothesis. *American Journal of Physical Anthropology* 84: 249–60.

Tyler, Edward. 1865. *Researches into the Early History of Mankind and the Development of Civilization.* London: J. Murray.

———. 1871. *Primitive Culture: Researches into the Development of Mythology, Philosophy, Religion, Language, Art, and Custom.* London: J. Murray.

Unger-Hamilton, Ramona. 1989. The epi-Paleolithic southern Levant and the origins of cultivation. *Current Anthropology* 30:88–103.

Valdes, Victoria Cabrera, and James L. Bischoff. 1989. Accelerator ^{14}C dates for early Upper Paleolithic (Basal Aurignacian) at El Castillo Cave (Spain). *Journal of Archaeological Science* 16:577–84.

Valladas, H., J. L. Reyss, J. L. Joron, G. Valladas, O. Bar-Yosef, and B. Vandermeersch. 1988. Thermoluminescence dating of Mousterian "Proto-Cro-Magnon" remains from Israel and the origin of modern man. *Nature* 331:614–16.

Van Peer, Philip, and Pierre M. Vermeersch. 1990. Middle to Upper Paleolithic transition: The evidence for the Nile Valley. In *The Emergence of Modern Humans: An Archaeological Perspective,* edited by P. Mellars. 139–59. Ithaca: Cornell University Press.

Van Riper, A. Bowdoin. 1993. *Men Among the Mammoths: Victorian Science and the Discovery of Human Prehistory.* Chicago: University of Chicago Press.

Vercors. [Jean Bruller]. 1953. *You Shall Know Them.* Translated by Rita Barisse. Boston: Little, Brown.

Vietmeyer, Noel. 1992. Forgotten roots of the Incas. In *Chilies to Chocolate: Food the Americas Gave the World,* edited by N. Foster and L. S. Cordell. 95–104. Tucson: University of Arizona Press.

Vigilant, L., Marc Stoneking, H. Hardpending, K. Hawkes, and Allan Wilson. 1991. African populations and the evolution of human mitochondrial DNA. *Science* 253: 1503–8.

Villa, Paola. 1990. Torralba and Aridos: Elephant exploitation in middle Pleistocene Spain. *Journal of Human Evolution* 19:299–309.

Vrba, Elisabeth. 1985. Ecological and adaptive changes associated with early hominid evolution. In *Ancestors: The Hard Evidence,* edited by E. Delson. 63–71. New York: Liss.

———. 1988. Late Pliocene climatic events and hominid evolution. In *The Evolutionary History of the "Robust" Australopithecines,* edited by F. E. Grine. 405–26. New York: Aldine de Gruyter.

———. 1993. The pulse that produced us. *Natural History* 102(5):47–51.

Walker, Alan, and Richard Leakey, eds. 1993. *The Narioko-tome* Homo erectus *Skeleton.* Cambridge: Harvard University Press.

Walker, A., R. E. Leakey, J. M. Harris, and F. H. Brown. 1986. 2.5 Myr *Australopithecus boisei* from west of Lake Turkana, Kenya. *Nature* 322:517–22.

Walker, A., and P. Shipman. 1996. *The Wisdom of the Bones.* New York: Vintage.

Walker, A. C., and M. Pickford. 1983. New post-cranial fossils of *Proconsul africanus* and *Proconsul nyanzae.* In *New Interpretations of Ape and Human Ancestry,* edited by R. L. Ciochon and R. S. Corruccini. 325–52. New York: Plenum.

Wallace, D. C., K. Garrison, and W. C. Knowler. 1985. Dramatic founder effects in Amerindian mitochondrial DNAs. *American Journal of Physical Anthropology* 68:149–55.

Ward, S. C., and D. R. Pilbeam. 1983. Maxillofacial morphology of Miocene hominoids from Africa and Indo-Pakistan. In *New Interpretations of Ape and Human Ancestry,* edited by R. L. Ciochon and R. S. Corruccini. 211–38. New York: Plenum.

Warren, Peter. 1984. Knossos: New excavations and discoveries. *Archaeology* 37(4):48–55.

———. 1987. Crete: The Minoans and their gods. In *Origins: The Roots of European Civilisation,* edited by B. Cunliffe. 30–41. Chicago: Dorsey Press.

Waters, M., S. L. Forman, and J. M. Pierson. 1997. Diring Yuriakh: A Lower Paleolithic site in central Siberia. *Science* 275:1281–83.

Weaver, Kenneth. 1985. The search for our ancestors. *National Geographic* 168(5): 560–623.

Weidenreich, Franz. 1943. The skull of *Sinanthropus pekinensis:* A comparative study on a primitive hominid skull. *Paleontologica Sinica,* New Series, D. 10.

Weiner, Steve, Qinqi Xu, Paul Goldberg, Jinyi Liu, and Ofer Bar-Yosef. 1998. Evidence for the use of fire at Zhoukoudian, China. *Science* 281:251–53.

Wendorf, Fred, Angela E. Close, Romuald Schild, Krystyna Wasylikowa, Rupert A. Housley, Jack R. Harlan, and Halina Królik. 1992. Saharan exploitation of plants 8000 years B.P. *Nature* 359:721–24.

Wendorf, Fred, Romuald Schild, and Angela E. Close. 1989. Loaves and fishes: *The Prehistory of Waddi, Kubbaniya.* Dallas: Southern Methodist University, Dept. of Anthropology.

Wendorf, Fred, R. Schild, N. El Hadidi, A. Close, M. Kobusiewicz, H. Wieckowska, B. Issawa, and H. Hass. 1979. Use of barley in the Egyptian Late Paleolithic. *Science* 205: 1341–47.

Wendt, W. E. 1976. Art mobiler from the Apollo 11 Cave, South West Africa: Africa's oldest dated works of art. *South African Archaeological Bulletin* 31:5–11.

West, Frederick Hadleigh. 1967. The Donnelly Ridge site and the definition of an early core and blade complex in central Alaska. *American Antiquity* 32:360–82.

———. 1975. Dating the Denali complex. *Arctic Anthropology* 11(1):76–81.

———. 1981. *The Archaeology of Beringia.* New York: Columbia University Press.

———. 1996. *American Beginnings: The Prehistory and Palaeoecology of Beringia.* Chicago: University of Chicago Press.

Wheat, Joe Ben. 1972. *The Olsen-Chubbuck Site: A Paleo Indian Bison Kill.* Salt Lake City: Memoir of the Society for American Archaeology 26.

Wheeler, M. 1968. *The Indus Civilization.* New York: Cambridge University Press.

Wheeler, P. E. 1991. The thermoregulatory advantages of hominid bipedalism in open equatorial environments: The contribution of increased convective heat loss and cutaneous evaporative cooling. *Journal of Human Evolution* 21:107–15.

Whiston, William. 1696. *A New Theory of the Earth.* London.

White, J. Peter. 1993. The settlement of ancient Australia. In *The First Humans: Human Origins and History to 10,000 B.C.,* edited by G. Burenhult. 147–51, 153–57, 160–65. San Francisco: HarperSanFrancisco.

White, J. Peter, and James F. O'Connell. 1982. *A Prehistory of Australia, New Guinea, and Sahul.* New York: Academic Press.

White, Leslie. 1959. *The Evolution of Culture: Civilization to the Fall of Rome.* New York: McGraw-Hill.

White, Peter W. 1986. The Temples of Angkor: Ancient glory in stone. *National Geographic* 161(5):552–89.

White, Randall. 1982. Rethinking the Middle/Upper Paleolithic transition. *Current Anthropology* 23:169–92.

———. 1986. *Dark Caves, Bright Visions: Life in Ice Age Europe.* New York: American Museum of Natural History.

———. 1993. Technological and social dimensions of "Aurignacian-age" body ornaments across Europe. In *Before Lascaux: The Complex Record of the Early Upper Paleolithic,* edited by H. Knecht, A. Pike-Tay, and R. White. 277–99. Boca Raton: CRC Press.

White, Tim. 1980. Evolutionary implications of Pliocene hominid footprints. *Science* 208:175–76.

White, Tim, and Pieter A. Folkens. 1991. *Human Osteology.* San Diego: Academic Press.

White, Tim D., and Gen Suwa. 1987. Hominid footprints at Laetoli: Facts and interpretations. *American Journal of Physical Anthropology* 72:485–514.

White, Tim D., Gen Suwa, and Berhane Asfaw. 1994. *Australopithecus ramidus,* a new species of early hominid from Aramis, Ethiopia. *Nature* 371:306–12.

Whittle, Alasdair. 1985. *Neolithic Europe: A Survey.* New York: Cambridge University Press.

Willey, Gordon R. 1966. *An Introduction to American Archaeology* 1: North and Middle America. Englewood Cliffs, N.J.: Prentice-Hall.

Williams, Stephen. 1991. *Fantastic Archaeology: The Wild Side of North American Prehistory.* Philadelphia: University of Pennsylvania Press.

Willis, Delta. 1989. *The Hominid Gang: Behind the Scenes in the Search for Human Origins.* New York: Viking.

Willoughby, C. C. 1935. *Antiquities of the New England Indians.* Cambridge, Mass.: Peabody Museum of Archaeology and Ethnology.

Wills, W. H. 1988. *Early Prehistoric Agriculture in the American Southwest.* Santa Fe: School of American Research.

Wilmsen, Edwin. 1974. *Lindenmeier: A Pleistocene Hunting Society.* New York: Harper and Row.

Wilson, Allan C., and Rebecca L. Cann. 1992. The recent African genesis of humans. *Scientific American* 266(4): 68–73.

Wing, Elizabeth. 1977. Animal domestication in the Andes. In *Origins of Agriculture,* edited by C. A. Reed. 837–60. The Hague: Mouton.

Wittfogel, Karl. 1957. *Oriental Despotism: A Comparative Study of Total Power.* New Haven: Yale University Press.

Wolpoff, Milford H. 1984. Evolution in *Homo erectus*: The question of stasis. *Paleobiology* 10(4):389–406.

———. 1989a. Multiregional evolution: The fossil alternative to Eden. In *The Human Revolution: Behavioural and Biological Perspectives in the Origins of Modern Humans,* edited by P. Mellars and C. Stringer. 62–108. Princeton: Princeton University Press.

———. 1989b. The place of the Neandertals in human evolution. In *The Emergence of Modern Humans: Biocultural Adaptations in the Later Pleistocene,* edited by E. Trinkaus. 97–141. Cambridge: Cambridge University Press.

———. 1992. Theories of modern human origins. In *Continuity or Replacement: Controversies in* Homo sapiens *Evolution,* edited by G. Bräuer and F. Smith. 25–64. Rotterdam: Balkema.

Wolpoff, Milford, and R. Caspari. 1997. *Race and Human Evolution.* New York: Simon and Schuster.

Wolpoff, Milford H., Alan G. Thorne, Fred H. Smith, David W. Frayer, and Geoffrey G. Pope. 1994. Multiregional evolution: A worldwide source for modern human populations. In *Origins of Anatomically Modern Humans,* edited by M. Nitecki and D. Nitecki. 175–99. New York: Plenum.

Wolpoff, Milford H., X. Z. Wu, and Alan G. Thorne. 1984. Modern *Homo sapiens* origins: A general theory of hominid evolution involving the fossil evidence from East Asia. In *The Origins of Modern Human: A World Survey of the Fossil Evidence,* edited by F. H. Smith and F. Spencer. 411–84. New York: Liss.

Wood, Bernard. 1992a. Early hominid species and speciation. *Journal of Human Evolution* 22:351–65.

———. 1992b. Origin and evolution of the genus *Homo. Nature* 355:783–90.

Woo Ju-kang (Wu-Rukang). 1966. The skull of Lantian Man. *Current Anthropology* 7(1):83–86.

———. 1985. New Chinese *Homo erectus* and recent work at Zhoukoudian. In *Ancestors: The Hard Evidence,* edited by E. Delson. 245–48. New York: Liss.

Wright, G. 1971. Origins of food production in southwestern Asia: A survey of current ideas. *Current Anthropology* 12: 447–77.

Wright, H. E., Jr. 1991. Environmental conditions for Paleoindian immigration. In *The First Americans: Search and Research,* edited by T. D. Dillehay and D. J. Meltzer. 113–35. Boca Raton: CRC Press.

Wu Rukang (Woo Ju-kang), and Xingren Dong. 1982. Preliminary study of *Homo erectus* remains from Hexian, Anhui. *Acta Anthropological Sinica* 1(1):2–13.

Yarnell, R. 1974. Plant food and cultivation of the Salts Caverns. In *Archaeology of the Mammoth Cave Area,* edited by P. J. Watson. 113–22. Orlando: Academic Press.

———. 1977. Native plant husbandry north of Mexico. In *Origins of Agriculture,* edited by C. A. Reed. 861–78. The Hague: Mouton.

Yellen, John E., Alison S. Brooks, Els Cornelissen, Michael J. Mehlman, and Kathlyn Stewart. 1995. A Middle Stone Age worked bone industry from Katanda, Upper Semliki Valley, Zaire. *Science* 268:553–56.

Yi Seonbonk, and Geoffrey Clark. 1985. The "Dyuktai Culture" and New World origins. *Current Anthropology* 26:1–13.

Yoffee, Norman, and George L. Cowgill, eds. 1988. *The Collapse of Ancient States and Civilizations.* Tucson: University of Arizona Press.

Zeder, Melinda A. 1994a. After the revolution: Post-Neolithic subsistence in northern Mesopotamia. *American Anthropologist* 96:97–126.

———. 1994b. New perspectives on agricultural origins in the ancient Near East. *AnthroNotes* 16(2):1–7.

Zihlman, Adrienne. 1979. Gathering and the hominid adaptation. In *Female Hierarchies,* edited by L. Tiger and H. M. Fowler. Chicago: Beresford Book Service.

Zohary, Daniel, and Maria Hopf. 1994. *Domestication of Plants in the Old World.* Oxford Scientific Publications. Oxford: Clarendon Press.

Zubrow, Ezra. 1989. The demographic modeling of Neanderthal extinction. In *The Human Revolution: Behavioural and Biological Perspectives in the Origins of Modern Humans,* edited by P. Mellars and C. Stringer. 212–31. Princeton: Princeton University Press.

Zun'e Lu. 1987. Cracking the evolutionary puzzle. Jinniushan Man. *China Pictorial.* 4:34–45.

Index